C   HOW TO PROGRAM

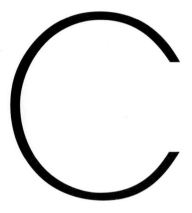

C HOW TO PROGRAM

SECOND EDITION

H. M. Deitel
Nova University
Deitel and Associates

P. J. Deitel
Deitel and Associates

PRENTICE HALL, Englewood Cliffs, New Jersey 07632

Library of Congress Cataloging-in-Publication Data

Deitel, Harvey M.
    C : how to program / H.M. Deitel, P.J. Deitel.. -- 2nd ed.
        p.   cm.
    Includes bibliographical references and index.
    ISBN 0-13-226119-7
    1. C (Computer program language)   I. Deitel, Paul J. II. Title.
    QA76.73.C15D44   1994
    005.13'3--dc20   93-33697
                                                               CIP

Acquisitions Editor: *Marcia Horton*
Production Editor: *Joe Scordato*
Copy Editor: *Michael Schiaparelli*
Chapter Opener and Cover Designer: *JeannetteJacobs*
Buyer: *Dave Dickey*
Supplements Editor: *Alice Dworkin*
Editorial Assistant: *Dolores Mars*

© 1994, 1992 by Prentice-Hall, Inc.
A Simon & Schuster Company
Englewood Cliffs, New Jersey 07632

The authors and publisher of this book have used their best efforts in preparing this book. These efforts include the development, research, and testing of the theories and programs to determine their effectiveness. The authors and publisher make no warranty of any kind, expressed or implied, with regard to these programs or to the documentation contained in this book. The authors and publisher shall not be liable in any event for incidental or consequential damages in connection with, or arising out of, the furnishing, performance, or use of these programs.

Printed in the United States of America

20 19 18 17 16

ISBN   0-13-226119-7

Prentice-Hall International (UK) Limited, London
Prentice-Hall of Australia Pty. Limited, Sydney
Prentice-Hall Canada Inc., Toronto
Prentice-Hall Hispanoamericana, S.A., Mexico
Prentice-Hall of India Private Limited, New Delhi
Prentice-Hall of Japan, Inc., Tokyo
Simon & Schuster of Asia Pte. Ltd., Singapore
Editora Prentice-Hall do Brasil, Ltda., Rio de Janeiro

TO

Dr. Stephen Feldman, President of Nova University and to Dr. Edward Lieblein, Dean of the Nova University Center for Computer and Information Sciences

For their vision of an institution for advanced scientific and computer science education and research in South Florida, and for their indefatigable efforts in realizing that vision in this young university.

H. M. D.

TO

My teachers at Lawrenceville and M.I.T.

For instilling in me a love of learning and writing.

P. J. D.

Contents

*Summary • Terminology • Common Programming Errors •
Good Programming Practices • Performance Tips •
Portability Tip • Software Engineering Observations • Self-
Review Exercises • Answers to Self-Review Exercises •
Exercises*

*Summary • Terminology • Common Programming Errors •
Good Programming Practices • Performance Tips • Software
Engineering Observations • Self-Review Exercises • Answers
to Self-Review Exercises • Exercises*

Illustrations

Preface

Welcome to C! This book is by an old guy and a young guy. The old guy (HMD; Massachusetts Institute of Technology 1967) has been programming and/or teaching programming for more than 30 years. The young guy (PJD; MIT 1991) has been programming for a dozen years and has caught the teaching and writing "bug." The old guy programs and teaches from experience. The young guy programs from an inexhaustible reserve of energy. The old guy wants clarity. The young guy wants performance. The old guy appreciates elegance and beauty. The young guy wants results. We got together to produce a book we hope you will find informative, interesting, and entertaining.

In most educational environments, C is taught to people who know how to program. Many educators believe that the complexity of C, and a number of other difficulties, make C unworthy for a first programming course—precisely the target course for this book. So why did we write this text?

C has in fact become the systems implementation language of choice in industry, and there is good reason to believe that its object-oriented variant, C++, will emerge as the dominant language of the mid-to-late 1990s. Harvey Deitel has been teaching Pascal in university environments for 13 years with an emphasis on developing clearly written, well-structured programs. Much of what is taught in an introductory Pascal course sequence is the basic principles of structured programming. We have presented this material exactly the way HMD has done in his university courses. There are some pitfalls, but where these occur, we point them out and explain procedures for dealing with them effectively. Our experience has been that students handle the course in about the same manner as they handle Pascal. There is one noticeable difference though: Students are highly motivated by the fact that they are learning a language that will be immediately useful to them as they leave the university environment. This increases their enthusiasm for the material—a big help when you consider that C is more difficult to learn.

Our goal was clear: Produce a C programming textbook for introductory university-level courses in computer programming for students with little or no programming experience, but produce a book that also offers the rigorous treatment of theory and practice demanded by traditional C courses. To meet these goals, we produced a book larger than other C texts—this because our text also patiently teaches structured programming principles. Approximately 1000 students have studied this material in our courses. Tens of thousands of students worldwide learned C from the first edition of this book.

The book contains a rich collection of examples, exercises, and projects drawn from many fields to provide the student with a chance to solve interesting real-world problems.

The book concentrates on the principles of good software engineering and stresses program clarity through use of the structured programming methodology. We avoid the use of arcane terminology and syntax specifications in favor of teaching by example.

Among the pedagogical devices of this text are complete programs and sample outputs to demonstrate the concepts; a set of objectives and an outline at the beginning of every chapter; common programming errors and good programming practices enumerated throughout each chapter and summarized at the end of each chapter; summary and terminology sections in each chapter; self-review exercises and answers in each chapter; and the richest collection of exercises in any C book. An instructor's manual is available on PC format disks and Macintosh format disks with the programs in the main text and answers to most of the exercises at the end of each chapter. The exercises range from simple recall questions to lengthy programming problems to major projects. Instructors requiring substantial term projects of their students will find many appropriate problems listed in the exercises for Chapters 5 through 21. We have put a great deal of effort into the exercises to enhance the value of this course for the student. The programs in the text were tested on ANSI C-compliant compilers on Sun SPARCstations, Apple Macintosh (Think C), IBM PC (Turbo C, Turbo C++, and Borland C++), and DEC VAX/VMS (VAX C).

This text follows the ANSI C standard. Many features of ANSI C will not work with pre-ANSI C versions. See the reference manuals for your particular system for more details about the language, or obtain a copy of ANSI/ISO 9899: 1990, "American National Standard for Information Systems—Programming Language C," from the American National Standards Institute, 11 West 42nd Street, New York, New York 10036.

About this Book

This book is loaded with features to help the student learn.

Objectives

Each chapter begins with a statement of objectives. This tells the student what to expect and gives the student a chance, after reading the chapter, to determine if he or she has met these objectives. It is a confidence builder and a source of positive reinforcement.

Quotations

The learning objectives are followed by a series of quotations. Some are humorous, some are philosophical, and some offer interesting insights. Our students have told us that they enjoy relating the quotes to the chapter material.

Outline

The chapter outline helps the student approach the material in top-down fashion. This, too, helps students anticipate what is to come and set a responsible pace.

Sections

Each chapter is organized into small sections that address key areas. C features are presented in the context of complete, working C programs. Each program is followed by a window containing the output produced when the program is run. This enables the student to confirm that the programs run as expected. Relating outputs back to the program statements that produce the outputs is an excellent way to learn and reinforce concepts. Our programs are designed to exercise the diverse features of C. Reading the book carefully is much like entering and running these programs on a computer.

Illustrations

An abundance of line drawings and charts is included. The discussion of structured flowcharting, which helps students appreciate the use of control structures and structured programming, features carefully drawn flowcharts. The chapter on data structures uses abundant line drawings to illustrate the creation and maintenance of important data structures such as linked lists, queues, stacks, and binary trees.

Helpful Design Elements

We have included four design elements to help students focus on important aspects of program development, testing and debugging, performance, and portability. We highlight scores of these in the form of Good Programming Practices, Common Programming Errors, Performance Tips, Portability Tips, and Software Engineering Observations.

Good Programming Practices

Good programming practices are highlighted in the text. They call the student's attention to techniques that help produce better programs. These practices represent the best we have been able to glean from a combined four decades of programming experience.

Common Programming Errors

Students learning a language—especially in their first programming course—tend to make certain common errors. Focusing the students' attention on these common programming errors is an enormous help. It also helps reduce the long lines outside instructors' offices during office hours!

Performance Tips

We find that writing clear and understandable programs is by far the most important goal for a first programming course. But students want to write the program that runs the fastest, uses the least memory, requires the smallest number of keystrokes, or dazzles in some other nifty way. Students really care about performance. They want to know what they can do to "turbo charge" their programs. So we have include Performance Tips to highlight opportunities for improving program performance.

Portability Tips

Software development is a complex and enormously expensive activity. Organizations that develop software must often produce versions customized to a variety of computers and operating systems. So there is a strong emphasis today on portability, i.e., on producing software that will run on many different computer systems without change. Many people tout C as the best language for developing portable software. Some people assume that if they implement an application in C, the application will automatically be portable. This is simply not the case. Achieving portability requires careful and cautious design. There are many pitfalls. The ANSI Standard C document itself lists 11 pages of potential difficulties. We include numerous Portability Tips. We have combined our own experience in building portable software with a careful study of the ANSI standard section on portability, as well as two excellent books on portability (see references Ja89 and Ra90 at the end of Chapter 1).

Software Engineering Observations

This design element is new in the second edition. We have summarized scores of observations that affect the architecture and construction of software systems, especially large-scale software systems.

Summary

Each of our chapters ends with a number of additional pedagogical devices. We present a detailed summary of the chapter in bullet-list fashion. This helps the students review and reinforce key concepts. We then collect and list in order all of the chapters Good Programming Practices, Common Programming Errors, Performance Tips, Portability Tips, and Software Engineering Observations.

Terminology

We include a Terminology section with an alphabetized list of the important terms defined in the chapter. Again, further confirmation. Then we summarize the Good Programming Practices, Common Programming Errors, Performance Tips, Portability Tips, and Software Engineering Observations.

Self-Review Exercises

Extensive Self-Review Exercises with complete answers are included for self-study. This gives the student a chance to build confidence with the material and prepare to attempt the regular exercises.

Exercises

Each chapter concludes with a substantial set of exercises spanning the range from simple recall of important terminology and concepts, to writing individual C statements, to writing small portions of C functions, to writing complete C functions and programs, to writ ing major term projects. The large number of exercises enables instructors to tailor their courses to the unique needs of their audiences and to vary course assignments each semester. Instructors can use these exercises to form homework assignments, short quizzes, and major examinations. The solutions for the exercises are included on the IBM-PC-format and Apple-Macintosh-format disks available to instructors through their Prentice-Hall representatives.

A Tour of the Book

The book is divided into three major parts. The first part, Chapters 1 through 14, presents a thorough treatment of the C programming language including a formal introduction to structured programming. The second part—unique among C textbooks—Chapters 15 through 21, presents a substantial treatment of C++ and object-oriented programming sufficient for an upper-level undergraduate college course. The third part, Appendices A through E, presents a variety of reference materials that support the main text.

Chapter 1, "Introduction," discusses what computers are, how they work, and how they are programmed. It introduces the notion of structured programming and explains why this set of techniques has fostered a revolution in the way programs are written. The chapter gives a brief history of the development of programming languages from machine languages, to assembly languages, to high-level languages. The origin of the C programming language is discussed. The chapter includes an introduction to the C programming environment.

Chapter 2, "Introduction to C Programming," gives a concise introduction to writing C programs. A detailed treatment of decision making and arithmetic operations in C is presented. After studying this chapter, the student will understand how to write simple, but complete, C programs.

Chapter 3, "Structured Programming," is probably the most important chapter in the text, especially for the serious student of computer science. It introduces the notion of algorithms (procedures) for solving problems. It explains the importance of structured programming in producing programs that are understandable, debuggable, maintainable, and more likely to work properly on the first try. It introduces the fundamental control structures of structured programming, namely the sequence, selection (if and if/else), and repetition (while) structures. It explains the technique of top-down, stepwise refinement that is critical to the production of properly structured programs. It presents the popular program design aid, structured pseudocode. The methods and approaches used in Chapter 3 are applicable to structured programming in any programming language, not just C. This chapter helps the student develop good programming habits in preparation for dealing with the more substantial programming tasks in the remainder of the text.

Chapter 4, "Program Control," refines the notions of structured programming and introduces additional control structures. It examines repetition in detail, and compares the alternatives of counter-controlled loops and sentinel-controlled loops. The `for` structure is introduced as a convenient means for implementing counter-controlled loops. The `switch` selection structure and the `do/while` repetition structure are presented. The chapter concludes with a discussion of logical operators.

Chapter 5, "Functions," discusses the design and construction of program modules. C includes standard library functions, programmer-defined functions, recursion, and call-by-value capabilities. The techniques presented in Chapter 5 are essential to the production and appreciation of properly structured programs, especially the kinds of larger programs and software that system programmers and application programmers are likely to develop in real-world applications. The "divide and conquer" strategy is presented as an effective means for solving complex problems; functions enable the programmer to divide complex programs into simpler interacting components. Students enjoy the treatment of random numbers and simulation, and they appreciate the discussion of the dice game craps which makes elegant use of control structures. The chapter offers a solid introduction to recursion and includes a table summarizing the 31 recursion examples and exercises distributed throughout the remainder of the book. Some books leave recursion for a chapter late in the book; but we feel this topic is best covered gradually throughout the text. The extensive collection of 39 exercises at the end of the Chapter 5 includes several classical recursion problems such as the Towers of Hanoi.

Chapter 6, "Arrays," discusses the structuring of data into arrays, or groups, of related data items of the same type. The chapter presents numerous examples of both single-subscripted arrays and double-subscripted arrays. It is widely recognized that structuring data is just as important as using control structures in the development of properly structured programs. Examples in the chapter investigate various common array manipulations, printing histograms, sorting data, passing arrays to functions, and an introduction to the field of survey data analysis. A feature of this chapter is the careful presentation of binary searching as a dramatic improvement over linear searching. The end-of-chapter exercises include an especially large selection of interesting and challenging problems. These include improved sorting techniques, the design of an airline reservations system, an introduction to the concept of turtle graphics (made famous in the LOGO language), and the Knight's Tour and Eight Queens problems that introduce the notions of heuristic programming so widely employed in the field of artificial intelligence.

Chapter 7, "Pointers," presents one of the most powerful features of the C language. The chapter provides detailed explanations of pointer operators, call by reference, pointer expressions, pointer arithmetic, the relationship between pointers and arrays, arrays of pointers, and pointers to functions. The chapter exercises include a simulation of the classic race between the tortoise and the hare, and card shuffling and dealing algorithms. A special section entitled "Building Your Own Computer" is also included. This section explains the notion of machine language programming and proceeds with a project involving the design and implementation of a computer simulator that allows the reader to write and run machine language programs. This unique feature of the text will be especially useful to the reader who wants to understand how computers really work. Our students enjoy this project and often implement substantial enhancements; many enhancements are suggested in the exercises. In Chapter 12, another special section guides the reader through building a compiler; the machine language produced by the compiler is then executed on the machine language simulator produced in Chapter 7.

Chapter 8, "Characters and Strings," deals with the fundamentals of processing non-numeric data. The chapter includes a complete walkthrough of the character and string processing functions available in C's libraries. The techniques discussed here are widely used in building word processors, page layout and typesetting software, and text-processing applications. The chapter includes an interesting collection of 33 exercises that explore text-processing applications. The student will enjoy the exercises on writing limericks, writing random poetry, converting English to pig Latin, generating seven-letter words that are equivalent to a given telephone number, text justification, check protection, writing a check amount in words, generating Morse Code, metric conversions, and dunning letters. The last exercise challenges the student to use a computerized dictionary to create a crossword puzzle generator!

Chapter 9, "Formatted Input/Output," presents all the powerful formatting capabilities of printf and scanf. We discuss `printf`'s output formatting capabilities such as rounding floating point values to a given number of decimal places, aligning columns of numbers, right justification and left justification, insertion of literal information, forcing a plus sign, printing leading zeros, using exponential notation, using octal and hexadecimal numbers, and controlling field widths and precisions. We discuss all of `printf`'s escape sequences for cursor movement, printing special characters, and causing an audible alert. We examine all of `scanf`'s input formatting capabilities including inputting specific types of data and skipping specific characters in an input stream. We discuss all of `scanf`'s conversion specifiers for reading decimal, octal, hexadecimal, floating point, character, and string values. We discuss scanning inputs to match (or not match) the characters in a scan set. The chapter exercises test virtually all of C's formatted input/output capabilities.

Chapter 10, "Structures, Unions, Bit Manipulations, and Enumerations," presents a variety of important features. Structures are like records in Pascal and other languages—they group data items of various types. Structures are used in Chapter 11 to form files consisting of records of information. Structures are used in conjunction with pointers and dynamic memory allocation in Chapter 12 to form dynamic data structures such as linked lists, queues, stacks, and trees. Unions enable an area of memory to be used for different types of data at different times; such sharing can reduce a program's memory requirements or secondary storage requirements. Enumerations provide a convenient means of defining useful symbolic constants; this helps make programs more self-documenting. C's powerful bit manipulation capabilities enable programmers to write programs that exercise lower-level hardware capabilities. This helps programs process bit strings, set individual bits on or off, and store information more compactly. Such capabilities, often found only in low-level assembly languages, are valued by programmers writing system software such as operating systems and networking software. A feature of the chapter is its revised, high-performance card shuffling and dealing simulation. This is an excellent opportunity for the instructor to emphasize the quality of algorithms.

Chapter 11, "File Processing," discusses the techniques used to process text files with sequential access and random access. The chapter begins with an introduction to the data hierarchy from bits, to bytes, to fields, to records, to files. Next, C's simple view of files and streams is presented. Sequential access files are discussed using a series of three programs that show how to open and close files, how to store data sequentially in a file, and how to read data sequentially from a file. Random access files are discussed using a series of four programs that show how to sequentially create a file for random access, how to read and write data to a file with random access, and how to read data sequentially from a randomly accessed file. The fourth random access program combines many of the techniques of accessing files both sequentially and randomly into a complete transaction processing program. Students in our industry seminars have told us that after studying the material on file processing, they were able to produce substantial file-processing programs that were immediately useful in their organizations.

Chapter 12, "Data Structures," discusses the techniques used to create dynamic data structures. The chapter begins with discussions of self-referential structures and dynamic memory allocation. The chapter proceeds with a discussion of how to create and maintain various dynamic data structures including linked lists, queues (or waiting lines), stacks, and trees. For each type of data structure, we present complete, working programs and show sample outputs. Chapter 12 helps the student truly master pointers. The chapter includes abundant examples using indirection and double indirection—a particularly difficult concept. One problem when working with pointers is that students have trouble visualizing the data structures and how their nodes are linked together. So we have included illustrations that show the links, and the sequence in which they are created. The binary tree example is a superb capstone for the study of pointers and dynamic data structures. This example creates a binary tree; enforces duplicate elimination; and introduces preorder, inorder, and postorder recursive tree traversals. Students have a real sense of accomplishment when they study and implement this example. They particularly appreciate seeing that the inorder traversal prints the node values in sorted order. The chapter includes a substantial collection of exercises. A highlight of the chapter is the special section "Building Your Own Compiler." The exercises walk the student through the development of an infix-to-postfix-conversion program and a postfix-expression-evaluation program. We then modify the postfix evaluation algorithm to generate machine language code. The compiler places this code in a file (using the techniques of Chapter 11). Students then run the machine language produced by their compilers on the software simulators they built in the exercises of Chapter 7!

Chapter 13, "The Preprocessor," provides detailed discussions of the preprocessor directives. The chapter includes more complete information on the `#include` directive that causes a copy of a specified file to be included in place of the directive before the file is compiled, and the `#define` directive that creates symbolic constants and macros. The chapter explains conditional compilation for enabling the programmer to control the execution of preprocessor directives, and the compilation of program code. The `#` operator that converts its operand to a string and the `##` operator that concatenates two tokens are discussed. The five predefined symbolic constants (`__LINE__`, `__FILE__`, `__DATE__`, `__TIME__`, and `__STDC__`) are presented. Finally, macro `assert` of the `assert.h` header is discussed. assert is valuable in program testing, debugging, verification, and validation.

Chapter 14, "Advanced Topics," presents several advanced topics not ordinarily covered in introductory courses. Section 14.2 shows how to redirect input to a program to come from a file, redirect output from a program to be placed in a file, redirect the output of one program to be the input of another program (piping), and append the output of a program to an existing file. Section 14.3 discusses how to develop functions that use variable-length argument lists. Section 14.4 shows how command-line arguments can be passed to function **main**, and used in a program. Section 14.5 discusses compiling programs whose components are spread across multiple files. Section 14.6 discusses registering functions with **atexit** to be executed at program termination, and terminating program execution with function **exit**. Section 14.7 discusses the **const** and **volatile** type qualifiers. Section 14.8 shows how to specify the type of a numeric constant using the integer and floating point suffixes. Section 14.9 explains binary files and the use of temporary files. Section 14.10 shows how to use signal handling library to trap unexpected events. Section 14.11 discusses the creation and use of dynamic arrays with **calloc** and **realloc**.

In the first edition of the text, we included a one-chapter introduction to C++ and Object-Oriented Programming. In the interim, many universities have decided to incorporate an introduction to C++ and Object-Oriented Programming into their C courses. So in this edition, we have expanded the treatment to seven chapters—sufficient text, exercises, and laboratories for a one-semester course.

Chapter 15, "C++ as a Better C," introduces the non-object-oriented features of C++. These features improve the process of writing conventional procedure-oriented programs. The chapter discusses single-line comments, stream input/output, declarations, creating new data types, function prototypes and type checking, inline functions (as a replacement for macros), reference parameters, the const qualifier, dynamic memory allocation, default arguments, the unary scope resolution operator, function overloading, linkage specifications, and function templates.

Chapter 16, "Classes and Data Abstraction," represents a wonderful opportunity for teaching data abstraction the "right way"—through a language (C++) expressly devoted to implementing abstract data types (ADTs). In recent years, data abstraction has become a major topic in introductory computing courses taught in Pascal. As we were writing this book, we considered presenting data abstraction in C, but we decided instead to include this detailed introduction to C++. Chapters 16, 17, and 18 include a solid treatment of data abstraction. Chapter 16 discusses implementing ADTs as **struct**s, implementing ADTs as C++-style classes, accessing class members, separating interface from implementation, using access functions and utility functions, initializing objects with constructors, destroying objects with destructors, assignment by default memberwise copy, and software reusability.

Chapter 17, "Classes: Part II," continues the study of classes and data abstraction. The chapter discusses declaring and using constant objects, constant member functions, composition—the process of building classes that have other classes as members, friend functions and friend classes that have special access rights to the private members of classes, the **this** pointer that enables an object to know its own address, dynamic memory allocation, static class members for containing and manipulating class-wide data, examples of popular abstract data types (arrays, strings, and queues), container classes, iterators, and template classes. Template classes are among the more recent additions to the evolving C++ language. Template classes enable the programmer to capture the essence of an abstract data type (such as a stack, an array, or a queue) and then create—with min imal additional code—versions of that ADT for particular types (such as a stack of int, a stack of float, a queue of int, etc.). For this reason, template classes are often called parameterized types.

Chapter 18, "Operator Overloading," is one of the most popular topics in C++ courses. Students really enjoy this material. They find it a perfect match with the discussion of abstract data types in Chapters 16 and 17. Operator overloading enables the programmer to tell the compiler how to use existing operators with objects of new types. C++ already knows how to use these operators with objects of built-in types such as integers, floats, and characters. But suppose we create a new string class. What does the plus sign mean? Many programmers use plus with strings to mean concatenation. In this chapter, the programmer will learn how to "overload" the plus sign so that when it is written between two string objects in an expression, the compiler will generate a function call to an "operator function" that will concatenate the two strings. The chapter discusses the fundamentals of operator overloading, restrictions in operator overloading, overloading with class member functions vs. with nonmember functions, overloading unary and binary operators, and converting between types. A feature of the chapter is the large number of substantial case studies, namely an array class, a string class, a date class, a huge integers class, and a complex numbers class (the last two appear with full source code in the exercises).

Chapter 19, "Inheritance," deals with one of the fundamental capabilities of object-oriented programming languages. Inheritance is a form of software reusability in which new classes are developed quickly by absorbing the capabilities of existing classes and then adding apropriate new capabilities. The chapter discusses the notions of base classes and derived classes, protected members, public inheritance, protected inheritance, private inheritance, direct base classes, indirect base classes, use of constructors and destructors in base classes and derived classes, and software engineering with inheritance. The chapter compares inheritance ("is a" relationships) with composition ("has a" relationships) and introduces "uses a" and "knows a" relationships. A feature of the chapter is its several substantial case studies. In particular, a lengthy case study implements a point, circle, cylinder class hierarchy. The chapter concludes with a case study on multiple inheritance—an advanced feature of C++ in which a derived class may be formed by inheriting attributes and behaviors from several base classes.

Chapter 20, "Virtual Functions and Polymorphism," deals with another of the fundamental capabilities of object-oriented programming, namely polymorphic behavior. When many classes are related through inheritance to a common base class, each derived-class object may be treated as a base-class object. This enables programs to be written in a rather general manner independent of the specific types of the derived-class objects. New kinds of objects can be handled by the same program, thus making systems more extensible. Polymorphism enables programs to eliminate complex switch logic in favor of simpler "straight-line" logic. A screen manager of a video game, for example, can simply send a draw message to every object in a linked list of objects to be drawn. Each object knows how to draw itself. A new object can be added to the program without modifying that program as long as that new object also knows how to draw itself. This style of programming is typically used to implement today's enormously popular graphical user in terfaces. The chapter discusses the mechanics of achieving polymorphic behavior through the use of virtual functions. The chapter distinguishes between abstract classes (from which no objects can be instantiated) and concrete classes (from which objects can be instantiated). Abstract classes are useful for providing an inheritable interface to classes throughout the hierarchy. A feature of the chapter is its two major polymorphism case studies—a payroll system and another version of the point, circle, cylinder shape hierarchy discussed in Chapter 19.

Chapter 21, "C++ Stream Input/Output," contains an extremely detailed treatment of the new object-oriented style of input/output introduced in C++. Many C courses are taught with C++ compilers, and the instructors often prefer to teach the new C++ style of I/O rather than continuing to use the older **printf/scanf** style. The chapter discusses the various I/O capabilities of C++ including output with the stream insertion operator, input with the stream extraction operator, type-safe I/O (a nice improvement over C), formatted I/O, unformatted I/O (for performance), stream manipulators for controlling the stream base (decimal, octal, or hexadecimal), floating-point numbers, controlling field widths, user-defined manipulators, stream format states, stream error states, I/O of objects of user-defined types, and tying output streams to input streams (to ensure that prompts actually appear before the user is expected to enter responses).

Several Appendices provide valuable reference material. In particular, we present the C syntax summary in Appendix A; a summary of all C standard library functions with explanations in Appendix B; a complete operator precedence and associativity chart in Appendix C; the set of ASCII character codes in Appendix D; and a discussion of the binary, octal, decimal, and hexadecimal number systems in Appendix E. Appendix B was condensed from the ANSI standard document with the express written permission of the American National Standards Institute; this appendix is a detailed and valuable reference for the practicing C programmer. Appendix E is a complete tutorial on number systems including many self-review exercises and answers.

Acknowledgments

One of the great pleasures of writing a textbook is acknowledging the efforts of the many people whose names may not appear on the cover, but without whose hard work, cooperation, friendship, and understanding producing this text would have been impossible.

HMD wants to thank his Nova University Colleagues Ed Simco, Clovis Tondo, Ed Lieblein, Phil Adams, Raisa Szabo, Raul Salazar, and Barbara Edge.

We would like to thank our friends at Digital Equipment Corporation (Stephanie Stosur Schwartz, Sue-Lane Garrett, Janet Hebert, Faye Napert, Betsy Mills, Jennie Connolly, Barbara Couturier and Paul Sandore), Sun Microsystems (Gary Morin), the Corporation for Open Systems International (Bill Horst, David Litwack, Steve Hudson, and Linc Faurer), Informative Stages (Don Hall), Semaphore Training (Clive Lee), and Cambridge Technology Partners (Gart Davis, Paul Sherman, and Wilberto Martinez), and our many other corporate clients who have made teaching this material in an industrial setting such a joy.

We are fortunate to have been able to work on this project with a talented and dedicated team of publishing professionals at Prentice Hall. Joe Scordato did a marvelous job as production editor. Dolores Mars coordinated the complex reviewer effort on the manuscript and was always incredibly helpful when we needed assistance—her ebullience and good cheer are sincerely appreciated.

This book happened because of the encouragement, enthusiasm, and persistence of Marcia Horton, Editor-in-Chief. It is a great credit to Prentice Hall that its top executives continue their editorial responsibilities. We have always been impressed with this and we are grateful to be able to continue to work closely with Marcia even as her administrative responsibilities increase.

We appreciate the efforts of our first and second edition reviewers (their affiliations at the time of review are listed in parentheses)

David Falconer (California State University at Fullerton)
David Finkel (Worcester Polytechnic)
H. E. Dunsmore (Purdue University)
Jim Schmolze (Tufts University)
Gene Spafford (Purdue University)
Clovis Tondo (IBM Corporation and visiting professor at Nova University)
Jeffrey Esakov (University of Pennsylvania)
Tom Slezak (University of California, Lawrence Livermore National Laboratory)
Gary A. Wilson (Gary A Wilson & Associates and University of California Berkeley Extension)
Mike Kogan (IBM Corporation; chief architect of 32-bit OS/2 2.0)
Don Kostuch (IBM Corporation retired; now worldwide instructor in C, C++, and object-oriented programming)
Ed Lieblein (Nova University)
John Carroll (San Diego State University)
Alan Filipski (Arizona State University)
Greg Hidley (University of California San Diego)
Daniel Hirschberg (University of California Irvine)
Jack Tan (University of Houston)
Richard Alpert (Boston University)
Eric Bloom (Bentley College).

These people scrutinized every aspect of the text and made dozens of valuable suggestions for improving the accuracy and completeness of the presentation.

We owe a special note of thanks to Dr. Graem Ringwood, Computer Science Dept., QMW University of London. Dr. Ringwood sent us a continuing stream of constructive suggestions while he was teaching from our book. His comments and criticisms played an important part in shaping the second edition.

Tem Nieto contributed long hours of painstaking effort helping us form the special section "Building Your Own Compiler" at the end of Chapter 12.

We would also like to thank the many professors, instructors, students, and professional people who sent us their comments on the first edition: MacRae, Joe, Sysop on the Autodesk AutoCad forum on CompuServe; McCarthy, Michael J., Director of Undergraduate Programs, University of Pittsburgh; Mahmoud Fath El-Den, Department of

Math and Computer Science, Ft. Hays State University; Rader, Cyndi, Wright State University; Soni, Manish, Tufts University (student); Bullock, Tom, Department of Electrical Engineering, University of Florida, Gainesville (Professor of EE); Derruks, Jan, Hogeschool van Amsterdam, Technische Maritieme Faculteit, Amsterdam; Duchan, Alan, Chair, MIS Department, Richard J. Wehle School of Business, Canisius College; Kenny, Barbara T., Department of Mathematics, Boise State University; Riegelhaupt-Herzig, Scott P., Boston University Metropolitan College, Computer Science Department; Yean, Leong Wai, Nanyang Technological University, Division of Computer Technology, School of Applied Science, Singapore (student); Abdullah, Rosni, Universiti Sains Malaysia, Computer Science Department; Willis, Bob; Cohoon, Jim, Department of Computer Science, University of Virginia; Tranchant, Mark, University of Southhampton, Great Britain (student); Martignoni, Stephane, Royal Insititute of Technology, Sweden (student); Spears, Marlene, Homebrewer (makes beer)(husband student using our book); French, Rev. Michael D.(SJ), Computer Science Department, Loyola College, Maryland; Wallace, Ted, Departments of Russian and Physics, Dartmouth College (student); Wright, Kevin, University of Nebraska (student); Elder, Scott, (student); Schneller, Jeffrey; Byrd, William, Department of Industrial and Systems Engineering, University of Florida (student); Naiman, E. J., Compuware; Sedgwick, Arthur E., Dr., Department of Mathematics, Statistics, and Computer Science, Dalhousie University, Halifax, Nova Scotia (user); Holsberg, Peter J., Professor, Engineering Technology, Computers and Math, Mecer County Community College; Pont, Michael J., DR., Lecturer, Department of Engineering, University of Leicester, England; Linney, John, Teaching Assistant, Department of Computer Science, Queen Mary and Westfield College, London; Zipper, Herbert J., Professor, Electrical Engineering Department, SUNY Farmingdale; Humenik, Keith, University of Maryland, Baltimore Campus; Beeson, Michael, Department of Mathematics and Computer Science, San Jose State University; Gingo, Peter J., Dr., Department of Mathematical Sciences, Buchtel College of Arts and Sciences; and Vaught, Lloyd, Computer Science Department, Modesto Junior College.

The authors would like to extend a special note of thanks to Ed Lieblein, one of the world's leading authorities on software engineering, for his extraordinary review of portions of the material on C++ and object-oriented programming. Dr. Lieblein is a friend and colleague of HMD at Nova University in Ft. Lauderdale, Florida where he is Full Professor of Computer Science. Dr. Lieblein was previously Chief Technical Officer of Tartan Laboratories, one of the leading compiler development organizations in the world. Before that, he served as Director of Computer Software and Systems in the Office of the Secretary of Defense. In that capacity, he managed the DoD Software Initiative, a special program to improve the nation's software capability for future mission-critical systems. He initiated the Pentagon's STARS program for software technology and reusability, guided the Ada program to international standardization, and played an important role in establishing the Software Engineering Institute at Carnegie Mellon University. It is indeed a special privilege for us to be able to work with Dr. Lieblein at Nova University.

We would also like to extend a special note of thanks to Dr. Clovis Tondo of IBM Corporation and visiting professor at Nova University. Dr. Tondo was the head of our review team. His meticulous and thorough reviews taught us much about the subtleties of C and C++. Dr. Tondo is the co-author of *The C Answer Book* which contains answers to the exercises in—and is widely used in conjunction with—*The C Programming Language*, the classic by Brian Kernighan and Dennis Ritchie.

This text is based on the version of C standardized through the American National Standards Institute (ANSI) in the United States and through the International Standards Organization (ISO) worldwide. We have used extensive materials from the ANSI standard document with the express written permission of the American National Standards Institute. We sincerely appreciate the cooperation of Mary Clare Lynch—Director of Publications for ANSI—for helping us obtain the necessary publication permissions. Figures 5.6, 8.1, 8.5, 8.12, 8.17, 8.20, 8.22, 8.30, 8.36, 9.1, 9.3, 9.6, 9.9, 9.16, 10.7, and 11.6, and Appendix A: C Syntax, and Appendix B: Standard Library have been condensed and adapted with permission from American National Standard for Information Systems—Programming Language C, ANSI/ISO 9899: 1990. Copies of this standard may be purchased from the American National Standards Institute at 11 West 42nd Street, New York, NY 10036.

Last, but certainly not least, we would like to thank Barbara and Abbey Deitel, for their love and understanding, and for their enormous efforts in helping prepare the manuscript. They contributed endless hours of effort; they tested every program in the text, assisted in every phase of the manuscript preparation, and proofread every draft of the text through to publication. Their sharp eyes prevented innumerable errors from finding a home in the manuscript. Barbara also researched the quotes, and Abbey suggested the title for the book.

We assume complete responsibility for any remaining flaws in this text. We would greatly appreciate your comments, criticisms, corrections, and suggestions for improving the text. Please send us your suggestions for improving and adding to our list of Good Programming Practices, Common Programming Errors, Performance Tips, Portability Tips, and Software Engineering Observations. We will acknowledge all contributors in the next edition of our book. Please address all correspondence to our email address:

`deitel@world.std.com`

or write us as follows:

Harvey M. Deitel (author)
Paul J. Deitel (author)
c/o Computer Science Editor
College Book Editorial
Prentice Hall
Englewood Cliffs, New Jersey 07632

We will respond immediately.

Harvey M. Deitel
Paul J. Deitel

C   HOW TO PROGRAM

1

Computing Concepts

Objectives
- To understand basic computer concepts.
- To become familiar with different types of programming languages.
- To become familiar with the history of the C programming language.
- To become aware of the C Standard Library.
- To understand the C program development environment.
- To appreciate why it is appropriate to learn C in a first programming course.
- To appreciate why C provides a foundation for further study of programming in general and C++ in particular.

Things are always at their best in their beginning.
Blaise Pascal

High thoughts must have high language.
Aristophanes

Our life is frittered away by detail ... Simplify, simplify.
Henry Thoreau

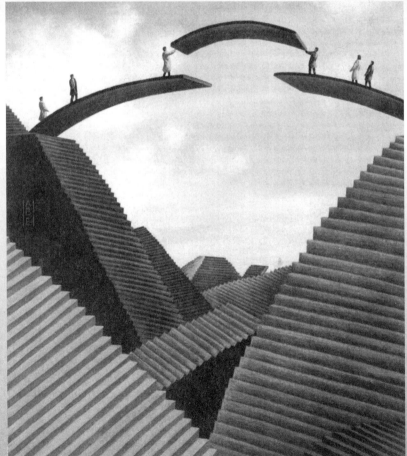

Outline

1.1 Introduction

Welcome to C! We have worked hard to create what we sincerely hope will be an informative and entertaining learning experience for you. C is a difficult language that is normally taught only to experienced programmers, so this book is unique among C textbooks:

- It is appropriate for technically oriented people with little or no programming experience.

- It is appropriate for experienced programmers who want a deep and rigorous treatment of the language.

How can one book appeal to both groups? The answer is that the common core of the book places an emphasis on achieving program *clarity* through the proven techniques of "structured programming." Nonprogrammers will learn programming the "right" way from the beginning. We have attempted to write in a clear and straightforward manner. The book is abundantly illustrated. Perhaps most importantly, the book presents a huge number of working C programs and shows the outputs produced when those programs are run on a computer.

The first four chapters introduce the fundamentals of computing, computer programming, and the C computer programming language. The discussions are wrapped in an introduction to computer programming using the structured approach. Novices who have taken our courses tell us that the material in these chapters presents a solid foundation for the deeper treatment of C in Chapters 5 through 14. Experienced programmers typically read the first four chapters quickly and then discover that the treatment of C in Chapters 5 through 14 is both rigorous and challenging. They particularly appreciate the detailed treatments of pointers, strings, files, and data structures in the later chapters.

Many experienced programmers have told us that they appreciate our treatment of structured programming. Often they have been programming in a structured language like Pascal, but because they were never formally introduced to structured programming, they are not writing the best possible code. As they learn C with this book, they are able to improve their programming style. So whether you are a novice or an experienced programmer, there is much here to inform, entertain, and challenge you.

Most people are familiar with the exciting things computers do. In this course, you will learn how to command computers to do those things. It is *software* (i.e., the instructions you write to command the computer to perform actions and make decisions) that controls computers (often referred to as *hardware*), and one of today's most popular software development languages is C. This text provides an introduction to programming in ANSI C, the version standardized in 1989 in both the United States through the American National Standards Institute (ANSI), and around the world through the International Standards Organization (ISO).

Use of computers is increasing in almost every field of endeavor. In an era of steadily rising costs, computing costs have been decreasing dramatically because of exciting developments in both hardware and software technology. Computers that might have filled large rooms and cost millions of dollars 25 years ago can now be inscribed on the surfaces of silicon chips smaller than a fingernail, and that cost perhaps a few dollars each. Ironically, silicon is one of the most abundant materials on the earth—it is an ingredient in common sand. Silicon chip technology has made computing so economical that approximately 150 million general-purpose computers are in use worldwide helping people in business, industry, government, and in their personal lives. That number could easily double in a few years.

Can C be taught in a first programming course, the intended audience for this book? We think so. Two years ago we took on this challenge when Pascal was the entrenched language in first computer science courses. We wrote *C How to Program,* the first edition of this text. Hundreds of universities worldwide have used *C How to Program.* Courses based on that book have proven to be equally effective to their Pascal-based predecessors. No significant differences have been observed, except that students are better motivated because they know they are more likely to use C rather than Pascal in their upper-level courses, and in their careers. Students learning C also know that they will be better prepared to learn C++ quickly. C++ is a superset of the C language intended for programmers who wish to write object-oriented programs. We will say more about C++ in Section 1.14.

Actually, C++ is receiving so much interest today that we have included a detailed introduction to C++ and object-oriented programming in Chapter 15. An interesting phenomenon occurring in the programming languages marketplace is that many of the key vendors now simply market a combined C/C++ product rather than offering separate products. This gives users the ability to continue programming in C if they wish, and then gradually migrate to C++ when appropriate.

So there you have it! You are about to start on a challenging and hopefully rewarding path. As you proceed, if you would like to communicate with us, send us email over the Internet at **deitel@world.std.com**. We will make every effort to respond quickly. Good luck!

1.2 What Is a Computer?

A *computer* is a device capable of performing computations and making logical decisions at speeds millions, and even billions, of times faster than human beings can. For example, many of today's personal computers can perform tens of millions of additions per second. A person operating a desk calculator might require decades to complete the same number of calculations that a powerful personal computer can perform in one second. (Points to ponder: How would you know whether the person added the numbers correctly? How would you know whether the computer added the numbers correctly?) Today's fastest *supercomputers* can perform hundreds of billions of additions per second—about as many calculations as hundreds of thousands of people could perform in one year! And trillion-instruction-per-second computers are already functioning in research laboratories.

Computers process *data* under the control of sets of instructions called *computer programs*. These computer programs guide the computer through orderly sets of actions specified by people called *computer programmers*.

The various devices (such as the keyboard, screen, disks, memory, and processing units) that comprise a computer system are referred to as *hardware*. The computer programs that run on a computer are referred to as *software*. Hardware costs have been decreasing dramatically in recent years, to the point that personal computers have become a commodity. Unfortunately, software development costs have been rising steadily as programmers develop ever more powerful and complex applications, without being able to make corresponding improvements in the technology of software development. In this book you will learn software development methods that can substantially reduce software development costs and speed the process of developing powerful, high-quality software applications. These methods include *structured programming*, *top-down stepwise refinement*, *functionalization* and, in the last chapter of the book, *object-oriented programming*.

1.3 Computer Organization

Regardless of differences in physical appearance, virtually every computer may be envisioned as being divided into six *logical units* or sections. These are:

1. *Input unit.* This is the "receiving" section of the computer. It obtains information (data and computer programs) from various *input devices* and places this information at the disposal of the other units so that the information may be pro-

cessed. Most information is entered into computers today through typewriter-like keyboards.

2. *Output unit.* This is the "shipping" section of the computer. It takes information that has been processed by the computer and places it on various *output devices* to make the information available for use outside the computer. Most information is output from computers today by displaying it on screens or by printing it on paper.

3. *Memory unit.* This is the rapid access, relatively low-capacity "warehouse" section of the computer. It retains information that has been entered through the input unit so that the information may be made immediately available for processing when it is needed. The memory unit also retains information that has already been processed until that information can be placed on output devices by the output unit. The memory unit is often called either *memory* or *primary memory.*

4. *Arithmetic and logic unit (ALU).* This is the "manufacturing" section of the computer. It is responsible for performing calculations such as addition, subtraction, multiplication, and division. It contains the decision mechanisms that allow the computer, for example, to compare two items from the memory unit to determine whether or not they are equal.

5. *Central processing unit (CPU).* This is the "administrative" section of the computer. It is the computer's coordinator and is responsible for supervising the operation of the other sections. The CPU tells the input unit when information should be read into the memory unit, tells the ALU when information from the memory unit should be utilized in calculations, and tells the output unit when to send information from the memory unit to certain output devices.

6. *Secondary storage unit.* This is the long-term, high-capacity "warehouse" section of the computer. Programs or data not actively being used by the other units are normally placed on secondary storage devices (such as disks) until they are again needed, possibly hours, days, months, or even years later.

1.4 Batch Processing, Multiprogramming, and Timesharing

Early computers were capable of performing only one *job* or *task* at a time. This form of computer operation is often called single-user *batch processing*. The computer runs a single program at a time while processing data in groups or *batches*. In these early systems, users generally submitted their jobs to the computer center on decks of punched cards. The users often had to wait hours or even days before printouts were returned to their desks.

As computers became more powerful, it became evident that single-user batch processing rarely utilized the computer's resources efficiently. Instead, it was thought that many jobs or tasks could be made to *share* the resources of the computer to achieve better utilization. This is called *multiprogramming*. Multiprogramming involves the "simultaneous" operation of many jobs on the computer—the computer shares its resources among the jobs competing for its attention. With early multiprogramming systems, users still submitted jobs on decks of punched cards and waited hours or days for results.

In the 1960s, several groups in industry and the universities pioneered the concept of *timesharing*. Timesharing is a special case of multiprogramming in which users access the computer through input/output devices or *terminals*. In a typical timesharing computer system, there may be dozens or even hundreds of users sharing the computer at once. The computer does not actually run all the users simultaneously. Rather, it runs a small portion of one user's job and then moves on to service the next user. The computer does this so quickly that it may provide service to each user several times per second. Thus the users *appear* to be running simultaneously.

1.5 Personal Computing, Distributed Computing, and Client/Server Computing

In 1977, Apple Computer popularized the phenomenon of *personal computing*. Initially, it was a hobbyist's dream. Computers became economical enough for people to buy them for their own personal or business use. In 1981, IBM, the world's largest computer vendor, introduced the IBM Personal Computer. Literally overnight, personal computing became legitimate in business, industry, and government organizations.

But these computers were "standalone" units—people did their work on their own machines and then transported disks back and forth to share information. Although early personal computers were not powerful enough to timeshare several users, these machines could be linked together in computer networks, sometimes over telephone lines and sometimes in local area networks within an organization. This led to the phenomenon of *distributed computing* in which an organization's computing workload, instead of being performed strictly at some central computer installation, is distributed over networks to the sites at which the real work of the organization is performed. Personal computers were powerful enough to handle the computing requirements of individual users, and to handle the basic communications tasks of passing information back and forth electronically.

Today's most powerful personal computers are as powerful as the million dollar machines of just a decade ago. The most powerful desktop machines—called *workstations*—provide individual users with enormous capabilities. Information is easily shared across computer networks where some computers called *file servers* offer a common store of programs and data that may be used by *client* computers distributed throughout the network, hence the term *client/server computing*. C and C++ have become the programming languages of choice for writing software for operating systems, for computer networking, and for distributed client/server applications.

1.6 Machine Languages, Assembly Languages, and High-level Languages

Programmers write instructions in various programming languages, some directly understandable by the computer and others that require intermediate *translation* steps. Hundreds of computer languages are in use today. These may be divided into three general types:

1. Machine languages

2.   Assembly languages

3.   High-level languages

Any computer can directly understand only its own *machine language.* Machine language is the "natural language" of a particular computer. It is closely related to the hardware design of that computer. Machine languages generally consist of strings of numbers (ultimately reduced to 1s and 0s) that instruct computers to perform their most elementary operations one at a time. Machine languages are *machine-dependent,* i.e., a particular machine language can be used on only one type of computer. Machine languages are cumbersome for humans, as can be seen by the following section of a machine language program that adds overtime pay to base pay and stores the result in gross pay.

```
+1300042774
+1400593419
+1200274027
```

As computers became more popular, it became apparent that machine language programming was simply too slow and tedious for most programmers. Instead of using the strings of numbers that computers could directly understand, programmers began using English-like abbreviations to represent the elementary operations of the computer. These English-like abbreviations formed the basis of *assembly languages. Translator programs* called *assemblers* were developed to convert assembly language programs to machine language at computer speeds. The following section of an assembly language program also adds overtime pay to base pay and stores the result in gross pay, but more clearly than its machine language equivalent:

```
LOAD      BASEPAY
ADD       OVERPAY
STORE     GROSSPAY
```

Computer usage increased rapidly with the advent of assembly languages, but these still required many instructions to accomplish even the simplest tasks. To speed the programming process, *high-level languages* were developed in which single statements could be written to accomplish substantial tasks. The translator programs that convert high-level language programs into machine language are called *compilers.* High-level languages allow programmers to write instructions that look almost like everyday English and contain commonly used mathematical notations. A payroll program written in a high-level language might contain a statement such as:

```
grossPay = basePay + overTimePay
```

Obviously, high-level languages are much more desirable from the programmer's standpoint than either machine languages or assembly languages. C and C++ are among the most powerful and most widely-used high-level languages.

1.7 The History of C

C evolved from two previous languages, BCPL and B. BCPL was developed in 1967 by Martin Richards as a language for writing operating systems software and compilers. Ken

Thompson modeled many features in his language B after their counterparts in BCPL and used B to create early versions of the UNIX operating system at Bell Laboratories in 1970 on a DEC PDP-7 computer. Both BCPL and B were "typeless" languages—every data item occupied one "word" in memory and the burden of treating a data item as a whole number or a real number, for example, fell on the shoulders of the programmer.

The C language was evolved from B by Dennis Ritchie at Bell Laboratories and was originally implemented on a DEC PDP-11 computer in 1972. C initially became widely known as the development language of the UNIX operating system. Today, virtually all new major operating systems are written in C and/or C++. Over the past two decades, C has become available for most computers. C is hardware independent. With careful design, it is possible to write programs in C that are *portable* to most computers. C uses many of the important concepts of BCPL and B while adding data typing and other powerful features.

By the late 1970s, C had evolved into what is now referred to as "traditional C." The publication in 1978 of Kernighan and Ritchie's book, *The C Programming Language,* brought wide attention to the language. This publication became one of the most successful computer science books of all time.

The rapid expansion of C over various types of computers (sometimes called *hardware platforms*) led to many variations. These were similar, but often incompatible. This was a serious problem for program developers who needed to develop code that would run on several platforms. It became clear that a standard version of C was needed. In 1983, the X3J11 technical committee was created under the American National Standards Committee on Computers and Information Processing (X3) to "provide an unambiguous and machine-independent definition of the language." In 1989, the standard was approved. The document is referred to as ANSI/ISO 9899: 1990. Copies of this document may be ordered from the American National Standards Institute whose address is listed in the Preface to this text. The second edition of Kernighan and Ritchie, published in 1988, reflects this version called ANSI C, now used worldwide (Ke88).

Portability Tip 1.1

Because C is a hardware-independent, widely available language, applications written in C can run with little or no modifications an a wide range of different computer systems.

1.8 The C Standard Library

As you will learn in Chapter 5, C programs consist of modules or pieces called *functions.* You can program all the functions you need to form a C program, but most C programmers take advantage of a rich collection of existing functions called the *C Standard Library.* Thus, there are really two pieces to learning the C "world." The first is learning the C language itself, and the second is learning how to use the functions in the C Standard Library. Throughout the book, we discuss many of these functions. Appendix B (condensed and adapted from the ANSI C standard document itself) enumerates all the functions available in the C standard library. The book by Plauger (Pl92) is must reading for programmers who need a deep understanding of the library functions, how to implement them, and how to use them to write portable code.

You will be encouraged in this course to use a *building block approach* to creating programs. Avoid reinventing the wheel. Use existing pieces—this is called *software reusability* and it is a key to the developing field of object-oriented programming as we will see in Chapter 15. When programming in C you will typically use the following building blocks:

- C Standard Library functions

- Functions you create yourself

- Functions other people have created and made available to you

The advantage of creating your own functions is that you will know exactly how they work. You will be able to examine the C code. The disadvantage is the time-consuming effort that goes into designing and developing new functions.

Using existing functions avoids reinventing the wheel. In the case of the ANSI standard functions, you know that they are carefully written, and you know that because you are using functions that are available on virtually all ANSI C implementations, your programs will have a greater chance of being portable.

Performance Tip 1.1

Using ANSI standard library functions instead of writing your own comparable versions can improve program performance because these functions are carefully written to perform efficiently.

Portability Tip 1.2

Using ANSI standard library functions instead of writing your own comparable versions can improve program portability because these functions are implemented on virtually all ANSI C implementations.

1.9　Other High-level Languages

Hundreds of high-level languages have been developed, but only a few have achieved broad acceptance. *FORTRAN* (FORmula TRANslator) was developed by IBM between 1954 and 1957 to be used for scientific and engineering applications that require complex mathematical computations. FORTRAN is still widely used.

COBOL (COmmon Business Oriented Language) was developed in 1959 by a group of computer manufacturers and government and industrial computer users. COBOL is used primarily for commercial applications that require precise and efficient manipulation of large amounts of data. Today, more than half of all business software is still programmed in COBOL. Over one million people are employed as COBOL programmers.

Pascal was designed at about the same time as C. It was intended for academic use. We will say more about Pascal in the next section.

1.10　Structured Programming

During the 1960s, many large software development efforts encountered severe difficulties. Software schedules were typically late, costs greatly exceeded budgets, and the finished products were unreliable. People began to realize that software development was a far more complex activity than they had imagined. Research activity in the 1960s resulted in the evolution of *structured programming*—a disciplined approach to writing programs that are clear, demonstrably correct, and easy to modify. Chapter 3 and Chapter 4 overview the principles of structured programming. The remainder of the text discusses the development of structured C programs.

One of the more tangible results of this research was the development of the Pascal programming language by Professor Nicklaus Wirth in 1971. Pascal, named after the seventeenth-century mathematician and philosopher Blaise Pascal, was designed for teaching structured programming in academic environments, and rapidly became the preferred introductory programming language in most universities. Unfortunately, the language lacks many features needed to make it useful in commercial, industrial, and government applications, so it has not been widely accepted in these environments. History may well record that the real significance of Pascal was its selection as the base of the *Ada* programming language.

Ada was developed under the sponsorship of the United States Department of Defense (DOD) during the 1970s and early 1980s. Hundreds of separate languages were being used to produce DOD's massive command and control software systems. DOD wanted a single language that would meet its needs. Pascal was chosen as a base, but the final Ada language is quite different from Pascal. The language was named after Lady Ada Lovelace, daughter of the poet Lord Byron. Lady Lovelace is generally credited with writing the world's first computer program in the early 1800s. One important capability of Ada is called *multitasking*; this allows programmers to specify that many activities are to occur in parallel. Other widely used high-level languages we have discussed—including C and C++—allow the programmer to write programs that perform only one activity at a time. It remains to be seen if Ada will meet its goals of producing reliable software and substantially reducing software development and maintenance costs.

1.11 The Basics of the C Environment

All C systems generally consist of three parts: the environment, the language, and the C Standard Library. The following discussion explains the typical C development environment shown in Figure 1.1.

C programs typically go through six phases to be executed (Fig. 1.1). These are: *edit, preprocess, compile, link, load,* and *execute.* We concentrate on a typical UNIX-based C system here. If you are not using a UNIX system, refer to the manuals for your system, or ask your instructor how to accomplish these tasks in your environment.

The first phase consists of editing a file. This is accomplished with an *editor program.* The programmer types a C program with the editor and makes corrections if necessary. The program is then stored on a secondary storage device such as a disk. C program file names should end with the **.c** extension. Two editors widely used on UNIX systems are **vi** and **emacs**. C/C++ software packages such as Borland C++ for IBM PCs and compatibles, and Symantec C++ for the Apple Macintosh have built-in editors that are smoothly integrated into the programming environment. We assume that the reader knows how to edit a program.

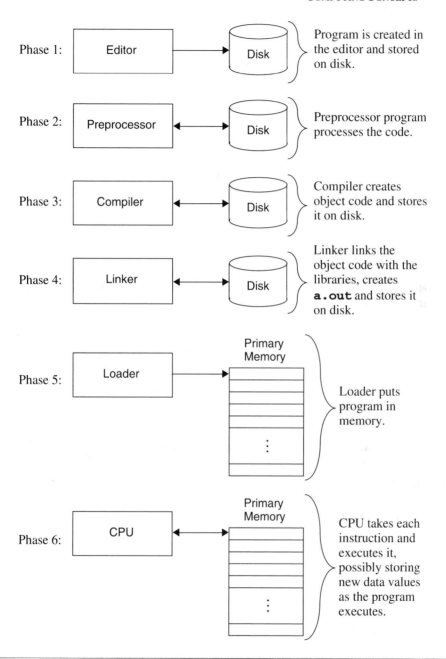

Fig. 1.1   A typical C environment.

Next, the programmer gives the command to *compile* the program. The compiler translates the C program into machine language code (also referred to as *object code*). In a C system, a *preprocessor* program automatically executes before the translation phase begins. The C preprocessor obeys special commands called *preprocessor directives* which indicate that certain manipulations are to be performed on the program before compilation. These manipulations usually consist of including other files in the file to be compiled and replacing special symbols with program text. The most common preprocessor directives are discussed in the early chapters; a detailed discussion of all the preprocessor features appears in Chapter 13. The preprocessor is automatically invoked by the compiler before the program is converted to machine language.

The fourth phase is called *linking*. C programs typically contain references to functions defined elsewhere such as in the standard libraries or in the libraries of a group of programmers working on a particular project. Thus, the object code produced by the C compiler typically contains "holes" due to these missing parts. A *linker* links the object code with the code for the missing functions to produce an *executable image* (with no missing pieces). On a typical UNIX-based system, the command to compile and link a program is **cc**. For example, to compile and link a program named **welcome.c** type

```
cc welcome.c
```

at the UNIX prompt and press the return key. If the program compiles and links correctly, a file called **a.out** is produced. This is the executable image of our **welcome.c** program.

The fifth phase is called *loading*. Before a program can be executed, the program must first be placed in memory. This is done by the *loader* which takes the executable image from disk and transfers it to memory.

Finally, the computer, under the control of its CPU, executes the program one instruction at a time. To load and execute the program on a UNIX system, we type **a.out** at the UNIX prompt and press the return key.

Most programs in C input and/or output data. Certain C functions take their input from **stdin** (the *standard input device*) which is normally assigned to the keyboard, but **stdin** can be connected to another device. Data is output to **stdout** (the *standard output device*) which is normally the computer screen, but can be connected to another device. When we say that a program prints a result, we normally mean that the result is displayed on a screen. Data may be output to other devices such as disks and hardcopy printers. There is also a *standard error device* referred to as **stderr**. The **stderr** device (normally connected to the screen) is used for displaying error messages. It is common to route regular output data, i.e., **stdout**, to a device other than the screen while keeping **stderr** assigned to the screen so that the user can immediately be informed of errors.

1.12 General Notes About C and this Book

C is a difficult language. Experienced C programmers sometimes take pride in being able to create weird, contorted, convoluted usages of the language. This is a poor programming practice. It makes programs difficult to read, more likely to behave strangely, and more difficult to test and debug. This book is geared for novice programmers, so we stress writing clear, well-structured programs. One of our key goals in this book is achieving program *clarity* through the proven techniques of structured programming and through the many related good programming practices.

Good Programming Practice 1.1

Write your C programs in a simple and straightforward manner. This is sometimes referred to as KIS ("keep it simple"). Do not "stretch" the language by trying "weirdisms."

You may hear that C is a portable language, and that programs written in C can run on many different computers. *Portability is an elusive goal.* The ANSI standard document (An90) lists 11 pages of subtle portability issues. Complete books have been written on the subject of portability in C (Ja89) (Ra90).

Portability Tip 1.3

Although it is possible to write portable programs, there are many problems between different C implementations and different computers that make portability difficult to achieve. Simply writing programs in C does not guarantee portability.

We have done a careful walkthrough of the ANSI C standard document and audited our presentation against it for completeness and accuracy. However, C is a very rich language, and there are some subtleties in the language and some advanced subjects we have not covered. If you need additional technical details on ANSI C, we suggest that you read the ANSI C standard document itself or the reference manual in Kernighan and Ritchie (Ke88).

We have limited our discussions to ANSI C. Many features of ANSI C are not compatible with older C implementations, so you may find that some of the programs in this text do not work on older C compilers.

Good Programming Practice 1.2

Read the manuals for the version of C you are using. Reference these manuals frequently to be sure you are aware of the rich collection of C features and that you are using these features correctly.

Good Programming Practice 1.3

Your computer and compiler are good teachers. If you are not sure how a feature of C works, write a sample program with that feature, compile and run the program, and see what happens.

1.13 Concurrent C

Other versions of C have been developed through continuing research efforts at Bell Laboratories. Gehani (Ge89) has developed *Concurrent C*—a C superset that includes capabilities for specifying that multiple activities can be performed in parallel. Languages like Concurrent C and operating systems features that support parallelism in user applications will become increasingly popular in the next decade as the use of *multiprocessors* (i.e., computers with more than one CPU) increases. As of this writing, Concurrent C is still primarily a research language. Operating systems courses and textbooks (De90) usually include substantial treatments of concurrent programming.

1.14 Object-Oriented Programming and C++

Another C superset, namely *C++*, was developed by Stroustrup (St86) at Bell Laboratories. C++ provides a number of features that "spruce up" the C language. But more importantly, it provides capabilities to do *object-oriented programming.*

Objects are essentially reusable software *components* that model items in the real world. There is a revolution brewing in the software community. Building software quickly, correctly, and economically remains an elusive goal, and this at a time when demands for new and more powerful software are soaring.

Software developers are discovering that using a modular, object-oriented design and implementation approach can make software development groups 10 to 100 times more productive than is possible with conventional programming techniques.

Many object-oriented languages have been developed. It is widely believed that C++ will become the dominant systems-implementation language in the mid-to-late 1990s.

Many people feel that the best educational strategy today is to master C, then study C++. Therefore, we have provided Chapters 15 through 21 introducing object-oriented programming and C++. We hope that the reader finds this valuable, and that the chapter will encourage the reader to pursue further study of C++ after completing this book.

Summary

- It is software (i.e., the instructions you write to command the computer to perform actions and make decisions) that controls computers (often referred to as hardware).

- ANSI C is the version of the C programming language standardized in 1989 in both the United States through the American National Standards Institute (ANSI), and around the world through the International Standards Organization (ISO).

- Computers that might have filled large rooms and cost millions of dollars 25 years ago can now be inscribed on the surfaces of silicon chips smaller than a fingernail, and that cost perhaps a few dollars each.

- Approximately 150 million general-purpose computers are in use worldwide helping people in business, industry, government, and in their personal lives. That number could easily double in a few years.

- A computer is a device capable of performing computations and making logical decisions at speeds millions, and even billions, of times faster than human beings can.

- Computers process data under the control of computer programs.

- The various devices (such as the keyboard, screen, disks, memory, and processing units) that comprise a computer system are referred to as hardware.

- The computer programs that run on a computer are referred to as software.

- The input unit is the "receiving" section of the computer. Most information is entered into computers today through typewriter-like keyboards.

- The output unit is the "shipping" section of the computer. Most information is output from computers today by displaying it on screens or by printing it on paper.

- The memory unit is the "warehouse" section of the computer, and is often called either memory or primary memory.

- The arithmetic and logic unit (ALU) performs calculations and makes decisions.

- The central processing unit (CPU) is the computer's coordinator and is responsible for supervising the operation of the other sections.

- Programs or data not actively being used by the other units are normally placed on secondary storage devices (such as disks) until they are again needed.

- In single-user batch processing, the computer runs a single program at a time while processing data in groups or batches.

- Multiprogramming involves the "simultaneous" operation of many jobs on the computer—the computer shares its resources among the jobs.

- Timesharing is a special case of multiprogramming in which users access the computer through terminals. The users appear to be running simultaneously.

- With distributed computing, an organization's computing is distributed via networking to the sites at which the real work of the organization is performed.

- File servers store programs and data that may be shared by client computers distributed throughout the network, hence the term client/server computing.

- Any computer can directly understand only its own machine language.

- Machine languages generally consist of strings of numbers (ultimately reduced to 1s and 0s) that instruct computers to perform their most elementary operations one at a time. Machine languages are machine-dependent.

- English-like abbreviations form the basis of assembly languages. Assemblers translate assembly language programs into machine language.

- Compilers translate high-level language programs into machine language. High-level languages contain English words and conventional mathematical notations.

- C is known as the development language of the UNIX operating system.

- It is possible to write programs in C that are portable to most computers.

- The ANSI C standard was approved in 1989.

- FORTRAN (FORmula TRANslator) is used for mathematical applications.

- COBOL (COmmon Business Oriented Language) is used primarily for commercial applications that require precise and efficient manipulation of large amounts of data.

- Structured programming is a disciplined approach to writing programs that are clear, demonstrably correct, and easy to modify.

- Pascal was designed for teaching structured programming in academic environments.

- Ada was developed under the sponsorship of the United States Department of Defense (DOD) using Pascal as a base.

- Ada *multitasking* allows programmers to specify parallel activities.

- All C systems consist of three parts: the environment, the language, and the standard libraries. Library functions are not part of the C language itself; these functions perform operations such as input/output and mathematical calculations.

- C programs typically go through six phases to be executed: edit, preprocess, compile, link, load, and execute.

- The programmer types a program with an editor, and makes corrections if necessary.

- A compiler translates a C program into machine language code (or object code).

- The C preprocessor obeys preprocessor directives which typically indicate that other files are to be included in the file to be compiled, and special symbols are to be replaced with program text.

- A linker links the object code with the code for missing functions to produce an executable image (with no missing pieces).

- A loader takes an executable image from disk and transfers it to memory.

- A computer, under the control of its CPU, executes a program one instruction at a time.

- Certain C functions (such as **scanf**) take their input from **stdin** (the standard input device) which is normally assigned to the keyboard.

- Data is output to **stdout** (the standard output device) which is normally the computer screen.

- There is also a standard error device referred to as **stderr**. The **stderr** device (normally the screen) is used for displaying error messages.

- Although it is possible to write portable programs, there are many problems between different C implementations and different computers than can make portability difficult to achieve.

- Concurrent C is a C superset that includes capabilities for specifying that multiple activities can be performed in parallel.

- C++ provides capabilities to do object-oriented programming.

- Objects are essentially reusable software components that model items in the real world.

- It is widely believed that C++ will become the dominant systems implementation language in the mid-to-late 1990s.

Terminology

.c extension	arithmetic and logic unit (ALU)
Ada	assembler
ALU	assembly language
ANSI C	batch processing

building block approach

C

C preprocessor

C Standard Library

C++

central processing unit (CPU)

clarity

client

client/server computing

COBOL

compiler

computer

computer program

computer programmer

Concurrent C

CPU

data

distributed computing

editor

environment

executable image

execute a program

file server

FORTRAN

function

functionalization

hardware

hardware platform

high-level language

input device

input unit

input/output (I/O)

linker

loader

logical units

machine dependent

machine independent

machine language

memory

memory unit

multiprocessor

multiprogramming

multitasking

natural language of a computer

object

object code

object-oriented programming

output device

output unit

Pascal

personal computer

portability

primary memory

programming language

run a program

screen

software

software reusability

standard error (**stderr**)

standard input (**stdin**)

standard output (**stdout**)

stored program

structured programming

supercomputer

task

terminal

timesharing

top-down, stepwise refinement

translator program

UNIX

workstation

Good Programming Practices

1.1   Write your C programs in a simple and straightforward manner. This is sometimes referred to as KIS ("keep it simple"). Do not "stretch" the language by trying "weirdisms."

1.2   Read the manuals for the version of C you are using. Reference these manuals frequently to be sure you are aware of the rich collection of C features and that you are using these features correctly.

1.3   Your computer and compiler are good teachers. If you are not sure how a feature of C works, write a sample program with that feature, compile and run the program, and see what happens.

Portability Tips

1.1   Because C is a hardware-independent, widely available language, applications written in C can run with little or no modifications on a wide range of different computer systems.

1.2   Using ANSI standard library functions instead of writing your own comparable versions can improve program portability because these functions are implemented on virtually all ANSI C implementations.

1.3   Although it is possible to write portable programs, there are many problems between different C implementations and different computers that make portability difficult to achieve. Simply writing programs in C does not guarantee portability.

Performance Tips

1.1   Using ANSI standard library functions instead of writing your own comparable versions can improve program performance because these functions are carefully written to perform efficiently.

Self-Review Exercises

1.1   Fill in the blanks in each of the following:

a) The company that brought the phenomenon of personal computing to the world was _____.

b) The computer that made personal computing legitimate in business and industry was the _____.

c) Computers process data under the control of sets of instructions called computer _____.

d) The six key logical units of the computer are the _____, _____, _____, _____, _____, and the _____.

e) _____ is a special case of multiprogramming in which users access the computer through devices called terminals.

f) The three classes of languages discussed in the chapter are _____, _____, and _____.

g) The programs that translate high-level language programs into machine language are called _____.

h) C is widely known as the development language of the _____ operating system.

i) This book presents the version of C called _____ C that was recently standardized through the American National Standards Institute.

j) The _____ language was developed by Wirth for teaching structured programming in universities.

k) The Department of Defense developed the Ada language with a capability called _____ which allows programmers to specify that many activities can proceed in parallel.

1.2   Fill in the blanks in each of the following sentences about the C environment.

a) C programs are normally typed into a computer using an _____ program.

b) In a C system, a _____ program automatically executes before the translation phase begins.

c) The two most common kinds of preprocessor directives are _____ and _____.

d) The _____ program combines the output of the compiler with various library functions to produce an executable image.

e) The _____ program transfers the executable image from disk to memory.

f) To load and execute the most recently compiled program on a UNIX system, type _____.

Answers to Self-Review Exercises

1.1   a) Apple. b) IBM Personal Computer. c) programs. d) input unit, output unit, memory unit, arithmetic and logic unit (ALU), central processing unit (CPU), secondary storage unit. e) timesharing. f) machine languages, assembly languages, high-level languages. g) compilers. h) UNIX. i) ANSI. j) Pascal. k) multitasking.

1.2   a) editor. b) preprocessor. c) including other files in the file to be compiled, replacing special symbols with program text. d) linker. e) loader. f) `a.out`.

Exercises

1.3.   Categorize each of the following items as either hardware or software:
  a) CPU
  b) C compiler
  c) ALU
  d) C preprocessor
  e) input unit
  f) a word processor program

1.4.   Why might you want to write a program in a machine-independent language instead of a machine-dependent language? Why might a machine-dependent language be more appropriate for writing certain types of programs?

1.5.   Translator programs such as assemblers and compilers convert programs from one language (referred to as the *source* language) to another language (referred to as the *object* language). Determine which of the following statements are true and which are false:
  a) A compiler translates high-level language programs into object language.
  b) An assembler translates source language programs into machine language programs.
  c) A compiler converts source language programs into object language programs.
  d) High-level languages are generally machine-dependent.
  e) A machine language program requires translation before the program can be run on a computer.

1.6.   Fill in the blanks in each of the following statements:
  a) Devices from which users access timesharing computer systems are usually called _____.
  b) A computer program that converts assembly language programs to machine language programs is called _____.
  c) The logical unit of the computer that receives information from outside the computer for use by the computer is called _____.
  d) The process of instructing the computer to solve specific problems is called _____.
  e) What type of computer language uses English-like abbreviations for machine language instructions? _____.
  f) What are the six logical units of the computer? _____.
  g) Which logical unit of the computer sends information that has already been processed by the computer to various devices so that the information may be used outside the computer? _____.

   h) The general name for a program that converts programs written in a certain computer language into machine language is _____.

   i) Which logical unit of the computer retains information? _____.

   j) Which logical unit of the computer performs calculations? _____.

   k) Which logical unit of the computer makes logical decisions? _____.

   l) The commonly used abbreviation for the computer's control unit is _____.

   m) The level of computer language most convenient to the programmer for writing programs quickly and easily is _____.

   n) The most common business-oriented language in wide use today is _____.

   o) The only language that a computer can directly understand is called that computer's _____.

   p) Which logical unit of the computer coordinates the activities of all the other logical units? _____.

1.7.   State whether each of the following is true or false. Explain your answers.

   a) Machine languages are generally machine-dependent.

   b) Timesharing truly runs several users simultaneously on a computer.

   c) Like other high-level languages, C is generally considered to be machine-independent.

1.8   Discuss the meaning of each of the following names in the UNIX environment:

   a) `stdin`

   b) `stdout`

   c) `stderr`

1.9   What key capability is provided in Concurrent C that is not available in ANSI C?

1.10   Why is so much attention today focused on object-oriented programming in general and C++ in particular?

Recommended Reading

(An90)   ANSI, *American National Standard for Information Systems—Programming Language C (ANSI Document ANSI/ISO 9899: 1990),* New York, NY: American National Standards Institute, 1990.

   This is the defining document for ANSI C. The document is available for sale from the American National Standards Institute, 1430 Broadway, New York, New York 10018.

(De90)   Deitel, H. M., *Operating Systems* (Second Edition), Reading, MA: Addison-Wesley Publishing Company, 1990.

   A textbook for the traditional computer science course in operating systems. Chapters 4 and 5 present an extensive discussion of concurrent programming.

(Ge89)   Gehani, N., and W. D. Roome, *The Concurrent C Programming Language,* Summit, NJ: Silicon Press, 1989.

   This is the defining book for Concurrent C—a C language superset that enables programmers to specify parallel execution of multiple activities. Also included is a summary of Concurrent C++.

(Ja89)   Jaeschke, R., *Portability and the C Language,* Indianapolis, IN: Hayden Books, 1989.

   This book discusses writing portable programs in C. Jaeschke served on both the ANSI and ISO C standards committees.

(Ke88)   Kernighan, B. W., and D. M. Ritchie, *The C Programming Language* (Second Edition), Englewood Cliffs, NJ: Prentice Hall, 1988.

This book is the classic in its field. The book is extensively used in C courses and seminars for established programmers, and includes an excellent reference manual. Ritchie is the author of the C language and one of the co-designers of the UNIX operating system.

(Pl92)   Plauger, P. J., *The Standard C Library,* Englewood Cliffs, NJ: Prentice Hall, 1992.

Defines and demonstrates the use of the functions in the C standard library. Plauger served as the head of the library subcommittee of the committee that developed the ANSI C standard, and he serves as the Convenor of the ISO committee evolving C.

(Ra90)   Rabinowitz, H., and C. Schaap, *Portable C,* Englewood Cliffs, NJ: Prentice Hall, 1990.

This book was developed for a course on portability taught at AT&T Bell Laboratories. Rabinowitz is with NYNEX Corporation's Artificial Intelligence Laboratory, and Schaap is a principal at Delft Consulting Corporation.

(Ri78)   Ritchie, D. M.; S. C. Johnson; M. E. Lesk; and B. W. Kernighan, "UNIX Time-Sharing System: The C Programming Language," *The Bell System Technical Journal,* Vol. 57, No. 6, Part 2, July–August 1978, pp. 1991–2019.

This is one of the classic articles introducing the C language. It appeared in a special issue of the *Bell System Technical Journal* devoted to the "UNIX Time-Sharing System."

(Ri84)   Ritchie, D. M., "The UNIX System: The Evolution of the UNIX Time-Sharing System," *AT&T Bell Laboratories Technical Journal,* Vol. 63, No. 8, Part 2, October 1984, pp. 1577–1593.

A classic article on the UNIX operating system. This article appeared in a special edition of the *Bell System Technical Journal* completely devoted to "The UNIX System."

(Ro84)   Rosler, L., "The UNIX System: The Evolution of C—Past and Future," *AT&T Bell Laboratories Technical Journal,* Vol. 63, No. 8, Part 2, October 1984, pp. 1685–1699.

An excellent article to follow (Ri78) for the reader interested in tracing the history of C and the roots of the ANSI C standardization effort. It appeared in a special edition of the *Bell System Technical Journal* devoted to "The UNIX System."

(St84)   Stroustrup, B., "The UNIX System: Data Abstraction in C," *AT&T Bell Laboratories Technical Journal,* Vol. 63, No. 8, Part 2, October 1984, pp. 1701–1732.

The classic article introducing C++. It appeared in a special edition of the *Bell System Technical Journal* devoted to "The UNIX System."

(St91)   Stroustrup, B. *The C++ Programming Language (*Second Edition*),* Reading, MA: Addison-Wesley Series in Computer Science, 1991.

This book is the defining reference for C++, a C superset that includes various enhancements to C, especially features for object-oriented programming. Stroustrup developed C++ at AT&T Bell Laboratories.

(To89)   Tondo, C. L., and S. E. Gimpel, *The C Answer Book,* Englewood Cliffs, NJ: Prentice Hall, 1989.

This unique book provides answers to the exercises in Kernighan and Ritchie (Ke88). The authors demonstrate an exemplary programming style, and provide insights into their problem solving approaches and design decisions. Tondo is with IBM Corporation and Nova University in Ft. Lauderdale, Florida. Gimpel is a consultant.

2

Introduction to C Programming

Objectives

- To be able to write simple computer programs in C.
- To be able to use simple input and output statements.
- To become familiar with fundamental data types.
- To understand computer memory concepts.
- To be able to use arithmetic operators.
- To understand the precedence of arithmetic operators.
- To be able to write simple decision-making statements.

What's in a name? That which we call a rose
By any other name would smell as sweet.
William Shakespeare
Romeo and Juliet

I only took the regular course ... the different branches of arithmetic—Ambition, Distraction, Uglification, and Derision.
Lewis Carroll

Precedents deliberately established by wise men are entitled to great weight.
Henry Clay

Outline

2.1 Introduction

The C language facilitates a structured and disciplined approach to computer program design. In this chapter we introduce C programming and present several examples that illustrate many important features of C. Each example is carefully analyzed one statement at a time. In Chapter 3 and Chapter 4 we present an introduction to *structured programming* in C. We then use the structured approach throughout the remainder of the text.

2.2 A Simple C Program: Printing a Line of Text

C uses some notations that may appear strange to people who have not programmed computers. We begin by considering a simple C program. Our first example prints a line of text. The program and the program's screen output are shown in Fig. 2.1.

Even though this program is simple, it illustrates several important features of the C language. We now consider each line of the program in detail. The line

```
/* A first program in C */

main()
{
    printf("Welcome to C!\n");
}
```

```
Welcome to C!
```

Fig. 2.1   Text printing program.

```
/* A first program in C */
```

begins with **/*** and ends with ***/** indicating that the line is a *comment*. Programmers insert comments to *document* programs and improve program readability. Comments do not cause the computer to perform any action when the program is run. Comments are ignored by the C compiler and do not cause any machine language object code to be generated. The comment **A first program in C** simply describes the purpose of the program. Comments also help other people read and understand your program, but too many comments can make a program difficult to read.

Common Programming Error 2.1

Forgetting to terminate a comment with ***/**.

Common Programming Error 2.2

Starting a comment with the characters ***/** *or ending a comment with the characters* **/***.

The line

```
main()
```

is a part of every C program. The parentheses after **main** indicate that **main** is a program building block called a *function*. C programs contain one or more functions, one of which must be **main**. Every program in C begins executing at the function **main**.

Good Programming Practice 2.1

Every function should be preceded by a comment describing the purpose of the function.

The *left brace,* **{**, must begin the *body* of every function. A corresponding *right brace* must end each function. This pair of braces and the portion of the program between the braces is also called a *block*. The block is an important program unit in C.

The line

```
printf("Welcome to C!\n");
```

instructs the computer to perform an *action*, namely to print on the screen the *string* of characters marked by the quotation marks. A string is sometimes called a *character string*, a *message* or a *literal*. The entire line, including **printf**, its *arguments* within the parentheses, and the *semicolon* (**;**), is called a *statement*. Every statement must end with a semicolon (also known as the *statement terminator*). When the preceding **printf** statement is executed, it prints the message **Welcome to C!** on the screen. The characters normally print exactly as they appear between the double quotes in the **printf** statement. Notice that the characters **\n** were not printed on the screen. The backslash (****) is called an *escape character*. It indicates that **printf** is supposed to do something out of the ordinary. When encountering a backslash, **printf** looks ahead at the next character and combines it with the backslash to form an *escape sequence*. The escape sequence **\n** means *newline,* and it causes the cursor to position to the beginning of the next line on the screen. Some other common escape sequences are listed in Fig. 2.2. The **printf** function is one of many functions provided in the *C Standard Library* (listed in Appendix B).

Escape Sequence	Description
`\n`	Newline. Position the cursor at the beginning of the next line.
`\t`	Horizontal tab. Move the cursor to the next tab stop.
`\r`	Carriage return. Position the cursor to the beginning of the current line; do not advance to the next line.
`\a`	Alert. Sound the system bell.
`\\`	Backslash. Print a backslash character in a `printf` statement.
`\"`	Double quote. Print a double quote character in a `printf` statement.

Fig. 2.2   Some common escape sequences.

The last two escape sequences in Fig. 2.2 may seem strange. Because the backslash has special meaning to `printf`, i.e., `printf` recognizes it as an escape character rather than as a character to be printed, we use a double backslash (`\\`) to indicate that a single backslash is to be printed. Printing a double quote also presents a problem to `printf` because it normally assumes the double quote is marking the boundary of a string, and that the double quote itself should not in fact be printed. By using the escape sequence `\"` we inform `printf` to print a double quote.

The *right brace*, `}`, indicates that the end of `main` has been reached.

Common Programming Error 2.3

Typing the name of the output function `printf` *as* `print` *in a program.*

We said that `printf` causes the computer to perform an *action.* As any program executes, it performs a variety of actions and the program makes *decisions*. At the end of this chapter, we discuss decision making. In Chapter 3, we will further explain this *action/decision model* of programming.

It is important to note that standard library functions like `printf` and `scanf` are not part of the C programming language. So the compiler can not find a spelling error in `printf` or `scanf` for example. When the compiler compiles a `printf` statement, it merely provides space in the object program for a "call" to the library function. But the compiler does not know where the library functions are. The linker does. So when the linker runs it locates the library functions and inserts the proper calls to these library functions in the object program. Now the object program is "complete" and ready to be executed. In fact, the linked program is often called an *executable.* If the function name is misspelled, it is the linker that will spot the error, because it will not be able to match the name in the C program with the name of any known function in the libraries.

Good Programming Practice 2.2

The last character printed by a function that does any printing should be a newline (`\n`*). This ensures that the function will leave the screen cursor positioned at the beginning of a new line. Conventions of this nature encourage software reusability—a key goal in software development environments.*

Good Programming Practice 2.3

Indent the entire body of each function one level of indentation (three spaces) within the braces that define the body of the function. This emphasizes the functional structure of programs and helps make programs easier to read.

Good Programming Practice 2.4

Set a convention for the size of indent you prefer and then uniformly apply that convention. The tab key may be used to create indents, but tab stops may vary. We recommend using either 1/4-inch tab stops or hand counting three spaces per level of indent.

The **printf** function can print **Welcome to C!** several different ways. For example, the program of Fig. 2.3 produces the same output as the program of Fig. 2.1. This works because each **printf** resumes printing where the previous **printf** stopped printing. The first **printf** prints **Welcome** followed by a space, and the second **printf** begins printing immediately following the space.

One **printf** can print several lines by using newline characters as in Fig. 2.4. Each time the **\n** (newline) escape sequence is encountered, **printf** positions to the beginning of the next line.

```
/* Printing on one line with two printf statements */

main()
{
   printf("Welcome ");
   printf("to C!\n");
}
```

```
Welcome to C!
```

Fig. 2.3   Printing on one line with separate **printf** statements.

```
/* Printing multiple lines with a single printf */

main()
{
   printf("Welcome\nto\nC!\n");
}
```

```
Welcome
to
C!
```

Fig. 2.4   Printing on multiple lines with a single **printf**.

2.3 Another Simple C Program: Adding Two Integers

Our next program uses the standard library function **scanf** to obtain two integers typed by a user at the keyboard, computes the sum of these values, and prints the result using **printf**. The program and sample output are shown in Fig. 2.5.

The comment **/* Addition program */** states the purpose of the program. The line

        #include <stdio.h>

is a directive to the *C preprocessor*. Lines beginning with **#** are processed by the preprocessor before the program is compiled. This specific line tells the preprocessor to include the contents of the *standard input/output header file* (**stdio.h**) in the program. This header file contains information and declarations used by the compiler when compiling standard input/output library functions such as **printf**. The header file also contains information that helps the compiler determine if calls to library functions have been written correctly. We will explain the contents of header files in more detail in Chapter 5.

Good Programming Practice 2.5

*Although the inclusion of **<stdio.h>** is optional, it should be done on every C program that uses any input/output standard library functions. This helps the compiler help you locate errors at the compile phase of your program rather than at the execution phase (when errors are usually more costly to correct).*

```
/* Addition program */
#include <stdio.h>

main()
{
    int integer1, integer2, sum;        /* declaration */

    printf("Enter first integer\n");    /* prompt */
    scanf("%d", &integer1);             /* read an integer */
    printf("Enter second integer\n");   /* prompt */
    scanf("%d", &integer2);             /* read an integer */
    sum = integer1 + integer2;          /* assignment of sum */
    printf("Sum is %d\n", sum);         /* print sum */

    return 0;  /* indicate that program ended successfully */
}
```

```
Enter first integer
45
Enter second integer
72
Sum is 117
```

Fig. 2.5   An addition program.

As we stated earlier, every program begins execution with **main**. The left brace **{** marks the beginning of the body of **main** and the corresponding right brace marks the end of **main**. The line

```
int integer1, integer2, sum;
```

is a *declaration*. The letters **integer1**, **integer2**, and **sum** are the names of *variables*. A variable is a location in memory where a value can be stored for use by a program. This declaration specifies that the variables **integer1**, **integer2**, and **sum** are of type **int** which means that these variables will hold *integer* values, i.e., whole numbers such as 7, -11, 0, 31914, and the like. All variables must be declared with a name and a data type immediately after the left brace that begins the body of **main** before they can be used in a program. There are other data types besides **int** in C. Several variables of the same type may be declared in one declaration. We could have written three declarations, one for each variable, but the preceding declaration is more concise.

Good Programming Practice 2.6

*Place a space after each comma (**,**) to make programs more readable.*

A variable name in C is any valid *identifier*. An identifier is a series of characters consisting of letters, digits, and underscores (_) that does not begin with a digit. An identifier can be any length, but only the first 31 characters are required to be recognized by C compilers according to the ANSI C standard. C is *case sensitive*—uppercase and lowercase letters are different in C, so **a1** and **A1** are different identifiers.

Common Programming Error 2.4

*Using a capital letter where a lowercase letter should be used (for example, typing **Main** instead of **main**).*

Portability Tip 2.1

Use identifiers of 31 or fewer characters. This helps ensure portability and can avoid some subtle programming errors.

Good Programming Practice 2.7

Choosing meaningful variable names helps make a program self documenting, i.e., fewer comments are needed.

Good Programming Practice 2.8

The first letter of an identifier used as a simple variable name should be a lowercase letter. Later in the text we will assign special significance to identifiers that begin with a capital letter and to identifiers that use all capital letters.

Good Programming Practice 2.9

Multiple-word variable names can help make a program be more readable. Avoid running the separate words together as in totalcommissions. *Rather separate the words with underscores as in* total_commissions, *or, if you do wish to run the words together, begin each word after the first with a capital letter as in* totalCommissions.

Declarations must be placed after the left brace of a function and before *any* executable statements. For example, in the program of Fig. 2.5, inserting the declaration after the first **printf** would cause a syntax error. A *syntax error* is caused when the compiler can not recognize a statement. The compiler normally issues an error message to help the programmer locate and fix the incorrect statement. Syntax errors are violations of the language. Syntax errors are also called *compile errors*, or *compile-time errors*.

Common Programming Error 2.5

Placing variable declarations among executable statements.

Good Programming Practice 2.10

Separate the declarations and executable statements in a function with one blank line to emphasize where the declarations end and the executable statements begin.

The statement

```
printf("Enter first integer\n");
```

prints the literal **Enter first integer** on the screen and positions to the beginning of the next line. This message is called a *prompt* because it tells the user to take a specific action.

The statement

```
scanf("%d", &integer1);
```

uses *scanf* to obtain a value from the user. The **scanf** function takes input from the standard input which is usually the keyboard. This **scanf** has two arguments, **"%d"** and **&integer1**. The first argument, the *format control string,* indicates the type of data that should be input by the user. The **%d** *conversion specifier* indicates that the data should be an integer (the letter **d** stands for "decimal integer"). The **%** in this context is treated by **scanf** (and **printf** as we will see) as an escape character (like ****) and the **%d** combination is an escape sequence (like **\n**). The second argument of **scanf** begins with an ampersand (**&**)—called the *address operator* in C—followed by the variable name. The ampersand, when combined with the variable name, tells **scanf** the location in memory in which the variable **integer1** is stored. The computer then stores the value for **integer1** at that location. The use of ampersand (**&**) is often confusing to novice programmers or to people who have programmed in other languages that do not require this notation. For now, just remember to precede each variable in every **scanf** statement with an ampersand. Some exceptions to this rule are discussed in Chapter 6 and Chapter 7. The real meaning of the use of the ampersand will become clear after we study pointers in Chapter 7.

When the computer executes the preceding **scanf**, it waits for the user to enter a value for variable **integer1**. The user responds by typing an integer and then pressing the *return key* (sometimes called the *enter key*) to send the number to the computer. The computer then assigns this number, or *value*, to the variable **integer1**. Any subsequent references to **integer1** in the program will use this same value. The **printf** and

scanf functions facilitate interaction between the user and the computer. Because this interaction resembles a dialogue, it is often called *conversational computing* or *interactive computing*.

The statement

```
printf("Enter second integer\n");
```

prints the message **Enter second integer** on the screen, then positions the cursor to the beginning of next line. This **printf** also prompts the user to take action.

The statement

```
scanf("%d", &integer2);
```

obtains a value for variable **integer2** from the user. The *assignment statement*

```
sum = integer1 + integer2;
```

calculates the sum of variables **integer1** and **integer2**, and assigns the result to variable **sum** using the *assignment operator* **=**. The statement is read as, "**sum** *gets* the value of **integer1 + integer2**." Most calculations are performed in assignment statements. The **=** operator and the **+** operator are called *binary operators* because they each have two *operands*. In the case of the **+** operator, the two operands are **integer1** and **integer2**. In the case of the **=** operator, the two operands are **sum** and the value of the expression **integer1 + integer2**.

Good Programming Practice 2.11

Place spaces on either side of a binary operator. This makes the operator stand out and makes the program more readable.

Common Programming Error 2.6

The calculation in an assignment statement must be on the right side of the = operator. It is a syntax error to place a calculation on the left side of an assignment operator.

The statement

```
printf("Sum is %d\n", sum);
```

uses the **printf** function to print the literal **Sum is** followed by the numerical value of variable **sum** on the screen. This **printf** has two arguments, **"Sum is %d\n"** and **sum**. The first argument is the format control string. It contains some literal characters to be displayed, and it contains the conversion specifier **%d** indicating that an integer will be printed. The second argument specifies the value to be printed. Notice that the conversion specifier for an integer is the same in both **printf** and **scanf**. This is the case for most data types in C.

Calculations can also be performed inside **printf** statements. We could have combined the previous two statements into the statement

```
printf("Sum is %d\n", integer1 + integer2);
```

The statement

```
return 0;
```

passes the value **0** back to the operating system environment in which the program is being executed. This indicates to the operating system that the program executed successfully. For information on how to report a program failure of some kind, see the manuals for your particular operating system environment.

The right brace, **}**, indicates that the end of function **main** has been reached.

Common Programming Error 2.7

Forgetting one or both of the double quotes surrounding the format control string in a **printf** *or* **scanf**.

Common Programming Error 2.8

Forgetting the **%** *in a conversion specification in the format control string of a* **printf** *or* **scanf**.

Common Programming Error 2.9

Placing an escape sequence such as **\n** *outside the format control string of a* **printf** *or* **scanf**.

Common Programming Error 2.10

Forgetting to include the expressions whose values are to be printed in a **printf** *containing conversion specifiers.*

Common Programming Error 2.11

Not providing in a **printf** *format control string a conversion specifier when one is needed to print an expression.*

Common Programming Error 2.12

Placing inside the format control string the comma that is supposed to separate the format control string from the expressions to be printed.

Common Programming Error 2.13

Forgetting to precede a variable in a **scanf** *statement with an ampersand when that variable should, in fact, be preceded by an ampersand.*

On many systems, this execution-time error is called a "segmentation fault" or "access violation." Such an error occurs when a user's program attempts to access a part of the computer's memory to which the user's program does not have access privileges. The precise cause of this error will be explained in Chapter 7.

Common Programming Error 2.14

Preceding a variable included in a **printf** *statement with an ampersand when, in fact, that variable should not be preceded by an ampersand.*

In Chapter 7, we will study pointers and will see cases where we will want to precede a variable name by an ampersand to print the address of that variable. For the next several chapters, however, **printf** statements should not include these ampersands.

2.4 Memory Concepts

Variable names such as **integer1**, **integer2**, and **sum** actually correspond to *locations* in the computer's memory. Every variable has a *name,* a *type,* and a *value.*

In the addition program of Fig. 2.5, when the statement

```
scanf("%d", &integer1);
```

is executed, the value typed by the user is placed into a memory location to which the name **integer1** has been assigned. Suppose the user enters the number **45** as the value for **integer1**. The computer will place **45** into location **integer1** as shown in Fig. 2.6.

Whenever a value is placed in a memory location, the value overrides the previous value in that location. Since this previous information is destroyed, the process of reading information into a memory location is called *destructive read-in.*

Returning to our addition program again, when the statement

```
scanf("%d", &integer2);
```

is executed, suppose the user enters the value **72**. This value is placed into location **integer2**, and memory appears as in Fig. 2.7. Note that these locations are not necessarily adjacent in memory.

Once the program has obtained values for **integer1** and **integer2**, it adds these values and places the sum into variable **sum**. The statement

```
sum = integer1 + integer2;
```

Fig. 2.6   A memory location showing the name and value of a variable.

integer1   45

integer2   72

Fig. 2.7   Memory locations after both variables are input.

that performs the addition also involves destructive read-in. This occurs when the calculated sum of **integer1** and **integer2** is placed into location **sum** (destroying the
value that may already be in **sum**). After **sum** is calculated, memory appears as in Fig.
2.8. Note that the values of **integer1** and **integer2** appear exactly as they did before
they were used in the calculation of **sum**. These values were used, but not destroyed, as
the computer performed the calculation. Thus, when a value is read out of a memory
location, the process is referred to as *nondestructive read-out*.

2.5 Arithmetic in C

Most C programs perform arithmetic calculations. The C *arithmetic operators* are summarized in Fig. 2.9. Note the use of various special symbols not used in algebra. The *asterisk (*)* indicates multiplication, and the *percent sign (%)* denotes the *modulus* operator
which is introduced below. In algebra, if we want to multiply *a* times *b* we can simply
place these single-letter variable names side by side as in *ab*. In C, however, if we were to
do this, **ab** would be interpreted as a single, two-letter name (or identifier). Therefore, C
(and other programming languages, in general) require that multiplication be explicitly
denoted by using the ***** operator as in **a * b**.

The arithmetic operators are all binary operators. For example, the expression **3 + 7**
contains the binary operator **+** and the operands **3** and **7**.

integer1	45
integer2	72
sum	117

Fig. 2.8   Memory locations after a calculation.

C operation	Arithmetic operator	Algebraic expression	C expression
Addition	+	f + 7	**f + 7**
Subtraction	–	p – c	**p - c**
Multiplication	*	bm	**b * m**
Division	/	x / y or $\frac{x}{y}$ or x ÷ y	**x / y**
Modulus	%	r mod s	**r % s**

Fig. 2.9   C arithmetic operators.

Integer division yields an integer result. For example, the expression **7 / 4** evaluates to **1**, and the expression **17 / 5** evaluates to **3**. C provides the modulus operator, **%**, which yields the remainder after integer division. The modulus operator is an integer operator that can be used only with integer operands. The expression **x % y** yields the remainder after **x** is divided by **y**. Thus, **7 % 4** yields **3**, and **17 % 5** yields **2**. We will discuss many interesting applications of the modulus operator.

Common Programming Error 2.15

An attempt to divide by zero is normally undefined on computer systems and generally results in a fatal error, i.e., an error that causes the program to terminate immediately without having successfully performed its job. Nonfatal errors allow programs to run to completion, often producing incorrect results.

Arithmetic expressions in C must be written in *straight-line form* to facilitate entering programs into the computer. Thus, expressions such as "**a** divided by **b**" must be written as **a/b** so that all operators and operands appear in a straight line. The algebraic notation

$$\frac{a}{b}$$

is generally not acceptable to compilers, although some special-purpose software packages do exist that support more natural notation for complex mathematical expressions.

Parentheses are used in C expressions in much the same manner as in algebraic expressions. For example, to multiply **a** times the quantity **b + c** we write:

```
a * (b + c)
```

C evaluates arithmetic expressions in a precise sequence determined by the following *rules of operator precedence,* which are generally the same as those followed in algebra:

1. Expressions or portions of expressions contained within pairs of parentheses are evaluated first. Thus, *parentheses may be used to force the order of evaluation to occur in any sequence desired by the programmer. Parentheses* are said to be at the "highest level of precedence." In cases of *nested,* or *embedded,* parentheses, the expression in the innermost pair of parentheses is evaluated first.

2. Multiplication, division, and modulus operations are evaluated next. If an expression contains several multiplication, division, and modulus operations, evaluation proceeds from left to right. Multiplication, division, and modulus are said to be on the same level of precedence.

3. Addition and subtraction operations are evaluated last. If an expression contains several addition and subtraction operations, evaluation proceeds from left to right. Addition and subtraction also have the same level of precedence.

The rules of operator precedence are guidelines that enable C to evaluate expressions in the correct order. When we say evaluation proceeds from left to right, we are referring to the *associativity* of the operators. We will see that some operators associate from right to left. Fig. 2.10 summarizes these rules of operator precedence.

Operator(s)	Operation(s)	Order of evaluation (precedence)
( )	Parentheses	Evaluated first. If the parentheses are nested, the expression in the innermost pair is evaluated first. If there are several pairs of parentheses "on the same level" (i.e., not nested), they are evaluated left to right.
*, /, or %	Multiplication Division Modulus	Evaluated second. If there are several, they are evaluated left to right.
+ or -	Addition Subtraction	Evaluated last. If there are several, they are evaluated left to right.

Fig. 2.10 Precedence of arithmetic operators.

Now let us consider several expressions in light of the rules of operator precedence. Each example lists an algebraic expression and its C equivalent.

The following example calculates the arithmetic mean (average) of five terms:

Algebra: $m = \dfrac{a + b + c + d + e}{5}$

C: `m = (a + b + c + d + e) / 5;`

The parentheses are required because division has higher precedence than addition. The entire quantity **(a + b + c + d + e)** is to be divided by **5**. If the parentheses are erroneously omitted, we obtain **a + b + c + d + e / 5** which evaluates incorrectly as

$$a + b + c + d + \frac{e}{5}$$

The following example is the equation of a straight line:

Algebra: $y = mx + b$

C: `y = m * x + b;`

No parentheses are required. The multiplication is evaluated first because multiplication has a higher precedence than addition.

The following example contains modulus (%), multiplication, division, addition, and subtraction operations:

Algebra: $z = pr\%q + w/x - y$

C:

The circled numbers under the statement indicate the order in which C evaluates the operators. The multiplication, modulus, and division are evaluated first in left-to-right order (i.e., they associate from left to right) since they have higher precedence than addition and subtraction. The addition and subtraction are evaluated next. These are also evaluated left to right.

Not all expressions with several pairs of parentheses contain nested parentheses. The expression

```
a * (b + c) + c * (d + e)
```

does not contain nested parentheses. Instead, the parentheses are said to be "on the same level." In this situation, C evaluates the parenthesized expressions first and in left-to-right order.

To develop a better understanding of the rules of operator precedence, let us see how C evaluates a second-degree polynomial.

The circled numbers under the statement indicate the order in which C performs the operations. There is no arithmetic operator for exponentiation in C, so we have represented x^2 as **x * x**. The C Standard Library includes the **pow** ("power") function to perform exponentiation. Because of some subtle issues related to the data types required by **pow**, we defer a detailed explanation of **pow** until Chapter 4.

Suppose **a = 2**, **b = 3**, **c = 7**, and **x = 5**. Figure 2.11 illustrates how the preceding second degree polynomial is evaluated.

2.6 Decision Making: Equality and Relational Operators

Executable C statements either perform *actions* (such as calculations or input or output of data), or they make *decisions* (we will soon see several examples of these). We might make a decision in a program, for example, to determine if a person's grade on an exam is greater than or equal to 60, and if it is to print the message "Congratulations! You passed." This section introduces a simple version of C's **if** *control structure* that allows a program to make a decision based on the truth or falsity of some statement of fact called a *condition.* If the condition is met (i.e., the condition is *true)* the statement in the body of the **if** structure is executed. If the condition is not met (i.e., the condition is *false)* the body statement is not executed. Whether the body statement is executed or not, after the **if** structure completes, execution proceeds with the next statement after the **if** structure.

Conditions in **if** structures are formed by using the *equality operators* and *relational operators* summarized in Fig. 2.12. The relational operators have the same level of precedence and they associate left to right. The equality operators have a lower level of precedence than the relational operators and they also associate left to right. (Note: In C, a condition may actually be any expression that generates a zero (false) or nonzero (true) value. We will see many applications of this throughout the book.)

Step 1.   `y = 2 * 5 * 5 + 3 * 5 + 7;`

`2 * 5 =` ⑩   (Leftmost multiplication first)

Step 2.   `y = 10 * 5 + 3 * 5 + 7;`

`10 * 5 =` ㊿   (Leftmost multiplication)

Step 3.   `y = 50 + 3 * 5 + 7;`

`3 * 5 =` ⑮   (Multiplication before addition)

Step 4.   `y = 50 + 15 + 7;`

`50 + 15 =` �65   (Leftmost addition)

Step 5.   `y = 65 + 7;`

`65 + 7 =` �72   (Last operation)

Fig. 2.11   Evaluation of a second degree polynomial.

Standard algebraic equality operator or relational operator	C equality or relational operator	Example of C condition	Meaning of C condition
Equality operators			
=	==	x == y	**x** is equal to **y**
≠	!=	x != y	**x** is not equal to **y**
Relational operators			
>	>	x > y	**x** is greater than **y**
<	<	x < y	**x** is less than **y**
≥	>=	x >= y	**x** is greater than or equal to **y**
≤	<=	x <= y	**x** is less than or equal to **y**

Fig. 2.12   Equality and relational operators.

Common Programming Error 2.16

A syntax error will occur if the two symbols in any of the operators ==, !=, >=, *and* <= *are separated by spaces.*

Common Programming Error 2.17

A syntax error will occur if the two symbols in any of the operators !=, >=, *and* <= *are reversed as in* =!, =>, *and* =<, *respectively.*

Common Programming Error 2.18

Confusing the equality operator == *with the assignment operator* =.

To avoid this confusion, the equality operator should be read "double equals" and the assignment operator should be read "gets." As we will soon see, confusing these operators may not necessarily cause an easy-to-recognize syntax error, but may cause extremely subtle logic errors.

Common Programming Error 2.19

Placing a semicolon immediately to the right of the right parenthesis after the condition in an if *structure.*

The example of Fig. 2.13 uses six **if** statements to compare two numbers input by the user. If the condition in any of these **if** statements is satisfied, the **printf** statement associated with that **if** is executed. The program and three sample execution outputs are shown in the figure.

Note that the program in Fig. 2.13 uses **scanf** to input two numbers. Each conversion specifier has a corresponding argument in which a value will be stored. The first **%d** converts a value to be stored in variable **num1** and the second **%d** converts a value to be stored in variable **num2**. Indenting the body of each **if** statement and placing blank lines above and below each **if** statement enhances program readability. Also, notice that each **if** statement in Fig. 2.13 has a single statement in its body. In Chapter 3 we show how to specify **if** statements with multiple-statement bodies.

Good Programming Practice 2.12

Indent the statement(s) in the body of an if *structure.*

Good Programming Practice 2.13

Place a blank line before and after every control structure in a program for readability.

Good Programming Practice 2.14

There should be no more than one statement per line in a program.

Common Programming Error 2.20

Placing commas (when none are needed) between conversion specifiers in the format control string of a **scanf** *statement.*

```
/* Using if statements, relational
   operators, and equality operators */
#include <stdio.h>

main()
{
   int num1, num2;

   printf("Enter two integers, and I will tell you\n");
   printf("the relationships they satisfy: ");
   scanf("%d%d", &num1, &num2);    /* read two integers */

   if (num1 == num2)
      printf("%d is equal to %d\n", num1, num2);

   if (num1 != num2)
      printf("%d is not equal to %d\n", num1, num2);

   if (num1 < num2)
      printf("%d is less than %d\n", num1, num2);

   if (num1 > num2)
      printf("%d is greater than %d\n", num1, num2);

   if (num1 <= num2)
      printf("%d is less than or equal to %d\n",
             num1, num2);

   if (num1 >= num2)
      printf("%d is greater than or equal to %d\n",
             num1, num2);

   return 0;    /* indicate program ended successfully */
}
```

Fig. 2.13   Using equality and relational operators (part 1 of 2).

The comment in Fig. 2.13 is split over two lines. In C programs, *white space* characters such as tabs, newlines, and spaces are normally ignored. So, statements and comments may be split over several lines. It is not correct, however, to split identifiers.

Good Programming Practice 2.15

A lengthy statement may be spread over several lines. If a statement must be split across lines, choose breaking points that make sense (such as after a comma in a comma-separated list). If a statement is split across two or more lines, indent all subsequent lines.

The chart in Fig. 2.14 shows the precedence of the operators introduced in this chapter. The operators are shown top to bottom in decreasing order of precedence. Note that the equals sign is also an operator. All these operators, with the exception of the assignment operator =, associate from left to right. The assignment operator (=) associates from right to left.

```
Enter two integers, and I will tell you
the relationships they satisfy: 3 7
3 is not equal to 7
3 is less than 7
3 is less than or equal to 7
```

```
Enter two integers, and I will tell you
the relationships they satisfy: 22 12
22 is not equal to 12
22 is greater than 12
22 is greater than or equal to 12
```

```
Enter two integers, and I will tell you
the relationships they satisfy: 7 7
7 is equal to 7
7 is less than or equal to 7
7 is greater than or equal to 7
```

Fig. 2.13   Using equality and relational operators (part 2 of 2).

Good Programming Practice 2.16

Refer to the operator precedence chart when writing expressions containing many operators. Confirm that the operators in the expression are performed in the proper order. If you are uncertain about the order of evaluation in a complex expression, use parentheses to force the order, exactly as you would do in algebraic expressions. Be sure to observe that some of C's operators such as the assignment operator (=) associate from right to left rather than from left to right.

Operators				Associativity
( )				left to right
*	/	%		left to right
+	–			left to right
<	<=	>	>=	left to right
==	!=			left to right
=				right to left

Fig. 2.14   Precedence and associativity of the operators discussed so far.

Some of the words we have used in the C programs in this chapter—in particular **int**, **return** and **if**—are keywords or reserved words of the language. The complete set of C keywords is shown in Fig. 2.15. These words have special meaning to the C compiler, so the programmer must be careful not to use these words as identifiers such as variable names. In this book, we will discuss all of these keywords.

In this chapter, we have introduced many important features of the C programming language, including printing data on the screen, inputting data from the user, performing calculations, and making decisions. In the next chapter, we build upon these techniques as we introduce *structured programming*. The student will become more familiar with indentation techniques. We will study how to specify the order in which statements are executed—this is called *flow of control.*

Summary

- Comments begin with **/*** and end with ***/**. Programmers insert comments to document programs and improve their readability. Comments do not cause the computer to perform any action when the program is run.

- The preprocessor directive **#include <stdio.h>** tells the compiler to include the standard input/output header file in the program. This file contains information used by the compiler to verify the accuracy of calls to input and output functions such as **scanf** and **printf**.

- C programs consist of functions one of which must be **main**. Every C program begins executing at the function **main**.

- The **printf** function can be used to print a string contained in quotation marks, and to print the values of expressions. When printing integer values, the first argument of the **printf** function—the format control string—contains the conversion specifier **%d** and any other characters that will be printed; the second argument is the expression whose value will be printed. If more than one integer will be printed, then the format control string contains a **%d** for each integer, and the comma-separated arguments following the format control string contain the expressions whose values are to be printed.

Keywords

auto	break	case	char
const	continue	default	do
double	else	enum	extern
float	for	goto	if
int	long	register	return
short	signed	sizeof	static
struct	switch	typedef	union
unsigned	void	volatile	while

Fig. 2.15 C's reserved keywords.

- The **scanf** function obtains values the user normally enters at the keyboard. Its first argument is the format control string that tells the computer what type of data should be input by the user. The conversion specifier **%d** indicates that the data should be an integer. Each of the remaining arguments corresponds to one of the conversion specifiers in the format control string. Each variable name is normally preceded by an ampersand (**&**), called the address operator in C. The ampersand, when combined with the variable name, tells the computer the location in memory where the value will be stored. The computer then stores the value at that location.

- All variables in a C program must be declared before they can be used in the program.

- A variable name in C is any valid identifier. An identifier is a series of characters consisting of letters, digits, and underscores (_). Identifiers cannot start with a digit. Identifiers can be any length; however, only the first 31 characters are significant according to the ANSI standard.

- C is case sensitive.

- Most calculations are performed in assignment statements.

- Every variable stored in the computer's memory has a name, a value, and a type.

- Whenever a new value is placed in a memory location, it overrides the previous value in that location. Since this previous information is destroyed, the process of reading information into a memory location is called destructive read-in.

- The process of reading a value from memory is referred to as nondestructive read-out.

- Arithmetic expressions in C must be written in straight-line form to facilitate entering programs into the computer.

- C evaluates arithmetic expressions in a precise sequence determined by the rules of operator precedence and associativity.

- The **if** statement allows the programmer to make a decision when a certain condition is met. The format for an **if** statement is

      if (*condition*)
          statement

If the condition is true, the statement in the body of the **if** is executed. If the condition is false, the body statement is skipped.

- Conditions in **if** statements are commonly formed by using equality operators and relational operators. The result of using these operators is always simply the observation of "true" or "false." Note that conditions may be any expression that generates a zero (false) or nonzero (true) value.

Terminology

action	ampersand (**&**)
action/decision model	argument
address operator	arithmetic operators

assignment operator (**=**)
assignment statement
associativity of operators
asterisk (*****)
backslash (****) escape character
binary operators
block
body of a function
braces **{}**
C
case sensitive
character string
C keywords
comment
compile error
compile-time error
condition
control string
conversational computing
conversion specifier
C preprocessor
C Standard Library
%d conversion specifier
decision
decision making
declaration
destructive read-in
division by zero
enter key
equal sign (**=**) assignment operator
equality operators
    == "is equal to"
    != "is not equal to"
escape character
escape sequence
false
fatal error
flow of control
format control string
function
identifier
if control structure
indentation
int
integer
integer division
interactive computing
keywords
left-to-right associativity

literal
location
main
memory
memory location
message
modulus operator (**%**)
multiplication operator (*****)
name
nested parentheses
newline character (**\n**)
nondestructive read-out
nonfatal error
nonzero (true)
operand
operator
parentheses (**)**
percent sign (**%**) escape character
precedence
printf function
prompt
relational operators
    > "is greater than"
    < "is less than"
    >= "is greater than or equal to"
    <= "is less than or equal to"
reserved words
return key
right-to-left associativity
rules of operator precedence
scanf function
semicolon (**;**) statement terminator
standard input/output header file
statement
statement terminator (**;**)
stdio.h
straight-line form
string
structured programming
syntax error
true
underscore (**_**)
value
variable
variable name
variable type
variable value
white space characters
zero (false)

Common Programming Errors

2.1   Forgetting to terminate a comment with `*/`.

2.2   Starting a comment with the characters `*/` or ending a comment with the characters `/*`.

2.3   Typing the name of the output function `printf` as `print` in a program.

2.4   Using a capital letter where a lowercase letter should be used (for example, typing `Main` instead of `main`).

2.5   Placing variable declarations among executable statements.

2.6   The calculation in an assignment statement must be on the right side of the `=` operator. It is a syntax error to place a calculation on the left side of an assignment operator.

2.7   Forgetting one or both of the double quotes surrounding the format control string in a `printf` or `scanf`.

2.8   Forgetting the `%` in a conversion specification in the format control string of a `printf` or `scanf`.

2.9   Placing an escape sequence such as `\n` outside the format control string of a `printf` or `scanf`.

2.10   Forgetting to include the expressions whose values are to be printed in a `printf` that contains conversion specifiers.

2.11   Not providing in a `printf` format control string a conversion specifier when one is needed to print an expression.

2.12   Placing inside the format control string the comma that is supposed to separate the format control string from the expressions to be printed.

2.13   Forgetting to precede a variable in a `scanf` statement with an ampersand when that variable should, in fact, be preceded by an ampersand.

2.14   Preceding a variable included in a `printf` statement with an ampersand when, in fact, that variable should not be preceded by an ampersand.

2.15   An attempt to divide by zero is normally undefined on computer systems and generally results in a fatal error, i.e., an error that causes the program to terminate immediately without having successfully performed its job. Nonfatal errors allow programs to run to completion, often producing incorrect results.

2.16   A syntax error will occur if the two symbols in any of the operators `==`, `!=`, `>=`, and `<=` are separated by spaces.

2.17   A syntax error will occur if the two symbols in any of the operators `!=`, `>=`, and `<=` are reversed as in `=!`, `=>`, and `=<`, respectively.

2.18   Confusing the equality operator `==` with the assignment operator `=`.

2.19   Placing a semicolon immediately to the right of the right parenthesis after the condition in an `if` structure.

2.20   Placing commas (when none are needed) between conversion specifiers in the format control string of a `scanf` statement.

Good Programming Practices

2.1   Every function should be preceded by a comment describing the purpose of the function.

2.2   The last character printed by a function that does any printing should be a newline (`\n`). This ensures that the function will leave the screen cursor positioned at the beginning of a new line. Conventions of this nature encourage software reusability—a key goal in software development environments.

2.3   Indent the entire body of each function one level of indentation (three spaces) within the braces that define the body of the function. This emphasizes the functional structure of programs and helps make programs easier to read.

2.4   Set a convention for the size of indent you prefer and then uniformly apply that convention. The tab key may be used to create indents, but tab stops may vary. We recommend using either 1/4-inch tab stops or hand counting three spaces per level of indent.

2.5   Although the inclusion of **<stdio.h>** is optional, it should be done on every C program that uses any input/output standard library functions. This helps the compiler help you locate errors at the compile phase of your program rather than at the execution phase (when errors are usually more costly to correct).

2.6   Place a space after each comma (**,**) to make programs more readable.

2.7   Choosing meaningful variable names helps make a program self documenting, i.e., fewer comments are needed.

2.8   The first letter of an identifier used as a simple variable name should be a lowercase letter. Later in the text we will assign special significance to identifiers that begin with a capital letter and to identifiers that use all capital letters.

2.9   Multiple-word variable names can help make a program be more readable. Avoid running the separate words together as in **totalcommissions**. Rather separate the words with underscores as in **total_commissions**, or, if you do wish to run the words together, begin each word after the first with a capital letter as in **totalCommissions**.

2.10   Separate the declarations and executable statements in a function with one blank line to emphasize where the declarations end and the executable statements begin.

2.11   Place spaces on either side of a binary operator. This makes the operator stand out and makes the program more readable.

2.12   Indent the statement(s) in the body of an **if** structure.

2.13   Place a blank line before and after every control structure in a program for readability.

2.14   There should be no more than one statement per line in a program.

2.15   A lengthy statement may be spread over several lines. If a statement must be split across lines, choose breaking points that make sense such as after a comma in a comma-separated list. If a statement is split across two or more lines, indent all subsequent lines.

2.16   Refer to the operator precedence chart when writing expressions containing many operators. Confirm that the operators in the expression are performed in the proper order. If you are uncertain about the order of evaluation in a complex expression, use parentheses to force the order, exactly as you would do in algebraic expressions. Be sure to observe that some of C's operators such as the assignment operator (**=**) associate from right to left rather than from left to right.

Portability Tip

2.1   Use identifiers of 31 or fewer characters. This helps ensure portability and can avoid some subtle programming errors.

Self-Review Exercises

2.1   Fill in the blanks in each of the following.
        a) Every C program begins execution at the function _____.
        b) The _____ begins the body of every function and the _____ ends the body of every function.
        c) Every statement ends with a _____.

d) The _____ standard library function displays information on the screen.

e) The escape sequence `\n` represents the _____ character which causes the cursor to position to the beginning of the next line on the screen.

f) The _____ standard library function is used to obtain data from the keyboard.

g) The conversion specifier _____ is used in a `scanf` format control string to indicate that an integer will be input and in a `printf` format control string to indicate that an integer will be output.

h) Whenever a new value is placed in a memory location, that value overrides the previous value in that location. This process is known as _____ read-in.

i) When a value is read out of a memory location the value in that location is preserved; this is called _____ read-out.

j) The _____ statement is used to make decisions.

2.2   State whether each of the following is true or false. If false, explain why.

a) When the `printf` function is called it always begins printing at the beginning of a new line.

b) Comments cause the computer to print the text enclosed between `/*` and `*/` on the screen when the program is executed.

c) The escape sequence `\n` when used in a `printf` format control string causes the cursor to position to the beginning of the next line on the screen.

d) All variables must be declared before they are used.

e) All variables must be given a type when they are declared.

f) C considers the variables `number` and `NuMbEr` to be identical.

g) Declarations can appear anywhere in the body of a function.

h) All arguments following the format control string in a `printf` function must be preceded by an ampersand (`&`).

i) The modulus operator (`%`) can be used only with integer operands.

j) The arithmetic operators `*`, `/`, `%`, `+`, and `-` all have the same level of precedence.

k) True or false: The following variable names are identical on all ANSI C systems.

   `thisisasuperduperlongname1234567`
   `thisisasuperduperlongname1234568`

l) True or false: A C program that prints three lines of output must contain three `printf` statements.

2.3   Write a single C statement to accomplish each of the following:

a) Declare the variables `c`, `thisVariable`, `q76354`, and `number` to be of type `int`.

b) Prompt the user to enter an integer. End your prompting message with a colon (`:`) followed by a space and leave the cursor positioned after the space.

c) Read an integer from the keyboard and store the value entered in integer variable `a`.

d) If the variable `number` is not equal to `7`, print `"The variable number is not equal to 7."`

e) Print the message `"This is a C program."` on one line.

f) Print the message `"This is a C program."` on two lines where the first line ends with `C`.

g) Print the message `"This is a C program."` with each word on a separate line.

h) Print the message `"This is a C program."` with each word separated by tabs.

2.4   Write a statement (or comment) to accomplish each of the following:

a) State that a program will calculate the product of three integers.

b) Declare the variables `x`, `y`, `z`, and `result` to be of type `int`.

c) Prompt the user to enter three integers.

d) Read three integers from the keyboard and store them in the variables **x**, **y**, and **z**.

e) Compute the product of the three integers contained in variables **x**, **y**, and **z**, and assign the result to the variable **result**.

f) Print **"The product is"** followed by the value of the variable **result.**

2.5   Using the statements you wrote in Exercise 2.4, write a complete program that calculates the product of three integers.

2.6   Identify and correct the errors in each of the following statements:

a) `printf("The value is %d\n", &number);`

b) `scanf("%d%d", &number1, number2);`

c) `if (c < 7);`
    `printf("C is less than 7\n");`

d) `if (c => 7)`
    `printf("C is equal to or less than 7\n");`

Answers to Self-Review Exercises

2.1   a) **main.** b) left brace (**{**), right brace (**}**). c) semicolon. d) **printf.** e) newline. f) **scanf.** g) **%d.** h) destructive. i) nondestructive. j) **if.**

2.2   a) False. The **printf** function always begins printing where the cursor is positioned, and this may be anywhere on a line of the screen.

b) False. Comments do not cause any action to be performed when the program is executed. They are used to document programs and improve their readability.

c) True.

d) True.

e) True.

f) False. C is case sensitive, so these variables are unique.

g) False. The declarations must appear after the left brace of the body of a function and before any executable statements.

h) False. Arguments in a **printf** function ordinarily should not be preceded by an ampersand. Arguments following the format control string in a **scanf** function ordinarily should be preceded by an ampersand. We will discuss exceptions in Chapters 6 and 7.

i) True.

j) False. The operators *****, **/**, and **%** are on the same level of precedence, and the operators **+** and **–** are on a lower level of precedence.

k) False. Some systems may distinguish between identifiers longer than 31 characters.

l) False. A **printf** statement with multiple **\n** escape sequences can print several lines.

2.3   a) `int c, thisVariable, q76354, number;`

b) `printf("Enter an integer: ");`

c) `scanf("%d", &a);`

d) `if (number != 7)`
    `printf("The variable number is not equal to 7.\n");`

e) `printf("This is a C program.\n");`

f) `printf("This is a C\nprogram.\n");`

g) `printf("This\nis\na\nC\nprogram.\n");`

h) `printf("This\tis\ta\tC\tprogram.\n");`

2.4   a) `/* Calculate the product of three integers */`

b) `int x, y, z, result;`

```
c) printf("Enter three integers: ");
d) scanf("%d%d%d", &x, &y, &z);
e) result = x * y * z;
f) printf("The product is %d\n", result);
```

2.5
```
/* Calculate the product of three integers */
#include <stdio.h>

main()
{
   int x, y, z, result;

   printf("Enter three integers: ");
   scanf("%d%d%d", &x, &y, &z);
   result = x * y * z;
   printf("The product is %d\n", result);

   return 0;
}
```

2.6 a) Error: **&number**. Correction: Eliminate the **&**. Later in the text we discuss exceptions to this.
  b) Error: **number2** does not have an ampersand. Correction: **number2** should be **&number2**. Later in the text we discuss exceptions to this.
  c) Error: Semicolon after the right parenthesis of the condition in the **if** statement. Correction: Remove the semicolon after the right parenthesis. Note: The result of this error is that the **printf** statement will be executed whether or not the condition in the **if** statement is true. The semicolon after the right parenthesis is considered an empty statement—a statement that does nothing.
  d) Error: The relational operator =>. should be changed to >=.

Exercises

2.7 Identify and correct the errors in each of the following statements (Note: there may be more than one error per statement):
```
a) scanf("d", value);
b) printf("The product of %d and %d is %d"\n, x, y);
c) firstNumber + secondNumber = sumOfNumbers
d) if (number => largest)
       largest == number;
e) */ Program to determine the largest of three integers /*
f) Scanf("%d", anInteger);
g) printf("Remainder of %d divided by %d is\n", x, y, x % y);
h) if (x = y);
       printf(%d is equal to %d\n", x, y);
i) print("The sum is %d\n," x + y);
j) Printf("The value you entered is: %d\n, &value);
```

2.8 Fill in the blanks in each of the following:
  a) _____ are used to document a program and improve its readability.
  b) The function used to print information on the screen is _____.
  c) A C statement that makes a decision is _____.

      d) Calculations are normally performed by _____ statements.

      e) The _____ function inputs values from the keyboard.

2.9   Write a single C statement or line that accomplishes each of the following:

      a) Print the message "**Enter two numbers**."

      b) Assign the product of variables **b** and **c** to variable **a**.

      c) State that a program performs a sample payroll calculation (i.e., use text that helps to document a program).

      d) Input three integer values from the keyboard and place these values in integer variables **a**, **b**, and **c**.

2.10   State which of the following are true and which are false. Explain your answers.

      a) C operators are evaluated from left to right.

      b) The following are all valid variable names: **_under_bar_**, **m928134**, **t5**, **j7**, **her_sales**, **his_account_total**, **a**, **b**, **c**, **z**, **z2**.

      c) The statement **printf("a = 5;");** is a typical example of an assignment statement.

      d) A valid C arithmetic expression containing no parentheses is evaluated from left to right.

      e) The following are all invalid variable names: **3g**, **87**, **67h2**, **h22**, **2h**.

2.11   Fill in the blanks in each of the following:

      a) What arithmetic operations are on the same level of precedence as multiplication? _____.

      b) When parentheses are nested, which set of parentheses is evaluated first in an arithmetic expression? _____.

      c) A location in the computer's memory that may contain different values at various times throughout the execution of a program is called a _____.

2.12   What, if anything, prints when each of the following C statements is performed? If nothing prints, then answer "nothing." Assume **x = 2** and **y = 3**.

      a) `printf("%d", x);`

      b) `printf("%d", x + x);`

      c) `printf("x=");`

      d) `printf("x=%d", x);`

      e) `printf("%d = %d", x + y, y + x);`

      f) `z = x + y;`

      g) `scanf("%d%d", &x, &y);`

      h) `/* printf("x + y = %d", x + y); */`

      i) `printf("\n");`

2.13   Which, if any, of the following C statements contain variables involved in destructive read-in?

      a) `scanf("%d%d%d%d%d", &b, &c, &d, &e, &f);`

      b) `p = i + j + k + 7;`

      c) `printf("Destructive read-in");`

      d) `printf("a = 5");`

2.14   Given the equation $y = ax^3 + 7$, which of the following, if any, are correct C statements for this equation?

      a) `y = a * x * x * x + 7;`

      b) `y = a * x * x * (x + 7);`

      c) `y = (a * x) * x * (x + 7);`

    d) `y = (a * x) * x * x + 7;`
    e) `y = a * (x * x * x) + 7;`
    f) `y = a * x * (x * x + 7);`

2.15   State the order of evaluation of the operators in each of the following C statements, and show the value of **x** after each statement is performed.
    a) `x = 7 + 3 * 6 / 2 - 1;`
    b) `x = 2 % 2 + 2 * 2 - 2 / 2;`
    c) `x = (3 * 9 * (3 + (9 * 3/ (3))));`

2.16   Write a program that asks the user to enter two numbers, obtains the two numbers from the user, and prints the sum, product, difference, quotient and modulus of the two numbers.

2.17   Write a program that prints the numbers 1 to 4 on the same line. Write the program using the following methods.
    a) Using one **printf** statement with no conversion specifiers.
    b) Using one **printf** statement with four conversion specifiers.
    c) Using four **printf** statements.

2.18   Write a program that asks the user to enter two integers, obtains the numbers from the user, and then prints the larger number followed by the words "**is larger.**" If the numbers are equal, print the message "**These numbers are equal.**" Use only the single-selection form of the **if** statement you learned in this chapter.

2.19   Write a C program that inputs three different integers from the keyboard, and then prints the sum, the average, the product, the smallest, and the largest of these numbers. Use only the single-selection form of the **if** statement you learned in this chapter. The screen dialogue should appear as follows:

```
Input three different integers: 13 27 14
Sum is 54
Average is 18
Product is 4914
Smallest is 13
Largest is 27
```

2.20   Write a program that reads in the radius of a circle and prints the circle's diameter, circumference, and area. Use the constant value 3.14159 for "pi." Do each of these calculations inside the **printf** statement(s) and use the conversion specifier **%f**. (Note: In this chapter, we have discussed only integer constants and variables. In Chapter 3 we will discuss floating point numbers, i.e., values that can have decimal points.)

2.21   Write a program that prints a box, an oval, an arrow, and a diamond as follows:

2.22 What does the following code print?

```
printf("*\n**\n***\n****\n*****\n");
```

2.23 Write a program that reads in five integers and then determines and prints the largest and the smallest integers in the group. Use only the programming techniques you have learned in this chapter.

2.24 Write a program that reads an integer and determines and prints whether it is odd or even. (Hint: Use the modulus operator. An even number is a multiple of two. Any multiple of two leaves a remainder of zero when divided by 2.)

2.25 Print your initials in block letters down the page. Construct each block letter out of the letter it represents as follows:

```
PPPPPPPPP
    P      P
    P      P
    P      P
     P P

     JJ
    J
   J
    J
    JJJJJJJ

DDDDDDDD
D            D
D            D
 D        D
    DDDDD
```

2.26 Write a program that reads in two integers and determines and prints if the first is a multiple of the second. (Hint: Use the modulus operator.)

2.27 Display a checkerboard pattern with eight **printf** statements, and then display the same pattern with as few **printf** statements as possible.

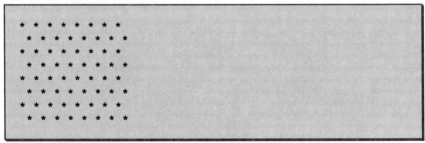

2.28 Distinguish between the terms fatal error and nonfatal error. Why might you prefer to experience a fatal error rather than a nonfatal error?

2.29 Here's a peek ahead. In this chapter you learned about integers and the type **int**. C can also represent uppercase letters, lowercase letters, and a considerable variety of special symbols. C uses small integers internally to represent each different character. The set of characters a computer uses and the corresponding integer representations for those characters is called that computer's character set. You can print the integer equivalent of uppercase **A** for example, by executing the statement

```
printf("%d", 'A');
```

Write a C program that prints the integer equivalents of some uppercase letters, lowercase letters, digits and special symbols. As a minimum, determine the integer equivalents of the following: **A B C a b c 0 1 2 $ * + /** and the blank character.

2.30   Write a program that inputs a five-digit number, separates the number into its individual digits and prints the digits separated from one another by three spaces each. For example, if the user types in **42339** the program should print

```
4    2    3    3    9
```

2.31   Using only the techniques you learned in this chapter, write a program that calculates the squares and cubes of the numbers from 0 to 10 and uses tabs to print the following table of values:

```
number   square   cube
0        0        0
1        1        1
2        4        8
3        9        27
4        16       64
5        25       125
6        36       216
7        49       343
8        64       512
9        81       729
10       100      1000
```

3

Structured Program Development

Objectives

- To understand basic problem solving techniques.
- To be able to develop algorithms through the process of top-down, stepwise refinement.
- To be able to use the if selection structure and if/else selection structure to select actions.
- To be able to use the while repetition structure to execute statements in a program repeatedly.
- To understand counter-controlled repetition and sentinel-controlled repetition.
- To understand structured programming.
- To be able to use the increment, decrement, and assignment operators.

The secret to success is constancy to purpose.
Benjamin Disraeli

Let's all move one place on.
Lewis Carroll

The wheel is come full circle.
William Shakespeare
King Lear

How many apples fell on Newton's head before he took the hint!
Robert Frost
Comment

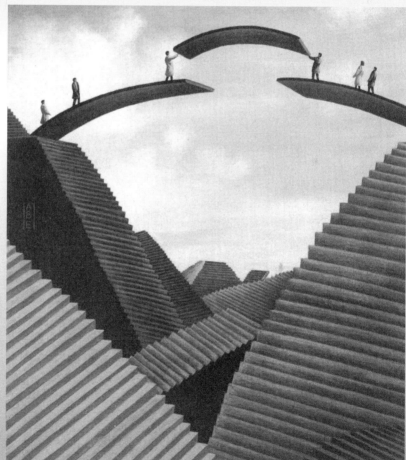

Outline

3.1 Introduction

Before writing a program to solve a particular problem, it is essential to have a thorough understanding of the problem, and a carefully planned approach to solving the problem. The next two chapters discuss techniques that facilitate the development of structured computer programs. In Section 4.11, we present a summary of structured programming that ties together the techniques developed here and in Chapter 4.

3.2 Algorithms

The solution to any computing problem involves executing a series of actions in a specific order. A *procedure* for solving a problem in terms of

1.   the *actions* to be executed, and

2.   the *order* in which these actions are to be executed

is called an *algorithm*. The following example demonstrates that correctly specifying the order in which the actions are to be executed is important.

Consider the "rise-and-shine algorithm" followed by one junior executive for getting out of bed and going to work:

Get out of bed.
Take off pajamas.
Take a shower.
Get dressed.
Eat breakfast.
Carpool to work.

This routine gets the executive to work well prepared to make critical decisions. Suppose, however, that the same steps are performed in a slightly different order:

Get out of bed.
Take off pajamas.
Get dressed.
Take a shower.
Eat breakfast.
Carpool to work.

In this case, our junior executive shows up for work soaking wet. Specifying the order in which statements are to be executed in a computer program is called *program control*. In this and the next chapter, we investigate the program control capabilities of C.

3.3 Pseudocode

Pseudocode is an artificial and informal language that helps programmers develop algorithms. The pseudocode we present here is particularly useful for developing algorithms that will be converted to structured C programs. Pseudocode is similar to everyday English; it is convenient and user-friendly although it is not an actual computer programming language.

Pseudocode programs are not actually executed on computers. Rather, they merely help the programmer "think out" a program before attempting to write it in a programming language such as C. In this chapter, we give several examples of how pseudocode may be used effectively in developing structured C programs.

Pseudocode consists purely of characters, so programmers may conveniently type pseudocode programs into a computer using an editor program. The computer can display or print a fresh copy of a pseudocode program on demand. A carefully prepared pseudocode program may be converted easily to a corresponding C program. This is done in many cases simply by replacing pseudocode statements with their C equivalents.

Pseudocode consists only of action statements—those that are executed when the program has been converted from pseudocode to C and is run in C. Declarations are not executable statements. They are messages to the compiler. For example, the declaration

```
int i;
```

simply tells the compiler the type of variable **i** and instructs the compiler to reserve space in memory for the variable. But this declaration does not cause any action—such as input, output, or a calculation—to occur when the program is executed. Some programmers choose to list each variable and briefly mention the purpose of each at the beginning of a pseudocode program. Again, pseudocode is an informal program development aid.

3.4 Control Structures

Normally, statements in a program are executed one after the other in the order in which they are written. This is called *sequential execution.* Various C statements we will soon discuss enable the programmer to specify that the next statement to be executed may be other than the next one in sequence. This is called *transfer of control.*

During the 1960s, it became clear that the indiscriminate use of transfers of control was the root of a great deal of difficulty experienced by software development groups. The finger of blame was pointed at the **goto** *statement* that allows the programmer to specify a transfer of control to one of a very wide range of possible destinations in a program. The notion of so-called *structured programming* became almost synonymous with *"**goto** elimination."*

The research of Bohm and Jacopini[1] had demonstrated that programs could be written without any **goto** statements. The challenge of the era became for programmers to shift their styles to "**goto**-less programming." It was not until well into the 1970s that the programming profession at large started taking structured programming seriously. The results have been impressive as software development groups have reported reduced development times, more frequent on-time delivery of systems, and more frequent within-budget completion of software projects. The key to these successes is simply that programs produced with structured techniques are clearer, easier to debug and modify, and more likely to be bug-free in the first place.

Bohm and Jacopini's work demonstrated that all programs could be written in terms of only three *control structures*, namely the *sequence structure*, the *selection structure*, and the *repetition structure*. The sequence structure is essentially built into C. Unless directed otherwise, the computer automatically executes C statements one after the other in the order in which they are written. The *flowchart* segment of Fig. 3.1 illustrates C's sequence structure.

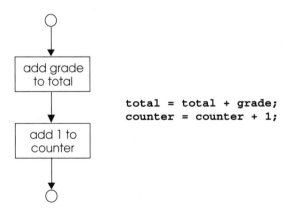

```
total = total + grade;
counter = counter + 1;
```

Fig. 3.1   Flowcharting C's sequence structure.

[1] Bohm, C. , and G. Jacopini, "Flow Diagrams, Turing Machines, and Languages with Only Two Formation Rules," *Communications of the ACM*, Vol. 9, No. 5, May 1966, pp. 336-371.

A flowchart is a graphical representation of an algorithm or of a portion of an algorithm. Flowcharts are drawn using certain special-purpose symbols such as rectangles, diamonds, ovals, and small circles; these symbols are connected by arrows called *flowlines*.

Like pseudocode, flowcharts are useful for developing and representing algorithms, although pseudocode is preferred by most programmers. Flowcharts clearly show how control structures operate; that is all we use them for in this text.

Consider the flowchart segment for the sequence structure in Fig. 3.1. We use the *rectangle symbol*, also called the *action symbol,* to indicate any type of action including a calculation or an input/output operation. The flowlines in the figure indicate the order in which the actions are to be performed—first, **grade** is to be added to **total** and then **1** is to be added to **counter**. C allows us to have as many actions as we want in a sequence structure. As we will soon see, anywhere a single action may be placed, we may place several actions in sequence.

When drawing a flowchart that represents a *complete* algorithm, an *oval symbol* containing the word "Begin" is the first symbol used in the flowchart; an oval symbol containing the word "End" is the last symbol used. When drawing only a portion of an algorithm as in Fig. 3.1, the oval symbols are omitted in favor of using *small circle symbols* also called *connector symbols*.

Perhaps the most important flowcharting symbol is the *diamond symbol*, also called the *decision symbol,* which indicates that a decision is to be made. We will discuss the diamond symbol in the next section.

C provides three types of selection structures. The **if** selection structure (Section 3.5) either performs (selects) an action if a condition is true or skips the action if the condition is false. The **if/else** selection structure (Section 3.6) performs an action if a condition is true and performs a different action if the condition is false. The **switch** selection structure (discussed in Chapter 4) performs one of many different actions depending on the value of an expression.

The **if** structure is called a *single-selection structure* because it selects or ignores a single action. The **if/else** structure is called a *double-selection structure* because it selects between two different actions. The **switch** structure is called a *multiple-selection structure* because it selects among many different actions.

C provides three types of repetition structures, namely the **while** (Section 3.7), and the **do/while** and the **for** (both discussed in Chapter 4).

That is all there is. C has only seven control structures: Sequence, three types of selection and three types of repetition. Each C program is formed by combining as many of each type of control structure as is appropriate for the algorithm the program implements. As with the sequence structure of Fig. 3.1, we will see that each control structure has two small circle symbols, one at the entry point to the control structure and one at the exit point. These *single-entry/single-exit control structures* make it easy to build programs. The control structures can be attached to one another by connecting the exit point of one control structure to the entry point of the next. This is very much like the way in which a child stacks building blocks, so we call this *control-structure stacking*. We will learn that there is only one other way control structures may be connected—a method called *control-structure nesting*. Thus, any C program we will ever need to build can be constructed from only seven different types of control structures combined in only two ways.

3.5 The If Selection Structure

A selection structure is used to choose among alternative courses of action. For example, suppose the passing grade on an exam is 60. The pseudocode statement

> *If student's grade is greater than or equal to 60*
>   *Print "Passed"*

determines if the condition "student's grade is greater than or equal to 60" is true or false. If the condition is true, then "Passed" is printed, and the next pseudocode statement in order is "performed" (remember that pseudocode is not a real programming language). If the condition is false, the printing is ignored, and the next pseudocode statement in order is performed. Note that the second line of this selection structure is indented. Such indentation is optional, but it is highly recommended as it helps emphasize the inherent structure of structured programs. We will apply indentation conventions carefully throughout this text. The C compiler ignores *whitespace characters* like blanks, tabs and newlines used for indentation and vertical spacing.

> *Good Programming Practice 3.1*
> ___
> *Consistently applying responsible indentation conventions greatly improves program readability. We suggest a fixed-size tab of about 1/4 inch or three blanks per indent.*

The preceding pseudocode *If* statement may be written in C as

```
if (grade >= 60)
    printf("Passed\n");
```

Notice that the C code corresponds closely to the pseudocode. This is one of the properties of pseudocode that makes it such a useful program development tool.

> *Good Programming Practice 3.2*
> ___
> *Pseudocode is often used to "think out" a program during the program design process. Then the pseudocode program is converted to C.*

The flowchart of Fig. 3.2 illustrates the single selection **if** structure. This flowchart contains what is perhaps the most important flowcharting symbol—the *diamond symbol*, also called the *decision symbol,* which indicates that a decision is to be made. The decision symbol contains an expression, such as a condition, that can be either true or false. The decision symbol has two flowlines emerging from it. One indicates the direction to be taken when the expression in the symbol is true; the other indicates the direction to be taken when the expression is false. We learned in Chapter 2 that decisions can be made based on conditions containing relational or equality operators. Actually, a decision can be made on any expression—if the expression evaluates to zero, it is treated as false, and if the expression evaluates to nonzero, it is treated as true.

Note that the **if** structure, too, is a single-entry/single-exit structure. We will soon learn that the flowcharts for the remaining control structures also contain (besides small circle symbols and flowlines) only rectangle symbols to indicate the actions to be performed, and diamond symbols to indicate decisions to be made. This is the action/decision model of programming we have been emphasizing.

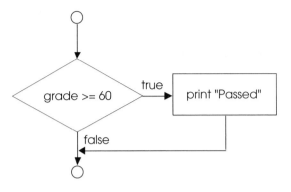

Fig. 3.2   Flowcharting C's single selection structure.

We can envision seven bins, each containing only control structures of one of the seven types. These control structures are empty. Nothing is written in the rectangles and nothing is written in the diamonds. The programmers task, then, is assembling a program from as many of each type of control structure as the algorithm demands, combining those control structures in only two possible ways (stacking or nesting), and then filling in the actions and decisions in a manner appropriate for the algorithm. We will discuss the variety of ways in which actions and decisions may be written.

3.6 The If/Else Selection Structure

The **if** selection structure performs an indicated action only when the condition is true; otherwise the action is skipped. The **if/else** selection structure allows the programmer to specify that different actions are to be performed when the condition is true than when the condition is false. For example, the pseudocode statement

> *If student's grade is greater than or equal to 60*
> > *Print "Passed"*
> *else*
> > *Print "Failed"*

prints *Passed* if the student's grade is greater than or equal to 60 and prints *Failed* if the student's grade is less than 60. In either case, after printing occurs, the next pseudocode statement in sequence is "performed." Note that the body of the *else* is also indented.

> **Good Programming Practice 3.3**
>
> *Indent both body statements of an **if/else** structure.*

Whatever indentation convention you choose should be carefully applied throughout your programs. It is difficult to read a program that does not obey uniform spacing conventions.

> **Good Programming Practice 3.4**
>
> *If there are several levels of indentation, each level should be indented the same additional amount of space.*

The preceding pseudocode *If/else* structure may be written in C as

```
if (grade >= 60)
    printf("Passed\n");
else
    printf("Failed\n");
```

The flowchart of Fig. 3.3 nicely illustrates the flow of control in the **if/else** structure. Once again, note that (besides small circles and arrows) the only symbols in the flowchart are rectangles (for actions) and a diamond (for a decision). We continue to emphasize this action/decision model of computing. Imagine again a deep bin containing as many empty double-selection structures as might be needed to build any C program. The programmer's job, again, is to assemble these selection structures (by stacking and nesting) with any other control structures required by the algorithm, and to fill in the empty rectangles and empty diamonds with actions and decisions appropriate to the algorithm being implemented.

C provides the *conditional operator (? :)* which is closely related to the **if/else** structure. The conditional operator is C's only *ternary operator*—it takes three operands. The operands together with the conditional operator form a *conditional expression*. The first operand is a condition, the second operand is the value for the entire conditional expression if the condition is true, and the third operand is the value for the entire conditional expression if the condition is false. For example, the **printf** statement

```
printf("%s\n", grade >= 60 ? "Passed" : "Failed");
```

contains a conditional expression that evaluates to the string literal **"Passed"** if the condition **grade >= 60** is true and evaluates to the string literal **"Failed"** if the condition

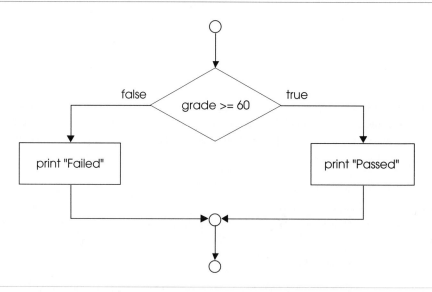

Fig. 3.3   Flowcharting C's double selection **if/else** structure.

is false. The format control string of the **printf** contains the conversion specification **%s** for printing a character string. So the preceding **printf** statement performs essentially the same as the preceding **if/else** statement.

The values in a conditional expression can also be actions to be executed. For example, the conditional expression

```
grade >= 60 ? printf("Passed\n") : printf("Failed\n");
```

is read, "If **grade** is greater than or equal to **60** then **printf("Passed\n")**, otherwise **printf("Failed\n")**." This, too, is comparable to the preceding **if/else** structure. We will see that conditional operators can be used in some situations where **if/else** statements can not.

Nested ***if/else*** *structures* test for multiple cases by placing **if/else** structures inside **if/else** structures. For example, the following pseudocode statement will print **A** for exam grades greater than or equal to **90**, **B** for grades greater than or equal to **80**, **C** for grades greater than or equal to **70**, **D** for grades greater than or equal to **60**, and **F** for all other grades.

> *If student's grade is greater than or equal to 90*
> > *Print "A"*
>
> *else*
> > *If student's grade is greater than or equal to 80*
> > > *Print "B"*
> >
> > *else*
> > > *If student's grade is greater than or equal to 70*
> > > > *Print "C"*
> > >
> > > *else*
> > > > *If student's grade is greater than or equal to 60*
> > > > > *Print "D"*
> > > >
> > > > *else*
> > > > > *Print "F"*

This pseudocode may be written in C as

```
if (grade >= 90)
   printf("A\n");
else
   if (grade >= 80)
      printf("B\n");
   else
      if (grade >= 70)
         printf("C\n");
      else
         if (grade >= 60)
            printf("D\n");
         else
            printf("F\n");
```

If the variable **grade** is greater than or equal to 90, the first four conditions will be true, but only the **printf** statement after the first test will be executed. After that **printf** is executed, the **else**-part of the "outer" **if/else** statement is skipped. Many C programmers prefer to write the preceding **if** structure as

```
if (grade >= 90)
    printf("A\n");
else if (grade >= 80)
    printf("B\n");
else if (grade >= 70)
    printf("C\n");
else if (grade >= 60)
    printf("D\n");
else
    printf("F\n");
```

As far as the C compiler is concerned, both forms are equivalent. The latter form is popular because it avoids the deep indentation of the code to the right. Such indentation often leaves little room on a line, forcing lines to be split and decreasing program readability.

The **if** selection structure expects only one statement in its body. To include several statements in the body of an **if**, enclose the set of statements in braces (**{** and **}**). A set of statements contained within a pair of braces is called a *compound statement*.

Software Engineering Observation 3.1

A compound statement can be placed anywhere in a program that a single statement can be placed.

The following example includes a compound statement in the **else** part of an **if/else** structure.

```
if (grade >= 60)
    printf("Passed.\n");
else {
    printf("Failed.\n");
    printf("You must take this course again.\n");
}
```

In this case, if grade is less than **60**, the program executes both **printf** statements in the body of the **else** and prints

```
Failed.
You must take this course again.
```

Notice the braces surrounding the two statements in the **else** clause. These braces are important. Without the braces, the statement

```
printf("You must take this course again.\n");
```

would be outside the body of the **else**-part of the **if**, and would execute regardless of whether the grade is less than 60.

Common Programming Error 3.1

Forgetting one or both of the braces that delimit a compound statement.

A syntax error is caught by the compiler. A logic error has its effect at execution time. A fatal logic error causes a program to fail and terminate prematurely. A nonfatal logic error allows a program to continue executing but to produce incorrect results.

Common Programming Error 3.2

*Placing a semicolon after the condition in an **if** structure leads to a logic error in single-selection **if** structures and a syntax error in double-selection **if** structures.*

Good Programming Practice 3.5

Some programmers prefer to type the beginning and ending braces of compound statements before typing the individual statements within the braces. This helps avoid omitting one or both of the braces.

Software Engineering Observation 3.2

*Just as a compound statement can be placed anywhere a single statement can be placed, it is also possible to have no statement at all, i.e., the empty statement. The empty statement is represented by placing a semicolon (**;**) where a statement would normally be.*

In this section, we introduced the notion of a compound statement. A compound statement may contain declarations (as does the body of **main**, for example). If so, the compound statement is called a *block*. The declarations in a block must be placed first in the block before any action statements. We will discuss the use of blocks in Chapter 5. The reader should avoid using blocks (other than the body of **main**, of course) until that time.

3.7 The While Repetition Structure

A *repetition structure* allows the programmer to specify that an action is to be repeated while some condition remains true. The pseudocode statement

> *While there are more items on my shopping list*
>> *Purchase next item and cross it off my list*

describes the repetition that occurs during a shopping trip. The condition, "there are more items on my shopping list" may be true or false. If it is true, then the action, "Purchase next item and cross it off my list" is performed. This action will be performed repeatedly while the condition remains true. The statement(s) contained in the *while* repetition structure constitute the body of the *while*. The *while* structure body may be a single statement or a compound statement.

Eventually, the condition will become false (when the last item on the shopping list has been purchased and crossed off the list). At this point, the repetition terminates, and the first pseudocode statement after the repetition structure is executed.

Common Programming Error 3.3

*Not providing in the body of a **while** structure an action that eventually causes the condition in the **while** to become false. Normally, such a repetition structure will never terminate—an error called an "infinite loop."*

Common Programming Error 3.4

Spelling the keyword **while** *with an uppercase* **W** *as in* **While** *(remember that C is a case-sensitive language). All of C's reserved keywords such as* **while***,* **if***, and* **else** *contain only lowercase letters.*

As an example of an actual **while**, consider a program segment designed to find the first power of 2 larger than 1000. Suppose the integer variable **product** has been initialized to 2. When the following **while** repetition structure finishes executing, **product** will contain the desired answer:

```
product = 2;

while (product <= 1000)
    product = 2 * product;
```

The flowchart of Fig. 3.4 nicely illustrates the flow of control in the **while** repetition structure. Once again, note that (besides small circles and arrows) the flowchart contains only a rectangle symbol and a diamond symbol. Imagine, again, a deep bin of empty **while** structures that may be stacked and nested with other control structures to form a structured implementation of an algorithm's flow of control. The empty rectangles and diamonds are then filled in with appropriate actions and decisions. The flowchart clearly shows the repetition. The flowline emerging from the rectangle wraps back to the decision which is tested each time through the loop until the decision eventually becomes false. At this point, the **while** structure is exited and control passes to the next statement in the program.

When the **while** structure is entered, the value of **product** is 2. The variable **product** is repeatedly multiplied by 2, taking on the values 4, 8, 16, 32, 64, 128, 256, 512, and 1024 successively. When **product** becomes 1024, the condition in the **while** structure, **product <= 1000**, becomes false. This terminates the repetition and the final value of **product** is 1024. Program execution continues with the next statement after the **while**.

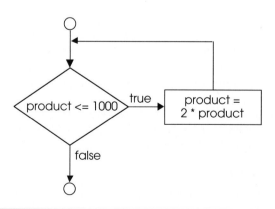

Fig. 3.4   Flowcharting the **while** repetition structure.

3.8 Formulating Algorithms: Case Study 1 (Counter-Controlled Repetition)

To illustrate how algorithms are developed, we solve several variations of a class averaging problem. Consider the following problem statement:

> *A class of ten students took a quiz. The grades (integers in the range 0 to 100) for this quiz are available to you. Determine the class average on the quiz.*

The class average is equal to the sum of the grades divided by the number of students. The algorithm for solving this problem on a computer must input each of the grades, perform the averaging calculation, and print the result.

Let us use pseudocode, list the actions to be executed, and specify the order in which these actions should be executed. We use *counter-controlled repetition* to input the grades one at a time. This technique uses a variable called a *counter* to specify the number of times a set of statements should execute. In this example, repetition terminates when the counter exceeds 10. In this section we simply present the pseudocode algorithm (Fig. 3.5) and the corresponding C program (Fig. 3.6). In the next section, we show how pseudocode algorithms are developed. Counter-controlled repetition is often called *definite repetition* because the number of repetitions is known before the loop begins executing.

Note the references in the algorithm to a total and a counter. A *total* is a variable used to accumulate the sum of a series of values. A counter is a variable used to count—in this case, to count the number of grades entered. Variables used to store totals should normally be initialized to zero before being used in a program; otherwise the sum would include the previous value stored in the total's memory location. Counter variables are normally initialized to zero or one, depending on their use (we will present examples showing each of these uses). An uninitialized variable contains a *"garbage" value*—the value last stored in the memory location reserved for that variable.

Common Programming Error 3.5

If a counter or total is not initialized, the results of your program will probably be incorrect. This is an example of a logic error.

Set total to zero
Set grade counter to one

While grade counter is less than or equal to ten
    Input the next grade
    Add the grade into the total
    Add one to the grade counter

Set the class average to the total divided by ten
Print the class average

Fig. 3.5   Pseudocode algorithm that uses counter-controlled repetition to solve the class average problem.

```
/* Class average program with
   counter-controlled repetition */
#include <stdio.h>

main()
{
   int counter, grade, total, average;

   /* initialization phase */
   total = 0;
   counter = 1;

   /* processing phase */
   while (counter <= 10) {
      printf("Enter grade: ");
      scanf("%d", &grade);
      total = total + grade;
      counter = counter + 1;
   }

   /* termination phase */
   average = total / 10;
   printf("Class average is %d\n", average);

   return 0;   /* indicate program ended successfully */
}
```

```
Enter grade: 98
Enter grade: 76
Enter grade: 71
Enter grade: 87
Enter grade: 83
Enter grade: 90
Enter grade: 57
Enter grade: 79
Enter grade: 82
Enter grade: 94
Class average is 81
```

Fig. 3.6   C program and sample execution for the class average problem with counter-controlled repetition.

Good Programming Practice 3.6

Initialize counters and totals.

Note that the averaging calculation in the program produced an integer result. Actually, the sum of the grades in this example is 817 which when divided by 10 should yield 81.7, i.e., a number with a decimal point. We will see how to deal with such numbers (called floating-point numbers) in the next section.

3.9 Formulating Algorithms with Top-down, Stepwise Refinement: Case Study 2 (Sentinel-Controlled Repetition)

Let us generalize the class average problem. Consider the following problem:

Develop a class averaging program that will process an arbitrary number of grades each time the program is run.

In the first class average example, the number of grades (10) was known in advance. In this example, no indication is given of how many grades are to be entered. The program must process an arbitrary number of grades. How can the program determine when to stop the input of grades? How will it know when to calculate and print the class average?

One way to solve this problem is to use a special value called a *sentinel value* (also called a *signal value*, a *dummy value*, or a *flag value*) to indicate "end of data entry." The user types grades in until all legitimate grades have been entered. The user then types the sentinel value to indicate that the last grade has been entered. Sentinel-controlled repetition is often called *indefinite repetition* because the number of repetitions is not known before the loop begins executing.

Clearly, the sentinel value must be chosen so that it cannot be confused with an acceptable input value. Since grades on a quiz are normally nonnegative integers, -1 is an acceptable sentinel value for this problem. Thus, a run of the class average program might process a stream of inputs such as 95, 96, 75, 74, 89, and -1. The program would then compute and print the class average for the grades 95, 96, 75, 74, and 89 (-1 is the sentinel value, so it should not enter into the averaging calculation).

Common Programming Error 3.6

Choosing a sentinel value that is also a legitimate data value.

We approach the class average program with a technique called *top-down, stepwise refinement*, a technique that is essential to the development of well-structured programs. We begin with a pseudocode representation of the *top:*

Determine the class average for the quiz

The top is a single statement that conveys the overall function of the program. As such, the top is, in effect, a complete representation of a program. Unfortunately, the top (as in this case) rarely conveys a sufficient amount of detail from which to write the C program.

So we now begin the refinement process. We divide the top into a series of smaller tasks and list these in the order in which they need to be performed. This results in the following *first refinement*.

Initialize variables
Input, sum, and count the quiz grades
Calculate and print the class average

Here, only the sequence structure has been used—the steps listed are to be executed in order, one after the other.

Software Engineering Observation 3.3

Each refinement, as well as the top itself, is a complete specification of the algorithm; only the level of detail varies.

To proceed to the next level of refinement, i.e., the *second refinement*, we commit to specific variables. We need a running total of the numbers, a count of how many numbers have been processed, a variable to receive the value of each grade as it is input, and a variable to hold the calculated average. The pseudocode statement

Initialize variables

may be refined as follows:

Initialize total to zero
Initialize counter to zero

Notice that only total and counter need to be initialized; the variables average and grade (for the calculated average and the user input, respectively) need not be initialized because their values will be written over by the process of destructive read-in discussed in Chapter 2. The pseudocode statement

Input, sum, and count the quiz grades

requires a repetition structure (i.e., a loop) that successively inputs each grade. Since we do not know in advance how many grades are to be processed, we will use sentinel-controlled repetition. The user will type legitimate grades in one at a time. After the last legitimate grade is typed, the user will type the sentinel value. The program will test for this value after each grade is input and will terminate the loop when the sentinel is entered. The refinement of the preceding pseudocode statement is then

Input the first grade
While the user has not as yet entered the sentinel
    Add this grade into the running total
    Add one to the grade counter
    Input the next grade (possibly the sentinel)

Notice that in pseudocode, we do not use braces around the set of statements that form the body of the *while* structure. We simply indent all these statements under the *while* to show that they all belong to the *while*. Again, pseudocode is only an informal program development aid.

The pseudocode statement

Calculate and print the class average

may be refined as follows:

If the counter is not equal to zero
    Set the average to the total divided by the counter
    Print the average
else
    Print "No grades were entered"

Notice that we are being careful here to test for the possibility of division by zero—a *fatal error* that if undetected would cause the program to fail (often called *"bombing"* or *"crashing"*). The complete second refinement is shown in Fig. 3.7.

Common Programming Error 3.7

An attempt to divide by zero causes a fatal error.

Initialize total to zero
Initialize counter to zero

Input the first grade
While the user has not as yet entered the sentinel
    Add this grade into the running total
    Add one to the grade counter
    Input the next grade (possibly the sentinel)

If the counter is not equal to zero
    Set the average to the total divided by the counter
    Print the average
else
    Print "No grades were entered"

Fig. 3.7   Pseudocode algorithm that uses sentinel-controlled repetition to solve
the class average problem.

Good Programming Practice 3.7

*When performing division by an expression whose value could be zero, explicitly test for
this case and handle it appropriately in your program (such as printing an error message)
rather than allowing the fatal error to occur.*

In Fig. 3.5 and Fig. 3.7, we include some completely blank lines in the pseudocode
for readability. Actually, the blank lines separate these programs into their various phases.

Software Engineering Observation 3.4

*Many programs can be divided logically into three phases: An initialization phase that
initializes the program variables; a processing phase that inputs data values and adjusts
program variables accordingly; and a termination phase that calculates and prints the final results.*

The pseudocode algorithm in Fig. 3.7 solves the more general class averaging problem. This algorithm was developed after only two levels of refinement. Sometimes more
levels are necessary.

Software Engineering Observation 3.5

*The programmer terminates the top-down, stepwise refinement process when the pseu-
docode algorithm is specified in sufficient detail for the programmer to be able to convert
the pseudocode to C. Implementing the C program is then normally straightforward.*

The C program and a sample execution are shown in Fig. 3.8. Although only integer
grades are entered, the averaging calculation is likely to produce a decimal number with a
decimal point. The type **int** can not represent such a number. The program introduces
the data type ***float*** to handle numbers with decimal points (called *floating-point numbers*) and introduces a special operator called a *cast operator* to handle the averaging calculation. These features are explained in detail after the program is presented.

```c
/* Class average program with
   sentinel-controlled repetition */
#include <stdio.h>

main()
{
   float average;                  /* new data type */
   int counter, grade, total;

   /* initialization phase */
   total = 0;
   counter = 0;

   /* processing phase */
   printf("Enter grade, -1 to end: ");
   scanf("%d", &grade);

   while (grade != -1) {
      total = total + grade;
      counter = counter + 1;
      printf("Enter grade, -1 to end: ");
      scanf("%d", &grade);
   }

   /* termination phase */
   if (counter != 0) {
      average = (float) total / counter;
      printf("Class average is %.2f", average);
   }
   else
      printf("No grades were entered\n");

   return 0;    /* indicate program ended successfully */
}
```

```
Enter grade, -1 to end: 75
Enter grade, -1 to end: 94
Enter grade, -1 to end: 97
Enter grade, -1 to end: 88
Enter grade, -1 to end: 70
Enter grade, -1 to end: 64
Enter grade, -1 to end: 83
Enter grade, -1 to end: 89
Enter grade, -1 to end: -1
Class average is 82.50
```

Fig. 3.8   C program and sample execution for the class average problem with sentinel-controlled repetition.

Notice the compound statement in the **while** loop in Fig 3.8. Once again, the braces are necessary for all four statements to be executed within the loop. Without the braces, the last three statements in the body of the loop would fall outside the loop, causing the computer to interpret this code incorrectly as follows.

```
while(grade != -1)
    total = total + grade;
counter = counter + 1;
printf("Enter grade, -1 to end: ");
scanf("%d", &grade);
```

This would cause an infinite loop if the user does not input -1 for the first grade.

Good Programming Practice 3.8

In a sentinel-controlled loop, the prompts requesting data entry should explicitly remind the user what the sentinel value is.

Averages do not always evaluate to integer values. Often, an average is a value such as 7.2 or -93.5 that contains a fractional part. These values are referred to as floating-point numbers and are represented by the data type **float**. The variable **average** is declared to be of type **float** to capture the fractional result of our calculation. However, the result of the calculation **total / counter** is an integer because **total** and **counter** are both integer variables. Dividing two integers results in *integer division* in which any fractional part of the calculation is lost (i.e., *truncated*). Since the calculation is performed first, the fractional part is lost before the result is assigned to **average**. To produce a floating-point calculation with integer values, we must create temporary values that are floating-point numbers for the calculation. C provides the *unary cast operator* to accomplish this task. The statement

```
average = (float) total / counter;
```

includes the cast operator (**float**) which creates a temporary floating point copy of its operand, **total**. Using a cast operator in this manner is called *explicit conversion*. The value stored in **total** is still an integer. The calculation now consists of a floating-point value (the temporary **float** version of **total**) divided by the integer value stored in **counter**. The C compiler only knows how to evaluate expressions in which the data types of the operands are identical. To ensure that the operands are of the same type, the compiler performs an operation called *promotion* (also called *implicit conversion*) on selected operands. For example, in an expression containing the data types **int** and **float**, the ANSI standard specifies that copies of **int** operands are made and *promoted* to **float**. In our example, after a copy of **counter** is made and promoted to **float**, the calculation is performed and the result of the floating-point division is assigned to **average**. The ANSI standard provides a set of rules for promotion of operands of different types. Chapter 5 presents a discussion of all the standard data types and their order of promotion.

Cast operators are available for any data type. The cast operator is formed by placing parentheses around a data type name. The cast operator is a *unary operator*, i.e., an operator that takes only one operand. In Chapter 2, we studied the binary arithmetic operators. C also supports unary versions of the plus (+) and minus (-) operators, so the programmer can write expressions like -7 or +5. Cast operators associate from right to left and have the same precedence as other unary operators such as unary **+** and unary **-**. This precedence is one level higher than that of the *multiplicative operators* *****, **/**, and **%**, and one level lower than that of parentheses.

The program in Fig. 3.8 uses the **printf** conversion specifier **%.2f** to print the value of **average**. The **f** specifies that a floating-point value will be printed. The **.2** is the *precision* with which the value will be displayed. It states that the value will be displayed with 2 decimal digits to the right of the decimal point. If the **%f** conversion specifier is used (without specifying the precision), the *default precision* of 6 is used—exactly as if the conversion specifier **%.6f** had been used. When floating-point values are printed with precision, the printed value is *rounded* to the indicated number of decimal positions. The value in memory is unaltered. When the following statements are executed, the values 3.45 and 3.4 are printed.

```
printf("%.2f\n", 3.446);    /* prints 3.45 */
printf("%.1f\n", 3.446);    /* prints 3.4  */
```

Common Programming Error 3.8

Using precision in a conversion specification in the format control string of a **scanf** *statement is wrong. Precisions are used only in* **printf** *conversion specifications.*

Common Programming Error 3.9

Using floating-point numbers in a manner that assumes they are represented precisely can lead to incorrect results. Floating-point numbers are represented only approximately by most computers.

Good Programming Practice 3.9

Do not compare floating-point values for equality.

Despite the fact that floating-point numbers are not always "100% precise," they have numerous applications. For example, when we speak of a "normal" body temperature of 98.6 we do not need to be precise to a large number of digits. When we view the temperature on a thermometer and read it as 98.6, it may actually be 98.5999473210643. The point here is that calling this number simply 98.6 is fine for most applications. We will say more about this issue later.

Another way floating-point numbers develop is through division. When we divide 10 by 3, the result is 3.3333333… with the sequence of 3s repeating infinitely. The computer allocates only a fixed amount of space to hold such a value, so clearly the stored floating-point value can only be an approximation.

3.10 Formulating Algorithms with Top-down, Stepwise Refinement: Case Study 3 (Nested Control Structures)

Let us work another complete problem. We will once again formulate the algorithm using pseudocode and top-down, stepwise refinement, and write a corresponding C program. We have seen that control structures may be stacked on top of one another (in sequence) just as a child stacks building blocks. In this case study we will see the only other struc-ed way control structures may be connected in C, namely through *nesting* of one control structure within another.

Consider the following problem statement:

A college offers a course that prepares students for the state licensing exam for real estate brokers. Last year, several of the students who completed this course took the licensing examination. Naturally, the college wants to know how well its students did on the exam. You have been asked to write a program to summarize the results. You have been given a list of these 10 students. Next to each name is written a 1 if the student passed the exam and a 2 if the student failed.

Your program should analyze the results of the exam as follows:

1. *Input each test result (i.e., a 1 or a 2). Display the message "Enter result" on the screen each time the program requests another test result.*

2. *Count the number of test results of each type.*

3. *Display a summary of the test results indicating the number of students who passed and the number of students who failed.*

4. *If more than 8 students passed the exam, print the message "Raise tuition."*

After reading the problem statement carefully, we make the following observations:

1. The program must process 10 test results. A counter-controlled loop will be used.

2. Each test result is a number—either a 1 or a 2. Each time the program reads a test result, the program must determine if the number is a 1 or a 2. We test for a 1 in our algorithm. If the number is not a 1, we assume that it is a 2. (An exercise at the end of the chapter considers the consequences of this assumption.)

3. Two counters are used—one to count the number of students who passed the exam and one to count the number of students who failed the exam.

4. After the program has processed all the results, it must decide if more than 8 students passed the exam.

Let us proceed with top-down, stepwise refinement. We begin with a pseudocode representation of the top:

Analyze exam results and decide if tuition should be raised

Once again, it is important to emphasize that the top is a complete representation of the program, but several refinements are likely to be needed before the pseudocode can be naturally evolved into a C program. Our first refinement is

Initialize variables
Input the ten quiz grades and count passes and failures
Print a summary of the exam results and decide if tuition should be raised

Here, too, even though we have a complete representation of the entire program, further refinement is necessary. We now commit to specific variables. Counters are needed to record the passes and failures, a counter will be used to control the looping process, and a variable is needed to store the user input. The pseudocode statement

Initialize variables

may be refined as follows:

Initialize passes to zero
Initialize failures to zero
Initialize student to one

Notice only the counters and totals are initialized. The pseudocode statement

Input the ten quiz grades and count passes and failures

requires a loop that successively inputs the result of each exam. Here it is known in advance that there are precisely ten exam results, so counter-controlled looping is appropriate. Inside the loop (i.e., *nested* within the loop) a double-selection structure will determine whether each exam result is a pass or a failure, and will increment the appropriate counters accordingly. The refinement of the preceding pseudocode statement is then

While student counter is less than or equal to ten
    Input the next exam result

    If the student passed
        Add one to passes
    else
        Add one to failures

    Add one to student counter

Notice the use of blank lines to set off the *If/else* control structure to improve program readability. The pseudocode statement

Print a summary of the exam results and decide if tuition should be raised

may be refined as follows:

Print the number of passes
Print the number of failures
If more than eight students passed
    Print "Raise tuition"

The complete second refinement appears in Fig. 3.9. Notice that blank lines are also used to set off the *while* structure for program readability.

This pseudocode is now sufficiently refined for conversion to C. The C program and two sample executions are shown in Fig. 3.10. Note that we have taken advantage of a feature of C that allows initialization to be incorporated into declarations. Such initialization occurs at compile-time.

Performance Tip 3.1
_____

Initializing variables when they are declared reduces a program's execution time.

Software Engineering Observation 3.6
_____

Experience has shown that the most difficult part of solving a problem on a computer is developing the algorithm for the solution. Once a correct algorithm has been specified, the process of producing a working C program is normally straightforward.

Initialize passes to zero
Initialize failures to zero
Initialize student to one

While student counter is less than or equal to ten
  Input the next exam result

  If the student passed
      Add one to passes
  else
      Add one to failures

  Add one to student counter

Print the number of passes
Print the number of failures
If more than eight students passed
  Print "Raise tuition"

Fig. 3.9   Pseudocode for examination results problem.

Software Engineering Observation 3.7

Many programmers write programs without ever using program development tools like pseudocode. They feel that their ultimate goal is to solve the problem on a computer, and that writing pseudocode merely delays the production of final outputs.

3.11 Assignment Operators

C provides several assignment operators for abbreviating assignment expressions. For example the statement

```
c = c + 3;
```

can be abbreviated with the *addition assignment operator* += as

```
c += 3;
```

The += operator adds the value of the expression on the right of the operator to the value of the variable on the left of the operator and stores the result in the variable on the left of the operator. Any statement of the form

  variable = *variable operator expression*;

where *operator* is one of the binary operators +, −, *, /, or % (or others we will discuss in Chapter 10), can be written in the form

  variable operator= *expression*;

```
/* Analysis of examination results */
#include <stdio.h>

main()
{
   /* initializing variables in declarations */
   int passes = 0, failures = 0, student = 1, result;

   /* process 10 students; counter-controlled loop */
   while (student <= 10) {
      printf("Enter result (1=pass,2=fail): ");
      scanf("%d", &result);

      if (result == 1)          /* if/else nested in while */
         passes = passes + 1;
      else
         failures = failures + 1;

      student = student + 1;
   }

   printf("Passed %d\n", passes);
   printf("Failed %d\n", failures);

   if (passes > 8)
      printf("Raise tuition\n");

   return 0;   /* successful termination */
}
```

```
Enter Result (1=pass,2=fail): 1
Enter Result (1=pass,2=fail): 2
Enter Result (1=pass,2=fail): 2
Enter Result (1=pass,2=fail): 1
Enter Result (1=pass,2=fail): 1
Enter Result (1=pass,2=fail): 1
Enter Result (1=pass,2=fail): 2
Enter Result (1=pass,2=fail): 1
Enter Result (1=pass,2=fail): 1
Enter Result (1=pass,2=fail): 2
Passed 6
Failed 4
```

Fig. 3.10   C program and sample executions for examination results problem (part 1 of 2).

Thus the assignment **c += 3** adds **3** to **c**. Figure 3.11 shows the arithmetic assignment operators, sample expressions using these operators, and explanations.

Performance Tip 3.2

An expression with an assignment operator (as in **c += 3***) compiles faster than the equivalent expanded expression (* **c = c + 3***) because* **c** *in the first expression is evaluated only once while in the second expression it is evaluated twice.*

```
Enter Result (1=pass,2=fail): 1
Enter Result (1=pass,2=fail): 1
Enter Result (1=pass,2=fail): 1
Enter Result (1=pass,2=fail): 2
Enter Result (1=pass,2=fail): 1
Enter Result (1=pass,2=fail): 1
Enter Result (1=pass,2=fail): 1
Enter Result (1=pass,2=fail): 1
Enter Result (1=pass,2=fail): 1
Enter Result (1=pass,2=fail): 1
Passed 9
Failed 1
Raise tuition
```

Fig. 3.10   C program and sample executions for examination results problem (part 2 of 2).

Assignment operator	Sample expression	Explanation	Assigns
Assume : `int c = 3, d = 5, e = 4, f = 6, g = 12;`			
`+=`	`c += 7`	`c = c + 7`	10 to `c`
`-=`	`d -= 4`	`d = d - 4`	1 to `d`
`*=`	`e *= 5`	`e = e * 5`	20 to `e`
`/=`	`f /= 3`	`f = f / 3`	2 to `f`
`%=`	`g %= 9`	`g = g % 9`	3 to `g`

Fig. 3.11   Arithmetic assignment operators.

Performance Tip 3.3

Many of the performance tips we mention in this text result in nominal improvements, so the reader may be tempted to ignore them. The point is that it is the cumulative effect of all these performance enhancements that can make a program perform significantly faster. Also, significant improvement is realized when a supposedly nominal improvement is placed in a loop that may repeat a large number of times.

3.12 Increment and Decrement Operators

C also provides the unary *increment operator*, **++**, and the unary *decrement operator*, **--**, which are summarized in Fig. 3.12. If a variable **c** is incremented by 1, the increment operator **++** can be used rather than the expressions **c = c + 1** or **c += 1**. If increment or decrement operators are placed before a variable, they are referred to as the *preincrement*

Operator	Sample expression	Explanation
++	++a	Increment **a** by 1 then use the new value of **a** in the expression in which **a** resides.
++	a++	Use the current value of **a** in the expression in which **a** resides, then increment **a** by 1.
--	--b	Decrement **b** by 1 then use the new value of **b** in the expression in which **b** resides.
--	b--	Use the current value of **b** in the expression in which **b** resides, then decrement **b** by 1.

Fig. 3.12   The increment and decrement operators.

or *predecrement operators,* respectively. If increment or decrement operators are placed after a variable, they are referred to as the *postincrement* or *postdecrement operators,* respectively. Preincrementing (predecrementing) a variable causes the variable to be incremented (decremented) by 1, then the new value of the variable is used in the expression in which it appears. Postincrementing (postdecrementing) the variable causes the current value of the variable to be used in the expression in which it appears, then the variable value is incremented (decremented) by 1.

The program of Fig. 3.13 demonstrates the difference between the preincrementing and the postincrementing versions of the **++** operator. Postincrementing the variable **c** causes it to be incremented after it is used in the **printf** statement. Preincrementing the variable **c** causes it to be incremented before it is used in the **printf** statement.

The program displays the value of **c** before and after the **++** operator is used. The decrement operator (**--**) works similarly.

Good Programming Practice 3.10

Unary operators should be placed directly next to their operands with no intervening spaces.

The three assignment statements in Fig 3.10

```
passes = passes + 1;
failures = failures + 1;
student = student + 1;
```

can be written more concisely with assignment operators as

```
passes += 1;
failures += 1;
student += 1;
```

with preincrement operators as

```
++passes;
++failures;
++student;
```

```
/* Preincrementing and postincrementing */
#include <stdio.h>

main()
{
   int c;

   c = 5;
   printf("%d\n", c);
   printf("%d\n", c++);          /* postincrement */
   printf("%d\n\n", c);

   c = 5;
   printf("%d\n", c);
   printf("%d\n", ++c);          /* preincrement */
   printf("%d\n", c);

   return 0;    /* successful termination */
}
```

```
5
5
6

5
6
6
```

Fig. 3.13 Showing the difference between preincrementing and postincrementing.

or with postincrement operators as

```
passes++;
failures++;
student++;
```

It is important to note here that when incrementing or decrementing a variable in a statement by itself, the preincrement and postincrement forms have the same effect. It is only when a variable appears in the context of a larger expression that preincrementing and postincrementing have different effects (and similarly for predecrementing and postdecrementing).

Only a simple variable name may be used as the operand of an increment or decrement operator.

Common Programming Error 3.10

Attempting to use the increment or decrement operator on an expression other than a simple variable name, e.g., writing ++(x + 1) is a syntax error.

Good Programming Practice 3.11

The ANSI standard generally does not specify the order in which an operator's operands will be evaluated (although we will see exceptions to this for a few operators in Chapter 4). Therefore the programmer should avoid using statements with increment or decrement operators in which a particular variable being incremented or decremented appears more than once.

The chart in Fig. 3.14 shows the precedence and associativity of the operators introduced to this point. The operators are shown top-to-bottom in decreasing order of precedence. The second column describes the associativity of the operators at each level of precedence. Notice that the conditional operator (**? :**), the unary operators increment (**++**), decrement (**--**), plus (**+**), minus (**-**) and casts, and the assignment operators **=**, **+=**, **-=**, ***=**, **/ =** and **%=** associate from right to left. The third column names the various groups of operators. All other operators in Fig. 3.14 associate from left to right.

Summary

- The solution to any computing problem involves performing a series of actions in a specific order. A procedure for solving a problem in terms of the actions to be executed and the order in which these actions should be executed is called an algorithm.

- Specifying the order in which statements are to be executed in a computer program is called program control.

- Pseudocode is an artificial and informal language that helps programmers develop algorithms. It is similar to everyday English. Pseudocode programs are not actually executed on computers. Rather, pseudocode merely helps the programmer to "think out" a program before attempting to write it in a programming language such as C.

- Pseudocode consists purely of characters, so programmers may type pseudocode programs into the computer, edit them, and save them.

Operators							Associativity	Type
( )							left to right	parentheses
++	--	+	-	(type)			right to left	unary
*	/	%					left to right	multiplicative
+	-						left to right	additive
<	<=	>	>=				left to right	relational
==	!=						left to right	equality
? :							right to left	conditional
=	+=	-=	*=	/=	%=		right to left	assignment

Fig. 3.14 Precedence of the operators encountered so far in the text.

- Pseudocode consists only of executable statements. Declarations are messages to the compiler telling it the attributes of variables and telling it to reserve space for variables.

- A selection structure is used to choose among alternative courses of action.

- The **if** selection structure executes an indicated action only when the condition is true.

- The **if/else** selection structure specifies separate actions to be executed when the condition is true and when the condition is false.

- A nested **if/else** selection structure can test for many different cases. If more than one condition is true, only the statements after the first true condition will be executed.

- Whenever more than one statement is to be executed where normally only a single statement is expected, these statements must be enclosed in braces forming a compound statement. A compound statement can be placed anywhere a single statement can be placed.

- An empty statement indicating that no action is to be taken is indicated by placing a semicolon (**;**) where a statement would normally be.

- A repetition structure specifies that an action is to be repeated while some condition remains true.

- The format for the **while** repetition structure is

      while (*condition*)
         statement

   The statement (or compound statement or block) contained in the **while** repetition structure constitutes the body of the loop.

- Normally, some action specified within the body of a **while** must eventually cause the condition to become false. Otherwise, the loop will never terminate—an error called an infinite loop.

- Counter-controlled looping uses a variable as a counter to determine when a loop should terminate.

- A total is a variable that accumulates the sum of a series of numbers. Totals should normally be initialized to zero before a program is run.

- A flowchart is a graphical representation of an algorithm. Flowcharts are drawn using certain special symbols such as ovals, rectangles, diamonds, and small circles connected by arrows called flowlines. Symbols indicate the actions to be performed. Flowlines indicate the order in which actions are to be performed.

- The oval symbol, also called the termination symbol, indicates the beginning and end of every algorithm.

- The rectangle symbol, also called the action symbol, indicates any type of calculation or input/output operation. Rectangle symbols correspond to the actions that are normally performed by assignment statements or to the input/output operations that are normally performed by standard library functions like **printf** and **scanf**.

- The diamond symbol, also called the decision symbol, indicates that a decision is to be made. The decision symbol contains an expression that can be either true or false. Two flowlines emerge from it. One flowline indicates the direction to be taken when the condition is true; the other indicates the direction to be taken when the condition is false.

- A value that contains a fractional part is referred to as a floating-point number and is represented by the data type **float**.

- Dividing two integers results in integer division in which any fractional part of the calculation is lost (i.e., truncated).

- C provides the unary cast operator **(float)** to create a temporary floating-point copy of its operand. Using a cast operator in this manner is called explicit conversion. Cast operators are available for any data type.

- The C compiler only knows how to evaluate expressions in which the data types of the operands are identical. To ensure that the operands are of the same type, the compiler performs an operation called promotion (also called implicit conversion) on selected operands. The ANSI standard specifies that copies of **int** operands are made and promoted to **float**. The ANSI standard provides a set of rules for promotion of operands of different types.

- Floating-point values are output with a specific number of digits following the decimal point by using a precision with the **%f** conversion specifier in a **printf** statement. The value **3.456** output with the conversion specifier **%.2f** is displayed as **3.46**. If the **%f** conversion specifier is used (without specifying the precision), the default precision of 6 is used.

- C provides various assignment operators that help abbreviate certain common types of arithmetic assignment expressions. These operators are: **+=**, **-=**, ***=**, **/=**, and **%=**. In general, any statement of the form

    variable **=** *variable operator expression***;**

  where **operator** is one of the operators **+**, **-**, *****, **/**, or **%**, can be written in the form

    *variable operator***=** *expression***;**

- C provides the increment operator, **++**, and the decrement operator, **--**, to increment or decrement a variable by 1. These operators can be prefixed or postfixed to a variable. If the operator is prefixed to the variable, the variable is incremented or decremented by 1 first, then used in its expression. If the operator is postfixed to the variable, the variable is used in its expression, then incremented or decremented by 1.

Terminology

action	arrow symbol
action symbol	block
algorithm	body of a loop
arithmetic assignment operators: +=, -=,	"bombing"
*=, /=, and %=	cast operator

compound statement
conditional operator (**?:**)
control structure
counter
counter-controlled repetition
"crashing"
decision
decision symbol
decrement operator (**--**)
default precision
definite repetition
diamond symbol
division by zero
double-selection structure
dummy value
empty statement (**;**)
"end of data entry"
end symbol
explicit conversion
fatal error
first refinement
flag value
float
floating-point number
flowchart
flowchart symbol
flowline
"garbage" value
goto elimination
goto statement
if/else selection structure
if selection structure
implicit conversion
increment operator (**++**)
indefinite repetition
infinite loop
initialization
initialization phase
integer division
logic error
looping
multiple-selection structure
multiplicative operators

nested control structures
nested **if/else** structures
nonfatal error
order of actions
oval symbol
postdecrement operator
postincrement operator
precision
predecrement operator
preincrement operator
processing phase
program control
promotion
pseudocode
rectangle symbol
repetition
repetition structures
rounding
second refinement
selection
selection structures
sentinel value
sequential execution
sequence structure
signal value
single-entry/single-exit control structures
single-selection structure
stacked control structures
steps
stepwise refinement
structured programming
syntax error
terminating condition
termination phase
termination symbol
ternary operator
top
top-down, stepwise refinement
total
transfer of control
truncation
while repetition structure
whitespace characters

Common Programming Errors

3.1   Forgetting one or both of the braces that delimit a compound statement.

3.2   Placing a semicolon after the condition in an **if** structure leads to a logic error in single selection **if** structures and a syntax error in double selection **if** structures.

3.3   Not providing in the body of a **while** structure an action that eventually causes the condition in the **while** to become false. Normally, such a repetition structure will never terminate—an error called an "infinite loop."

3.4   Spelling the keyword **while** with an uppercase **W** as in **While** (remember that C is a case-sensitive language). All of C's reserved keywords such as **while**, **if**, and **else** contain only lowercase letters.

3.5   If a counter or total is not initialized, the results of your program will probably be incorrect. This is an example of a logic error.

3.6   Choosing a sentinel value that is also a legitimate data value.

3.7   An attempt to divide by zero causes a fatal error.

3.8   Using precision in a conversion specification in the format control string of a **scanf** statement. Precisions are used only in **printf** conversion specifications.

3.9   Using floating-point numbers in a manner that assumes they are represented precisely can lead to incorrect results. Floating-point numbers are represented only approximately by most computers.

3.10   Attempting to use the increment or decrement operator on an expression other than a simple variable name,e.g., writing **++(x + 1)** is a syntax error.

Good Programming Practices

3.1   Consistently applying responsible indentation conventions greatly improves program readability. We suggest a fixed-size tab of about 1/4 inch or three blanks per indent.

3.2   Pseudocode is often used to "think out" a program during the program design process. Then the pseudocode program is converted to C.

3.3   Indent both body statements of an **if/else** structure.

3.4   If there are several levels of indentation, each level should be indented the same additional amount of space.

3.5   Some programmers prefer to type the beginning and ending braces of compound statements before typing the individual statements within the braces. This helps avoid omitting one or both of the braces.

3.6   Initialize counters and totals.

3.7   When performing division by an expression whose value could be zero, explicitly test for this case and handle it appropriately in your program (such as printing an error message) rather than allowing the fatal error to occur.

3.8   In a sentinel-controlled loop, the prompts requesting data entry should explicitly remind the user what the sentinel value is.

3.9   Do not compare floating-point values for equality.

3.10   Unary operators should be placed directly next to their operands with no intervening spaces.

3.11   The ANSI standard generally does not specify the order in which an operator's operands will be evaluated (although we will see exceptions to this for a few operators in Chapter 4). Therefore the programmer should avoid using statements with increment or decrement operators in which a particular variable being incremented or decremented appears more than once.

Performance Tips

3.1   Initializing variables when they are declared reduces a program's execution time.

3.2   An expression with an assignment operator (as in `c += 3`) compiles faster than the equivalent expanded expression (`c = c + 3`) because `c` in the first expression is evaluated only once while in the second expression it is evaluated twice.

3.3   Many of the performance tips we mention in this text result in nominal improvements, so the reader may be tempted to ignore them. The point is that it is the cumulative effect of all these performance enhancements that can make a program perform significantly faster. Also, significant improvement is realized when a supposedly nominal improvement is placed in a loop that may repeat a large number of times.

Software Engineering Observations

3.1   A compound statement can be placed anywhere in a program that a single statement can be placed.

3.2   Just as a compound statement can be placed anywhere a single statement can be placed, it is also possible to have no statement at all, i.e., the empty statement. The empty statement is represented by placing a semicolon (`;`) where a statement would normally be.

3.3   Each refinement, as well as the top itself, is a complete specification of the algorithm; only the level of detail varies.

3.4   Many programs can be divided logically into three phases: An initialization phase that initializes the program variables; a processing phase that inputs data values and adjusts program variables accordingly; and a termination phase that calculates and prints the final results.

3.5   The programmer terminates the top-down, stepwise refinement process when the pseudocode algorithm is specified in sufficient detail for the programmer to be able to convert the pseudocode to C. Implementing the C program is then normally straightforward.

3.6   Experience has shown that the most difficult part of solving a problem on a computer is developing the algorithm for the solution. Once a correct algorithm has been specified, the process of producing a working C program is normally straightforward.

3.7   Many programmers write programs without ever using program development tools like pseudocode. They feel that their ultimate goal is to solve the problem on a computer, and that writing pseudocode merely delays the production of final outputs.

Self-Review Exercises

3.1   Answer each of the following questions.
   a) A procedure for solving a problem in terms of the actions to be executed and the order in which the actions should be executed is called an _____.
   b) Specifying the execution order of statements by the computer is called _____.
   c) All programs can be written in terms of three control structures:_____, _____, and _____.
   d) The _____ selection structure is used to execute one action when a condition is true and another action when that condition is false.
   e) Several statements grouped together in braces (`{` and `}`) are called a _____.
   f) The _____ repetition structure specifies that a statement or group of statements is to be executed repeatedly while some condition remains true.
   g) Repetition of a set of instructions a specific number of times is called _____ repetition.
   h) When it is not known in advance how many times a set of statements will be repeated, a _____ value can be used to terminate the repetition.

3.2   Write four different C statements that each add 1 to integer variable **x**.

3.3   Write a single C statement to accomplish each of the following:
a) Assign the sum of **x** and **y** to **z** and increment the value of **x** by 1 after the calculation.
b) Multiply the variable **product** by 2 using the ***=** operator.
c) Multiply the variable **product** by 2 using the **=** and ***** operators.
d) Test if the value of the variable **count** is greater than 10. If it is, print "**Count is greater than 10.**"
e) Decrement the variable **x** by 1 then subtract it from the variable **total**.
f) Add the variable **x** to the variable **total**, then decrement **x** by 1.
g) Calculate the remainder after **q** is divided by **divisor** and assign the result to **q**. Write this statement two different ways.
h) Print the value **123.4567** with **2** digits of precision. What value is printed?
i) Print the floating point value **3.14159** with three digits to the right of the decimal point. What value is printed?

3.4   Write a C statement to accomplish each of the following tasks.
a) Declare variables **sum** and **x** to be of type **int**.
b) Initialize variable **x** to **1**.
c) Initialize variable **sum** to **0**.
d) Add variable **x** to variable **sum** and assign the result to variable **sum**.
e) Print **"The sum is: "** followed by the value of variable **sum**.

3.5   Combine the statements that you wrote in Exercise 3.4 into a program that calculates the sum of the integers from 1 to 10. Use the **while** structure to loop through the calculation and increment statements. The loop should terminate when the value of **x** becomes 11.

3.6   Determine the values of each variable after the calculation is performed. Assume that when each statement begins executing all variables have the value 5.
a) **product *= x++;**
b) **result = ++x + x;**

3.7   Write single C statements that
a) Input integer variable **x** with **scanf**.
b) Input integer variable **y** with **scanf**.
c) Initialize integer variable **i** to **1**.
d) Initialize integer variable **power** to **1**.
e) Multiply variable **power** by **x** and assign the result to **power**.
f) Increment variable **y** by **1**.
g) Test **y** to see if it is less than or equal to **x**.
h) Output integer variable **power** with **printf**.

3.8   Write a C program that uses the statements in Exercise 3.7 to calculate **x** raised to the **y** power. The program should have a **while** repetition control structure.

3.9   Identify and correct the errors in each of the following:
a) **while (c <= 5) {**
       product *= c;
       ++c;
b) **scanf("%.4f", &value);**
c) **if (gender == 1)**
       printf("Woman\n");
   else;
       printf("Man\n");

3.10   What is wrong with the following **while** repetition structure:
```
while (z >= 0)
    sum += z;
```

Answers to Self-Review Exercises

3.1   a) Algorithm. b) Program control. c) Sequence, selection, repetition. d) **if/else**. e) Compound statement. f) **while**. g) Counter-controlled. h) Sentinel.

3.2
```
x = x + 1;
x += 1;
++x;
x++;
```

3.3   a) ```z = x++ + y;```
            b) ```product *= 2;```
            c) ```product = product * 2;```
            d) ```if (count > 10)```
                   ```printf("Count is greater than 10.\n");```
            e) ```total -= --x;```
            f) ```total += x--;```
            g) ```q %= divisor;```
               ```q = q % divisor;```
            h) ```printf("%.2f", 123.4567);```
               ```123.46``` is displayed.
            i) ```printf("%.3f\n", 3.14159);```
               ```3.142``` is displayed.

3.4   a) ```int sum, x;```
            b) ```x = 1;```
            c) ```sum = 0;```
            d) ```sum += x;``` or ```sum = sum + x;```
            e) ```printf("The sum is: %d\n", sum);```

3.5
```
/* Calculate the sum of the integers from 1 to 10 */
#include <stdio.h>

main()
{
    int sum, x;

    x = 1;
    sum = 0;
    while (x <= 10) {
        sum += x;
        ++x;
    }

    printf("The sum is: %d\n", sum);
}
```

3.6   a) ```product = 25, x = 6;```
            b) ```result = 12, x = 6;```

3.7   a) `scanf("%d", &x);`
b) `scanf("%d", &y);`
c) `i = 1;`
d) `power = 1;`
e) `power *= x;`
f) `y++;`
g) `if(y <= x)`
h) `printf("%d", power);`

3.8
```
/* raise x to the y power */
#include <stdio.h>

main()
   int x,y,i,power;

   i = 1;
   power = 1;
   scanf("%d", &x);
   scanf("%d", &y);

   while (i <= y) {
      power *= x;
      ++i;
   }

   printf("%d", power);
   return 0;
}
```

3.9   a) Error: Missing the closing right brace of the **while** body.
Correction: Add closing right brace after the statement **++c;**.
b) Error: Precision used in a **scanf** conversion specification.
Correction: Remove **.4** from the conversion specification.
c) Error: Semicolon after the **else** part of the **if/else** structure results in a logic error. The second **printf** will always be executed.
Correction: Remove the semicolon after **else**.

3.10   The value of the variable **z** is never changed in the **while** structure. Therefore, an infinite loop is created. To prevent the infinite loop, **z** must be decremented so that it eventually becomes **0**.

Exercises

3.11   Identify and correct the errors in each of the following (Note: there may be more than one error in each piece of code):
a)
```
if (age >= 65);
   printf("Age is greater than or equal to 65\n");
else
   printf("Age is less than 65\n");
```
b)
```
int x = 1, total;

while (x <= 10) {
   total += x;
   ++x;
}
```

```
c) While (x <= 100)
      total += x;
      ++x;
d) while (y > 0) {
      printf("%d\n", y);
      ++y;
   }
```

3.12   Fill in the blanks in each of the following:

   a) The solution to any problem involves performing a series of actions in a specific
      _____.

   b) A synonym for procedure is _____.

   c) A variable that accumulates the sum of several numbers is a _____.

   d) The process of setting certain variables to specific values at the beginning of a program
      is called _____.

   e) A special value used to indicate "end of data entry" is called a _____, a
      _____, a _____, or a _____ value.

   f) A _____ is a graphical representation of an algorithm.

   g) In a flowchart, the order in which the steps should be performed is indicated by
      _____symbols.

   h) The termination symbol indicates the _____ and _____ of every algorithm.

   i) Rectangle symbols correspond to calculations that are normally performed by
      _____ statements and input/output operations that are normally performed by
      calls to the_____ and _____ standard library functions.

   j) The item written inside a decision symbol is called a _____.

3.13   What does the following program print?

```
#include <stdio.h>

main()
{
   int x = 1, total = 0, y;

   while (x <= 10) {
      y = x * x;
      printf("%d\n", y);
      total += y;
      ++x;
   }

   printf("Total is %d\n", total);
   return 0;
}
```

3.14   Write a single pseudocode statement that indicates each of the following:

   a) Display the message "**Enter two numbers**".

   b) Assign the sum of variables **x**, **y**, and **z** to variable **p**.

   c) The following condition is to be tested in an **if/else** selection structure: The current
      value of variable **m** is greater than twice the current value of variable **v**.

   d) Obtain values for variables **s**, **r**, and **t** from the keyboard.

3.15   Formulate a pseudocode algorithm for each of the following :

   a) Obtain two numbers from the keyboard, compute the sum of the numbers, and display
      the result.

b) Obtain two numbers from the keyboard, and determine and display which (if either) is the larger of the two numbers.

c) Obtain a series of positive numbers from the keyboard, and determine and display the sum of the numbers. Assume that the user types the sentinel value **-1** to indicate "end of data entry."

3.16   State which of the following are true and which are false. If a statement is false, explain why.

a) Experience has shown that the most difficult part of solving a problem on a computer is producing a working C program.

b) A sentinel value must be a value that cannot be confused with a legitimate data value.

c) Flowlines indicate the actions to be performed.

d) Conditions written inside decision symbols always contain arithmetic operators (i.e., **+**, **-**, *****, **/**, and **%**).

e) In top-down, stepwise refinement, each refinement is a complete representation of the algorithm.

For Exercises 3.17 to 3.21, perform each of these steps:

1. Read the problem statement.
2. Formulate the algorithm using pseudocode and top-down, stepwise refinement.
3. Write a C program.
4. Test, debug, and execute the C program.

3.17   Because of the high price of gasoline, drivers are concerned with the mileage obtained by their automobiles. One driver has kept track of several tankfuls of gasoline by recording miles driven and gallons used for each tankful. Develop a C program that will input the miles driven and gallons used for each tankful. The program should calculate and display the miles per gallon obtained for each tankful. After processing all input information, the program should calculate and print the combined miles per gallon obtained for all tankfuls.

```
Enter the gallons used (-1 to end): 12.8
Enter the miles driven: 287
The miles / gallon for this tank was 22.421875

Enter the gallons used (-1 to end): 10.3
Enter the miles driven: 200
The miles / gallon for this tank was 19.417475

Enter the gallons used (-1 to end): 5
Enter the miles driven: 120
The miles / gallon for this tank was 24.000000

Enter the gallons used (-1 to end): -1

The overall average miles/gallon was 21.601423
```

3.18   Develop a C program that will determine if a department store customer has exceeded the credit limit on a charge account. For each customer, the following facts are available:

1. Account number
2. Balance at the beginning of the month
3. Total of all items charged by this customer this month
4. Total of all credits applied to this customer's account this month

5. Allowed credit limit

The program should input each of these facts, calculate the new balance (= beginning balance + charges - credits), and determine if the new balance exceeds the customer's credit limit. For those customers whose credit limit is exceeded, the program should display the customer's account number, credit limit, new balance, and the message "Credit limit exceeded."

```
Enter account number (-1 to end): 100
Enter beginning balance: 5394.78
Enter total charges: 1000.00
Enter total credits: 500.00
Enter credit limit: 5500.00
Account:      100
Credit limit: 5500.00
Balance:      5894.78
Credit Limit Exceeded.

Enter account number (-1 to end): 200
Enter beginning balance: 1000.00
Enter total charges: 123.45
Enter total credits: 321.00
Enter credit limit: 1500.00

Enter account number (-1 to end): 300
Enter beginning balance: 500.00
Enter total charges: 274.73
Enter total credits: 100.00
Enter credit limit: 800.00

Enter account number (-1 to end): -1
```

3.19   One large chemical company pays its salespeople on a commission basis. The salespeople receive $200 per week plus 9 percent of their gross sales for that week. For example, a salesperson who sells $5000 worth of chemicals in a week receives $200 plus 9 percent of $5000, or a total of $650. Develop a C program that will input each salesperson's gross sales for last week and will calculate and display that salesperson's earnings. Process one salesperson's figures at a time.

```
Enter sales in dollars (-1 to end): 5000.00
Salary is: $650.00

Enter sales in dollars (-1 to end): 1234.56
Salary is: $311.11

Enter sales in dollars (-1 to end): 1088.89
Salary is: $298.00

Enter sales in dollars (-1 to end): -1
```

3.20   The simple interest on a loan is calculated by the formula

```
interest = principal * rate * days / 365
```

The preceding formula assumes that **rate** is the annual interest rate, and therefore includes the division by 365 (days). Develop a C program that will input **principal**, **rate**, and **days** for several loans, and will calculate and display the simple interest for each loan, using the preceding formula.

```
Enter loan principal (-1 to end): 1000.00
Enter interest rate: .1
Enter term of the loan in days: 365
The interest charge is $100.00

Enter loan principal (-1 to end): 1000.00
Enter interest rate: .08375
Enter term of the loan in days: 224
The interest charge is $51.40

Enter loan principal (-1 to end): 10000.00
Enter interest rate: .09
Enter term of the loan in days: 1460
The interest charge is $3600.00

Enter loan principal (-1 to end): -1
```

3.21   Develop a C program that will determine the gross pay for each of several employees. The company pays "straight-time" for the first 40 hours worked by each employee and pays "time-and-a-half" for all hours worked in excess of 40 hours. You are given a list of the employees of the company, the number of hours each employee worked last week, and the hourly rate of each employee. Your program should input this information for each employee, and should determine and display the employee's gross pay.

```
Enter # of hours worked (-1 to end): 39
Enter hourly rate of the worker ($00.00): 10.00
Salary is $390.00

Enter # of hours worked (-1 to end): 40
Enter hourly rate of the worker ($00.00): 10.00
Salary is $400.00

Enter # of hours worked (-1 to end): 41
Enter hourly rate of the worker ($00.00): 10.00
Salary is $415.00

Enter # of hours worked (-1 to end): -1
```

3.22   Write a C program that demonstrates the difference between predecrementing and postdecrementing using the decrement operator --.

3.23   Write a C program that utilizes looping to print the numbers from 1 to 10 side-by-side on the same line with 3 spaces between each number.

3.24   The process of finding the largest number (i.e., the maximum of a group of numbers) is used frequently in computer applications. For example, a program that determines the winner of a sales contest would input the number of units sold by each salesperson. The salesperson who sells the most units wins the contest. Write a pseudocode program and then a C program that inputs a series of 10 numbers, and determines and prints the largest of the numbers. Hint: Your program should use three variables as follows:

counter: A counter to count to 10 (i.e., to keep track of how many numbers have been input, and to determine when all 10 numbers have been processed).

number: The current number input to the program.

largest: The largest number found so far.

3.25 Write a C program that utilizes looping to print the following table of values:

N	10*N	100*N	1000*N
1	10	100	1000
2	20	200	2000
3	30	300	3000
4	40	400	4000
5	50	500	5000
6	60	600	6000
7	70	700	7000
8	80	800	8000
9	90	900	9000
10	100	1000	10000

The tab character, **\t**, may be used in the **printf** statement to separate the columns with tabs.

3.26 Write a C program that utilizes looping to produce the following table of values:

A	A+2	A+4	A+6
3	5	7	9
6	8	10	12
9	11	13	15
12	14	16	18
15	17	19	21

3.27 Using an approach similar to Exercise 3.24, find the *two* largest values of the 10 numbers. Note: You may input each number only once.

3.28 Modify the program in Fig. 3.10 to validate its inputs. On any input, if the value entered is other than 1 or 2, keep looping until the user enters a correct value.

3.29 What does the following program print?

```
#include <stdio.h>

main()
{
    int count = 1;

    while (count <= 10) {
        printf("%s\n", count % 2 ? "****" : "++++++++");
        ++count;
    }

    return 0;
}
```

3.30 What does the following program print?

```
#include <stdio.h>

main()
{
   int row = 10, column;

   while (row >= 1) {
      column = 1;

      while (column <= 10) {
         printf("%s", row % 2 ? "<" : ">");
         ++column;
      }

      --row;
      printf("\n");
   }

   return 0;
}
```

3.31 *(Dangling Else Problem)* Determine the output for each of the following when **x** is **9** and **y** is **11** and when **x** is **11** and **y** is **9**. Note that the compiler ignores the indentation in a C program. Also, the C compiler always associates an **else** with the previous **if** unless told to do otherwise by the placement of braces **{}**. Because, on first glance, the programmer may not be sure which **if** an **else** matches, this is referred to as the "dangling else" problem. We have eliminated the indentation from the following code to make the problem more challenging. (Hint: Apply indentation conventions you have learned.)

a)
```
if (x < 10)
if (y > 10)
printf("*****\n");
else
printf("#####\n");
printf("$$$$$\n");
```

b)
```
if (x < 10) {
if (y > 10)
printf("*****\n");
}
else {
printf("#####\n");
printf("$$$$$\n");
}
```

3.32 *(Another Dangling Else Problem)* Modify the following code to produce the output shown. Use proper indentation techniques. You may not make any changes other than inserting braces. The compiler ignores the indentation in a C program. We have eliminated the indentation from the following code to make the problem more challenging. Note: It is possible that no modification is necessary.

```
if (y == 8)
if (x == 5)
printf("@@@@@\n");
else
printf("#####\n");
printf("$$$$$\n");
printf("&&&&&\n");
```

a) Assuming **x** = **5** and **y** = **8**, the following output is produced.

```
@@@@@
$$$$$
&&&&&
```

b) Assuming **x** = **5** and **y** = **8**, the following output is produced.

```
@@@@@
```

c) Assuming **x** = **5** and **y** = **8**, the following output is produced.

```
@@@@@
&&&&&
```

d) Assuming **x** = **5** and **y** = **7**, the following output is produced. Note: The last three **printf** statements are all part of a compound statement.

```
#####
$$$$$
&&&&&
```

3.33   Write a program that reads in the side of a square and then prints that square out of asterisks. Your program should work for squares of all side sizes between 1 and 20. For example, if your program reads a size of 4, it should print

```
****
****
****
****
```

3.34   Modify the program you wrote in Exercise 3.33 so that it prints a hollow square. For example, if your program reads a size of 5, it should print

```
*****
*   *
*   *
*   *
*****
```

3.35 A palindrome is a number or a text phrase that reads the same backwards as forwards. For example, each of the following five-digit integers are palindromes: 12321, 55555, 45554 and 11611. Write a program that reads in a five-digit integer and determines whether or not it is a palindrome. (Hint: Use the division and modulus operators to separate the number into its individual digits.)

3.36 Input an integer containing only 0s and 1s (i.e., a "binary" integer) and print its decimal equivalent. (Hint: Use the modulus and division operators to pick off the "binary" number's digits one at a time from right to left. Just as in the decimal number system where the rightmost digit has a positional value of 1, and the next digit left has a positional value of 10, then 100, then 1000, etc., in the binary number system the rightmost digit has a positional value of 1, the next digit left has a positional value of 2, then 4, then 8, etc. Thus the decimal number 234 can be interpreted as 4 * 1 + 3 * 10 + 2 * 100. The decimal equivalent of binary 1101 is 1 * 1 + 0 * 2 + 1 * 4 + 1 * 8 or 1 + 0 + 4 + 8 or 13.)

3.37 We keep hearing how fast computers are. How can you determine how fast your own machine really operates? Write a program with a **while** loop that counts from 1 to 3,000,000 by 1s. Every time the count reaches a multiple of 1,000,000 print that number on the screen. Use your watch to time how long each million repetitions of the loop takes.

3.38 Write a program that prints 100 asterisks, one at a time. After every tenth asterisk, your program should print a newline character. (Hint: Count from 1 to 100. Use the modulus operator to recognize each time the counter reaches a multiple of 10.)

3.39 Write a program that reads an integer and determines and prints how many digits in the integer are 7s.

3.40 Write a program that displays the following checkerboard pattern

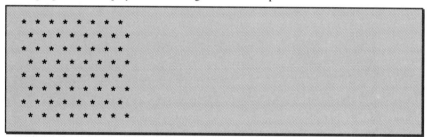

Your program may use only three **printf** statements, one of the form

```
printf("* ");
```

one of the form

```
printf(" ");
```

and one of the form

```
printf("\n");
```

3.41 Write a program that keeps printing the multiples of the integer 2 , namely 2, 4, 8, 16, 32, 64, etc. Your loop should not terminate (i.e., you should create an infinite loop). What happens when you run this program?

3.42 Write a program that reads the radius of a circle (as a **float** value) and computes and prints the diameter, the circumference, and the area. Use the value 3.14159 for π.

3.43 What's wrong with the following statement? Rewrite the statement to accomplish what the programmer was probably trying to do.

```
printf ("%d", ++(x + y));
```

3.44   Write a program that reads three nonzero **float** values and determines and prints if they could represent the sides of a triangle.

3.45   Write a program that reads three nonzero integers and determines and prints if they could be the sides of a right triangle.

3.46   A company wants to transmit data over the telephone, but they are concerned that their phones may be tapped. All of their data is transmitted as four-digit integers. They have asked you to write a program that will encrypt their data so that it may be transmitted more securely. Your program should read a four-digit integer and encrypt it as follows: Replace each digit by *(the sum of that digit plus 7) modulus 10.* Then, swap the first digit with the third, and swap the second digit with the fourth. Then print the encrypted integer. Write a separate program that inputs an encrypted four-digit integer, and decrypts it to form the original number.

3.47   The factorial of a nonnegative integer n is written $n!$ (pronounced "n factorial") and is defined as follows:

$$n! = n \cdot (n - 1) \cdot (n - 2) \cdot ... \cdot 1 \quad \text{(for values of } n \text{ greater than or equal to 1)}$$

and

$$n! = 1 \quad \text{(for } n = 0\text{)}.$$

For example, $5! = 5 \cdot 4 \cdot 3 \cdot 2 \cdot 1$ which is 120.

   a) Write a program that reads a nonegative integer and computes and prints its factorial.

   b) Write a program that estimates the value of the mathematical constant e by using the formula:

$$e = 1 + \frac{1}{1!} + \frac{1}{2!} + \frac{1}{3!} + ...$$

   c) Write a program that computes the value of e^x by using the formula

$$e^x = 1 + \frac{x}{1!} + \frac{x^2}{2!} + \frac{x^3}{3!} + ...$$

4

Program Control

Objectives

- To be able to use the `for` and `do/while` repetition structures.
- To understand multiple selection using the `switch` selection structure.
- To be able to use the `break` and `continue` program control statements.
- To be able to use the logical operators.

Who can control his fate?
William Shakespeare
Othello

The used key is always bright.
Benjamin Franklin

Man is a tool-making animal.
Benjamin Franklin

Intelligence ... is the faculty of making artificial objects, especially tools to make tools.
Henry Bergson

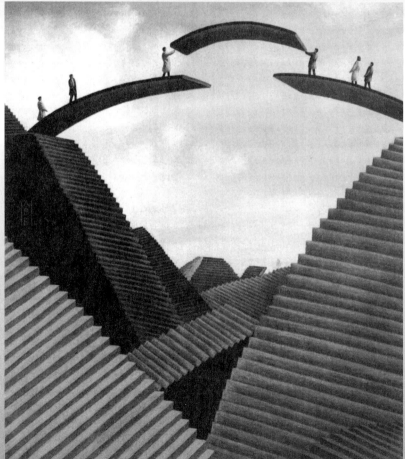

Outline

4.1 Introduction

At this point, the reader should be comfortable with the process of writing simple but complete C programs. In this chapter, repetition is considered in greater detail, and additional repetition control structures, namely the **for** structure and the **do/while** structure, are presented. The **switch** multiple selection structure is introduced. We discuss the **break** statement for exiting immediately and rapidly from certain control structures, and the **continue** statement for skipping the remainder of the body of a repetition structure and proceeding with the next iteration of the loop. The chapter discusses logical operators used for combining conditions, and concludes with a summary of the principles of structured programming as presented in Chapter 3 and Chapter 4.

4.2 The Essentials of Repetition

Most programs involve repetition or *looping*. A *loop* is a group of instructions the computer executes repeatedly while some *loop-continuation condition* remains true. We have discussed two means of repetition:

1. Counter-controlled repetition

2. Sentinel-controlled repetition

Counter-controlled repetition is sometimes called *definite repetition* because we know in advance exactly how many times the loop will be executed. Sentinel-controlled repetition is sometimes called *indefinite repetition* because it is not known in advance how many times the loop will be executed.

In counter-controlled repetition, a *control variable* is used to count the number of repetitions. The control variable is incremented (usually by 1) each time the group of instructions is performed. When the value of the control variable indicates that the correct number of repetitions has been performed, the loop terminates and the computer continues executing with the statement after the repetition structure.

Sentinel values are used to control repetition when:

1. The precise number of repetitions is not known in advance, and

2. The loop includes statements that obtain data each time the loop is performed.

The sentinel value indicates "end of data." The sentinel is entered after all regular data items have been supplied to the program. Sentinels must be distinct from regular data items.

4.3 Counter-Controlled Repetition

Counter-controlled repetition requires:

1. The *name* of a control variable (or loop counter).

2. The *initial value* of the control variable.

3. The *increment* (or *decrement*) by which the control variable is modified each time through the loop.

4. The condition that tests for the *final value* of the control variable (i.e., whether looping should continue).

Consider the simple program shown in Fig. 4.1, which prints the numbers from 1 to 10. The declaration

```
int counter = 1;
```

names the control variable (**counter**), declares it to be an integer, reserves space for it, and sets it to an *initial value* of **1**. This declaration is not an executable statement.

The declaration and initialization of **counter** could also have been accomplished with the statements

```
int counter;

counter = 1;
```

The declaration is not executable, but the assignment is. We use both methods of initializing variables.

The statement

```
++counter;
```

```
/* Counter-controlled repetition */
#include <stdio.h>

main()
{
   int counter = 1;                    /* initialization */

   while (counter <= 10) {        /* repetition condition */
      printf ("%d\n", counter);
      ++counter;                       /* increment */
   }

   return 0;
}
```

Fig. 4.1   Counter-controlled repetition.

increments the loop counter by 1 each time the loop is performed. The loop-continuation condition in the **while** structure tests if the value of the control variable is less than or equal to **10** (the last value for which the condition is true). Note that the body of this **while** is performed even when the control variable is **10**. The loop terminates when the control variable exceeds **10** (i.e., **counter** becomes **11**).

   C programmers would normally make the program in Fig. 4.1 more concise by initializing **counter** to **0** and by replacing the **while** structure with

```
while (++counter <= 10)
   printf ("%d\n", counter);
```

This code saves a statement because the incrementing is done directly in the **while** condition before the condition is tested. Also, this code eliminates the braces around the body of the **while** because the **while** now contains only one statement. Coding in such a condensed fashion takes some practice.

   Common Programming Error 4.1

   Because floating-point values may be approximate, controlling counting loops with floating-point variables may result in imprecise counter values and inaccurate tests for termination.

Good Programming Practice 4.1

Control counting loops with integer values.

Good Programming Practice 4.2

Indent the statements in the body of each control structure.

Good Programming Practice 4.3

Put a blank line before and after each major control structure to make it stand out in the program.

Good Programming Practice 4.4

Too many levels of nesting can make a program difficult to understand. As a general rule, try to avoid using more than three levels of indentation.

Good Programming Practice 4.5

The combination of vertical spacing before and after control structures and indentation of the bodies of control structures within the control structure headers gives programs a two-dimensional appearance that greatly improves program readability.

4.4 The For Repetition Structure

The **for** repetition structure handles all the details of counter-controlled repetition automatically. To illustrate the power of **for**, let us rewrite the program of Fig. 4.1. The result is shown in Fig. 4.2.

The program operates as follows. When the **for** structure begins executing, the control variable **counter** is initialized to **1**. Then, the loop-continuation condition **counter <= 10** is checked. Because the initial value of **counter** is **1**, the condition is satisfied, so the **printf** statement prints the value of **counter**, namely **1**. The control

```
/* Counter-controlled repetition with the for structure */
#include <stdio.h>

main()
{
   int counter;

   /* initialization, repetition condition, and increment */
   /* are all included in the for structure header        */
   for (counter = 1; counter <= 10; counter++)
      printf("%d\n", counter);

   return 0;
}
```

Fig. 4.2   Counter-controlled repetition with the **for** structure.

variable **counter** is then incremented by the expression **counter++**, and the loop begins again with the loop-continuation test. Since the control variable is now equal to **2**, the final value is not exceeded, so the program performs the **printf** statement again. This process continues until the control variable **counter** is incremented to its final value of 11—this causes the loop-continuation test to fail and repetition terminates. The program continues by performing the first statement after the **for** structure (in this case, the **return** statement at the end of the program).

Fig. 4.3 takes a closer look at the **for** structure of Fig. 4.2. Notice that the **for** structure "does it all"—it specifies each of the items needed for counter-controlled repetition with a control variable. If there is more than one statement in the body of the **for**, braces are required to define the body of the loop.

Notice that Fig. 4.2 uses the loop-continuation condition **counter <= 10**. If the programmer incorrectly wrote **counter < 10**, then the loop would only be executed 9 times. This is a common logic error called an *off-by-one error*.

Common Programming Error 4.2

*Using an incorrect relational operator or using an incorrect final value of a loop counter in the condition of a **while** or **for** structure can cause off-by-one errors.*

Good Programming Practice 4.6

*Using the final value in the condition of a **while** or **for** structure and using the **<=** relational operator will help avoid off-by-one errors. For a loop used to print the values 1 to 10, for example, the loop-continuation condition should be **counter <= 10** rather than **counter < 11** or **counter < 10**.*

The general format of the **for** structure is

    for (*expression1; expression2; expression3*)
      statement

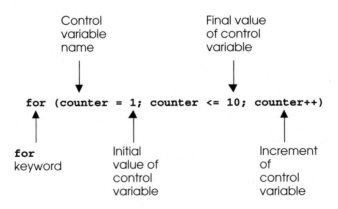

Fig. 4.3   Components of a typical **for** header.

where *expression1* initializes the loop's control variable, *expression2* is the loop-continuation condition, and *expression3* increments the control variable. In most cases the **for** structure can be represented with an equivalent **while** structure as follows:

```
expression1;
while (expression2) {
    statement
    expression3;
}
```

There is an exception to this rule which we will discuss in Section 4.9.

Often, *expression1* and *expression3* are comma-separated lists of expressions. The commas as used here are actually *comma operators* that guarantee lists of expressions evaluate from left to right. The value and type of a comma-separated list of expressions is the value and type of the rightmost expression in the list. The comma operator is most often used in a **for** structure. Its primary use is to enable the programmer to use multiple initialization and/or multiple increment expressions. For example, there may be two control variables in a single **for** structure that must be initialized and incremented.

Good Programming Practice 4.7

*Place only expressions involving the control variables in the initialization and increment sections of a **for** structure. Manipulations of other variables should appear either before the loop (if they execute only once like initialization statements) or in the loop body (if they execute once per repetition like incrementing or decrementing statements).*

The three expressions in the **for** structure are optional. If *expression2* is omitted, C assumes that the condition is true, thus creating an infinite loop. One might omit *expression1* if the control variable is initialized elsewhere in the program. *expression3* might be omitted if the increment is calculated by statements in the body of the **for** structure or if no increment is needed. The increment expression in the **for** structure acts like a standalone C statement at the end of the body of the **for**. Therefore, the expressions

```
counter = counter + 1
counter += 1
++counter
counter++
```

are all equivalent in the incrementing portion of the **for** structure. Many C programmers prefer the form **counter++** because the incrementing occurs after the loop body is executed. So, the postincrementing form seems more natural. Because the variable being preincremented or postincremented here does not appear in an expression, both forms of incrementing have the same effect. The two semicolons in the **for** structure are required.

Common Programming Error 4.3

*Using commas instead of semicolons in a **for** header.*

Common Programming Error 4.4

*Placing a semicolon immediately to the right of a **for** header makes the body of that **for** structure an empty statement. This is normally a logic error.*

4.5 The For Structure: Notes and Observations

1. The initialization, loop-continuation condition, and increment can contain arithmetic expressions. For example, assume that **x = 2** and **y = 10**, the statement

   ```
   for (j = x; j <= 4 * x * y; j += y / x)
   ```

   is equivalent to the statement

   ```
   for (j = 2; j <= 80; j += 5)
   ```

2. The "increment" may be negative (in which case it is really a decrement and the loop actually counts downwards).

3. If the loop-continuation condition is initially false, the body portion of the loop is not performed. Instead, execution proceeds with the statement following the **for** structure.

4. The control variable is frequently printed or used in calculations in the body of a loop, but it does not need to be. It is common to use the control variable for controlling repetition while never mentioning it in the body of the loop.

5. The **for** structure is flowcharted much like the **while** structure. For example, the flowchart of the **for** statement

   ```
   for (counter = 1; counter <= 10; counter++)
      printf("%d", counter);
   ```

   is shown in Fig. 4.4. This flowchart makes it clear that the initialization occurs only once and that incrementing occurs after the body statement is performed. Note that (besides small circles and arrows) the flowchart contains only rectangle symbols and a diamond symbol. Imagine, again, that the programmer has access to a deep bin of empty **for** structures—as many as the programmer might need to stack and nest with other control structures to form a structured implementation of an algorithm's flow of control. And again, the rectangles and diamonds are then filled with actions and decisions appropriate to the algorithm.

Good Programming Practice 4.8

*Although the value of the control variable can be changed in the body of a **for** loop, this can lead to subtle errors. It is best not to change it.*

4.6 Examples Using the For Structure

The following examples show methods of varying the control variable in a **for** structure.

a) Vary the control variable from **1** to **100** in increments of **1**.

   ```
   for (i = 1; i <= 100; i++)
   ```

b) Vary the control variable from **100** to **1** in increments of **−1** (decrements of **1**).

   ```
   for (i = 100; i >= 1; i--)
   ```

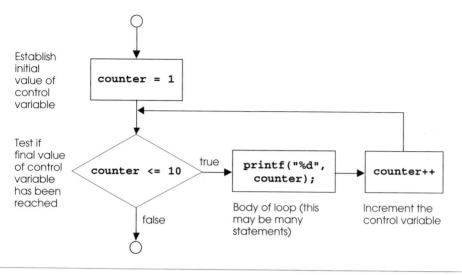

Fig. 4.4   Flowcharting a typical **for** structure.

c) Vary the control variable from **7** to **77** in steps of **7**.

```
for (i = 7; i <= 77; i += 7)
```

d) Vary the control variable from **20** to **2** in steps of **-2**.

```
for (i = 20; i >= 2; i -= 2)
```

e) Vary the control variable over the following sequence of values: **2, 5, 8, 11, 14, 17, 20**.

```
for (j = 2; j <= 20; j += 3)
```

f) Vary the control variable over the following sequence of values: **99, 88, 77, 66, 55, 44, 33, 22, 11, 0**.

```
for (j = 99; j >= 0; j -= 11)
```

The next two examples provide simple applications of the **for** structure. The program of Fig. 4.5 uses the **for** structure to sum all the even integers from **2** to **100**.

Note that the body of the **for** structure in Fig. 4.5 could actually be merged into the rightmost portion of the **for** header by using the comma operator as follows:

```
for (number = 2; number <= 100; sum += number, number += 2)
    ;
```

The initialization **sum = 0** could also be merged into the initialization section of the **for**.

Good Programming Practice 4.9

*Although statements preceding a **for** and statements in the body of a **for** can often be merged into the **for** header, avoid doing so because it makes the program more difficult to read.*

```
/* Summation with for */
#include <stdio.h>

main()
{
    int sum = 0, number;

    for (number = 2; number <= 100; number += 2)
        sum += number;

    printf("Sum is %d\n", sum);

    return 0;
}
```

```
Sum is 2550
```

Fig. 4.5   Summation with `for`.

Good Programming Practice 4.10

Limit the size of control structure headers to a single line if possible.

The next example computes compound interest using the **for** structure. Consider the following problem statement:

A person invests $1000.00 in a savings account yielding 5 percent interest. Assuming that all interest is left on deposit in the account, calculate and print the amount of money in the account at the end of each year for 10 years. Use the following formula for determining these amounts:

$$a = p(1 + r)^n$$

where

p is the original amount invested (i.e., the principal)
r is the annual interest rate
n is the number of years
a is the amount on deposit at the end of the nth year.

This problem involves a loop that performs the indicated calculation for each of the 10 years the money remains on deposit. The solution is shown in Fig. 4.6.

The **for** structure executes the body of the loop 10 times, varying a control variable from 1 to 10 in increments of 1. Although C does not include an exponentiation operator, we can, however, use the standard library function **pow** for this purpose. The function **pow(x, y)** calculates the value of **x** raised to the **y**th power. It takes two arguments of type **double** and returns a **double** value. The type **double** is a floating-point type much like **float**, but a variable of type **double** can store a value of much greater magnitude with greater precision than **float**. Note that the header file **math.h** should be included whenever a math function such as **pow** is used. Actually, this program would

```
/* Calculating compound interest */
#include <stdio.h>
#include <math.h>

main()
{
    int year;
    double amount, principal = 1000.0, rate = .05;

    printf("%4s%21s\n", "Year", "Amount on deposit");

    for (year = 1; year <= 10; year++) {
        amount = principal * pow(1.0 + rate, year);
        printf("%4d%21.2f\n", year, amount);
    }

    return 0;
}
```

Year	Amount on deposit
1	1050.00
2	1102.50
3	1157.62
4	1215.51
5	1276.28
6	1340.10
7	1407.10
8	1477.46
9	1551.33
10	1628.89

Fig. 4.6   Calculating compound interest with **for**.

malfunction without the inclusion of **math.h**. Function **pow** requires two **double** arguments. Note that **year** is an integer. The **math.h** file includes information that tells the compiler to convert the value of **year** to a temporary **double** representation before calling the function. This information is contained in something called **pow**'s *function prototype*. Function prototypes are an important new feature of ANSI C and are explained in Chapter 5. We provide a summary of the **pow** function and other math library functions in Chapter 5.

Notice that we have declared the variables **amount**, **principal**, and **rate** to be of type **double**. We have done this for simplicity because we are dealing with fractional parts of dollars.

Good Programming Practice 4.11

*Do not use variables of type **float** or **double** to perform monetary calculations. The impreciseness of floating point numbers can cause errors that will result in incorrect monetary values. In the exercises, we explore the use of integers to perform monetary calculations.*

Here is a simple explanation of what can go wrong when using **float** or **double** to represent dollar amounts.

Two **float** dollar amounts stored in the machine could be 14.234 (which prints as 14.23 with **%.2f**) and 18.673 (which with **%.2f** prints as 18.67). When these amounts are added, they produce the sum 32.907 which with **%.2f** prints as 32.91. Thus your printout could appear as

```
   14.23
+ 18.67
-------
   32.91
```

but clearly the sum of the individual numbers as printed should be 32.90! You have been warned!

The conversion specifier **%21.2f** is used to print the value of the variable **amount** in the program. The **21** in the conversion specifier denotes the *field width* in which the value will be printed. A field width of **21** specifies that the value printed will appear in **21** print positions. The **2** specifies the precision (i.e., the number of decimal positions). If the number of characters displayed is less than the field width, then the value will automatically be *right justified* in the field. This is particularly useful for aligning floating-point values with the same precision. To *left justify* a value in a field, place a – (minus sign) between the **%** and the field width. Note that the minus sign may also be used to left justify integers (such as in **%-6d**) and character strings (such as in **%-8s**). We will discuss the powerful formatting capabilities of **printf** and **scanf** in detail in Chapter 9.

4.7 The Switch Multiple-Selection Structure

In Chapter 3, we discussed the **if** single-selection structure and the **if/else** double-selection structure. Occasionally, an algorithm will contain a series of decisions in which a variable or expression is tested separately for each of the constant integral values it may assume, and different actions are taken. C provides the **switch** multiple-selection structure to handle such decision making.

The **switch** structure consists of a series of **case** labels, and an optional **default** case. The program in Fig. 4.7 uses **switch** to count the number of each different letter grade that students earned on an exam.

In the program, the user enters letter grades for a class. Inside the **while** header,

```
while ( ( grade = getchar() ) != EOF)
```

the parenthesized assignment **(grade = getchar())** is executed first. The **getchar** function (from the standard input/output library) reads one character from the keyboard and stores that character in integer variable **grade**. Characters are normally stored in variables of type *char*. However, an important feature of C is that characters can be stored in any integer data type because they are represented as 1 byte integers in the computer. Thus, we can treat a character as either an integer or a character depending on its use. For example, the statement

```
printf("The character (%c) has the value %d.\n", 'a', 'a');
```

```
/* Counting letter grades */
#include <stdio.h>
main()
{
    int grade;
    int aCount = 0, bCount = 0, cCount = 0,
        dCount = 0, fCount = 0;

    printf("Enter the letter grades.\n");
    printf("Enter the EOF character to end input.\n");

    while ( ( grade = getchar() ) != EOF) {

        switch (grade) {     /* switch nested in while */

            case 'A': case 'a':  /* grade was uppercase A */
                ++aCount;           /* or lowercase a */
                break;

            case 'B': case 'b':  /* grade was uppercase B */
                ++bCount;           /* or lowercase b */
                break;

            case 'C': case 'c':  /* grade was uppercase C */
                ++cCount;           /* or lowercase c */
                break;

            case 'D': case 'd':  /* grade was uppercase D */
                ++dCount;           /* or lowercase d */
                break;

            case 'F': case 'f':  /* grade was uppercase F */
                ++fCount;           /* or lowercase f */
                break;

            case '\n': case ' ': /* ignore these in input */
                break;

            default:            /* catch all other characters */
                printf("Incorrect letter grade entered.");
                printf(" Enter a new grade.\n");
                break;
        }
    }

    printf("\nTotals for each letter grade are:\n");
    printf("A: %d\n", aCount);
    printf("B: %d\n", bCount);
    printf("C: %d\n", cCount);
    printf("D: %d\n", dCount);
    printf("F: %d\n", fCount);

    return 0;
}
```

Fig. 4.7   An example using **switch** (part 1 of 2).

```
Enter the letter grades.
Enter the EOF character to end input.
A
B
C
C
A
D
F
C
E
Incorrect letter grade entered. Enter a new grade.
D
A
B

Totals for each letter grade are:
A: 3
B: 2
C: 3
D: 2
F: 1
```

Fig. 4.7   An example using **switch** (part 2 of 2).

uses the conversion specifiers **%c** and **%d** to print the character **a** and its integer value, respectively. The result is

The character (a) has the value 97.

The integer 97 is the character's numerical representation in the computer. Many computers today use the *ASCII (American Standard Code for Information Interchange) character set* in which 97 represents the lower case letter **'a'**. A list of the ASCII characters and their decimal values is presented in Appendix D. Characters can be read with **scanf** by using the conversion specifier **%c**.

Assignment statements as a whole actually have a value. This is precisely the value that is assigned to the variable on the left side of the **=**. The value of the assignment **grade = getchar()** is the character that is returned by **getchar** and assigned to the variable **grade**.

The fact that assignment statements have values can be useful for initializing several variables to the same value. For example,

a = b = c = 0;

first evaluates the assignment **c = 0** (because the **=** operator associates from right to left). The variable **b** is then assigned the value of the assignment **c = 0** (which is 0). Then, the variable **a** is assigned the value of the assignment **b = (c = 0)** (which is also 0). In the program, the value of the assignment **grade = getchar()** is compared with the value of **EOF** (a symbol whose acronym stands for "end of file"). We use **EOF** (which normally has the value -1) as the sentinel value. The user types a system-dependent keystroke combination to mean "end of file," i.e., "I have no more data to enter." EOF is a symbolic integer constant defined in the **<stdio.h>** header file (we will see how symbolic constants are defined in Chapter 6). If the value assigned to **grade** is equal to **EOF**, the program terminates. We have chosen to represent characters in this program as **int**s because **EOF** has an integer value (again, normally -1).

Portability Tip 4.1

---

*The keystroke combinations for entering **EOF** (end of file) are system dependent.*

Portability Tip 4.2

---

*Testing for the symbolic constant **EOF** rather than -1 makes programs more portable. The ANSI standard states that **EOF** is a negative integral value (but not necessarily -1). Thus, **EOF** could have different values on different systems.*

On UNIX systems and many others, the **EOF** indicator is entered by typing the sequence

>   *<return> <ctrl-d>*

This notation means to press the return key and then simultaneously press both the **ctrl** key and the **d** key. On other systems such as Digital Equipment Corporation's VAX VMS or Microsoft Corporation's MS-DOS, the **EOF** indicator can be entered by typing

>   *<ctrl-z>*

The user enters grades at the keyboard. When the return (or enter) key is pressed, the characters are read by the **getchar** function one character at a time. If the character entered is not equal to **EOF**, the **switch** structure is entered. The keyword **switch** is followed by the variable name **grade** in parentheses. This is called the *controlling expression.* The value of this expression is compared with each of the *case* labels. Assume the user has entered the letter **C** as a grade. **C** is automatically compared to each **case** in the **switch**. If a match occurs (**case 'C':**), the statements for that **case** are executed. In the case of the letter **C**, **cCount** is incremented by **1**, and the **switch** structure is exited immediately with the **break** statement.

The **break** statement causes program control to continue with the first statement after the **switch** structure. The **break** statement is used because the **case**s in a **switch** statement would otherwise run together. If **break** is not used anywhere in a **switch** structure, then each time a match occurs in the structure, the statements for all the remaining **case**s will be executed. (This feature is rarely useful, although it is perfect for programming the iterative song "The Twelve Days of Christmas!") If no match occurs, the **default** case is executed and an error message is printed.

Each **case** can have one or more actions. The **switch** structure is different from all other structures in that braces are not required around multiple actions in a **case** of a **switch**. The general **switch** multiple-selection structure (using a **break** in each **case**) is flowcharted in Fig. 4.8.

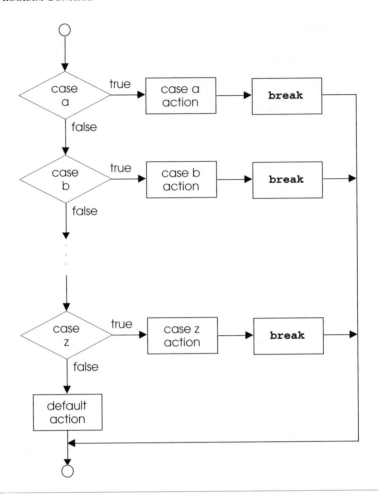

Fig. 4.8   The **switch** multiple-selection structure.

The flowchart makes it clear that each **break** statement at the end of a **case** causes control to immediately exit the **switch** structure. Again, note that (besides small circles and arrows) the flowchart contains only rectangle symbols and diamond symbols. Imagine, again, that the programmer has access to a deep bin of empty **switch** structures—as many as the programmer might need to stack and nest with other control structures to form a structured implementation of an algorithm's flow of control. And again, the rectangles and diamonds are then filled with actions and decisions appropriate to the algorithm.

Common Programming Error 4.5

*Forgetting a **break** statement when one is needed in a **switch** structure.*

Good Programming Practice 4.12

Provide a `default` *case in* `switch` *statements. Cases not explicitly tested in a* `switch` *are ignored. The* `default` *case helps prevent this by focusing the programmer on the need to process exceptional conditions. There are situations in which no* `default` *processing is needed.*

Good Programming Practice 4.13

Although the `case` *clauses and the* `default` *case clause in a* `switch` *structure can occur in any order, it is considered a good programming practice to place the* `default` *clause last.*

Good Programming Practice 4.14

In a `switch` *structure when the* `default` *clause is listed last, the* `break` *statement is not required. But some programmers include this* `break` *for clarity and symmetry with other* `cases`*.*

In the `switch` structure of Fig. 4.7, the lines

```
case '\n': case ' ':
    break;
```

cause the program to skip newline and blank characters. Reading characters one at a time can cause some problems. To have the program read the characters, they must be sent to the computer by pressing the *return key* on the keyboard. This causes the newline character to be placed in the input after the character we wish to process. Often, this newline character must be specially processed to make the program work correctly. By including the preceding cases in our `switch` structure, we prevent the error message in the **default** case from being printed each time a newline or space is encountered in the input.

Common Programming Error 4.6

Not processing newline characters in the input when reading characters one at a time can cause logic errors.

Good Programming Practice 4.15

Remember to provide processing capabilities for newline characters in the input when processing characters one at a time.

Note that several case labels listed together (such as **case 'D': case 'd':** in Fig. 4.7) simply means that the same set of actions is to occur for either of these cases.

When using the **switch** structure, remember that it can only be used for testing a *constant integral expression,* i.e., any combination of character constants and integer constants that evaluates to a constant integer value. A character constant is represented as the specific character in single quotes such as **'A'**. Characters must be enclosed within single quotes to be recognized as character constants. Integer constants are simply integer values. In our example we have used character constants. Remember that characters are actually small integer values.

Portable languages like C must have flexible data type sizes. Different applications may need integers of different sizes. C provides several data types to represent integers. The range of integer values for each type depends on the particular computer's hardware. In addition to the types **int** and **char**, C provides the types **short** (an abbreviation of **short int**) and **long** (an abbreviation of **long int**). The ANSI standard specifies that the minimum range of values for **short** integers is ±32767. For the vast majority of integer calculations, **long** integers are sufficient. The standard specifies that the minimum range of values for **long** integers is ±2147483647. On most computers, **int**s are equivalent either to **short** or to **long**. The standard states that the range of values for an **int** is at least the same as the range for **short** integers and no larger than the range for **long** integers. The data type **char** can be used to represent integers in the range ±127 or any of the characters in the computer's character set.

Portability Tip 4.3

*Since **int**s vary in size between systems, use **long** integers if you expect to process integers outside the range ±32767 and you would like to be able to run the program on several different computer systems.*

Performance Tip 4.1

In performance-oriented situations where memory is at a premium or speed is necessary, it may be desirable to use smaller integer sizes.

4.8 The Do/While Repetition Structure

The **do/while** repetition structure is similar to the **while** structure. In the **while** structure, the loop-continuation condition is tested at the beginning of the loop before the body of the loop is performed. The **do/while** structure tests the loop-continuation condition *after* the loop body is performed, therefore the loop body will be executed at least once. When a **do/while** terminates, execution continues with the statement after the **while** clause. Note that it is not necessary to use braces in the **do/while** structure if there is only one statement in the body. However, the braces are usually included to avoid confusion between the **while** and **do/while** structures. For example,

    while(*condition*)

is normally regarded as the header to a **while** structure. A **do/while** with no braces around the single statement body appears as

    do
        statement
    while(*condition*);

which can be confusing. The last line—**while**(*condition*); may be misinterpreted by the reader as a **while** structure containing an empty statement. Thus, the **do/while** with one statement is often written as follows to avoid confusion:

```
do {
    statement
} while (condition);
```

Good Programming Practice 4.16

*Some programmers always include braces in a **do/while** structure even if the braces are not necessary. This helps eliminate ambiguity between the **do/while** structure containing one statement and the **while** structure.*

Common Programming Error 4.7

*Infinite loops are caused when the loop-continuation condition in a **while**, **for**, or **do/while** structure never becomes false. To prevent this, make sure there is not a semicolon immediately after the header of a **while** or **for** structure. In a counter-controlled loop, make sure the control variable is incremented (or decremented) in the body of the loop. In a sentinel-controlled loop, make sure the sentinel value is eventually input.*

The program in Fig. 4.9 uses a **do/while** structure to print the numbers from 1 to 10. Note that the control variable **counter** is preincremented in the loop-continuation test. Note also the use of the braces to enclose the single-statement body of the **do/while**.

The **do/while** structure is flowcharted in Fig. 4.10. This flowchart makes it clear that the loop-continuation condition is not executed until after the action is performed at least once. Again, note that (besides small circles and arrows) the flowchart contains only a rectangle symbol and a diamond symbol. Imagine, again, that the programmer has access to a deep bin of empty **do/while** structures—as many as the programmer might need to stack and nest with other control structures to form a structured implementation of an algorithm's flow of control. And again, the rectangles and diamonds are then filled with actions and decisions appropriate to the algorithm.

```
/* Using the do/while repetition structure */
#include <stdio.h>

main()
{
    int counter = 1;

    do {
        printf("%d  ", counter);
    } while (++counter <= 10);

    return 0;
}
```

```
1  2  3  4  5  6  7  8  9  10
```

Fig. 4.9   Using the **do/while** structure.

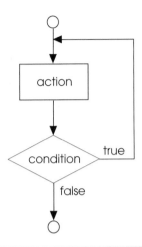

Fig. 4.10 The **do/while** repetition structure.

4.9 The Break and Continue Statements

The **break** and **continue** statements are used to alter the flow of control. The **break** statement, when executed in a **while**, **for**, **do/while**, or **switch** structure, causes immediate exit from that structure. Program execution continues with the first statement after the structure. Common uses of the **break** statement are to escape early from a loop, or to skip the remainder of a **switch** structure (as in Fig. 4.7). Figure 4.11 demonstrates the break statement in a **for** repetition structure. When the **if** structure detects that **x** has become **5**, **break** is executed. This terminates the **for** statement and the program continues with the **printf** after the **for**. The loop only fully executes four times.

The **continue** statement, when executed in a **while**, **for**, or **do/while** structure, skips the remaining statements in the body of that structure, and performs the next iteration of the loop. In **while** and **do/while** structures, the loop-continuation test is evaluated immediately after the **continue** statement is executed. In the **for** structure, the increment expression is executed, then the loop-continuation test is evaluated. Earlier, we stated that the **while** structure could be used in most cases to represent the **for** structure. The one exception occurs when the increment expression in the **while** structure follows the **continue** statement. In this case, the increment is not executed before the repetition-continuation condition is tested, and the **while** does not execute in the same manner as the **for**. Figure 4.12 uses the **continue** statement in a **for** structure to skip the **printf** statement in the structure and begin the next iteration of the loop.

> ***Good Programming Practice 4. 17***
>
> *Some programmers feel that **break** and **continue** violate the norms of structured programming. Because the effects of these statements can be achieved by structured programming techniques we will soon learn, these programmers do not use **break** and* **continue***.*

```
/* Using the break statement in a for structure */
#include <stdio.h>

main()
{
   int x;

   for (x = 1; x <= 10; x++) {

      if (x == 5)
         break;     /* break loop only if x == 5 */

      printf("%d ", x);
   }

   printf("\nBroke out of loop at x == %d\n", x);
   return 0;
}
```

```
1 2 3 4
Broke out of loop at x == 5
```

Fig. 4.11   Using the **break** statement in a **for** structure.

```
/* Using the continue statement in a for structure */
#include <stdio.h>

main()
{
   int x;

   for (x = 1; x <= 10; x++) {

      if (x == 5)
         continue;  /* skip remaining code in loop only
                       if x == 5 */

      printf("%d ", x);
   }

   printf("\nUsed continue to skip printing the value 5\n");
   return 0;
}
```

```
1 2 3 4 6 7 8 9 10
Used continue to skip printing the value 5
```

Fig. 4.12   Using the **continue** statement in a **for** structure.

Performance Tip 4.2

The **break** *and* **continue** *statements, when used properly, perform faster than the corresponding structured techniques which we will soon learn.*

Software Engineering Observation 4.1

There is a tension between achieving quality software engineering and achieving the best performing software. Often one of these goals is achieved at the expense of the other.

4.10 Logical Operators

So far we have studied only *simple conditions* such as **counter <= 10, total > 1000**, and **number != sentinelValue**. We have expressed these conditions in terms of the relational operators **>, <, >=**, and **<=**, and the equality operators **==** and **!=**. Each decision tested precisely one condition. If we wanted to test multiple conditions in the process of making a decision, we had to perform these tests in separate statements or in nested **if** or **if/else** structures.

C provides *logical operators* that may be used to form more complex conditions by combining simple conditions. The logical operators are **&&** *(logical AND),* **||** *(logical OR),* and **!** *(logical NOT* also called *logical negation).* We will consider examples of each of these.

Suppose we wish to ensure at some point in a program that two conditions are *both* true before we choose a certain path of execution. In this case we can use the logical **&&** operator as follows:

```
if (gender == 1 && age >= 65)
    ++seniorFemales;
```

This **if** statement contains two simple conditions. The condition **gender == 1** might be evaluated, for example, to determine if a person is a female. The condition **age >= 65** is evaluated to determine if a person is a senior citizen. The two simple conditions are evaluated first because the precedences of **==** and **>=** are both higher than the precedence of **&&**. The **if** statement then considers the combined condition

```
gender == 1 && age >= 65
```

This condition is true if and only if both of the simple conditions are true. Finally, if this combined condition is indeed true, then the count of **seniorFemales** is incremented by **1**. If either or both of the simple conditions are false, then the program skips the incrementing and proceeds to the statement following the **if**.

The table of Fig. 4.13 summarizes the **&&** operator. The table shows all four possible combinations of zero (false) and nonzero (true) values for expression1 and expression2. Such tables are often called *truth tables*. C evaluates all expressions that include relational operators, equality operators, and/or logical operators to 0 or 1. Although C sets a true value to 1, it accepts *any* nonzero value as true.

Now let us consider the **||** (logical OR) operator. Suppose we wish to ensure at some point in a program that either *or* both of two conditions are true before we choose a

expression1	expression2	expression1 && expression2
0	0	0
0	nonzero	0
nonzero	0	0
nonzero	nonzero	1

Fig. 4.13 Truth table for the **&&** (logical AND) operator.

certain path of execution. In this case we use the | | operator as in the following program segment:

```
if (semesterAverage >= 90 || finalExam >= 90)
    printf("Student grade is A\n");
```

This statement also contains two simple conditions. The condition **semesterAverage >= 90** is evaluated to determine if the student deserves an "A" in the course because of a solid performance throughout the semester. The condition **finalExam >= 90** is evaluated to determine if the student deserves an "A" in the course because of an outstanding performance on the final exam. The **if** statement then considers the combined condition

```
semesterAverage >= 90 || finalExam >= 90
```

and awards the student an "A" if either or both of the simple conditions are true. Note that the message "**Student grade is A**" is not printed only when both of the simple conditions are false (zero). Figure 4.14 is a truth table for the logical OR operator (| |).

The **&&** operator has a higher precedence than | |. Both operators associate from left to right. An expression containing **&&** or | | operators is evaluated only until truth or falsehood is known. Thus, evaluation of the condition

```
gender == 1 && age >= 65
```

will stop if **gender** is not equal to **1** (i.e., the entire expression is false), and continue if **gender** is equal to **1** (i.e., the entire expression could still be true if **age >= 65**).

expression1	expression2	expression1 || expression2
0	0	0
0	nonzero	1
nonzero	0	1
nonzero	nonzero	1

Fig. 4.14 Truth table for the logical OR (| |) operator.

Performance Tip 4.3

In expressions using operator **&&**, *make the condition that is most likely to be false the leftmost condition. In expressions using operator* | |, *make the condition that is most likely to be true the leftmost condition. This can reduce a program's execution time.*

C provides **!** (logical negation) to enable a programmer to "reverse" the meaning of a condition. Unlike the **&&** and | | operators, which combine two conditions (and are therefore binary operators), the logical negation operator has only a single condition as an operand (and is therefore a unary operator). The logical negation operator is placed before a condition when we are interested in choosing a path of execution if the original condition (without the logical negation operator) is false, such as in the following program segment:

```
if (!(grade == sentinelValue))
    printf("The next grade is %f\n", grade);
```

The parentheses around the condition **grade == sentinelValue** are needed because the logical negation operator has a higher precedence than the equality operator. Figure 4.15 is a truth table for the logical negation operator.

In most cases, the programmer can avoid using logical negation by expressing the condition differently with an appropriate relational operator. For example, the preceding statement may also be written as follows:

```
if (grade != sentinelValue)
    printf("The next grade is %f\n", grade);
```

The chart in Fig. 4.16 shows the precedence and associativity of the various C operators introduced to this point. The operators are shown from top to bottom in decreasing order of precedence.

4.11 Confusing Equality (==) and Assignment (=) Operators

There is one type of error that C programmers, no matter how experienced, tend to make so frequently that we felt it was worth a separate section. That error is accidentally swapping the operators **==** (equality) and **=** (assignment). What makes these swaps so damaging is the fact that they do not ordinarily cause syntax errors. Rather, statements with these errors ordinarily compile correctly, and the programs run to completion probably generating incorrect results through run-time logic errors.

expression	!expression
0	1
nonzero	0

Fig. 4.15 Truth table for operator **!** (logical negation).

Operators						Associativity	Type
( )						left to right	parentheses
++	--	+	-	!	(*type*)	right to left	unary
*	/	%				left to right	multiplicative
+	-					left to right	additive
<	<=	>	>=			left to right	relational
==	!=					left to right	equality
&&						left to right	logical AND
||						left to right	logical OR
?:						right to left	conditional
=	+=	-=	*=	/=	%=	right to left	assignment
,						left to right	comma

Fig. 4.16 Operator precedence and associativity.

There are two aspects of C that cause these problems. One is that any expression in C that produces a value can be used in the decision portion of any control structure. If the value is 0, it is treated as false, and if the value is nonzero, it is treated as true. The second is that assignments in C produce a value, namely the value that is assigned to the variable on the left side of the assignment operator. For example, suppose we intend to write

```
if (payCode == 4)
    printf("You get a bonus!");
```

but we accidentally write

```
if (payCode = 4)
    printf ("You get a bonus!");
```

The first **if** statement properly awards a bonus to the person whose paycode is equal to 4. The second **if** statement—the one with the error—evaluates the assignment expression in the **if** condition. This expression is a simple assignment whose value is the constant 4 . Because any nonzero value is interpreted as "true," the condition in this **if** statement is always true, and the person always receives a bonus regardless of what the actual paycode is!

Common Programming Error 4.8

Using operator == for assignment, or using operator = for equality.

Programmers normally write conditions such as **x == 7** with the variable name on the left and the constant on the right. By reversing these so that the constant is on the left and the variable name is on the right as in **7 == x**, the programmer who accidentally replaces the **==** operator with **=** will be protected by the compiler. The compiler will treat this as a syntax error because only a variable name can be placed on the left-hand side of an assignment statement. At least this will prevent the potential devastation of a run-time logic error.

Variable names are said to be *lvalues* (for "left values") because they can be used on the left side of an assignment operator. Constants are said to be *rvalues* (for "right values") because they can be used on only the right side of an assignment operator. Note that lvalues can also be used as rvalues, but not vice versa.

> **Good Programming Practice 4.18**
>
> *When an equality expression has a variable and a constant as in* **x == 1**, *some programmers prefer to write the expression with the constant on the left and the variable name on the right as protection against the logic error that occurs when the programmer accidentally replaces the* **==** *operator with* **=**.

The other side of the coin can be equally unpleasant. Suppose the programmer wants to assign a value to a variable with a simple statement like

```
x = 1;
```

but instead writes

```
x == 1;
```

Here, too, this is not a syntax error. Rather the compiler simply evaluates the conditional expression. If **x** is equal to **1**, the condition is true and the expression returns the value 1. If **x** is not equal to **1**, the condition is false and the expression returns the value 0. Regardless of what value is returned, there is no assignment operator, so the value is simply lost, and the value of **x** remains unaltered, probably causing an execution-time logic error. Unfortunately, we do not have a handy trick available to help you with this problem!

4.12 Structured Programming Summary

Just as architects design buildings by employing the collective wisdom of their profession, so should programmers design programs. Our field is younger than architecture is, and our collective wisdom is considerably sparser. We have learned a great deal in a mere five decades. Perhaps most importantly, we have learned that structured programming produces programs that are easier (than unstructured programs) to understand and hence are easier to test, debug, modify, and even prove correct in a mathematical sense.

Chapters 3 and 4 have concentrated on C's control structures. Each structure has been presented, flowcharted, and discussed separately with examples. Now, we summarize the results of Chapters 3 and 4 and introduce a simple set of rules for the formation and properties of structured programs.

Figure 4.17 summarizes the control structures discussed in Chapters 3 and 4. Small circles are used in the figure to indicate the single entry point and the single exit point of each structure. Connecting individual flowchart symbols arbitrarily can lead to unstructured programs. Therefore, the programming profession has chosen to combine flowchart symbols to form a limited set of control structures, and to build only structured programs by properly combining control structures in only two simple ways. For simplicity, only

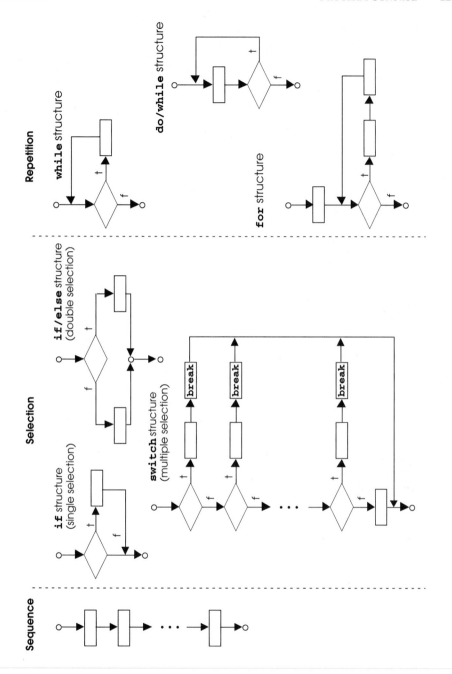

Fig. 4.17   C's single-entry/single-exit sequence, selection, and repetition structures.

single-entry/single-exit control structures are used—there is only one way to enter and only one way to exit each control structure. Connecting control structures in sequence to form structured programs is simple—the exit point of one control structure is connected directly to the entry point of the next control structure, i.e., the control structures are simply placed one after another in a program; we have called this "control structure stacking." The rules for forming structured programs also allow for control structures to be nested.

Fig. 4.18 shows the rules for forming properly structured programs. The rules assume that the rectangle flowchart symbol may be used to indicate any action including input/output.

Applying the rules of Fig. 4.18 always results in a structured flowchart with a neat, building-block appearance. For example, repeatedly applying rule 2 to the simplest flowchart results in a structured flowchart containing many rectangles in sequence (Fig. 4.20). Notice that rule 2 generates a stack of control structures; so let us call rule 2 the *stacking rule*.

Rule 3 is called the *nesting rule*. Repeatedly applying rule 3 to the simplest flowchart results in a flowchart with neatly nested control structures. For example, in Fig. 4.21, the rectangle in the simplest flowchart is first replaced with a double-selection (**if/else**) structure. Then rule 3 is applied again to both of the rectangles in the double-selection structure, replacing each of these rectangles with double-selection structures. The dashed boxes around each of the double-selection structures represent the rectangle that was replaced.

Rules for Forming Structured Programs

---

1) Begin with the "simplest flowchart" (Fig. 4.19).
2) Any rectangle (action) can be replaced by two rectangles (actions) in sequence.
3) Any rectangle (action) can be replaced by any control structure (sequence, **if**, **if/else**, **switch**, **while**, **do/while**, or **for**).
4) Rules 2 and 3 may be applied as often as you like and in any order.

Fig. 4.18   Rules for forming structured programs.

Fig. 4.19   The simplest flowchart.

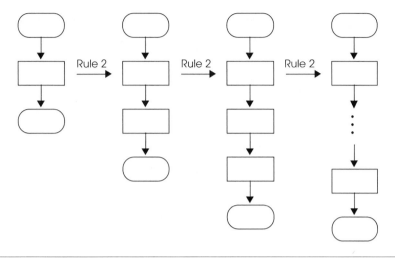

Fig. 4.20   Repeatedly applying rule 2 of Fig. 4.18 to the simplest flowchart.

Rule 4 generates larger, more involved, and more deeply nested structures. The flowcharts that emerge from applying the rules in Fig. 4.18 constitute the set of all possible structured flowcharts and hence the set of all possible structured programs.

It is because of the elimination of the **goto** statement that these building blocks never overlap one another. The beauty of the structured approach is that we use only a small number of simple single-entry/single-exit pieces, and we assemble them in only two simple ways. Figure 4.22 shows the kinds of stacked building blocks that emerge from applying rule 2 and the kinds of nested building blocks that emerge from applying rule 3. The figure also shows the kind of overlapped building blocks that cannot appear in structured flowcharts (because of the elimination of the **goto** statement).

If the rules in Fig. 4.18 are followed, an unstructured flowchart (such as that in Fig. 4.23) cannot be created. If you are uncertain if a particular flowchart is structured, apply the rules of Fig. 4.18 in reverse to try to reduce the flowchart to the simplest flowchart. If the flowchart is reducible to the simplest flowchart, the original flowchart is structured; otherwise, it is not.

Structured programming promotes simplicity. Bohm and Jacopini have given us the result that only three forms of control are needed:

- Sequence
- Selection
- Repetition

Sequence is trivial. Selection is implemented in one of three ways:

- **if** structure (single selection)
- **if/else** structure (double selection)
- **switch** structure (multiple selection)

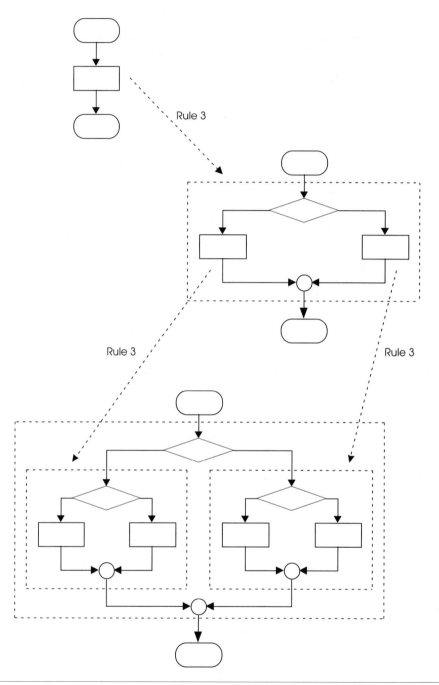

Fig. 4.21   Applying rule 3 of Fig. 4.18 to the simplest flowchart.

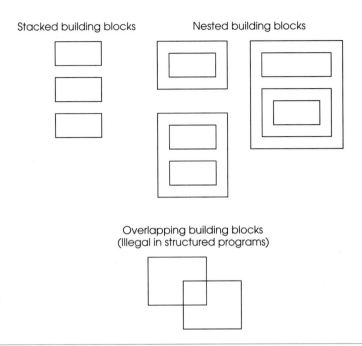

Fig. 4.22   Stacked building blocks, nested building blocks, and overlapped building blocks.

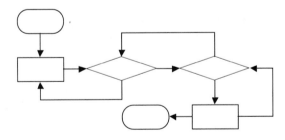

Fig. 4.23   An unstructured flowchart.

In fact, it is straightforward to prove that the simple **if** structure is sufficient to provide any form of selection—everything that can be done with the **if/else** structure and the **switch** structure can be implemented with the **if** structure.

Repetition is implemented in one of three ways:

- **while** structure
- **do/while** structure
- **for** structure

It is straightforward to prove that the **while** structure is sufficient to provide any form of repetition. Everything that can be done with the **do/while** structure and the **for** structure can be done with the **while** structure.

Combining these results illustrates that any form of control ever needed in a C program can be expressed in terms of only three forms of control:

- sequence
- **if** structure (selection)
- **while** structure (repetition)

And these control structures can be combined in only two ways—stacking and nesting. Indeed, structured programming promotes simplicity.

In Chapters 3 and 4, we discussed how to compose programs from control structures containing actions and decisions. In Chapter 5, we introduce another program structuring unit called the *function*. We will learn to compose large programs by combining functions which, in turn, are composed of control structures. We will also discuss how using functions promotes software reusability.

Summary

- A loop is a group of instructions the computer executes repeatedly until some terminating condition is satisfied. Two forms of repetition are counter-controlled repetition and sentinel-controlled repetition.

- A loop counter is used to count the number of times a group of instructions should be repeated. It is incremented (usually by 1) each time the group of instructions is performed.

- Sentinel values are generally used to control repetition when the precise number of repetitions is not known in advance and the loop includes statements that obtain data each time the loop is performed.

- A sentinel value is entered after all valid data items have been supplied to the program. Sentinels must be chosen carefully so that there is no possibility of confusing them with valid data items.

- The **for** repetition structure handles all the details of counter-controlled repetition automatically. The general format of the **for** structure is

    for (*expression1*; *expression2*; *expression3*)
        statement

  where *expression1* initializes the loop's control variable, *expression2* is the loop-continuation condition, and *expression3* increments the control variable.

- The **do/while** repetition structure is similar to the **while** repetition structure, but the **do/while** structure tests the loop-continuation condition at the end of the loop, so the body of the loop will be executed at least once. The format for the **do/while** statement is

```
do
    statement
while (condition);
```

- The **break** statement, when executed in one of the repetition structures (**for**, **while**, and **do/while**), causes immediate exit from the structure. Execution continues with the first statement after the loop.

- The **continue** statement, when executed in one of the repetition structures (**for**, **while**, and **do/while**), skips any remaining statements in the body of the structure, and proceeds with the next iteration of the loop.

- The **switch** statement handles a series of decisions in which a particular variable or expression is tested for each of the values it may assume, and different actions are taken. Each **case** in a **switch** statement may cause many statements to be performed. In most programs, it is necessary to include a **break** statement after the statements for each **case**, otherwise the program will execute the statements in each **case** until a **break** statement is encountered or the end of the **switch** statement is reached. Several **case**s can execute the same statements by listing the **case** labels together before the statements. The **switch** structure can only test constant integral expressions.

- The **getchar** function returns one character from the keyboard (the standard input) as an integer.

- On UNIX systems and many others, the **EOF** character is entered by typing the sequence

    <return> <ctrl-d>

On VMS and DOS, the **EOF** character is entered by typing

    <ctrl-z>

- Logical operators may be used to form complex conditions by combining conditions. The logical operators are **&&**, **||**, and **!**, meaning logical AND, logical OR, and logical NOT (negation), respectively.

- A true value is any nonzero value.

- A false value is 0 (zero).

Terminology

ASCII character set
body of a loop
break
case label
char
continue
control variable
counter-controlled repetition
<ctrl-z>

decrement
default case in **switch**
definite repetition
double
do/while repetition structure
end of file
EOF
field width
final value of control variable

for repetition structure
getchar function
increment of control variable
indefinite repetition
infinite loop
initial value of control variable
left justify
logical AND (**&&**)
logical negation (**!**)
logical operators
logical OR (**||**)
long
loop-continuation condition
loop-control variable
loop counter
lvalue ("left value")
minus sign for left justification

multiple selection
nested control structures
nesting rule
off-by-one error
pow function
repetition structures
<return> <ctrl-d>
right justify
rvalue("right value")
short
simple condition
single-entry/single-exit control structures
stacking rule
switch selection structure
truth table
unary operator
while repetition structure

Common Programming Errors

4.1 Because floating point values may be approximate, controlling counting loops with floating point variables may result in imprecise counter values and inaccurate tests for termination.

4.2 Using an incorrect relational operator or using an incorrect final value of a loop counter in the condition of a **while** or **for** structure can cause off-by-one errors.

4.3 Using commas instead of semicolons in a **for** header.

4.4 Placing a semicolon immediately to the right of a **for** header makes the body of that **for** structure an empty statement. This is normally a logic error.

4.5 Forgetting a **break** statement when one is needed in a **switch** structure.

4.6 Not processing newline characters in the input when reading characters one at a time can cause logic errors.

4.7 Infinite loops are caused when the loop-continuation condition in a **while**, **for**, or **do/while** structure never becomes false. To prevent this, make sure there is not a semicolon immediately after the header of a **while** or **for** structure. In a counter-controlled loop, make sure the control variable is incremented (or decremented) in the body of the loop. In a sentinel-controlled loop, make sure the sentinel value is eventually input.

4.8 Using operator **==** for assignment, or using operator **=** for equality.

Good Programming Practices

4.1 Control counting loops with integer values.

4.2 Indent the statements in the body of each control structure.

4.3 Put a blank line before and after each major control structure to make it stand out in the program.

4.4 Too many levels of nesting can make a program difficult to understand. As a general rule, try to avoid using more than three levels of indentation.

4.5 The combination of vertical spacing before and after control structures and indentation of the bodies of control structures within the control structure headers gives programs a two-dimensional appearance that greatly improves program readability.

4.6   Using the final value in the condition of a `while` or `for` structure and using the `<=` relational operator will help avoid off-by-one errors. For a loop used to print the values 1 to 10, for example, the loop-continuation condition should be `counter <= 10` rather than `counter < 11` or `counter < 10`.

4.7   Place only expressions involving the control variables in the initialization and increment sections of a `for` structure. Manipulations of other variables should appear either before the loop (if they are to be executed only once like initialization statements) or in the loop body (if they are to executed once per repetition like incrementing or decrementing statements).

4.8   Although the value of the control variable can be changed in the body of a `for` loop, this can lead to subtle errors; so it is best not to change it.

4.9   Although statements preceding a `for` and statements in the body of a `for` can often be merged into the `for` header, avoid doing so because it makes the program more difficult to read.

4.10   Limit the size of control structure headers to a single line if possible.

4.11   Do not use variables of type `float` or `double` to perform monetary calculations. The impreciseness of floating point numbers can cause errors that will result in incorrect monetary values. In the exercises, we explore the use of integers to perform monetary calculations.

4.12   Provide a `default` case in `switch` statements. As occurs with single selection `if` structures, cases not explicitly tested are ignored. The `default` case helps prevent this by focusing the programmer on the need to process exceptional conditions. There will be cases in which no default processing is needed.

4.13   Although the `case` clauses and the `default` case clause in a `switch` structure can occur in any order, it is considered a good programming practice to place the `default` clause last.

4.14   In a `switch` structure when the `default` clause is listed last, the `break` statement is not required. But some programmers include this `break` for clarity and symmetry with other `case`s.

4.15   Remember to provide processing capabilities for newline characters in the input when processing characters one at a time.

4.16   Some programmers always include braces in a `do/while` structure even if the braces are not necessary. This helps eliminate ambiguity between the `do/while` structure containing one statement and the `while` structure.

4.17   Some programmers feel that `break` and `continue` violate the norms of structured programming. Because the effects of these statements can be achieved by structured programming techniques we will soon learn, these programmers do not use `break` and `continue`.

4.18   When an equality expression has a variable and a constant as in `x == 1`, some programmers prefer to write the expression with the constant on the left and the variable name on the right as protection against the logic error that occurs when the programmer accidentally replaces the `==` operator with `=`.

Performance Tips

4.1   In performance-oriented situations where memory is at a premium or speed is necessary, it may be desirable to use smaller integer sizes.

4.2   The `break` and `continue` statements, when used properly, perform faster than the corresponding structured techniques which we will soon learn.

4.3 In expressions using operator **&&**, make the condition that is most likely to be false the leftmost condition. In expressions using operator **||**, make the condition that is most likely to be true the leftmost condition. This can reduce a program's execution time.

Portability Tips

4.1 The keystroke combinations for entering **EOF** (end of file) are system dependent.

4.2 Testing for the symbolic constant **EOF** rather than -1 makes programs more portable. The ANSI standard states that **EOF** is a negative integral value (but not necessarily -1). Thus, **EOF** could have different values on different systems.

4.3 Since **int**s vary in size between systems, use **long** integers if you expect to process integers outside the range ±32767, and you would like to be able to run the program on several different computer systems.

Software Engineering Observation

4.1 There is a tension between achieving quality software engineering and achieving the best performing software. Often one of these goals is achieved at the expense of the other.

Self-Review Exercises

4.1 Fill in the blanks in each of the following statements.
   a) Counter-controlled repetition is also known as _____ repetition because it is known in advance how many times the loop will be executed.
   b) Sentinel-controlled repetition is also known as _____ repetition because it is not known in advance how many times the loop will be executed.
   c) In counter-controlled repetition, a _____ is used to count the number of times a group of instructions should be repeated.
   d) The _____ statement, when executed in a repetition structure causes the next iteration of the loop to be performed immediately.
   e) The _____ statement, when executed in a repetition structure or a **switch** causes immediate exit from the structure.
   f) The _____ is used to test a particular variable or expression for each of the constant integral values it may assume.

4.2 State whether the following are true or false. If the answer is false, explain why.
   a) The **default** case is required in the **switch** selection structure.
   b) The **break** statement is required in the **default** case of a **switch** selection structure.
   c) The expression **(x > y && a < b)** is true if either **x > y** is true or **a < b** is true.
   d) An expression containing the **||** operator is true if either or both of its operands is true.

4.3 Write a C statement or a set of C statements to accomplish each of the following tasks:
   a) Sum the odd integers between 1 and 99 using a **for** structure. Assume the integer variables **sum** and **count** have been declared.
   b) Print the value **333.546372** in a field width of **15** characters with precisions of **1**, **2**, **3**, **4**, and **5**. Left justify the output. What are the five values that print?
   c) Calculate the value of **2.5** raised to the power of **3** using the **pow** function. Print the result with a precision of **2** in a field width of **10** positions. What is the value that prints?

d) Print the integers from 1 to 20 using a **while** loop and the counter variable **x**. Assume that the variable **x** has been declared, but not initialized. Print only 5 integers per line. Hint: Use the calculation **x % 5**. When the value of this is 0, print a newline character, otherwise print a tab character.

e) Repeat Exercise 4.3 (d) using a **for** structure.

4.4 Find the error in each of the following code segments and explain how to correct it.

a)
```
x = 1;
while (x <= 10);
    x++;
}
```

b)
```
for (y = .1; y != 1.0; y += .1)
    printf("%f\n", y);
```

c)
```
switch (n) {
    case 1:
        printf("The number is 1\n");
    case 2:
        printf("The number is 2\n");
        break;
    default:
        printf("The number is not 1 or 2\n");
        break;
}
```

d) The following code should print the values 1 to 10.
```
n = 1;
while (n < 10)
    printf("%d ", n++);
```

Answers to Self-Review Exercises

4.1 a) definite. b) indefinite. c) control variable or counter. d) **continue**. e) **break**. f) **switch** selection structure.

4.2
a) False. The **default** case is optional. If no default action is needed, then there is no need for a **default** case.

b) False. The **break** statement is used to exit the **switch** structure. The **break** statement is not required when the **default** case is the last case.

c) False. Both of the relational expressions must be true in order for the entire expression to be true when using the **&&** operator.

d) True.

4.3
a)
```
sum = 0;
for (count = 1; count <= 99; count += 2)
    sum += count;
```
b)
```
printf("%-15.1f\n", 333.546372);   /* prints 333.5     */
printf("%-15.2f\n", 333.546372);   /* prints 333.55    */
printf("%-15.3f\n", 333.546372);   /* prints 333.546   */
printf("%-15.4f\n", 333.546372);   /* prints 333.5464  */
printf("%-15.5f\n", 333.546372);   /* prints 333.54637 */
```
c)
```
printf("%10.2f\n", pow(2.5, 3));   /* prints 15.63     */
```

d)
```
x = 1;
while (x <= 20) {
   printf("%d", x);
   if (x % 5 == 0)
      printf("\n");
   else
      printf("\t");
   x++;
}
```

or

```
x = 1;
while (x <= 20)
   if (x % 5 == 0)
      printf("%d\n", x++);
   else
      printf("%d\t", x++);
```

or

```
x = 0;
while (++x <= 20)
   if (x % 5 == 0)
      printf("%d\n", x);
   else
      printf("%d\t", x);
```

e)
```
for (x = 1; x <= 20; x++) {
   printf("%d", x);
   if (x % 5 == 0)
      printf("\n");
   else
      printf("\t");
}
```

or

```
for (x = 1; x <= 20; x++)
   if (x % 5 == 0)
      printf("%d\n", x);
   else
      printf("%d\t", x);
```

4.4   a) Error: The semicolon after the **while** header causes an infinite loop.
Correction: Replace the semicolon by a **{** or remove both the **;** and the **}**.

b) Error: Using a floating-point number to control a **for** repetition structure.
Correction: Use an integer, and perform the proper calculation in order to get the values you desire.

```
for (y = 1; y != 10; y++)
   printf("%f\n", (float) y / 10);
```

c) Error: Missing **break** statement in the statements for the first **case**.
Correction: Add a **break** statement at the end of the statements for the first **case**.
Note that this is not necessarily an error if the programmer wants the statement of
case 2: to execute every time the **case 1:** statement executes.

d) Error: Improper relational operator used in the while repetition-continuation condition.
Correction: Use **<=** rather than **<**.

Exercises

4.5   Find the error in each of the following (Note: there may be more than one error):

a)
```
For (x = 100, x >= 1, x++)
    printf("%d\n", x);
```

b) The following code should print whether a given integer is odd or even:
```
switch (value % 2) {
   case 0:
      printf("Even integer\n");
   case 1:
      printf("Odd integer\n");
}
```

c) The following code should input an integer and a character and print them. Assume the
user types as input **100 A**.
```
scanf("%d", &intVal);
charVal = getchar();
printf("Integer: %d\nCharacter: %c\n", intVal, charVal);
```

d)
```
for (x = .000001; x <= .0001; x += .000001)
    printf("%.7f\n", x);
```

e) The following code should output the odd integers from 999 to 1:
```
for (x = 999; x >= 1; x += 2)
    printf("%d\n", x);
```

f) The following code should output the even integers from 2 to 100:
```
counter = 2;

Do {
   if (counter % 2 == 0)
      printf("%d\n", counter);

   counter += 2;
} While (counter < 100);
```

g) The following code should sum the integers from 100 to 150 (assume **total** is initialized to 0):
```
for (x = 100; x <= 150; x++);
    total += x;
```

4.6   State which values of the control variable **x** are printed by each of the following **for**
statements:

a)
```
for (x = 2; x <= 13; x += 2)
    printf("%d\n", x);
```

b)
```
for (x = 5; x <= 22; x += 7)
    printf("%d\n", x);
```

    c) `for(x = 3; x <= 15; x += 3)`
       `printf("%d\n", x);`
    d) `for(x = 1; x <= 5; x += 7)`
       `printf("%d\n", x);`
    e) `for(x = 12; x >= 2; x -= 3)`
       `printf("%d\n", x);`

4.7   Write **for** statements that print the following sequences of values:
    a) 1, 2, 3, 4, 5, 6, 7
    b) 3, 8, 13, 18, 23
    c) 20, 14, 8, 2, -4, -10
    d) 19, 27, 35, 43, 51

4.8   What does the following program do?

```
#include <stdio.h>

main()
{
   int i, j, x, y;

   printf("Enter integers in the range 1-20: ");
   scanf("%d%d", &x, &y);

   for (i = 1; i <= y; i++) {

      for (j = 1; j <= x; j++)
         printf("@");

      printf("\n");
   }

   return 0;
}
```

4.9   Write a program that sums a sequence of integers. Assume that the first integer read with **scanf** specifies the number of values remaining to be entered. Your program should read only one value each time **scanf** is executed. A typical input sequence might be

    5 100 200 300 400 500

where the **5** indicates that the subsequent **5** values are to be summed.

4.10   Write a program that calculates and prints the average of several integers. Assume the last value read with **scanf** is the sentinel **9999**. A typical input sequence might be

    10 8 11 7 9 9999

indicating that the average of all the values preceding **9999** is to be calculated.

4.11   Write a program that finds the smallest of several integers. Assume that the first value read specifies the number of values remaining.

4.12   Write a program that calculates and prints the sum of the even integers from 2 to 30.

4.13   Write a program that calculates and prints the product of the odd integers from 1 to 15.

4.14   The *factorial* function is used frequently in probability problems. The factorial of a positive integer n (written $n!$ and pronounced "n factorial") is equal to the product of the positive integers from 1 to n. Write a program that evaluates the factorials of the integers from 1 to 5. Print the results in tabular format. What difficulty might prevent you from calculating the factorial of 20?

4.15   Modify the compound interest program of Section 4.6 to repeat its steps for interest rates of 5 percent, 6 percent, 7 percent, 8 percent, 9 percent, and 10 percent. Use a **for** loop to vary the interest rate.

4.16   Write a program that prints the following patterns separately one below the other. Use **for** loops to generate the patterns. All asterisks (*) should be printed by a single **printf** statement of the form **printf("*");** (this causes the asterisks to print side by side). Hint: The last two patterns require that each line begin with an appropriate number of blanks.

```
      (A)              (B)              (C)              (D)

       *           **********       **********               *
       **          *********         *********              **
       ***         ********           ********             ***
       ****        *******             *******            ****
       *****       ******               ******           *****
       ******      *****                 *****          ******
       *******     ****                   ****         *******
       ********    ***                     ***        ********
       *********   **                       **       *********
       **********  *                         *      **********
```

4.17   Collecting money becomes increasingly difficult during periods of recession, so companies may tighten their credit limits to prevent their accounts receivable (money owed to them) from becoming too large. In response to a prolonged recession, one company has cut its customer's credit limits in half. Thus, if a particular customer had a credit limit of $2000, this customer's credit limit is now $1000. If a customer had a credit limit of $5000, this customer's credit limit is now $2500. Write a program that analyzes the credit status of three customers of this company. For each customer you are given:

1. The customer's account number
2. The customer's credit limit before the recession
3. The customer's current balance (i.e., the amount the customer owes the company).

Your program should calculate and print the new credit limit for each customer, and should determine (and print) which customers have current balances that exceed their new credit limits.

4.18   One interesting application of computers is drawing graphs and bar charts (sometimes called "histograms"). Write a program that reads five numbers (each between 1 and 30). For each number read, your program should print a line containing that number of adjacent asterisks. For example, if your program reads the number seven, it should print *******.

4.19   A mail order house sells five different products whose retail prices are shown in the following table:

Product number	Retail price
1	$ 2.98
2	4.50
3	9.98
4	4.49
5	6.87

Write a program that reads a series of pairs of numbers as follows:

1. Product number
2. Quantity sold for one day

Your program should use a **switch** statement to help determine the retail price for each product. Your program should calculate and display the total retail value of all products sold last week.

4.20   Complete the following truth tables by filling in each blank with 0 or 1.

Condition1	Condition2	Condition1 && Condition2
0	0	0
0	nonzero	0
nonzero	0	_____
nonzero	nonzero	_____

Condition1	Condition2	Condition1 || Condition2
0	0	0
0	nonzero	1
nonzero	0	_____
nonzero	nonzero	_____

Condition1	!Condition1
0	1
nonzero	_____

4.21   Rewrite the program of Fig. 4.2 so that the initialization of the variable **counter** is done in the declaration instead of the **for** structure.

4.22   Modify the program of Fig. 4.7 so that it calculates the average grade for the class.

4.23   Modify the program in Fig. 4.6 so that it uses only integers to calculate the compound interest. (Hint: Treat all monetary amounts as integral numbers of pennies. Then "break" the result into its dollar portion and cents portion by using the division and modulus operations respectively. Insert a period.)

4.24   Assume **i = 1, j = 2, k = 3**, and **m = 2**. What does each of the following statements print?
```
a) printf("%d", i == 1);
b) printf("%d", j == 3);
```

```
c)  printf("%d", i >= 1 && j < 4);
d)  printf("%d", m < = 99 && k < m);
e)  printf("%d", j >= i || k == m);
f)  printf("%d", k + m < j || 3 - j >= k);
g)  printf("%d", !m);
h)  printf("%d", !(j - m));
i)  printf("%d", !(k > m));
j)  printf("%d", !(j > k));
```

4.25   Print a table of decimal, binary, octal, and hexadecimal equivalents. If you are not familiar with these number systems, read Appendix E first if you would like to attempt this exercise.

4.26   Calculate the value of π from the infinite series

$$\pi = 4 - \frac{4}{3} + \frac{4}{5} - \frac{4}{7} + \frac{4}{9} - \frac{4}{11} + \dots$$

Print a table that show the value of π approximated by 1 term of this series, by two terms, by three terms, etc. How many terms of this series do you have to use before you first get 3.14? 3.141? 3.1415? 3.14159?

4.27   *(Pythagorean Triples)* A right triangle can have sides that are all integers. The set of three integer values for the sides of a right triangle is called a Pythagorean triple. These three sides must satisfy the relationship that the sum of the squares of two of the sides is equal to the square of the hypotenuse. Find all Pythagorean triples for side1, side2, and the hypotenuse all no larger than 500. Use a triple-nested **for**-loop that simply tries all possibilities. This is an example of "brute force" computing. It is not aesthetically pleasing to many people. But there are many reasons why these techniques are important. First, with computing power increasing at such a phenomenal pace, solutions that would have taken years or even centuries of computer time to produce with the technology of just a few years ago, can now be produced in hours, minutes or even seconds. Recent microprocessor chips can process more than 100 million instructions per second! And billion-instruction-per-second microprocessor chips are likely to appear in the 1990s. Second, as you will learn in more advanced computer science courses, there are large numbers of interesting problems for which there is no known algorithmic approach other than sheer brute force. We investigate many kinds of problem-solving methodologies in this book. We will consider many brute force approaches to various interesting problems.

4.28   A company pays its employees as managers (who receive a fixed weekly salary), hourly workers (who receive a fixed hourly wage for up to the first 40 hours they work and "time-and-a-half," i.e., 1.5 times their hourly wage, for overtime hours worked), commission workers (who receive a $250 plus 5.7% of their gross weekly sales), or pieceworkers (who receive a fixed amount of money per item for each of the items they produce—each pieceworker in this company works on only one type of item). Write a program to compute the weekly pay for each employee. You do not know the number of employees in advance. Each type of employee has its own pay code: Managers have paycode 1, hourly workers have code 2, commission workers have code 3 and pieceworkers have code 4. Use a **switch** to compute each employee's pay based on that employee's paycode. Within the **switch**, prompt the user (i.e., the payroll clerk) to enter the appropriate facts your program needs to calculate each employee's pay based on that employee's paycode.

4.29   *(De Morgan's Laws)* In this chapter, we discussed the logical operators **&&**, **||**, and **!**. De Morgan's Laws can sometimes make it more convenient for us to express a logical expression. These laws state that the expression **!** *(condition1* **&&** *condition2)* is logically equivalent to the expression **(** **!** *condition1* **||** **!** *condition2)* . Also, the expression **!** *(condition1* **||**   *condition2)* is logically equivalent to the expression **(** **!** *condition1* **&&** !*condition2)*. Use De Morgan's Laws to write equivalent expressions for each of the following and then write a program to show that both the original expression and the new expression in each case are equivalent:.

a) `!(x < 5) && !(y >= 7)`
b) `!(a == b) || !(g != 5)`
c) `!((x <= 8) && (Y > 4))`
d) `!((i > 4) || (j <= 6))`

4.30   Rewrite the program of Fig. 4.7 by replacing the **switch** statement with a nested **if/else** statement; be careful to deal with the **default** case properly. Then rewrite this new version by replacing the nested **if/else** statement with a series of **if** statements; here, too, be careful to deal with the **default** case properly (this is more difficult than in the nested **if/else** version). This exercise demonstrates that **switch** is a convenience and that any **switch** statement can be written with only single-selection statements.

4.31   Write a program that prints the following diamond shape. You may use **printf** statements that print either a single asterisk (*) or a single blank. Maximize your use of repetition (with nested **for** structures) and minimize the number of **printf** statements.

4.32   Modify the program you wrote in Exercise 4.31 to read an odd number in the range 1 to 19 to specify the number of rows in the diamond. Your program should then display a diamond of the appropriate size.

4.33   If you are familiar with Roman Numerals, write a program that prints a table of all the Roman number equivalents of the decimal numbers in the range 1 to 100.

4.34   Write a program that prints a table of the binary, octal, and hexadecimal equivalents of the decimal numbers in the range 1 through 256. If you are not familiar with these number systems, read Appendix E first if you would like to attempt this exercise.

4.35   Describe the process you would use to replace a **do/while** loop with an equivalent **while** loop. What problem occurs when you try to replace a **while** loop with an equivalent **do/while** loop? Suppose you have been told that you must remove a **while** loop and replace it with a **do/while**. What additional control structure would you need to use and how would you use it to ensure that the resulting program behaves exactly as the original.

4.36   Write a program that inputs the year in the range 1994 through 1999 and uses **for**-loop repetition to produce a condensed, neatly printed calendar. Watch out for leap years.

4.37   A criticism of the **break** statement and the **continue** statement is that each is unstructured. Actually **break** statements and **continue** statements can always be replaced by structured statements, although doing so can be awkward. Describe in general how you would remove any **break** statement from a loop in a program and replace that statement with some structured equivalent. (Hint: The **break** statement leaves a loop from within the body of the loop. The other way to leave is by failing the loop-continuation test. Consider using in the loop-continuation test a second test that indicates "early exit because of a 'break' condition.") Use the technique you developed here to remove the break statement from the program of Fig. 4.11.

4.38   What does the following program segment do?

```
for (i = 1; i <= 5; i++) {
    for (j = 1; j <= 3; j++) {
        for (k = 1, k <= 4; k++)
            printf("*");
        printf("\n");
    }
    printf("\n");
}
```

4.39   Describe in general how you would remove any **continue** statement from a loop in a program and replace that statement with some structured equivalent. Use the technique you developed here to remove the **continue** statement from the program of Fig. 4.12.

4.40   Describe in general how you would remove **break** statements from a **switch** structure and replace them with structured equivalents. Use the (perhaps awkward) technique you developed here to remove the **break** statements from the program of Fig. 4.7.

5

Functions

Objectives

- To understand how to construct programs modularly from small pieces called functions.
- To introduce the common math functions available in the C standard library.
- To be able to create new functions.
- To understand the mechanisms used to pass information between functions.
- To introduce simulation techniques using random number generation.
- To understand how to write and use functions that call themselves.

Form ever follows function.
Louis Henri Sullivan

E pluribus unum. (One composed of many.)
Virgil

O! call back yesterday, bid time return.
William Shakespeare
Richard II

Call me Ishmael.
Herman Melville
Moby Dick

When you call me that, smile.
Owen Wister

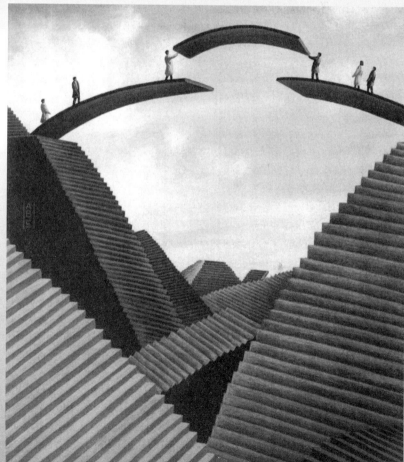

Outline

5.1 Introduction

Most computer programs that solve real-world problems are much larger than the programs presented in the first few chapters. Experience has shown that the best way to develop and maintain a large program is to construct it from smaller pieces or *modules* each of which is more manageable than the original program. This technique is called *divide and conquer*. This chapter describes the features of the C language that facilitate the design, implementation, operation, and maintenance of large programs.

5.2 Program Modules in C

Modules in C are called *functions*. C programs are typically written by combining new functions the programmer writes with "pre-packaged" functions available in the *C standard library*. We discuss both kinds of functions in this chapter. The C standard library provides a rich collection of functions for performing common mathematical calculations, string manipulations, character manipulations, input/output, and many other useful operations. This makes the programmer's job easier because these functions provide many of the capabilities programmers need.

Good Programming Practice 5.1

Familiarize yourself with the rich collection of functions in the ANSI C standard library.

Software Engineering Observation 5.1

Avoid reinventing the wheel. When possible, use ANSI C standard library functions instead of writing new functions. This reduces program development time.

Portability Tip 5.1

Using the functions in the ANSI C standard library helps make programs more portable.

Although the standard library functions are technically not a part of the C language, they are invariably provided with ANSI C systems. The functions **printf**, **scanf**, and **pow** that we have used in previous chapters are standard library functions.

The programmer can write functions to define specific tasks that may be used at many points in a program. These are sometimes referred to as *programmer-defined functions*. The actual statements defining the function are written only once, and the statements are hidden from other functions.

Functions are *invoked* by a *function call*. The function call specifies the function name and provides information (as *arguments*) that the called function needs in order to perform its designated task. A common analogy for this is the hierarchical form of management. A boss (the *calling function* or *caller*) asks a worker (the *called function*) to perform a task and report back when the task is done. For example, a function that wants to display information on the screen calls the worker function **printf** to perform that task, then **printf** displays the information and reports back—or *returns*—to the calling function when its task is completed. The boss function does not know how the worker function performs its designated tasks. The worker may call other worker functions, and the boss will be unaware of this. We will soon see how this "hiding" of implementation details promotes good software engineering. Figure 5.1 shows the **main** function communicating with several worker functions in a hierarchical manner. Note that **worker1** acts as a boss function to **worker4** and **worker5**. Relationships among functions may be other than the hierarchical structure shown in this figure.

5.3 Math Library Functions

Math library functions allow the programmer to perform certain common mathematical calculations. We use various math library functions here to introduce the concept of functions. Later in the book, we will discuss many of the other functions in the C standard library. A complete list of the C standard library functions is provided in Appendix B.

Functions are normally used in a program by writing the name of the function followed by a left parenthesis followed by the *argument* (or a comma separated list of arguments) of the function followed by a right parenthesis. For example, a programmer desiring to calculate and print the square root of **900.0** might write

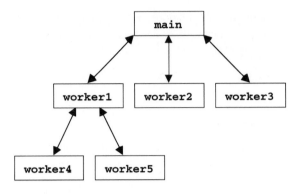

Fig. 5.1   Hierarchical boss function/worker function relationship.

```
printf("%.2f", sqrt(900.0));
```

When this statement is executed, the math library function **sqrt** is called to calculate the square root of the number contained in the parentheses (**900.0**). The number **900.0** is the argument of the **sqrt** function. The preceding statement would print **30.00**. The **sqrt** function takes an argument of type **double** and returns a result of type **double**. All functions in the math library return the data type **double**.

> **Good Programming Practice 5.2**
>
> *Include the math header file by using the preprocessor directive **#include <math.h>** when using functions in the math library.*

> **Common Programming Error 5.1**
>
> *Forgetting to include the math header file when using math library functions can cause strange results.*

Function arguments may be constants, variables, or expressions. If **c1 = 13.0**, **d = 3.0**, and **f = 4.0**, then the statement

```
printf("%.2f", sqrt(c1 + d * f));
```

calculates and prints the square root of **13.0 + 3.0 * 4.0 = 25.0**, namely **5.00**.

Some C math library functions are summarized in Fig. 5.2. In the figure, the variables **x** and **y** are of type **double**.

5.4 Functions

Functions allow the programmer to modularize a program. All variables declared in function definitions are *local variables*—they are known only in the function in which they are defined. Most functions have a list of *parameters*. The parameters provide the means for communicating information between functions. A function's parameters are also local variables.

Function	Description	Example
`sqrt(x)`	square root of *x*	`sqrt(900.0)` is `30.0` `sqrt(9.0)` is `3.0`
`exp(x)`	exponential function e^x	`exp(1.0)` is `2.718282` `exp(2.0)` is `7.389056`
`log(x)`	natural logarithm of *x* (base e)	`log(2.718282)` is `1.0` `log(7.389056)` is `2.0`

`log10(x)`	logarithm of *x* (base 10)	`log10(1.0)` is `0.0`
		`log10(10.0)` is `1.0`
		`log10(100.0)` is `2.0`

`fabs(x)`	absolute value of *x*	if `x > 0` then `fabs(x)` is `x` if `x = 0` then `fabs(x)` is `0.0` if `x < 0` then `fabs(x)` is `-x`
`ceil(x)`	rounds *x* to the smallest integer not less than *x*	`ceil(9.2)` is `10.0` `ceil(-9.8)` is `-9.0`
`floor(x)`	rounds *x* to the largest integer not greater than *x*	`floor(9.2)` is `9.0` `floor(-9.8)` is `-10.0`
`pow(x, y)`	*x* raised to power *y* (x^y)	`pow(2, 7)` is `128.0` `pow(9, .5)` is `3.0`
`fmod(x, y)`	remainder of *x/y* as a floating point number	`fmod(13.657, 2.333)` is `1.992`
`sin(x)`	trigonometric sine of *x* (*x* in radians)	`sin(0.0)` is `0.0`
`cos(x)`	trigonometric cosine of *x* (*x* in radians)	`cos(0.0)` is `1.0`
`tan(x)`	trigonometric tangent of *x* (*x* in radians)	`tan(0.0)` is `0.0`

Fig. 5.2   Commonly used math library functions.

Software Engineering Observation 5.2

In programs containing many functions, **main** *should be implemented as a group of calls to functions that perform the bulk of the program's work.*

There are several motivations for "functionalizing" a program. The divide-and-conquer approach makes program development more manageable. Another motivation is *software reusability*—using existing functions as building blocks to create new programs. Software reusability is a major factor in the object-oriented programming movement. With good function naming and definition, programs can be created from standardized functions that accomplish specific tasks, rather than being built by using customized code. This technique is known as *abstraction.* We use abstraction each time we write programs including standard library functions like **printf**, **scanf**, and **pow**. A third motivation is to avoid repeating code in a program. Packaging code as a function allows the code to be executed from several locations in a program simply by calling the function.

Software Engineering Observation 5.3

Each function should be limited to performing a single, well-defined task, and the function name should effectively express that task. This facilitates abstraction and promotes software reusability.

Software Engineering Observation 5.4

If you can not choose a concise name that expresses what the function does, it is possible that your function is attempting to perform too many diverse tasks. It is usually best to break such a function into several smaller functions.

5.5 Function Definitions

Each program we have presented has consisted of a function called **main** that called standard library functions to accomplish its tasks. We now consider how programmers write their own customized functions.

Consider a program that uses a function **square** to calculate the squares of the integers from 1 to 10 (Fig. 5.3).

```
/* A programmer-defined square function */
#include <stdio.h>

int square(int);    /* function prototype */

main()
{
   int x;

   for (x = 1; x <= 10; x++)
      printf("%d  ", square(x));

   printf("\n");
   return 0;
}

/* Function definition */
int square(int y)
{
   return y * y;
}
```

```
1   4   9   16   25   36   49   64   81   100
```

Fig. 5.3   Using a programmer-defined function.

```c
/* Finding the maximum of three integers */
#include <stdio.h>

int maximum(int, int, int);   /* function prototype */

main()
{
   int a, b, c;

   printf("Enter three integers: ");
   scanf("%d%d%d", &a, &b, &c);
   printf("Maximum is: %d\n", maximum(a, b, c));

   return 0;
}

/* Function maximum definition */
int maximum(int x, int y, int z)
{
   int max = x;

   if (y > max)
      max = y;

   if (z > max)
      max = z;

   return max;
}
```

```
Enter three integers: 22 85 17
Maximum is: 85
```

```
Enter three integers: 85 22 17
Maximum is: 85
```

```
Enter three integers: 22 17 85
Maximum is: 85
```

Fig. 5.4   Programmer-defined **maximum** function.

Good Programming Practice 5.8

*Include function prototypes for all functions to take advantage of C's type checking capabilities. Use **#include** preprocessor directives to obtain function prototypes for the standard library functions from the header files for the appropriate libraries. Also use **#include** to obtain header files containing function prototypes used by you and/or your group members.*

Software Engineering Observation 5.5

A function should be no longer than one page. Better yet, a function should be no longer than half a page. Small functions promote software reusability.

Software Engineering Observation 5.6

Programs should be written as collections of small functions. This makes programs easier to write, debug, maintain and modify.

Software Engineering Observation 5.7

A function requiring a large number of parameters may be performing too many tasks. Consider dividing the function into smaller functions that perform the separate tasks. The function header should fit on one line if possible.

Software Engineering Observation 5.8

The function prototype, function header, and function calls should all agree in the number, type, and order of arguments and parameters, and in the type of return value.

There are three ways to return control to the point at which a function was invoked. If the function does not return a result, control is returned simply when the function-ending right brace is reached, or by executing the statement

```
return;
```

If the function does return a result, the statement

```
return expression;
```

returns the value of *expression* to the caller.

Our second example uses a programmer-defined function **maximum** to determine and return the largest of three integers (Fig. 5.4). The three integers are input with **scanf**. Next, the integers are passed to **maximum** which determines the largest integer. This value is returned to main by the **return** statement in **maximum**. The value returned is assigned to the variable **largest** which is then printed in the **printf** statement.

5.6 Function Prototypes

One of the most important features of ANSI C is the *function prototype*. This feature was borrowed by the ANSI C committee from the developers of C++. A function prototype tells the compiler the type of data returned by the function, the number of parameters the function expects to receive, the types of the parameters, and the order in which these parameters are expected. The compiler uses function prototypes to validate function calls. Previous versions of C did not perform this kind of checking, so it was possible to call functions improperly without the compiler detecting the errors. Such calls could result in fatal execution-time errors or nonfatal errors that caused subtle, difficult to detect logic errors. ANSI C function prototypes correct this deficiency.

Common Programming Error 5.4

Returning a value from a function whose return type has been declared **void** *causes a syntax error.*

Good Programming Practice 5.4

Even though an omitted return type defaults to **int**, *always state the return type explicitly. The return type for* **main**, *however, is normally omitted.*

The *parameter-list* is a comma-separated list containing the declarations of the parameters received by the function when it is called. If a function does not receive any values, *parameter-list* is **void** A type must be listed explicitly for each parameter unless the parameter is of type **int**. If a type is not listed, **int** is assumed.

Common Programming Error 5.5

Declaring function parameters of the same type as **float x, y** *instead of* **float x, float y**. *The parameter declaration* **float x, y** *would actually make* **y** *a parameter of type* **int** *because* **int** *is the default.*

Common Programming Error 5.6

Placing a semicolon after the right parenthesis enclosing the parameter list of a function definition is a syntax error.

Common Programming Error 5.7

Defining a function parameter again as a local variable within the function is a syntax error.

Good Programming Practice 5.5

Include the type of each parameter in the parameter list, even if that parameter is of the default type **int**.

Good Programming Practice 5.6

Although it is not incorrect to do so, do not use the same names for the arguments passed to a function and the corresponding parameters in the function definition. This helps avoid ambiguity.

The *declarations* and *statements* within braces form the *function body*. The function body is also referred to as a *block*. A block is simply a compound statement that includes declarations. Variables can be declared in any block, and blocks can be nested. *A function can not be defined inside another function under any circumstances.*

Common Programming Error 5.8

Defining a function inside another function is a syntax error.

Good Programming Practice 5.7

Choosing meaningful function names and meaningful parameter names makes programs more readable and helps avoid excessive use of comments.

Good Programming Practice 5.3

Place a blank line between function definitions to separate the functions and enhance program readability.

Function **square** is *invoked* or *called* in **main** within the **printf** statement

```
printf("%d  ", square(x));
```

Function **square** receives a copy of the value of **x** in the *parameter* **y**. Then **square** calculates **y * y**. The result is passed back to the **printf** function in **main** where **square** was invoked, and **printf** displays the result. This process is repeated ten times using the **for** repetition structure.

The definition of **square** shows that **square** expects an integer parameter **y**. The keyword **int** preceding the function name indicates that **square** returns an integer result. The **return** statement in **square** passes the result of the calculation back to the calling function.

The line

```
int square(int);
```

is a *function prototype*. The **int** in parentheses informs the compiler that **square** expects to receive an integer value from the caller. The **int** to the left of the function name **square** informs the compiler that **square** returns an integer result to the caller. The compiler refers to the function prototype to check that calls to **square** contain the correct return type, the correct number of arguments, the correct argument types, and that the arguments are in the correct order. Function prototypes are discussed in detail in Section 5.6.

The format of a function definition is

return-value-type function-name (parameter-list)
    {
       declarations

       statements
    }

The *function-name* is any valid identifier. The *return-value-type* is the data type of the result returned to the caller. The *return-value-type* **void** indicates that a function does not return a value. An unspecified *return-value-type* is always assumed by the compiler to be **int**.

Common Programming Error 5.2

Omitting the return-value-type in a function definition causes a syntax error if the function prototype specifies a return type other than **int**.

Common Programming Error 5.3

Forgetting to return a value from a function that is supposed to return a value can lead to unexpected errors. The ANSI standard states that the result of this omission is undefined.

The function prototype for **maximum** in Fig. 5.4 is

```
int maximum(int, int, int);
```

This function prototype states that **maximum** takes three arguments of type **int**, and returns a result of type **int**. Notice that the function prototype is the same as the first line of the function definition of **maximum** except the names of the parameters (**x**, **y**, and **z**) are not included.

Good Programming Practice 5.9

Parameter names are sometimes included in function prototypes for documentation purposes. The compiler ignores these names.

Common Programming Error 5.9

Forgetting the semicolon at the end of a function prototype causes a syntax error.

A function call that does not match the function prototype causes a syntax error. An error is also generated if the function prototype and the function definition disagree. For example, in Fig. 5.4, if the function prototype had been written

```
void maximum(int, int, int);
```

the compiler would generate an error because the **void** return type in the function prototype would differ from the **int** return type in the function header.

Another important feature of function prototypes is the *coercion of arguments,* i.e., the forcing of arguments to the appropriate type. For example, the math library function **sqrt** can be called with an integer argument even though the function prototype in **math.h** specifies a **double** argument, and the function will still work correctly. The statement

```
printf("%.3f\n", sqrt(4));
```

correctly evaluates **sqrt(4)**, and prints the value **2.000**. The function prototype causes the compiler to convert the integer value **4** to the **double** value **4.0** before the value is passed to **sqrt**. In general, argument values that do not correspond precisely to the parameter types in the function prototype are converted to the proper type before the function is called. These conversions can lead to incorrect results if C's *promotion rules* are not followed. The promotion rules specify how types can be converted to other types without losing data. In our **sqrt** example above, an **int** is automatically converted to a **double** without changing its value. However, a **double** converted to an **int** truncates the fractional part of the **double** value. Converting large integer types to small integer types (e.g., **long** to **short**) may also result in changed values.

The promotion rules automatically apply to expressions containing values of two or more data types (also referred to as *mixed-type* expressions). The type of each value in a mixed-type expression is automatically promoted to the highest type in the expression (actually a temporary version of each value is created and used for the expression—the original values remain unchanged). Figure 5.5 lists the data types in order from highest type to lowest type with each type's **printf** and **scanf** conversion specifications.

Data types	printf conversion specifications	scanf conversion specifications
long double	%Lf	%Lf
double	%f	%lf
float	%f	%f
unsigned long int	%lu	%lu
long int	%ld	%ld
unsigned int	%u	%u
int	%d	%d
short	%hd	%hd
char	%c	%c

Fig. 5.5 Promotion hierarchy for data types.

Converting values to lower types normally results in an incorrect value. Therefore, a value can only be converted to a lower type by explicitly assigning the value to a variable of lower type, or by using a cast operator. Function argument values are converted to the parameter types in a function prototype as if they are being assigned directly to variables of those types. If our **square** function that uses an integer parameter (Fig. 5.3) is called with a floating point argument, the argument is converted to **int** (a lower type), and **square** usually returns an incorrect value. For example, **square(4.5)** would return **16** not **20.25**.

Common Programming Error 5.10

Converting from a higher data type in the promotion hierarchy to a lower type can change the data value.

If the function prototype for a function has not been included in a program, the compiler forms its own function prototype using the first occurrence of the function—either the function definition or a call to the function. By default, the compiler assumes the function returns an **int**, and nothing is assumed about the arguments. Therefore, if the arguments passed to the function are incorrect, the errors are not detected by the compiler.

Common Programming Error 5.11

*Forgetting a function prototype causes a syntax error if the return type of the function is not **int** and the function definition appears after the function call in the program. Otherwise, forgetting a function prototype may cause a run-time error or an unexpected result.*

Software Engineering Observation 5.9

A function prototype placed outside any function definition applies to all calls to the function appearing after the function prototype in the file. A function prototype placed in a function applies only to calls made in that function.

5.7 Header Files

Each standard library has a corresponding *header file* containing the function prototypes for all the functions in that library and definitions of various data types and constants needed by those functions. Fig. 5.6 lists alphabetically the standard library header files that may be included in programs. The term "macros" that is used several times in Fig. 5.6 is discussed in detail in Chapter 13, "Preprocessor."

Standard library header file	Explanation
`<assert.h>`	Contains macros and information for adding diagnostics that aid program debugging.
`<ctype.h>`	Contains function prototypes for functions that test characters for certain properties, and function prototypes for functions that can be used to convert lowercase letters to uppercase letters and vice versa.
`<errno.h>`	Defines macros that are useful for reporting error conditions.
`<float.h>`	Contains the floating point size limits of the system.
`<limits.h>`	Contains the integral size limits of the system.
`<locale.h>`	Contains function prototypes and other information that enables a program to be modified for the current locale on which it is running. The notion of locale enables the computer system to handle different conventions for expressing data like dates, times, dollar amounts, and large numbers in different areas throughout the world.
`<math.h>`	Contains function prototypes for math library functions.
`<setjmp.h>`	Contains function prototypes for functions that allow bypassing of the usual function call and return sequence.
`<signal.h>`	Contains function prototypes and macros to handle various conditions that may arise during program execution.
`<stdarg.h>`	Defines macros for dealing with a list of arguments to a function whose number and types are unknown.
`<stddef.h>`	Contains common definitions of types used by C for performing certain calculations.
`<stdio.h>`	Contains function prototypes for the standard input/output library functions, and information used by them.
`<stdlib.h>`	Contains function prototypes for conversions of numbers to text and text to numbers, memory allocation, random numbers, and other utility functions.
`<string.h>`	Contains function prototypes for string processing functions.
`<time.h>`	Contains function prototypes and types for manipulating the time and date.

Fig. 5.6   The standard library header files.

The programmer can create custom header files. Programmer-defined header files should also end in **.h**. A programmer-defined header file can be included by using the **#include** preprocessor directive. For example, the header file **square.h** can be included in our program by the directive

```
#include "square.h"
```

at the top of the program. Section 13.2 presents additional information on including header files.

5.8 Calling Functions: Call by Value and Call by Reference

Two ways to invoke functions in many programming languages are *call by value* and *call by reference*. When arguments are passed call by value, a *copy* of the argument's value is made and passed to the called function. Changes to the copy do not affect an original variable's value in the caller. When an argument is passed call by reference, the caller actually allows the called function to modify the original variable's value.

Call by value should be used whenever the called function does not need to modify the value of the caller's original variable. This prevents the accidental *side effects* that so greatly hinder the development of correct and reliable software systems. Call by reference should only be used with trusted called functions that need to modify the original variable.

In C, all calls are call by value. As we will see in Chapter 7, it is possible to *simulate* call by reference by using address operators and indirection operators. In Chapter 6, we will see that arrays are automatically passed simulated call by reference. We will have to wait until Chapter 7 for a full understanding of this complex issue. For now, we concentrate on call by value.

5.9 Random Number Generation

We now take a brief and, it is hoped, entertaining diversion into a popular programming application, namely simulation and game playing. In this section and the next section, we will develop a nicely structured game-playing program that includes multiple functions. The program uses most of the control structures we have studied.

There is something in the air of a gambling casino that invigorates every type of person from the high-rollers at the plush mahogany-and-felt craps tables to the quarter-poppers at the one-armed bandits. It is the *element of chance,* the possibility that luck will convert a mere pocketful of money into a mountain of wealth. The element of chance can be introduced into computer applications by using the **rand** function in the C standard library.

Consider the following statement:

```
i = rand();
```

The **rand** function generates an integer between 0 and **RAND_MAX** (a symbolic constant defined in the **<stdlib.h>** header file). The ANSI standard states that the value of **RAND_MAX** must be at least 32767 which is the maximum value for a two-byte (i.e., 16-

bit) integer. The programs in this section were tested on a C system with a maximum value of 32767 for **RAND_MAX**. If **rand** truly produces integers at random, every number between 0 and **RAND_MAX** has an equal *chance* (or *probability*) of being chosen each time **rand** is called.

The range of values produced directly by **rand** is often different than what is needed in a specific application. For example, a program that simulates coin tossing might require only 0 for "heads" and 1 for "tails." A dice-rolling program that simulates a six-sided die would require random integers in range 1 to 6.

To demonstrate **rand**, let us develop a program to simulate 20 rolls of a six-sided die and print the value of each roll. The function prototype for the **rand** function can be found in **<stdlib.h>**. We use the modulus operator (**%**) in conjunction with **rand** as follows

    rand() % 6

to produce integers in the range 0 to 5. This is called *scaling*. The number 6 is called the *scaling factor*. We then *shift* the range of numbers produced by adding 1 to our previous result. Fig. 5.7 confirms that the results are in the range 1 to 6.

To show that these numbers occur approximately with equal likelihood, let us simulate 6000 rolls of a die with the program of Fig. 5.8. Each integer from 1 to 6 should appear approximately 1000 times.

```c
/* Shifted, scaled integers produced by 1 + rand() % 6 */
#include <stdio.h>
#include <stdlib.h>

main()
{
    int i;

    for (i = 1; i <= 20; i++) {
        printf("%10d", 1 + (rand() % 6));

        if (i % 5 == 0)
            printf("\n");
    }

    return 0;
}
```

5	5	3	5	5
2	4	2	5	5
5	3	2	2	1
5	1	4	6	4

Fig. 5.7   Shifted, scaled integers produced by **1 + rand() % 6**.

```
/* Roll a six-sided die 6000 times */
#include <stdio.h>
#include <stdlib.h>

main()
{
   int face, roll, frequency1 = 0, frequency2 = 0,
       frequency3 = 0, frequency4 = 0,
       frequency5 = 0, frequency6 = 0;

   for (roll = 1; roll <= 6000; roll++) {
      face = 1 + rand() % 6;

      switch (face) {
         case 1:
            ++frequency1;
            break;
         case 2:
            ++frequency2;
            break;
         case 3:
            ++frequency3;
            break;
         case 4:
             ++frequency4;
            break;
         case 5:
            ++frequency5;
            break;
         case 6:
            ++frequency6;
            break;
      }
   }

   printf("%s%13s\n", "Face", "Frequency");
   printf("    1%13d\n", frequency1);
   printf("    2%13d\n", frequency2);
   printf("    3%13d\n", frequency3);
   printf("    4%13d\n", frequency4);
   printf("    5%13d\n", frequency5);
   printf("    6%13d\n", frequency6);
   return 0;
}
```

```
Face     Frequency
   1          987
   2          984
   3         1029
   4          974
   5         1004
   6         1022
```

Fig. 5.8   Rolling a six-sided die 6000 times.

As the program output shows, by scaling and shifting we have utilized the **rand** function to realistically simulate the rolling of a six-sided die. Note that *no* **default** case is provided in the **switch** structure. Also note the use of the **%s** conversion specifier to print the character strings **"Face"** and **"Frequency"** as column headers. After we study arrays in Chapter 6, we will show how to replace the entire **switch** structure elegantly with a single-line statement.

Executing the program of Fig. 5.7 again produces

5	5	3	5	5
2	4	2	5	5
5	3	2	2	1
5	1	4	6	4

Notice that exactly the same sequence of values was printed. How can these be random numbers? Ironically, this repeatability is an important characteristic of the **rand** function. When debugging a program, this repeatability is essential for proving that corrections to a program work properly.

The **rand** function actually generates *pseudo-random numbers.* Calling **rand** repeatedly produces a sequence of numbers that appears to be random. However, the sequence repeats itself each time the program is executed. Once a program has been thoroughly debugged, it can be conditioned to produce a different sequence of random numbers for each execution. This is called *randomizing,* and is accomplished with the standard library function **srand**. The **srand** function takes an **unsigned** integer argument and *seeds* the **rand** function to produce a different sequence of random numbers for each execution of the program.

The use of **srand** is demonstrated in Fig. 5.9. In the program, we use the data type **unsigned** which is short for **unsigned int**. An **int** is stored in at least two bytes of memory, and can have positive and negative values. A variable of type **unsigned** is also stored in at least two bytes of memory. A two-byte **unsigned int** can have only positive values in the range 0 to 65535. A four-byte **unsigned int** can have only positive values in the range 0 to 4294967295. The **srand** function takes an **unsigned** value as an argument. The conversion specifier **%u** is used to read an **unsigned** value with **scanf**. The function prototype for **srand** is found in **<stdlib.h>**.

Let us run the program several times and observe the results. Notice that a *different* sequence of random numbers is obtained each time the program is run provided that a different seed is supplied.

If we wish to randomize without the need for entering a seed each time, we may use a statement like

```
srand(time(NULL));
```

This causes the computer to read its clock to obtain the value for the seed automatically. The **time** function returns the current time of day in seconds. This value is converted to an unsigned integer and used as the seed to the random number generator. Function **time** takes **NULL** as an argument (**time** is capable of providing the programmer with a string

```
/* Randomizing die-rolling program */
#include <stdlib.h>
#include <stdio.h>

main()
{
   int i;
   unsigned seed;

   printf("Enter seed: ");
   scanf("%u", &seed);
   srand(seed);

   for (i = 1; i <= 10; i++) {
     printf("%10d", 1 + (rand() % 6));

     if (i % 5 == 0)
        printf("\n");
   }

   return 0;
}
```

```
Enter seed: 67
         1         6         5         1         4
         5         6         3         1         2
```

```
Enter seed: 432
         4         2         5         4         3
         2         5         1         4         4
```

```
Enter seed: 67
         1         6         5         1         4
         5         6         3         1         2
```

Fig. 5.9   Randomizing the die-rolling program.

representing the time of day; **NULL** disables this capability for a specific call to **time**). The function prototype for **time** is in **<time.h>**.

The values produced directly by **rand** are always in the range:

$$0 \leq rand() \leq RAND\_MAX$$

Previously we demonstrated how to write a single C statement to simulate the rolling of a six-sided die:

```
face = 1 + rand() % 6;
```

This statement always assigns an integer value (at random) to the variable **face** in the range 1 ≤ **face** ≤ 6. Note that the width of this range (i.e., the number of consecutive integers in the range) is 6 and the starting number in the range is 1. Referring to the preceding statement, we see that the width of the range is determined by the number used to scale **rand** with the modulus operator (i.e., 6), and the starting number of the range is equal to the number (i.e., 1) that is added to **rand % 6**. We can generalize this result as follows

```
n = a + rand() % b;
```

where **a** is the *shifting value* (which is equal to the first number in the desired range of consecutive integers), and **b** is the scaling factor (which is equal to the width of the desired range of consecutive integers). In the exercises, we will see that it is possible to choose integers at random from sets of values other than ranges of consecutive integers.

Common Programming Error 5.12

*Using **srand** in place of **rand** to generate random numbers.*

5.10 Example: A Game of Chance

One of the most popular games of chance is a dice game known as "craps," which is played in casinos and back alleys throughout the world. The rules of the game are straightforward:

> *A player rolls two dice. Each die has six faces. These faces contain 1, 2, 3, 4, 5, and 6 spots. After the dice have come to rest, the sum of the spots on the two upward faces is calculated. If the sum is 7 or 11 on the first throw, the player wins. If the sum is 2, 3, or 12 on the first throw (called "craps"), the player loses (i.e., the "house" wins). If the sum is 4, 5, 6, 8, 9, or 10 on the first throw, then that sum becomes the player's "point." To win, you must continue rolling the dice until you "make your point." The player loses by rolling a 7 before making the point.*

The program in Fig. 5.10 simulates the game of craps. Figure 5.11 shows several sample executions.

Notice that the player must roll two dice on the first roll, and must do so later on all subsequent rolls. We define a function **rollDice** to roll the dice and compute and print their sum. Function **rollDice** is defined once, but it is called from two places in the program. Interestingly, **rollDice** takes no arguments, so we have indicated **void** in the parameter list. The function **rollDice** does return the sum of the two dice, so a return type of **int** is indicated in the function header.

The game is reasonably involved. The player may win or lose on the first roll, or may win or lose on any subsequent roll. The variable **gameStatus** is used to keep track of all this.

When the game is won, either on the first roll or on a subsequent roll, **gameStatus** is set to 1. When the game is lost, either on the first roll or on a subsequent roll, **gameStatus** is set to 2. Otherwise **gameStatus** is zero and the game should continue.

```
/* Craps */
#include <stdio.h>
#include <stdlib.h>
#include <time.h>

int rollDice(void);

main()
{
   int gameStatus, sum, myPoint;

   srand(time(NULL));
   sum = rollDice();               /* first roll of the dice */

   switch(sum) {
      case 7: case 11:             /* win on first roll */
         gameStatus = 1;
         break;
      case 2: case 3: case 12:     /* lose on first roll */
         gameStatus = 2;
         break;
      default:                     /* remember point */
         gameStatus = 0;
         myPoint = sum;
         printf("Point is %d\n", myPoint);
         break;
   }

   while (gameStatus == 0) {    /* keep rolling */
      sum = rollDice();

      if (sum == myPoint)          /* win by making point */
         gameStatus = 1;
      else
         if (sum == 7)             /* lose by rolling 7 */
            gameStatus = 2;
   }

   if (gameStatus == 1)
      printf("Player wins\n");
   else
      printf("Player loses\n");

   return 0;
}

int rollDice(void)
{
   int die1, die2, workSum;

   die1 = 1 + (rand() % 6);
   die2 = 1 + (rand() % 6);
   workSum = die1 + die2;
   printf("Player rolled %d + %d = %d\n", die1, die2, workSum);
   return workSum;
}
```

Fig. 5.10 Program to simulate the game of craps.

```
Player rolled 6 + 5 = 11
Player wins
```

```
Player rolled 6 + 6 = 12
Player loses
```

```
Player rolled 4 + 6 = 10
Point is 10
Player rolled 2 + 4 = 6
Player rolled 6 + 5 = 11
Player rolled 3 + 3 = 6
Player rolled 6 + 4 = 10
Player wins
```

```
Player rolled 1 + 3 = 4
Point is 4
Player rolled 1 + 4 = 5
Player rolled 5 + 4 = 9
Player rolled 4 + 6 = 10
Player rolled 6 + 3 = 9
Player rolled 1 + 2 = 3
Player rolled 5 + 2 = 7
Player loses
```

Fig. 5.11 Sample runs for the game of craps.

After the first roll, if the game is over, the **while** structure is skipped because **gameStatus** is not equal to zero. The program proceeds to the **if/else** structure which prints "**Player wins**" if **gameStatus** is **1** and "**Player loses**" if **game-Status** is **2**.

After the first roll, if the game is not over, then **sum** is saved in **myPoint**. Execution proceeds with the **while** structure because **gameStatus** is **0**. Each time through the **while**, **rollDice** is called to produce a new **sum**. If **sum** matches **myPoint**, **game-Status** is set to **1** to indicate that the player won, the **while**-test fails, the **if/else** structure prints "**Player wins**" and execution terminates. If **sum** is equal to **7**, **game-Status** is set to **2** to indicate that the player lost, the **while**-test fails, the **if/else** statement prints "**Player loses**" and execution terminates.

Note the interesting control structure of the program. We have used two functions—**main** and **rollDice**—and the **switch**, **while**, **if/else**, and nested **if** structures. In the exercises, we will investigate various interesting characteristics of the game of craps.

5.11 Storage Classes

In Chapters 2 through 4, we used identifiers for variable names. The attributes of variables include name, type, and value. In this chapter, we also use identifiers as names for user-defined functions. Actually, each identifier in a program has other attributes including *storage class*, *storage duration*, *scope* and *linkage*.

C provides four storage classes indicated by the *storage class specifiers:* **auto**, **register**, **extern**, and **static**. An identifier's *storage class* helps determine its storage duration, scope, and linkage. An identifier's *storage duration* is the period during which that identifier exists in memory. Some identifiers exist briefly, some are repeatedly created and destroyed, and others exist for the entire execution of a program. An identifier's *scope* is where the identifier can be referenced in a program. Some identifiers can be referenced throughout a program, others from only portions of a program. An identifier's *linkage* determines for a multiple-source-file program (a topic we will investigate in Chapter 14) whether an identifier is known only in the current source file or in any source file with proper declarations. This section discusses the four storage classes and storage duration. Section 5.12 discusses the scope of identifiers. Chapter 14, Advanced Topics, discusses identifier linkage and programming with multiple source files.

The four storage class specifiers can be split into two storage durations: *automatic storage duration* and *static storage duration*. The **auto** and **register** keywords are used to declare variables of automatic storage duration. Variables with automatic storage duration are created when the block in which they are declared is entered, they exist while the block is active, and they are destroyed when the block is exited.

Only variables can have automatic storage duration. A function's local variables (those declared in the parameter list or in the function body) normally have automatic storage duration. The keyword **auto** explicitly declares variables of automatic storage duration. For example, the following declaration indicates that **float** variables **x** and **y** are automatic local variables and they exist only in the body of the function in which the declaration appears:

```
auto float x, y;
```

Local variables have automatic storage duration by default, so the **auto** keyword is rarely used. For the remainder of the text, we will refer to variables with automatic storage duration simply as automatic variables.

Performance Tip 5.1

Automatic storage is a means of conserving memory because automatic variables only exist when they are needed. They are created when the function in which they are declared is entered, and they are destroyed when the function is exited.

Software Engineering Observation 5.10

Automatic storage is yet another example of the principle of least privilege. Why have variables stored in memory and accessible when in fact they are not needed?

Data in the machine language version of a program are normally loaded into registers for calculations and other processing.

Performance Tip 5.2

The storage class specifier **register** *can be placed before an automatic variable declaration to suggest that the compiler maintain the variable in one of the computer's high-speed hardware registers. If intensely used variables such as counters or totals can be maintained in hardware registers, the overhead of repeatedly loading the variables from memory into the registers and storing the results back into memory can be eliminated.*

The compiler may ignore **register** declarations. For example, there may not be a sufficient number of registers available for the compiler to use. The following declaration suggests that the integer variable **counter** be placed in one of the computer's registers and initialized to 1:

```
register int counter = 1;
```

The **register** keyword can be used only with variables of automatic storage duration.

Performance Tip 5.3

Often, **register** *declarations are unnecessary. Today's optimizing compilers are capable of recognizing frequently used variables and can decide to place them in registers without the need for a* **register** *declaration from the programmer.*

The keywords **extern** and **static** are used to declare identifiers for variables and functions of static storage duration. Identifiers of static storage duration exist from the point at which the program begins execution. For variables, storage is allocated and initialized once when the program begins execution. For functions, the name of the function exists when the program begins execution. However, even though the variables and the function names exist from the start of program execution, this does not mean that the these identifiers can be used throughout the program. Storage duration and scope (where a name can be used) are separate issues as we will see in Section 5.12.

There are two types of identifiers with static storage duration: external identifiers (such as global variables and function names) and local variables declared with the storage class specifier **static**. Global variables and function names are of storage class **extern** by default. Global variables are created by placing variable declarations outside any function definition, and they retain their values throughout the execution of the program. Global variables and functions can be referenced by any function that follows their declarations or definitions in the file. This is one reason for using function prototypes. When we include **stdio.h** in a program that calls **printf**, the function prototype is placed at the start of our file to make the name **printf** known to the rest of the file.

Software Engineering Observation 5.11

Declaring a variable as global rather than local allows unintended side effects to occur when a function that does not need access to the variable accidentally or maliciously modifies it. In general, use of global variables should be avoided except in certain situations with unique performance requirements (as discussed in Chapter 14).

Good Programming Practice 5.10

Variables used only in a particular function should be declared as local variables in that function rather than as external variables.

Local variables declared with the keyword **static** are still known only in the function in which they are defined, but unlike automatic variables, **static** local variables retain their value when the function is exited. The next time the function is called, the **static** local variable contains the value it had when the function last exited. The following statement declares local variable **count** to be **static** and to be initialized to 1.

```
static int count = 1;
```

All numeric variables of static storage duration are initialized to zero if they are not explicitly initialized by the programmer. (Pointer variables, discussed in Chapter 7, are initialized to **NULL**.)

Common Programming Error 5.13

Using multiple storage class specifiers for an identifier. Only one storage class specifier can be applied to an identifier.

The keywords **extern** and **static** have special meaning when explicitly applied to external identifiers. In Chapter 14, Advanced Topics, we discuss the explicit use of **extern** and **static** with external identifiers and multiple-source-file programs.

5.12 Scope Rules

The *scope* of an identifier is the portion of the program in which the identifier can be referenced. For example, when we declare a local variable in a block, it can be referenced only in that block or in blocks nested within that block. The four scopes for an identifier are *function scope, file scope, block scope,* and *function-prototype scope.*

Labels (an identifier followed by a colon such as **start:**) are the only identifiers with *function scope.* Labels can be used anywhere in the function in which they appear, but can not be referenced outside the function body. Labels are used in **switch** structures (as **case** labels) and in **goto** statements (see Chapter 14, Advanced Topics). Labels are implementation details that functions hide from one another. This hiding—more formally called *information hiding*—is one of the most fundamental principles of good software engineering.

An identifier declared outside any function has *file scope.* Such an identifier is "known" in all functions from the point at which the identifier is declared until the end of the file. Global variables, function definitions, and function prototypes placed outside a function all have file scope.

Identifiers declared inside a block have *block scope.* Block scope ends at the terminating right brace (**}**) of the block. Local variables declared at the beginning of a function have block scope as do function parameters, which are considered local variables by the function. Any block may contain variable declarations. When blocks are nested, and an identifier in an outer block has the same name as an identifier in an inner block, the identifier in the outer block is "hidden" until the inner block terminates. This means that while executing in the inner block, the inner block sees the value of its own local identifier and not the value of the identically named identifier in the enclosing block. Local variables declared **static** still have block scope even though they exist from the time the program begins execution. Thus, storage duration does not affect the scope of an identifier.

The only identifiers with *function-prototype scope* are those used in the parameter list of a function prototype. As mentioned previously, function prototypes do not require names in the parameter list—only types are required. If a name is used in the parameter list of a function prototype, the compiler ignores the name. Identifiers used in a function prototype can be reused elsewhere in the program without ambiguity.

Common Programming Error 5.14

Accidentally using the same name for an identifier in an inner block as is used for an identifier in an outer block, when in fact, the programmer wants the identifier in the outer block to be active for the duration of the inner block.

Good Programming Practice 5.11

Avoid variable names that hide names in outer scopes. This can be accomplished simply by avoiding the use of duplicate identifiers in a program.

The program of Fig. 5.12 demonstrates scoping issues with global variables, automatic local variables, and **static** local variables. A global variable **x** is declared and initialized to 1. This global variable is hidden in any block (or function) in which a variable named **x** is declared. In **main**, a local variable **x** is declared and initialized to 5. This variable is then printed to show that the global **x** is hidden in **main**. Next, a new block is defined in **main** with another local variable **x** initialized to 7. This variable is printed to show that it hides **x** in the outer block of **main**. The variable **x** with value 7 is automatically destroyed when the block is exited, and the local variable **x** in the outer block of **main** is printed again to show that it is no longer hidden. The program defines three functions that each take no arguments and return nothing. Function **a** defines an automatic variable **x** and initializes it to 25. When **a** is called, the variable is printed, incremented, and printed again before exiting the function. Each time this function is called, automatic variable **x** is reinitialized to 25. Function **b** declares a **static** variable **x** and initializes it to 50. Local variables declared as **static** retain their values even when they are out of scope. When **b** is called, **x** is printed, incremented, and printed again before exiting the function. In the next call to this function, **static** local variable **x** will contain the value 51. Function **c** does not declare any variables. Therefore, when it refers to variable **x**, the global **x** is used. When **c** is called, the global variable is printed, multiplied by 10, and printed again before exiting the function. The next time function **c** is called, the global variable still has its modified value, 10. Finally, the program prints the local variable **x** in **main** again to show that none of the function calls modified the value of **x** because the functions all referred to variables in other scopes.

5.13 Recursion

The programs we have discussed are generally structured as functions that call one another in a disciplined, hierarchical manner. For some types of problems, it is useful to have functions call themselves. A *recursive function* is a function that calls itself either directly or indirectly through another function. Recursion is a complex topic discussed at length in upper-level computer science courses. In this section and the next, simple examples of recursion are presented. This book contains an extensive treatment of recursion

```c
/* A scoping example */
#include <stdio.h>
void a(void);    /* function prototype */
void b(void);    /* function prototype */
void c(void);    /* function prototype */

int x = 1;       /* global variable */

main()
{
   int x = 5;    /* local variable to main */

   printf("local x in outer scope of main is %d\n", x);

   {             /* start new scope */
      int x = 7;

      printf("local x in inner scope of main is %d\n", x);
   }             /* end new scope */

   printf("local x in outer scope of main is %d\n", x);

   a();          /* a has automatic local x */
   b();          /* b has static local x */
   c();          /* c uses global x */
   a();          /* a reinitializes automatic local x */
   b();          /* static local x retains its previous value */
   c();          /* global x also retains its value */

   printf("local x in main is %d\n", x);
   return 0;
}

void a(void)
{
   int x = 25;   /* initialized each time a is called */

   printf("\nlocal x in a is %d after entering a\n", x);
   ++x;
   printf("local x in a is %d before exiting a\n", x);
}

void b(void)
{
   static int x = 50;   /* static initialization only */
                        /* first time b is called */
   printf("\nlocal static x is %d on entering b\n", x);
   ++x;
   printf("local static x is %d on exiting b\n", x);
}

void c(void)
{
   printf("\nglobal x is %d on entering c\n", x);
   x *= 10;
   printf("global x is %d on exiting c\n", x);
}
```

Fig. 5.12   A scoping example (part 1 of 2).

```
local x in outer scope of main is 5
local x in inner scope of main is 7
local x in outer scope of main is 5

local x in a is 25 after entering a
local x in a is 26 before exiting a

local static x is 50 on entering b
local static x is 51 on exiting b

global x is 1 on entering c
global x is 10 on exiting c

local x in a is 25 after entering a
local x in a is 26 before exiting a

local static x is 51 on entering b
local static x is 52 on exiting b

global x is 10 on entering c
global x is 100 on exiting c
local x in main is 5
```

Fig. 5.12   A scoping example (part 2 of 2).

which is spread throughout Chapters 5 through 12. Fig. 5.17, located at the end of Section 5.15, summarizes the 31 recursion examples and exercises in the book.

We consider recursion conceptually first, and then examine several programs containing recursive functions. Recursive problem solving approaches have a number of elements in common. A recursive function is called to solve a problem. The function actually knows how to solve only the simplest case(s), or so-called *base case(s)*. If the function is called with a base case, the function simply returns a result. If the function is called with a more complex problem, the function divides the problem into two conceptual pieces: A piece that the function knows how to do and a piece that the function does not know how to do. To make recursion feasible, the latter piece must resemble the original problem, but be a slightly simpler or slightly smaller version of the original problem. Because this new problem looks like the original problem, the function launches (calls) a fresh copy of itself to go to work on the smaller problem—this is referred to as a *recursive call* and is also called the *recursion step*. The recursion step also includes the keyword **return** because its result will be combined with the portion of the problem the function knew how to solve to form a result that will be passed back to the original caller, possibly **main**.

The recursion step executes while the original call to the function is still open, i.e., it has not yet finished executing. The recursion step can result in many more such recursive calls as the function keeps dividing each problem it is called with into two conceptual pieces. In order for the recursion to eventually terminate, each time the function calls itself with a slightly simpler version of the original problem, this sequence of smaller and smaller problems must eventually converge on the base case. At that point, the function recognizes the base case, returns a result to the previous copy of the function, and a sequence of returns ensues all the way up the line until the original call of the function eventually returns the final result to **main**. All of this sounds quite exotic compared to the kind of conventional problem solving we have been using to this point. Indeed, it takes a great deal of practice writing recursive programs before the process will appear natural. As an example of these concepts at work, let us write a recursive program to perform a popular mathematical calculation.

The factorial of a nonnegative integer *n,* written *n!* (and pronounced "*n* factorial"), is the product

$$n \cdot (n-1) \cdot (n-2) \cdot \ldots \cdot 1$$

with 1! equal to 1, and 0! defined to be 1. For example, 5! is the product $5 * 4 * 3 * 2 * 1$, which is equal to 120.

The factorial of an integer, **number**, greater than or equal to 0, can be calculated *iteratively* (nonrecursively) using **for** as follows:

```
factorial = 1;
for (counter = number; counter >= 1; counter--)
    factorial *= counter;
```

A recursive definition of the factorial function is arrived at by observing the following relationship:

$$n! = n \cdot (n-1)!$$

For example, 5! is clearly equal to $5 * 4!$ as is shown by the following:

$$5! = 5 \cdot 4 \cdot 3 \cdot 2 \cdot 1$$
$$5! = 5 \cdot (4 \cdot 3 \cdot 2 \cdot 1)$$
$$5! = 5 \cdot (4!)$$

The evaluation of 5! would proceed as shown in Fig. 5.13. Figure 5.13a shows how the succession of recursive calls proceeds until 1! is evaluated to be 1, which terminates the recursion. Figure 5.13b shows the values returned from each recursive call to its caller until the final value is calculated and returned.

The program of Fig. 5.14 uses recursion to calculate and print the factorials of the integers 0 to 10 (the choice of the data type **long** will be explained momentarily). The recursive function **factorial** first tests to see if a terminating condition is true, i.e., is **number** less than or equal to 1. If **number** is indeed less than or equal to 1, **factorial** returns 1, no further recursion is necessary, and the program terminates. If **number** is greater than 1, the statement

```
return number * factorial(number - 1);
```

expresses the problem as the product of **number** and a recursive call to **factorial** evaluating the factorial of **number - 1**. Note that **factorial(number - 1)** is a slightly simpler problem than the original calculation **factorial(number)**.

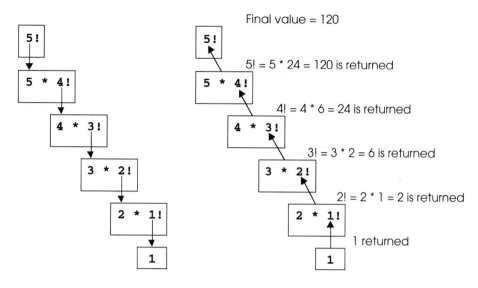

a) Procession of recursive calls.   b) Values returned from each recursive call.

Fig. 5.13   Recursive evaluation of 5!.

Function **factorial** has been declared to receive a parameter of type **long** and return a result of type **long**. This is shorthand notation for **long int**. The ANSI standard specifies that a variable of type **long int** is stored in at least 4 bytes, and thus may hold a value as large as +2147483647. As can be seen in Fig. 5.14, factorial values become large quickly. We have chosen the data type **long** so the program can calculate factorials greater than 7! on computers with small (such as 2-byte) integers. The conversion specifier **%ld** is used to print **long** values. Unfortunately, the **factorial** function produces large values so quickly that even **long int** does not help us print many factorial values before the size of a **long int** variable is exceeded.

As we explore in the exercises, **float** and **double** may ultimately be needed by the user desiring to calculate factorials of larger numbers. This points to a weakness in C (and most other programming languages), namely that the language is not easily extended to handle the unique requirements of various applications. As we will see later, C++ is an extensible language that allows us to create arbitrarily large integers if we wish.

Common Programming Error 5.15

Forgetting to return a value from a recursive function when one is needed.

Common Programming Error 5.16

Either omitting the base case, or writing the recursion step incorrectly so that it does not converge on the base case, will cause infinite recursion, eventually exhausting memory. This is analogous to the problem of an infinite loop in an iterative (nonrecursive) solution. Infinite recursion can also be caused by providing an unexpected input.

```
/* Recursive factorial function */
#include <stdio.h>

long factorial(long);

main()
{
   int i;

   for (i = 1; i <= 10; i++)
      printf("%2d! = %ld\n", i, factorial(i));

   return 0;
}

/* Recursive definition of function factorial */
long factorial(long number)
{
   if (number <= 1)
      return 1;
   else
      return (number * factorial(number - 1));
}
```

```
 1! = 1
 2! = 2
 3! = 6
 4! = 24
 5! = 120
 6! = 720
 7! = 5040
 8! = 40320
 9! = 362880
10! = 3628800
```

Fig. 5.14   Calculating factorials with a recursive function.

5.14 Example Using Recursion: The Fibonacci Series

The Fibonacci series

$$0, 1, 1, 2, 3, 5, 8, 13, 21, \ldots$$

begins with 0 and 1 and has the property that each subsequent Fibonacci number is the sum of the previous two Fibonacci numbers.

The series occurs in nature and, in particular, describes a form of spiral. The ratio of successive Fibonacci numbers converges on a constant value of 1.618.... This number, too, repeatedly occurs in nature and has been called the *golden ratio* or the *golden mean*.

Humans tend to find the golden mean aesthetically pleasing. Architects often design windows, rooms, and buildings whose length and width are in the ratio of the golden mean. Postcards are often designed with a golden mean length/width ratio.

The Fibonacci series may be defined recursively as follows:

$fibonacci(0) = 0$
$fibonacci(1) = 1$
$fibonacci(n) = fibonacci(n – 1) + fibonacci(n – 2)$

The program of Fig. 5.15 calculates the ith Fibonacci number recursively using function **fibonacci**. Notice that Fibonacci numbers tend to become large quickly. Therefore, we have chosen the data type **long** for the parameter type and the return type in function **fibonacci**. In Fig. 5.15, each pair of output lines shows a separate run of the program.

The call to **fibonacci** from **main** is not a recursive call, but all subsequent calls to **fibonacci** are recursive. Each time **fibonacci** is invoked, it immediately tests for the base case—**n** is equal to 0 or 1. If this is true, **n** is returned. Interestingly, if **n** is greater than 1, the recursion step generates *two* recursive calls, each of which is for a slightly simpler problem than the original call to **fibonacci**. Figure 5.16 shows how function **fibonacci** would evaluate **fibonacci(3)**—we abbreviate **fibonacci** simply as **f** to make the figure more readable.

```
/* Recursive fibonacci function */
#include <stdio.h>

long fibonacci(long);

main()
{
   long result, number;

   printf("Enter an integer: ");
   scanf("%ld", &number);
   result = fibonacci(number);
   printf("Fibonacci(%ld) = %ld\n", number, result);
   return 0;
}

/* Recursive definition of function fibonacci */
long fibonacci(long n)
{
   if (n == 0 || n == 1)
      return n;
   else
      return fibonacci(n - 1) + fibonacci(n - 2);
}
```

Fig. 5.15 Recursively generating Fibonacci numbers (part 1 of 2).

```
Enter an integer: 0
Fibonacci(0) = 0

Enter an integer: 1
Fibonacci(1) = 1

Enter an integer: 2
Fibonacci(2) = 1

Enter an integer: 3
Fibonacci(3) = 2

Enter an integer: 4
Fibonacci(4) = 3

Enter an integer: 5
Fibonacci(5) = 5

Enter an integer: 6
Fibonacci(6) = 8

Enter an integer: 10
Fibonacci(10) = 55

Enter an integer: 20
Fibonacci(20) = 6765

Enter an integer: 30
Fibonacci(30) = 832040

Enter an integer: 35
Fibonacci(35) = 9227465
```

Fig. 5.15 Recursively generating Fibonacci numbers (part 2 of 2).

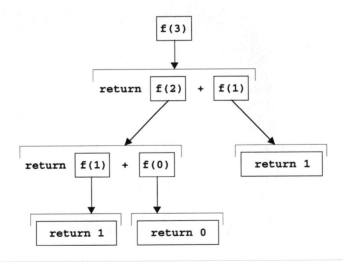

Fig. 5.16 Set of recursive calls to function **fibonacci**.

This figure raises some interesting issues about the order in which C compilers will evaluate the operands of operators. This is a different issue from the order in which operators are applied to their operands, namely the order dictated by the rules of operator precedence. From the Fig. 5.16 it appears that while evaluating **f(3)**, two recursive calls will be made, namely **f(2)** and **f(1)**. But in what order will these calls be made? Most programmers simply assume the operands will be evaluated left to right. Strangely, the ANSI standard does not specify the order in which the operands of most operators (including **+**) are to be evaluated. Therefore, the programmer may make no assumption about the order in which these calls will execute. The calls could in fact execute **f(2)** first and then **f(1)**, or the calls could execute in the reverse order, **f(1)** then **f(2)**. In this program and in most other programs, it turns out the final result would be the same. But in some programs the evaluation of an operand may have side effects that could affect the final result of the expression. Of C's many operators, the ANSI standard specifies the order of evaluation of the operands of only four operators—namely **&&**, **||**, the comma (**,**) operator, and **?:**. The first three of these are binary operators whose two operands are guaranteed to be evaluated left to right. The last operator is C's only ternary operator. Its leftmost operand is always evaluated first; if the leftmost operand evaluates to nonzero, the middle operand is evaluated next and the last operand is ignored; if the leftmost operand evaluates to zero, the third operand is evaluated next and the middle operand is ignored.

Common Programming Error 5.17

*Writing programs that depend on the order of evaluation of the operands of operators other than **&&**, **||**, **?:**, and the comma (**,**) operator can lead to errors because compilers may not necessarily evaluate the operands in the order the programmer expects.*

Portability Tip 5.2

*Programs that depend on the order of evaluation of the operands of operators other than **&&**, **||**, **?:**, and the comma (,) operator can function differently on systems with different compilers.*

A word of caution is in order about recursive programs like the one we use here to generate Fibonacci numbers. Each level of recursion in the **fibonacci** function has a doubling effect on the number of calls, i.e., the number of recursive calls that will be executed to calculate the nth Fibonacci number is on the order of 2^n. This rapidly gets out of hand. Calculating only the 20th Fibonacci number would require on the order of 2^{20} or about a million calls, calculating the 30th Fibonacci number would require on the order of 2^{30} or about a billion calls, and so on. Computer scientists refer to this as *exponential complexity*. Problems of this nature humble even the world's most powerful computers! Complexity issues in general, and exponential complexity in particular, are discussed in detail in the upper-level computer science curriculum course generally called "Algorithms."

Performance Tip 5.4

Avoid fibonacci-style recursive programs which result in an exponential "explosion" of calls.

5.15 Recursion vs. Iteration

In the previous sections, we studied two functions that can easily be implemented either recursively or iteratively. In this section we compare the two approaches and discuss why the programmer might choose one approach over the other in a particular situation.

Both iteration and recursion are based on a control structure: Iteration uses a repetition structure; recursion uses a selection structure. Both iteration and recursion involve repetition: Iteration explicitly uses a repetition structure; recursion achieves repetition through repeated function calls. Iteration and recursion each involve a termination test: Iteration terminates when the loop-continuation condition fails; recursion terminates when a base case is recognized. Iteration with counter-controlled repetition and recursion each gradually approach termination: Iteration keeps modifying a counter until the counter assumes a value that makes the loop-continuation condition fail; recursion keeps producing simpler versions of the original problem until the base case is reached. Both iteration and recursion can occur infinitely: An infinite loop occurs with iteration if the loop-continuation test never becomes false; infinite recursion occurs if the recursion step does not reduce the problem each time in a manner that converges on the base case.

Recursion has many negatives. It repeatedly invokes the mechanism, and consequently the overhead, of function calls. This can be expensive in both processor time and memory space. Each recursive call causes another copy of the function (actually only the function's variables) to be created; this can consume considerable memory. Iteration normally occurs within a function so the overhead of repeated function calls and extra memory assignment is omitted. So why choose recursion?

> ### Software Engineering Observation 5.12
> *Any problem that can be solved recursively can also be solved iteratively (nonrecursively). A recursive approach is normally chosen in preference to an iterative approach when the recursive approach more naturally mirrors the problem and results in a program that is easier to understand and debug. Another reason to choose a recursive solution is that an iterative solution may not be apparent.*

> ### Performance Tip 5.5
> *Avoid using recursion in performance situations. Recursive calls take time and consume additional memory.*

> ### Common Programming Error 5.18
> *Accidentally having a nonrecursive function call itself either directly, or indirectly through another function.*

Most programming textbooks introduce recursion much later than we have done here. We feel that recursion is a sufficiently rich and complex topic that it is better to introduce it earlier and spread the examples over the remainder of the text. Figure 5.17 summarizes by chapter the 31 recursion examples and exercises in the text.

Let us close this chapter with some observations that we make repeatedly throughout the book. Good software engineering is important. High performance is important. Unfortunately, these goals are often at odds with one another. Good software engineering is key to making more manageable the task of developing the larger and more complex software systems we need. High performance is key to realizing the systems of the future that will place ever greater computing demands on hardware. Where do functions fit in here?

Software Engineering Observation 5.13

Functionalizing programs in a neat, hierarchical manner promotes good software engineering. But it has a price.

Performance Tip 5.6

A heavily functionalized program—as compared to a monolithic (i.e., one-piece) program without functions—makes potentially large numbers of function calls and these consume execution time on a computer's processor(s). But monolithic programs are difficult to program, test, debug, maintain, and evolve.

So functionalize your programs judiciously, always keeping in mind the delicate balance between performance and good software engineering.

Summary

- The best way to develop and maintain a large program is to divide it into several smaller program modules each of which is more manageable than the original program. Modules are written as functions in C.

- A function is invoked by a function call. The function call mentions the function by name and provides information (as arguments) that the called function needs to perform its task.

- The purpose of information hiding is for functions to have access only to the information they need to complete their tasks. This is a means of implementing the principle of least privilege, one of the most important principles of good software engineering.

- Functions are normally invoked in a program by writing the name of the function followed by a left parenthesis followed by the *argument* (or a comma separated list of arguments) of the function followed by a right parenthesis.

- Data type **double** is a floating point type like **float**. A variable of type **double** can store a value of much greater magnitude and precision than **float** can store.

- Each argument of a function may be a constant, a variable, or an expression.

- A local variable is known only in a function definition. Other functions are not allowed to know the names of a function's local variables, nor is any function allowed to know the implementation details of any other function.

- The general format for a function definition is

  return-value-type function-name (*parameter-list*)
  {
      declarations

      statements
  }

Chapter	Recursion Examples and Exercises
Chapter 5	Factorial function Fibonacci functions Greatest common divisor Sum of two integers Multiply two integers Raising an integer to an integer power Towers of Hanoi Recursive **main** Printing keyboard inputs in reverse Visualizing recursion
Chapter 6	Sum the elements of an array Print an array Print an array backwards Print a string backwards Check if a string is a palindrome Minimum value in an array Selection sort Quicksort Linear search Binary search
Chapter 7	Eight Queens Maze traversal
Chapter 8	Printing a string input at the keyboard backwards
Chapter 12	Linked list insert Linked list delete Search a linked list Print a linked list backwards Binary tree insert Preorder traversal of a binary tree Inorder traversal of a binary tree Postorder traversal of a binary tree

Fig. 5.17 Summary of recursion examples and exercises in the text.

The *return-value-type* states the type of the value returned to the calling function. If a function does not return a value, the *return-value-type* is declared as **void**. The *function-name* is any valid identifier. The *parameter-list* is a comma-separated list containing the declarations of the variables that will be passed to the function. If a function does not receive any values, *parameter-list* is declared as **void**. The *function-body* is the set of declarations and statements that constitute the function.

• The arguments passed to a function should match in number, type, and order with the parameters in the function definition.

- When a program encounters a function, control is transferred from the point of invocation to the called function, the statements of the called function are executed, and control returns to the caller.

- A called function can return control to the caller in one of three ways. If the function does not return a value, control is returned when the function-ending right brace is reached, or by executing the statement

  ```
  return;
  ```

  If the function does return a value, the statement

  ```
  return expression;
  ```

  returns the value of **expression**.

- A function prototype declares the return-type of the function and declares the number, the types, and order of the parameters the function expects to receive.

- Function prototypes enable the compiler to verify that functions are called correctly.

- The compiler ignores variable names mentioned in the function prototype.

- Each standard library has a corresponding header file containing the function prototypes for all the functions in that library, as well as definitions of various symbolic constants needed by those functions.

- Programmers can create and include their own header files.

- When an argument is passed call by value, a *copy* of the variable's value is made and the copy is passed to the called function. Changes to the copy in the called function do not affect the original variable's value.

- All calls in C are call by value.

- The **rand** function generates an integer between 0 and **RAND_MAX** which is defined by the ANSI C standard to be at least 32767.

- The function prototypes for **rand** and **srand** are contained in **<stdlib.h>**.

- Values produced by **rand** can be scaled and shifted to produce values in a specific range.

- To randomize a program, use the C standard library function **srand**.

- The **srand** statement is ordinarily inserted in a program only after the program has been thoroughly debugged. While debugging, it is better to omit **srand**. This ensures repeatability, which is essential to proving that corrections to a random number generation program work properly.

- To randomize without the need for entering a seed each time, we may use **srand(time(NULL))**. The **time** function returns the number of seconds since the start of the day. The **time** function prototype is located in the header **<time.h>**.

- The general equation for scaling and shifting a random number is

  ```
  n = a + rand() % b;
  ```

where **a** is the shifting value (which is equal to the first number in the desired range of consecutive integers), and **b** is the scaling factor (which is equal to the width of the desired range of consecutive integers).

- Each identifier in a program has the attributes storage class, storage duration, scope and linkage.

- C provides four storage classes indicated by the storage class specifiers: **auto**, **register**, **extern**, and **static**.

- An identifier's storage duration is when that identifier exists in memory.

- An identifier's scope is where the identifier can be referenced in a program.

- An identifier's linkage determines for a multiple-source-file program if an identifier is known only in the current source file or in any source file with proper declarations.

- Variables with automatic storage duration are created when the block in which they are declared is entered, exist while the block is active, and are destroyed when the block is exited. A function's local variables normally have automatic storage duration.

- The storage class specifier **register** can be placed before an automatic variable declaration to suggest that the compiler maintain the variable in one of the computer's high-speed hardware registers. The compiler may ignore **register** declarations. The **register** keyword can be used only with variables of automatic storage duration.

- The keywords **extern** and **static** are used to declare identifiers for variables and functions of static storage duration.

- Variables with static storage duration are allocated and initialized once when the program begins execution.

- There are two types of identifiers with static storage duration: External identifiers (such as global variables and function names) and local variables declared with the storage class specifier **static**.

- Global variables are created by placing variable declarations outside any function definition, and they retain their values throughout the execution of the program.

- Local variables declared **static** retain their value when the function in which they are declared is exited.

- All numeric variables of static storage duration are initialized to zero if they are not explicitly initialized by the programmer.

- The four scopes for an identifier are function scope, file scope, block scope, and function-prototype scope.

- Labels are the only identifiers with function scope. Labels can be used anywhere in the function in which they appear, but can not be referenced outside the function body.

- An identifier declared outside any function has file scope. Such an identifier is "known" in all functions from the point at which the identifier is declared until the end of the file.

- Identifiers declared inside a block have block scope. Block scope ends at the terminating right brace (**}**) of the block.

- Local variables declared at the beginning of a function have block scope as do function parameters, which are considered local variables by the function.

- Any block may contain variable declarations. When blocks are nested, and an identifier in an outer block has the same name as an identifier in an inner block, the identifier in the outer block is "hidden" until the inner block terminates.

- The only identifiers with function-prototype scope are those used in the parameter list of a function prototype. Identifiers used in a function prototype can be reused elsewhere in the program without ambiguity.

- A recursive function is a function that calls itself either directly or indirectly.

- If a recursive function is called with a base case, the function simply returns a result. If the function is called with a more complex problem, the function divides the problem into two conceptual pieces: A piece that the function knows how to do and a slightly smaller version of the original problem. Because this new problem looks like the original problem, the function launches a recursive call to work on the smaller problem.

- For recursion to terminate, each time the recursive function calls itself with a slightly simpler version of the original problem, the sequence of smaller and smaller problems must converge on the base case. When the function recognizes the base case, the result is returned to the previous function call, and a sequence of returns ensues all the way up the line until the original call of the function eventually returns the final result.

- The ANSI standard does not specify the order in which the operands of most operators (including **+**) are to be evaluated. Of C's many operators, the standard specifies the order of evaluation of the operands of the operators **&&**, **||**, the comma (**,**) operator, and **?:**. The first three of these are binary operators whose two operands are evaluated left to right. The last operator is C's only ternary operator. Its leftmost operand is evaluated first; if the leftmost operand evaluates to nonzero, the middle operand is evaluated next and the last operand is ignored; if the leftmost operand evaluates to zero, the third operand is evaluated next and the middle operand is ignored.

- Both iteration and recursion are based on a control structure: Iteration uses a repetition structure; recursion uses a selection structure.

- Both iteration and recursion involve repetition: Iteration explicitly uses a repetition structure; recursion achieves repetition through repeated function calls.

- Iteration and recursion each involve a termination test: Iteration terminates when the loop-continuation condition fails; recursion terminates when a base case is recognized.

- Iteration and recursion can occur infinitely: An infinite loop occurs with iteration if the loop-continuation test never becomes false; infinite recursion occurs if the recursion step does not reduce the problem in a manner that converges on the base case.

- Recursion repeatedly invokes the mechanism, and consequently the overhead, of function calls. This can be expensive in both processor time and memory space.

Terminology

abstraction	math library functions
argument in a function call	mixed-type expression
automatic storage	modular program
automatic storage duration	optimizing compiler
automatic variable	parameter in a function definition
auto storage class specifier	principle of least privilege
base case in recursion	programmer-defined function
block	promotion hierarchy
block scope	pseudo-random numbers
C standard library	**rand**
call a function	**RAND_MAX**
call by reference	randomize
call by value	random number generation
called function	recursion
caller	recursive call
calling function	recursive function
clock	**register** storage class specifier
coercion of arguments	**return**
copy of a value	return-value-type
divide and conquer	scaling
element of chance	**%s** conversion specifier
extern storage class specifier	scope
factorial function	shifting
file scope	side effects
function	simulation
function call	software engineering
function declaration	software reusability
function definition	**srand**
function prototype	standard library header files
function prototype scope	**static** storage class specifier
function scope	static storage duration
global variable	**static** variable
header file	storage classes
information hiding	storage class specifier
invoke a function	storage duration
iteration	**time**
linkage	**unsigned**
local variable	**void**

Common Programming Errors

5.1 Forgetting to include the math header file when using math library functions can cause strange results.

5.2 Omitting the return-value-type in a function definition causes a syntax error if the function prototype specifies a return type other than **int**.

5.3 Forgetting to return a value from a function that is supposed to return a value can lead to unexpected errors. The ANSI standard states that the result of this omission is undefined.

5.4   Returning a value from a function whose return type has been declared **void** causes a syntax error.

5.5   Declaring function parameters of the same type as *float x, y* instead of *float x, float y*. The parameter declaration *float x, y* would actually make *y* a parameter of type *int* because *int* is the default.

5.6   Placing a semicolon after the right parenthesis enclosing the parameter list of a function definition is a syntax error.

5.7   Defining a function parameter again as a local variable within the function is a syntax error.

5.8   Defining a function inside another function is a syntax error.

5.9   Forgetting the semicolon at the end of a function prototype causes a syntax error.

5.10   Converting from a higher data type in the promotion hierarchy to a lower type can change the data value.

5.11   Forgetting a function prototype causes a syntax error if the return type of the function is not **int** and the function definition appears after the function call in the program. Otherwise, forgetting a function prototype may cause a run-time error or an unexpected result.

5.12   Using *srand* in place of *rand* to generate random numbers.

5.13   Using multiple storage class specifiers for an identifier. Only one storage class specifier can be applied to an identifier.

5.14   Accidentally using the same name for an identifier in an inner block as is used for an identifier in an outer block, when in fact, the programmer wants the identifier in the outer block to be active for the duration of the inner block.

5.15   Forgetting to return a value from a recursive function when one is needed.

5.16   Either omitting the base case or writing the recursion step incorrectly so that it does not converge on the base case will cause infinite recursion, eventually exhausting memory. This is analogous to the problem of an infinite loop in an iterative (nonrecursive) solution. Infinite recursion can also be caused by providing an unexpected input.

5.17   Writing programs that depend on the order of evaluation of the operands of operators other than **&&**, **||**, **?:**, and the comma **(,)** operator can lead to errors because compilers may not necessarily evaluate the operands in the order the programmer expects.

5.18   Accidentally having a nonrecursive function call itself either directly or indirectly through another function.

Good Programming Practices

5.1   Familiarize yourself with the rich collection of functions in the ANSI C standard library.

5.2   Include the math header file by using the preprocessor directive **#include <math.h>** when using functions in the math library.

5.3   Place a blank line between function definitions to separate the functions and enhance program readability.

5.4   Even though an omitted return type defaults to **int**, always state the return type explicitly. The return type for **main**, however, is normally omitted.

5.5   Include the type of each parameter in the parameter list, even if that parameter is of the default type **int**.

5.6   Although it is not incorrect to do so, do not use the same names for the arguments passed to a function and the corresponding parameters in the function definition. This helps avoid ambiguity.

5.7   Choosing meaningful function names and meaningful parameter names makes programs more readable and helps avoid excessive use of comments.

5.8   Include function prototypes for all functions to take advantage of C's type checking capabilities. Use **#include** preprocessor directives to obtain function prototypes for the standard library functions from the header files for the appropriate libraries. Also use **#include** to obtain header files containing function prototypes used by you and/or your group members.

5.9   Parameter names are sometimes included in function prototypes for documentation purposes. The compiler ignores these names.

5.10   Variables used only in a particular function should be declared as local variables in that function rather than as global variables.

5.11   Avoid variable names that hide names in outer scopes. This can be accomplished simply by avoiding the use of duplicate identifiers in a program.

Portability Tips

5.1   Using the functions in the ANSI C standard library helps make programs more portable.

5.2   Programs that depend on the order of evaluation of the operands of operators other than **&&**, **||**, **?:**, and the comma (**,**) operator can function differently on systems with different compilers.

Performance Tips

5.1   Automatic storage is a means of conserving memory because automatic variables only exist when they are needed. They are created when the function in which they are declared is entered, and they are destroyed when the function is exited.

5.2   The storage class specifier **register** can be placed before an automatic variable declaration to suggest that the compiler maintain the variable in one of the computer's high-speed hardware registers. If intensely used variables such as counters or totals can be maintained in hardware registers, the overhead of repeatedly loading the variables from memory into the registers and storing the results back into memory can be eliminated.

5.3   Often, **register** declarations are unnecessary. Today's optimizing compilers are capable of recognizing frequently used variables and can decide to place them in registers without the need for a **register** declaration from the programmer.

5.4   Avoid fibonacci-style recursive programs which result in an exponential "explosion" of calls.

5.5   Avoid using recursion in performance situations. Recursive calls take time and consume additional memory.

5.6   A heavily functionalized program—as compared to a monolithic (i.e., one-piece) program without functions—makes potentially large numbers of function calls and these consume execution time on a computer's processor(s). But monolithic programs are difficult to program, test, debug, maintain, and evolve.

Software Engineering Observations

5.1   Avoid reinventing the wheel. When possible, use ANSI C standard library functions instead of writing new functions. This reduces program development time.

5.2   In programs containing many functions, **main** should be implemented as a group of calls to functions that perform the bulk of the program's work.

5.3   Each function should be limited to performing a single, well-defined task, and the function name should effectively express that task. This facilitates abstraction and promotes software reusability.

5.4   If you can not choose a concise name that expresses what the function does, it is possible that your function is attempting to perform too many diverse tasks. It is usually best to break such a function into several smaller functions.

5.5   A function should be no longer than one page. Better yet, a function should be no longer than half a page. Small functions promote software reusability.

5.6   Programs should be written as collections of small functions. This makes programs easier to write, debug, maintain and modify.

5.7   A function requiring a large number of parameters may be performing too many tasks. Consider dividing the function into smaller functions that perform the separate tasks. The function header should fit on one line if possible.

5.8   The function prototype, function header, and function calls should all agree in the number, type, and order of arguments and parameters, and in the type of return value.

5.9   A function prototype placed outside any function definition applies to all calls to the function appearing after the function prototype in the file. A function prototype placed in a function applies only to calls made in that function.

5.10   Automatic storage is yet another example of the principle of least privilege. Why have variables stored in memory and accessible when in fact they are not needed?

5.11   Declaring a variable as global rather than local allows unintended side effects to occur when a function that does not need access to the variable accidentally or maliciously modifies it. In general, use of global variables should be avoided except in certain situations with unique performance requirements (as discussed in Chapter 14).

5.12   Any problem that can be solved recursively can also be solved iteratively (nonrecursively). A recursive approach is normally chosen in preference to an iterative approach when the recursive approach more naturally mirrors the problem and results in a program that is easier to understand and debug. Another reason to choose a recursive solution is that an iterative solution may not be apparent.

5.13   Functionalizing programs in a neat, hierarchical manner promotes good software engineering. But it has a price.

Self-Review Exercises

5.1   Answer each of the following:

a) A program module in C is called a _____.

b) A function is invoked with a _____.

c) A variable that is known only within the function in which it is defined is called a _____.

d) The _____ statement in a called function is used to pass the value of an expression back to the calling function.

e) The keyword _____ is used in a function header to indicate that a function does not return a value or to indicate that a function contains no parameters.

f) The _____ of an identifier is the portion of the program in which the identifier can be used.

g) The three ways to return control from a called function to a caller are _____, _____, and _____.

h) A _____ allows the compiler to check the number, types, and order of the arguments passed to a function.

i) The _____ function is used to produce random numbers.

j) The _____ function is used to set the random number seed to randomize a program.

k) The storage class specifiers are _____, _____, _____, and_____.
l) Variables declared in a block or in the parameter list of a function are assumed to be of storage class _____ unless specified otherwise.
m) The storage class specifier _____ is a recommendation to the compiler to store a variable in one of the computer's registers.
n) A variable declared outside any block or function is an _____ variable.
o) For a local variable in a function to retain its value between calls to the function, it must be declared with the _____ storage class specifier.
p) The four possible scopes of an identifier are _____, _____, _____, and _____.
q) A function that calls itself either directly or indirectly is a _____ function.
r) A recursive function typically has two components: One that provides a means for the recursion to terminate by testing for a _____ case, and one that expresses the problem as a recursive call for a slightly simpler problem than the original call.

5.2   For the following program, state the scope (either function scope, file scope, block scope, or function prototype scope) of each of the following elements.
a) The variable **x** in **main**.
b) The variable **y** in **cube**.
c) The function **cube**.
d) The function **main**.
e) The function prototype for **cube**.
f) The identifier **y** in the function prototype for **cube**.

```
#include <stdio.h>
int cube(int y);

main()
{
   int x;

   for (x = 1; x <= 10; x++)
      printf("%d\n", cube(x));
}

int cube(int y)
{
   return y * y * y;
}
```

5.3   Write a program that tests if the examples of the math library function calls shown in Fig. 5.2 actually produce the indicated results.

5.4   Give the function header for each of the following functions.
a) Function **hypotenuse** that takes two double-precision floating point arguments, **side1** and **side2**, and returns a double-precision floating point result.
b) Function **smallest** that takes three integers, **x**, **y**, **z**, and returns an integer.
c) Function **instructions** that does not receive any arguments and does not return a value. (Note: Such functions are commonly used to display instructions to a user.)
d) Function **intToFloat** that takes an integer argument, **number**, and returns a floating point result.

5.5   Give the function prototype for each of the following:
a) The function described in Exercise 5.4a.

b) The function described in Exercise 5.4b.

c) The function described in Exercise 5.4c.

d) The function described in Exercise 5.4d.

5.6   Write a declaration for each of the following:

a) Integer **count** that should be maintained in a register. Initialize **count** to **0**.

b) Floating point variable **lastVal** that is to retain its value between calls to the function in which it is defined.

c) External integer **number** whose scope should be restricted to the remainder of the file in which it is defined.

5.7   Find the error in each of the following program segments and explain how the error can be corrected (see also Exercise 5.50):

a)
```c
int g(void) {
    printf("Inside function g\n");

    int h(void) {
        printf("Inside function h\n");
    }
}
```

b)
```c
int sum(int x, int y) {
    int result;

    result = x + y;
}
```

c)
```c
int sum(int n) {
    if (n == 0)
        return 0;
    else
        n + sum(n - 1);
}
```

d)
```c
void f(float a); {
    float a;

    printf("%f", a);
}
```

e)
```c
void product(void) {
    int a, b, c, result;

    printf("Enter three integers: ")
    scanf("%d%d%d", &a, &b, &c);
    result = a * b * c;
    printf("Result is %d", result);
    return result;
}
```

Answers to Self-Review Exercises

5.1   a) Function. b) Function call. c) Local variable. d) **return**. e) **void** f) Scope. g) **return;** or **return expression;** or encountering the closing left brace of a function. h) Function prototype. i) **rand**. j) **srand**. k) **auto, register, extern, static**. l) Automatic. m) **register**. n) External, global. o) **static**. p) Function scope, file scope, block scope, function prototype scope. q) Recursive. r) Base.

5.2 a) Block scope. b) Block Scope. c) File scope. d) File scope. e) File scope. f) Function prototype scope.

5.3
```
/* Testing the math library functions */
#include <stdio.h>
#include <math.h>

main()
{
    printf("sqrt(%.1f) = %.1f\n", 900.0, sqrt(900.0));
    printf("sqrt(%.1f) = %.1f\n", 9.0, sqrt(9.0));
    printf("exp(%.1f) = %f\n", 1.0, exp(1.0));
    printf("exp(%.1f) = %f\n", 2.0, exp(2.0));
    printf("log(%f) = %.1f\n", 2.718282, log(2.718282));
    printf("log(%f) = %.1f\n", 7.389056, log(7.389056));
    printf("log10(%.1f) = %.1f\n", 1.0, log10(1.0));
    printf("log10(%.1f) = %.1f\n", 10.0, log10(10.0));
    printf("log10(%.1f) = %.1f\n", 100.0, log10(100.0));
    printf("fabs(%.1f) = %.1f\n", 13.5, fabs(13.5));
    printf("fabs(%.1f) = %.1f\n", 0.0, fabs(0.0));
    printf("fabs(%.1f) = %.1f\n", -13.5, fabs(-13.5));
    printf("ceil(%.1f) = %.1f\n", 9.2, ceil(9.2));
    printf("ceil(%.1f) = %.1f\n", -9.8, ceil(-9.8));
    printf("floor(%.1f) = %.1f\n", 9.2, floor(9.2));
    printf("floor(%.1f) = %.1f\n", -9.8, floor(-9.8));
    printf("pow(%.1f, %.1f) = %.1f\n", 2.0, 7.0, pow(2.0, 7.0));
    printf("pow(%.1f, %.1f) = %.1f\n", 9.0, 0.5, pow(9.0, 0.5));
    printf("fmod(%.3f/%.3f) = %.3f\n",
        13.675, 2.333, fmod(13.675, 2.333));
    printf("sin(%.1f) = %.1f\n", 0.0, sin(0.0));
    printf("cos(%.1f) = %.1f\n", 0.0, cos(0.0));
    printf("tan(%.1f) = %.1f\n", 0.0, tan(0.0));
}
```

```
sqrt(900.0) = 30.0
sqrt(9.0) = 3.0
exp(1.0) = 2.718282
exp(2.0) = 7.389056
log(2.718282) = 1.0
log(7.389056) = 2.0
log10(1.0) = 0.0
log10(10.0) = 1.0
log10(100.0) = 2.0
fabs(13.5) = 13.5
fabs(0.0) = 0.0
fabs(-13.5) = 13.5
ceil(9.2) = 10.0
ceil(-9.8) = -9.0
floor(9.2) = 9.0
floor(-9.8) = -10.0
pow(2.0, 7.0) = 128.0                          continued
```

```
pow(9.0, 0.5) = 3.0                          continued
fmod(13.675/2.333) = 2.010
sin(0.0) = 0.0
cos(0.0) = 1.0
tan(0.0) = 0.0
```

5.4   a) `double hypotenuse(double side1, double side2)`
       b) `int smallest(int x, int y, int z)`
       c) `void instructions(void)`
       d) `float intToFloat(int number)`

5.5   a) `double hypotenuse(double, double);`
       b) `int smallest(int, int, int);`
       c) `void instructions(void);`
       d) `float intToFloat(int);`

5.6   a) `register int count = 0;`
       b) `static float lastVal;`
       c) `static int number;`
          Note: This would appear outside any function definition.

5.7   a) Error: Function **h** is defined in function **g**.
          Correction: Move the definition of **h** out of the definition of **g**.
       b) Error: The function is supposed to return an integer, but does not.
          Correction: Delete variable **result** and place the following statement in the function:

              `return x + y;`

       c) Error: The result of **n + sum(n - 1)** is not returned; **sum** returns an improper result.
          Correction: Rewrite the statement in the **else** clause as

              `return n + sum(n - 1);`

       d) Error: Semicolon after the right parenthesis that encloses the parameter list, and re-
          defining the parameter **a** in the function definition.
          Correction: Delete the semicolon after the right parenthesis of the parameter list, and
          delete the declaration **float a;**.
       e) Error: The function returns a value when it is not supposed to.
          Correction: Eliminate the **return** statement.

Exercises

5.8   Show the value of x after each of the following statements is performed:
       a) `x = fabs(7.5)`
       b) `x = floor(7.5)`
       c) `x = fabs(0.0)`
       d) `x = ceil(0.0)`
       e) `x = fabs(-6.4)`
       f) `x = ceil(-6.4)`
       g) `x = ceil(-fabs(-8+floor(-5.5)))`

5.9   A parking garage charges a $2.00 minimum fee to park for up to three hours. The garage
charges an additional $0.50 per hour for each hour *or part thereof* in excess of three hours. The
maximum charge for any given 24-hour period is $10.00. Assume that no car parks for longer than

24 hours at a time. Write a program that will calculate and print the parking charges for each of 3 customers who parked their cars in this garage yesterday. You should enter the hours parked for each customer. Your program should print the results in a neat tabular format, and should calculate and print the total of yesterday's receipts. The program should use the function **calculate-Charges** to determine the charge for each customer. Your outputs should appear in the following format:

```
Car       Hours        Charge
1           1.5          2.00
2           4.0          2.50
3          24.0         10.00
TOTAL      29.5         14.50
```

5.10   An application of function **floor** is rounding a value to the nearest integer. The statement

```
y = floor(x + .5);
```

will round the number **x** to the nearest integer, and assign the result to **y**. Write a program that reads several numbers and uses the preceding statement to round each of these numbers to the nearest integer. For each number processed, print both the original number and the rounded number.

5.11   Function **floor** may be used to round a number to a specific decimal place. The statement

```
y = floor(x * 10 + .5) / 10;
```

rounds **x** to the tenths position (the first position to the right of the decimal point). The statement

```
y = floor(x * 100 + .5) / 100;
```

rounds **x** to the hundredths position (i.e., the second position to the right of the decimal point). Write a program that defines four functions to round a number **x** in various ways

    a) **roundToInteger(number)**
    b) **roundToTenths(number)**
    c) **roundToHundreths(number)**
    d) **roundToThousandths(number)**

For each value read, your program should print the original value, the number rounded to the nearest integer, the number rounded to the nearest tenth, the number rounded to the nearest hundredth, and the number rounded to the nearest thousandth.

5.12   Answer each of the following questions.
    a) What does it mean to choose numbers "at random?"
    b) Why is the **rand** function useful for simulating games of chance?
    c) Why would you randomize a program by using **srand**? Under what circumstances is it desirable not to randomize?
    d) Why is it often necessary to scale and/or shift the values produced by **rand**?
    e) Why is computerized simulation of real-world situations a useful technique?

5.13   Write statements that assign random integers to the variable n in the following ranges:
    a) $1 \le n \le 2$
    b) $1 \le n \le 100$
    c) $0 \le n \le 9$
    d) $1000 \le n \le 1112$
    e) $-1 \le n \le 1$
    f) $-3 \le n \le 11$

5.14   For each of the following sets of integers, write a single statement that will print a number at random from the set.

     a)   2, 4, 6, 8, 10.

     b)   3, 5, 7, 9, 11.

     c)   6, 10, 14, 18, 22.

5.15   Define a function **hypotenuse** that calculates the length of the hypotenuse of a right triangle when the other two sides are given. Use this function in a program to determine the length of the hypotenuse for each of the following triangles. The function should take two arguments of type **double** and return the hypotenuse as a **double**.

Triangle	Side 1	Side 2
1	3.0	4.0
2	5.0	12.0
3	8.0	15.0

5.16   Write a function **integerPower(base, exponent)** that returns the value of

    $base^{exponent}$

For example, **integerPower(3,4) = 3 * 3 * 3 * 3**. Assume that **exponent** is a positive, nonzero integer, and **base** is an integer. The function **integerPower** should use **for** to control the calculation. Do not use any math library functions.

5.17   Write a function **multiple** that determines for a pair of integers whether the second integer is a multiple of the first. The function should take two integer arguments and return **1** (true) if the second is a multiple of the first, and **0** (false) otherwise. Use this function in a program that inputs a series of pairs of integers.

5.18   Write a program that inputs a series of integers and passes them one at a time to function **even** which uses the modulus operator to determine if an integer is even. The function should take an integer argument and return **1** if the integer is even and **0** otherwise.

5.19   Write a function that displays at the left margin of the screen a solid square of asterisks whose side is specified in integer parameter **side**. For example, if **side** is **4**, the function displays

```
****
****
****
****
```

5.20   Modify the function created in Exercise 5.19 to form the square out of whatever character is contained in character parameter **fillCharacter**. Thus if **side** is **5** and **fillCharacter** is "**#**" then this function should print

```
#####
#####
#####
#####
#####
```

5.21   Use techniques similar to those developed in Exercises 5.19 and 5.20 to produce a program that graphs a wide range of shapes.

5.22   Write program segments that accomplish each of the following:
a) Calculate the integer part of the quotient when integer **a** is divided by integer **b**.
b) Calculate the integer remainder when integer **a** is divided by integer **b**.
c) Use the program pieces developed in a) and b) to write a function that inputs an integer between **1** and **32767** and prints it as a series of digits, each pair of which is separated by two spaces. For example, the integer **4562** should be printed as

```
4   5   6   2
```

5.23   Write a function that takes the time as three integer arguments (for hours, minutes, and seconds), and returns the number of seconds since the last time the clock "struck 12." Use this function to calculate the amount of time in seconds between two times, both of which are within one 12-hour cycle of the clock.

5.24   Implement the following integer functions:
a) Function **celsius** returns the Celsius equivalent of a Fahrenheit temperature.
b) Function **fahrenheit** returns the Fahrenheit equivalent of a Celsius temperature.
c) Use these functions to write a program that prints charts showing the Fahrenheit equivalents of all Celsius temperatures from 0 to 100 degrees, and the Celsius equivalents of all Fahrenheit temperatures from 32 to 212 degrees. Print the outputs in a neat tabular format that minimizes the number of lines of output while remaining readable.

5.25   Write a function that returns the smallest of three floating point numbers.

5.26   An integer number is said to be a *perfect number* if its factors, including 1 (but not the number itself), sum to the number. For example, 6 is a perfect number because $6 = 1 + 2 + 3$. Write a function **perfect** that determines if parameter **number** is a perfect number. Use this function in a program that determines and prints all the perfect numbers between 1 and 1000. Print the factors of each perfect number to confirm that the number is indeed perfect. Challenge the power of your computer by testing numbers much larger than 1000.

5.27   An integer is said to be *prime* if it is divisible only by 1 and itself. For example, 2, 3, 5, and 7 are prime, but 4, 6, 8, and 9 are not.
a) Write a function that determines if a number is prime.
b) Use this function in a program that determines and prints all the prime numbers between 1 and 10,000. How many of these 10,000 numbers do you really have to test before being sure that you have found all the primes?
c) Initially you might think that $n/2$ is the upper limit for which you must test to see if a number is prime, but you need only go as high as the square root of n. Why? Rewrite the program, and run it both ways. Estimate the performance improvement.

5.28   Write a function that takes an integer value and returns the number with its digits reversed. For example, given the number 7631, the function should return 1367.

5.29   The *greatest common divisor (GCD)* of two integers is the largest integer that evenly divides each of the two numbers. Write a function **gcd** that returns the greatest common divisor of two integers.

5.30   Write a function **qualityPoints** that inputs a student's average and returns 4 if a student's average is 90-100, 3 if the average is 80-89, 2 if the average is 70-79, 1 if the average is 60-69, and 0 if the average is lower than 60.

5.31   Write a program that simulates coin tossing. For each toss of the coin the program should print **Heads** or **Tails**. Let the program toss the coin 100 times, and count the number of times each side of the coin appears. Print the results. The program should call a separate function **flip** that takes no arguments and returns **0** for tails and **1** for heads. *Note:* If the program realistically simulates the coin tossing, then each side of the coin should appear approximately half the time for a total of approximately 50 heads and 50 tails.

5.32   Computers are playing an increasing role in education. Write a program that will help an elementary school student learn multiplication. Use **rand** to produce two positive one-digit integers. It should then type a question such as:

> How much is 6 times 7?

The student then types the answer. Your program checks the student's answer. If it is correct, print **"Very good!"** and then ask another multiplication question. If the answer is wrong, print **"No. Please try again."** and then let the student try the same question again repeatedly until the student finally gets it right.

5.33   The use of computers in education is referred to as *computer-assisted instruction* (CAI). One problem that develops in CAI environments is student fatigue. This can be eliminated by varying the computer's dialogue to hold the student's attention. Modify the program of Exercise 5.32 so the various comments are printed for each correct answer and each incorrect answer as follows:

> Responses to a correct answer
>
> > Very good!
> > Excellent!
> > Nice work!
> > Keep up the good work!
>
> Responses to an incorrect answer
>
> > No. Please try again.
> > Wrong. Try once more.
> > Don't give up!
> > No. Keep trying.

Use the random number generator to choose a number from 1 to 4 to select an appropriate response to each answer. Use a **switch** structure with **printf** statements to issue the responses.

5.34   More sophisticated computer-aided instructions systems monitor the student's performance over a period of time. The decision to begin a new topic is often based on the student's success with previous topics. Modify the program of Exercise 5.33 to count the number of correct and incorrect responses typed by the student. After the student types 10 answers, your program should calculate the percentage of correct responses. If the percentage is lower than 75 percent, your program should print **"Please ask your instructor for extra help"** and then terminate.

5.35   Write a C program that plays the game of "guess the number" as follows: Your program chooses the number to be guessed by selecting an integer at random in the range 1 to 1000. The program then types:

```
I have a number between 1 and 1000.
Can you guess my number?
Please type your first guess.
```

The player then types a first guess. The program responds with one of the following:

```
1. Excellent! You guessed the number!
   Would you like to play again (y or n)?
2. Too low. Try again.
3. Too high. Try again.
```

If the player's guess is incorrect, your program should loop until the player finally gets the number right. Your program should keep telling the player **Too high** or **Too low** to help the player "zero in" on the correct answer. Note: The searching technique employed in this problem is called *binary search*. We will say more about this in the next problem.

5.36   Modify the program of Exercise 5.35 to count the number of guesses the player makes. If the number is 10 or fewer, print **Either you know the secret or you got lucky!** If the player guesses the number in 10 tries, then print **Ahah! You know the secret!** If the player makes more than 10 guesses, then print **You should be able to do better!** Why should it take no more than 10 guesses? Well with each "good guess" the player should be able to eliminate half of the numbers. Now show why any number 1 to 1000 can be guessed in 10 or fewer tries.

5.37   Write a recursive function **power (base, exponent)** that when invoked returns

$$base^{exponent}$$

For example, **power(3, 4) = 3 * 3 * 3 *3**. Assume that **exponent** is an integer greater than or equal to 1. *Hint:* The recursion step would use the relationship

$$base^{exponent} = base \cdot base^{exponent - 1}$$

and the terminating condition occurs when **exponent** is equal to **1** because

$$base^1 = base$$

5.38   The Fibonacci series

0, 1, 1, 2, 3, 5, 8, 13, 21, ...

begins with the terms 0 and 1 and has the property that each succeeding term is the sum of the two preceding terms. a) Write a *nonrecursive* function **fibonacci(n)** that calculates the **n**th Fibonacci number. b) Determine the largest Fibonacci number that can be printed on your system. Modify the program of part a) to use **double** instead of **int** to calculate and return Fibonacci numbers. Let the program loop until it fails because of an excessively high value.

5.39   *(Towers of Hanoi)* Every budding computer scientist must grapple with certain classic problems, and the Towers of Hanoi (see Fig. 5.18) is one of the most famous of these. Legend has it that in a temple in the Far East, priests are attempting to move a stack of disks from one peg to another. The initial stack had 64 disks threaded onto one peg and arranged from bottom to top by decreasing size. The priests are attempting to move the stack from this peg to a second peg under the constraints that exactly one disk is moved at a time, and at no time may a larger disk be placed above a smaller disk. A third peg is available for temporarily holding the disks. Supposedly the world will end when the priests complete their task, so there is little incentive for us to facilitate their efforts.

Let us assume that the priests are attempting to move the disks from peg 1 to peg 3. We wish to develop an algorithm that will print the precise sequence of disk-to-disk peg transfers.

If we were to approach this problem with conventional methods, we would rapidly find ourselves hopelessly knotted up in managing the disks. Instead, if we attack the problem with recursion in mind, it immediately becomes tractable. Moving *n* disks can be viewed in terms of moving only *n* - 1 disks (and hence the recursion) as follows:

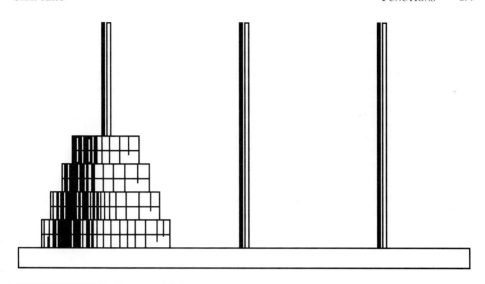

Fig. 5.18 The Towers of Hanoi for the case with four disks.

1. Move n - 1 disks from peg 1 to peg 2, using peg 3 as a temporary holding area.
2. Move the last disk (the largest) from peg 1 to peg 3.
3. Move the n - 1 disks from peg 2 to peg 3, using peg 1 as a temporary holding area.

The process ends when the last task involves moving $n = 1$ disk, i.e., the base case. This is accomplished by trivially moving the disk without the need for a temporary holding area.

Write a program to solve the Towers of Hanoi problem. Use a recursive function with four parameters:

1. The number of disks to be moved
2. The peg on which these disks are initially threaded
3. The peg to which this stack of disks is to be moved
4. The peg to be used as a temporary holding area

Your program should print the precise instructions it will take to move the disks from the starting peg to the destination peg. For example, to move a stack of three disks from peg 1 to peg 3, your program should print the following series of moves:

$1 \rightarrow 3$ (This means move one disk from peg 1 to peg 3.)

$1 \rightarrow 2$

$3 \rightarrow 2$

$1 \rightarrow 3$

$2 \rightarrow 1$

$2 \rightarrow 3$

$1 \rightarrow 3$

5.40   Any program that can be implemented recursively can be implemented iteratively, although sometimes with considerably more difficulty and considerably less clarity. Try writing an iterative version of the Towers of Hanoi. If you succeed, compare your iterative version with the recursive version you developed in Exercise 5.39. Investigate issues of performance, clarity, and your ability to demonstrate the correctness of the programs.

5.41   (Visualizing Recursion) It is interesting to watch recursion "in action." Modify the factorial function of Fig. 5.14 to print its local variable and recursive call parameter. For each recursive call, display the outputs on a separate line and add a level of indentation. Do your utmost to make the outputs clear, interesting, and meaningful. Your goal here is to design and implement an output format that helps a person understand recursion better. You may want to add such display capabilities to the many other recursion examples and exercises throughout the text.

5.42   The greatest common divisor of integers **x** and **y** is the largest integer that evenly divides both **x** and **y**. Write a recursive function **gcd** that returns the greatest common divisor of **x** and **y**. The **gcd** of **x** and **y** is defined recursively as follows: If **y** is equal to **0**, then **gcd(x, y)** is **x**; otherwise **gcd(x, y)** is **gcd(y, x % y)** where **%** is the modulus operator.

5.43   Can **main** be called recursively? Write a program containing a function **main**. Include **static** local variable **count** initialized to 1. Postincrement and print the value of **count** each time **main** is called. Run your program. What happens?

5.44   Exercises 5.32 through 5.34 developed a computer-assisted instruction program to teach an elementary school student multiplication. This exercise suggests enhancements to that program.

a)   Modify the program to allow the user to enter a grade-level capability. A grade level of 1 means to use only single-digit numbers in the problems, a grade level of two means to use numbers as large as two-digits, etc.

b)   Modify the program to allow the user to pick the type of arithmetic problems he or she wishes to study. An option of 1 means addition problems only, 2 means subtraction problems only, 3 means multiplication problems only, 4 means division problems only, and 5 means to randomly intermix problems of all these types.

5.45   Write function **distance** that calculates the distance between two points (x1, y1) and (x2, y2). All numbers and return values should be of type **float**.

5.46   What does the following program do?

```
main()
{
   int c;

   if ((c = getchar()) != EOF) {
      main();
      printf("%c", c);
   }

   return 0;
}
```

5.47   What does the following program do?

```
int mystery(int, int);

main()
{
   int x, y;

   printf("Enter two integers: ");
   scanf("%d%d", &x, &y);
   printf("The result is %d\n", mystery(x, y));
   return 0;
}
```

```
/* Parameter b must be a positive
   integer to prevent infinite recursion */
int mystery(int a, int b)
{
   if (b == 1)
      return a;
   else
      return a + mystery(a, b - 1);
}
```

5.48   After you determine what the program of Exercise 5.47 does, modify the program to function properly after removing the restriction of the second argument being nonnegative.

5.49   Write a program that tests as many of the math library functions in Fig. 5.2 as you can. Exercise each of these functions by having your program print out tables of return values for a diversity of argument values.

5.50   Find the error in each of the following program segments and explain how to correct it:

a)
```
float cube(float);    /* function prototype */
...
cube(float number)    /* function definition */
{
   return number * number * number;
}
```

b)
```
register auto int x = 7;
```

c)
```
int randomNumber = srand();
```

d)
```
float y = 123.45678;
int x;

x = y;
printf("%f\n", (float) x);
```

e)
```
double square(double number)
{
   double number;

   return number * number;
}
```

f)
```
int sum(int n)
{
   if (n == 0)
      return 0;
   else
      return n + sum(n);
}
```

5.51   Modify the craps program of Fig. 5.10 to allow wagering. Package as a function the portion of the program that runs one game of craps. Initialize variable **bankBalance** to 1000 dollars. Prompt the player to enter a **wager**. Use a **while** loop to check that **wager** is less than or equal to **bankBalance** and if not prompt the user to reenter **wager** until a valid **wager** is entered. After a correct **wager** is entered, run one game of craps. If the player wins, increase **bankBalance** by **wager** and print the new **bankBalance**. If the player loses, decrease **bankBalance** by **wager**, print the new **bankBalance**, check if **bankBalance** has become zero, and if so print the message **"Sorry. You busted!"** As the game progresses, print various messages to create some "chatter" such as **"Oh, you're going for broke, huh?"**, or **"Aw cmon, take a chance!"**, or **"You're up big. Now's the time to cash in your chips!"**.

6

Arrays

Objectives

- To introduce the array data structure.
- To understand the use of arrays to store, sort, and search lists and tables of values.
- To understand how to declare an array, initialize an array, and refer to individual elements of an array.
- To be able to pass arrays to functions.
- To understand basic sorting techniques.
- To be able to declare and manipulate multiple subscript arrays.

With sobs and tears he sorted out
Those of the largest size ...
Lewis Carroll

Attempt the end, and never stand to doubt;
Nothing's so hard, but search will find it out.
Robert Herrick

Now go, write it before them in a table,
and note it in a book.
Isaiah 30:8

'Tis in my memory lock'd,
And you yourself shall keep the key of it.
William Shakespeare

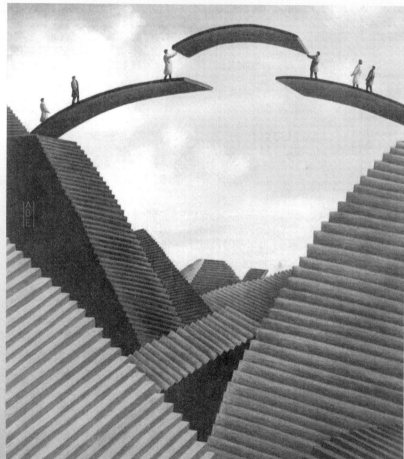

Outline

6.1 Introduction

This chapter serves as an introduction to the important topic of data structures. *Arrays* are data structures consisting of related data items of the same type. In Chapter 10, we discuss C's notion of **struct** (structure)—a data structure consisting of related data items of possibly different types. Arrays and structures are "static" entities in that they remain the same size throughout program execution (they may, of course, be of automatic storage class and hence created and destroyed each time the blocks in which they are defined are entered and exited). In Chapter 12, we introduce dynamic data structures such as lists, queues, stacks, and trees that may grow and shrink as programs execute.

6.2 Arrays

An array is a group of memory locations related by the fact that they all have the same name and the same type. To refer to a particular location or element in the array, we specify the name of the array and the *position number* of the particular element in the array.

Fig. 6.1 shows an integer array called **c**. This array contains twelve *elements*. Any one of these elements may be referred to by giving the name of the array followed by the position number of the particular element in square brackets (**[]**). The first element in every array is the *zeroth element*. Thus, the first element of array **c** is referred to as **c[0]**, the second element of array **c** is referred to as **c[1]**, the seventh element of array **c** is referred to as **c[6]**, and, in general, the *i*th element of array **c** is referred to as **c[i-1]**. Array names follow the same conventions as other variable names.

Name of array (Note that
all elements of this array
have the same name, c)

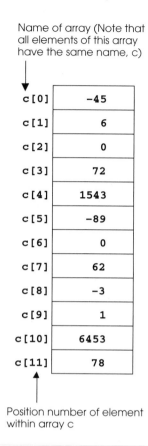

Position number of element
within array c

Fig. 6.1   A 12-element array.

The position number contained within square brackets is more formally called a *subscript*. A subscript must be an integer or an integer expression. If a program uses an expression as a subscript, then the expression is evaluated to determine the subscript. For example, if **a = 5** and **b = 6**, then the statement

```
c[a + b] += 2;
```

adds 2 to array element **c[11]**. Note that a subscripted array name is an lvalue—it can be used on the left side of an assignment.

Let us examine array **c** in Fig. 6.1 more closely. The *name* of the array is **c**. Its twelve elements are referred to as **c[0]**, **c[1]**, **c[2]**, ..., **c[11]**. The *value* of **c[0]** is **-45**, the value of **c[1]** is **6**, the value of **c[2]** is **0**, the value of **c[7]** is **62**, and the value of **c[11]** is **78**. To print the sum of the values contained in the first three elements of array **c**, we would write

```
printf("%d", c[0] + c[1] + c[2]);
```

To divide the value of the seventh element of array **c** by **2** and assign the result to the variable **x**, we would write

```
x = c[6] / 2;
```

Common Programming Error 6.1

It is important to note the difference between the "seventh element of the array" and "array element seven." Because array subscripts begin at 0, the "seventh element of the array" has a subscript of 6, while "array element seven" has a subscript of 7 and is actually the eighth element of the array. This is a source of "off-by-one" errors.

The brackets used to enclose the subscript of an array are actually considered to be an operator in C. They have the same level of precedence as parentheses. The chart in Fig. 6.2 shows the precedence and associativity of the operators introduced to this point in the text. They are shown top to bottom in decreasing order of precedence.

6.3 Declaring Arrays

Arrays occupy space in memory. The programmer specifies the type of each element and the number of elements required by each array so that the computer may reserve the appropriate amount of memory. To tell the computer to reserve 12 elements for integer array **c**, the declaration

```
int c[12];
```

is used. Memory may be reserved for several arrays with a single declaration. To reserve 100 elements for integer array **b** and 27 elements for integer array **x**, the following declaration is used:

Operators						Associativity	Type
( )	[ ]					left to right	highest
++	--	!	(*type*)			right to left	unary
*	/	%				left to right	multiplicative
+	-					left to right	additive
<	<=	>	>=			left to right	relational
==	!=					left to right	equality
&&						left to right	logical and
||						left to right	logical or
?:						right to left	conditional
=	+=	-=	*=	/=	%=	right to left	assignment
,						left to right	comma

Fig. 6.2   Operator precedence.

```
int b[100], x[27];
```

Arrays may be declared to contain other data types. For example, an array of type **char** can be used to store a character string. Character strings and their similarity to arrays are discussed in Chapter 8. The relationship between pointers and arrays is discussed in Chapter 7.

6.4 Examples Using Arrays

The program in Fig. 6.3 uses a **for** repetition structure to initialize the elements of a ten-element integer array **n** to zeros, and prints the array in tabular format.

Note that we chose not to place a blank line between the first **printf** statement and the **for** structure in Fig. 6.3 because they are closely related. In this case, the **printf** statement displays the column heads for the two columns printed in the **for** structure. Programmers often omit the blank line between a **for** structure and a closely related **printf** statement.

```
/* initializing an array */
#include <stdio.h>

main()
{
    int n[10], i;

    for (i = 0; i <= 9; i++)          /* initialize array */
        n[i] = 0;

    printf("%s%13s\n", "Element", "Value");
    for(i = 0; i <= 9; i++)           /* print array */
        printf("%7d%13d\n", i, n[i]);

    return 0;
}
```

```
Element        Value
      0            0
      1            0
      2            0
      3            0
      4            0
      5            0
      6            0
      7            0
      8            0
      9            0
```

Fig. 6.3   Initializing the elements of an array to zeros.

The elements of an array can also be initialized in the array declaration by following the declaration with an equals sign and a comma-separated list (enclosed in braces) of *initializers*. The program in Fig. 6.4 initializes an integer array with ten values and prints the array in tabular format.

If there are fewer initializers than elements in the array, the remaining elements are automatically initialized to zero. For example, the elements of the array **n** in Fig. 6.3 could have been initialized to zero with the declaration

```
int n[10] = {0};
```

which explicitly initializes the first element to zero, and automatically initializes the remaining nine elements to zero because there are fewer initializers than there are elements in the array. It is important to remember that arrays are not automatically initialized to zero. The programmer must at least initialize the first element to zero for the remaining elements to be automatically zeroed. This method of initializing the array elements to **0** is performed at compile time. The method used in Fig. 6.3 can be done repeatedly as a program executes.

```
/* Initializing an array with a declaration */
#include <stdio.h>

main()
{
    int i, n[10] = {32, 27, 64, 18, 95, 14, 90, 70, 60, 37};

    printf("%s%13s\n", "Element", "Value");

    for(i = 0; i <= 9; i++)
        printf("%7d%13d\n", i, n[i]);

    return 0;
}
```

```
Element        Value
      0           32
      1           27
      2           64
      3           18
      4           95
      5           14
      6           90
      7           70
      8           60
      9           37
```

Fig. 6.4   Initializing the elements of an array with a declaration.

Common Programming Error 6.2

Forgetting to initialize the elements of an array whose elements should be initialized.

The following array declaration

```
int n[5] = {32, 27, 64, 18, 95, 14};
```

would cause a syntax error because there are 6 initializers and only 5 array elements.

Common Programming Error 6.3

Providing more initializers in an array initializer list than there are elements in the array is a syntax error.

If the array size is omitted from a declaration with an initializer list, the number of elements in the array will be the number of elements in the initializer list. For example,

```
int n[] = {1, 2, 3, 4, 5};
```

would create a five-element array.

The program in Fig. 6.5 initializes the elements of a ten-element array **s** to the values **2, 4, 6,** ..., **20**, and prints the array in tabular format. The values are generated by multiplying the loop counter by **2** and adding **2**.

The **#define** preprocessor directive is introduced in this program. The line

```
#define SIZE 10
```

defines a *symbolic constant* **SIZE** whose value is **10**. A symbolic constant is an identifier that is replaced with *replacement text* by the C preprocessor before the program is compiled. When the program is preprocessed, all occurrences of the symbolic constant **SIZE** are replaced with the replacement text **10**. Using symbolic constants to specify array sizes makes programs more *scalable*. In Fig. 6.5, the first **for** loop could fill a 1000-element array by simply changing the value of **SIZE** in the **#define** directive from **10** to **1000**. If the symbolic constant **SIZE** had not been used, we would have to change the program in three separate places to scale the program to handle 1000 array elements. As programs get larger, this technique becomes more useful for writing clear programs.

Common Programming Error 6.4

*Ending a **#define** or **#include** preprocessor directive with a semicolon. Remember that preprocessor directives are not C statements.*

If the preceding **#define** preprocessor directive is terminated with a semicolon, all occurrences of the symbolic constant **SIZE** in the program are replaced with the text **10;** by the preprocessor. This may lead to syntax errors at compile time, or logic errors at execution time. Remember that the preprocessor is not C—it is only a text manipulator.

Common Programming Error 6.5

Assigning a value to a symbolic constant in an executable statement is a syntax error. A symbolic constant is not a variable. No space is reserved for it by the compiler as with variables that hold values at execution time.

```
/* Initialize the elements of array s to
   the even integers from 2 to 20 */
#include <stdio.h>
#define SIZE 10

main()
{
   int s[SIZE], j;

   for (j = 0; j <= SIZE - 1; j++)    /* set the values */
      s[j] = 2 + 2 * j;

   printf("%s%13s\n", "Element", "Value");

   for (j = 0; j <= SIZE - 1; j++)    /* print the values */
      printf("%7d%13d\n", j, s[j]);

   return 0;
}
```

Element	Value
0	2
1	4
2	6
3	8
4	10
5	12
6	14
7	16
8	18
9	20

Fig. 6.5   Generating the values to be placed into elements of an array.

Software Engineering Observation 6.1

Defining the size of each array as a symbolic constant makes programs more scalable.

Good Programming Practice 6.1

Use only uppercase letters for symbolic constant names. This makes these constants stand out in a program and reminds the programmer that symbolic constants are not variables.

The program in Fig. 6.6 sums the values contained in the twelve-element integer array **a**. The statement in the body of the **for** loop does the totaling.

Our next example uses arrays to summarize the results of data collected in a survey. Consider the problem statement.

Forty students were asked to rate the quality of the food in the student cafeteria on a scale of 1 to 10 (1 means awful and 10 means excellent). Place the forty responses in an integer array and summarize the results of the poll.

```
/* Compute the sum of the elements of the array */
#include <stdio.h>
#define SIZE 12

main()
{
   int a[SIZE] = {1, 3, 5, 4, 7, 2, 99, 16, 45, 67, 89, 45},
      i, total = 0;

   for (i = 0; i <= SIZE - 1; i++)
      total += a[i];

   printf("Total of array element values is %d\n", total);
   return 0;
}
```

> Total of array element values is 383

Fig. 6.6   Computing the sum of the elements of an array.

This is a typical array application (see Fig. 6.7). We wish to summarize the number of responses of each type (i.e., 1 through 10). The array **responses** is a 40-element array of the students' responses. We use an eleven-element array, **frequency** to count the number of occurrences of each response. We ignore the first element, **frequency[0]**, because it is more logical to have the response 1 increment **frequency[1]** than **frequency[0]**. This allows us to use each response directly as the subscript in the **frequency** array.

Good Programming Practice 6.2

Strive for program clarity. Sometimes it may be worthwhile to trade off the most efficient use of memory or processor time in favor of writing clearer programs.

Performance Tip 6.1

Sometimes performance considerations far outweigh clarity considerations.

The first **for** loop takes the responses one at a time from the array **response** and increments one of the ten counters (**frequency[1]** to **frequency[10]**) in the **frequency** array. The key statement in the loop is

```
++frequency[responses[answer]];
```

This statement increments the appropriate **frequency** counter depending on the value of **responses[answer]**. For example, when the counter variable **answer** is 0, **responses[answer]** is **1**, so **++frequency[responses[answer]];** is actually interpreted as

```
++frequency[1];
```

```
/* Student poll program */
#include <stdio.h>
#define RESPONSE_SIZE 40
#define FREQUENCY_SIZE 11

main()
{
   int answer, rating;
   int responses[RESPONSE_SIZE] = {1, 2, 6, 4, 8, 5, 9, 7, 8,
      10, 1, 6, 3, 8, 6, 10, 3, 8, 2, 7, 6, 5, 7, 6, 8, 6, 7,
      5, 6, 6, 5, 6, 7, 5, 6, 4, 8, 6, 8, 10};
   int frequency[FREQUENCY_SIZE] = {0};

   for (answer = 0; answer <= RESPONSE_SIZE - 1; answer++)
      ++frequency[responses[answer]];

   printf("%s%17s\n", "Rating", "Frequency");

   for (rating = 1; rating <= FREQUENCY_SIZE - 1; rating++)
      printf("%6d%17d\n", rating, frequency[rating]);

   return 0;
}
```

Rating	Frequency
1	2
2	2
3	2
4	2
5	5
6	11
7	5
8	7
9	1
10	3

Fig. 6.7   A simple student poll analysis program.

which increments array element one. When **answer** is 1, **responses[answer]** is 2, so **++frequency[responses[answer]];** is interpreted as

```
++frequency[2];
```

which increments array element two. When **answer** is 2, **responses[answer]** is 6, so **++frequency[responses[answer]];** is interpreted as

```
++frequency[6];
```

which increments array element six, and so on. Note that regardless of the number of responses processed in the survey, only an eleven-element array is required (ignoring element zero) to summarize the results. If the data contained invalid values such as 13, the program would attempt to add **1** to **frequency[13]**. This would be outside the bounds of the array. *C has no array bounds checking to prevent the computer from referring to an element that does not exist.* Thus, an executing program can walk off the end of an array without warning. The programmer should ensure that all array references remain within the bounds of the array.

Common Programming Error 6.6

Referring to an element outside the array bounds.

Good Programming Practice 6.3

When looping through an array, the array subscript should never go below 0 and should always be less than the total number of elements in the array (size – 1). Make sure the loop terminating condition prevents accessing elements outside this range.

Good Programming Practice 6.4

Mention the high array subscript in a for *structure to help eliminate off-by-one errors.*

Good Programming Practice 6.5

Programs should validate the correctness of all input values to prevent erroneous information from affecting a program's calculations.

Performance Tip 6.2

The (normally serious) effects of referencing elements outside the array bounds are system dependent.

Our next example (Fig. 6.8) reads numbers from an array and graphs the information in the form of a bar chart or histogram—each number is printed, and then a bar consisting of that many asterisks is printed beside the number. The nested **for** loop actually draws the bars. Note the use of **printf("\n")** to end a histogram bar.

In Chapter 5 we stated that we would show a more elegant method of writing the dice-rolling program of Fig. 5.10. The problem was to roll a single six-sided die 6000 times to test whether the random number generator actually produces random numbers. An array version of this program is shown in Fig. 6.9.

To this point we have discussed only integer arrays. However, arrays are capable of holding data of any type. We now discuss storing strings in character arrays. So far, the only string processing capability we have is outputting a string with **printf**. A string such as "**hello**" is really an array of individual characters in C.

Character arrays have several unique features. A character array can be initialized using a string literal. For example, the declaration

```
char string1[] = "first";
```

initializes the elements of array **string1** to the individual characters in the string literal **"first"**. The size of array **string1** in the preceding declaration is determined by the

```
/* Histogram printing program */
#include <stdio.h>
#define SIZE 10

main()
{
   int n[SIZE] = {19, 3, 15, 7, 11, 9, 13, 5, 17, 1};
   int i, j;

   printf("%s%13s%17s\n", "Element", "Value", "Histogram");

   for (i = 0; i <= SIZE - 1; i++) {
      printf("%7d%13d        ", i, n[i]);

      for (j = 1; j <= n[i]; j++)     /* print one bar */
         printf("%c", '*');

      printf("\n");
   }

   return 0;
}
```

```
Element          Value        Histogram
      0             19        *******************
      1              3        ***
      2             15        ***************
      3              7        *******
      4             11        ***********
      5              9        *********
      6             13        *************
      7              5        *****
      8             17        *****************
      9              1        *
```

Fig. 6.8   A program that prints histograms.

compiler based on the length of the string. It is important to note that the string **"first"** contains five characters *plus* a special string termination character called the *null character*. Thus, array **string1** actually contains six elements. The character constant representation of the null character is **'\0'**. All strings in C end with this character. A character array representing a string should always be declared large enough to hold the number of characters in the string and the terminating null character.

Character arrays also can be initialized with individual character constants in an initializer list. The preceding declaration is equivalent to

```
char string1[] = {'f', 'i', 'r', 's', 't', '\0'};
```

Because a string is really an array of characters, we can access individual characters in a string directly using array subscript notation. For example, **string1[0]** is the character **'f'** and **string1[3]** is the character **'s'**.

```
/* Roll a six-sided die 6000 times */
#include <stdio.h>
#include <stdlib.h>
#include <time.h>
#define SIZE 7

main()
{
    int face, roll, frequency[SIZE] = {0};

    srand(time(NULL));

    for (roll = 1; roll <= 6000; roll++) {
        face = rand() % 6 + 1;
        ++frequency[face];       /* replaces 20-line switch */
    }                            /* of Fig. 5.8 */

    printf("%s%17s\n", "Face", "Frequency");

    for (face = 1; face <= SIZE - 1; face++)
        printf("%4d%17d\n", face, frequency[face]);

    return 0;
}
```

```
Face        Frequency
  1            1037
  2             987
  3            1013
  4            1028
  5             952
  6             983
```

Fig. 6.9   Dice-rolling program using arrays instead of `switch`.

We also can input a string directly into a character array from the keyboard using **scanf** and the conversion specification **%s**. For example, the declaration

```
char string2[20];
```

creates a character array capable of storing a string of 19 characters and a terminating null character. The statement

```
scanf("%s", string2);
```

reads a string from the keyboard into **string2**. Note that the name of the array is passed to **scanf** without the preceding **&** used with other variables. The **&** is normally used to provide **scanf** with a variable's location in memory so a value can be stored there. In Section 6.5, we discuss passing arrays to functions. We will see that an array name is the address of the start of the array; therefore, the **&** is not necessary.

It is the programmer's responsibility to ensure that the array into which the string is read is capable of holding any string that the user types at the keyboard. Function **scanf** reads characters from the keyboard until the first whitespace character is encountered—it does not care how large the array is. Thus, **scanf** can write beyond the end of the array.

Common Programming Error 6.7

*Not providing **scanf** with a character array large enough to store a string typed at the keyboard can result in loss of data in a program and other run-time errors.*

A character array representing a string can be output with **printf** and the **%s** conversion specifier. The array **string2** is printed with the statement

```
printf("%s\n", string2);
```

Note that **printf**, like **scanf**, does not care how large the character array is. The characters of the string are printed until a terminating null character is encountered.

Figure 6.10 demonstrates initializing a character array with a string literal, reading a string into a character array, printing a character array as a string, and accessing individual characters of a string.

```
/* Treating character arrays as strings */
#include <stdio.h>

main()
{
   char string1[20], string2[] = "string literal";
   int i;

   printf("Enter a string: ");
   scanf("%s", string1);
   printf("string1 is: %s\nstring2: is %s\n"
          "string1 with spaces between characters is:\n",
          string1, string2);

   for (i = 0; string1[i] != '\0'; i++)
      printf("%c ", string1[i]);

   printf("\n");
   return 0;
}
```

```
Enter a string: Hello there
string1 is: Hello
string2 is: string literal
string1 with spaces between characters is:
H e l l o
```

Fig. 6.10   Treating character arrays as strings.

Figure 6.10 uses a **for** structure to loop through the **string1** array and print the individual characters separated by spaces using the **%c** conversion specification. The condition in the **for** structure, **string1[i] != '\0'**, is true while the terminating null character has not been encountered in the string.

Chapter 5 discussed the storage class specifier **static**. A **static** local variable in a function definition exists for the duration of the program, but is only visible in the function body. We can apply **static** to a local array declaration so the array is not created and initialized each time the function is called, and the array is not destroyed each time the function is exited in the program. This reduces program execution time particularly for programs with frequently called functions that contain large arrays.

Performance Tip 6.3

*In functions that contain automatic arrays where the function is in and out of scope frequently, make the array **static** so it is not created each time the function is called.*

Arrays that are declared **static** are automatically initialized once at compile time. If a **static** array is not explicitly initialized by the programmer, that array is initialized to zero by the compiler.

Figure 6.11 demonstrates function **staticArrayInit** with a local array declared **static** and function **automaticArrayInit** with an automatic local array. Function **staticArrayInit** is called twice. The **static** local array in the function is initialized to zero by the compiler. The function prints the array, adds 5 to each element, and prints the array again. The second time the function is called, the **static** array contains the values stored during the first function call. Function **automaticArrayInit** is also called twice. The elements of the automatic local array in the function are initialized with the values 1, 2, and 3. The function prints the array, adds 5 to each element, and prints the array again. The second time the function is called, the array elements are initialized to 1, 2, and 3 again because the array has automatic storage duration.

Common Programming Error 6.8

*Assuming that elements of a local array that is declared **static** are initialized to zero every time the function is called in which the array is declared.*

6.5 Passing Arrays to Functions

To pass an array argument to a function, specify the name of the array without any brackets. For example, if array **hourlyTemperatures** has been declared as

```
int hourlyTemperatures[24];
```

the function call statement

```
modifyArray(hourlyTemperatures, 24);
```

passes array **hourlyTemperatures** and its size to function **modifyArray**. When passing an array to a function, the array size is often passed so the function can process the specific number of elements in the array.

```
/* Static arrays are initialized to zero */
#include <stdio.h>

void staticArrayInit(void);
void automaticArrayInit(void);

main()
{
   printf("First call to each function:\n");
   staticArrayInit();
   automaticArrayInit();
   printf("\n\nSecond call to each function:\n");
   staticArrayInit();
   automaticArrayInit();
   return 0;
}

/* function to demonstrate a static local array */
void staticArrayInit(void)
{
   static int a[3];
   int i;

   printf("\nValues on entering staticArrayInit:\n");

   for (i = 0; i <= 2; i++)
      printf("array1[%d] = %d   ", i, a[i]);

   printf("\nValues on exiting staticArrayInit:\n");

   for (i = 0; i <= 2; i++)
      printf("array1[%d] = %d   ", i, a[i] += 5);
}

/* function to demonstrate an automatic local array */
void automaticArrayInit(void)
{
   int a[3] = {1, 2, 3};
   int i;

   printf("\n\nValues on entering automaticArrayInit:\n");

   for (i = 0; i <= 2; i++)
      printf("array1[%d] = %d   ", i, a[i]);

   printf("\nValues on exiting automaticArrayInit:\n");

   for (i = 0; i <= 2; i++)
      printf("array1[%d] = %d   ", i, a[i] += 5);
}
```

Fig. 6.11   Static arrays are automatically initialized to zero if not explicitly initialized by the programmer (part 1 of 2).

```
First call to each function:

Values on entering staticArrayInit:
array1[0] = 0  array1[1] = 0  array1[2] = 0
Values on exiting staticArrayInit:
array1[0] = 5  array1[1] = 5  array1[2] = 5

Values on entering automaticArrayInit:
array1[0] = 1  array1[1] = 2  array1[2] = 3
Values on exiting automaticArrayInit:
array1[0] = 6  array1[1] = 7  array1[2] = 8

Second call to each function:

Values on entering staticArrayInit:
array1[0] = 5  array1[1] = 5  array1[2] = 5
Values on exiting staticArrayInit:
array1[0] = 10  array1[1] = 10  array1[2] = 10

Values on entering automaticArrayInit:
array1[0] = 1  array1[1] = 2  array1[2] = 3
Values on exiting automaticArrayInit:
array1[0] = 6  array1[1] = 7  array1[2] = 8
```

Fig. 6.11 Static arrays are automatically initialized to zero if not explicitly initialized by the programmer (part 2 of 2).

C automatically passes arrays to functions using simulated call by reference—the called functions can modify the element values in the callers' original arrays. The name of the array is actually the address of the first element of the array! Because the starting address of the array is passed, the called function knows precisely where the array is stored. Therefore, when the called function modifies array elements in its function body, it is modifying the actual elements of the array in their original memory locations.

Figure 6.12 demonstrates that an array name is really the address of the first element of an array by printing **array** and **&array[0]** using the **%p** conversion specification—a special conversion specification for printing addresses. The **%p** conversion specification normally outputs addresses as hexadecimal numbers. Hexadecimal (base 16) numbers consist of the digits 0 through 9 and the letters A through F. They are often used as shorthand notation for large integer values. Appendix E: Number Systems provides an in-depth discussion of the relationships between binary (base 2), octal (base 8), decimal (base 10; standard integers), and hexadecimal integers. The output shows that both **array** and **&array[0]** have the same value, namely **FFF0**. The output of this program is system dependent, but the addresses will always be identical.

Performance Tip 6.4

Passing arrays simulated call by reference makes sense for performance reasons. If arrays were passed call by value, a copy of each element would be passed. For large, frequently passed arrays, this would be time consuming and would consume considerable storage for the copies of the arrays.

```
/* The name of an array is the same as &array[0] */
#include <stdio.h>

main()
{
   char array[5];

   printf("    array = %p\n&array[0] = %p\n",
          array, &array[0]);
   return 0;
}
```

```
     array = FFF0
&array[0] = FFF0
```

Fig. 6.12   The name of an array is the same as the address of the array's first element.

Software Engineering Observation 6.2

It is possible to pass an array by value by using a simple trick we explain in Chapter 10.

Although entire arrays are passed simulated call by reference, individual array elements are passed call by value exactly as simple variables are. Such simple single pieces of data are called *scalars* or *scalar quantities*. To pass an element of an array to a function, use the subscripted name of the array element as an argument in the function call. In Chapter 7, we show how to simulate call by reference for scalars (i.e., individual variables and array elements).

For a function to receive an array through a function call, the function's parameter list must specify that an array will be received. For example, the function header for function **modifyArray** might be written as

```
void modifyArray(int b[], int size)
```

indicating that **modifyArray** expects to receive an array of integers in parameter **b** and the number of array elements in parameter **size**. The size of the array is not required between the array brackets. If it is included, the compiler will ignore it. Because arrays are automatically passed simulated call by reference, when the called function uses the array name **b**, it will in fact be referring to the actual array in the caller (array **hourlyTemperatures** in the preceding call). In Chapter 7, we introduce other notations for indicating that an array is being received by a function. As we will see, these notations are based on the intimate relationship between arrays and pointers in C.

Note the strange appearance of the function prototype for **modifyArray**

```
void modifyArray(int [], int);
```

This prototype could have been written

```
void modifyArray(int anyArrayName[], int anyVariableName)
```

but as we learned in Chapter 5, the C compiler ignores variable names in prototypes.

Good Programming Practice 6.6

Some programmers include variable names in function prototypes to make programs clearer. The compiler ignores these names.

Remember, the prototype tells the compiler the number of arguments and the types of each argument (in the order in which the arguments are executed) to appear.

The program in Fig. 6.13 demonstrates the difference between passing an entire array and passing an array element. The program first prints the five elements of integer array **a**. Next, **a** and its size are passed to function **modifyArray** where each of **a**'s elements is multiplied by 2. Then **a** is reprinted in **main**. As the output shows, the elements of **a** are indeed modified by **modifyArray**. Now the program prints the value of **a[3]** and passes it to function **modifyElement**. Function **modifyElement** multiplies its argument by 2 and prints the new value. Note that when **a[3]** is reprinted in **main**, it has not been modified because individual array elements are passed call by value.

```
/* Passing arrays and individual array elements to functions */
#include <stdio.h>
#define SIZE 5

void modifyArray(int [], int);   /* appears strange */
void modifyElement(int);

main()
{
   int a[SIZE] = {0, 1, 2, 3, 4};
   int i;

   printf("Effects of passing entire array call "
          "by reference:\n\nThe values of the "
          "original array are:\n");

   for (i = 0; i <= SIZE - 1; i++)
      printf("%3d", a[i]);

   printf("\n");
   modifyArray(a, SIZE);   /* array a passed call by reference */
   printf("The values of the modified array are:\n");

   for (i = 0; i <= SIZE - 1; i++)
      printf("%3d", a[i]);

   printf("\n\n\nEffects of passing array element call "
          "by value:\n\nThe value of a[3] is %d\n", a[3]);
   modifyElement(a[3]);
   printf("The value of a[3] is %d\n", a[3]);
   return 0;
}
```

Fig. 6.13 Passing arrays and individual array elements to functions (part 1 of 2).

```
void modifyArray(int b[], int size)
{
   int j;

   for (j = 0; j <= size - 1; j++)
      b[j] *= 2;
}

void modifyElement(int e)
{
   printf("Value in modifyElement is %d\n", e *= 2);
}
```

```
Effects of passing entire array call by reference:

The values of the original array are:
   0   1   2   3   4
The values of the modified array are:
   0   2   4   6   8


Effects of passing array element call by value:

The value of a[3] is 6
Value in modifyElement is 12
The value of a[3] is 6
```

Fig. 6.13   Passing arrays and individual array elements to functions (part 2 of 2).

There may be situations in your programs in which a function should not be allowed to modify array elements. Because arrays are always passed simulated call by reference, modification of values in an array is difficult to control. C provides the special type qualifier **const** to prevent modification of array values in a function. When an array parameter is preceded by the **const** qualifier, the elements of the array become constant in the function body, and any attempt to modify an element of the array in the function body results in a compile time error. This enables the programmer to correct a program so it does not attempt to modify array elements. Although the **const** qualifier is well defined in the ANSI standard, C systems vary in their ability to enforce it.

Figure 6.14 demonstrates the **const** qualifier. Function **tryToModifyArray** is defined with parameter **const int b[]** which specifies that array **b** is constant and cannot be modified. The output shows the error messages produced by the Borland C++ compiler. Each of the three attempts by the function to modify array elements results in the compiler error "**Cannot modify a const object**." The **const** qualifier will be discussed again in Chapter 7.

Software Engineering Observation 6.3

*The **const** type qualifier can be applied to an array parameter in a function definition to prevent the original array from being modified in the function body. This is another example of the principle of least privilege. Functions should not be given the capability to modify an array unless it is absolutely necessary.*

```
/* Demonstrating the const type qualifier */
#include <stdio.h>

void tryToModifyArray(const int []);

main()
{
    int a[] = {10, 20, 30};

    tryToModifyArray(a);
    printf("%d %d %d\n", a[0], a[1], a[2]);
    return 0;
}

void tryToModifyArray(const int b[])
{
    b[0] /= 2;     /* error */
    b[1] /= 2;     /* error */
    b[2] /= 2;     /* error */
}
```

```
Compiling FIG6_14.C:
Error FIG6_14.C 16: Cannot modify a const object
Error FIG6_14.C 17: Cannot modify a const object
Error FIG6_14.C 18: Cannot modify a const object
Warning FIG6_14.C 19: Parameter 'b' is never used
```

Fig. 6.14　Demonstrating the const type qualifier.

6.6 Sorting Arrays

Sorting data (i.e., placing the data into some particular order such as ascending or descending) is one of the most important computing applications. A bank sorts all checks by account number so that it can prepare individual bank statements at the end of each month. Telephone companies sort their lists of accounts by last name and, within that, by first name to make it easy to find phone numbers. Virtually every organization must sort some data and in many cases massive amounts of data. Sorting data is an intriguing problem which has attracted some of the most intense research efforts in the field of computer science. In this chapter we discuss what is perhaps the simplest known sorting scheme. In the exercises and in Chapter 12, we investigate more complex schemes that yield far superior performance.

Performance Tip 6.5

Often, the simplest algorithms perform poorly. Their virtue is that they are easy to write, test and debug. However, more complex algorithms are often needed to realize maximum performance.

The program in Fig. 6.15 sorts the values in the elements of the ten-element array **a** into ascending order. The technique we use is called the *bubble sort* or the *sinking sort* because the smaller values gradually "bubble" their way upward to the top of the array like air bubbles rising in water, while the larger values sink to the bottom of the array. The technique is to make several passes through the array. On each pass, successive pairs of elements are compared. If a pair is in increasing order (or if the values are identical), we leave the values as they are. If a pair is in decreasing order, their values are swapped in the array.

```
/* This program sorts an array's values into
   ascending order */
#include <stdio.h>
#define SIZE 10

main()
{
    int a[SIZE] = {2, 6, 4, 8, 10, 12, 89, 68, 45, 37};
    int i, pass, hold;

    printf("Data items in original order\n");

    for (i = 0; i <= SIZE - 1; i++)
       printf("%4d", a[i]);

    for (pass = 1; pass <= SIZE - 1; pass++)   /* passes */

        for (i = 0; i <= SIZE - 2; i++)        /* one pass */

            if (a[i] > a[i + 1]) {        /* one comparison */
                hold = a[i];              /* one swap */
                a[i] = a[i + 1];
                a[i + 1] = hold;
            }

    printf("\nData items in ascending order\n");

    for (i = 0; i <= SIZE - 1; i++)
       printf("%4d", a[i]);

    printf("\n");

    return 0;
}
```

```
Data items in original order
   2    6    4    8   10   12   89   68   45   37
Data items in ascending order
   2    4    6    8   10   12   37   45   68   89
```

Fig. 6.15 Sorting an array with bubble sort.

First the program compares **a[0]** to **a[1]**, then **a[1]** to **a[2]**, then **a[2]** to **a[3]**, and so on until it completes the pass by comparing **a[8]** to **a[9]**. Note that although there are 10 elements, only nine comparisons are performed. Because of the way the successive comparisons are made, a large value may move down the array many positions on a single pass, but a small value may move up only one position. On the first pass, the largest value is guaranteed to sink to the bottom element of the array, **a[9]**. On the second pass, the second largest value is guaranteed to sink to **a[8]**. On the ninth pass, the ninth largest value sinks to **a[1]**. This leaves the smallest value in **a[0]**, so only nine passes of the array are needed to sort the array even though there are ten elements.

The sorting is performed by the nested **for** loop. If a swap is necessary, it is performed by the three assignments

```
hold = a[i];
a[i] = a[i + 1];
a[i + 1] = hold;
```

where the extra variable **hold** temporarily stores one of the two values being swapped. The swap cannot be performed with only the two assignments

```
a[i] = a[i + 1];
a[i + 1] = a[i];
```

If, for example, **a[i]** is **7** and **a[i + 1]** is **5**, after the first assignment both values will be **5** and the value **7** will be lost. Hence the need for the extra variable **hold**.

The chief virtue of the bubble sort is that it is easy to program. However, the bubble sort runs slowly. This becomes apparent when sorting large arrays. In the exercises, we will develop more efficient versions of the bubble sort. Far more efficient sorts than the bubble sort have been developed. We will investigate a few of these later in the text. More advanced courses investigate sorting and searching in greater depth.

6.7 Case Study: Computing Mean, Median, and Mode Using Arrays

We now consider a larger example. Computers are commonly used to compile and analyze the results of surveys and opinion polls. The program in Fig. 6.16 uses array **response** initialized with 99 (represented by symbolic constant **SIZE**) responses to a survey. Each of the responses is a number from 1 to 9. The program computes the mean, median, and mode of the 99 values.

The mean is the arithmetic average of the 99 values. Function **mean** computes the mean by totaling the 99 elements and dividing the result by 99.

The median is the "middle value." Function **median** determines the median by calling function **bubbleSort** to sort the array of responses into ascending order, and picking the middle element, **answer[SIZE / 2]**, of the sorted array. Note that when there is an even number of elements, the median should be calculated as the mean of the two middle elements. Function **median** does not currently provide this capability. Function **printArray** is called to output the **response** array.

The mode is the value that occurs most frequently among the 99 responses. Function **mode** determines the mode by counting the number of responses of each type, then selecting the value with the greatest count. This version of function **mode** does not handle a tie (see Exercise 6.14). Function **mode** also produces a histogram to aid in determining the mode graphically. Fig. 6.17 contains a sample run of this program. This example includes most of the common manipulations usually required in array problems, including passing arrays to functions.

```c
/* This program introduces the topic of survey data analysis.
   It computes the mean, median, and  mode of the data */
#include <stdio.h>
#define SIZE 99

void mean(int []);
void median(int []);
void mode(int [], int []);
void bubbleSort(int[]);
void printArray(int[]);

main()
{
   int frequency[10] = {0},
       response[SIZE] = {6, 7, 8, 9, 8, 7, 8, 9, 8, 9,
                         7, 8, 9, 5, 9, 8, 7, 8, 7, 8,
                         6, 7, 8, 9, 3, 9, 8, 7, 8, 7,
                         7, 8, 9, 8, 9, 8, 9, 7, 8, 9,
                         6, 7, 8, 7, 8, 7, 9, 8, 9, 2,
                         7, 8, 9, 8, 9, 8, 9, 7, 5, 3,
                         5, 6, 7, 2, 5, 3, 9, 4, 6, 4,
                         7, 8, 9, 6, 8, 7, 8, 9, 7, 8,
                         7, 4, 4, 2, 5, 3, 8, 7, 5, 6,
                         4, 5, 6, 1, 6, 5, 7, 8, 7};
   mean(response);
   median(response);
   mode(frequency, response);
   return 0;
}

void mean(int answer[])
{
   int j, total = 0;

   printf("%s\n%s\n%s\n", "********", "  Mean", "********");

   for (j = 0; j <= SIZE - 1; j++)
      total += answer[j];

   printf("The mean is the average value of the data\n"
          "items. The mean is equal to the total of\n"
          "all the data items divided by the number\n"
          "of data items (%d). The mean value for\n"
          "this run is: %d / %d = %.4f\n\n",
          SIZE, total, SIZE, (float) total / SIZE);
}
```

Fig. 6.16 Survey data analysis program (part 1 of 3).

```c
void median(int answer[])
{
   printf("\n%s\n%s\n%s\n%s",
          "********", " Median", "********",
          "The unsorted array of responses is");

   printArray(answer);
   bubbleSort(answer);
   printf("\n\nThe sorted array is");
   printArray(answer);
   printf("\n\nThe median is element %d of\n"
          "the sorted %d element array.\n"
          "For this run the median is %d\n\n",
          SIZE / 2, SIZE, answer[SIZE / 2]);
}


void mode(int freq[], int answer[])
{
   int rating, j, h, largest = 0, modeValue = 0;

   printf("\n%s\n%s\n%s\n",
          "********", "  Mode", "********");

   for (rating = 1; rating <= 9; rating++)
      freq[rating] = 0;

   for (j = 0; j <= SIZE - 1; j++)
      ++freq[answer[j]];

   printf("%s%11s%19s\n\n%54s\n%54s\n\n",
          "Response", "Frequency", "Histogram",
          "1    1    2    2", "5    0    5    0    5");

   for (rating = 1; rating <= 9; rating++) {
      printf("%8d%11d          ", rating, freq[rating]);

      if (freq[rating] > largest) {
         largest = freq[rating];
         modeValue = rating;
      }

      for (h = 1; h <= freq[rating]; h++)
         printf("*");

      printf("\n");
   }

   printf("The mode is the most frequent value.\n"
          "For this run the mode is %d which occurred"
          " %d times.\n", modeValue, largest);
}
```

Fig. 6.16   Survey data analysis program (part 2 of 3).

```
void bubbleSort(int a[])
{
    int pass, j, hold;

    for (pass = 1; pass <= SIZE - 1; pass++)

        for (j = 0; j <= SIZE - 2; j++)

            if (a[j] > a[j+1]) {
                hold = a[j];
                a[j] = a[j+1];
                a[j+1] = hold;
            }
}

void printArray(int a[])
{
    int j;

    for (j = 0; j <= SIZE - 1; j++) {

        if (j % 20 == 0)
            printf("\n");

        printf("%2d", a[j]);
    }
}
```

Fig. 6.16 Survey data analysis program (part 3 of 3).

6.8 Searching Arrays

Often, a programmer will be working with large amounts of data stored in arrays. It may be necessary to determine whether an array contains a value that matches a certain *key value*. The process of finding a particular element of an array is called *searching*. In this section we discuss two searching techniques—the simple *linear search* technique and the more efficient *binary search* technique. Exercises 6.34 and 6.35 at the end of this chapter ask you to implement recursive versions of the linear search and the binary search.

The linear search (Fig. 6.18) compares each element of the array with the *search key*. Since the array is not in any particular order, it is just as likely that the value will be found in the first element as the last. On average, therefore, the program will have to compare the search key with half the elements of the array.

The linear searching method works well for small arrays or for unsorted arrays. However, for large arrays linear searching is inefficient. If the array is sorted, the high-speed binary search technique can be used.

The binary search algorithm eliminates one half of the elements in the array being searched after each comparison. The algorithm locates the middle element of the array and compares it to the search key. If they are equal, the search key is found and the array subscript of that element is returned. If they are not equal, the problem is reduced to

```
********
  Mean
********
The mean is the average value of the data
items. The mean is equal to the total of
all the data items divided by the number
of data items (99). The mean value for
this run is: 681 / 99 = 6.8788


********
  Median
********
The unsorted array of responses is
  6 7 8 9 8 7 8 9 8 9 7 8 9 5 9 8 7 8 7 8
  6 7 8 9 3 9 8 7 8 7 7 8 9 8 9 8 9 7 8 9
  6 7 8 7 8 7 9 8 9 2 7 8 9 8 9 8 9 7 5 3
  5 6 7 2 5 3 9 4 6 4 7 8 9 6 8 7 8 9 7 8
  7 4 4 2 5 3 8 7 5 6 4 5 6 1 6 5 7 8 7

The sorted array is
  1 2 2 2 3 3 3 3 4 4 4 4 4 5 5 5 5 5 5 5
  5 6 6 6 6 6 6 6 6 6 6 7 7 7 7 7 7 7 7 7
  7 7 7 7 7 7 7 7 7 7 7 7 7 8 8 8 8 8 8 8
  8 8 8 8 8 8 8 8 8 8 8 8 8 8 8 8 8 8 8 8
  9 9 9 9 9 9 9 9 9 9 9 9 9 9 9 9 9 9 9

The median is element 49 of
the sorted 99 element array.
For this run the median is 7


********
  Mode
********
Response  Frequency          Histogram

                                  1   1   2   2
                              5   0   5   0   5

        1          1        *
        2          3        ***
        3          4        ****
        4          5        *****
        5          8        ********
        6          9        *********
        7         23        ***********************
        8         27        ***************************
        9         19        *******************
The mode is the most frequent value.
For this run the mode is 8 which occurred 27 times.
```

Fig. 6.17 Sample run for the survey data analysis program.

```
/* Linear search of an array */
#include <stdio.h>
#define SIZE 100

int linearSearch(int [], int, int);

main()
{
   int a[SIZE], x, searchKey, element;

   for (x = 0; x <= SIZE - 1; x++)   /* create some data */
      a[x] = 2 * x;

   printf("Enter integer search key:\n");
   scanf("%d", &searchKey);
   element = linearSearch(a, searchKey, SIZE);

   if (element != -1)
      printf("Found value in element %d\n", element);
   else
      printf("Value not found\n");

   return 0;
}

int linearSearch(int array[], int key, int size)
{
   int n;

   for (n = 0; n <= size - 1; n++)
      if (array[n] == key)
         return n;

   return -1;
}
```

```
Enter integer search key:
36
Found value in element 18
```

```
Enter integer search key:
37
Value not found
```

Fig. 6.18   Linear search of an array.

searching one half of the array. If the search key is less than the middle element of the array, the first half of the array is searched, otherwise the second half of the array is searched. If the search key is not found in the specified subarray (piece of the original array), the algorithm is repeated on one quarter of the original array. The search continues until the search key is equal to the middle element of a subarray, or until the subarray consists of one element that is not equal to the search key (i.e., the search key is not found).

In a worst case scenario, searching an array of 1024 elements will take only 10 comparisons using a binary search. Repeatedly dividing 1024 by 2 yields the values 512, 256, 128, 64, 32, 16, 8, 4, 2, and 1. The number 1024 (2^{10}) is divided by 2 only ten times to get the value 1. Dividing by 2 is equivalent to one comparison in the binary search algorithm. An array of 1048576 (2^{20}) elements takes a maximum of 20 comparisons to find the search key. An array of one billion elements takes a maximum of 30 comparisons to find the search key. This is a tremendous increase in performance over the linear search that required comparing the search key to an average of half the elements in the array. For a one billion element array, this is a difference between an average of 500 million comparisons and a maximum of 30 comparisons! The maximum comparisons for any array can be determined by finding the first power of 2 greater than the number of elements in the array.

Figure 6.19 presents the iterative version of function **binarySearch**. The function receives four arguments—an integer array **b**, an integer **searchKey**, the **low** array subscript, and the **high** array subscript. If the search key does not match the middle element of a subarray, the **low** subscript or **high** subscript is modified so a smaller subarray can be searched. If the search key is less than the middle element, the **high** subscript is set to **middle - 1**, and the search is continued on the elements from **low** to **middle - 1**. If the search key is greater than the middle element, the **low** subscript is set to **middle + 1**, and the search is continued on the elements from **middle + 1** to **high**. The program uses an array of 15 elements. The first power of 2 greater than the number of elements in this array is 16 (2^4), so a maximum of 4 comparisons are required to find the search key. The program uses function **printHeader** to output the array subscripts and function **printRow** to output each subarray during the binary search process. The middle element in each subarray is marked with an asterisk (*****) to indicate the element to which the search key is compared.

6.9 Multiple-Subscripted Arrays

Arrays in C can have multiple subscripts. A common use of multiple-subscripted arrays is to represent *tables* of values consisting of information arranged in *rows* and *columns*. To identify a particular table element, we must specify two subscripts: The first (by convention) identifies the element's row, and the second (by convention) identifies the element's column. Tables or arrays that require two subscripts to identify a particular element are called *double-subscripted arrays*. Note that multiple-subscripted arrays can have more than two subscripts. The ANSI standard states that an ANSI C system must support at least 12 array subscripts.

Fig. 6.20 illustrates a double-subscripted array, **a**. The array contains three rows and four columns, so it is said to be a 3-by-4 array. In general, an array with *m* rows and *n* columns is called an *m-by-n array*.

```
/* Binary search of an array */

#include <stdio.h>
#define SIZE 15

int binarySearch(int [], int, int, int);
void printHeader(void);
void printRow(int [], int, int, int);


main()
{
   int a[SIZE], i, key, result;

   for (i = 0; i <= SIZE - 1; i++)
      a[i] = 2 * i;

   printf("Enter a number between 0 and 28: ");
   scanf("%d", &key);

   printHeader();
   result = binarySearch(a, key, 0, SIZE - 1);

   if (result != -1)
      printf("\n%d found in array element %d\n", key, result);
   else
      printf("\n%d not found\n", key);

   return 0;
}


int binarySearch(int b[], int searchKey, int low, int high)
{
   int middle;

   while (low <= high) {
      middle = (low + high) / 2;

      printRow(b, low, middle, high);

      if (searchKey == b[middle])
         return middle;
      else if (searchKey < b[middle])
         high = middle - 1;
      else
         low = middle + 1;
   }

   return -1;    /* searchKey not found */
}
```

Fig. 6.19 Binary search of a sorted array (part 1 of 3).

```
/* Print a header for the output */
void printHeader(void)
{
   int i;

   printf("\nSubscripts:\n");

   for (i = 0; i <= SIZE - 1; i++)
      printf("%3d ", i);

   printf("\n");

   for (i = 1; i <= 4 * SIZE; i++)
      printf("-");

   printf("\n");
}

/* Print one row of output showing the current
   part of the array being processed. */
void printRow(int b[], int low, int mid, int high)
{
   int i;

   for (i = 0; i <= SIZE - 1; i++)
      if (i < low || i > high)
         printf("    ");
      else if (i == mid)
         printf("%3d*", b[i]);  /* mark middle value */
      else
         printf("%3d ", b[i]);

   printf("\n");
}
```

Fig. 6.19 Binary search of a sorted array (part 2 of 3).

Every element in array **a** is identified in Fig. 6.20 by an element name of the form **a[i][j]**; **a** is the name of the array, and **i** and **j** are the subscripts that uniquely identify each element in **a**. Notice that the names of the elements in the first row all have a first subscript of **0**; the names of the elements in the fourth column all have a second subscript of **3**.

Common Programming Error 6.9

*Referencing a double-subscripted array element **a[x][y]** incorrectly as **a[x, y]**.*

A multiple-subscripted array can be initialized in its declaration much like a single subscripted array. For example, a double-subscripted array **b[2][2]** could be declared and initialized with

```
int b[2][2] = {{1, 2}, {3, 4}};
```

```
Enter a number between 0 and 28: 25

Subscripts:
 0   1   2   3   4   5   6   7   8   9  10  11  12  13  14
-----------------------------------------------------------
 0   2   4   6   8  10  12  14* 16  18  20  22  24  26  28
                            16  18  20  22* 24  26  28
                                            24  26* 28
                                            24*

25 not found
```

```
Enter a number between 0 and 28: 8

Subscripts:
 0   1   2   3   4   5   6   7   8   9  10  11  12  13  14
-----------------------------------------------------------
 0   2   4   6   8  10  12  14* 16  18  20  22  24  26  28
 0   2   4   6*  8  10  12
             8  10* 12
             8*

8 found in array element 4
```

```
Enter a number between 0 and 28: 6

Subscripts:
 0   1   2   3   4   5   6   7   8   9  10  11  12  13  14
-----------------------------------------------------------
 0   2   4   6   8  10  12  14* 16  18  20  22  24  26  28
 0   2   4   6*  8  10  12

6 found in array element 3
```

Fig. 6.19   Binary search of a sorted array (part 3 of 3).

The values are grouped by row in braces. So, **1** and **2** initialize **b[0][0]** and **b[0][1]**, and **3** and **4** initialize **b[1][0]** and **b[1][1]**. If there are not enough initializers for a given row, the remaining elements of that row are initialized to **0**. Thus, the declaration

```
int b[2][2] = {{1}, {3, 4}};
```

would initialize **b[0][0]** to **1**, **b[0][1]** to **0**, **b[1][0]** to **3** and **b[1][1]** to **4**.

Figure 6.21 demonstrates initializing double-subscripted arrays in declarations. The program declares three arrays of two rows and three columns (six elements each). The

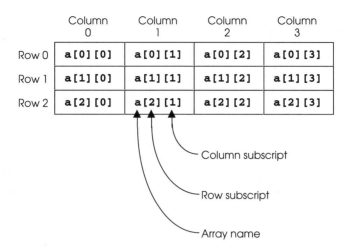

Fig. 6.20   A double-subscripted array with three rows and four columns.

declaration of **array1** provides six initializers in two sublists. The first sublist initializes the first row of the array to the values 1, 2, and 3; and the second sublist initializes the second row of the array to the values 4, 5, and 6. If the braces around each sublist are removed from the **array1** initializer list, the compiler automatically initializes the elements of the first row followed by the elements of the second row. The declaration of **array2** provides five initializers. The initializers are assigned to the first row then the second row. Any elements that do not have an explicit initializer are initialized to zero automatically, so **array2[1][2]** is initialized to 0. The declaration of **array3** provides three initializers in two sublists. The sublist for the first row explicitly initializes the first two elements of the first row to 1 and 2. The third element is automatically initialized to zero. The sublist for the second row explicitly initializes the first element to 4. The last two elements are automatically initialized to zero.

The program calls function **printArray** to output each array's elements. Notice that the function definition specifies the array parameter as **int a[][3]**. When we receive a single-subscripted array as an argument to a function, the array brackets are empty in the function's parameter list. The first subscript of a multiple-subscripted array is not required either, but all subsequent subscripts are required. The compiler uses these subscripts to determine the locations in memory of elements in multiple-subscripted arrays. All array elements are stored consecutively in memory regardless of the number of subscripts. In a double-subscripted array, the first row is stored in memory followed by the second row.

Providing the subscript values in a parameter declaration enables the compiler to tell the function how to locate an element in the array. In a double-subscripted array, each row is basically a single-subscripted array. To locate an element in a particular row, the compiler must know exactly how many elements are in each row so it can skip the proper number of memory locations when accessing the array. Thus, when accessing **a[1][2]** in our example, the compiler knows to skip the three elements of the first row in memory

```
/* Initializing multidimensional arrays */
#include <stdio.h>

void printArray(int [][3]);

main()
{
    int array1[2][3] = { {1, 2, 3}, {4, 5, 6} },
        array2[2][3] = { 1, 2, 3, 4, 5 },
        array3[2][3] = { {1, 2}, {4} };

    printf("Values in array1 by row are:\n");
    printArray(array1);

    printf("Values in array2 by row are:\n");
    printArray(array2);

    printf("Values in array3 by row are:\n");
    printArray(array3);

    return 0;
}

void printArray(int a[][3])
{
    int i, j;

    for (i = 0; i <= 1; i++) {

        for (j = 0; j <= 2; j++)
            printf("%d ", a[i][j]);

        printf("\n");
    }
}
```

```
Values in array1 by row are:
1 2 3
4 5 6
Values in array2 by row are:
1 2 3
4 5 0
Values in array3 by row are:
1 2 0
4 0 0
```

Fig. 6.21 Initializing multidimensional arrays.

to get to the second row (row 1). Then, the compiler accesses the third element of that row (element 2).

Many common array manipulations use **for** repetition structures. For example, the following structure sets all the elements in the third row of array **a** in Fig. 6.20 to zero:

```
for (column = 0; column <= 3; column++)
    a[2][column] = 0;
```

We specified the *third* row, therefore we know that the first subscript is always **2** (**0** is the first row, and **1** is the second row). The **for** loop varies only the second subscript (i.e., the column subscript). The preceding **for** structure is equivalent to the assignment statements:

```
a[2][0] = 0;
a[2][1] = 0;
a[2][2] = 0;
a[2][3] = 0;
```

The following nested **for** structure determines the total of all the elements in array **a**.

```
total = 0;

for (row = 0; row <= 2; row++)

    for (column = 0; column <= 3; column++)
        total += a[row][column];
```

The **for** structure totals the elements of the array one row at a time. The outer **for** structure begins by setting **row** (i.e., the row subscript) to **0** so the elements of the first row may be totaled by the inner **for** structure. The outer **for** structure increments **row** to **1**, so the elements of the second row can be totaled. Then, the outer **for** structure increments **row** to **2**, so the elements of the third row can be totaled. The result is printed when the nested **for** structure terminates.

The program of Fig. 6.22 performs several other common array manipulations on 3-by-4 array **studentGrades** using **for** structures. Each row of the array represents a student and each column represents a grade on one of the four exams the students took during the semester. The array manipulations are performed by four functions. Function **minimum** determines the lowest grade of any student for the semester. Function **maximum** determines the highest grade of any student for the semester. Function **average** determines a particular student's semester average. Function **printArray** outputs the double-subscripted array in a neat, tabular format.

Functions **minimum**, **maximum**, and **printArray** each receive three arguments—the **studentGrades** array (called **grades** in each function), the number of students (rows of the array), and the number of exams (columns of the array). Each function loops through array **grades** using nested **for** structures. The following nested **for** structure is from the function **minimum** definition:

```
for (i = 0; i <= pupils - 1; i++)
    for (j = 0; j <= tests - 1; j++)
        if (grades[i][j] < lowGrade)
            lowGrade = grades[i][j];
```

```
/* Double-subscripted array example */
#include <stdio.h>
#define STUDENTS 3
#define EXAMS 4

int minimum(int [][EXAMS], int, int);
int maximum(int [][EXAMS], int, int);
float average(int [], int);
void printArray(int [][EXAMS], int, int);

main()
{
   int student,
       studentGrades[STUDENTS][EXAMS] = {{77, 68, 86, 73},
                                         {96, 87, 89, 78},
                                         {70, 90, 86, 81}};

   printf("The array is:\n");
   printArray(studentGrades, STUDENTS, EXAMS);
   printf("\n\nLowest grade: %d\nHighest grade: %d\n",
          minimum(studentGrades, STUDENTS, EXAMS),
          maximum(studentGrades, STUDENTS, EXAMS));

   for (student = 0; student <= STUDENTS - 1; student++)
      printf("The average grade for student %d is %.2f\n",
             student, average(studentGrades[student], EXAMS));

   return 0;
}

/* Find the minimum grade */
int minimum(int grades[][EXAMS], int pupils, int tests)
{
   int i, j, lowGrade = 100;

   for (i = 0; i <= pupils - 1; i++)
      for (j = 0; j <= tests - 1; j++)
         if (grades[i][j] < lowGrade)
            lowGrade = grades[i][j];

   return lowGrade;
}

/* Find the maximum grade */
int maximum(int grades[][EXAMS], int pupils, int tests)
{
   int i, j, highGrade = 0;

   for (i = 0; i <= pupils - 1; i++)
      for (j = 0; j <= tests - 1; j++)
         if (grades[i][j] > highGrade)
            highGrade = grades[i][j];

   return highGrade;
}
```

Fig. 6.22   Example of using double-subscripted arrays (part 1 of 2).

```
/* Determine the average grade for a particular exam */
float average(int setOfGrades[], int tests)
{
   int i, total = 0;

   for (i = 0; i <= tests - 1; i++)
      total += setOfGrades[i];

   return (float) total / tests;
}

/* Print the array */
void printArray(int grades[][EXAMS], int pupils, int tests)
{
   int i, j;

   printf("                    [0]   [1]   [2]   [3]");

   for (i = 0; i <= pupils - 1; i++) {
      printf("\nstudentGrades[%d] ", i);

      for (j = 0; j <= tests - 1; j++)
         printf("%-5d", grades[i][j]);
   }
}
```

```
The array is:
                  [0]   [1]   [2]   [3]
studentGrades[0]  77    68    86    73
studentGrades[1]  96    87    89    78
studentGrades[2]  70    90    86    81

Lowest grade: 68
Highest grade: 96
The average grade for student 0 is 76.00
The average grade for student 1 is 87.50
The average grade for student 2 is 81.75
```

The outer **for** structure begins by setting **i** (i.e., the row subscript) to **0** so the elements of the first row can be compared to variable **lowGrade** in the body of the inner **for** structure. The inner **for** structure loops through the four grades of a particular row and compares each grade to **lowGrade**. If a grade is less than **lowGrade**, **lowGrade** is set to that grade. The outer **for** structure then increments the row subscript to **1**. The elements of the second row are compared to variable **lowGrade**. The outer **for** structure then increments the row subscript to **2**. The elements of the third row are compared to variable **lowGrade**. When execution of the nested structure is complete, **lowGrade** contains the smallest grade in the double-subscripted array. Function **maximum** works similarly to function **minimum**.

Function **average** takes two arguments—a single-subscripted array of test results for a particular student called **setOfGrades** and the number of test results in the array. When **average** is called, the first argument passed is **studentGrades[student]**. This causes the address of one row of the double-subscripted array to be passed to **average**. The argument **studentGrades[1]** is the starting address of the second row of the array. Remember that a double-subscripted array is basically an array of single-subscripted arrays, and that the name of a single-subscripted array is the address of the array in memory. Function **average** calculates the sum of the array elements, divides the total by the number of test results, and returns the floating-point result.

Summary

- C stores lists of values in arrays. An array is a group of related memory locations. These locations are related by the fact that they all have the same name and the same type. To refer to a particular location or element within the array, we specify the name of the array and the subscript.

- A subscript may be an integer or an integer expression. If a program uses an expression as a subscript, then the expression is evaluated to determine the particular element of the array.

- It is important to note the difference when referring to the seventh element of the array as opposed to array element seven. The seventh element has a subscript of **6**, while array element seven has a subscript of **7** (actually the eighth element of the array). This is a source of "off-by-one" errors.

- Arrays occupy space in memory. To reserve 100 elements for integer array **b** and 27 elements for integer array **x**, the programmer writes

      ```
      int b[100], x[27];
      ```
- An array of type **char** can be used to store a character string.

- The elements of an array can be initialized three ways: by declaration, by assignment, and by input.

- If there are fewer initializers than elements in the array, C automatically initializes the remaining elements to zero.

- C does not prevent referencing elements beyond the bounds of an array.

- A character array can be initialized using a string literal.

- All strings in C end with the null character. The character constant representation of the null character is **'\0'**.

- Character arrays can be initialized with character constants in an initializer list.

- Individual characters in a string stored in an array can be accessed directly using array subscript notation.

- A string can be input directly into a character array from the keyboard using **scanf** and the conversion specification **%s**.

- A character array representing a string can be output with **printf** and the **%s** conversion specifier.

- Apply **static** to a local array declaration so the array is not created each time the function is called and the array is not destroyed each time the function exits.

- Arrays that are declared **static** are automatically initialized once at compile time. If the programmer does not explicitly initialize a **static** array, it is initialized to zero by the compiler.

- To pass an array to a function, the name of the array is passed. To pass a single element of an array to a function, simply pass the name of the array followed by the subscript (contained in square brackets) of the particular element.

- C passes arrays to functions using simulated call by reference—the called functions can modify the element values in the callers' original arrays. The name of the array is actually the address of the first element of the array! Because the starting address of the array is passed, the called function knows precisely where the array is stored.

- To receive an array argument, the function's parameter list must specify that an array will be received. The size of the array is not required in the array brackets.

- The **%p** conversion specification normally outputs addresses as hexadecimal numbers.

- C provides the special type qualifier **const** to prevent modification of array values in a function. When an array parameter is preceded by the **const** qualifier, the elements of the array become constant in the function body, and any attempt to modify an element of the array in the function body results in a compile time error.

- An array can be sorted using the bubble sort technique. Several passes of the array are made. On each pass, successive pairs of elements are compared. If a pair is in order (or if the values are identical), it is left as is. If a pair is out of order, the values are swapped. For small arrays, the bubble sort is acceptable, but for larger arrays it is inefficient compared to other more sophisticated sorting algorithms.

- The linear search compares each element of the array with the search key. Since the array is not in any particular order, it is just as likely that the value will be found in the first element as the last. On average, therefore, the program will have to compare the search key with half the elements of the array. The linear searching method works well for small arrays or for unsorted arrays.

- The binary search algorithm eliminates one half of the elements in the array being searched after each comparison. The algorithm locates the middle element of the array and compares it to the search key. If they are equal, the search key is found and the array subscript of that element is returned. If they are not equal, the problem is reduced to searching one half of the array.

- In a worst case scenario, searching an array of 1024 elements will take only 10 comparisons using a binary search. An array of 1048576 (2^{20}) elements takes a maximum of 20 comparisons to find the search key. An array of one billion elements takes a maximum of 30 comparisons to find the search key.

- Arrays may be used to represent tables of values consisting of information arranged in rows and columns. To identify a particular element of a table, two subscripts are specified: The first (by convention) identifies the row in which the element is contained, and the second (by convention) identifies the column in which the element is contained. Tables or arrays that require two subscripts to identify a particular element are called double-subscripted arrays.

- The standard states that an ANSI C system must support at least 12 array subscripts.

- A multiple-subscripted array can be initialized in its declaration using an initializer list.

- When we receive a single-subscripted array as an argument to a function, the array brackets are empty in the function's parameter list. The first subscript of a multiple-subscripted array is not required either, but all subsequent subscripts are required. The compiler uses these subscripts to determine the locations in memory of elements in mulitple-subscripted arrays.

- To pass one row of a double-subscripted array to a function that receives a single-subscripted array, simply pass the name of the array followed by the first subscript.

Terminology

a[i]
a[i][j]
array
array initializer list
bar chart
bounds checking
bubble sort
column subscript
declare an array
#define preprocessor directive
double precision
double-subscripted array
element of an array
expression as a subscript
histogram
initialize an array
linear search
m-by-n array
mean
median
mode
multiple-subscripted array
name of an array
null character '\0'
off-by-one error
pass-by-reference
passing arrays to functions

%p conversion specification
position number
replacement text
row subscript
scalability
scalar
scalar quantity
search key
searching an array
single-subscripted array
sinking sort
sorting
sorting pass
sorting the elements of an array
square brackets
string
subscript
survey data analysis
symbolic constant
table of values
tabular format
temporary area for exchange of values
totaling the elements of an array
triple-subscripted array
value of an element
walk off an array
zeroth element

Common Programming Errors

6.1   It is important to note the difference between the "seventh element of the array" and "array element seven." Because array subscripts begin at 0, the "seventh element of the array" has a subscript of *6*, while "array element seven" has a subscript of *7* and is actually the eighth element of the array. This is a source of "off-by-one" errors.

6.2   Forgetting to initialize the elements of an array whose elements should be initialized.

6.3   Providing more initializers in an array initializer list than there are elements in the array is a syntax error.

6.4   Ending a **#define** or **#include** preprocessor directive with a semicolon. Remember that preprocessor directives are not C statements.

6.5   Assigning a value to a symbolic constant in an executable statement is a syntax error. A symbolic constant is not a variable. No space is reserved for it by the compiler as with variables that hold values at execution time.

6.6   Referring to an element outside the array bounds.

6.7   Not providing **scanf** with a character array large enough to store a string typed at the keyboard can result in loss of data in a program and other run-time errors.

6.8   Assuming that elements of a local array that is declared *static* are initialized to zero every time the function is called in which the array is declared.

6.9   Referencing a double-subscripted array element as **a[x, y]** instead of **a[x][y]**.

Good Programming Practices

6.1   Use only uppercase letters for symbolic constant names. This makes these constants stand out in a program and reminds the programmer that symbolic constants are not variables.

6.2   Strive for program clarity. Sometimes it may be worthwhile to trade off the most efficient use of memory or processor time in favor of writing clearer programs.

6.3   When looping through an array, the array subscript should never go below 0 and should always be less than the total number of elements in the array (size − 1). Make sure the loop terminating condition prevents accessing elements outside this range.

6.4   Mention the high array subscript in a **for** structure to help eliminate off-by-one errors.

6.5   Programs should validate the correctness of all input values to prevent erroneous information from affecting a program's calculations.

6.6   Some programmers include variable names in function prototypes to make programs clearer. The compiler ignores these names.

Performance Tips

6.1   Sometimes performance considerations far outweigh clarity considerations.

6.2   The (normally serious) effects of referencing elements outside the array bounds are system dependent.

6.3   In functions that contain automatic arrays where the function is in and out of scope frequently, make the array *static* so it is not created each time the function is called.

6.4   Passing arrays simulated call by reference makes sense for performance reasons. If arrays were passed call by value, a copy of each element would be passed. For large, frequently passed arrays, this would be time consuming and would consume considerable storage for the copies of the arrays.

6.5   Often, the simplest algorithms perform poorly. Their virtue is that they are easy to write, test and debug. However, more complex algorithms are often needed to realize maximum performance.

Software Engineering Observations

6.1   Defining the size of your arrays as a symbolic constant makes your programs more scalable.

6.2   It is possible to pass an array by value by using a simple trick we explain in Chapter 10.

6.3   The `const` type qualifier can be applied to an array parameter in a function definition to prevent the original array from being modified in the function body. This is another example of the principle of least privilege. Functions should not be given the capability to modify an array unless it is absolutely necessary.

Self-Review Exercises

6.1   Answer each of the following:
a) Lists and tables of values are stored in _____.
b) The elements of an array are related by the fact that they have the same _____ and _____.
c) The number used to refer to a particular element of an array is called its _____.
d) A _____ should be used to declare the size of an array because it makes the program more scalable.
e) The process of placing the elements of an array in order is called _____ the array.
f) The process of determining if an array contains a certain key value is called _____ the array.
g) An array that uses two subscripts is referred to as a _____ array.

6.2   State whether the following are true or false. If the answer is false, explain why.
a) An array can store many different types of values.
b) An array subscript can be of data type `float`.
c) If there are fewer initializers in an initializer list than the number of elements in the array, C automatically initializes the remaining elements to the last value in the list of initializers.
d) It is an error if an initializer list contains more initializers than there are elements in the array.
e) An individual array element that is passed to a function and modified in the called function will contain the modified value in the calling function.

6.3   Answer the following questions regarding an array called `fractions`.
a) Define a symbolic constant `SIZE` to be replaced with the replacement text 10.
b) Declare an array with `SIZE` elements of type `float` and initialize the elements to `0`.
c) Name the fourth element from the beginning of the array.
d) Refer to array element 4.
e) Assign the value `1.667` to array element nine.
f) Assign the value `3.333` to the seventh element of the array.
g) Print array elements 6 and 9 with two digits of precision to the right of the decimal point, and show the output that is actually displayed on the screen.
h) Print all the elements of the array using a `for` repetition structure. Assume the integer variable `x` has been defined as a control variable for the loop. Show the output.

6.4   Answer the following questions regarding an array called `table`.
a) Declare the array to be an integer array and to have 3 rows and 3 columns. Assume the symbolic constant `SIZE` has been defined to be 3.

b) How many elements does the array contain?

c) Use a **for** repetition structure to initialize each element of the array to the sum of its subscripts. Assume the integer variables **x** and **y** are declared as control variables.

d) Print the values of each element of array **table**. Assume the array was initialized with the declaration,

`int table[SIZE][SIZE] = {{1, 8}, {2, 4, 6}, {5}};`

and the integer variables **x** and **y** are declared as control variables. Show the output.

6.5   Find the error in each of the following program segments and correct the error.

a) `#define SIZE 100;`

b) `SIZE = 10;`

c) Assume `int b[10] = {0}, i;`
```
for (i = 0; i <= 10; i++)
    b[i] = 1;
```

d) `#include <stdio.h>;`

e) Assume `int a[2][2] = {{1, 2}, {3, 4}};`
```
a[1, 1] = 5;
```

Answers to Self-Review Exercises

6.1   a) Arrays. b) Name, type. c) Subscript. d) Symbolic constant. e) Sorting. f) Searching. g) Double-subscripted.

6.2
a) False. An array can store only values of the same type.

b) False. An array subscript must be an integer or an integer expression.

c) False. C automatically initializes the remaining elements to zero.

d) True.

e) False. Individual elements of an array are passed call by value. If the entire array is passed to a function, then any modifications will be reflected in the original.

6.3
a) `#define SIZE 10`

b) `float fractions[SIZE] = {0};`

c) `fractions[3]`

d) `fractions[4]`

e) `fractions[9] = 1.667;`

f) `fractions[6] = 3.333;`

g) `printf("%.2f %.2f\n", fractions[6], fractions[9]);`
Output: `3.33 1.67`.

h) `for (x = 0; x <= SIZE - 1; x++)`
    `printf("fractions[%d] = %f\n", x, fractions[x]);`
Output:
```
fractions[0] = 0.000000
fractions[1] = 0.000000
fractions[2] = 0.000000
fractions[3] = 0.000000
fractions[4] = 0.000000
fractions[5] = 0.000000
fractions[6] = 3.333000
fractions[7] = 0.000000
fractions[8] = 0.000000
fractions[9] = 1.667000
```

6.4   a) `int table[SIZE][SIZE];`
      b) Nine elements.
      c)
```
for (x = 0; x <= SIZE - 1; x++)
    for (y = 0; y <= SIZE - 1; y++)
        table[x][y] = x + y;
```
      d)
```
for (x = 0; x <= SIZE - 1; x++)
    for (y = 0; y <= SIZE - 1; y++)
        printf("table[%d][%d] = %d\n", x, y, table[x][y]);
```
        Output:
```
table[0][0] = 1
table[0][1] = 8
table[0][2] = 0
table[1][0] = 2
table[1][1] = 4
table[1][2] = 6
table[2][0] = 5
table[2][1] = 0
table[2][2] = 0
```

6.5   a) Error: Semicolon at end of **#define** preprocessor directive.
        Correction: Eliminate semicolon.
      b) Error: Assigning a value to a symbolic constant using an assignment statement.
        Correction: Assign a value to the symbolic constant in a **#define** preprocessor directive without using the assignment operator as in **#define SIZE 10**.
      c) Error: Referencing an array element outside the bounds of the array (**b[10]**).
        Correction: Change the final value of the control variable to **9**.
      d) Error: Semicolon at end of **#include** preprocessor directive.
        Correction: Eliminate semicolon.
      e) Error: Array subscripting done incorrectly.
        Correction: Change the statement to **a[1][1] = 5;**

Exercises

6.6   Fill in the blanks in each of the following:
      a) C stores lists of values in _____.
      b) The elements of an array are related by the fact that they _____.
      c) When referring to an array element, the position number contained within parentheses is called a _____.
      d) The names of the five elements of array **p** are _____, _____, _____, _____, and _____.
      e) The contents of a particular element of an array is called the _____ of that element.
      f) Naming an array, stating its type, and specifying the number of elements in the array is called _____ the array.
      g) The process of placing the elements of an array into either ascending or descending order is called _____.
      h) In a double-subscripted array, the first subscript (by convention) identifies the _____ of an element, and the second subscript (by convention) identifies the _____ of an element.
      i) An m-by-n array contains _____ rows, _____ columns, and _____ elements.

	1	2	3	4	5	6
1	2	3	4	5	6	7
2	3	4	5	6	7	8
3	4	5	6	7	8	9
4	5	6	7	8	9	10
5	6	7	8	9	10	11
6	7	8	9	10	11	12

Fig. 6.23   The 36 possible outcomes of rolling two dice.

6.20   Write a program that runs 1000 games of craps and answers each of the following questions:

   a) How many games are won on the first roll, second roll, ..., twentieth roll, and after the twentieth roll?
   b) How many games are lost on the first roll, second roll, ..., twentieth roll, and after the twentieth roll?
   c) What are the chances of winning at craps? (*Note:* You should discover that craps is one of the fairest casino games. What do you suppose this means?)
   d) What is the average length of a game of craps?
   e) Do the chances of winning improve with the length of the game?

6.21   (*Airline Reservations System*) A small airline has just purchased a computer for its new automated reservations system. The president has asked you to program the new system in C. You are to write a program to assign seats on each flight of the airline's only plane (capacity: 10 seats).

   Your program should display the following menu of alternatives:

   Please type 1 for "smoking"
   Please type 2 for "nonsmoking"

If the person types 1, then your program should assign a seat in the smoking section (seats 1-5). If the person types 2, then your program should assign a seat in the nonsmoking section (seats 6-10). Your program should then print a boarding pass indicating the person's seat number and whether it is in the smoking or nonsmoking section of the plane.

   Use a single-subscripted array to represent the seating chart of the plane. Initialize all the elements of the array to 0 to indicate that all seats are empty. As each seat is assigned, set the corresponding elements of the array to 1 to indicate that the seat is no longer available.

   Your program should, of course, never assign a seat that has already been assigned. When the smoking section is full, your program should ask the person if it is acceptable to be placed in the nonsmoking section (and vice versa). If yes, then make the appropriate seat assignment. If no, then print the message **"Next flight leaves in 3 hours."**

6.22   Use a double-subscripted array to solve the following problem. A company has four salespeople (1 to 4) who sell five different products (1 to 5). Once a day, each salesperson passes in a slip for each different type of product sold. Each slip contains:

   1. The salesperson number
   2. The product number
   3. The total dollar value of that product sold that day

6.17   What does the following program do?

```
#include <stdio.h>
#define SIZE 10

int whatIsThis(int [], int);

main()
{
    int total, a[SIZE] = {1, 2, 3, 4, 5, 6, 7, 8, 9, 10};

    total = whatIsThis(a, SIZE);
    printf("Total of array element values is %d\n", total);
    return 0;
}

int whatIsThis(int b[], int size)
{
    if (size == 1)
        return b[0];
    else
        return b[size - 1] + whatIsThis(b, size - 1);
}
```

6.18   What does the following program do?

```
#include <stdio.h>
#define SIZE 10

void someFunction(int [], int);

main()
{
    int a[SIZE] = {32, 27, 64, 18, 95, 14, 90, 70, 60, 37};

    printf("The values in the array are:\n");
    someFunction(a, SIZE);
    printf("\n");
    return 0;
}

void someFunction(int b[], int size)
{
    if (size > 0) {
        someFunction(&b[1], size - 1);
        printf("%d  ", b[0]);
    }
}
```

6.19   Write a C program that simulates the rolling of two dice. The program should use **rand** to roll the first die, and should use **rand** again to roll the second die. The sum of the two values should then be calculated. *Note:* Since each die can show an integer value from 1 to 6, then the sum of the two values will vary from 2 to 12 with 7 being the most frequent sum and 2 and 12 being the least frequent sums. Fig. 6.23 shows the 36 possible combinations of the two dice. Your program should roll the two dice 36,000 times. Use a single-subscripted array to tally the numbers of times each possible sum appears. Print the results in a tabular format. Also, determine if the totals are reasonable, i.e., there are six ways to roll a 7, so approximately one sixth of all the rolls should be 7.

1. $200-$299
2. $300-$399
3. $400-$499
4. $500-$599
5. $600-$699
6. $700-$799
7. $800-$899
8. $900-$999
9. $1000 and over

6.11 The bubble sort presented in Fig. 6.15 is inefficient for large arrays. Make the following simple modifications to improve the performance of the bubble sort.

a) After the first pass, the largest number is guaranteed to be in the highest-numbered element of the array; after the second pass, the two highest numbers are "in place," and so on. Instead of making nine comparisons on every pass, modify the bubble sort to make eight comparisons on the second pass, seven on the third pass, and so on.

b) The data in the array may already be in the proper order or near-proper order, so why make nine passes if fewer will suffice? Modify the sort to check at the end of each pass if any swaps have been made. If none has been made, then the data must already be in the proper order, so the program should terminate. If swaps have been made, then at least one more pass is needed.

6.12 Write single statements that perform each of the following single-subscripted array operations:

a) Initialize the 10 elements of integer array **counts** to zeros.

b) Add 1 to each of the 15 elements of integer array **bonus**.

c) Read the 12 values of floating point array **monthlyTemperatures** from the keyboard.

d) Print the 5 values of integer array **bestScores** in column format.

6.13 Find the error(s) in each of the following statements:

a) Assume: **char str[5];**
   scanf("%s", str); /* User types hello */

b) Assume: **int a[3];**
   printf("$d %d %d\n", a[1], a[2], a[3]);

c) **float f[3] = {1.1, 10.01, 100.001, 1000.0001};**

d) Assume: **double d[2][10];**
   d[1, 9] = 2.345;

6.14 Modify the program of Fig. 6.16 so function **mode** is capable of handling a tie for the mode value. Also modify function **median** so the two middle elements are averaged in an array with an even number of elements.

6.15 Use a single-subscripted array to solve the following problem. Read in 20 numbers, each of which is between 10 and 100, inclusive. As each number is read, print it only if it is not a duplicate of a number already read. Provide for the "worst case" in which all 20 numbers are different. Use the smallest possible array to solve this problem.

6.16 Label the elements of 3-by-5 double-subscripted array **sales** to indicate the order in which they are set to zero by the following program segment:

```
for (row = 0; row <= 2; row++)
   for (column = 0; column <= 4; column++)
      sales[row][column] = 0;
```

     j)   The name of the element in row 3 and column 5 of array **d** is _____.

6.7   State which of the following are true and which are false; for those that are false, explain why they are false.

     a)   To refer to a particular location or element within an array, we specify the name of the array and the value of the particular element.

     b)   An array declaration reserves space for the array.

     c)   To indicate that 100 locations should be reserved for integer array **p**, the programmer writes the declaration

```
p[100];
```

     d)   A C program that initializes the elements of a 15-element array to zero must contain one **for** statement.

     e)   A C program that totals the elements of a double-subscripted array must contain nested **for** statements.

     f)   The mean, median, and mode of the following set of values are 5, 6, and 7, respectively: 1, 2, 5, 6, 7, 7, 7.

6.8   Write C statements to accomplish each of the following:

     a)   Display the value of the seventh element of character array **f**.

     b)   Input a value into element 4 of single-subscripted floating-point array **b**.

     c)   Initialize each of the 5 elements of single-subscripted integer array **g** to **8**.

     d)   Total the elements of floating-point array **c** of 100 elements.

     e)   Copy array **a** into the first portion of array **b**. Assume **float a[11], b[34];**

     f)   Determine and print the smallest and largest values contained in 99-element floating-point array **w**.

6.9   Consider a 2-by-5 integer array **t**.

     a)   Write a declaration for **t**.

     b)   How many rows does **t** have?

     c)   How many columns does **t** have?

     d)   How many elements does **t** have?

     e)   Write the names of all the elements in the second row of **t**.

     f)   Write the names of all the elements in the third column of **t**.

     g)   Write a single C statement that sets the element of **t** in row 1 and column 2 to zero.

     h)   Write a series of C statements that initializes each element of **t** to zero. Do not use a repetition structure.

     i)   Write a nested **for** structure that initializes each element of **t** to zero.

     j)   Write a C statement that inputs the values for the elements of **t** from the terminal.

     k)   Write a series of C statements that determines and prints the smallest value in array **t**.

     l)   Write a C statement that displays the elements of the first row of **t**.

     m)   Write a C statement that totals the elements of the fourth column of **t**.

     n)   Write a series of C statements that prints the array **t** in neat, tabular format. List the column subscripts as headings across the top, and list the row subscripts at the left of each row.

6.10   Use a single-subscripted array to solve the following problem. A company pays its salespeople on a commission basis. The salespeople receive $200 per week plus 9 percent of their gross sales for that week. For example, a salesperson who grosses $3000 in sales in a week receives $200 plus 9 percent of $3000, or a total of $470. Write a C program (using an array of counters) that determines how many of the salespeople earned salaries in each of the following ranges (assume that each salesperson's salary is truncated to an integer amount):

Thus, each salesperson passes in between 0 and 5 sales slips per day. Assume that the information from all of the slips for last month is available. Write a program that will read all this information for last month's sales, and summarize the total sales by salesperson by product. All totals should be stored in the double-subscripted array **sales**. After processing all the information for last month, print the results in tabular format with each of the columns representing a particular salesperson and each of the rows representing a particular product. Cross total each row to get the total sales of each product for last month; cross total each column to get the total sales by salesperson for last month. Your tabular printout should include these cross totals to the right of the totaled rows and to the bottom of the totaled columns.

6.23   (*Turtle Graphics*) The Logo language, which is particularly popular among personal computer users, made the concept of *turtle graphics* famous. Imagine a mechanical turtle that walks around the room under the control of a C program. The turtle holds a pen in one of two positions, up or down. While the pen is down, the turtle traces out shapes as it moves; while the pen is up, the turtle moves about freely without writing anything. In this problem you will simulate the operation of the turtle and create a computerized sketchpad as well.

Use a 50-by-50 array **floor** which is initialized to zeros. Read commands from an array that contains them. Keep track of the current position of the turtle at all times and whether the pen is currently up or down. Assume that the turtle always starts at position 0,0 of the floor with its pen up. The set of turtle commands your program must process are as follows:

Command	Meaning
1	Pen up
2	Pen down
3	Turn right
4	Turn left
5,10	Move forward 10 spaces
	(or a number other than 10)
6	Print the 50-by-50 array
9	End of data (sentinel)

Suppose that the turtle is somewhere near the center of the floor. The following "program" would draw and print a 12-by 12-square:

```
        2
        5,12
        3
        5,12
        3
        5,12
        3
        5,12
        1
        6
        9
```

As the turtle moves with the pen down, set the appropriate elements of array **floor** to **1**s. When the **6** command (print) is given, wherever there is a **1** in the array, display an asterisk, or some other character you choose. Wherever there is a zero display a blank. Write a C program to implement the turtle graphics capabilities discussed here. Write several turtle graphics programs to draw interesting shapes. Add other commands to increase the power of your turtle graphics language.

6.24.   (*Knight's Tour*) One of the more interesting puzzlers for chess buffs is the Knight's Tour problem, originally proposed by the mathematician Euler. The question is this: Can the chess piece called the knight move around an empty chessboard and touch each of the 64 squares once and only once? We study this intriguing problem in depth here.

The knight makes L-shaped moves (over two in one direction and then over one in a perpendicular direction). Thus, from a square in the middle of an empty chessboard, the knight can make eight different moves (numbered 0 through 7) as shown in Fig. 6.24.

a) Draw an 8-by-8 chessboard on a sheet of paper and attempt a Knight's Tour by hand. Put a **1** in the first square you move to, a **2** in the second square, a **3** in the third, etc. Before starting the tour, estimate how far you think you will get, remembering that a full tour consists of 64 moves. How far did you get? Were you close to the estimate?

Fig. 6.24 The eight possible moves of the knight.

b) Now let us develop a program that will move the knight around a chessboard. The board itself is represented by an 8-by-8 double-subscripted array **board**. Each of the squares is initialized to zero. We describe each of the eight possible moves in terms of both their horizontal and vertical components. For example, a move of type 0 as shown in Fig. 6.24 consists of moving two squares horizontally to the right and one square vertically upward. Move 2 consists of moving one square horizontally to the left and two squares vertically upward. Horizontal moves to the left and vertical moves upward are indicated with negative numbers. The eight moves may be described by two single-subscripted arrays, **horizontal** and **vertical**, as follows:

```
horizontal[0] = 2
horizontal[1] = 1
horizontal[2] = -1
horizontal[3] = -2
horizontal[4] = -2
horizontal[5] = -1
horizontal[6] = 1
horizontal[7] = 2

vertical[0] = -1
vertical[1] = -2
vertical[2] = -2
vertical[3] = -1
vertical[4] = 1
vertical[5] = 2
vertical[6] = 2
vertical[7] = 1
```

Let the variables **currentRow** and **currentColumn** indicate the row and column of the knight's current position. To make a move of type **moveNumber**, where **moveNumber** is between 0 and 7, your program uses the statements

```
currentRow += vertical[moveNumber];
currentColumn += horizontal[moveNumber];
```

Keep a counter that varies from 1 to 6 4. Record the latest count in each square the knight moves to. Remember to test each potential move to see if the knight has already visited that square. And, of course, test every potential move to make sure that the knight does not land off the chessboard. Now write a program to move the knight around the chessboard. Run the program. How many moves did the knight make?

c) After attempting to write and run a Knight's Tour program, you have probably developed some valuable insights. We will use these to develop a *heuristic* (or strategy) for moving the knight. Heuristics do not guarantee success, but a carefully developed heuristic greatly improves the chance of success. You may have observed that the outer squares are in some sense more troublesome than the squares nearer the center of the board. In fact, the most troublesome, or inaccessible, squares are the four corners.

Intuition may suggest that you should attempt to move the knight to the most troublesome squares first, and leave open those that are easiest to get to so that when the board gets congested near the end of the tour there will be a greater chance of success.

We may develop an "accessibility heuristic" by classifying each of the squares according to how accessible they are, and then always moving the knight to the square (within the knight's L-shaped moves, of course) that is most inaccessible. We label a double-subscripted array **accessibility** with numbers indicating from how many squares each particular square is accessible. On a blank chessboard, the center squares are therefore rated as **8**s, the corner squares are rated as **2**s, and the other squares have accessibility numbers of **3**, **4**, or **6** as follows:

```
2  3  4  4  4  4  3  2
3  4  6  6  6  6  4  3
4  6  8  8  8  8  6  4
4  6  8  8  8  8  6  4
4  6  8  8  8  8  6  4
4  6  8  8  8  8  6  4
3  4  6  6  6  6  4  3
2  3  4  4  4  4  3  2
```

Now write a version of the Knight's Tour program using the accessibility heuristic. At any time, the knight should move to the square with the lowest accessibility number. In case of a tie, the knight may move to any of the tied squares. Therefore, the tour may begin in any of the four corners. (*Note:* As the knight moves around the chessboard, your program should reduce the accessibility numbers as more and more squares become occupied. In this way, at any given time during the tour, each available square's accessibility number will remain equal to precisely the number of squares from which that square may be reached.) Run this version of your program. Did you get a full tour? Now modify the program to run 64 tours, one from each square of the chessboard. How many full tours did you get?

d) Write a version of the Knight's Tour program which, when encountering a tie between two or more squares, decides what square to choose by looking ahead to those squares reachable from the "tied" squares. Your program should move to the square for which the next move would arrive at a square with the lowest accessibility number.

6.25   (*Knight's Tour: Brute Force Approaches*) In Exercise 6.24 we developed a solution to the Knight's Tour problem. The approach used, called the "accessibility heuristic," generates many solutions and executes efficiently.

As computers continue increasing in power, we will be able to solve many problems with sheer computer power and relatively unsophisticated algorithms. Let us call this approach "brute force" problem solving.

a) Use random number generation to enable the knight to walk around the chess board (in its legitimate L-shaped moves, of course) at random. Your program should run one tour and print the final chessboard. How far did the knight get?

b) Most likely, the preceding program produced a relatively short tour. Now modify your program to attempt 1000 tours. Use a single-subscripted array to keep track of the number of tours of each length. When your program finishes attempting the 1000 tours, it should print this information in neat tabular format. What was the best result?

c) Most likely, the preceding program gave you some "respectable" tours but no full tours. Now "pull all the stops out" and simply let your program run until it produces a full tour. (*Caution.* This version of the program could run for hours on a powerful computer.) Once again, keep a table of the number of tours of each length, and print this table when the first full tour is found. How many tours did your program attempt before producing a full tour? How much time did it take?

d) Compare the brute force version of the Knight's Tour with the accessibility heuristic version. Which required a more careful study of the problem? Which algorithm was more difficult to develop? Which required more computer power? Could we be certain (in advance) of obtaining a full tour with the accessibility heuristic approach? Could we be certain (in advance) of obtaining a full tour with the brute force approach? Argue the pros and cons of brute force problem solving in general.

6.26.   (*Eight Queens*) Another puzzler for chess buffs is the Eight Queens problem. Simply stated: Is it possible to place eight queens on an empty chessboard so that no queen is "attacking" any other, that is, so that no two queens are in the same row, the same column, or along the same diagonal? Use the kind of thinking developed in Exercise 6.24 to formulate a heuristic for solving the Eight Queens problem. Run your program. (*Hint:* It is possible to assign a numeric value to each square of the chessboard indicating how many squares of an empty chessboard are "eliminated" once a queen is placed in that square. For example, each of the four corners would be assigned the value 22, as in Fig. 6.25.)

Once these "elimination numbers" are placed in all 64 squares, an appropriate heuristic might be: Place the next queen in the square with the smallest elimination number. Why is this strategy intuitively appealing?

6.27   (*Eight Queens: Brute Force Approaches*) In this problem you will develop several brute force approaches to solving the Eight Queens problem introduced in Exercise 6.26.

   a) Solve the Eight Queens problem, using the random brute force technique developed in Problem 6.25.
   b) Use an exhaustive technique, i.e., try all possible combinations of eight queens on the chessboard.
   c) Why do you suppose the exhaustive brute force approach may not be appropriate for solving the Knight's Tour problem?
   d) Compare and contrast the random brute force and exhaustive brute force approaches in general.

6.28   (*Duplicate elimination*) In Chapter 12 we explore the high-speed binary search tree data structure. One feature of a binary search tree is that duplicate values are discarded when insertions are made into the tree. This is referred to as duplicate elimination. Write a program that produces 20 random numbers between 1 and 20. The program should store all non-duplicate values in an array. Use the smallest possible array to accomplish this task.

6.29   (*Knight's Tour: Closed Tour Test*) In the Knight's Tour, a full tour is when the knight makes 64 moves touching each square of the chess board once and only once. A closed tour occurs when the 64th move is one move away from the location in which the knight started the tour. Modify the Knight's Tour program you wrote in Exercise 6.24 to test for a closed tour if a full tour has occurred.

6.30   (*The Sieve of Eratosthenes*) A prime integer is any integer that can be divided evenly only by itself and 1. The Sieve of Eratosthenes is a method of finding prime numbers. It works as follows:

Fig. 6.25   The 22 squares eliminated by placing a queen in the upper left corner.

1) Create an array with all elements initialized to 1 (true). Array elements with prime subscripts will remain 1. All other array elements will eventually be set to zero.
2) Starting with array subscript 2 (subscript 1 must be prime), every time an array element is found whose value is 1, loop through the remainder of the array and set to zero every element whose subscript is a multiple of the subscript for the element with value 1. For array subscript 2, all elements beyond 2 in the array that are multiples of 2 will be set to zero (subscripts 4, 6, 8, 10, etc.). For array subscript 3, all elements beyond 3 in the array that are multiples of 3 will be set to zero (subscripts 6, 9, 12, 15, etc.).

When this process is complete, the array elements that are still set to one indicate that the subscript is a prime number. These subscripts can then be printed. Write a program that uses an array of 1000 elements to determine and print the prime numbers between 1 and 999. Ignore element 0 of the array.

6.31   (*Bucket Sort*) A bucket sort begins with an single-subscripted array of positive integers to be sorted, and a double-subscripted array of integers with rows subscripted from 0 to 9 and columns subscripted from 0 to $n - 1$ where n is the number of values in the array to be sorted. Each row of the double-subscripted array is referred to as a bucket. Write a function **bucketSort** that takes an integer array and the array size as arguments.

The algorithm is as follows:
1) Loop through the single-subscripted array and place each of its values in a row of the bucket array based on its ones digit. For example, 97 is placed in row 7, 3 is placed in row 3, and 100 is placed in row 0.
2) Loop through the bucket array and copy the values back to the original array. The new order of the above values in the single-subscripted array is 100, 3, and 97.
3) Repeat this process for each subsequent digit position (tens, hundreds, thousands, etc.), and stop when the leftmost digit of the largest number has be processed.

On the second pass of the array, 100 is placed in row 0, 3 is placed in row 0 (it had only one digit), and 97 is placed in row 9. The order of the values in the single-subscripted array is 100, 3, and 97. On the third pass, 100 is placed in row 1, 3 is placed in row zero and 97 is placed in row zero (after 3). The bucket sort is guaranteed to have all the values properly sorted after processing the leftmost digit of the largest number. The bucket sort knows it is done when all the values are copied into row zero of the double-subscripted array.

Note that the double-subscripted array of buckets is ten times the size of the integer array being sorted. This sorting technique provides better performance than a bubble sort, but requires much larger storage capacity. Bubble sort requires only one additional memory location for the type of data being sorted. Bucket sort is an example of a space-time tradeoff. It uses more memory, but performs better. This version of the bucket sort requires copying all the data back to the original array on each pass. Another possibility is to create a second double-subscripted bucket array and repeatedly move the data between the two bucket arrays until all the data is copied into row zero of one of the arrays. Row zero then contains the sorted array.

Recursion Exercises

6.32   (*Selection Sort*) A selection sort searches an array looking for the smallest element in the array. When the smallest element is found, it is swapped with the first element of the array. The process is then repeated for the subarray beginning with the second element of the array. Each pass of the array results in one element being placed in its proper location. This sort requires similar processing capabilities to the bubble sort—for an array of n elements, $n - 1$ passes must be made, and for each subarray, $n - 1$ comparisons must be made to find the smallest value. When the subarray being processed contains one element, the array is sorted. Write a recursive function **selection-Sort** to perform this algorithm.

6.33   (*Palindromes*) A palindrome is a string that is spelled the same way forwards and backwards. Some examples of palindromes are: "radar," "able was i ere i saw elba," and "a man a plan a canal panama." Write a recursive function **testPalindrome** that returns 1 if the string stored in the array is a palindrome, and 0 otherwise. The function should ignore spaces and punctuation in the string.

6.34   (*Linear Search*) Modify the program of Fig. 6.18 to use a recursive function **linearSearch** to perform the linear search of the array. The function should receive an integer array and the size of the array as arguments. If the search key is found, return the array subscript; otherwise, return -1.

6.35   (*Binary Search*) Modify the program of Fig. 6.19 to use a recursive function **binarySearch** to perform the binary search of the array. The function should receive an integer array and the starting subscript and ending subscript as arguments. If the search key is found, return the array subscript; otherwise, return -1.

6.36   (*Eight Queens*) Modify the Eight Queens program you created in Exercise 6.26 to solve the problem recursively.

6.37   (*Print an array*) Write a recursive function **printArray** that takes an array and the size of the array as arguments and returns nothing. The function should stop processing and return when it receives an array of size zero.

6.38   (*Print a string backwards*) Write a recursive function **stringReverse** that takes a character array as an argument and returns nothing. The function should stop processing and return when the terminating null character of the string is encountered.

6.39   (*Find the minimum value in an array*) Write a recursive function **recursiveMinimum** that takes an integer array and the array size as arguments and returns the smallest element of the array. The function should stop processing and return when it receives an array of 1 element.

7

Pointers

Objectives

- To be able to use pointers.
- To be able to use pointers to pass arguments to functions call by reference.
- To understand the close relationships among pointers, arrays and strings.
- To understand the use of pointers to functions.
- To be able to declare and use arrays of strings.

Addresses are given to us to conceal our whereabouts.
Saki (H. H. Munro)

By indirections find directions out.
William Shakespeare
Hamlet

Many things, having full reference
To one consent, may work contrariously.
William Shakespeare
King Henry V

You will find it a very good practice always to verify your
references, sir!
Dr. Routh
You can't trust code that you did not totally create yourself.
(Especially code from companies that employ people like me.)
Ken Thompson
1983 Turing Award Lecture
Association for Computing Machinery, Inc.

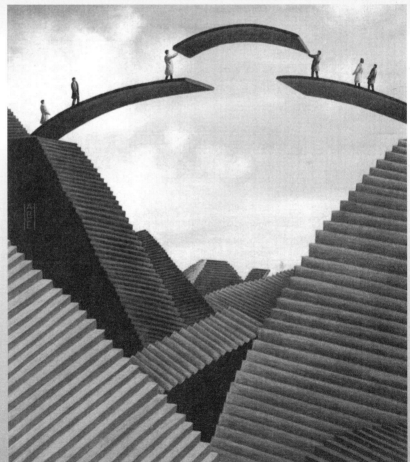

259

Outline

7.1 Introduction

In this chapter, we discuss one of the most powerful features of the C programming language, the *pointer.* Pointers are among C's most difficult capabilities to master. Pointers enable programs to simulate call by reference, and to create and manipulate dynamic data structures, i.e., data structures that can grow and shrink, such as linked lists, queues, stacks, and trees. This chapter explains basic pointer concepts. Chapter 10 examines the use of pointers with structures. Chapter 12 introduces dynamic memory management techniques and presents examples of creating and using dynamic data structures.

7.2 Pointer Variable Declarations and Initialization

Pointers are variables that contain memory addresses as their values. Normally a variable directly contains a specific value. A pointer, on the other hand, contains an address of a variable that contains a specific value. In this sense, a variable name *directly* references a value and a pointer *indirectly* references a value (Fig. 7.1). Referencing a value through a pointer is called *indirection.*

Pointers, like any other variables, must be declared before they can be used. The declaration

```
int *countPtr, count;
```

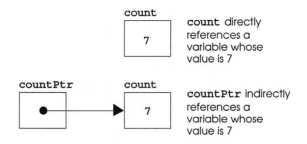

Fig. 7.1   Directly and indirectly referencing a variable.

declare the variable **countPtr** to be of type **int *** (i.e., a pointer to an integer value) and is read, "**countPtr** is a pointer to **int**" or "**countPtr** points to an object of type integer." Also, variable **count** is declared to be an integer, not a pointer to an integer. The ***** only applies to **countPtr** in the declaration. When ***** is used in this manner in a declaration, it indicates that the variable being declared is a pointer. Pointers can be declared to point to objects of any data type.

Common Programming Error 7.1

The indirection operator * does not distribute to all variable names in a declaration. Each pointer must be declared with the * prefixed to the name.

Good Programming Practice 7.1

Include the letters ptr in pointer variable names to make it clear that these variables are pointers and need to be handled appropriately.

Pointers should be initialized either when they are declared or in an assignment statement. A pointer may be initialized to **0**, **NULL**, or an address. A pointer with the value **NULL** points to nothing. **NULL** is a symbolic constant defined in the **<stdio.h>** header file (and in several other header files). Initializing a pointer to **0** is equivalent to initializing a pointer to **NULL**, but **NULL** is preferred. When **0** is assigned, it is first converted to a pointer of the appropriate type. The value **0** is the only integer value that can be assigned directly to a pointer variable. Assigning a variable's address to a pointer is discussed in Section 7.3.

Good Programming Practice 7.2

Initialize pointers to prevent unexpected results.

7.3 Pointer Operators

The **&**, or *address operator*, is a unary operator that returns the address of its operand. For example, assuming the declarations

```
int y = 5;
int *yPtr;
```

the statement

```
yPtr = &y;
```

assigns the address of the variable **y** to pointer variable **yPtr**. Variable **yPtr** is then said to "point to" **y**. Figure 7.2 shows a schematic representation of memory after the preceding assignment is executed.

Figure 7.3 shows the representation of the pointer in memory assuming that integer variable **y** is stored at location **600000**, and pointer variable **yPtr** is stored at location **500000**. The operand of the address operator must be a variable; the address operator can not be applied to constants, to expressions, or to variables declared with the storage class **register**.

The ***** operator, commonly referred to as the *indirection operator* or *dereferencing operator*, returns the value of the object to which its operand (i.e., a pointer) points. For example, the statement

```
printf("%d", *yPtr);
```

prints the value of variable **y**, namely 5. Using ***** in this manner is called *dereferencing a pointer*.

Common Programming Error 7.2

Dereferencing a pointer that has not been properly initialized, or that has not been assigned to point to a specific location in memory. This could cause a fatal execution time error, or it could accidentally modify important data and allow the program to run to completion providing incorrect results.

The program in Fig. 7.4 demonstrates the pointer operators. The **printf** conversion specification **%p** outputs the memory location as a hexadecimal integer (see Appendix E, Number Systems, for more information on hexadecimal integers). Notice that the address

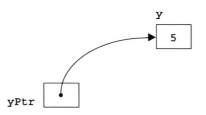

Fig. 7.2   Graphical representation of a pointer pointing to an integer variable in memory.

yPtr		y	
500000	600000	600000	5

Fig. 7.3   Representation of **y** and **yPtr** in memory.

of **a** and the value of **aPtr** are identical in the output, thus confirming that the address of **a** is indeed assigned to the pointer variable **aPtr**. The **&** and ***** operators are complements of one another—when they are both applied consecutively to **aPtr** in either order, the same result is printed. The chart in Fig. 7.5 shows the precedence and associativity of the operators introduced to this point.

7.4 Calling Functions by Reference

There are two ways to pass arguments to a function—call by value and call by reference. All function calls in C are call by value. As we saw in Chapter 5, **return** may be used to return one value from a called function to a caller (or to return control from a called function without passing back a value). Many functions require the capability to modify one or more variables in the caller, or to pass a pointer to a large data object to avoid the

```
/* Using the & and * operators */
#include <stdio.h>

main()
{
    int a;        /* a is an integer */
    int *aPtr;    /* aPtr is a pointer to an integer */

    a = 7;
    aPtr = &a;    /* aPtr set to address of a */

    printf("The address of a is %p\n"
           "The value of aPtr is %p\n\n", &a, aPtr);

    printf("The value of a is %d\n"
           "The value of *aPtr is %d\n\n", a, *aPtr);

    printf("Proving that * and & are complements of "
           "each other.\n&*aPtr = %p\n*&aPtr = %p\n",
           &*aPtr, *&aPtr);
    return 0;
}
```

```
The address of a is FFF4
The value of aPtr is FFF4

The value of a is 7
The value of *aPtr is 7

Proving that * and & are complements of each other.
&*aPtr = FFF4
*&aPtr = FFF4
```

Fig. 7.4   The **&** and ***** pointer operators.

Operators								Associativity	Type
( )	[]							left to right	highest
+	-	++	--	!	*	&	(type)	right to left	unary
*	/	%						left to right	multiplicative
+	-							left to right	additive
<	<=	>	>=					left to right	relational
==	!=							left to right	equality
&&								left to right	logical and
||								left to right	logical or
?:								right to left	conditional
=	+=	-=	*=	/=	%=			right to left	assignment
,								left to right	comma

Fig. 7.5   Operator precedence.

overhead of passing the object call by value (which, of course, requires making a copy of the object). For these purposes, C provides the capabilities for simulating call by reference.

In C, programmers use pointers and the indirection operator to simulate call by reference. When calling a function with arguments that should be modified, the addresses of the arguments are passed. This is normally accomplished by applying the address operator (**&**) to the variable whose value will be modified. As we saw in Chapter 6, arrays are not passed using operator **&** because C automatically passes the starting location in memory of the array (the name of an array is equivalent to **&arrayName[0]**). When the address of a variable is passed to a function, the indirection operator (*****) may be used in the function to modify the value at that location in the caller's memory.

The programs in Fig. 7.6 and Fig. 7.7 present two versions of a function that cubes an integer—**cubeByValue** and **cubeByReference**. The program in Fig. 7.6 passes the variable **number** to function **cubeByValue** using call by value. Function **cubeByValue** cubes its argument and passes the new value back to **main** using a **return** statement. The new value is assigned to **number** in **main**.

The program of Fig. 7.7 passes the variable **number** using call by reference—the address of **number** is passed—to function **cubeByReference**. Function **cubeByReference** takes a pointer to **int** called **nPtr** as an argument. The function dereferences the pointer and cubes the value to which **nPtr** points. This changes the value of **number** in **main**. Figures 7.8 and 7.9 analyze graphically the programs in Fig. 7.6 and Fig. 7.7, respectively.

Common Programming Error 7.3

Not dereferencing a pointer when it is necessary to do so to obtain the value to which the pointer points.

```c
/* Cube a variable using call by value */
#include <stdio.h>

int cubeByValue(int);

main()
{
   int number = 5;

   printf("The original value of number is %d\n", number);
   number = cubeByValue(number);
   printf("The new value of number is %d\n", number);
   return 0;
}

int cubeByValue(int n)
{
   return n * n * n;    /* cube local variable n */
}
```

```
The original value of number is 5
The new value of number is 125
```

Fig. 7.6 Cube a variable using call by value.

```c
/* Cube a variable using call by reference */
#include <stdio.h>

void cubeByReference(int *);

main()
{
   int number = 5;

   printf("The original value of number is %d\n", number);
   cubeByReference(&number);
   printf("The new value of number is %d\n", number);
   return 0;
}

void cubeByReference(int *nPtr)
{
   *nPtr = *nPtr * *nPtr * *nPtr;   /* cube number in main */
}
```

```
The original value of number is 5
The new value of number is 125
```

Fig. 7.7 Cube a variable using call by reference.

Before **main** calls **cubeByValue**:

```
main()                  number        int cubeByValue(int n)
{                       ┌─────┐        {
    int number = 5;     │  5  │            return n * n * n;
                        └─────┘        }
    number = cubeByValue(number);                      n
}                                                  ┌─────────┐
                                                   │undefined│
                                                   └─────────┘
```

After **cubeByValue** receives the call:

```
main()                  number        int cubeByValue(int n)
{                       ┌─────┐        {
    int number = 5;     │  5  │            return n * n * n;
                        └─────┘        }
    number = cubeByValue(number);                      n
}                                                  ┌─────────┐
                                                   │    5    │
                                                   └─────────┘
```

After **cubeByValue** cubes the parameter **n**:

```
main()                  number        int cubeByValue(int n)
{                       ┌─────┐        {              125
    int number = 5;     │  5  │            return (n * n * n;)
                        └─────┘        }
    number = cubeByValue(number);                      n
}                                                  ┌─────────┐
                                                   │    5    │
                                                   └─────────┘
```

After **cubeByValue** returns to **main**:

```
main()                  number        int cubeByValue(int n)
{                       ┌─────┐        {
    int number = 5;     │  5  │            return n * n * n;
                        └─────┘        }
            125                                        n
    number = (cubeByValue(number);)                ┌─────────┐
}                                                  │undefined│
                                                   └─────────┘
```

After **main** completes the assignment to **number**:

```
main()                  number        int cubeByValue(int n)
{                       ┌─────┐        {
    int number = 5;     │ 125 │            return n * n * n;
                        └─────┘        }
    number = cubeByValue(number);                      n
}                                                  ┌─────────┐
                                                   │undefined│
                                                   └─────────┘
```

Fig. 7.8   Analysis of a typical call by value.

A function receiving an address as an argument must define a pointer parameter to receive the address. For example, the header for function **cubeByReference** is

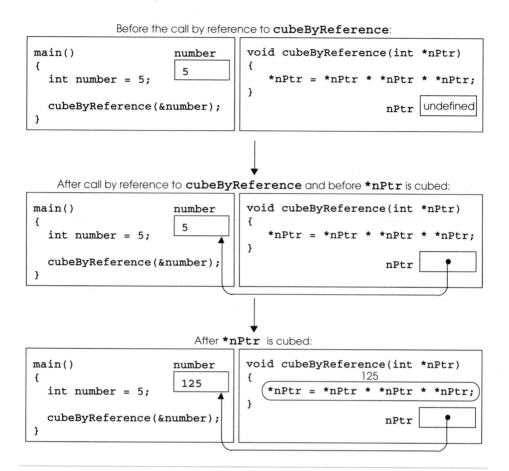

Fig. 7.9   Analysis of a typical call by reference.

```
void cubeByReference(int *nPtr)
```

The header specifies that **cubeByReference** receives the address of an integer variable as an argument, stores the address locally in **nPtr**, and does not return a value.

The function prototype for **cubeByReference** contains **int *** in parentheses. As with other variable types, it is not necessary to include names of pointers in function prototypes. Names included for documentation purposes are ignored by the C compiler.

In the function header and in the prototype for a function that expects a single-subscripted array as an argument, the pointer notation in the parameter list of **cubeByReference** may be used. The compiler does not differentiate between a function that receives a pointer and a function that receives a single-subscripted array. This, of course, means that the function must "know" when it is receiving an array or simply a single variable for which it is to perform call by reference. When the compiler encounters a function parameter for a single-subscripted array of the form **int b[]**, the compiler converts the parameter to the pointer notation **int *b**. The two forms are interchangeable.

Good Programming Practice 7.3

Use call by value to pass arguments to a function unless the caller explicitly requires that the called function modify the value of the argument variable in the caller's environment. This is another example of the principle of least privilege.

7.5 Using the Const Qualifier with Pointers

The *const qualifier* enables the programmer to inform the compiler that the value of a particular variable should not be modified. The **const** qualifier did not exist in early versions of C; it was added to the language by the ANSI C committee.

Software Engineering Observation 7.1

The **const** *qualifier can be used to enforce the principle of least privilege. Using the principle of least privilege to properly design software tremendously reduces debugging time and improper side effects, and makes a program easier to modify and maintain.*

Portability Tip 7.1

Although **const** *is well defined in ANSI C, some systems do not enforce it.*

Over the years, a large base of legacy code was written in early versions of C that did not use **const** because it was not available. For this reason, there are tremendous opportunities for improvement in the software engineering of old C code. Also, many programmers currently using ANSI C do not use **const** in their programs because they began programming in early versions of C. These programmers are omitting many opportunities for good software engineering.

Six possibilities exist for using (or not using) **const** with function parameters—two with call-by-value parameter passing and four with call-by-reference parameter passing. How do you choose one of the six possibilities? Let the principle of least privilege be your guide. Always award a function enough access to the data in its parameters to accomplish its specified task, but no more.

In Chapter 5, we explained that all calls in C are call by value—a copy of the argument in the function call is made and passed to the function. If the copy is modified in the function, the original value is maintained without change in the caller. In many cases, a value passed to a function is modified so the function can accomplish its task. However, in some instances, the value should not be altered in the called function even though the called function manipulates a copy of the original value.

Consider a function that takes a single-subscripted array and its size as arguments and prints the array. Such a function should loop through the array and output each array element individually. The size of the array is used in the function body to determine the high subscript of the array so the loop can terminate when the printing is completed. The size of the array does not change in the function body.

Software Engineering Observation 7.2

If a value does not (or should not) change in the body of a function to which it is passed, the value should be declared **const** *to ensure that it is not accidentally modified.*

If an attempt is made to modify a value that is declared **const**, the compiler catches it and issues either a warning or an error depending on the particular compiler.

Software Engineering Observation 7.3

Only one value can be altered in a calling function when call by value is used. That value must be assigned from the return value of the function. To modify multiple values in a calling function, call by reference must be used.

Good Programming Practice 7.4

Before using a function, check the function prototype for the function to determine if the function is able to modify the values passed to it.

Common Programming Error 7.4

Being unaware that a function is expecting pointers as arguments for call-by-reference and passing arguments call by value. Some compilers take the values assuming they are pointers and dereference the values as pointers. At run-time, memory access violations or segmentation faults are often generated. Other compilers catch the mismatch in types between arguments and parameters and generate error messages.

There are four ways to pass a pointer to a function: a non-constant pointer to non-constant data, a constant pointer to non-constant data, a non-constant pointer to constant data, and a constant pointer to constant data. Each of the four combinations provides a different level of access privileges.

The highest level of data access is granted by a non-constant pointer to non-constant data. In this case, the data can be modified through the dereferenced pointer, and the pointer can be modified to point to other data items. A declaration for a non-constant pointer to non-constant data does not include **const**. Such a pointer might be used to receive a string as an argument to a function that uses pointer arithmetic to process (and possibly modify) each character in the string. Function **convertToUppercase** of Fig. 7.10 declares as its argument a non-constant pointer to non-constant data called **s** (**char *s**). The function processes the string **s** one character at a time using pointer arithmetic. If a character is in the range **a** to **z**, it is converted to its corresponding uppercase letter **A** to **Z** using a calculation based on its ASCII code; otherwise it is skipped, and the next character in the string is processed. Note that all uppercase letters in the ASCII character set have integer values that are equivalent to their corresponding lowercase letter's ASCII value minus 32 (see Appendix D for a table of ASCII character values). In Chapter 8, we present function **toupper** of the C standard library for converting letters to uppercase.

A non-constant pointer to constant data is a pointer that can be modified to point to any data item of the appropriate type, but the data to which it points cannot be modified. Such a pointer might be used to receive an array argument to a function that will process each element of the array without modifying the data. For example, function **printCharacters** of Fig. 7.11 declares parameters **s** to be of type **const char ***. The declaration is read from right to left as "**s** is a pointer to a character constant." The body of the function uses a **for** structure to output each character in the string until the null character is encountered. After each character is printed, pointer **s** is incremented to point to the next character in the string.

```
/* Converting lowercase letters to uppercase letters */
/* using a non-constant pointer to non-constant data */
#include <stdio.h>

void convertToUppercase(char *);

main()
{
   char string[] = "characters";

   printf("The string before conversion is: %s\n", string);
   convertToUppercase(string);
   printf("The string after conversion is:  %s\n", string);
   return 0;
}

void convertToUppercase(char *s)
{
   while (*s != '\0') {

      if (*s >= 'a' && *s <= 'z')
         *s -= 32;   /* convert to ASCII uppercase letter */

      ++s;   /* increment s to point to the next character */
   }
}
```

```
The string before conversion is: characters
The string after conversion is:  CHARACTERS
```

Fig. 7.10   Converting a string to uppercase using a non-constant pointer to non-constant data.

Figure 7.12 demonstrates the error messages produced by the Borland C++ compiler when attempting to compile a function that receives a non-constant pointer to constant data, and that function uses the pointer to modify data.

As we know, arrays are aggregate data types that store many related data items of the same type under one name. In Chapter 10, we will discuss another form of aggregate data type called a *structure* (sometimes called a *record* in other languages). A structure is capable of storing many related data items of different data types under one name (e.g., storing information about each employee of a company). When a function is called with an array as an argument, the array is automatically passed to the function call by reference. However, structures are always passed call by value—a copy of the entire structure is passed. This requires the execution-time overhead of making a copy of each data item in the structure and storing it on the computer's function call stack. When structure data must be passed to a function, we can use pointers to constant data to get the performance of call by reference and the protection of call by value. When a pointer to a structure is passed, only a copy of the address at which the structure is stored must be

```
/* Printing a string one character at a time using */
/* a non-constant pointer to constant data          */
#include <stdio.h>

void printCharacters(const char *);

main()
{
    char string[] = "print characters of a string";

    printf("The string is:\n");
    printCharacters(string);
    putchar('\n');
    return 0;
}

void printCharacters(const char *s)
{
    for ( ; *s != '\0'; s++)    /* no initialization */
        putchar(*s);
}
```

```
The string is:
print characters of a string
```

Fig. 7.11   Printing a string one character at a time using a non-constant pointer to constant data.

made. On a machine with 4-byte addresses, a copy of 4 bytes of memory is made rather than a copy of possibly hundreds or thousands of bytes of the structure.

Performance Tip 7.1

Pass large objects such as structures using pointers to constant data to obtain the performance benefits of call by reference and the security of call by value.

Using pointers to constant data in this manner is an example of *time/space tradeoff.* If memory is low and execution efficiency is a major concern, pointers should be used. If memory is in abundance and efficiency is not a major concern, data should be passed call by value to enforce the principle of least privilege. Remember that some systems do not enforce **const** well, so call by value is still the best way to prevent data from being modified.

A constant pointer to non-constant data is a pointer that always points to the same memory location, and the data at that location can be modified through the pointer. This is the default for an array name. An array name is a constant pointer to the beginning of the array. All data in the array can be accessed and changed by using the array name and array subscripting. A constant pointer to non-constant data can be used to receive an array as an argument to a function that accesses array elements using only array subscript notation. Pointers that are declared **const** must be initialized when they are declared (if

```
/* Attempting to modify data through a    */
/* non-constant pointer to constant data */
#include <stdio.h>

void f(const int *);

main()
{
   int y;

   f(&y);      /* f attempts illegal modification */
   return 0;
}

void f(const int *x)
{
   *x = 100;   /* cannot modify a const object */
}
```

```
Compiling FIG7_12.C:
Error FIG7_12.C 17: Cannot modify a const object
Warning FIG7_12.C 18: Parameter 'x' is never used
```

Fig. 7.12   Attempting to modify data through a non-constant pointer to constant data.

the pointer is a function parameter, it is initialized with a pointer that is passed to the function). The program of Fig. 7.13 attempts to modify a constant pointer. Pointer **ptr** is declared to be of type **int * const**. The declaration is read from right to left as "**ptr** is a constant pointer to an integer." The pointer is initialized with the address of integer variable **x**. The program attempts to assign the address of **y** to **ptr**, but an error message is generated.

The least access privilege is granted by a constant pointer to constant data. Such a pointer always points to the same memory location, and the data at that memory location cannot be modified. This is how an array should be passed to a function that only looks at the array using array subscript notation and does not modify the array. The program of Fig. 7.14 declares pointer variable **ptr** to be of type **const int * const**. This declaration is read from right to left as "**ptr** is a constant pointer to an integer constant." The figure shows the error messages generated when an attempt is made to modify the data to which **ptr** points, and when an attempt is made to modify the address stored in the pointer variable.

7.6 Bubble Sort Using Call by Reference

Let us modify the bubble sort program of Fig. 6.15 to use two functions—**bubbleSort** and **swap**. Function **bubbleSort** performs the sort of the array. It calls function **swap** to exchange the array elements **array[j]** and **array[j + 1]** (see Fig. 7.15). Remem-

```
/* Attempting to modify a constant pointer to */
/* non-constant data                          */
#include <stdio.h>

main()
{
    int x, y;
    int * const ptr = &x;

    ptr = &y;
    return 0;
}
```

```
Compiling FIG7_13.C:
Error FIG7_13.C 10: Cannot modify a const object
Warning FIG7_13.C 12: 'ptr' is assigned a value that is
    never used
Warning FIG7_13.C 12: 'y' is declared but never used
```

Fig. 7.13 Attempting to modify a constant pointer to non-constant data.

```
/* Attempting to modify a constant pointer to */
/* constant data                              */
#include <stdio.h>

main()
{
    int x = 5, y;
    const int *const ptr = &x;

    *ptr = 7;
    ptr = &y;
    return 0;
}
```

```
Compiling FIG7_14.C:
Error FIG7_14.C 10: Cannot modify a const object
Error FIG7_14.C 11: Cannot modify a const object
Warning FIG7_14.C 13: 'ptr' is assigned a value that is
    never used
Warning FIG7_14.C 13: 'y' is declared but never used
```

Fig. 7.14 Attempting to modify a constant pointer to constant data.

ber that C enforces information hiding between functions, so **swap** does not have access to individual array elements in **bubbleSort**. Because **bubbleSort** *wants* **swap** to have access to the array elements to be swapped, **bubbleSort** passes each of these elements call by reference to **swap**—the address of each array element is passed explicitly. Although entire arrays are automatically passed call by reference, individual array elements are scalars, and are ordinarily passed call by value. Therefore, **bubbleSort** uses the address operator (**&**) on each of the array elements in the **swap** call as follows

```
swap(&array[j], &array[j + 1]);
```

to effect call by reference. Function **swap** receives **&array[j]** in pointer variable **element1Ptr**. Even though **swap**—because of information hiding—is not allowed to know the name **array[j]**, **swap** may use ***element1Ptr** as a synonym for **array[j]**. Therefore, when **swap** references ***element1Ptr**, it is actually referencing **array[j]** in **bubbleSort**. Similarly, when **swap** references ***element2Ptr**, it is actually referencing **array[j + 1]** in **bubbleSort**. Even though **swap** is not allowed to say

```
temp = array[j];
array[j] = array[j + 1];
array[j + 1] = temp;
```

precisely the same effect is achieved by

```
temp = *element1Ptr;
*element1Ptr = *element2Ptr;
*element2Ptr = temp;
```

in the **swap** function of Fig. 7.15.

Several features of function **bubbleSort** should be noted. The function header declares **array** as **int *array** rather than **int array[]** to indicate that **bubbleSort** receives a single-subscripted array as an argument (again, these notations are interchangeable). Parameter **size** is declared **const** to enforce the principle of least privilege. Although parameter **size** receives a copy of a value in **main**, and modifying the copy cannot change the value in **main**, **bubbleSort** does not need to alter **size** to accomplish its task. The size of the array remains fixed during the execution of **bubbleSort**. Therefore, **size** is declared **const** to ensure that it is not modified. If the size of the array is modified during the sorting process, it is possible that the sorting algorithm would not run correctly.

The prototype for function **swap** is included in the body of function **bubbleSort** because it is the only function that calls **swap**. Placing the prototype in **bubbleSort** restricts proper calls of **swap** to those made from **bubbleSort**. Other functions that attempt to call **swap** do not have access to a proper function prototype, so the compiler generates one automatically. This normally results in a prototype that does not match the function header (and generates a compiler error) because the compiler assumes **int** for the return type and the parameter types.

Software Engineering Observation 7.4

Placing function prototypes in the definitions of other functions enforces the principle of least privilege by restricting proper function calls to the functions in which the prototypes appear.

```
/* This program puts values into an array, sorts
   the values into ascending order, and prints the
   resulting array */
#include <stdio.h>
#define SIZE 10

void bubbleSort(int *, int);

main()
{
   int i, a[SIZE] = {2, 6, 4, 8, 10, 12, 89, 68, 45, 37};

   printf("Data items in original order\n");

   for (i = 0; i <= SIZE - 1; i++)
      printf("%4d", a[i]);

   bubbleSort(a, SIZE);              /* sort the array */
   printf("\nData items in ascending order\n");

   for (i = 0; i <= SIZE - 1; i++)
      printf("%4d", a[i]);

   printf("\n");
   return 0;
}

void bubbleSort(int *array, int size)
{
   int pass, j;
   void swap(int *, int *);

   for (pass = 1; pass <= size - 1; pass++)

      for (j = 0; j <= size - 2; j++)

         if (array[j] > array[j + 1])
            swap(&array[j], &array[j + 1]);
}

void swap(int *element1Ptr, int *element2Ptr)
{
   int temp;

   temp = *element1Ptr;
   *element1Ptr = *element2Ptr;
   *element2Ptr = temp;
}
```

```
Data items in original order
   2   6   4   8  10  12  89  68  45  37
Data items in ascending order
   2   4   6   8  10  12  37  45  68  89
```

Fig. 7.15 Bubble sort with call by reference.

Note that function **bubbleSort** receives the size of the array as a parameter. The function must know the size of the array to sort the array. When an array is passed to a function, the address in memory of the first element of the array is received by the function. The address does not provide any information to the function regarding the number of elements in the array. Therefore, the programmer must provide the function with the array size.

In the program, function **bubbleSort** was explicitly passed the size of the array. There are two main benefits to this approach—software reusability and proper software engineering. By defining the function so it receives the array size as an argument, we enable the function to be used by any program that sorts single-subscripted integer arrays, and the arrays can be any size.

Software Engineering Observation 7.5
___

When passing an array to a function, also pass the size of the array. This helps make the function more general. General functions are often reusable in many programs.

We could have stored the size of the array in a global variable that is accessible to the entire program. This would be more efficient because a copy of the size is not made to pass to the function. However, other programs that require an integer array sorting capability may not have the same global variable, so the function can not be used in those programs.

Software Engineering Observation 7.6
___

Global variables violate the principle of least privilege and are an example of poor software engineering.

Performance Tip 7.2
___

Passing the size of an array to a function takes time and requires additional stack space because a copy of the size is made to pass to the function. Global variables, however, require no additional time or space because they can be accessed directly by any function.

The size of the array could have been programmed directly into the function. This restricts the use of the function to an array of a specific size and reduces its reusability tremendously. Only programs processing single-subscripted integer arrays of the specific size coded into the function can use the function.

C provides the special *unary operator* **sizeof** to determine the size in bytes of an array (or any other data type) during program compilation. When applied to the name of an array as in Fig. 7.16, the **sizeof** operator returns the total number of bytes in the array as an integer. Note that variables of type **float** are normally stored in 4 bytes of memory, and **array** is declared to have 20 elements. Therefore, there are a total of 80 bytes in **array**.

The number of elements in an array also can be determined at compile time. For example, consider the following array declaration:

```
double real[22];
```

```
/* sizeof operator when used on an array name */
/* returns the number of bytes in the array   */
#include <stdio.h>

main()
{
   float array[20];

   printf("The number of bytes in the array is %d\n",
           sizeof(array));

   return 0;
}
```

```
The number of bytes in the array is 80
```

Fig. 7.16   The `sizeof` operator when applied to an array name returns the number of bytes in the array.

Variables of type **double** normally are stored in 8 bytes of memory. Thus, array **real** contains a total of 176 bytes. To determine the number of elements in the array, the following expression can be used:

```
sizeof(real) / sizeof(double)
```

The expression determines the number of bytes in array **real**, and divides that value by the number of bytes used in memory to store a **double** value.

The program of Fig. 7.17 calculates the number of bytes used to store each of the standard data types on a PC compatible.

Portability Tip 7.2

The number of bytes used to store a particular data type may vary between systems. When writing programs that depend on data type sizes, and that will run on several computer systems, use sizeof *to determine the number of bytes used to store the data types.*

Operator **sizeof** can be applied to any variable name, type, or constant. When applied to a variable name (that is not an array name) or a constant, the number of bytes used to store the specific type of variable or constant is returned. Note that the parentheses used with **sizeof** are required if a type name is supplied as its operand. Omitting the parenthese results in a syntax error. The parentheses are not required if a variable name is supplied as its operand.

7.7 Pointer Expressions and Pointer Arithmetic

Pointers are valid operands in arithmetic expressions, assignment expressions, and comparison expressions. However, not all the operators normally used in these expressions are valid in conjunction with pointer variables. This section describes the operators that can have pointers as operands, and how these operators are used.

```
/* Demonstrating the sizeof operator */
#include <stdio.h>

main()
{
    printf("         sizeof(char) = %d\n"
           "        sizeof(short) = %d\n"
           "          sizeof(int) = %d\n"
           "         sizeof(long) = %d\n"
           "        sizeof(float) = %d\n"
           "       sizeof(double) = %d\n"
           "sizeof(long double) = %d\n",
           sizeof(char), sizeof(short), sizeof(int),
           sizeof(long), sizeof(float), sizeof(double),
           sizeof(long double));
    return 0;
}
```

```
          sizeof(char) = 1
         sizeof(short) = 2
           sizeof(int) = 2
          sizeof(long) = 4
         sizeof(float) = 4
        sizeof(double) = 8
   sizeof(long double) = 10
```

Fig. 7.17   Using the **sizeof** operator to determine standard data type sizes.

A limited set of arithmetic operations may be performed on pointers. A pointer may be incremented (**++**) or decremented (**--**), an integer may be added to a pointer (**+** or **+=**), an integer may be subtracted from a pointer (**-** or **-=**), or one pointer may be subtracted from another.

Assume that array **int v[10]** has been declared and its first element is at location **3000** in memory. Assume pointer **vPtr** has been initialized to point to **v[0]**, i.e., the value of **vPtr** is **3000**. Figure 7.18 diagrams this situation for a machine with 4-byte integers. Note that **vPtr** can be initialized to point to array **v** with either of the statements

```
vPtr = v;
vPtr = &v[0];
```

Portability Tip 7.3

Most computers today have 2-byte or 4-byte integers. Some of the newer machines use 8-byte integers. Because the results of pointer arithmetic depends on the size of the objects a pointer points to, pointer arithmetic is machine dependent.

In conventional arithmetic, the addition **3000 + 2** yields the value **3002**. This is normally not the case with pointer arithmetic. When an integer is added to or subtracted from a pointer, the pointer is not simply incremented or decremented by that integer, but

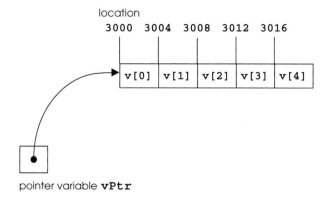

Fig. 7.18   The array **v** and a pointer variable **vPtr** that points to **v**.

by that integer times the size of the object to which the pointer refers. The number of bytes depends on the object's data type. For example, the statement

        vPtr += 2;

would produce **3008** (**3000 + 2 * 4**) assuming an integer is stored in 4 bytes of memory. In the array **v**, **vPtr** would now point to **v[2]** (Fig. 7.19). If an integer is stored in 2 bytes of memory, then the preceding calculation would result in memory location **3004** (**3000 + 2 * 2**). If the array were of a different data type, the preceding statement would increment the pointer by twice the number of bytes that it takes to store an object of that data type. When performing pointer arithmetic on a character array, the results will be consistent with regular arithmetic because each character is one byte long.

        If **vPtr** had been incremented to **3016**, which points to **v[4]**, the statement

        vPtr -= 4;

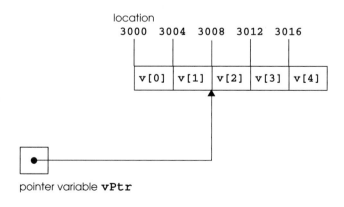

Fig. 7.19   The pointer **vPtr** after pointer arithmetic.

would set **vPtr** back to **3000**—the beginning of the array. If a pointer is being incremented or decremented by one, the increment (**++**) and decrement (**--**) operators can be used. Either of the statements

```
++vPtr;
vPtr++;
```

increment the pointer to point to the next location in the array. Either of the statements

```
--vPtr;
vPtr--;
```

decrement the pointer to point to the previous element of the array.

Pointer variables may be subtracted from one another. For example, if **vPtr** contains the location **3000**, and **v2Ptr** contains the address **3008**, the statement

```
x = v2Ptr - vPtr;
```

would assign to **x** the number of array elements from **vPtr** to **v2Ptr**, in this case, **2**. Pointer arithmetic is meaningless unless performed on an array. We can not assume that two variables of the same type are stored contiguously in memory unless they are adjacent elements of an array.

Common Programming Error 7.5

Using pointer arithmetic on a pointer that does not refer to an array of values.

Common Programming Error 7.6

Subtracting or comparing two pointers that do not refer to the same array.

Common Programming Error 7.7

Running off either end of an array when using pointer arithmetic.

A pointer can be assigned to another pointer if both pointers are of the same type. Otherwise, a cast operator must be used to convert the pointer on the right of the assignment to the pointer type on the left of the assignment. The exception to this rule is the pointer to **void** (i.e., **void ***) which is a generic pointer that can represent any pointer type. All pointer types can be assigned a pointer to **void**, and a pointer to **void** can be assigned a pointer of any type. In both cases, a cast operation is not required.

A pointer to **void** can not be dereferenced. For example, the compiler knows that a pointer to **int** refers to four bytes of memory on a machine with 4-byte integers, but a pointer to **void** simply contains a memory location for an unknown data type—the precise number of bytes to which the pointer refers is not known by the compiler. The compiler must know the data type to determine the number of bytes to be dereferenced for a particular pointer. In the case of a pointer to **void**, this number of bytes cannot be determined from the type.

Common Programming Error 7.8

*Assigning a pointer of one type to a pointer of another type if neither is of type **void *** causes a syntax error.*

Common Programming Error 7.9

Dereferencing a **void** * *pointer.*

Pointers can be compared using equality and relational operators, but such comparisons are meaningless unless the pointers point to members of the same array. Pointer comparisons compare the addresses stored in the pointers. A comparison of two pointers pointing to the same array could show, for example, that one pointer points to a higher-numbered element of the array than the other pointer does. A common use of pointer comparison is determining whether a pointer is **NULL**.

7.8 The Relationship between Pointers and Arrays

Arrays and pointers are intimately related in C and may be used *almost* interchangeably. An array name can be thought of as a constant pointer. Pointers can be used to do any operation involving array subscripting.

Performance Tip 7.3

Array subscripting notation is converted to pointer notation during compilation, so writing array subscripting expressions with pointer notation can save compile time.

Good Programming Practice 7.5

Use array notation instead of pointer notation when manipulating arrays. Although the program may take slightly longer to compile, it will probably be much clearer.

Assume that integer array **b[5]** and integer pointer variable **bPtr** have been declared. Since the array name (without a subscript) is a pointer to the first element of the array, we can set **bPtr** equal to the address of the first element in array **b** with the statement

```
bPtr = b;
```

This statement is equivalent to taking the address of the first element of the array as follows

```
bPtr = &b[0];
```

Array element **b[3]** can alternatively be referenced with the pointer expression

```
*(bPtr + 3)
```

The **3** in the above expression is the *offset* to the pointer. When the pointer points to the beginning of an array, the offset indicates which element of the array should be referenced, and the offset value is identical to the array subscript. The preceding notation is referred to as *pointer/offset notation*. The parentheses are necessary because the precedence of * is higher than the precedence of +. Without the parentheses, the above expression would add **3** to the value of the expression ***bPtr** (i.e., **3** would be added to **b[0]** assuming **bPtr** points to the beginning of the array). Just as the array element can be referenced with a pointer expression, the address

```
&b[3]
```

can be written with the pointer expression

```
bPtr + 3
```

The array itself can be treated as a pointer and used in pointer arithmetic. For example, the expression

```
*(b + 3)
```

also refers to the array element **b[3]**. In general, all subscripted array expressions can be written with a pointer and an offset. In this case, pointer/offset notation was used with the name of the array as a pointer. Note that the preceding statement does not modify the array name in any way; **b** still points to the first element in the array.

Pointers can be subscripted exactly as arrays can. For example, the expression

```
bPtr[1]
```

refers to the array element **b[1]**. This is referred to as *pointer/subscript notation.*

Remember that an array name is essentially a constant pointer; it always points to the beginning of the array. Thus, the expression

```
b += 3
```

is invalid because it attempts to modify the value of the array name with pointer arithmetic.

Common Programming Error 7.10

Attempting to modify an array name with pointer arithmetic is a syntax error.

The program in Fig. 7.20 uses the four methods we have discussed for referring to array elements—array subscripting, pointer/offset with the array name as a pointer, pointer subscripting, and pointer/offset with a pointer—to print the four elements of the integer array **b**.

To further illustrate the interchangeability of arrays and pointers, let us look at the two string copying functions—**copy1** and **copy2**—in the program of Fig. 7.21. Both functions copy a string (possibly a character array) into a character array. After a comparison of the function prototypes for **copy1** and **copy2**, the functions appear identical. They accomplish the same task; however, they are implemented differently.

Function **copy1** uses array subscript notation to copy the string in **s2** to the character array **s1**. The function declares an integer counter variable **i** to use as the array subscript. The **for** structure header performs the entire copy operation—its body is the empty statement. The header specifies that **i** is initialized to zero and incremented by one on each iteration of the loop. The condition in the **for** structure, **s1[i] = s2[i]**, performs the copy operation character by character from **s2** to **s1**. When the null character is encountered in **s2**, it is assigned to **s1**, and the loop terminates because the integer value of the null character is zero (false). Remember that the value of an assignment statement is the value assigned to the left argument.

```
/* Using subscripting and pointer notations with arrays */
#include <stdio.h>

main()
{
   int i, offset, b[] = {10, 20, 30, 40};
   int *bPtr = b;    /* set bPtr to point to array b */

   printf("Array b printed with:\n"
          "Array subscript notation\n");

   for (i = 0; i <= 3; i++)
      printf("b[%d] = %d\n", i, b[i]);

   printf("\nPointer/offset notation where \n"
          "the pointer is the array name\n");

   for (offset = 0; offset <= 3; offset++)
      printf("*(b + %d) = %d\n", offset, *(b + offset));

   printf("\nPointer subscript notation\n");

   for (i = 0; i <= 3; i++)
      printf("bPtr[%d] = %d\n", i, bPtr[i]);

   printf("\nPointer/offset notation\n");

   for (offset = 0; offset <= 3; offset++)
      printf("*(bPtr + %d) = %d\n", offset, *(bPtr + offset));

   return 0;
}
```

Fig. 7.20   Using four methods of referencing array elements (part 1 of 2).

Function **copy2** uses pointers and pointer arithmetic to copy the string in **s2** to the character array **s1**. Again, the **for** structure header performs the entire copy operation. The header does not include any variable initialization. As in function **copy1**, the condition (***s1 = *s2**) performs the copy operation. Pointer **s2** is dereferenced and the resulting character is assigned to the dereferenced pointer **s1**. After the assignment in the condition, the pointers are incremented to point to the next element of array **s1** and the next character of string **s2**, respectively. When the null character is encountered in **s2**, it is assigned to the dereferenced pointer **s1** and the loop terminates.

Note that the first argument to both **copy1** and **copy2** must be an array large enough to hold the string in the second argument. Otherwise, an error may occur when an attempt is made to write into a memory location that is not part of the array. Also, note that the second parameter of each function is declared as **const char *** (a constant string). In both functions, the second argument is copied into the first argument—characters are read from it one at a time, but the characters are never modified. Therefore, the second parameter is declared to point to a constant value so the principle of least privilege

```
Array b printed with:
Array subscript notation
b[0] = 10
b[1] = 20
b[2] = 30
b[3] = 40

Pointer/offset notation where
the pointer is the array name
*(b + 0) = 10
*(b + 1) = 20
*(b + 2) = 30
*(b + 3) = 40

Pointer subscript notation
bPtr[0] = 10
bPtr[1] = 20
bPtr[2] = 30
bPtr[3] = 40

Pointer/offset notation
*(bPtr + 0) = 10
*(bPtr + 1) = 20
*(bPtr + 2) = 30
*(bPtr + 3) = 40
```

Fig. 7.20   Using four methods of referencing array elements (part 2 of 2).

is enforced. Neither function requires the capability of modifying the second argument, so neither function is provided with that capability.

7.9 Arrays of Pointers

Arrays may contain pointers. A common use of such a data structure is to form an array of strings, referred to simply as a *string array*. Each entry in the array is a string, but in C a string is essentially a pointer to its first character. So each entry in an array of strings is actually a pointer to the first character of a string. Consider the declaration of string array **suit** that might be useful in representing a deck of cards.

```
char *suit[4] = {"Hearts", "Diamonds", "Clubs", "Spades"};
```

The **suit[4]** portion of the declaration indicates an array of 4 elements. The **char *** portion of the declaration indicates that each element of array **suit** is of type "pointer to **char**." The four values to be placed in the array are **"Hearts"**, **"Diamonds"**, **"Clubs"**, and **"Spades"**. Each of these is stored in memory as a NULL-terminated character string that is one character longer than the number of characters between quotes. The four strings are 7, 9, 6, and 7 characters long, respectively. Although it appears as though these strings are being placed in the **suit** array, only pointers are actually stored

```
/* Copying a string using array notation
   and pointer notation */
#include <stdio.h>

void copy1(char *, const char *);
void copy2(char *, const char *);

main()
{
    char string1[10], *string2 = "Hello",
         string3[10], string4[] = "Good Bye";

    copy1(string1, string2);
    printf("string1 = %s\n", string1);

    copy2(string3, string4);
    printf("string3 = %s\n", string3);
    return 0;
}

/* copy s2 to s1 using array notation */
void copy1(char *s1, const char *s2)
{
    int i;

    for (i = 0; s1[i] = s2[i]; i++)
        ;    /* do nothing in body */
}

/* copy s2 to s1 using pointer notation */
void copy2(char *s1, const char *s2)
{
    for ( ; *s1 = *s2; s1++, s2++)
        ;    /* do nothing in body */
}
```

```
string1 = Hello
string3 = Good Bye
```

Fig. 7.21   Copying a string using array notation and pointer notation.

in the array (Fig. 7.22). Each pointer points to the first character of its corresponding string. Thus, even though the **suit** array is fixed in size, it provides access to character strings of any length. This flexibility is one example of C's powerful data structuring capabilities.

The suits could have been placed into a double array in which each row would represent one suit, and each column would represent one of the letters of a suit name. Such a data structure would have to have a fixed number of columns per row, and that number would have to be as large as the largest string. Therefore, considerable memory could be

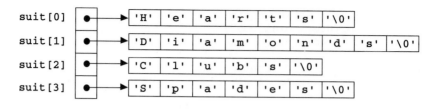

Fig. 7.22   A graphical example of the array `suit`.

wasted when a large number of strings being stored with most strings shorter than the longest string. We use arrays of strings to represent a deck of cards in the next section.

7.10 Case Study: A Card Shuffling and Dealing Simulation

In this section, we use random number generation to develop a card shuffling and dealing simulation program. This program can then be used to implement programs that play specific card games. To reveal some subtle performance problems, we have intentionally used sub-optimal shuffling and dealing algorithms. In the exercises and in Chapter 10, we develop more efficient algorithms.

Using the top-down, stepwise refinement approach, we develop a program that will shuffle a deck of 52 playing cards, and then deal each of the 52 cards. The top-down approach is particularly useful in attacking larger, more complex problems than we have seen in the early chapters.

We use a 4-by-13 double-subscripted array `deck` to represent the deck of playing cards (Fig. 7.23). The rows correspond to the suits—row 0 corresponds to hearts, row 1 to diamonds, row 2 to clubs, and row 3 to spades. The columns correspond to the face values of the cards—columns 0 through 9 correspond to faces ace through ten respectively, and columns 10 through 12 correspond to jack, queen, and king. We shall load string array `suit` with character strings representing the four suits, and string array `face` with character strings representing the thirteen face values.

This simulated deck of cards may be shuffled as follows. First the array `deck` is cleared to zeros. Then, a `row` (0–3) and a `column` (0–12) are chosen at random. The number 1 is inserted in array element `deck[row][column]` to indicate that this card is going to be the first one dealt from the shuffled deck. This process continues with the numbers 2, 3, ..., 52 being randomly inserted in the `deck` array to indicate which cards are to be placed second, third, ..., and fifty-second in the shuffled deck. As the `deck` array begins to fill with card numbers, it is possible that a card will be selected twice, i.e., `deck[row][column]` will be nonzero when it is selected. This selection is simply ignored and other `row`s and `column`s are repeatedly chosen at random until an unselected card is found. Eventually, the numbers 1 through 52 will occupy the 52 slots of the `deck` array. At this point, the deck of cards is fully shuffled.

This shuffling algorithm could execute indefinitely if cards that have already been shuffled are repeatedly selected at random. This phenomenon is known as *indefinite postponement*. In the exercises we discuss a better shuffling algorithm that eliminates the possibility of indefinite postponement.

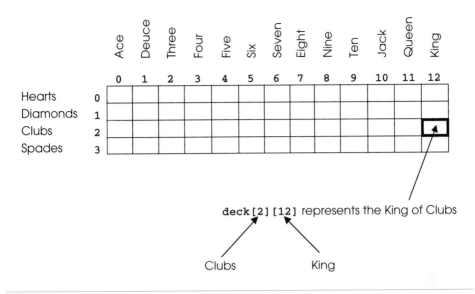

Fig. 7.23 Double-subscripted array representation of a deck of cards.

Performance Tip 7.4

Sometimes an algorithm that emerges in a "natural" way can contain subtle performance problems such as indefinite postponement. Seek algorithms that avoid indefinite postponement.

To deal the first card we search the array for `deck[row][column]` `= 1`. This is accomplished with a nested `for` structure that varies `row` from 0 to 3 and `column` from 0 to 12. What card does that slot of the array correspond to? The `suit` array has been preloaded with the four suits, so to get the suit we print the character string `suit[row]`. Similarly, to get the face value of the card, we print the character string `face[column]`. We also print the character string `" of "`. Printing this information in the proper order enables us to print each card in the form `"King of Clubs"`, `"Ace of Diamonds"`, and so on.

Let us proceed with the top-down, stepwise refinement process. The top is simply

Shuffle and deal 52 cards

Our first refinement yields:

Initialize the suit array
Initialize the face array
Initialize the deck array
Shuffle the deck
Deal 52 cards

"Shuffle the deck" may be expanded as follows:

For each of the 52 cards
    Place card number in randomly selected unoccupied slot of deck

"Deal 52 cards" may be expanded as follows:

For each of the 52 cards
    Find card number in deck array and print face and suit of card

Incorporating these expansions yields our complete second refinement:

Initialize the suit array
Initialize the face array
Initialize the deck array

For each of the 52 cards
    Place card number in randomly selected unoccupied slot of deck

For each of the 52 cards
    Find card number in deck array and print face and suit of card

"Place card number in randomly selected unoccupied slot of deck" may be expanded as follows:

Choose slot of deck randomly
While chosen slot of deck has been previously chosen
    Choose slot of deck randomly
Place card number in chosen slot of deck

"Find card number in deck array and print face and suit of card" may be expanded as follows:

For each slot of the deck array
    If slot contains card number
        Print the face and suit of the card

Incorporating these expansions yields our third refinement:

Initialize the suit array
Initialize the face array
Initialize the deck array

For each of the 52 cards
    Choose slot of deck randomly
    While slot of deck has been previously chosen
        Choose slot of deck randomly
    Place card number in chosen slot of deck

For each of the 52 cards
    For each slot of deck array
        If slot contains desired card number
            Print the face and suit of the card

This completes the refinement process. Note that this program is more efficient if the shuffle and deal portions of the algorithm are combined so each card is dealt as it is placed in the deck. We have chosen to program these operations separately because normally cards are dealt after they are shuffled (not while they are shuffled).

The card shuffling and dealing program is shown in Fig. 7.24 and a sample execution is shown in Fig. 7.25. Note the use of the conversion specifier `%s` to print strings of characters in the calls to `printf`. The corresponding argument in the `printf` call must be a pointer to `char` (or a `char` array). In the `deal` function, the format specification `"%5s of %-8s"` prints a character string right-justified in a field of five characters followed by `" of "` and a character string left-justified in a field of eight characters. The minus sign in `%-8s` signifies that the string is left-justified in a field of width 8.

```c
/* Card dealing program */

#include <stdio.h>
#include <stdlib.h>
#include <time.h>

void shuffle(int [][13]);
void deal(const int [][13], const char *[], const char *[]);

main()
{
   char *suit[4] = {"Hearts", "Diamonds", "Clubs", "Spades"};
   char *face[13] = {"Ace", "Deuce", "Three", "Four",
                     "Five", "Six", "Seven", "Eight",
                     "Nine", "Ten", "Jack", "Queen", "King"};
   int deck[4][13] = {0};

   srand(time(NULL));

   shuffle(deck);
   deal(deck, face, suit);

   return 0;
}

void shuffle(int wDeck[][13])
{
   int card, row, column;

   for (card = 1; card <= 52; card++) {
      row = rand() % 4;
      column = rand() % 13;

      while (wDeck[row][column] != 0) {
         row = rand() % 4;
         column = rand() % 13;
      }

      wDeck[row][column] = card;
   }
}
```

Fig. 7.24 Card dealing program (part 1 of 2).

```
void deal(const int wDeck[][13], const char *wFace[],
        const char *wSuit[])
{
   int card, row, column;

   for (card = 1; card <= 52; card++)

      for (row = 0; row <= 3; row++)

         for (column = 0; column <= 12; column++)

            if (wDeck[row][column] == card)
               printf("%5s of %-8s%c",
                      wFace[column], wSuit[row],
                      card % 2 == 0 ? '\n' : '\t');
}
```

Fig. 7.24   Card dealing program (part 2 of 2).

Six of Clubs	Seven of Diamonds
Ace of Spades	Ace of Diamonds
Ace of Hearts	Queen of Diamonds
Queen of Clubs	Seven of Hearts
Ten of Hearts	Deuce of Clubs
Ten of Spades	Three of Spades
Ten of Diamonds	Four of Spades
Four of Diamonds	Ten of Clubs
Six of Diamonds	Six of Spades
Eight of Hearts	Three of Diamonds
Nine of Hearts	Three of Hearts
Deuce of Spades	Six of Hearts
Five of Clubs	Eight of Clubs
Deuce of Diamonds	Eight of Spades
Five of Spades	King of Clubs
King of Diamonds	Jack of Spades
Deuce of Hearts	Queen of Hearts
Ace of Clubs	King of Spades
Three of Clubs	King of Hearts
Nine of Clubs	Nine of Spades
Four of Hearts	Queen of Spades
Eight of Diamonds	Nine of Diamonds
Jack of Diamonds	Seven of Clubs
Five of Hearts	Five of Diamonds
Four of Clubs	Jack of Hearts
Jack of Clubs	Seven of Spades

Fig. 7.25   Sample run of card dealing program.

There is a weakness in the dealing algorithm. Once a match is found, even if it is found on the first try, the two inner **for** structures continue searching the remaining ele ments of **deck** for a match. In the exercises and in a case study in Chapter 10, we correct this deficiency.

7.11 Pointers to Functions

A pointer to a function contains the address of the function in memory. In Chapter 6, we saw that an array name is really the address in memory of the first element of the array. Similarly, a function name is really the starting address in memory of the code that performs the function's task. Pointers to functions can be passed to functions, returned from functions, stored in arrays, and assigned to other function pointers.

To illustrate the use of pointers to functions, we have modified the bubble sort program of Fig. 7.15 to form the program of Fig. 7.26. Our new program consists of **main**, and the functions **bubble**, **swap**, **ascending**, and **descending**. Function **bubbleSort** receives a pointer to a function—either function **ascending** or function **descending**—as an argument in addition to an integer array and the size of the array. The program prompts the user to choose if the array should be sorted in ascending order or in descending order. If the user enters 1, a pointer to function **ascending** is passed to function **bubble** causing the array to be sorted into increasing order. If the user enters 2, a pointer to function **descending** is passed to function **bubble** causing the array to be sorted into decreasing order. The output of the program is shown in Fig. 7.27.

The following parameter appears in the function header for **bubble**:

```
int (*compare)(int, int)
```

This tells **bubble** to expect a parameter that is a pointer to a function that receives two integer parameters and returns an integer result. Parentheses are needed around ***compare** because ***** has a lower precedence than the parentheses enclosing the function parameters. If we had not included the parentheses, the declaration would have been

```
int *compare(int, int)
```

which declares a function that receives two integers as parameters and returns a pointer to an integer.

The corresponding parameter in the function prototype of **bubble** is

```
int (*)(int, int)
```

Note that only types have been included, but for documentation purposes the programmer can include names that the compiler will ignore.

The function passed to **bubble** is called in an **if** statement as follows

```
if ((*compare)(work[count], work[count + 1]))
```

Just as a pointer to a variable is dereferenced to access the value of the variable, a pointer to a function is dereferenced to use the function.

The call to the function could have been made without dereferencing the pointer as in

```
if (compare(work[count], work[count + 1]))
```

```c
/* Multipurpose sorting program using function pointers */
#include <stdio.h>
#define SIZE 10

void bubble(int *, const int, int (*)(int, int));
int ascending(const int, const int);
int descending(const int, const int);

main()
{
   int a[SIZE] = {2, 6, 4, 8, 10, 12, 89, 68, 45, 37};
   int counter, order;

   printf("Enter 1 to sort in ascending order,\n");
   printf("Enter 2 to sort in descending order: ");
   scanf("%d", &order);

   printf("\nData items in original order\n");

   for (counter = 0; counter <= SIZE - 1; counter++)
      printf("%4d", a[counter]);

   if (order == 1) {
      bubble(a, SIZE, ascending);
      printf("\nData items in ascending order\n");
   }
   else {
      bubble(a, SIZE, descending);
      printf("\nData items in descending order\n");
   }

   for (counter = 0; counter <= SIZE - 1; counter++)
      printf("%4d", a[counter]);

   printf("\n");

   return 0;
}

void bubble(int *work, const int size, int (*compare)(int, int))
{
   int pass, count;
   void swap(int *, int *);

   for (pass = 1; pass <= size - 1; pass++)

      for (count = 0; count <= size - 2; count++)

         if ((*compare)(work[count], work[count + 1]))
            swap(&work[count], &work[count + 1]);
}
```

Fig. 7.26   Multipurpose sorting program using function pointers (part 1 of 2).

```
void swap(int *element1Ptr, int *element2Ptr)
{
   int temp;

   temp = *element1Ptr;
   *element1Ptr = *element2Ptr;
   *element2Ptr = temp;
}

int ascending(const int a, const int b)
{
   return b < a;
}

int descending(const int a, const int b)
{
   return b > a;
}
```

Fig. 7.26   Multipurpose sorting program using function pointers (part 2 of 2).

which uses the pointer directly as the function name. We prefer the first method of calling a function through a pointer because it explicitly illustrates that **compare** is a pointer to a function that is dereferenced to call the function. The second method of calling a function through a pointer makes it appear as though **compare** is an actual function. This may be confusing to a user of the program who would like to see the definition of function **compare** and finds that it is never defined in the file.

```
Enter 1 to sort in ascending order,
Enter 2 to sort in descending order: 1

Data items in original order
   2    6    4    8   10   12   89   68   45   37
Data items in ascending order
   2    4    6    8   10   12   37   45   68   89
```

```
Enter 1 to sort in ascending order,
Enter 2 to sort in descending order: 2

Data items in original order
   2    6    4    8   10   12   89   68   45   37
Data items in descending order
  89   68   45   37   12   10    8    6    4    2
```

Fig. 7.27   The outputs of the bubble sort program in Fig. 7.26.

A common use of function pointers is in so-called menu driven systems. A user is prompted to select an option from a menu (possibly from 1 to 5). Each option is serviced by a different function. Pointers to each function are stored in an array of pointers to functions. The user's choice is used as a subscript into the array, and the pointer in the array is used to call the function.

The program of Fig. 7.28 provides a generic example of the mechanics of declaring and using an array of pointers to functions. Three functions are defined—**function1**, **function2**, and **function3**— that each take an integer argument and return nothing. Pointers to these three functions are stored in array **f** which is declared as follows:

```
void (*f[3])(int) = {function1, function2, function3};
```

The declaration is read beginning in the leftmost set of parentheses, "**f** is an array of 3 pointers to functions that take an **int** as an argument and that return **void**." The array is initialized with the names of the three functions. When the user enters a value between 0 and 2, the value is used as the subscript into the array of pointers to functions. The function call is made as follows:

```
(*f[choice])(choice);
```

In the call, **f[choice]** selects the pointer at location **choice** in the array. The pointer is dereferenced to call the function, and **choice** is passed as the argument to the function. Each function prints its argument's value and its function name to indicate that the function is called correctly. In the exercises, you will develop a menu-driven system.

Summary

- Pointers are variables that contain as their values addresses of other variables.

- Pointers must be declared before they can be used.

- The declaration

    ```
    int *ptr;
    ```

    declares **ptr** to be a pointer to an object of type **int**, and is read, "**ptr** is a pointer to **int**." The ***** as used here in a declaration indicates that the variable is a pointer.

- There are three values that can be used to initialize a pointer; **0**, **NULL**, or an address. Initializing a pointer to **0** and initializing that same pointer to **NULL** are identical.

- The only integer that can be assigned to a pointer is 0.

- The **&** (address) operator returns the address of its operand.

- The operand of the address operator must be a variable; the address operator can not be applied to constants, to expressions, or to variables declared with the storage class **register**.

- The ***** operator, referred to as the indirection or dereferencing operator, returns the value of the object that its operand points to in memory. This is called dereferencing the pointer.

```
/* Demonstrating an array of pointers to functions */
#include <stdio.h>

void function1(int);
void function2(int);
void function3(int);

main()
{
    void (*f[3])(int) = {function1, function2, function3};
    int choice;

    printf("Enter a number between 0 and 2, 3 to end: ");
    scanf("%d", &choice);

    while (choice >= 0 && choice < 3) {
        (*f[choice])(choice);
        printf("Enter a number between 0 and 2, 3 to end: ");
        scanf("%d", &choice);
    }

    printf("You entered 3 to end\n");
    return 0;
}

void function1(int a)
{
    printf("You entered %d so function1 was called\n\n", a);
}

void function2(int b)
{
    printf("You entered %d so function2 was called\n\n", b);
}

void function3(int c)
{
    printf("You entered %d so function3 was called\n\n", c);
}
```

```
Enter a number between 0 and 2, 3 to end: 0
You entered 0 so function1 was called

Enter a number between 0 and 2, 3 to end: 1
You entered 1 so function2 was called

Enter a number between 0 and 2, 3 to end: 2
You entered 2 so function3 was called

Enter a number between 0 and 2, 3 to end: 3
You entered 3 to end
```

Fig. 7.28   Demonstrating an array of pointers to functions.

- When calling a function with an argument that the caller wants the called function to modify, the address of the argument is passed. The called function then uses the indirection operator (*****) to modify the value of the argument in the calling function.

- A function receiving an address as an argument must include a pointer as its corresponding formal parameter.

- It is not necessary to include the names of pointers in function prototypes; it is only necessary to include the pointer types. Pointer names may be included for documentation reasons, but the compiler ignores them.

- The **const** qualifier enables the programmer to inform the compiler that the value of a particular variable should not be modified.

- If an attempt is made to modify a value that is declared **const**, the compiler catches it and issues either a warning or an error depending on the particular compiler.

- There are four ways to pass a pointer to a function: a non-constant pointer to non-constant data, a constant pointer to non-constant data, a constant pointer to non-constant data, and a constant pointer to constant data.

- Arrays are automatically passed by reference because the value of the array name is the address of the array.

- To pass a single element of an array call by reference, the address of the specific array element must be passed.

- C provides the special unary operator **sizeof** to determine the size in bytes of an array (or any other data type) during program compilation.

- When applied to the name of an array, the **sizeof** operator returns the total number of bytes in the array as an integer.

- Operator **sizeof** can be applied to any variable name, type, or constant.

- The arithmetic operations that may be performed on pointers are incrementing (**++**) a pointer, decrementing (**--**) a pointer, adding (**+** or **+=**) a pointer and an integer, subtracting (**-** or **-=**) a pointer and an integer, and subtracting one pointer from another.

- When an integer is added or subtracted from a pointer, the pointer is incremented or decremented by that integer times the size of the object pointed to.

- Pointer arithmetic operations should only be performed on contiguous portions of memory such as an array. All elements of an array are stored contiguously in memory.

- When performing pointer arithmetic on a character array, the results are like regular arithmetic because each character is stored in one byte of memory.

- Pointers can be assigned to one another if both pointers are of the same type. Otherwise, a cast must be used. The exception to this is a pointer to **void** which is a generic pointer type that can hold pointers of any type. Pointers to **void** can be assigned pointers of other types and can be assigned to pointers of other types without a cast.

- A pointer to **void** may not be dereferenced.

- Pointers can be compared using the equality and relational operators. Pointer comparisons are normally meaningful only if the pointers point to members of the same array.

- Pointers can be subscripted exactly as array names can.

- An array name without a subscript is a pointer to the first element of the array.

- In pointer/offset notation, the offset is the same as an array subscript.

- All subscripted array expressions can be written with a pointer and an offset using either the name of the array as a pointer, or a separate pointer that points to the array.

- An array name is a constant pointer that always points to the same location in memory. Array names can not be modified as conventional pointers can.

- It is possible to have arrays of pointers.

- It is possible to have pointers to functions.

- A pointer to a function is the address where the code for the function resides.

- Pointers to functions can be passed to functions, returned from functions, stored in arrays, and assigned to other pointers.

- A common use of function pointers is in so called menu-driven systems.

Terminology

adding a pointer and an integer
address operator (`&`)
array of pointers
array of strings
call by reference
call by value
character pointer
`const`
constant pointer
constant pointer to constant data
constant pointer to non-constant data
decrement a pointer
dereference a pointer
dereferencing operator (`*`)
directly reference a variable
dynamic memory allocation
function pointer
increment a pointer
indefinite postponement
indirection
indirection operator (`*`)
indirectly reference a variable
initializing pointers
linked list

non-constant pointer to constant data
non-constant pointer to non-constant data
`NULL` pointer
offset
pointer
pointer arithmetic
pointer assignment
pointer comparison
pointer expression
pointer indexing
pointer/offset notation
pointer subscripting
pointer to a function
pointer to `void` (`void *`)
pointer types
principle of least privilege
simulated call by reference
`sizeof`
string array
subtracting an integer from a pointer
subtracting two pointers
top-down, stepwise refinement
`void *` (pointer to `void`)

Common Programming Errors

7.1   The indirection operator * does not distribute to all variable names in a declaration. Each pointer must be declared with the * prefixed to the name.

7.2   Dereferencing a pointer that has not been initialized, or that has not been assigned to point to a specific location in memory. This could cause a fatal execution time error, or it could accidentally modify important data and allow the program to run to completion providing incorrect results.

7.3   Not dereferencing a pointer when it is necessary to do so to obtain the value to which the pointer points.

7.4   Being unaware that a function is expecting pointers as arguments for call-by-reference and passing arguments call by value. Some compilers take the values assuming they are pointers and dereference the values as pointers. At run-time, memory access violations or segmentation faults are often generated. Other compilers catch the mismatch in types between arguments and parameters and generate error messages.

7.5   Using pointer arithmetic on a pointer that does not refer to an array of values.

7.6   Subtracting or comparing two pointers that do not refer to the same array.

7.7   Running off either end of an array when using pointer arithmetic.

7.8   Assigning a pointer of one type to a pointer of another type if neither is of type **void *** causes a syntax error.

7.9   Dereferencing a **void *** pointer.

7.10   Although array names are pointers to the beginning of the array, and pointers can be modified in arithmetic expressions, array names can not be modified in arithmetic expressions.

Good Programming Practices

7.1   Include the letters **ptr** in pointer variable names to make it clear that these variables are pointers and thus need to be handled appropriately.

7.2   Initialized pointers to prevent unexpected results.

7.3   Use call by value to pass arguments to a function unless the value of the variable must be modified. This is an example of the principle of least privilege. Some people prefer call by reference for performance reasons because the overhead of copying values is avoided.

7.4   Before using a function, check the function prototype for the function to determine if the function is able to modify the values passed to it.

7.5   Use array notation instead of pointer notation when manipulating arrays. Although the program may take slightly longer to compile, it will probably be much clearer.

Performance Tips

7.1   Pass large objects such as structures using pointers to constant data to obtain the performace benefits of call by reference and the security of call by value.

7.2   Passing the size of an array to a function takes time and requires additional stack space because a copy of the size is made to pass to the function. Global variables, however, require no additional time or space because they can be accessed directly by any function.

7.3   Array subscripting notation is converted to pointer notation during compilation, so writing array subscripting expressions with pointer notation can save compile time.

7.4   Sometimes an algorithm that emerges in a "natural" way can contain subtle performance problems such as indefinite postponement. Seek algorithms that avoid indefinite postponement.

Portability Tips

7.1   Although **const** is well defined in ANSI C, some systems do not enforce it.

7.2   The number of bytes used to store a particular data type may vary between systems. When writing programs that depend on data type sizes, and that will run on several computer systems, be sure to use **sizeof** to determine the number of bytes used to store the data types.

7.3   Most computers today have 2-byte or 4-byte integers. Some of the newer machines use 8-byte integers. Because the results of pointer arithmetic depends on the size of the objects a pointer points to, pointer arithmetic is machine dependent.

Software Engineering Observations

7.1   The **const** qualifier can be used to enforce the principle of least privilege. Using the principle of least privilege to properly design software tremendously reduces debugging time and improper side effects, and makes a program easier to modify and maintain.

7.2   If a value does not (or should not) change in the body of a function to which it is passed, the value should be declared **const** to ensure that it is not accidentally modified.

7.3   Only one value can be altered in a calling function when call by value is used. That value must be assigned from the return value of the function. To modify multiple values in a calling function, call by reference must be used.

7.4   Placing function prototypes in function definitions enforces the principle of least privilege by restricting proper function calls to the functions in which the prototypes appear.

7.5   When passing an array to a function, also pass the size of the array. This helps make the function more general. General functions are often reusable in many programs.

7.6   Global variables violate the principle of least privilege and are an example of poor software engineering.

Self-Review Exercises

7.1   Answer each of the following:
  a) A pointer is a variable that contains as its value the _____ of another variable.
  b) The three values that can be used to initialize a pointer are _____, _____, or an _____.
  c) The only integer that can be assigned to a pointer is _____.

7.2   State whether the following are true or false. If the answer is false, explain why.
  a) The address operator **&** can only be applied to constants, to expressions, and to variables declared with the storage class **register**.
  b) A pointer that is declared to be **void** can be dereferenced.
  c) Pointers of different types may not be assigned to one another without a cast operation.

7.3   Answer each of the following. Assume that single-precision floating-point numbers are stored in 4 bytes, and that the starting address of the array is at location 1002500 in memory. Each part of the exercise should use the results of previous parts where appropriate.
  a) Declare an array of type **float** called **numbers** with 10 elements, and initialize the elements to the values **0.0**, **1.1**, **2.2**, ..., **9.9**. Assume the symbolic constant **SIZE** has been defined as **10**.
  b) Declare a pointer **nPtr** that points to an object of type **float**.
  c) Print the elements of array **numbers** using array subscript notation. Use a **for** structure, and assume the integer control variable **i** has been declared. Print each number with 1 position of precision to the right of the decimal point.

    d) Give two separate statements that assign the starting address of array **numbers** to the pointer variable **nPtr**.

    e) Print the elements of array **numbers** using pointer/offset notation with the pointer **nPtr**.

    f) Print the elements of array **numbers** using pointer/offset notation with the array name as the pointer.

    g) Print the elements of array **numbers** by subscripting pointer **nPtr**.

    h) Refer to element 4 of array **numbers** using array subscript notation, pointer/offset notation with the array name as the pointer, pointer subscript notation with **nPtr**, and pointer/offset notation with **nPtr**.

    i) Assuming that **nPtr** points to the beginning of array **numbers**, what address is referenced by **nPtr + 8**? What value is stored at that location?

    j) Assuming that **nPtr** points to **numbers[5]**, what address is referenced by **nPtr -= 4**. What is the value stored at that location?

7.4 For each of the following, write a single statement that performs the indicated task. Assume that floating-point variables **number1** and **number2** have been declared, and that **number1** has been initialized to **7.3**.

    a) Declare the variable **fPtr** to be a pointer to an object of type **float**.

    b) Assign the address of variable **number1** to pointer variable **fPtr**.

    c) Print the value of the object pointed to by **fPtr**.

    d) Assign the value of the object pointed to by **fPtr** to variable **number2**.

    e) Print the value of **number2**.

    f) Print the address of **number1**. Use the **%p** conversion specifier.

    g) Print the address stored in **fPtr**. Use the **%p** conversion specifier. Is the value printed the same as the address of **number1**?

7.5 Do each of the following.

    a) Write the function header for a function called **exchange** that takes two pointers to floating-point numbers **x** and **y** as parameters, and does not return a value.

    b) Write the function prototype for the function in part (a).

    c) Write the function header for a function called **evaluate** that returns an integer and that takes as parameters integer **x** and a pointer to function **poly**. Function **poly** takes an integer parameter and returns an integer.

    d) Write the function prototype for the function in part (c).

7.6 Find the error in each of the following program segments. Assume

```
int *zPtr;    /* zPtr will reference array z */
int *aPtr = NULL;
void *sPtr = NULL;
int number, i;
int z[5] = {1, 2, 3, 4, 5};

sPtr = z;
```

    a) ++zptr;

    b) `/* use pointer to get first value of array */`
```
number = zPtr;
```

    c) `/* assign array element 2 (the value 3) to number */`
```
number = *zPtr[2];
```

    d) `/* print entire array z */`
```
for (i = 0; i <= 5; i++)
    printf("%d ", zPtr[i]);
```

```
e)  /* assign the value pointed to by sPtr to number */
    number = *sPtr;
f)  ++z;
```

Answers to Self-Review Exercises

7.1   a) address. b) 0, NULL, an address. c) 0.

7.2
a) False. The address operator can only be applied to variables, and it can not be applied to variables declared with storage class **register**.
b) False. A pointer to **void** cannot be dereferenced because there is no way to know exactly how many bytes of memory should be dereferenced.
c) False. Pointers of type **void** can be assigned pointers of other types, and pointers of type **void** can be assigned to pointers of other types.

7.3
```
a)  float numbers[SIZE] = {0.0, 1.1, 2.2, 3.3, 4.4, 5.5,
                           6.6, 7.7, 8.8, 9.9};
b)  float *nPtr;
c)  for (i = 0; i <= SIZE - 1; i++)
        printf("%.1f ", numbers[i]);
d)  nPtr = numbers;
    nPtr = &numbers[0];
e)  for (i = 0; i <= SIZE - 1; i++)
        printf("%.1f ", *(nPtr + i));
f)  for (i = 0; i <= SIZE - 1; i++)
        printf("%.1f ", *(numbers + i));
g)  for (i = 0; i <= SIZE - 1; i++)
        printf("%.1f ", nPtr[i]);
h)  numbers[4]
    *(numbers + 4)
    nPtr[4]
    *(nPtr + 4)
```
i) The address is 1002500 + 8 * 4 = 1002532. The value is 8.8.
j) The address of numbers[5] is 1002500 + 5 * 4 = 1002520. The address of nPtr -= 4 is 1002520 - 4 * 4 = 1002504. The value at that location is 1.1.

7.4
```
a)  float *fPtr;
b)  fPtr = &number1;
c)  printf("The value of *fPtr is %f\n", *fPtr);
d)  number2 = *fPtr;
e)  printf("The value of number2 is %f\n", number2);
f)  printf("The address of number1 is %p\n", &number1);
g)  printf("The address stored in fptr is %p\n", fPtr);
```
Yes, the value is the same.

7.5
```
a)  void exchange(float *x, float *y)
b)  void exchange(float *, float *);
c)  int evaluate(int x, int (*poly)(int))
d)  int evaluate(int, int (*)(int));
```

7.6
a) Error: zPtr has not been initialized.
  Correction: Initialize zPtr with zPtr = z;
b) Error: The pointer is not dereferenced.
  Correction: Change the statement to number = *zPtr;
c) Error: zPtr[2] is not a pointer and should not be dereferenced.

Correction: Change `*zPtr[2]` to `zPtr[2]`.

d) Error: Referring to an array element outside the array bounds with pointer subscripting.
Correction: Change the final value of the control variable in the `for` structure to **4**.

e) Error: Dereferencing a void pointer.
Correction: In order to dereference the pointer, it must first be cast to an integer pointer. Change the above statement to `number = *(int *)sPtr;`

f) Error: Trying to modify an array name with pointer arithmetic.
Correction: Use a pointer variable instead of the array name to accomplish pointer arithmetic, or subscript the array name to refer to a specific element.

Exercises

7.7   Answer each of the following:

a) The _____ operator returns the location in memory where its operand is stored.

b) The _____ operator returns the value of the object to which its operand points.

c) To simulate call by reference when passing a non-array variable to a function, it is necessary to pass the _____ of the variable to the function.

7.8   State whether the following are true or false. If false, explain why.

a) Two pointers that point to different arrays cannot be compared meaningfully.

b) Because the name of an array is a pointer to the first element of the array, array names may be manipulated in precisely the same manner as pointers.

7.9   Answer each of the following. Assume that unsigned integers are stored in 2 bytes, and that the starting address of the array is at location 1002500 in memory.

a) Declare an array of type `unsigned int` called `values` with 5 elements, and initialize the elements to the even integers from 2 to 10. Assume the symbolic constant `SIZE` has been defined as **5**.

b) Declare a pointer `vPtr` that points to an object of type `unsigned int`.

c) Print the elements of array `values` using array subscript notation. Use a `for` structure and assume integer control variable `i` has been declared.

d) Give two separate statements that assign the starting address of array `values` to pointer variable `vPtr`.

e) Print the elements of array `values` using pointer/offset notation.

f) Print the elements of array `values` using pointer/offset notation with the array name as the pointer.

g) Print the elements of array `values` by subscripting the pointer to the array.

h) Refer to element 5 of array `values` using array subscript notation, pointer/offset notation with the array name as the pointer, pointer subscript notation, and pointer/offset notation.

i) What address is referenced by `vPtr + 3`? What value is stored at that location?

j) Assuming `vPtr` points to `values[4]`, what address is referenced by `vPtr -= 4`. What value is stored at that location?

7.10   For each of the following, write a single statement that performs the indicated task. Assume that long integer variables `value1` and `value2` have been declared, and that `value1` has been initialized to **200000**.

a) Declare the variable `lPtr` to be a pointer to an object of type `long`.

b) Assign the address of variable `value1` to pointer variable `lPtr`.

c) Print the value of the object pointed to by **1Ptr**.
d) Assign the value of the object pointed to by **1Ptr** to variable **value2**.
e) Print the value of **value2**.
f) Print the address of **value1**.
g) Print the address stored in **1Ptr**. Is the value printed the same as the address of **value1**?

7.11   Do each of the following.
a) Write the function header for function **zero** which takes a long integer array parameter **bigIntegers** and does not return a value.
b) Write the function prototype for the function in part **(a)**.
c) Write the function header for function **add1AndSum** which takes an integer array parameter **oneTooSmall** and returns an integer.
d) Write the function prototype for the function described in part **(c)**.

Note: Exercises 7.12 through 7.15 are reasonably challenging. Once you have done these problems, you ought to be able to implement most popular card games easily.

7.12   Modify the program in Fig. 7.24 so that the card dealing function deals a five card poker hand. Then write the following additional functions:
a) Determine if the hand contains a pair.
b) Determine if the hand contains two pairs.
c) Determine if the hand contains three of a kind (e.g., three jacks).
d) Determine if the hand contains four of a kind (e.g., four aces).
e) Determine if the hand contains a flush (i.e., all five cards of the same suit).
f) Determine if the hand contains a straight (i.e., five cards of consecutive face values).

7.13   Use the functions developed in Exercise 7.12 to write a program that deals two five-card poker hands, evaluates each hand, and determines which is the better hand.

7.14   Modify the program developed in Exercise 7.13 so that it can simulate the dealer. The dealer's five-card hand is dealt "face down" so the player cannot see it. The program should then evaluate the dealer's hand and, based on the quality of the hand, the dealer should draw one, two, or three more cards to replace the corresponding number of unneeded cards in the original hand. The program should then reevaluate the dealer's hand. (*Caution:* This is a difficult problem!)

7.15   Modify the program developed in Exercise 7.14 so that it can handle the dealer's hand automatically, but the player is allowed to decide which cards of the player's hand to replace. The program should then evaluate both hands and determine who wins. Now use this new program to play 20 games against the computer. Who wins more games, you or the computer? Have one of your friends play 20 games against the computer. Who wins more games? Based on the results of these games, make appropriate modifications to refine your poker playing program (this, too, is a difficult problem). Play 20 more games. Does your modified program play a better game?

7.16   In the card shuffling and dealing program of Fig. 7.24, we intentionally used an inefficient shuffling algorithm that introduced the possibility of indefinite postponement. In this problem, you will create a high-performance shuffling algorithm that avoids indefinite postponement.

Modify the program of Fig. 7.24 as follows. Begin by initializing the **deck** array as shown in Fig. 7.29. Modify the **shuffle** function to loop row-by-row and column-by-column through the array touching every element once. Each element should be swapped with a randomly selected element of the array.

Print the resulting array to determine if the deck is satisfactorily shuffled (as in Fig. 7.30, for example). You may want your program to call the **shuffle** function several times to ensure a satisfactory shuffle.

	0	1	2	3	4	5	6	7	8	9	10	11	12
0	1	2	3	4	5	6	7	8	9	10	11	12	13
1	14	15	16	17	18	19	20	21	22	23	24	25	26
2	27	28	29	30	31	32	33	34	35	36	37	38	39
3	40	41	42	43	44	45	46	47	48	49	50	51	52

Fig. 7.29   Unshuffled **deck** array.

	0	1	2	3	4	5	6	7	8	9	10	11	12
0	19	40	27	25	36	46	10	34	35	41	18	2	44
1	13	28	14	16	21	30	8	11	31	17	24	7	1
2	12	33	15	42	43	23	45	3	29	32	4	47	26
3	50	38	52	39	48	51	9	5	37	49	22	6	20

Fig. 7.30   Sample shuffled **deck** array.

Note that although the approach in this problem improves the shuffling algorithm, the dealing algorithm still requires searching the **deck** array for card 1, then card 2, then card 3, and so on. Worse yet, even after the dealing algorithm locates and deals the card, the algorithm continues searching through the remainder of the deck. Modify the program of Fig. 7.24 so that once a card is dealt, no further attempts are made to match that card number, and the program immediately proceeds with dealing the next card. In Chapter 10 we develop a dealing algorithm that requires only one operation per card.

7.17   (*Simulation: The Tortoise and the Hare*) In this problem you will recreate one of the truly great moments in history, namely the classic race of the tortoise and the hare. You will use random number generation to develop a simulation of this memorable event.

Our contenders begin the race at "square 1" of 70 squares. Each square represents a possible position along the race course. The finish line is at square 70. The first contender to reach or pass square 70 is rewarded with a pail of fresh carrots and lettuce. The course weaves its way up the side of a slippery mountain, so occasionally the contenders lose ground.

There is a clock that ticks once per second. With each tick of the clock, your program should adjust the position of the animals according to the following rules:

Animal	Move type	Percentage of the time	Actual move
Tortoise	Fast plod	50%	3 squares to the right
	Slip	20%	6 squares to the left
	Slow plod	30%	1 square to the right
Hare	Sleep	20%	No move at all
	Big hop	20%	9 squares to the right
	Big slip	10%	12 squares to the left
	Small hop	30%	1 square to the right
	Small slip	20%	2 squares to the left

Use variables to keep track of the positions of the animals (i.e., position numbers are 1-70). Start each animal at position 1 (i.e., the "starting gate"). If an animal slips left before square 1, move the animal back to square 1.

Generate the percentages in the preceding table by producing a random integer, i, in the range $1 \leq i \leq 10$. For the tortoise, perform a "fast plod" when $1 \leq i \leq 5$, a "slip" when $6 \leq i \leq 7$, or a "slow plod" when $8 \leq i \leq 10$. Use a similar technique to move the hare.

Begin the race by printing

```
BANG !!!!!
AND THEY'RE OFF !!!!!
```

Then, for each tick of the clock (i.e., each repetition of a loop), print a 70 position line showing the letter **T** in the position of the tortoise and the letter **H** in the position of the hare. Occasionally, the contenders will land on the same square. In this case, the tortoise bites the hare and your program should print **OUCH!!!** beginning at that position. All print positions other than the **T**, the **H**, or the **OUCH!!!** (in case of a tie) should be blank.

After each line is printed, test if either animal has reached or passed square 70. If so, then print the winner and terminate the simulation. If the tortoise wins, print **TORTOISE WINS!!! YAY!!!** If the hare wins, print **Hare wins. Yuch.** If both animals win on the same tick of the clock, you may want to favor the turtle (the "underdog"), or you may want to print **It's a tie**. If neither animal wins, perform the loop again to simulate the next tick of the clock. When you are ready to run your program, assemble a group of fans to watch the race. You'll be amazed at how involved your audience gets!

Special Section: Building Your Own Computer

In the next several problems, we take a temporary diversion away from the world of high-level language programming. We "peel open" a computer and look at its internal structure. We introduce machine language programming and write several machine language programs. To make this an especially valuable experience, we then build a computer (through the technique of software-based *simulation*) on which you can execute your machine language programs!

7.18 (*Machine Language Programming*) Let us create a computer we will call the Simpletron. As its name implies, it is a simple machine, but, as we will soon see, a powerful one as well. The Simpletron runs programs written in the only language it directly understands, that is, Simpletron Machine Language, or SML for short.

The Simpletron contains an *accumulator*—a "special register" in which information is put before the Simpletron uses that information in calculations or examines it in various ways. All information in the Simpletron is handled in terms of *words*. A word is a signed four-digit decimal number such as **+3364**, **-1293**, **+0007**, **-0001**, etc. The Simpletron is equipped with a 100-word memory, and these words are referenced by their location numbers **00**, **01**, ..., **99**.

Before running an SML program, we must *load* or place the program into memory. The first instruction (or statement) of every SML program is always placed in location **00**.

Each instruction written in SML occupies one word of the Simpletron's memory (and hence instructions are signed four-digit decimal numbers). We shall assume that the sign of an SML instruction is always plus, but the sign of a data word may be either plus or minus. Each location in the Simpletron's memory may contain either an instruction, a data value used by a program, or an unused (and hence undefined) area of memory. The first two digits of each SML instruction are the *operation code,* which specifies the operation to be performed. SML operation codes are summarized in Fig. 7.31.

The last two digits of an SML instruction are the *operand,* which is the address of the memory location containing the word to which the operation applies. Now let us consider several simple SML programs.

Operation code	Meaning
Input/output operations:	
#define READ 10	Read a word from the terminal into a specific location in memory.
#define WRITE 11	Write a word from a specific location in memory to the terminal.
Load/store operations:	
#define LOAD 20	Load a word from a specific location in memory into the accumulator.
#define STORE 21	Store a word from the accumulator into a specific location in memory.
Arithmetic operations:	
#define ADD 30	Add a word from a specific location in memory to the word in the accumulator (leave result in accumulator).
#define SUBTRACT 31	Subtract a word from a specific location in memory from the word in the accumulator (leave result in accumulator).
#define DIVIDE 32	Divide a word from a specific location in memory into the word in the accumulator (leave result in accumulator).
#define MULTIPLY 33	Multiply a word from a specific location in memory by the word in the accumulator (leave result in accumulator).
Transfer of control operations:	
#define BRANCH 40	Branch to a specific location in memory.
#define BRANCHNEG 41	Branch to a specific location in memory if the accumulator is negative.
#define BRANCHZERO 42	Branch to a specific location in memory if the accumulator is zero.
#define HALT 43	Halt, i.e., the program has completed its task.

Fig. 7.31   Simpletron Machine Language (SML) operation codes.

Example 1 Location	Number	Instruction
00	+1007	(Read A)
01	+1008	(Read B)
02	+2007	(Load A)
03	+3008	(Add B)
04	+2109	(Store C)
05	+1109	(Write C)
06	+4300	(Halt)
07	+0000	(Variable A)
08	+0000	(Variable B)
09	+0000	(Result C)

This SML program reads two numbers from the keyboard and computes and prints their sum. The instruction +1007 reads the first number from the keyboard and places it into location 07 (which has been initialized to zero). Then +1008 reads the next number into location 08. The *load* instruction, +2007, puts the first number into the accumulator, and the *add* instruction, +3008, adds the second number to the number in the accumulator. *All SML arithmetic instructions leave their results in the accumulator.* The *store* instruction, +2109, places the result back into memory location 09 from which the *write* instruction, +1109, takes the number and prints it (as a signed four-digit decimal number). The *halt* instruction, +4300, terminates execution.

Example 2 Location	Number	Instruction
00	+1009	(Read A)
01	+1010	(Read B)
02	+2009	(Load A)
03	+3110	(Subtract B)
04	+4107	(Branch negative to 07)
05	+1109	(Write A)
06	+4300	(Halt)
07	+1110	(Write B)
08	+4300	(Halt)
09	+0000	(Variable A)
10	+0000	(Variable B)

This SML program reads two numbers from the keyboard and determines and prints the larger value. Note the use of the instruction +4107 as a conditional transfer of control, much the same as C's `if` statement. Now write SML programs to accomplish each of the following tasks.

a) Use a sentinel-controlled loop to read 10 positive numbers and compute and print their sum.

b) Use a counter-controlled loop to read seven numbers, some positive and some negative, and compute and print their average.

c) Read a series of numbers and determine and print the largest number. The first number read indicates how many numbers should be processed.

7.19   (*A Computer Simulator*) It may at first seem outrageous, but in this problem you are going to build your own computer. No, you will not be soldering components together. Rather, you will use the powerful technique of *software-based simulation* to create a *software model* of the Simpletron. You will not be disappointed. Your Simpletron simulator will turn the computer you are using into a Simpletron, and you will actually be able to run, test, and debug the SML programs you wrote in Exercise 7.18.

When you run your Simpletron simulator, it should begin by printing:

```
*** Welcome to Simpletron! ***

*** Please enter your program one instruction ***
*** (or data word) at a time. I will type the ***
*** location number and a question mark (?).  ***
*** You then type the word for that location. ***
*** Type the sentinel -99999 to stop entering ***
*** your program. ***
```

Simulate the memory of the Simpletron with a single-subscripted array **memory** that has 100 elements. Now assume that the simulator is running, and let us examine the dialog as we enter the program of Example 2 of Exercise 7.18:

```
00 ? +1009
01 ? +1010
02 ? +2009
03 ? +3110
04 ? +4107
05 ? +1109
06 ? +4300
07 ? +1110
08 ? +4300
09 ? +0000
10 ? +0000
11 ? -99999

*** Program loading completed ***
*** Program execution begins   ***
```

The SML program has now been placed (or loaded) into the array **memory**. Now the Simpletron executes your SML program. Execution begins with the instruction in location **00** and, like C, continues sequentially, unless directed to some other part of the program by a transfer of control.

Use the variable **accumulator** to represent the accumulator register. Use the variable **instructionCounter** to keep track of the location in memory that contains the instruction being performed. Use the variable **operationCode** to indicate the operation currently being performed, i.e., the left two digits of the instruction word. Use the variable **operand** to indicate the memory location on which the current instruction operates. Thus, **operand** is the rightmost two digits of the instruction currently being performed. Do not execute instructions directly from memory. Rather, transfer the next instruction to be performed from memory to a variable called **instructionRegister**. Then "pick off" the left two digits and place them in **operationCode**, and "pick off" the right two digits and place them in **operand**.

When Simpletron begins execution, the special registers are initialized as follows:

```
accumulator          +0000
instructionCounter      00
instructionRegister +0000
operationCode           00
operand                 00
```

Now let us "walk through" the execution of the first SML instruction, **+1009** in memory location **00**. This is called an *instruction execution cycle.*

The **instructionCounter** tells us the location of the next instruction to be performed. We *fetch* the contents of that location from **memory** by using the C statement

```
instructionRegister = memory[instructionCounter];
```

The operation code and the operand are extracted from the instruction register by the statements

```
operationCode = instructionRegister / 100;
operand = instructionRegister % 100;
```

Now the Simpletron must determine that the operation code is actually a *read* (versus a *write*, a *load*, etc.). A **switch** differentiates among the twelve operations of SML.

In the **switch** structure, the behavior of various SML instructions is simulated as follows (we leave the others to the reader):

read:	`scanf("%d", &memory[operand]);`
load:	`accumulator = memory[operand];`
add:	`accumulator += memory[operand];`

Various branch instructions: We'll discuss these shortly.

halt: This instruction prints the message
*** Simpletron execution terminated ***

and then prints the name and contents of each register as well as the complete contents of memory. Such a printout is often called a *computer dump* (and, no, a computer dump is not a place where old computers go). To help you program your dump function, a sample dump format is shown in Fig. 7.32. Note that a dump after executing a Simpletron program would show the actual values of instructions and data values at the moment execution terminated.

Let us proceed with the execution of our program's first instruction, namely the **+1009** in location **00**. As we have indicated, the **switch** statement simulates this by performing the C statement

```
scanf("%d", &memory[operand]);
```

A question mark (**?**) should be displayed on the screen before the **scanf** is executed to prompt the user for input. The Simpletron waits for the user to type a value and then press the *Return key.* The value is then read into location **09**.

At this point, simulation of the first instruction is completed. All that remains is to prepare the Simpletron to execute the next instruction. Since the instruction just performed was not a transfer of control, we need merely increment the instruction counter register as follows:

```
++instructionCounter;
```

This completes the simulated execution of the first instruction. The entire process (i.e., the instruction execution cycle) begins anew with the fetch of the next instruction to be executed.

Now let us consider how the branching instructions—the transfers of control—are simulated. All we need to do is adjust the value in the instruction counter appropriately. Therefore, the unconditional branch instruction (**40**) is simulated within the **switch** as

```
instructionCounter = operand;
```

```
REGISTERS:
accumulator          +0000
instructionCounter      00
instructionRegister  +0000
operationCode           00
operand                 00

MEMORY:
           0      1      2      3      4      5      6      7      8      9
  0    +0000  +0000  +0000  +0000  +0000  +0000  +0000  +0000  +0000  +0000
 10    +0000  +0000  +0000  +0000  +0000  +0000  +0000  +0000  +0000  +0000
 20    +0000  +0000  +0000  +0000  +0000  +0000  +0000  +0000  +0000  +0000
 30    +0000  +0000  +0000  +0000  +0000  +0000  +0000  +0000  +0000  +0000
 40    +0000  +0000  +0000  +0000  +0000  +0000  +0000  +0000  +0000  +0000
 50    +0000  +0000  +0000  +0000  +0000  +0000  +0000  +0000  +0000  +0000
 60    +0000  +0000  +0000  +0000  +0000  +0000  +0000  +0000  +0000  +0000
 70    +0000  +0000  +0000  +0000  +0000  +0000  +0000  +0000  +0000  +0000
 80    +0000  +0000  +0000  +0000  +0000  +0000  +0000  +0000  +0000  +0000
 90    +0000  +0000  +0000  +0000  +0000  +0000  +0000  +0000  +0000  +0000
```

Fig. 7.32   A sample dump.

The conditional "branch if accumulator is zero" instruction is simulated as

```
if (accumulator == 0)
    instructionCounter = operand;
```

At this point you should implement your Simpletron simulator and run each of the SML programs you wrote in Exercise 7.18. You may embellish SML with additional features and provide for these in your simulator.

Your simulator should check for various types of errors. During the program loading phase, for example, each number the user types into the Simpletron's **memory** must be in the range **-9999** to **+9999**. Your simulator should use a **while** loop to test that each number entered is in this range, and, if not, keep prompting the user to reenter the number until the user enters a correct number.

During the execution phase, your simulator should check for various serious errors, such as attempts to divide by zero, attempts to execute invalid operation codes, accumulator overflows (i.e., arithmetic operations resulting in values larger than **+9999** or smaller than **-9999**), and the like. Such serious errors are called *fatal errors*. When a fatal error is detected, your simulator should print an error message such as:

```
*** Attempt to divide by zero ***
*** Simpletron execution abnormally terminated ***
```

and should print a full computer dump in the format we have discussed previously. This will help the user locate the error in the program.

7.20   Modify the card shuffling and dealing program of Fig. 7.24 so the shuffling and dealing operations are performed by the same function (**shuffleAndDeal**). The function should contain one nested looping structure that is similar to function **shuffle** in Fig. 7.24.

7.21   What does this program do?

```c
#include <stdio.h>

void mystery1(char *, const char *);

main()
{
   char string1[80], string2[80];

   printf("Enter two strings: ");
   scanf("%s%s", string1, string2);
   mystery1(string1, string2);
   printf("%s\n", string1);
   return 0;
}

void mystery1(char *s1, const char *s2)
{
   while (*s1 != '\0')
      ++s1;

   for ( ; *s1 = *s2; s1++, s2++)
      ;    /* empty statement */
}
```

7.22   What does this program do?

```c
#include <stdio.h>

int mystery2(const char *);

main()
{
   char string[80];

   printf("Enter a string: ");
   scanf("%s", string);
   printf("%d\n", mystery2(string));
   return 0;
}

int mystery2(const char *s)
{
   int x = 0;

   for ( ; *s != '\0'; s++)
      ++x;

   return x;
}
```

7.23   Find the error in each of the following program segments. If the error can be corrected, explain how.

    a) `int *number;`
       `printf("%d\n", *number);`

b) ```
float *realPtr;
long *integerPtr;
integerPtr = realPtr;
```
c) ```
int * x, y;
x = y;
```
d) ```
char s[] = "this is a character array";
int count;
for (; *s != '\0'; s++)
    printf("%c ", *s);
```
e) ```
short *numPtr, result;
void *genericPtr = numPtr;
result = *genericPtr + 7;
```
f) ```
float x = 19.34;
float xPtr = &x;
printf("%f\n", xPtr);
```
g) ```
char *s;
printf("%s\n", s);
```

7.24 (*Quicksort*) In the examples and exercises of Chapter 6, we discussed the sorting techniques of bubble sort, bucket sort, and selection sort. We now present the recursive sorting technique called Quicksort. The basic algorithm for a single-subscripted array of values is as follows:

1) *Partitioning Step:* Take the first element of the unsorted array and determine its final location in the sorted array. This occurs when all values to the left of the element in the array are less than the element, and all values to the right of the element in the array are greater than the element. We now have one element in its proper location and two unsorted subarrays.

2) *Recursive Step:* Perform step 1 on each unsorted subarray.

Each time step 1 is performed on a subarray, another element is placed in its final location of the sorted array, and two unsorted subarrays are created. When a subarray consists of one element, it must be sorted, therefore that element is in its final location.

The basic algorithm seems simple enough, but how do we determine the final position of the first element of each subarray. As an example, consider the following set of values (the element in bold is the partitioning element—it will be placed in its final location in the sorted array):

37   2   6   4   89   8   10   12   68   45

1) Starting from the rightmost element of the array, compare each element to **37** until an element less than **37** is found, then swap **37** and that element. The first element less than **37** is 12, so **37** and 12 are swapped. The new array is:

12   2   6   4   89   8   10   **37**   68   45

Element 12 is in italic to indicate that it was just swapped with **37**.

2) Starting from the left of the array, but beginning with the element after 12, compare each element to **37** until an element greater than **37** is found, then swap **37** and that element. The first element greater than **37** is 89, so **37** and 89 are swapped. The new array is:

12   2   6   4   **37**   8   10   *89*   68   45

3) Starting from the right, but beginning with the element before 89, compare each element to **37** until an element less than **37** is found, then swap **37** and that element. The first element less than **37** is 10, so **37** and 10 are swapped. The new array is:

$$12 \quad 2 \quad 6 \quad 4 \quad \textit{10} \quad 8 \quad \textbf{37} \quad 89 \quad 68 \quad 45$$

4) Starting from the left, but beginning with the element after 10, compare each element to **37** until an element greater than **37** is found, then swap **37** and that element. There are no more elements greater than **37** , so when we compare **37** to itself we know that **37** has been placed in its final location of the sorted array.

Once the partition has been applied on the above array, there are two unsorted subarrays. The subarray with values less than 37 contains 12, 2, 6, 4, 10, and 8. The subarray with values greater than 37 contains 89, 68, and 45. The sort continues with both subarrays being partitioned in the same manner as the original array.

Based on the preceding discussion, write recursive function `quicksort` to sort a single subscripted integer array. The function should receive as arguments an integer array, a starting subscript, and an ending subscript. Function `partition` should be called by `quicksort` to perform the partitioning step.

7.25 (*Maze Traversal*) The following grid of ones and zeros is a double-subscripted array representation of a maze.

```
1 1 1 1 1 1 1 1 1 1 1 1
1 0 0 0 1 0 0 0 0 0 0 1
0 0 1 0 1 0 1 1 1 1 0 1
1 1 1 0 1 0 0 0 0 1 0 1
1 0 0 0 0 1 1 1 0 1 0 0
1 1 1 1 0 1 0 1 0 1 0 1
1 0 0 1 0 1 0 1 0 1 0 1
1 1 0 1 0 1 0 1 0 1 0 1
1 0 0 0 0 0 0 0 0 1 0 1
1 1 1 1 1 1 0 1 1 1 0 1
1 0 0 0 0 0 0 1 0 0 0 1
1 1 1 1 1 1 1 1 1 1 1 1
```

The ones represent the walls of the maze, and the zeros represent squares in the possible paths through the maze.

There is a simple algorithm for walking through a maze that guarantees finding the exit (assuming there is an exit). If there is not an exit, you will arrive at the starting location again. Place your right hand on the wall to your right and begin walking forward. Never remove your hand from the wall. If the maze turns to the right, you follow the wall to the right. As long as you do not remove your hand from the wall, eventually you will arrive at the exit of the maze. There may be a shorter path than the one you have taken, but you are guaranteed to get out of the maze.

Write recursive function `mazeTraverse` to walk through the maze. The function should receive as arguments a 12-by-12 character array representing the maze, and the starting location of the maze. As `mazeTraverse` attempts to locate the exit from the maze, it should place the character **X** in each square in the path. The function should display the maze after each move so the user can watch as the maze is solved.

7.26 (*Generating Mazes Randomly*) Write a function `mazeGenerator` that takes as an argument a double-subscripted 12-by-12 character array and randomly produces a maze. The function should also provide the starting and ending locations of the maze. Try your function `mazeTraverse` from Exercise 7.25 using several randomly generated mazes.

7.27 (*Mazes of Any Size*) Generalize functions `mazeTraverse` and `mazeGenerator` of Exercises 7.25 and 7.26 to process mazes of any width and height.

7.28   (*Arrays of Pointers to Functions*) Rewrite the program of Fig. 6.22 to use a menu driven interface. The program should offer the user 4 options as follows:

```
Enter a choice:
  0  Print the array of grades
  1  Find the minimum grade
  2  Find the maximum grade
  3  Print the average on all tests for each student
  4  End program
```

One restriction on using arrays of pointers to functions is that all the pointers must have the same type. The pointers must be to functions of the same return type that receive arguments of the same type. For this reason, the functions in Fig. 6.22 must be modified so they each return the same type and take the same parameters. Modify functions **minimum** and **maximum** to print the minimum or maximum value and return nothing. For option 3, modify function **average** of Fig. 6.22 to output the average for each student (not a specific student). Function **average** should return nothing and take the same parameters as **printArray**, **minimum**, and **maximum**. Store the pointers to the four functions in array **processGrades** and use the choice made by the user as the subscript into the array for calling each function.

7.29   (*Modifications to the Simpletron Simulator*) In Exercise 7.19, you wrote a software simulation of a computer that executes programs written in Simpletron Machine Language (SML). In this exercise, we propose several modifications and enhancements to the Simpletron Simulator. In Exercises 12.26 and 12.27, we propose building a compiler that converts programs written in a high-level programming language (a variation of BASIC) to Simpletron Machine Language. Some of the following modifications and enhancements may be required to execute the programs produced by the compiler.

   a) Extend the Simpletron Simulator's memory to contain 1000 memory locations to enable the Simpletron to handle larger programs.

   b) Allow the simulator to perform modulus calculations. This requires an additional Simpletron Machine Language instruction.

   c) Allow the simulator to perform exponentiation calculations. This requires an additional Simpletron Machine Language instruction.

   d) Modify the simulator to use hexadecimal values rather than integer values to represent Simpletron Machine Language instructions.

   e) Modify the simulator to allow output of a newline. This requires an additional Simpletron Machine Language instruction.

   f) Modify the simulator to process floating point values in addition to integer values.

   g) Modify the simulator to handle string input. Hint: Each Simpletron word can be divided into two groups, each holding a two-digit integer. Each two-digit integer represents the ASCII decimal equivalent of a character. Add a machine language instruction that will input a string and store the string beginning at a specific Simpletron memory location. The first half of the word at that location will be a count of the number of characters in the string (i.e., the length of the string). Each succeeding half word contains one ASCII character expressed as two decimal digits. The machine language instruction converts each character into its ASCII equivalent and assigns it to a half word.

   h) Modify the simulator to handle output of strings stored in the format of part (g). Hint: Add a machine language instruction that will print a string beginning at a certain Simpletron memory location. The first half of the word at that location is a count of the number of characters in the string (i.e., the length of the string). Each succeeding half word contains one ASCII character expressed as two decimal digits. The machine language instruction checks the length and prints the string by translating each two-digit number into its equivalent character.

7.30 What does this program do?

```
#include <stdio.h>

int mystery3(const char *, const char *);

main()
{
    char string1[80], string2[80];

    printf("Enter two strings: ");
    scanf("%s%s", string1, string2);
    printf("The result is %d\n", mystery3(string1, string2));

    return 0;
}

int mystery3(const char *s1, const char *s2)
{
    for ( ; *s1 != '\0' && *s2 != '\0'; s1++, s2++)

        if (*s1 != *s2)
            return 0;

    return 1;
}
```

8

Characters
and Strings

Objectives

- To be able to use the functions of the character handling library (`ctype`).
- To be able to use the string and character input/output functions of the standard input/output library (`stdio`).
- To be able to use the string conversion functions of the general utilities library (`stdlib`).
- To be able to use the string processing functions of the string handling library (`string`).
- To appreciate the power of function libraries as a means of achieving software reuseability.

The chief defect of Henry King
Was chewing little bits of string.
Hilaire Belloc

Suit the action to the word, the word to the action.
William Shakespeare

Vigorous writing is concise. A sentence should contain no
unnecessary words, a paragraph no unnecessary sentences.
William Strunk, Jr.

In a concatenation accordingly.
Oliver Goldsmith

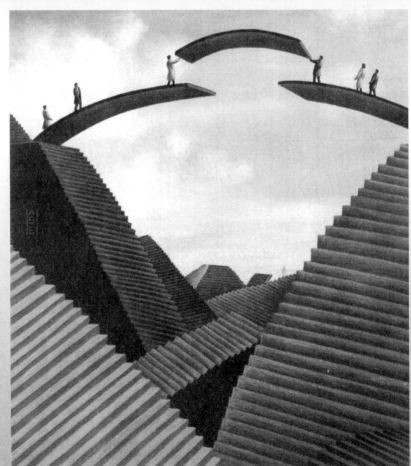

Outline

8.1 Introduction

In this chapter, we introduce the C standard library functions that facilitate string and character processing. The functions enable programs to process characters, strings, lines of text, and blocks of memory.

The chapter discusses the techniques used to develop editors, word processors, page layout software, computerized typesetting systems, and other kinds of text-processing software. The text manipulations performed by formatted input/output functions like **printf** and **scanf** can be implemented using the functions discussed in this chapter.

8.2 Fundamentals of Strings and Characters

Characters are the fundamental building blocks of source programs. Every program is composed of a sequence of characters that—when grouped together meaningfully—is interpreted by the computer as a series of instructions used to accomplish a task. A program may contain *character constants*. A character constant is an **int** value represented as a character in single quotes. The value of a character constant is the integer value of the character in the machine's character set. For example, **'z'** represents the integer value of z, and **'\n'** represents the integer value of newline.

A string is a series of characters treated as a single unit. A string may include letters, digits, and various *special characters* such as **+**, **-**, *****, **/**, **$**, and others. *String literals* or *string constants* in C are written in double quotation marks as follows:

"John Q. Doe"   (a name)
"99999 Main Street"   (a street address)
"Waltham, Massachusetts"   (a city and state)
"(201) 555-1212"   (a telephone number)

A string in C is an array of characters ending in the *null character (' \ 0 ')*. A string is accessed via a pointer to the first character in the string. The value of a string is the address of its first character. Thus in C it is appropriate to say that *a string is a pointer*—in fact a pointer to the string's first character. In this sense, strings are like arrays, because an array is also a pointer to its first element.

A string may be assigned in a declaration to either a character array or a variable of type **char ***. The declarations

```
char color[] = "blue";
char *colorPtr = "blue";
```

each initialize a variable to the string **"blue"**. The first declaration creates a 5-element array **color** containing the characters **'b'**, **'l'**, **'u'**, **'e'**, and **'\0'**. The second declaration creates pointer variable **colorPtr** that points to the string **"blue"** somewhere in memory.

Portability Tip 8.1

*When a variable of type **char *** is initialized with a string literal, some compilers may place the string in a location in memory where the string cannot be modified. If you may need to modify a string literal, it should be stored in a character array to ensure modifiability on all systems.*

The preceding array declaration could also have been written

```
char color[] = {'b', 'l', 'u', 'e', '\0'};
```

When declaring a character array to contain a string, the array must be large enough to store the string and its terminating **NULL** character. The preceding declaration determines the size of the array automatically based on the number of initializers in the initializer list.

Common Programming Error 8.1

*Not allocating sufficient space in a character array to store the **NULL** character that terminates a string.*

Common Programming Error 8.2

*Printing a "string" that does not contain a terminating **NULL** character.*

Good Programming Practice 8.1

When storing a string of characters in a character array, be sure the array is large enough to hold the largest string that will be stored. C allows strings of any length to be stored. If a string is longer than the character array in which it is to be stored, characters beyond the end of the array will overwrite data in memory following the array.

A string can be assigned to an array using **scanf**. For example, the following statement assigns a string to character array **word[20]**.

```
scanf("%s", word);
```

The string entered by the user is stored in **word** (note that **word** is an array which is, of course, a pointer so the **&** is not needed with argument **word**). Function **scanf** will read characters until a space, newline, or end-of-file indicator is encountered. Note that the string should be no longer than 19 characters to leave room for the terminating **NULL** character. For a character array to be printed as a string, the array must contain a terminating **NULL** character.

Common Programming Error 8.3

Processing a single character as a string. A string is a pointer—probably a respectably large integer. However, a character is a small integer (ASCII values range 0-255). On many systems this causes an error because low memory addresses are reserved for special purposes such as operating system interrupt handlers—so, "access violations" occur.

Common Programming Error 8.4

Passing a character as an argument to a function when a string is expected.

Common Programming Error 8.5

Passing a string as an argument to a function when a character is expected.

8.3 Character Handling Library

The character handling library includes several functions that perform useful tests and manipulations of character data. Each function receives a character—represented as an **int**—or **EOF** as an argument. As we discussed in Chapter 4, characters are often manipulated as integers because a character in C is a one-byte integer. Remember that **EOF** normally has the value -1 and some hardware architectures do not allow negative values to be stored in **char** variables. Therefore, the character handling functions manipulate characters as integers. Figure 8.1 summarizes the functions of the character handling library.

Good Programming Practice 8.2

*When using functions from the character handling library, include the **<ctype.h>** header file.*

The program of Fig. 8.2 demonstrates functions *isdigit*, *isalpha*, *isalnum*, and *isxdigit*. Function **isdigit** determines whether its argument is a digit (**0-9**). Function **isalpha** determines whether its argument is an uppercase letter (**A-Z**) or a lowercase letter (**a-z**). Function **isalnum** determines whether its argument is an uppercase letter, a lowercase letter, or a digit. Function **isxdigit** determines whether its argument is a hexadecimal digit (**A-F, a-f, 0-9**).

The program of Fig. 8.2 uses the conditional operator (**?:**) with each function to determine whether the string **" is a "** or the string **" is not a "** should be printed in the output for each character tested. For example, the expression

```
isdigit('8') ? "8 is a " : "8 is not a "
```

Prototype	Function description
int isdigit(int c)	Returns a true value if c is a digit, and 0 (false) otherwise.
int isalpha(int c)	Returns a true value if c is a letter, and 0 otherwise.
int isalnum(int c)	Returns a true value if c is a digit or a letter, and 0 otherwise.
int isxdigit(int c)	Returns a true value if c is a hexadecimal digit character, and 0 otherwise. (See Appendix E, "Number Systems," for a detailed explanation of binary numbers, octal numbers, decimal numbers, and hexadecimal numbers.)
int islower(int c)	Returns a true value if c is a lowercase letter, and 0 otherwise.
int isupper(int c)	Returns a true value if c is an uppercase letter, and 0 otherwise.
int tolower(int c)	If c is an uppercase letter, tolower returns c as a lowercase letter. Otherwise, tolower returns the argument unchanged.
int toupper(int c)	If c is a lowercase letter, toupper returns c as an uppercase letter. Otherwise, toupper returns the argument unchanged.
int isspace(int c)	Returns a true value if c is a white-space character—newline ('\n'), space (' '), form feed ('\f'), carriage return ('\r'), horizontal tab ('\t'), or vertical tab ('\v')—and 0 otherwise
int iscntrl(int c)	Returns a true value if c is a control character, and 0 otherwise.
int ispunct(int c)	Returns a true value if c is a printing character other than a space, a digit, or a letter, and 0 otherwise.
int isprint(int c)	Returns a true value if c is a printing character including space (' '), and 0 otherwise.
int isgraph(int c)	Returns a true value if c is a printing character other than space (' '), and 0 otherwise.

Fig. 8.1   Summary of the character handling library functions.

indicates that if '8' is a digit, i.e., isdigit returns a true (nonzero) value, the string "8 is a " is printed, and if '8' is not a digit, i.e., isdigit returns 0, the string "8 is not a " is printed.

The program of Fig. 8.3 demonstrates functions *islower*, *isupper*, *tolower*, and *toupper*. Function islower determines whether its argument is a lowercase letter (a-z). Function isupper determines whether its argument is an uppercase letter (A-Z). Function tolower converts an uppercase letter to a lowercase letter, and returns the lowercase letter. If the argument is not an uppercase letter, tolower returns the argument unchanged. Function toupper converts a lowercase letter to an uppercase letter, and returns the uppercase letter. If the argument is not a lowercase letter, toupper returns the argument unchanged.

```c
/* Using functions isdigit, isalpha, isalnum, and isxdigit */
#include <stdio.h>
#include <ctype.h>

main()
{
    printf("%s\n%s%s\n%s%s\n\n", "According to isdigit: ",
        isdigit('8') ? "8 is a " : "8 is not a ", "digit",
        isdigit('#') ? "# is a " : "# is not a ", "digit");
    printf("%s\n%s%s\n%s%s\n%s%s\n%s%s\n\n", "According to isalpha:",
        isalpha('A') ? "A is a " : "A is not a ", "letter",
        isalpha('b') ? "b is a " : "b is not a ", "letter",
        isalpha('&') ? "& is a " : "& is not a ", "letter",
        isalpha('4') ? "4 is a " : "4 is not a ", "letter");
    printf("%s\n%s%s\n%s%s\n%s%s\n\n", "According to isalnum:",
        isalnum('A') ? "A is a " : "A is not a ", "digit or a letter",
        isalnum('8') ? "8 is a " : "8 is not a ", "digit or a letter",
        isalnum('#') ? "# is a " : "# is not a ", "digit or a letter");
    printf("%s\n%s%s\n%s%s\n%s%s\n%s%s\n%s%s\n",
        "According to isxdigit:",
        isxdigit('F') ? "F is a " : "F is not a ", "hexadecimal digit",
        isxdigit('J') ? "J is a " : "J is not a ", "hexadecimal digit",
        isxdigit('7') ? "7 is a " : "7 is not a ", "hexadecimal digit",
        isxdigit('$') ? "$ is a " : "$ is not a ", "hexadecimal digit",
        isxdigit('f') ? "f is a " : "f is not a ", "hexadecimal digit");
    return 0;
}
```

```
According to isdigit:
8 is a digit
# is not a digit

According to isalpha:
A is a letter
b is a letter
& is not a letter
4 is not a letter

According to isalnum:
A is a digit or a letter
8 is a digit or a letter
# is not a digit or a letter

According to isxdigit:
F is a hexadecimal digit
J is not a hexadecimal digit
7 is a hexadecimal digit
$ is not a hexadecimal digit
f is a hexadecimal digit
```

Fig. 8.2   Using isdigit, isalpha, isalnum, and isxdigit.

```c
/* Using functions islower, isupper, tolower, toupper */
#include <stdio.h>
#include <ctype.h>

main()
{
   printf("%s\n%s%s\n%s%s\n%s%s\n%s%s\n\n",
          "According to islower:",
          islower('p') ? "p is a " : "p is not a ",
          "lowercase letter",
          islower('P') ? "P is a " : "P is not a ",
          "lowercase letter",
          islower('5') ? "5 is a " : "5 is not a ",
          "lowercase letter",
          islower('!') ? "! is a " : "! is not a ",
          "lowercase letter");
   printf("%s\n%s%s\n%s%s\n%s%s\n%s%s\n\n",
          "According to isupper:",
          isupper('D') ? "D is an " : "D is not an ",
          "uppercase letter",
          isupper('d') ? "d is an " : "d is not an ",
          "uppercase letter",
          isupper('8') ? "8 is an " : "8 is not an ",
          "uppercase letter",
          isupper('$') ? "$ is an " : "$ is not an ",
          "uppercase letter");
   printf("%s%c\n%s%c\n%s%c\n%s%c\n",
          "u converted to uppercase is ", toupper('u'),
          "7 converted to uppercase is ", toupper('7'),
          "$ converted to uppercase is ", toupper('$'),
          "L converted to lowercase is ", tolower('L'));
   return 0;
}
```

```
According to islower:
p is a lowercase letter
P is not a lowercase letter
5 is not a lowercase letter
! is not a lowercase letter

According to isupper:
D is an uppercase letter
d is not an uppercase letter
8 is not an uppercase letter
$ is not an uppercase letter

u converted to uppercase is U
7 converted to uppercase is 7
$ converted to uppercase is $
L converted to lowercase is l
```

Fig. 8.3   Using `islower`, `isupper`, `tolower`, and `toupper`.

Figure 8.4 demonstrates functions *isspace*, *iscntrl*, *ispunct*, *isprint*, and *isgraph*. Function **isspace** determines whether its argument is one of the following white-space characters: space (' '), form feed ('\f'), newline ('\n'), carriage return ('\r'), horizontal tab ('\t'), or vertical tab ('\v'). Function **iscntrl** determines whether its argument is one of the following control characters: horizontal tab ('\t'), vertical tab ('\v'), form feed ('\f'), alert ('\a'), backspace ('\b'), carriage return ('\r'), or newline ('\n'). Function **ispunct** determines whether its argument is a printing character other than a space, a digit, or a letter such as $, #, (,), [,], {, }, ;, :, %, etc. Function **isprint** determines whether its argument is a character that can be displayed on the screen (including the space character). Function **isgraph** tests for the same characters as **isprint**, however the space character is not included.

```
/* Using functions isspace, iscntrl, ispunct, isprint, isgraph */
#include <stdio.h>
#include <ctype.h>

main()
{
    printf("%s\n%s%s%s\n%s%s%s\n%s%s\n\n", "According to isspace:",
        "Newline", isspace('\n') ? " is a " : " is not a ",
        "whitespace character", "Horizontal tab",
        isspace('\t') ? " is a " : " is not a ",
        "whitespace character",
        isspace('%') ? "% is a " : "% is not a ",
        "whitespace character");
    printf("%s\n%s%s%s\n%s%s\n\n", "According to iscntrl:",
        "Newline", iscntrl('\n') ? " is a " : " is not a ",
        "control character", iscntrl('$') ? "$ is a " : "$ is not a ",
        "control character");
    printf("%s\n%s%s\n%s%s\n%s%s\n\n", "According to ispunct:",
        ispunct(';') ? "; is a " : "; is not a ",
        "punctuation character",
        ispunct('Y') ? "Y is a " : "Y is not a ",
        "punctuation character",
        ispunct('#') ? "# is a " : "# is not a ",
        "punctuation character");
    printf("%s\n%s%s%s\n%s%s%s\n\n", "According to isprint:",
        isprint('$') ? "$ is a " : "$ is not a ", "printing character",
        "Alert", isprint('\a') ? " is a " : " is not a ",
        "printing character");
    printf("%s\n%s%s\n%s%s%s\n", "According to isgraph:",
        isgraph('Q') ? "Q is a " : "Q is not a ",
        "printing character other than a space",
        "Space", isgraph(' ') ? " is a " : " is not a ",
        "printing character other than a space");
    return 0;
}
```

Fig. 8.4   Using `isspace`, `iscntrl`, `ispunct`, `isprint`, and `isgraph`
(part 1 of 2).

```
According to isspace:
Newline is a whitespace character
Horizontal tab is a whitespace character
% is not a whitespace character

According to iscntrl:
Newline is a control character
$ is not a control character

According to ispunct:
; is a punctuation character
Y is not a punctuation character
# is a punctuation character

According to isprint:
$ is a printing character
Alert is not a printing character

According to isgraph:
Q is a printing character other than a space
Space is not a printing character other than a space
```

Fig. 8.4   Using `isspace`, `iscntrl`, `ispunct`, `isprint`, and `isgraph`
(part 2 of 2).

8.4 String Conversion Functions

This section presents the *string conversion functions* from the *general utilities library*
(*`stdlib`*). These functions convert strings of digits to integer and floating-point values.
Figure 8.5 summarizes the string conversion functions. Note the use of **const** to declare
variable **nPtr** in the function headers (read from right to left as "**nPtr** is a pointer to a
character constant"); **const** declares that the argument value will not be modified.

Function prototype	Function description
`double atof(const char *nPtr)`	Converts the string `nPtr` to `double`.
`int atoi(const char *nPtr)`	Converts the string `nPtr` to `int`.
`long atol(const char *nPtr)`	Converts the string `nPtr` to long `int`.
`double strtod(const char *nPtr, char **endPtr)`	Converts the string `nPtr` to `double`.
`long strtol(const char *nPtr, char **endPtr, int base)`	Converts the string `nPtr` to `long`.
`unsigned long strtoul(const char *nPtr, char **endPtr, int base)`	Converts the string `nPtr` to `unsigned long`.

Fig. 8.5   Summary of the string conversion functions of the general utilities library.

Good Programming Practice 8.3

When using functions from the general utilities library, include the `<stdlib.h>` header file.

Function *atof* (Fig. 8.6) converts its argument—a string that represents a floating point number—to a **double** value. The function returns the **double** value. If the converted value cannot be represented—for example, if the first character of the string is not a digit—the behavior of function **atof** is undefined.

Function *atoi* (Fig. 8.7) converts its argument—a string of digits that represents an integer—to an **int** value. The function returns the **int** value. If the converted value cannot be represented, the behavior of function **atoi** is undefined.

Function *atol* (Fig. 8.8) converts its argument—a string of digits representing a long integer—to a **long** value. The function returns the **long** value. If the converted value cannot be represented, the behavior of function **atol** is undefined. If **int** and **long** are both stored in 4 bytes, function **atoi** and function **atol** work identically.

Function *strtod* (Fig. 8.9) converts a sequence of characters representing a floating point value to **double**. The function receives two arguments—a string (**char ***) and a pointer to a string. The string contains the character sequence to be converted to **double**. The pointer is assigned the location of the first character after the converted portion of the string. The statement

```
d = strtod(string, &stringPtr);
```

from the program of Fig. 8.9 indicates that **d** is assigned the **double** value converted from **string**, and **stringPtr** is assigned the location of the first character after the converted value (**51.2**) in **string**.

```
/* Using atof */
#include <stdio.h>
#include <stdlib.h>

main()
{
   double d;

   d = atof("99.0");
   printf("%s%.3f\n%s%.3f\n",
          "The string \"99.0\" converted to double is ", d,
          "The converted value divided by 2 is ", d / 2.0);
   return 0;
}
```

```
The string "99.0" converted to double is 99.000
The converted value divided by 2 is 49.500
```

Fig. 8.6   Using `atof`.

```
/* Using atoi */
#include <stdio.h>
#include <stdlib.h>

main()
{
    int i;

    i = atoi("2593");
    printf("%s%d\n%s%d\n",
            "The string \"2593\" converted to int is ", i,
            "The converted value minus 593 is ", i - 593);
    return 0;
}
```

```
The string "2593" converted to int is 2593
The converted value minus 593 is 2000
```

Fig. 8.7   Using `atoi`.

```
/* Using atol */
#include <stdio.h>
#include <stdlib.h>

main()
{
    long l;

    l = atol("1000000");
    printf("%s%ld\n%s%ld\n",
        "The string \"1000000\" converted to long int is ", l,
        "The converted value divided by 2 is ", l / 2);
    return 0;
}
```

```
The string "1000000" converted to long int is 1000000
The converted value divided by 2 is 500000
```

Fig. 8.8   Using `atol`.

Function *strtol* (Fig. 8.10) converts to **long** a sequence of characters representing an integer. The function receives three arguments—a string (**char ***), a pointer to a string, and an integer. The string contains the character sequence to be converted. The pointer is assigned the location of the first character after the converted portion of the string. The integer specifies the *base* of the value being converted. The statement

```
x = strtol(string, &remainderPtr, 0);
```

```
/* Using strtod */
#include <stdio.h>
#include <stdlib.h>

main()
{
   double d;
   char *string = "51.2% are admitted";
   char *stringPtr;

   d = strtod(string, &stringPtr);
   printf("The string \"%s\" is converted to the\n",
          string);
   printf("double value %.2f and the string \"%s\"\n",
          d, stringPtr);

   return 0;
}
```

```
The string "51.2% are admitted" is converted to the
double value 51.20 and the string "% are admitted"
```

Fig. 8.9 Using `strtod`.

in the program of Fig. 8.10 indicates that **x** is assigned the **long** value converted from **string**. The second argument, **remainderPtr**, is assigned the remainder of **string** after the conversion. Using **NULL** for the second argument causes the remainder of the string to be ignored. The third argument, **0**, indicates that the value to be converted can be in octal (base 8), decimal (base 10), or hexadecimal (base 16) format. The base can be specified as 0 or any value between 2 and 36. See Appendix E, "Number Systems," for a detailed explanation of the octal, decimal, and hexadecimal number systems. Numeric representations of integers from base 11 to base 36 use the characters A–Z to represent the values 10 to 35. For example, hexadecimal values can consist of the digits 0–9 and the characters A–F. A base 11 integer can consist of the digits 0–9 and the character A. A base 24 integer can consist of the digits 0–9 and the characters A–N. A base 36 integer can consist of the digits 0–9 and the characters A–Z.

Function *strtoul* (Fig. 8.11) converts to **unsigned long** a sequence of characters representing an **unsigned long** integer. The function works identically to function **strtol**. The statement

```
x = strtoul(string, &remainderPtr, 0);
```

in the program of Fig. 8.11 indicates that **x** is assigned the **unsigned long** value converted from **string**. The second argument, **&remainderPtr**, is assigned the remainder of **string** after the conversion. The third argument, 0, indicates that the value to be converted can be in octal, decimal, or hexadecimal format.

```
/* Using strtol */
#include <stdio.h>
#include <stdlib.h>

main()
{
    long x;
    char *string = "-1234567abc", *remainderPtr;

    x = strtol(string, &remainderPtr, 0);
    printf("%s\"%s\"\n%s%ld\n%s\"%s\"\n%s%ld\n",
        "The original string is ", string,
        "The converted value is ", x,
        "The remainder of the original string is ",
        remainderPtr,
        "The converted value plus 567 is ", x + 567);
    return 0;
}
```

```
The original string is "-1234567abc"
The converted value is -1234567
The remainder of the original string is "abc"
The converted value plus 567 is -1234000
```

Fig. 8.10   Using strtol.

```
/* Using strtoul */
#include <stdio.h>
#include <stdlib.h>

main()
{
    unsigned long x;
    char *string = "1234567abc", *remainderPtr;

    x = strtoul(string, &remainderPtr, 0);
    printf("%s\"%s\"\n%s%lu\n%s\"%s\"\n%s%lu\n",
        "The original string is ", string,
        "The converted value is ", x,
        "The remainder of the original string is ",
        remainderPtr,
        "The converted value minus 567 is ", x - 567);
    return 0;
}
```

```
The original string is "1234567abc"
The converted value is 1234567
The remainder of the original string is "abc"
The converted value minus 567 is 1234000
```

Fig. 8.11   Using strtoul.

8.5 Standard Input/Output Library Functions

This section presents several functions from the standard input/output library (**stdio**) specifically for manipulating character and string data. Figure 8.12 summarizes the character and string input/output functions of the standard input/output library.

Good Programming Practice 8.4

When using functions from the standard input/output library, include the **<stdio.h>** *header file.*

The program of Fig. 8.13 uses functions ***gets*** and ***putchar*** to read a line of text from the standard input (keyboard), and recursively output the characters of the line in reverse order. Function **gets** reads characters from the standard input into its argument—an array of type **char**—until a newline character or the end-of-file indicator is encountered. A **NULL** character (**'\0'**) is appended to the array when reading terminates. Function **putchar** prints its character argument. The program calls recursive function **reverse** to print the line of text backwards. If the first character of the array received by **reverse** is the **NULL** character **'\0'**, **reverse** returns. Otherwise, **reverse** is called again with the address of the subarray beginning at element **s[1]**, and character **s[0]** is output with **putchar** when the recursive call is completed. The order of the two statements in the **else** portion of the **if** structure causes **reverse** to walk to the terminating **NULL** character of the string before a character is printed. As the recursive calls are completed the characters are output in reverse order.

The program of Fig. 8.14 uses functions ***getchar*** and ***puts*** to read characters from the standard input into character array **sentence**, and print the array of characters as a string. Function **getchar** reads a character from the standard input and returns the

Function prototype	Function description
int getchar(void)	Input the next character from the standard input and return it as an integer.
char *gets(char *s)	Input characters from the standard input into the array **s** until a newline or end-of-file character is encountered. A terminating **NULL** character is appended to the array.
int putchar(int c)	Print the character stored in **c**.
int puts(const char *s)	Print the string **s** followed by a newline character.
int sprintf(char *s, const char *format, ...)	
	Equivalent to **printf** except the output is stored in the array **s** instead of printing on the screen.
int sscanf(char *s, const char *format, ...)	
	Equivalent to **scanf** except the input is read from the array **s** instead of reading from the keyboard.

Fig. 8.12   The standard input/output library character and string functions.

```
/* Using gets and putchar */
#include <stdio.h>

main()
{
    char sentence[80];
    void reverse(char *);

    printf("Enter a line of text:\n");
    gets(sentence);

    printf("\nThe line printed backwards is:\n");
    reverse(sentence);

    return 0;
}

void reverse(char *s)
{
    if (s[0] == '\0')
        return;
    else {
        reverse(&s[1]);
        putchar(s[0]);
    }
}
```

```
Enter a line of text:
Characters and Strings

The line printed backwards is:
sgnirtS dna sretcarahC
```

```
Enter a line of text:
able was I ere I saw elba

The line printed backwards is:
able was I ere I saw elba
```

Fig. 8.13   Using `gets` and `putchar`.

character as an integer. Function **puts** takes a string (**char ***) as an argument and prints the string followed by a newline character.

The program stops inputting characters when **getchar** reads the newline character entered by the user to end the line of text. A **NULL** character is appended to array **sentence** so that the array may be treated as a string. Function **puts** prints the string contained in **sentence**.

```
/* Using getchar and puts */
#include <stdio.h>

main()
{
   char c, sentence[80];
   int i = 0;

   puts("Enter a line of text:");
   while ( ( c = getchar() ) != '\n')
      sentence[i++] = c;

   sentence[i] = '\0';  /* insert NULL at end of string */
   puts("\nThe line entered was:");
   puts(sentence);
   return 0;
}
```

```
Enter a line of text:
This is a test.

The line entered was:
This is a test.
```

Fig. 8.14 Using `getchar` and `puts`.

The program of Fig. 8.15 uses function *sprintf* to print formatted data into array **s**—an array of characters. The function uses the same conversion specifications as **printf** (see Chapter 9 for a detailed discussion of all print formatting features). The program inputs an **int** value and a **float** value to be formatted and printed to array **s**. Array **s** is the first argument of **sprintf**.

```
/* Using sprintf */
#include <stdio.h>

main()
{
   char s[80];
   int x;
   float y;

   printf("Enter an integer and a float:\n");
   scanf("%d%f", &x, &y);
   sprintf(s, "Integer:%6d\nFloat:%8.2f", x, y);
   printf("%s\n%s\n",
           "The formatted output stored in array s is:", s);
   return 0;
}
```

Fig. 8.15 Using `sprintf` (part 1 of 2).

```
Enter an integer and a float:
298 87.375
The formatted output stored in array s is:
Integer:   298
Float:    87.38
```

Fig. 8.15 Using `sprintf` (part 2 of 2).

The program of Fig. 8.16 uses function ***sscanf*** to read formatted data from character array **s**. The function uses the same conversion specifications as **scanf**. The program reads an **int** and a **float** from array **s**, and stores the values in **x** and **y**, respectively. The values of **x** and **y** are printed. Array **s** is the first argument of **sscanf**.

8.6 String Manipulation Functions of the String Handling Library

The string handling library provides many useful functions for manipulating string data, comparing strings, searching strings for characters and other strings, tokenizing strings (separating strings into logical pieces), and determining the length of strings. This section presents the string manipulation functions of the string handling library. The functions are summarized in Fig. 8.17.

Good Programming Practice 8.5

When using functions from the string handling library, include the ***<string.h>*** *header file.*

```
/* Using sscanf */
#include <stdio.h>

main()
{
    char s[] = "31298 87.375";
    int x;
    float y;

    sscanf(s, "%d%f", &x, &y);
    printf("%s\n%s%6d\n%s%8.3f\n",
            "The values stored in character array s are:",
            "Integer:", x, "Float:", y);
    return 0;
}
```

```
The values stored in character array s are:
Integer: 31298
Float:    87.375
```

Fig. 8.16 Using `sscanf`.

Function prototype	Function description

`char *strcpy(char *s1, const char *s2)`
> Copies the string **s2** into the array **s1**. The value of **s1** is returned.

`char *strncpy(char *s1, const char *s2, size_t n)`
> Copies at most **n** characters of the string **s2** into the array **s1**. The value of **s1** is returned.

`char *strcat(char *s1, const char *s2)`
> Appends the string **s2** to the array **s1**. The first character of **s2** overwrites the terminating **NULL** character of **s1**. The value of **s1** is returned.

`char *strncat(char *s1, const char *s2, size_t n)`
> Appends at most **n** characters of string **s2** to array **s1**. The first character of **s2** overwrites the terminating **NULL** character of **s1**. The value of **s1** is returned.

Fig. 8.17   The string manipulation functions of the string handling library.

Function *strcpy* copies its second argument—a string—into its first argument—a character array that must be large enough to store the string and its terminating **NULL** character which is also copied. Function *strncpy* is equivalent to **strcpy** except that **strncpy** specifies the number of characters to be copied from the string into the array. Note that function **strncpy** does not necessarily copy the terminating **NULL** character of its second argument. A terminating **NULL** character is written only if the number of characters to be copied is at least one more than the length of the string. For example, if **"test"** is the second argument, a terminating **NULL** character is written only if the third argument to **strncpy** is at least 5 (4 characters in **"test"** plus 1 terminating **NULL** character). If the third argument is larger than 5, **NULL** characters are appended to the array until the total number of characters specified by the third argument are written.

Common Programming Error 8.6

*Not appending a terminating **NULL** character to the first argument of a **strncpy** when the third argument is less than or equal to the length of the string in the second argument.*

The program in Fig. 8.18 uses **strcpy** to copy the entire string in array **x** into array **y**, and uses **strncpy** to copy the first **14** characters of array **x** into array **z**. A **NULL** character (**'\0'**) is appended to array **z** because the call to **strncpy** in the program does not write a terminating **NULL** character (the third argument is less than the string length of the second argument).

Function *strcat* appends its second argument—a string—to its first argument—a character array containing a string. The first character of the second argument replaces the **NULL** (**'\0'**) that terminates the string in the first argument. The programmer must ensure that the array used to store the first string is large enough to store the first string, the

```
/* Using strcpy and strncpy */
#include <stdio.h>
#include <string.h>

main()
{
   char x[] = "Happy Birthday to You";
   char y[25], z[15];

   printf("%s%s\n%s%s\n",
          "The string in array x is: ", x,
          "The string in array y is: ", strcpy(y, x));

   strncpy(z, x, 14);
   z[14] = '\0';
   printf("The string in array z is: %s\n", z);
   return 0;
}
```

```
The string in array x is: Happy Birthday to You
The string in array y is: Happy Birthday to You
The string in array z is: Happy Birthday
```

Fig. 8.18 Using `strcpy` and `strncpy`.

second string, and the terminating **NULL** character (copied from the second string). Function *strncat* appends a specified number of characters from the second string to the first string. A terminating **NULL** character is automatically appended to the result. The program of Fig. 8.19 demonstrates function `strcat` and function `strncat`.

```
/* Using strcat and strncat */
#include <stdio.h>
#include <string.h>

main()
{
   char s1[20] = "Happy ";
   char s2[] = "New Year ";
   char s3[40] = "";

   printf("s1 = %s\ns2 = %s\n", s1, s2);
   printf("strcat(s1, s2) = %s\n", strcat(s1, s2));
   printf("strncat(s3, s1, 6) = %s\n", strncat(s3, s1, 6));
   printf("strcat(s3, s1) = %s\n", strcat(s3, s1));
   return 0;
}
```

Fig. 8.19 Using `strcat` and `strncat` (part 1 of 2).

```
s1 = Happy
s2 = New Year
strcat(s1, s2) = Happy New Year
strncat(s3, s1, 6) = Happy
strcat(s3, s1) = Happy Happy New Year
```

Fig. 8.19   Using **strcat** and **strncat** (part 2 of 2).

8.7 Comparison Functions of the String Handling Library

This section presents the string comparison functions, **strcmp** and **strncmp**, of the string handling library. The function headers and a brief description of each function appear in Fig. 8.20.

The program of Fig. 8.21 compares three strings using functions *strcmp* and *strncmp*. Function **strcmp** compares its first string argument to its second string argument character by character. The function returns 0 if the strings are equal, a negative value if the first string is less than the second string, and a positive value if the first string is greater than the second string. Function **strncmp** is equivalent to **strcmp** except that **strncmp** compares up to a specified number of characters. Function **strncmp** does not compare characters following a **NULL** character in a string. The program prints the integer value returned by each function call.

Common Programming Error 8.7

Assuming that **strcmp** *and* **strncmp** *return 1 when their arguments are equal. Both functions return 0 (C's false value) for equality. Therefore, when testing two strings for equality, the result of the* **strcmp** *or* **strncmp** *function should be compared with 0 to determine if the strings are equal.*

Function prototype	Function description
int strcmp(const char *s1, const char *s2)	Compares the string **s1** to the string **s2**. The function returns 0, less than 0, or greater than 0 if **s1** is equal to, less than, or greater than **s2**, respectively.
int strncmp(const char *s1, const char *s2, size_t n)	Compares up to **n** characters of the string **s1** to the string **s2**. The function returns 0, less than 0, or greater than 0 if **s1** is equal to, less than, or greater than **s2**, respectively.

Fig. 8.20   The string comparison functions of the string handling library.

```
/* Using strcmp and strncmp */
#include <stdio.h>
#include <string.h>

main()
{
    char *s1 = "Happy New Year";
    char *s2 = "Happy New Year";
    char *s3 = "Happy Holidays";

    printf("%s%s\n%s%s\n%s%s\n\n%s%2d\n%s%2d\n%s%2d\n\n",
           "s1 = ", s1, "s2 = ", s2, "s3 = ", s3,
           "strcmp(s1, s2) = ", strcmp(s1, s2),
           "strcmp(s1, s3) = ", strcmp(s1, s3),
           "strcmp(s3, s1) = ", strcmp(s3, s1));

    printf("%s%2d\n%s%2d\n%s%2d\n",
           "strncmp(s1, s3, 6) = ", strncmp(s1, s3, 6),
           "strncmp(s1, s3, 7) = ", strncmp(s1, s3, 7),
           "strncmp(s3, s1, 7) = ", strncmp(s3, s1, 7));
    return 0;
}
```

```
s1 = Happy New Year
s2 = Happy New Year
s3 = Happy Holidays

strcmp(s1, s2) =   0
strcmp(s1, s3) =   1
strcmp(s3, s1) =  -1

strncmp(s1, s3, 6) =   0
strncmp(s1, s3, 7) =   1
strncmp(s3, s1, 7) =  -1
```

Fig. 8.21   Using `strcmp` and `strncmp`.

To understand just what it means for one string to be "greater than" or "less than" another string, consider the process of alphabetizing a series of last names. The reader would, no doubt, place "Jones" before "Smith" because the first letter of "Jones" comes before the first letter of "Smith" in the alphabet. But the alphabet is more than just a list of 26 letters—it is an ordered list of characters. Each letter occurs in a specific position within the list. "Z" is more than merely a letter of the alphabet; "Z" is specifically the twenty-sixth letter of the alphabet.

How does the computer know that one particular letter comes before another? All characters are represented inside the computer as numeric codes; when the computer compares two strings, it actually compares the numeric codes of the characters in the strings.

In an effort at standardizing character representations, most computer manufacturers have designed their machines to utilize one of two popular coding schemes—*ASCII* or *EBCDIC*. ASCII stands for "American Standard Code for Information Interchange," and EBCDIC stands for "Extended Binary Coded Decimal Interchange Code." There are other coding schemes, but these two are the most popular.

ASCII and EBCDIC are called *character codes* or *character sets*. String and character manipulations actually involve the manipulation of the appropriate numeric codes and not the characters themselves. This explains the interchangeability of characters and small integers in C. Since it is meaningful to say that one numeric code is greater than, less than, or equal to another numeric code, it becomes possible to relate various characters or strings to one another by referring to the character codes. Appendix D contains a list of ASCII character codes.

8.8 Search Functions of the String Handling Library

This section presents the functions of the string handling library used to search strings for characters and other strings. The functions are summarized in Fig. 8.22. Note that functions `strcspn` and `strspn` specify return type `size_t`. Type `size_t` is a type defined by the standard as the integral type of the value returned by operator `sizeof`.

Function prototype	Function description
`char *strchr(const char *s, int c)`	Locates the first occurrence of character `c` in string `s`. If `c` is found, a pointer to `c` in s is returned. Otherwise a `NULL` pointer is returned.
`size_t strcspn(const char *s1, const char *s2)`	Determines and returns the length of the initial segment of string `s1` consisting of characters not contained in string `s2`.
`size_t strspn(const char *s1, const char *s2)`	Determines and returns the length of the initial segment of string `s1` consisting only of characters contained in string `s2`.

Fig. 8.22 String manipulation functions of the string handling library (part 1 of 2).

Function prototype	Function description
`char *strpbrk(const char *s1, const char *s2)`	Locates the first occurrence in string **s1** of any character in string **s2**. If a character from string **s2** is found, a pointer to the character in string **s1** is returned. Otherwise a **NULL** pointer is returned.
`char *strrchr(const char *s, int c)`	Locates the last occurrence of **c** in string **s**. If c is found, a pointer to c in string **s** is returned. Otherwise a **NULL** pointer is returned.
`char *strstr(const char *s1, const char *s2)`	Locates the first occurrence in string **s1** of string **s2**. If the string is found, a pointer to the string in **s1** is returned. Otherwise a **NULL** pointer is returned.
`char *strtok(char *s1, const char *s2)`	A sequence of calls to **strtok** breaks string **s1** into "tokens"—logical pieces such as words in a line of text—separated by characters contained in string **s2**. The first call contains **s1** as the first argument, and subsequent calls to continue tokenizing the same string contain **NULL** as the first argument. A pointer to the current token is returned by each call. If there are no more tokens when the function is called, **NULL** is returned.

Fig. 8.22   String manipulation functions of the string handling library (part 2 of 2).

Function ***strchr*** searches for the first occurrence of a character in a string. If the character is found, **strchr** returns a pointer to the character in the string, otherwise **strchr** returns **NULL**. The program of Fig. 8.23 uses **strchr** to search for the first occurrences of `'a'` and `'z'` in the string `"This is a test"`.

Function ***strcspn*** (Fig. 8.24) determines the length of the initial part of the string in its first argument that does not contain any characters from the string in its second argument. The function returns the length of the segment.

Function ***strpbrk*** searches for the first occurrence in its first string argument of any character in its second string argument. If a character from the second argument is found, **strpbrk** returns a pointer to the character in the first argument, otherwise **strpbrk** returns **NULL**. The program of Fig. 8.25 locates the first occurrence in **string1** of any character from **string2**.

Function ***strrchr*** searches for the last occurrence of the specified character in a string. If the character is found, **strrchr** returns a pointer to the character in the string, otherwise **strrchr** returns **NULL**. The program of Fig. 8.26 searches for the last occurrence of the character `'z'` in the string `"A zoo has many animals including zebras"`.

```
/* Using strchr */
#include <stdio.h>
#include <string.h>

main()
{
   char *string = "This is a test";
   char character1 = 'a', character2 = 'z';

   if (strchr(string, character1) != NULL)
      printf("\'%c\' was found in \"%s\".\n",
             character1, string);
   else
      printf("\'%c\' was not found in \"%s\".\n",
             character1, string);

   if (strchr(string, character2) != NULL)
      printf("\'%c\' was found in \"%s\".\n",
             character2, string);
   else
      printf("\'%c\' was not found in \"%s\".\n",
             character2, string);
   return 0;
}
```

```
'a' was found in "This is a test".
'z' was not found in "This is a test".
```

Fig. 8.23 Using strchr.

```
/* Using strcspn */
#include <stdio.h>
#include <string.h>

main()
{
   char *string1 = "The value is 3.14159";
   char *string2 = "1234567890";

   printf("%s%s\n%s%s\n\n%s\n%s%u",
          "string1 = ", string1, "string2 = ", string2,
          "The length of the initial segment of string1",
          "containing no characters from string2 = ",
          strcspn(string1, string2));
   return 0;
}
```

```
string1 = The value is 3.14159
string2 = 1234567890

The length of the initial segment of string1
containing no characters from string2 = 13
```

Fig. 8.24 Using strcspn.

```
/* Using strpbrk */
#include <stdio.h>
#include <string.h>

main()
{
    char *string1 = "This is a test";
    char *string2 = "beware";

    printf("%s\"%s\"\n'%c'%s\n\"%s\"\n",
           "Of the characters in ", string2,
           *strpbrk(string1, string2),
           " is the first character to appear in ", string1);
    return 0;
}
```

```
Of the characters in "beware"
'a' is the first character to appear in
"This is a test"
```

Fig. 8.25 Using `strpbrk`.

```
/* Using strrchr */
#include <stdio.h>
#include <string.h>

main()
{
    char *string1 = "A zoo has many animals including zebras";
    int c = 'z';

    printf("%s\n%s'%c'%s\"%s\"\n",
           "The remainder of string1 beginning with the",
           "last occurrence of character ", c,
           " is: ", strrchr(string1, c));
    return 0;
}
```

```
The remainder of string1 beginning with the
last occurrence of character 'z' is: "zebras"
```

Fig. 8.26 Using `strrchr`.

Function *strspn* (Fig. 8.27) determines the length of the initial part of the string in its first argument that contains only characters from the string in its second argument. The function returns the length of the segment.

```
/* Using strspn */
#include <stdio.h>
#include <string.h>

main()
{
   char *string1 = "The value is 3.14159";
   char *string2 = "aehilsTuv ";

   printf("%s%s\n%s%s\n\n%s\n%s%u\n",
          "string1 = ", string1, "string2 = ", string2,
          "The length of the initial segment of string1",
          "containing only characters from string2 = ",
          strspn(string1, string2));
   return 0;
}
```

```
string1 = The value is 3.14159
string2 = aehilsTuv

The length of the initial segment of string1
containing only characters from string2 = 13
```

Fig. 8.27   Using `strspn`.

Function **strstr** searches for the first occurrence of its second string argument in its first string argument. If the second string is found in the first string, a pointer to the location of the string in the first argument is returned. The program of Fig. 8.28 uses **strstr** to find the string **"def"** in the string **"abcdefabcdef"**.

Function **strtok** is used to break a string into a series of *tokens*. A token is a sequence of characters separated by *delimiting characters* (usually spaces or punctuation marks). For example, in a line of text, each word can be considered a token and the spaces separating the words can be considered delimiters.

Multiple calls to **strtok** are required to break a string into tokens (assuming the string contains more than one token). The first call to **strtok** contains two arguments, a string to be tokenized, and a string containing characters that separate the tokens. In the program of Fig. 8.29, the statement

```
tokenPtr = strtok(string, " ");
```

assigns **tokenPtr** a pointer to the first token in **string**. The second argument of **strtok**, **" "**, indicates that tokens in **string** are separated by spaces. Function **strtok** searches for the first character in **string** that is not a delimiting character (space). This begins the first token. The function then finds the next delimiting character in the string and replaces it with a null (**'\0'**) character. This terminates the current token. Function **strtok** saves a pointer to the next character following the token in **string**, and returns a pointer to the current token.

```
/* Using strstr */
#include <stdio.h>
#include <string.h>

main()
{
   char *string1 = "abcdefabcdef";
   char *string2 = "def";

   printf("%s%s\n%s%s\n\n%s\n%s%s\n",
          "string1 = ", string1, "string2 = ", string2,
          "The remainder of string1 beginning with the",
          "first occurrence of string2 is: ",
          strstr(string1, string2));

   return 0;
}
```

```
string1 = abcdefabcdef
string2 = def

The remainder of string1 beginning with the
first occurrence of string2 is: defabcdef
```

Fig. 8.28 Using `strstr`.

```
/* Using strtok */
#include <stdio.h>
#include <string.h>

main()
{
   char string[] = "This is a sentence with 7 tokens";
   char *tokenPtr;

   printf("%s\n%s\n\n%s\n",
          "The string to be tokenized is:", string,
          "The tokens are:");

   tokenPtr = strtok(string, " ");

   while (tokenPtr != NULL) {
      printf("%s\n", tokenPtr);
      tokenPtr = strtok(NULL, " ");
   }

   return 0;
}
```

Fig. 8.29 Using `strtok` (part 1 of 2).

```
The string to be tokenized is:
This is a sentence with 7 tokens

The tokens are:
This
is
a
sentence
with
7
tokens
```

Fig. 8.29   Using **strtok** (part 2 of 2).

Subsequent calls to **strtok** to continue tokenizing **string** contain **NULL** as the first argument. The **NULL** argument indicates that the call to **strtok** should continue tokenizing from the location in **string** saved by the last call to **strtok**. If no tokens remain when **strtok** is called, **strtok** returns **NULL**. The program of Fig. 8.29 uses **strtok** to tokenize the string **"This is a sentence with 7 tokens"**. Each token is printed separately. Note that **strtok** modifies the input string, therefore a copy of the string should be made if the string will be used again in the program after the calls to **strtok**.

8.9 Memory Functions of the String Handling Library

The string handling library functions presented in this section facilitate manipulating, comparing, and searching blocks of memory. The functions treat blocks of memory as character arrays. These functions can manipulate any block of data. Figure 8.30 summarizes the memory functions of the string handling library. In the function discussions, "object" refers to a block of data.

The pointer parameters to these functions are declared **void ***. In Chapter 7, we saw that a pointer to any data type can be assigned directly to a pointer of type **void ***, and a pointer of type **void *** can be assigned directly to a pointer to any data type. For this reason, these functions can receive pointers to any data type. Because a **void *** pointer cannot be dereferenced, each function receives a size argument that specifies the number of characters (bytes) the function will process. For simplicity, the examples in this section manipulate character arrays (blocks of characters).

Function *memcpy* copies a specified number of characters from the object pointed to by its second argument into the object pointed to by its first argument. The function can receive a pointer to any type of object. The result of this function is undefined if the two objects overlap in memory, i.e., they are parts of the same object. The program of Fig. 8.31 uses **memcpy** to copy the string in array **s2** to array **s1**.

Function *memmove*, like function **memcpy**, copies a specified number of bytes from the object pointed to by its second argument into the object pointed to by its first argument. Copying is accomplished as if the bytes are first copied from the second argument

Function prototype	Function description

```
void *memcpy(void *s1, const void *s2, size_t n)
```
Copies n characters from the object pointed to by **s2** into the object pointed to by **s1**. A pointer to the resulting object is returned.

```
void *memmove(void *s1, const void *s2, size_t n)
```
Copies n characters from the object pointed to by **s2** into the object pointed to by **s1**. The copy is performed as if the characters are first copied from the object pointed to by **s2** into a temporary array, then from the temporary array into the object pointed to by **s1**. A pointer to the resulting object is returned.

```
int memcmp(const void *s1, const void *s2, size_t n)
```
Compares the first n characters of the objects pointed to by **s1** and **s2**. The function returns **0**, less than **0**, or greater than **0** if **s1** is equal to, less than, or greater than **s2**.

```
void *memchr(const void *s, int c, size_t n)
```
Locates the first occurrence of **c** (converted to **unsigned char**) in the first n characters of the object pointed to by **s**. If **c** is found, a pointer to **c** in the object is returned. Otherwise **NULL** is returned.

```
void *memset(void *s, int c, size_t n)
```
Copies **c** (converted to **unsigned char**) into the first n characters of the object pointed to by **s**. A pointer to the result is returned.

Fig. 8.30   The memory functions of the string handling library.

```
/* Using memcpy */
#include <stdio.h>
#include <string.h>

main()
{
   char s1[17], s2[]  = "Copy this string";

   memcpy(s1, s2, 17);
   printf("%s\n%s\"%s\"\n",
          "After s2 is copied into s1 with memcpy,",
          "s1 contains ", s1);
   return 0;
}
```

```
After s2 is copied into s1 with memcpy,
s1 contains "Copy this string"
```

Fig. 8.31   Using **memcpy**.

into a temporary array of characters, then copied from the temporary array into the first argument. This allows characters from one part of a string to be copied into another part of the same string.

Common Programming Error 8.8

String manipulation functions other than **memmove** *that copy characters have undefined results when copying takes place between parts of the same string.*

The program in Fig. 8.32 uses **memmove** to copy the last **10** bytes of array **x** into the first **10** bytes of array **x**.

Function *memcmp* (Fig. 8.33) compares the specified number of characters of its first argument to the corresponding characters of its second argument. The function returns a value greater than 0 if the first argument is greater than the second argument, returns 0 if the arguments are equal, and returns a value less than zero if the first argument is less than the second argument.

Function *memchr* searches for the first occurrence of a byte, represented as **unsigned char**, in the specified number of bytes of an object. If the byte is found, a pointer to the byte in the object is returned, otherwise a **NULL** pointer is returned. The program of Fig. 8.34 searches for the character (byte) **'r'** in the string **"This is a string"**.

Function *memset* copies the value of the byte in its second argument into a specified number of bytes of the object pointed to by its first argument. The program in Fig. 8.35 uses **memset** to copy **'b'** into the first **7** bytes of **string1**.

```
/* Using memmove */
#include <stdio.h>
#include <string.h>

main()
{
   char x[] = "Home Sweet Home";

   printf("%s%s\n",
          "The string in array x before memmove is: ", x);
   printf("%s%s\n",
          "The string in array x after memmove is:  ",
          memmove(x, &x[5], 10));

   return 0;
}
```

```
The string in array x before memmove is: Home Sweet Home
The string in array x after memmove is:   Sweet Home Home
```

Fig. 8.32 Using **memmove**.

```
/* Using memcmp */
#include <stdio.h>
#include <string.h>

main()
{
   char s1[] = "ABCDEFG", s2[] = "ABCDXYZ";

   printf("%s%s\n%s%s\n\n%s%2d\n%s%2d\n%s%2d\n",
          "s1 = ", s1, "s2 = ", s2,
          "memcmp(s1, s2, 4) = ", memcmp(s1, s2, 4),
          "memcmp(s1, s2, 7) = ", memcmp(s1, s2, 7),
          "memcmp(s2, s1, 7) = ", memcmp(s2, s1, 7));
   return 0;
}
```

```
s1 = ABCDEFG
s2 = ABCDXYZ

memcmp(s1, s2, 4) =  0
memcmp(s1, s2, 7) = -1
memcmp(s2, s1, 7) =  1
```

Fig. 8.33   Using `memcmp`.

```
/* Using memchr */
#include <stdio.h>
#include <string.h>

main()
{
   char *s = "This is a string";

   printf("%s\'%c\'%s\"%s\"\n",
          "The remainder of s after character ", 'r',
          " is found is ", memchr(s, 'r', 16));
   return 0;
}
```

```
The remainder of s after character 'r' is found is "ring"
```

Fig. 8.34   Using `memchr`.

8.10 Other Functions of the String Handling Library

The two remaining functions of the string handling library are **strerror** and **strlen**.
Figure 8.36 summarizes the **strerror** and **strlen** functions.

```
/* Using memset */
#include <stdio.h>
#include <string.h>

main()
{
   char string1[15] = "BBBBBBBBBBBBBB";

   printf("string1 = %s\n", string1);
   printf("string1 after memset = %s\n",
          memset(string1, 'b', 7));
   return 0;
}
```

```
string1 = BBBBBBBBBBBBBB
string1 after memset = bbbbbbbBBBBBBB
```

Fig. 8.35 Using `memset`.

Function *strerror* takes an error number and creates an error message string. A pointer to the string is returned. The program of Fig. 8.37 demonstrates `strerror`.

Portability Tip 8.4

The message generated by `strerror` *is system dependent.*

Function *strlen* takes a string as an argument, and returns the number of characters in a string—the terminating **NULL** character is not included in the length. The program of Fig. 8.38 demonstrates function `strlen`.

Summary

• Function `islower` determines whether its argument is a lowercase letter (`a-z`).

• Function `isupper` determines if its argument is an uppercase letter (`A-Z`).

Function prototype	Function description
`char *strerror(int errornum)`	Maps `errornum` into a full text string in a system dependent manner. A pointer to the string is returned.
`size_t strlen(const char *s)`	Determines the length of string `s`. The number of characters preceding the terminating **NULL** character is returned.

Fig. 8.36 The string manipulation functions of the string handling library.

```
/* Using strerror */
#include <stdio.h>
#include <string.h>

main()
{
   printf("%s\n", strerror(2));
   return 0;
}
```

```
Error 2
```

Fig. 8.37 Using `strerror`.

```
/* Using strlen */
#include <stdio.h>
#include <string.h>

main()
{
   char *string1 = "abcdefghijklmnopqrstuvwxyz";
   char *string2 = "four";
   char *string3 = "Boston";

   printf("%s\"%s\"%s%lu\n%s\"%s\"%s%lu\n%s\"%s\"%s%lu\n",
           "The length of ", string1, " is ", strlen(string1),
           "The length of ", string2, " is ", strlen(string2),
           "The length of ", string3, " is ", strlen(string3));
   return 0;
}
```

```
The length of "abcdefghijklmnopqrstuvwxyz" is 26
The length of "four" is 4
The length of "Boston" is 6
```

Fig. 8.38 Using `strlen`.

- Function `isdigit` determines whether its argument is a digit (`0-9`).

- Function `isalpha` determines whether its argument is an uppercase letter (`A-Z`) or a lowercase letter (`a-z`).

- Function `isalnum` determines whether its argument is an uppercase letter (`A-Z`), a lowercase letter (`a-z`), or a digit (`0-9`).

- Function `isxdigit` determines whether its argument is a hexadecimal digit (`A-F`, `a-f`, `0-9`).

- Function **toupper** converts a lowercase letter to an uppercase letter, and returns the uppercase letter.

- Function **tolower** converts an uppercase letter to a lowercase letter, and returns the lowercase letter.

- Function **isspace** determines whether its argument is one of the following white-space characters: `' '` (space), `'\f'`, `'\n'`, `'\r'`, `'\t'`, or `'\v'`.

- Function **iscntrl** determines whether its argument is one of the following control characters: `'\t'`, `'\v'`, `'\f'`, `'\a'`, `'\b'`, `'\r'`, or `'\n'`.

- Function **ispunct** determines whether its argument is a printing character other than a space, a digit, or a letter.

- Function **isprint** determines whether its argument is any printing character including the space character.

- Function **isgraph** determines whether its argument is a printing character other than the space character.

- Function **atof** converts its argument—a string beginning with a series of digits that represents a floating-point number—to a **double** value.

- Function **atoi** converts its argument—a string beginning with a series of digits that represents an integer—to an **int** value.

- Function **atol** converts its argument—a string beginning with a series of digits that represents a long integer—to a **long** value.

- Function **strtod** converts a sequence of characters representing a floating-point value to **double**. The function receives two arguments—a string (**char ***) and a pointer to **char ***. The string contains the character sequence to be converted, and the pointer to **char *** is assigned the remainder of the string after the conversion.

- Function **strtol** converts a sequence of characters representing an integer to **long**. The function receives three arguments—a string (**char ***), a pointer to **char ***, and an integer. The string contains the character sequence to be converted, the pointer to **char *** is assigned the remainder of the string after the conversion, and the integer specifies the base of the value being converted.

- Function **strtoul** converts a sequence of characters representing an integer to **unsigned long**. The function receives three arguments—a string (**char ***), a pointer to **char ***, and an integer. The string contains the character sequence to be converted, the pointer to **char *** is assigned the remainder of the string after the conversion, and the integer specifies the base of the value being converted.

- Function **gets** reads characters from the standard input (keyboard) until a newline character or the end-of-file indicator is encountered. The argument to **gets** is an array of type **char**. A **NULL** character (`'\0'`) is appended to the array after reading terminates.

- Function **putchar** prints its character argument.

- Function **getchar** reads a single character from the standard input and returns the character as an integer. If the end-of-file indicator is encountered, **getchar** returns **EOF**.

- Function **puts** takes a string (**char ***) as an argument and prints the string followed by a newline character.

- Function **sprintf** uses the same conversion specifications as **printf** to print formatted data into an array of type **char**.

- Function **sscanf** uses the same conversion specifications as function **scanf** to read formatted data from a string.

- Function **strcpy** copies its second argument—a string—into its first argument—a character. The programmer must ensure that the array is large enough to store the string and its terminating **NULL** character.

- Function **strncpy** is equivalent to **strcpy** except that a call to **strncpy** specifies the number of characters to be copied from the string into the array. The terminating **NULL** character will only be copied if the number of characters to be copied is one more than the length of the string.

- Function **strcat** appends its second string argument—including the terminating **NULL** character—to its first string argument. The first character of the second string replaces the **NULL** (**'\0'**) character of the first string. The programmer must ensure that the array used to store the first string is large enough to store both the first string and the second string.

- Function **strncat** appends a specified number of characters from the second string to the first string. A terminating **NULL** character is appended to the result.

- Function **strcmp** compares its first string argument to its second string argument character-by-character. The function returns 0 if the strings are equal, returns a negative value if the first string is less than the second string, and returns a positive value if the first string is greater than the second string.

- Function **strncmp** is equivalent to **strcmp** except that **strncmp** compares a specified number of characters. If the number of characters in one of the strings is less than the number of characters specified, **strncmp** compares characters until the **NULL** character in the shorter string is encountered.

- Function **strchr** searches for the first occurrence of a character in a string. If the character is found, **strchr** returns a pointer to the character in the string, otherwise **strchr** returns **NULL**.

- Function **strcspn** determines the length of the initial part of the string in its first argument that does not contain any characters from the string in its second argument. The function returns the length of the segment.

- Function **strpbrk** searches for the first occurrence in its first argument of any character in its second argument. If a character from the second argument is found, **strpbrk** returns a pointer to the character, otherwise **strpbrk** returns **NULL**.

- Function **strrchr** searches for the last occurrence of a character in a string. If the character is found, **strrchr** returns a pointer to the character in the string, otherwise **strrchr** returns **NULL**.

- Function **strspn** determines the length of the initial part of the string in its first argument that contains only characters from the string in its second argument. The function returns the length of the segment.

- Function **strstr** searches for the first occurrence of its second string argument in its first string argument. If the second string is found in the first string, a pointer to the location of the string in the first argument is returned.

- A sequence of calls to **strtok** breaks the string **s1** into tokens that are separated by characters contained in the string **s2**. The first call contains **s1** as the first argument, and subsequent calls to continue tokenizing the same string contain **NULL** as the first argument. A pointer to the current token is returned by each call. If there are no more tokens when the function is called, a **NULL** pointer is returned.

- Function **memcpy** copies a specified number of characters from the object to which its second argument points into the object to which its first argument points. The function can receive a pointer to any type of object. The pointers are received by **memcpy** as **void** pointers, and converted to **char** pointers for use in the function. Function **memcpy** manipulates the bytes of the object as characters.

- Function **memmove**, copies a specified number of bytes from the object pointed to by its second argument to the object pointed to by its first argument. Copying is accomplished as if the bytes are copied from the second argument to a temporary character array, then copied from the temporary array to the first argument.

- Function **memcmp** compares the specified number of characters of its first and second arguments.

- Function **memchr** searches for the first occurrence of a byte, represented as **unsigned char**, in the specified number of bytes of an object. If the byte is found, a pointer to the byte is returned, otherwise a **NULL** pointer is returned.

- Function **memset** copies its second argument, treated as an **unsigned char**, to a specified number of bytes of the object pointed to by the first argument.

- Function **strerror** maps an integer error number into a full text string in a system dependent manner. A pointer to the string is returned.

- Function **strlen** takes a string as an argument, and returns the number of characters in a string—the terminating **NULL** character is not included in the length of the string.

Terminology

appending strings to other strings	character constant
ASCII	character set
atof	
atoi	
atol	
character code	

Common Programming Errors

8.1 Not allocating sufficient space in a character array to store the **NULL** character that terminates a string.

8.2 Printing a "string" that does not contain a terminating **NULL** character.

8.3 Processing a single character as a string. A string is a pointer—probably a respectably large integer. However, a character is a small integer (ASCII values range 0-255). On many systems this causes an error because low memory addresses are reserved for special purposes such as operating system interrupt handlers—so, "access violations" occur.

8.4 Passing a character as an argument to a function when a string is expected.

8.5 Passing a string as an argument to a function when a character is expected.

8.6 Not appending a terminating **NULL** character to the first argument of a **strncpy** when the third argument is less than or equal to the length of the string in the second argument.

8.7   Assuming that **strcmp** and **strncmp** return 1 when their arguments are equal. Both functions return 0 (C's false value) for equality. Therefore, when testing two strings for equality, the result of the **strcmp** or **strncmp** function should be compared with 0 to determine if the strings are equal.

8.8   String manipulation functions other than **memmove** that copy characters have undefined results when copying takes place between parts of the same string.

Good Programming Practices

8.1   When storing a string of characters in a character array, be sure the array is large enough to hold the largest string that will be stored. C allows strings of any length to be stored. If a string is longer than the character array in which it is to be stored, characters beyond the end of the array will overwrite data in memory following the array.

8.2   When using functions from the character handling library, include the **<ctype.h>** header file.

8.3   When using functions from the general utilities library, include the **<stdlib.h>** header file.

8.4   When using functions from the standard input/output library, include the **<stdio.h>** header file.

8.5   When using functions from the string handling library, include the **<string.h>** header file.

Portability Tips

8.1   When a variable of type **char *** is initialized with a string literal, some compilers may place the string in a location in memory where the string cannot be modified. If you may need to modify a string literal, it should be stored in a character array to ensure modifiability on all systems.

8.2   The internal numeric codes used to represent characters may be different on different computers.

8.3   Type **size_t** is a system dependent synonym for either **unsigned long** or **unsigned int**.

8.4   The message generated by **strerror** is system dependent.

Self-Review Exercises

8.1   Write a single statement to accomplish each of the following. Assume that variables **c** (which stores a character), **x**, **y**, and **z** are of type **int**, variables **d**, **e**, and **f** are of type **float**, variable **ptr** is of type **char ***, and arrays **s1[100]** and **s2[100]** are of type **char**.

a) Convert the character stored in variable **c** to an uppercase letter. Assign the result to variable **c**.

b) Determine if the value of variable **c** is a digit. Use the conditional operator as shown in Fig. 8.2, 8.3, and 8.4 to print " **is a** " or " **is not a** " when the result is displayed.

c) Convert the string **"1234567"** to **long** and print the value.

d) Determine if the value of variable **c** is a control character. Use the conditional operator to print " **is a** " or " **is not a** " when the result is displayed.

e) Read a line of text into array **s1** from the keyboard. Do not use **scanf**.

f) Print the line of text stored in array **s1**. Do not use **printf**.

g) Assign **ptr** the location of the last occurrence of **c** in **s1**.

h) Print the value of variable **c**. Do not use **printf**.

i) Convert the string **"8.63582"** to **double** and print the value.

j) Determine if the value of **c** is a letter. Use the conditional operator to print **" is a "** or **" is not a "** when the result is displayed.

k) Read a character from the keyboard and store the character in variable **c**.

l) Assign **ptr** the location of the first occurrence of **s2** in **s1**.

m) Determine if the value of variable **c** is a printing character. Use the conditional operator to print **" is a "** or **" is not a "** when the result is displayed.

n) Read three **float** values into variables **d**, **e**, and **f** from the string **"1.27 10.3 9.432"**.

o) Copy the string stored in array **s2** into array **s1**.

p) Assign **ptr** the location of the first occurrence in **s1** of any character from **s2**.

q) Compare the string in **s1** to the string in **s2**. Print the result.

r) Assign **ptr** the location of the first occurrence of **c** in **s1**.

s) Use **sprintf** to print the values of integer variables **x**, **y**, and **z** into array **s1**. Each value should be printed with a field width of 7.

t) Append 10 characters from the string in **s2** to the string in **s1**.

u) Determine the length of the string in **s1**. Print the result.

v) Convert the string **"-21"** to **int** and print the value.

w) Assign **ptr** to the location of the first token in **s2**. Tokens in **s2** are separated by commas (**,**).

8.2 Show two different methods of initializing character array **vowel** with the string of vowels, **"AEIOU"**.

8.3 What, if anything, prints when each of the following C statements is performed? If the statement contains an error, describe the error and indicate how to correct it. Assume the following variable declarations:

```
char s1[50] = "jack", s2[50] = " jill", s3[50], *sptr;
```

a) `printf("%c%s", toupper(s1[0]), &s1[1]);`

b) `printf("%s", strcpy(s3, s2));`

c) `printf("%s", strcat(strcat(strcpy(s3, s1), " and "), s2));`

d) `printf("%u", strlen(s1) + strlen(s2));`

e) `printf("%u", strlen(s3));`

8.4 Find the error in each of the following program segments and explain how to correct it:

a)
```
char s[10];
strncpy(s, "hello", 5);
printf("%s\n", s);
```

b) `printf("%s", 'a');`

c)
```
char s[12];
strcpy(s, "Welcome Home");
```

d)
```
if (strcmp(string1, string2))
    printf("The strings are equal\n");
```

Answers to Self-Review Exercises

8.1 a) `c = toupper(c);`

b)
```
printf("'%c'%sdigit\n",
        c, isdigit(c) ? " is a " : " is not a ");
```

c) `printf("%ld\n", atol("1234567"));`

d) `printf("'%c'%scontrol character\n",`
        `c, iscntrl(c) ? " is a " : " is not a ");`
e) `gets(s1);`
f) `puts(s1);`
g) `ptr = strrchr(s1, c);`
h) `putchar(c);`
i) `printf("%f\n", atof("8.63582"));`
j) `printf("'%c'%sletter\n",`
        `c, isalpha(c) ? " is a " : " is not a ");`
k) `c = getchar();`
l) `ptr = strstr(s1, s2);`
m) `printf("'%c'%sprinting character\n",`
        `c, isprint(c) ? " is a " : " is not a ");`
n) `sscanf("1.27 10.3 9.432", "%f%f%f", &d, &e, &f);`
o) `strcpy(s1, s2);`
p) `ptr = strpbrk(s1, s2);`
q) `printf("strcmp(s1, s2) = %d\n", strcmp(s1, s2));`
r) `ptr = strchr(s1, c);`
s) `sprintf(s1, "%7d%7d%7d", x, y, z);`
t) `strncat(s1, s2, 10);`
u) `printf("strlen(s1) = %u\n", strlen(s1));`
v) `printf("%d\n", atoi("-21"));`
w) `ptr = strtok(s2, ",");`

8.2   `char vowel[] = "AEIOU";`
        `char vowel[] = {'A', 'E', 'I', 'O', 'U', '\0'};`

8.3   a) `Jack`
        b) `jill`
        c) `jack and jill`
        d) `8`
        e) `13`

8.4   a) Error: Function **strncpy** does not write a terminating **NULL** character to array **s** be-
        cause its third argument is equal to the length of the string **"hello"**.
        Correction: Make the third argument of **strncpy** 6, or assign `'\0'` to `s[5]`.
        b) Error: Attempting to print a character constant as a string.
        Correction: Use **%c** to output the character, or replace `'a'` with `"a"`.
        c) Error: Character array **s** is not large enough to store the terminating **NULL** character.
        Correction: Declare the array with more elements.
        d) Error: Function **strcmp** will return 0 if the strings are equal, therefore the condition in
        the **if** structure will be false, and the **printf** will not be executed.
        Correction: Compare the result of **strcmp** with **0** in the condition.

Exercises

8.5   Write a program that inputs a character from the keyboard, and tests the character with
each of the functions in the character handling library. The program should print the value returned
by each function.

8.6   Write a program that inputs a line of text with function **gets** into character array
`s[100]`. Output the line in uppercase letters and in lowercase letters.

8.7   Write a program that inputs 4 strings that represent integers, converts the strings to integers, sums the values, and prints the total of the 4 values.

8.8   Write a program that inputs 4 strings that represent floating-point values, converts the strings to double values, sums the values, and prints the total of the 4 values.

8.9   Write a program that uses function `strcmp` to compare two strings input by the user. The program should state whether the first string is less than, equal to, or greater than the second string.

8.10   Write a program that uses function `strncmp` to compare two strings input by the user. The program should input the number of characters to be compared. The program should state whether the first string is less than, equal to, or greater than the second string.

8.11   Write a program that uses random number generation to create sentences. The program should use four arrays of pointers to `char` called `article`, `noun`, `verb`, and `preposition`. The program should create a sentence by selecting a word at random from each array in the following order: `article`, `noun`, `verb`, `preposition`, `article`, and `noun`. As each word is picked, it should be concatenated to the previous words in an array which is large enough to hold the entire sentence. The words should be separated by spaces. When the final sentence is output, it should start with a capital letter and end with a period. The program should generate 20 such sentences.

The arrays should be filled as follows: the `article` array should contain the articles `"the"`, `"a"`, `"one"`, `"some"`, and `"any"`; the `noun` array should contain the nouns `"boy"`, `"girl"`, `"dog"`, `"town"`, and `"car"`; the `verb` array should contain the verbs `"drove"`, `"jumped"`, `"ran"`, `"walked"`, and `"skipped"`; the `preposition` array should contain the prepositions `"to"`, `"from"`, `"over"`, `"under"`, and `"on"`.

After the preceding program is written and working, modify the program to produce a short story consisting of several of these sentences. (How about the possibility of a random term paper writer!)

8.12   *(Limericks)* A limerick is a humorous five-line verse in which the first and second lines rhyme with the fifth, and the third line rhymes with the fourth. Using techniques similar to those developed in Exercise 8.10, write a C program that produces random limericks. Polishing this program to produce good limericks is a challenging problem, but the result will be worth the effort!

8.13   Write a program that encodes English language phrases into pig Latin. Pig Latin is a form of coded language often used for amusement. Many variations exist in the methods used to form pig Latin phrases. For simplicity, use the following algorithm:

To form a pig Latin phrase from an English language phrase, tokenize the phrase into words with function `strtok`. To translate each English word into a pig Latin word, place the first letter of the English word at the end of the English word, and add the letters "`ay`." Thus the word "`jump`" becomes "`umpjay`," the word "`the`" becomes "`hetay`," and the word "`computer`" becomes "`omputercay`." Blanks between words remain as blanks. Assume the following: The English phrase consists of words separated by blanks, there are no punctuation marks, and all words have two or more letters. Function `printLatinWord` should display each word. Hint: Each time a token is found in a call to `strtok`, pass the token pointer to function `printLatinWord`, and print the pig Latin word.

8.14   Write a program that inputs a telephone number as a string in the form `(555) 555-5555`. The program should use function `strtok` to extract the area code as a token, the first three digits of the phone number as a token, and the last four digits of the phone number as a token. The seven digits of the phone number should be concatenated into one string. The program should convert the area code string to `int` and convert the phone number string to `long`. Both the area code and the phone number should be printed.

8.15   Write a program that inputs a line of text, tokenizes the line with function `strtok`, and outputs the tokens in reverse order.

8.16   Write a program that inputs a line of text and a search string from the keyboard. Using function `strstr`, locate the first occurrence of the search string in the line of text, and assign the location to variable `searchPtr` of type `char *`. If the search string is found, print the remainder of the line of text beginning with the search string. Then, use `strstr` again to locate the next occurrence of the search string in the line of text. If a second occurrence is found, print the remainder of the line of text beginning with the second occurrence. Hint: The second call to `strstr` should contain `searchPtr + 1` as its first argument.

8.17   Write a program based on the program of Exercise 8.16 that inputs several lines of text and a search string, and uses function `strstr` to determine the total occurrences of the string in the lines of text. Print the result.

8.18   Write a program that inputs several lines of text and a search character, and uses function `strchr` to determine the total occurrences of the character in the lines of text.

8.19   Write a program based on the program of Exercise 8.18 that inputs several lines of text and uses function `strchr` to determine the total occurrences of each letter of the alphabet in the lines of text. Uppercase and lowercase letters should be counted together. Store the totals for each letter in an array, and print the values in tabular format after the totals have been determined.

8.20   Write a program that inputs several lines of text and uses `strtok` to count the total number of words. Assume that the words are separated by either spaces or newline characters.

8.21   Use the string comparison functions discussed in Section 8.6 and the techniques for sorting arrays developed in Chapter 6 to write a program that alphabetizes a list of strings. Use the names of 10 or 15 towns in your area as data for your program.

8.22   The chart in Appendix D shows the numeric code representations for the characters in the ASCII character set. Study this chart and then state whether each of the following is true or false.
   a) The letter "A" comes before the letter "B."
   b) The digit "9" comes before the digit "0."
   c) The commonly used symbols for addition, subtraction, multiplication, and division all come before any of the digits.
   d) The digits come before the letters.
   e) If a sort program sorts strings into ascending sequence, then the program will place the symbol for a right parenthesis before the symbol for a left parenthesis.

8.23   Write a program that reads a series of strings and prints only those strings beginning with the letter "b."

8.24   Write a program that reads a series of strings and prints only those strings that end with the letters "ED."

8.25   Write a program that inputs an ASCII code and prints the corresponding character. Modify this program so that it generates all possible three-digit codes in the range 000 to 255 and attempts to print the corresponding characters. What happens when this program is run?

8.26   Using the ASCII character chart in Appendix D as a guide, write your own versions of the character handling functions in Fig. 8.1.

8.27   Write your own versions of the functions in Fig. 8.5 for converting strings to numbers.

8.28   Write two versions of each of the string copy and string concatenation functions in Fig. 8.17. The first version should use array subscripting, and the second version should use pointers and pointer arithmetic.

8.29   Write your own versions of the functions `getchar`, `gets`, `putchar`, and `puts` described in Fig. 8.12.

8.30   Write two versions of each string comparison function in Fig. 8.20. The first version should use array subscripting, and the second version should use pointers and pointer arithmetic.

8.31   Write your own versions of the functions in Fig. 8.22 for searching strings.

8.32   Write your own versions of the functions in Fig. 8.30 for manipulating blocks of memory.

8.33   Write two versions of function `strlen` in Fig. 8.36. The first version should use array subscripting, and the second version should use pointers and pointer arithmetic.

Special Section: Advanced String Manipulation Exercises

The preceding exercises are keyed to the text and designed to test the reader's understanding of fundamental string manipulation concepts. This section includes a collection of intermediate and advanced problems. The reader should find these problems challenging yet enjoyable. The problems vary considerably in difficulty. Some require an hour or two of program writing and implementation. Others are useful for lab assignments that might require two or three weeks of study and implementation. Some are challenging term projects.

8.34   *(Text Analysis)* The availability of computers with string manipulation capabilities has resulted in some rather interesting approaches to analyzing the writings of great authors. Much attention has been focused on whether William Shakespeare ever lived. Some scholars believe there is substantial evidence indicating that Christopher Marlowe actually penned the masterpieces attributed to Shakespeare. Researchers have used computers to find similarities in the writings of these two authors. This exercise examines three methods for analyzing texts with a computer.

    a) Write a program that reads several lines of text and prints a table indicating the number of occurrences of each letter of the alphabet in the text. For example, the phrase

```
To be, or not to be: that is the question:
```

       contains one "a," two "b's," no "c's," etc.

    b) Write a program that reads several lines of text and prints a table indicating the number of one-letter words, two-letter words, three-letter words, etc. appearing in the text. For example, the phrase

```
Whether 'tis nobler in the mind to suffer
```

       contains

Word length	Occurrences
1	0
2	2
3	2
4	2 (including 'tis)
5	0
6	2
7	1

c) Write a program that reads several lines of text and prints a table indicating the number of occurrences of each different word in the text. The first version of your program should include the words in the table in the same order in which they appear in the text. A more interesting (and useful) printout should then be attempted in which the words are sorted alphabetically. For example, the lines

```
To be, or not to be: that is the question:
Whether 'tis nobler in the mind to suffer
```

contain the words "to" three times, the word "be" two times, the word "or" once, etc.

8.35   *(Word Processing)* The detailed treatment of string manipulation in this text is greatly attributable to the exciting growth in word processing in recent years. One important function in word processing systems is *type-justification*—the alignment of words to both the left and right margins of a page. This generates a professional-looking document that gives the appearance of being set in type rather than prepared on a typewriter. Type-justification can be accomplished on computer systems by inserting one or more blank characters between each of the words in a line so that the rightmost word aligns with the right margin.

Write a program that reads several lines of text and prints this text in type-justified format. Assume that the text is to be printed on 8 1/2-inch-wide paper, and that one-inch margins are to be allowed on both the left and right sides of the printed page. Assume that the computer prints 10 characters to the horizontal inch. Therefore, your program should print 6 1/2 inches of text or 65 characters per line.

8.36   *(Printing Dates in Various Formats)* Dates are commonly printed in several different formats in business correspondence. Two of the more common formats are:

```
07/21/55 and July 21, 1955
```

Write a program that reads a date in the first format and prints that date in the second format.

8.37   *(Check Protection)* Computers are frequently employed in check-writing systems such as payroll and accounts payable applications. Many strange stories circulate regarding weekly paychecks being printed (by mistake) for amounts in excess of $1 million. Weird amounts are printed by computerized check-writing systems because of human error and/or machine failure. Systems designers, of course, make every effort to build controls into their systems to prevent erroneous checks from being issued.

Another serious problem is the intentional alteration of a check amount by someone who intends to cash a check fraudulently. To prevent a dollar amount from being altered, most computerized check-writing systems employ a technique called *check protection*.

Checks designed for imprinting by computer contain a fixed number of spaces in which the computer may print an amount. Suppose a paycheck contains eight blank spaces in which the computer is supposed to print the amount of a weekly paycheck. If the amount is large, then all eight of those spaces will be filled, for example:

```
1,230.60 (check amount)
--------
12345678   (position numbers)
```

On the other hand, if the amount is less than $1000, then several of the spaces would ordinarily be left blank. For example,

```
  99.87
--------
12345678
```

contains three blank spaces. If a check is printed with blank spaces, it is easier for someone to alter the amount of the check. To prevent a check from being altered, many check-writing systems insert *leading asterisks* to protect the amount as follows:

```
***99.87
--------
12345678
```

Write a program that inputs a dollar amount to be printed on a check, and then prints the amount in check-protected format with leading asterisks if necessary. Assume that nine spaces are available for printing an amount.

8.38   *(Writing the Word Equivalent of a Check Amount)* Continuing the discussion of the previous example, we reiterate the importance of designing check-writing systems to prevent alteration of check amounts. One common security method requires that the check amount be written both in numbers, and "spelled out" in words as well. Even if someone is able to alter the numerical amount of the check, it is extremely difficult to change the amount in words.

Many computerized check-writing systems do not print the amount of the check in words. Perhaps the main reason for this omission is the fact that most high-level languages used in commercial applications do not contain adequate string manipulation features. Another reason is that the logic for writing word equivalents of check amounts is somewhat involved.

Write a C program that inputs a numeric check amount and writes the word equivalent of the amount. For example, the amount 112.43 should be written as

```
ONE HUNDRED TWELVE and 43/100
```

8.39   *(Morse Code)* Perhaps the most famous of all coding schemes is the Morse code, developed by Samuel Morse in 1832 for use with the telegraph system. The Morse code assigns a series of dots and dashes to each letter of the alphabet, each digit, and a few special characters (such as period, comma, colon, and semicolon). In sound-oriented systems, the dot represents a short sound and the dash represents a long sound. Other representations of dots and dashes are used with light-oriented systems and signal-flag systems.

Separation between words is indicated by a space, or, quite simply, the absence of a dot or dash. In a sound-oriented system, a space is indicated by a short period of time during which no sound is transmitted. The international version of the Morse code appears in Fig. 8.39.

Write a program that reads an English language phrase and encodes the phrase into Morse code. Also write a program that reads a phrase in Morse code and converts the phrase into the English language equivalent. Use one blank between each Morse-coded letter and three blanks between each Morse-coded word.

8.40   *(A Metric Conversion Program)* Write a program that will assist the user with metric conversions. Your program should allow the user to specify the names of the units as strings (i.e., centimeters, liters, grams, etc. for the metric system and inches, quarts, pounds, etc. for the English system) and should respond to simple questions such as

```
"How many inches are in 2 meters?"
"How many liters are in 10 quarts?"
```

Your program should recognize invalid conversions. For example, the question

```
"How many feet in 5 kilograms?"
```

is not meaningful because `"feet"` are units of length while a `"kilogram"` is a unit of weight.

8.41   *(Dunning Letters)* Many businesses spend a great deal of time and money collecting overdue debts. *Dunning* is the process of making repeated and insistent demands upon a debtor in an attempt to collect a debt.

Character	Code	Character	Code
A	.-	T	-
B	-...	U	..-
C	-.-.	V	...-
D	-..	W	.--
E	.	X	-..-
F	..-.	Y	-.--
G	--.	Z	--..
H	....		
I	..	**Digits**	
J	.---	1	.----
K	-.-	2	..---
L	.-..	3	...--
M	--	4	....-
N	-.	5	.....
O	---	6	-....
P	.--.	7	--...
Q	--.-	8	---..
R	.-.	9	----.
S	...	0	-----

Fig. 8.39   The letters of the alphabet as expressed in international Morse code.

Computers are often used to generate dunning letters automatically and in increasing degrees of severity as a debt ages. The theory is that as a debt becomes older it becomes more difficult to collect, and therefore the dunning letters must become more threatening.

Write a C program that contains the texts of five dunning letters of increasing severity. Your program should accept as input:

1. Debtor's name
2. Debtor's address
3. Debtor's account
4. Amount owed
5. Age of the amount owed (i.e., one month overdue, two months overdue, etc.).

Use the age of the amount owed to select one of the five message texts, and then print the dunning letter inserting the other user-supplied information where appropriate.

A challenging string manipulation project

8.42   (*A Crossword Puzzle Generator*) Most people have worked a crossword puzzle at one time or another, but few have ever attempted to generate one. Generating a crossword puzzle is a diffi cult problem. It is suggested here as a string manipulation project requiring substantial sophistication and effort. There are many issues the programmer must resolve to get even the simplest crossword puzzle generator program working. For example, how does one represent the grid of a crossword puzzle inside the computer? Should one use a series of strings, or should double-subscripted arrays be used? The programmer needs a source of words (i.e., a computerized dictionary) that can be directly referenced by the program. In what form should these words be stored to facilitate the complex manipulations required by the program? The really ambitious reader will want to generate the "clues" portion of the puzzle in which the brief hints for each "across" word and each "down" word are printed for the puzzle worker. Merely printing a version of the blank puzzle itself is not a simple problem.

9

Formatted Input/Output

Objectives

- To understand input and output streams.
- To be able to use all print formatting capabilities.
- To be able to use all input formatting capabilities.

All the news that's fit to print.
Adolph S. Ochs

What mad pursuit? What struggle to escape?
John Keats

Remove not the landmark on the boundary of the fields.
Amenemope

The end must justify the means.
Matthew Prior

Outline

9.1 Introduction

An important part of the solution to any problem is the presentation of the results. In this chapter we discuss in depth the formatting features of **printf** and **scanf**. These functions input data from the *standard input stream,* and output data to the *standard output stream,* respectively. Four other functions that use the standard input and standard output—**gets**, **puts**, **getchar**, and **putchar**—were discussed Chapter 8. Include the header file **<stdio.h>** in programs that call these functions.

Many features of **printf** and **scanf** were discussed earlier in the text. This chapter summarizes those features and introduces many others. Chapter 11 discusses several other functions included in the standard input/output (**stdio**) library.

9.2 Streams

All input and output is performed with *streams*—sequences of characters organized into lines. Each line consists of zero or more characters and ends with the newline character. The standard states that ANSI C implementations must support lines of at least 254 characters including a terminating newline character.

When program execution begins, three streams are connected to the program automatically. Normally, the standard input stream is connected to the keyboard and the standard output stream is connected to the screen. Operating systems often allow these streams to be *redirected* to other devices. A third stream, *standard error,* is connected to the screen. Error messages are output to the standard error stream. Streams are discussed in detail in Chapter 11, "File Processing."

9.3 Formatting Output with Printf

Precise output formatting is accomplished with `printf`. Every `printf` call contains a *format control string* that describes the output format. The format control string consists of *conversion specifiers, flags, field widths, precisions,* and *literal characters.* Together with the percent sign (%), these form *conversion specifications.* Function `printf` can perform the following formatting capabilities, each of which is discussed in this chapter.

1. *Rounding* floating-point values to an indicated number of decimal places.
2. *Aligning* a column of numbers with decimal points appearing one above the other.
3. *Right-justification* and *left-justification* of outputs.
4. *Inserting literal characters* at precise locations in a line of output.
5. Representing floating-point numbers in exponential format.
6. Representing unsigned integers in octal and hexadecimal format. See Appendix E, "Number Systems," for more information on octal and hexadecimal values.
7. Displaying all types of data with fixed-size field widths and precisions.

The `printf` function has the form:

> `printf`(*format-control-string, other-arguments*)`;`

The *format-control-string* describes the output format, and *other-arguments* (these are optional) correspond to each conversion specification in the *format-control-string*. Each conversion specification begins with a percent sign and ends with a conversion specifier. There can be many conversion specifications in one format-control-string.

> ### Common Programming Error 9.1
>
> *Forgetting to enclose a format-control-string in quotation marks.*

> ### Good Programming Practice 9.1
>
> *Edit outputs neatly for presentation. This makes program outputs more readable and reduces user errors.*

9.4 Printing Integers

An integer is a whole number, such as 776 or –52, that contains no decimal point. Integer values are displayed in one of several formats. Figure 9.1 describes each of the integer conversion specifiers.

The program in Fig. 9.2 prints an integer using each of the integer conversion specifiers. Note that only the minus sign prints; plus signs are suppressed. Later in this chapter we will see how to force plus signs to print. Also note that the value `-455` is read by `%u` and converted to the unsigned value `65081` on a computer with 2-byte integers.

Conversion Specifier	Description
d	Display a signed decimal integer.
i	Display a signed decimal integer. (Note: The i and d specifiers are different when used with **scanf**.)
o	Display an unsigned octal integer.
u	Display an unsigned decimal integer.
x or X	Display an unsigned hexadecimal integer. **X** causes the digits 0-9 and the letters A-F to be displayed, and **x** causes the digits 0-9 and a-f to be displayed.
h or l (letter l)	Place before any integer conversion specifier to indicate that a **short** or **long** integer is displayed respectively.

Fig. 9.1   Integer conversion specifiers.

```
/* Using the integer conversion specifiers */
#include <stdio.h>

main()
{
    printf("%d\n", 455);
    printf("%i\n", 455);   /* i same as d in printf */
    printf("%d\n", +455);
    printf("%d\n", -455);
    printf("%hd\n", 32000);
    printf("%ld\n", 2000000000);
    printf("%o\n", 455);
    printf("%u\n", 455);
    printf("%u\n", -455);
    printf("%x\n", 455);
    printf("%X\n", 455);
    return 0;
}
```

```
455
455
455
-455
32000
2000000000
707
455
65081
1c7
1C7
```

Fig. 9.2   Using integer conversion specifiers.

Common Programming Error 9.2

Printing a negative value with a conversion specifier that expects an unsigned value.

9.5 Printing Floating-Point Numbers

A floating-point value contains a decimal point as in **33.5** or **657.983**. Floating-point values are displayed in one of several formats. Figure 9.3 describes the floating-point conversion specifiers.

The conversion specifiers **e** and **E** display floating-point values in *exponential notation*. Exponential notation is the computer equivalent of *scientific notation* used in mathematics. For example, the value 150.4582 is represented in scientific notation as

$$1.504582 \times 10^2$$

and is represented in exponential notation as

    1.504582E+02

by the computer. This notation indicates that **1.504582** is multiplied by **10** raised to the second power (**E+02**). The **E** stands for "exponent."

Values printed with the conversion specifiers **e**, **E**, and **f** are output with 6 digits of precision to the right of the decimal point by default; other precisions can be specified explicitly. Conversion specifier **f** always prints at least one digit to the left of the decimal point. Conversion specifiers **e** and **E** print lowercase **e** and uppercase **E** preceding the exponent respectively and always print exactly one digit to the left of the decimal point.

Conversion specifier **g** (**G**) prints in either **e** (**E**) or **f** format with no trailing zeros (i.e., **1.234000** is printed as **1.234**). Values are printed with **e** (**E**) if after converting the value to exponential notation, the value's exponent is less than **-4**, or it is greater than or equal to the specified precision (6 significant digits by default for **g** and **G**). Otherwise conversion specifier **f** is used to print the value. Trailing zeros are not printed in the fractional part of a value output with **g** or **G**. At least one decimal digit is required for the decimal point to be output. The values **0.0000875**, **8750000.0**, **8.75**, **87.50** and **875**

Conversion specifier	Description
e or E	Display a floating-point value in exponential notation.
f	Display floating-point values.
g or G	Display a floating-point value in either the floating-point form **f** or the exponential form **e** (or **E**).
L	Place before any floating-point conversion specifier to indicate that a **long double** floating-point value is displayed.

Fig. 9.3   Floating-point conversion specifiers.

are printed as **8.75e-05**, **8.75e+06**, **8.75**, **87.5**, and **875** with the **%g** conversion specification. The value **0.0000875** uses **e** notation because, when it is converted to exponential notation its exponent is less than **-4**. The value **8750000.0** uses **e** notation because its exponent is equal to the default precision.

The precision for conversion specifiers **g** and **G** indicates the maximum number of significant digits printed including the digit to the left of the decimal point. The value **1234567.0** is printed as **1.23457e+06** using conversion specification **%g** (remember that all floating point conversion specifiers have a default precision of 6). Note that there are 6 significant digits in the result. The difference between **g** and **G** is identical to the difference between **e** and **E** when the value is printed in exponential notation—lowercase **g** casues a lowercase **e** to be output, and uppercase **G** casues an uppercase **E** to be output.

Good Programming Practice 9.2

When outputting data, be sure that the user is aware of situations in which data may be imprecise due to formatting (e.g., rounding errors from specifying precisions).

The program in Fig. 9.4 demonstrates each of the three floating-point conversion specifications. Note that the **%E** and **%g** conversion specifications cause the value to be rounded in the output.

```
/* Printing floating-point numbers with
   floating-point conversion specifiers */

#include <stdio.h>

main()
{
    printf("%e\n", 1234567.89);
    printf("%e\n", +1234567.89);
    printf("%e\n", -1234567.89);
    printf("%E\n", 1234567.89);
    printf("%f\n", 1234567.89);
    printf("%g\n", 1234567.89);
    printf("%G\n", 1234567.89);

    return 0;
}
```

```
1.234568e+06
1.234568e+06
-1.234568e+06
1.234568E+06
1234567.890000
1.23457e+06
1.23457E+06
```

Fig. 9.4   Using floating-point conversion specifiers.

9.6 Printing Strings and Characters

The **c** and **s** conversion specifiers are used to print individual characters and strings respectively. Conversion specifier **c** requires a **char** argument. Conversion specifier **s** requires a pointer to **char** as an argument. Conversion specifier **s** causes characters to be printed until a terminating **NULL** (**'\0'**) character is encountered. The program shown in Fig. 9.5 displays characters and strings with conversion specifiers **c** and **s**.

Common Programming Error 9.3

Using %c to print the first character of a string. The conversion specification %c expects a char argument. A string is a pointer to char, i.e., a char *.

Common Programming Error 9.4

Using %s to print a char argument. The conversion specification %s expects an argument of type pointer to char. On some systems, this causes a fatal execution-time error called an access violation.

Common Programming Error 9.5

Using single quotes around character strings is a syntax error. Character strings must be enclosed in double quotes.

Common Programming Error 9.6

Using double quotes around a character constant. This actually creates a string consisting of two characters, the second of which is the terminating NULL. A character constant is a single character enclosed in single quotes.

```
/* Printing strings and characters */
#include <stdio.h>

main()
{
    char character = 'A';
    char string[] = "This is a string";
    char *stringPtr = "This is also a string";

    printf("%c\n", character);
    printf("%s\n", "This is a string");
    printf("%s\n", string);
    printf("%s\n", stringPtr);
    return 0;
}
```

```
A
This is a string
This is a string
This is also a string
```

Fig. 9.5   Using the character and string conversion specifiers.

9.7 Other Conversion Specifiers

The three remaining conversion specifiers are **p**, **n**, and **%** (Fig. 9.6).

Portability Tip 9.1

The conversion specifier p displays a pointer address in an implementation-defined manner (on many systems, hexadecimal notation is used rather than decimal notation).

The conversion specifier **n** stores the number of characters already output in the current **printf** statement—the corresponding argument is a pointer to an integer variable in which the value is stored. Nothing is printed by a **%n** conversion specification. The conversion specifier **%** causes a percent sign to be output.

In the program of Fig. 9.7, **%p** prints the value of **ptr** and the address of **x**; these values are identical because **ptr** is assigned the address of **x**. Next, **%n** stores the number of characters output by the third **printf** statement in integer variable **y**, and the value of **y** is printed. The last **printf** statement uses **%%** to print the **%** character in a character string. Note that every **printf** call returns a value—either the number of characters output, or a negative value if an output error occurs.

Common Programming Error 9.7

Trying to print a literal percent character using % rather than %% in the format control string. When % appears in a format control string, it must be followed by a conversion specifier.

9.8 Printing with Field Widths and Precisions

The exact size of a field in which data is printed is specified by a *field width*. If the field width is larger than the data being printed, the data will normally be right-justified within that field. An integer representing the field width is inserted between the percent sign (%) and the conversion specifier in the conversion specification. The program in Fig. 9.8 prints two groups of five numbers each, right-justifying those numbers that contain fewer digits than the field width. Note that the field width is automatically increased to print

Conversion specifier	Description
p	Display a pointer value in an implementation defined manner.
n	Store the number of characters already output in the current **printf** statement. A pointer to an integer is supplied as the corresponding argument. Nothing is displayed.
%	Display the percent character.

Fig. 9.6   Other conversion specifiers.

```
/* Using the p, n, and % conversion specifiers */
#include <stdio.h>

main()
{
   int *ptr;
   int x = 12345, y;

   ptr = &x;
   printf("The value of ptr is %p\n", ptr);
   printf("The address of x is %p\n\n", &x);

   printf("Total characters printed on this line is:%n", &y);
   printf(" %d\n\n", y);

   y = printf("This line has 28 characters\n");
   printf("%d characters were printed\n\n", y);

   printf("Printing a %% in a format control string\n");
   return 0;
}
```

```
The value of ptr is 001F2BB4
The address of x is 001F2BB4

Total characters printed on this line is: 41

This line has 28 characters
28 characters were printed

Printing a % in a format control string
```

Fig. 9.7   Using the **p**, **n**, and **%** conversion specifiers.

values wider than the field, and that the minus sign for a negative value uses one character position in the field width. Field widths can be used with all conversion specifiers.

Common Programming Error 9.8

Not providing a sufficiently large field width to handle a value to be printed. This can offset other data being printed and can produce confusing outputs. Know your data!

Function **printf** also provides the ability to specify the *precision* with which data is printed. Precision has different meanings for different data types. When used with integer conversion specifiers, precision indicates the minimum number of digits to be printed. If the printed value contains fewer digits than the specified precision, zeros are prefixed to the printed value until the total number of digits is equivalent to the precision. The default precision for integers is 1. When used with floating-point conversion specifiers **e**, **E**, and **f**, the precision is the number of digits to appear after the decimal point. When used with conversion specifiers **g** and **G**, the precision is the maximum number of significant

```
/* Printing integers right-justified */
#include <stdio.h>

main()
{
    printf("%4d\n", 1);
    printf("%4d\n", 12);
    printf("%4d\n", 123);
    printf("%4d\n", 1234);
    printf("%4d\n\n", 12345);

    printf("%4d\n", -1);
    printf("%4d\n", -12);
    printf("%4d\n", -123);
    printf("%4d\n", -1234);
    printf("%4d\n", -12345);

    return 0;
}
```

```
   1
  12
 123
1234
12345

  -1
 -12
-123
-1234
-12345
```

Fig. 9.8   Right-justifying integers in a field.

digits to be printed. When used with conversion specifier **s**, the precision is the maximum number of characters to be written from the string. To use precision, place a decimal point (**.**) followed by an integer representing the precision between the percent sign and the conversion specifier. The program of Fig. 9.9 demonstrates the use of precision in format control strings. Note that when a floating-point value is printed with a precision smaller than the original number of decimal places in the value, the value is rounded.

The field width and the precision can be combined by placing the field width followed by a decimal point followed by a precision between the percent sign and the conversion specifier, as in the statement

```
printf("%9.3f", 123.456789);
```

that displays **123.457** with 3 digits to the right of the decimal point, and right justified in a 9-digit field.

```
/* Using precision while printing integers,
   floating-point numbers, and strings */
#include <stdio.h>

main()
{
   int i = 873;
   float f = 123.94536;
   char s[] = "Happy Birthday";

   printf("Using precision for integers\n");
   printf("\t%.4d\n\t%.9d\n\n", i, i);
   printf("Using precision for floating-point numbers\n");
   printf("\t%.3f\n\t%.3e\n\t%.3g\n\n", f, f, f);
   printf("Using precision for strings\n");
   printf("\t%.11s\n", s);
   return 0;
}
```

```
Using precision for integers
        0873
        000000873

Using precision for floating-point numbers
        123.945
        1.239e+02
        124

Using precision for strings
        Happy Birth
```

Fig. 9.9   Using precisions to display information of several types.

It is possible to specify the field width and the precision using integer expressions in the argument list following the format control string. To use this feature, insert an ***** (asterisk) in place of the field width or precision (or both). The matching argument in the argument list is evaluated and used in place of the asterisk. The value of the argument can be negative for the field width, but must be positive for the precision. A negative value for the field width causes the output to be left justified in the field as described in the next section. The statement

```
printf("%*.*f", 7, 2, 98.736);
```

uses **7** for the field width, **2** for the precision and outputs the value **98.74** right justified.

9.9 Using Flags in the Printf Format Control String

Function **printf** also provides *flags* to supplement its output formatting capabilities. Five flags are available to the user for use in format control strings (Fig. 9.10).

Flag	Description
− (minus sign)	Left-justify the output within the specified field.
+ (plus sign)	Display a plus sign preceding positive values and a minus sign preceding negative values.
space	Print a space before a positive value not printed with the + flag.
#	Prefix **0** to the output value when used with the octal conversion specifier **o**. Prefix **0x** or **0X** to the output value when used with the hexadecimal conversion specifiers **x** or **X**. Force a decimal point for a floating-point number printed with **e**, **E**, **f**, **g**, or **G** that does not contain a fractional part. (Normally the decimal point is only printed if a digit follows it.) For **g** and **G** specifiers, trailing zeros are not eliminated.
0 (zero)	Pad a field with leading zeros.

Fig. 9.10   Format control string flags.

To use a flag in a format control string, place the flag immediately to the right of the percent sign. Several flags may be combined in one conversion specification.

The program of Fig. 9.11 demonstrates right justification and left justification of a string, an integer, a character, and a floating-point number.

The program in Fig. 9.12 prints a positive number and a negative number, each with and without the + flag. Note that the minus sign is displayed in both cases, but the plus sign is only displayed when the + flag is used.

The program in Fig. 9.13 prefixes a space to the positive number with the space flag. This is useful for aligning positive and negative numbers with the same number of digits.

```
/* Right justifying and left justifying values */
#include <stdio.h>

main()
{
   printf("%10s%10d%10c%10f\n\n", "hello", 7, 'a', 1.23);
   printf("%-10s%-10d%-10c%-10f\n", "hello", 7, 'a', 1.23);
   return 0;
}
```

```
        hello         7         a  1.230000

hello     7         a         1.230000
```

Fig. 9.11   Left-justifying strings in a field.

```
/* Printing numbers with and without the + flag */
#include <stdio.h>

main()
{
    printf("%d\n%d\n", 786, -786);
    printf("%+d\n%+d\n", 786, -786);
    return 0;
}
```

```
786
-786
+786
-786
```

Fig. 9.12   Printing positive and negative numbers with and without the + flag.

```
/* Printing a space before signed values
   not preceded by + or - */
#include <stdio.h>

main()
{
    printf("% d\n% d\n", 547, -547);
    return 0;
}
```

```
 547
-547
```

Fig. 9.13   Using the space flag.

The program in Fig. 9.14 uses the # flag to prefix 0 to the octal value, 0x and 0X to the hexadecimal values, and to force the decimal point on a value printed with g.

The program in Fig. 9.15 combines the + flag and the 0 (zero) flag to print 452 in a 9-space field with a + sign and leading zeros, then prints 452 again using only the 0 flag and a 9-space field.

9.10 Printing Literals and Escape Sequences

Most literal characters to be printed in a **printf** statement can simply be included in the format control string. However, there are several "problem" characters such as the quotation mark (**"**) that delimits the format control string itself. Various control characters, such as newline and tab, must be represented by *escape sequences*. An escape sequence is represented by a backslash (\) followed by a particular *escape character*. The table in Fig. 9.16 lists all the escape sequences and the actions they cause.

```
/* Using the # flag with conversion specifiers
   o, x, X, and any floating-point specifier */
#include <stdio.h>

main()
{
   int c = 1427;
   float p = 1427.0;

   printf("%#o\n", c);
   printf("%#x\n", c);
   printf("%#X\n", c);
   printf("\n%g\n", p);
   printf("%#g\n", p);
   return 0;
}
```

```
02623
0x593
0X593

1427
1427.00
```

Fig. 9.14   Using the # flag.

```
/* Printing with the 0(zero) flag fills in leading zeros */
#include <stdio.h>

main()
{
   printf("%+09d", 452);
   printf("%09d", 452);
   return 0;
}
```

```
+00000452
000000452
```

Fig. 9.15   Using the 0 (zero) flag.

Common Programming Error 9.9

Attempting to print as literal data in a **printf** *statement a single quote, double quote, question mark, or backslash character without preceding that character by a backslash to form a proper escape sequence.*

Escape sequence	Description
\'	Output the single quote (') character.
\"	Output the double quote (") character.
\?	Output the question mark (?) character.
\\	Output the backslash (\ ) character.
\a	Cause an audible (bell) or visual alert.
\b	Move the cursor back one position on the current line.
\f	Move the cursor to the start of the next logical page.
\n	Move the cursor to the beginning of the next line.
\r	Move the cursor to the beginning of the current line.
\t	Move the cursor to the next horizontal tab position.
\v	Move the cursor to the next vertical tab position.

Fig. 9.16   Escape sequences.

9.11 Formatting Input with Scanf

Precise input formatting is accomplished with **scanf**. Every **scanf** statement contains a format control string that describes the format of the data to be input. The format control string consists of conversion specifications and literal characters. Function **scanf** has the following input formatting capabilities:

1. Inputting all types of data.

2. Inputting specific characters from an input stream.

3. Skipping specific characters in the input stream.

The **scanf** function is written in the following form:

> **scanf**(*format-control-string,   other-arguments*);

The *format-control-string* describes the formats of the input, and the *other-arguments* are pointers to variables in which the input will be stored.

Good Programming Practice 9.3

When inputting data, prompt the user for one data item or a few data items at a time. Avoid asking the user to enter many data items in response to a single prompt.

Figure 9.17 summarizes the conversion specifiers used to input all types of data. The remainder of this section provides programs that demonstrate reading data with the various **scanf** conversion specifiers.

The program in Fig. 9.18 reads integers with the various integer conversion specifiers, and displays the integers as decimal numbers. Note that **%i** is capable of inputting decimal, octal, and hexadecimal integers.

Conversion specifier	Description
Integers	
d	Read an optionally signed decimal integer. The corresponding argument is a pointer to integer.
i	Read an optionally signed decimal, octal, or hexadecimal integer. The corresponding argument is a pointer to integer.
o	Read an octal integer. The corresponding argument is a pointer to unsigned integer.
u	Read an unsigned decimal integer. The corresponding argument is a pointer to unsigned integer.
x or **X**	Read a hexadecimal integer. The corresponding argument is a pointer to unsigned integer.
h or **l**	Place before any of the integer conversion specifiers to indicate that a **short** or **long** integer is to be input.
Floating-point numbers	
e, E, f, g or G	Read a floating-point value. The corresponding argument is a pointer to a floating-point variable.
l or **L**	Place before any of the floating-point conversion specifiers to indicate that a **double** or **long double** value is to be input.
Characters and strings	
c	Read a character. The corresponding argument is a pointer to **char**, no null (' \0 ') is added.
s	Read a string. The corresponding argument is a pointer to an array of type **char** that is large enough to hold the string and a terminating null (' \0 ') character.
Scan set	
[*scan characters*]	Scan a string for a set of characters that are stored in an array.
Miscellaneous	
p	Read a pointer address of the same form produced when an address is output with **%p** in a **printf** statement.
n	Store the number of characters input so far in this **scanf**. The corresponding argument is a pointer to integer
%	Skip a percent sign (**%**) in the input.

Fig. 9.17 Conversion specifiers for **scanf**.

When inputting floating-point numbers, any of the floating-point conversion specifiers **e**, **E**, **f**, **g**, or **G**, can be used. The program in Fig. 9.19 demonstrates reading three floating-point numbers, one with each of the three types of floating conversion specifiers, and displays all three numbers with conversion specifier **f**. Note that the program output confirms the fact that floating-point values are imprecise—this fact is highlighted by the second value printed.

```
/* Reading integers */
#include <stdio.h>

main()
{
   int a, b, c, d, e, f, g;

   printf("Enter seven integers: ");
   scanf("%d%i%i%i%o%u%x", &a, &b, &c, &d, &e, &f, &g);
   printf("The input displayed as decimal integers is:\n");
   printf("%d %d %d %d %d %d %d\n", a, b, c, d, e, f, g);
   return 0;
}
```

```
Enter seven integers: -70 -70 070 0x70 70 70 70
The input displayed as decimal integers is:
-70 -70 56 112 56 70 112
```

Fig. 9.18   Reading input with integer conversion specifiers.

```
/* Reading floating-point numbers */
#include <stdio.h>

main()
{
   float a, b, c;

   printf("Enter three floating-point numbers: \n");
   scanf("%e%f%g", &a, &b, &c);
   printf("Here are the numbers entered in plain\n");
   printf("floating-point notation:\n");
   printf("%f %f %f\n", a, b, c);
   return 0;
}
```

```
Enter three floating-point numbers:
1.27987 1.27987e+03 3.38476e-06
Here are the numbers entered in plain
floating-point notation:
1.279870
1279.869995
0.000003
```

Fig. 9.19   Reading input with floating-point conversion specifiers.

Characters and strings are input using the conversion specifiers **c** and **s**, respectively. The program in Fig. 9.20 prompts the user to enter a string. The program inputs the first character of the string with **%c** and stores it in the character variable **x**, then inputs the remainder of the string with **%s** and stores it in character array **y**.

A sequence of characters can be input using a *scan set*. A scan set is a set of characters enclosed in square brackets **[]** and preceded by a percent sign in the format control string. A scan set scans the characters in the input stream looking only for those characters that match characters contained in the scan set. Each time a character is matched, it is stored in the scan set's corresponding argument—a pointer to a character array. The scan set stops inputting characters when a character that is not contained in the scan set is encountered. If the first character in the input stream does not match a character in the scan set, only the null character is stored in the array. The program in Fig. 9.21 uses the scan set **[aeiou]** to scan the input stream for vowels. Notice that the first seven letters of the input are read. The eighth letter (**h**) is not in the scan set and therefore the scanning is terminated.

The scan set can also be used to scan for characters not contained in the scan set by using an *inverted scan set*. To create an inverted scan set, place a *caret (^)* in the square brackets before the scan characters. This causes characters not appearing in the scan set to be stored. When a character contained in the inverted scan set is encountered, input terminates. The program in Fig. 9.22 uses the inverted scan set **[^aeiou]** to search for consonants more properly—to search for "non-vowels."

A field width can be used in a **scanf** conversion specification to read a specific number of characters from the input stream. The program of Fig. 9.23 inputs a series of consecutive digits as a two digit-integer and an integer consisting of the remaining digits in the input stream.

```
/* Reading characters and strings */
#include <stdio.h>

main()
{
   char x, y[9];

   printf("Enter a string: ");
   scanf("%c%s", &x, y);

   printf("The input was:\n");
   printf("the character \"%c\" ", x);
   printf("and the string \"%s\"\n", y);
   return 0;
}
```

```
Enter a string: Sunday
The input was:
the character "S" and the string "unday"
```

Fig. 9.20   Inputting characters and strings.

```
/* Using a scan set */
#include <stdio.h>

main()
{
   char z[9];

   printf("Enter string: ");
   scanf("%[aeiou]", z);
   printf("The input was \"%s\"\n", z);
   return 0;
}
```

```
Enter String: ooeeooahah
The input was "ooeeooa"
```

Fig. 9.21   Using a scan set.

```
/* Using an inverted scan set */
#include <stdio.h>

main()
{
   char z[9];

   printf("Enter a string: ");
   scanf("%[^aeiou]", z);
   printf("The input was \"%s\"\n", z);
   return 0;
}
```

```
Enter a string: String
The input was "Str"
```

Fig. 9.22   Using an inverted scan set.

Often it is necessary to skip certain characters in the input stream. For example, a date could be entered as

```
7-9-91
```

Each number in the date needs to be stored, but the dashes that separate the numbers can be discarded. To eliminate unnecessary characters, include them in the format control string of **scanf** (whitespace characters—such as space, newline, and tab—skip all leading whitespace). For example, to skip the dashes in the input, use the statement

```
scanf("%d-%d-%d", &month, &day, &year);
```

```
/* inputting data with a field width */
#include <stdio.h>

main()
{
   int x, y;

   printf("Enter a six digit integer: ");
   scanf("%2d%d", &x, &y);
   printf("The integers input were %d and %d\n", x, y);
   return 0;
}
```

```
Enter a six digit integer: 123456
The integers input were 12 and 3456
```

Fig. 9.23 Inputting data with a field width.

Although, this **scanf** does eliminate the dashes in the preceding input, it is possible that the date could be entered as

    7/9/91

In this case the preceding **scanf** would not eliminate the unnecessary characters. For this reason, **scanf** provides the *assignment suppression character* *****. The assignment suppression character enables **scanf** to read any type of data from the input and discard it without assigning it to a variable. The program in Fig. 9.24 uses the assignment suppression character in the **%c** conversion specification to indicate that a character appearing in the input stream should be read and discarded. Only the month, day, and year are stored. The values of the variables are printed to demonstrate that they are in fact input correctly. Note that no variables in the argument list correspond to the conversion specifications that use the assignment suppression character because no assignments are performed for those conversion specifications.

Summary

* All input and output is dealt with in streams—sequences of characters organized into lines. Each line consists of zero or more characters and ends with a newline character.

* Normally, the standard input steam is connected to the keyboard, and the standard output stream is connected to the computer screen.

* Operating systems often allow the standard input and standard output streams to be redirected to other devices.

* The **printf** format control string describes the formats in which the output values appear. The format control string consists of conversion specifiers, flags, field widths, precisions, and literal characters.

```
/* Reading and discarding characters from the input stream */
#include <stdio.h>

main()
{
    int month1, day1, year1, month2, day2, year2;

    printf("Enter a date in the form mm-dd-yy: ");
    scanf("%d%*c%d%*c%d", &month1, &day1, &year1);
    printf("month = %d  day = %d  year = %d\n\n",
        month1, day1, year1);
    printf("Enter a date in the form mm/dd/yy: ");
    scanf("%d%*c%d%*c%d", &month2, &day2, &year2);
    printf("month = %d  day = %d  year = %d\n",
        month2, day2, year2);
    return 0;
}
```

```
Enter a date in the form mm-dd-yy: 11-18-71
month = 11  day = 18  year = 71

Enter a date in the form mm/dd/yy: 11/18/71
month = 11  day = 18  year = 71
```

Fig. 9.24   Reading and discarding characters from the input stream.

- Integers are printed with the following conversion specifiers: **d** or **i** for optionally signed integers, **o** for unsigned integers in octal form, **u** for unsigned integers in decimal form, and **x** or **X** for unsigned integers in hexadecimal form. The modifier **h** or **l** is prefixed to the preceding conversion specifiers to indicate a **short** or **long** integer respectively.

- Floating-point values are printed with the following conversion specifiers: **e** or **E** for exponential notation, **f** for regular floating-point notation, and **g** or **G** for either **e** (or **E**) notation or **f** notation. When the **g** (or **G**) conversion specifier is indicated, the **e** (or **E**) conversion specifier is used if the value's exponent is less than –**4** or greater than or equal to the precision with which the value is printed.

- The precision for the **g** and **G** conversion specifiers indicates the maximum number of significant digits printed.

- The **c** conversion specifier prints a character.

- The **s** conversion specifier prints a string of characters ending in the null character.

- The conversion specifier **p** displays a pointer address in an implementation-defined manner (on many systems, hexadecimal notation is used).

- The conversion specifier **n** stores the number of characters already output in the current **printf** statement. The corresponding argument is a pointer to an integer.

- The conversion specification %% causes a literal % to be output.

- If the field width is larger than the object being printed, the object is normally right-justified in the field.

- Field widths can be used with all conversion specifiers.

- Precision used with integer conversion specifiers indicates the minimum number of digits printed. If the value contains fewer digits than the precision specified, zeros are prefixed to the printed value until the number of digits is equivalent to the precision.

- Precision used with floating-point conversion specifiers e, E, and f indicates the number of digits that appear after the decimal point.

- Precision used with floating-point conversion specifiers g and G indicates the number of significant digits to appear.

- Precision used with conversion specifier s indicates the number of characters to be printed.

- The field width and the precision can be combined by placing the field width followed by a decimal point followed by the precision between the percent sign and the conversion specifier.

- It is possible to specify the field width and the precision through integer expressions in the argument list following the format control string. To use this feature, insert an * (asterisk) in place of the field width or precision. The matching argument in the argument list is evaluated and used in place of the asterisk. The value of the argument can be negative for the field width, but must be positive for the precision.

- The – flag left-justifies its argument in a field.

- The + flag prints a plus sign for positive values and a minus sign for negative values.

- The space flag prints a space preceding a positive value not displayed with the + flag.

- The # flag prefixes 0 to octal values, 0x or 0X to hexadecimal values, and forces the decimal point to be printed for floating-point values printed with e, E, f, g, or G (normally the decimal point is only displayed if the value contains a fractional part).

- The 0 flag prints leading zeros for a value that does not occupy its entire field width.

- Precise input formatting is accomplished with the **scanf** library function.

- Integers are input with the conversion specifiers d and i for optionally signed integers, and o, u, x, or X for unsigned integers. The modifiers h and l are placed before an integer conversion specifier to input a **short** or **long** integer respectively.

- Floating-point values are input with the conversion specifiers e, E, f, g, or G. The modifiers l and L are placed before any of the floating-point conversion specifiers to indicate that the input value is a **double** or **long double** value respectively.

- Characters are input with the conversion specifier c.

- Strings are input with the conversion specifier s.

- A scan set scans the characters in the input looking only for those characters that match characters contained in the scan set. When a character is matched, it is stored in a character array. The scan set stops inputting characters when a character not contained in the scan set is encountered.

- To create an inverted scan set, place a caret (^) in the square brackets before the scan characters. This causes characters not appearing in the scan set to be stored until a character contained in the inverted scan set is encountered.

- Address values are input with the conversion specifier **p**.

- Conversion specifier **n** stores the number of characters input previously in the current **scanf**. The corresponding argument is a pointer to **int**.

- The conversion specification %% matches a single % character in the input.

- The assignment suppression character is used to read data from the input stream and discard the data.

- A field width is used in a **scanf** to read a specific number of characters from the input stream.

Terminology

flag
% conversion specifier
* in field width
* in precision
+ (plus sign) flag
– (minus sign) flag
0 (zero) flag
`<stdio.h>`
\" escape sequence
\' escape sequence
\? escape sequence
\\ escape sequence
\a escape sequence
\b escape sequence
\f escape sequence
\n escape sequence
\r escape sequence
\t escape sequence
\v escape sequence
alignment
assignment suppression character (*)
blank insertion
c conversion specifier
caret (^)
conversion specification
conversion specifiers
d conversion specifier

e or E conversion specifier
escape sequence
exponential floating-point format
f conversion specifier
field width
flag
floating-point
format control string
g or G conversion specifier
h conversion specifier
hexadecimal format
i conversion specifier
integer conversion specifiers
inverted scan set
L conversion specifier
l conversion specifier
left justification
literal characters
long integer
n conversion specifier
o conversion specifier
octal format
p conversion specifier
precision
printf
printing character insertion
redirect a stream

right justification
rounding
s conversion specifier
scan set
scanf
scientific notation
short integer
signed integer format
space flag

standard error stream
standard input stream
standard output stream
stream
u conversion specifier
unsigned integer format
white space
x (or **X**) conversion specifier

Common Programming Errors

9.1 Forgetting to enclose a format control string in quotation marks.

9.2 Printing a negative value with a conversion specifier that expects an unsigned value.

9.3 Using **%c** to print the first character of a string. The conversion specification **%c** expects a **char** argument. A string is a pointer to **char**, i.e., a **char ***.

9.4 Using **%s** to print a **char** argument. The conversion specification **%s** expects an argument of type pointer to **char**. On some systems, this causes a fatal execution-time error called an access violation.

9.5 Using single quotes around character strings is a syntax error. Character strings must be enclosed in double quotes.

9.6 Using double quotes around a character constant. This actually creates a string consisting of two characters, the second of which is the terminating **NULL**. A character constant is a single character enclosed in single quotes.

9.7 Trying to print a literal percent character using **%** rather than **%%** in the format control string. When **%** appears in a format control string, it must be followed by a conversion specifier.

9.8 Not providing a sufficiently large field width to handle a value to be printed. This can offset other data being printed and can produce confusing outputs. Know your data!

9.9 Attempting to print as literal data in a **printf** statement a single quote, double quote, question mark, or backslash character without preceding that character by a backslash to form a proper escape sequence.

Good Programming Practices

9.1 Edit outputs neatly for presentation. This makes program outputs more readable and reduces user errors.

9.2 When outputting data, be sure that the user is aware of situations in which data may be imprecise due to formatting (e.g., rounding errors from specifying precisions).

9.3 When inputting data, prompt the user for one data item or a few data items at a time. Avoid asking the user to enter many data items in response to a single prompt.

Portability Tip

9.1 The conversion specifier **p** displays a pointer address in an implementation-defined manner (on many systems, hexadecimal notation is used rather than decimal notation).

Self-Review Exercises

9.1   Fill in the blanks in each of the following:
   a) All input and output is dealt with in the form of _____.
   b) The _____ stream is normally connected to the keyboard.
   c) The _____ stream is normally connected to the computer screen.
   d) Precise output formatting is accomplished with the _____ function.
   e) The format control string may contain _____, _____, _____, _____, and _____.
   f) The conversion specifier _____ or _____ may be used to output a signed decimal integer.
   g) The conversion specifiers _____, _____, and _____ are used to display unsigned integers in octal, decimal, and hexadecimal form respectively.
   h) The modifiers _____ and _____ are placed before the integer conversion specifiers to indicate that **short** or **long** integer values are to be displayed.
   i) The conversion specifier _____ is used to display a floating-point value in exponential notation.
   j) The modifier _____ is placed before any floating-point conversion specifier to indicate that a **long double** value is to be displayed.
   k) The conversion specifiers **e**, **E**, and **f** are displayed with _____ digits of precision to the right of the decimal point if no precision is specified.
   l) The conversion specifiers _____ and _____ are used to print strings and characters respectively.
   m) All strings end in the _____ character.
   n) The field width and precision in a **printf** conversion specification can be controlled with integer expressions by substituting an _____ for the field width or for the precision, and placing an integer expression in the corresponding argument of the argument list.
   o) The _____ flag causes output to be left-justified in a field.
   p) The _____ flag causes values to be displayed with either a plus sign or a minus sign.
   q) Precise input formatting is accomplished with the _____ function.
   r) A _____ is used to scan a string for specific characters and store the characters in an array.
   s) The conversion specifier _____ can be used to input optionally signed octal, decimal, and hexadecimal integers.
   t) The conversion specifier _____ can be used to input a **double** value.
   u) The _____ is used to read data from the input stream and discard it without assigning it to a variable.
   v) A _____ can be used in a **scanf** conversion specification to indicate that a specific number of characters or digits should be read from the input stream.

9.2   Find the error in each of the following and explain how the error can be corrected.
   a) The following statement should print the character **'c'**
```
printf("%s\n", 'c');
```
   b) The following statement should print **9.375%**.
```
printf("%.3f%", 9.375);
```
   c) The following statement should print the first character of the string **"Monday"**
```
printf("%c\n", "Monday");
```
   d) `printf(""A string in quotes"");`

e) `printf(%d%d, 12, 20);`

f) `printf("%c", "x");`

g) `printf("%s\n", 'Richard');`

9.3   Write a statement for each of the following:

a) Print **1234** right-justified in a **10** digit field.

b) Print **123.456789** in exponential notation with a sign (**+** or **-**) and **3** digits of precision.

c) Read a **double** value into variable **number**.

d) Print **100** in octal form preceded by **0**.

e) Read a string into character array **string**.

f) Read characters into array **n** until a non-digit character is encountered.

g) Use integer variables **x** and **y** to specify the field width and precision used to display the **double** value **87.4573**.

h) Read a value of the form **3.5%**. Store the percentage in **float** variable **percent**, and eliminate the **%** from the input stream. Do not use the assignment suppression character.

i) Print **3.333333** as a **long double** value with a sign (**+** or **-**)in a field of **20** characters with a precision of **3**.

Answers to Self-Review Exercises

9.1   a) Streams. b) Standard input. c) Standard output. d) **printf**. e) Conversion specifiers, flags, field widths, precisions, and literal characters. f) **d, i**. g) **o, u, x** (or **X**). h) **h, l**. i) **e** (or **E**). j) **L**. k) 6. l) **s, c**. m) **NULL** (**'\0'**). n) asterisk (*****). o) - (minus). p) + (plus). q) **scanf**. r) Scan set. s) **i**. t) **1e, 1E, 1f, 1g**, or **1G**. u) Assignment suppression character (*****). v) Field width.

9.2   a) Error: Conversion specifier **s** expects an argument of type pointer to **char**.
Correction: To print the character **'c'**, use the conversion specification **%c** or change **'c'** to **"c"**.

b) Error: Trying to print the literal character **%** without using the conversion specification **%%**.
Correction: Use **%%** to print a literal **%** character.

c) Error: Conversion specifier **c** expects an argument of type **char**.
Correction: To print the first character of **"Monday"** use the conversion specification **%1s**.

d) Error: Trying to print the literal character **"** without using the **\"** escape sequence.
Correction: Replace each quote in the inner set of quotes with **\"**.

e) Error: The format control string is not enclosed in double quotes.
Correctio: Enclose **%d%d** in double quotes.

f) Error: The character **x** is enclosed in double quotes.
Correction: Character constants to be printed with **%c** must be enclosed in single quotes.

g) Error: The string to be printed is enclosed in single quotes.
Correction: Use double quotes instead of single quotes to represent a string.

9.3   a) `printf("%10d\n", 1234);`

b) `printf("%+.3e\n", 123.456789);`

c) `scanf("%lf", &number);`

d) `printf("%#o\n", 100);`

```
e)  scanf("%s", string);
f)  scanf("%[^0123456789]", n);
g)  printf("%*.*f\n", x, y, 87.4573);
h)  scanf("%f%%", &percent);
i)  printf("%+20.3Lf\n", 3.333333);
```

Exercises

9.4   Write a `printf` or `scanf` statement for each of the following:
   a) Print unsigned integer **40000** left justified in a **15**-digit field with **8** digits.
   b) Read a hexadecimal value into variable **hex**.
   c) Print **200** with and without a sign.
   d) Print **100** in hexadecimal form preceded by **0x**.
   e) Read characters into array **s** until the letter **p** is encountered.
   f) Print **1.234** in a **9**-digit field with preceding zeros.
   g) Read a time of the form **hh:mm:ss** storing the parts of the time in the integer variables **hour, minute,** and **second**. Skip the colons (**:**) in the input stream. Use the assignment-suppression character.
   h) Read a string of the form **"characters"** from the standard input. Store the string in character array **s**. Eliminate the quotation marks from the input stream.
   i) Read a time of the form **hh:mm:ss** storing the parts of the time in the integer variables **hour, minute,** and **second**. Skip the colons (**:**) in the input stream. Do not use the assignment-suppression character.

9.5   Show what is printed by each of the following statements. If a statement is incorrect, indicate why.
   a) `printf("%-10d\n", 10000);`
   b) `printf("%c\n", "This is a string");`
   c) `printf("%*.*lf\n", 8, 3, 1024.987654);`
   d) `printf("%#o\n%#X\n%#e\n", 17, 17, 1008.83689);`
   e) `printf("% ld\n%+ld\n", 1000000, 1000000);`
   f) `printf("%10.2E\n", 444.93738);`
   g) `printf("%10.2g\n", 444.93738);`
   h) `printf("%d\n", 10.987);`

9.6   Find the error(s) in each of the following program segments. Explain how each error can be corrected
   a) `printf("%s\n", 'Happy Birthday');`
   b) `printf("%c\n", 'Hello');`
   c) `printf("%c\n", "This is a string");`
   d) The following statement should print **"Bon Voyage"**.
           `printf(""%s"", "Bon Voyage");`
   e) `char day[] = "Sunday";`
       `printf("%s\n", day[3]);`
   f) `printf('Enter your name: ');`
   g) `printf(%f, 123.456);`
   h) The following statement should print the characters **'O'** and **'K'**.
           `printf("%s%s\n", 'O', 'K');`
   i) `char s[10];`
       `scanf("%c", s[7]);`

9.7   Write a program that loads 10-element array **number** with random integers from 1 to 1000. For each value, print the value and a running total of the number of characters printed. Use the **%n** conversion specification to determine the number of characters output for each value. Print the total number of characters output for all values up to and including the current value each time the current value is printed. The output should have the following format:

```
Value        Total characters
342          3
1000         7
963          10
6            11
etc.
```

9.8   Write a program to test the difference between the **%d** and **%i** conversion specifiers when used in **scanf** statements. Use the statements

```
scanf("%i%d", &x, &y);
printf("%d %d\n", x, y);
```

to input and print the values. Test the program with the following sets of input data:

```
      10       10
     -10      -10
     010      010
    0x10     0x10
```

9.9   Write a program that prints pointer values using all the integer conversion specifiers and the **%p** conversion specification. Which ones print strange values? Which ones cause errors? In which format does the **%p** conversion specification display the address on your system?

9.10   Write a program to test the results of printing the integer value **12345** and the floating-point value **1.2345** in various size fields. What happens when the values are printed in fields containing fewer digits than the values?

9.11   Write a program that prints the value **100.453627** rounded to the nearest digit, tenth, hundredth, thousandth, and ten thousandth.

9.12   Write a program that inputs a string from the keyboard and determines the length of the string. Print the string using twice the length as the field width.

9.13   Write a program that converts integer Fahrenheit temperatures from **0** to **212** degrees to floating-point Celsius temperatures with **3** digits of precision. Use the formula

```
celcius = 5.0 / 9.0 * (fahrenheit - 32);
```

to perform the calculation. The output should be printed in two right-justified columns of 10 characters each, and the Celsius temperatures should be preceded by a sign for both positive and negative values.

9.14   Write a program to test all the escape sequences in Fig. 9.16. For the escape sequences that move the cursor, print a character before and after printing the escape sequence so it is clear where the cursor has moved.

9.15   Write a program that determines whether **?** can be printed as part of a **printf** format control string as a literal character rather than using the **\?** escape sequence.

9.16   Write a program that inputs the value **437** using each of the **scanf** integer conversion specifiers. Print each input value using all the integer conversion specifiers.

9.17 Write a program that uses each of the conversion specifiers **e**, **f**, and **g** to input the value **1.2345**. Print the values of each variable to prove that each conversion specifier can be used to input this same value.

9.18 In some programming languages, strings are entered surrounded by either single *or* double quotation marks. Write a program that reads the three strings **suzy**, **"suzy"**, and **'suzy'**. Are the single and double quotes ignored by C or read as part of the string?

9.19 Write a program that determines whether **?** can be printed as the character constant **'?'** rather than the character constant escape sequence **'\?'** using conversion specifier **%c** in the format control string of a **printf** statement.

9.20 Write a program that uses the conversion specifier **g** to output the value **9876.12345**. Print the value with precisions ranging from **1** to **9**.

10

Structures, Unions, Bit Manipulations, and Enumerations

Objectives

- To be able to create and use structures, unions, and enumerations.
- To be able to pass structures to functions call by value and call by reference.
- To be able to manipulate data with the bitwise operators.
- To be able to create bit fields for storing data compactly.

I could never make out what those damned dots meant.
Winston Churchill

But yet an union in partition;
William Shakespeare

You can include me out.
Samuel Goldwyn

The same old charitable lie
Repeated as the years scoot by
Perpetually makes a hit—
"You really haven't changed a bit!"
Margaret Fishback

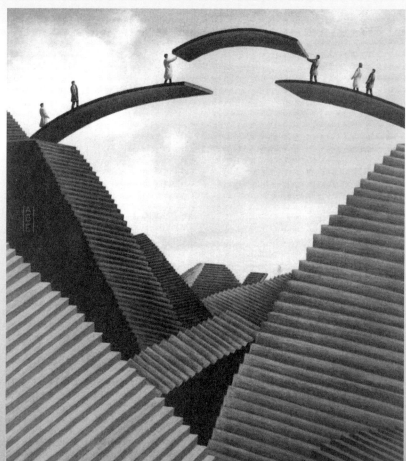

Outline

10.1 Introduction

Structures are collections of related variables—sometimes referred to as *aggregates*—under one name. Structures may contain variables of many different data types—in contrast to arrays that contain only elements of the same data type. Structures are commonly used to define records to be stored in files (see Chapter 11, "File Processing"). Pointers and structures facilitate the formation of more complex data structures such as linked lists, queues, stacks, and trees (see Chapter 12, "Data Structures").

10.2 Structure Definitions

Structures are *derived data types*—they are constructed using objects of other types. Consider the following structure definition:

```
struct card {
    char *face;
    char *suit;
};
```

The keyword **struct** introduces the structure definition. The identifier **card** is the *structure tag*. The structure tag names the structure definition, and is used with the keyword **struct** to declare variables of the *structure type*. In this example, the structure type is **struct card**. Variables declared within the braces of the structure definition are the structure's *members*. Members of the same structure must have unique names, but two different structures may contain members of the same name without conflict (we will soon see why). Each structure definition must end with a semicolon.

Common Programming Error 10.1

Forgetting the semicolon that terminates a structure definition.

The definition of **struct card** contains two members of type **char *—face** and **suit**. Structure members can be variables of the basic data types (e.g., **int**, **float**, etc.), or aggregates, such as arrays and other structures. As we saw in Chapter 6, each element of an array must be of the same type. Structure members, however, can be of a variety of data types. For example, a **struct employee** might contain character string members for the first and last names, an **int** member for the employee's age, a **char** member containing **'M'** or **'F'** for the employee's gender, a **float** member for the employee's hourly salary, and so on. A structure cannot contain an instance of itself. For example, a variable of type **struct card** cannot be declared in the definition for **struct card**. A pointer to **struct card**, however, may be included. A structure containing a member that is a pointer to the same structure type is referred to as a *self-referential structure*. Self-referential structures are used in Chapter 12 to build various kinds of linked data structures.

The preceding structure definition does not reserve any space in memory, rather the definition creates a new data type that is used to declare variables. Structure variables are declared like variables of other types. The declaration

```
struct card a, deck[52], *cPtr;
```

declares **a** to be a variable of type **struct card**, declares **deck** to be an array with 52 elements of type **struct card**, and declares **cPtr** to be a pointer to **struct card**. Variables of a given structure type may also be declared by placing a comma-separated list of the variable names between the closing brace of the structure definition and the semi-colon that ends the structure definition. For example, the preceding declaration could have been incorporated into the **struct card** structure definition as follows:

```
struct card {
   char *face;
   char *suit;
} a, deck[52], *cPtr;
```

The structure tag name is optional. If a structure definition does not contain a structure tag name, variables of the structure type may be declared only in the structure definition—not in a separate declaration.

Good Programming Practice 10.1

Provide a structure tag name when creating a structure type. The structure tag name is convenient for declaring new variables of the structure type later in the program.

Good Programming Practice 10.2

Choosing a meaningful structure tag name helps make a program self-documenting.

The only valid operations that may be performed on structures are: Assigning structure variables to structure variables of the same type, taking the address (**&**) of a structure variable, accessing the members of a structure variable (see Section 10.4), and using the **sizeof** operator to determine the size of a structure variable.

Common Programming Error 10.2

Assigning a structure of one type to a structure of a different type.

Structures may not be compared because structure members are not necessarily stored in consecutive bytes of memory. Sometimes there are "holes" in a structure because computers may store specific data types only on certain memory boundaries such as halfword, word, or doubleword boundaries. A word is a standard memory unit used to store data in a computer—usually 2 bytes or 4 bytes. Consider the following structure definition in which **sample1** and **sample2** of type **struct example** are declared:

```
struct example {
    char c;
    int i;
} sample1, sample2;
```

A computer with 2-byte words, may require that each of the members of **struct example** be aligned on a word boundary, i.e., at the beginning of a word (this is machine dependent). Figure 10.1 shows a sample storage alignment for a variable of type **struct example** that has been assigned the character **'a'** and the integer **97** (the bit representations of the values are shown). If the members are stored beginning at word boundaries, there is a 1-byte hole (byte **1** in the figure) in the storage for variables of type **struct example**. The value in the 1-byte hole is undefined. If the member values of **sample1** and **sample2** are in fact equal, the structures do not necessarily compare equal because the undefined 1-byte holes are not likely to contain identical values.

Common Programming Error 10.3

Comparing structures is a syntax error because of the different alignment requirements on various systems.

Portability Tip 10.1

Because the size of data items of a particular type is machine dependent, and because storage alignment considerations are machine dependent, so too is the representation of a structure.

Byte **0**   1   2   3

| 01100001 | | 00000000 | 01100001 |

Fig. 10.1 A possible storage alignment for a variable of type **struct example** showing an undefined area in memory.

10.3 Initializing Structures

Structures can be initialized using initializer lists as with arrays. To initialize a structure, follow the variable name in the structure declaration with an equal sign and a brace-enclosed, comma-separated list of initializers. For example, the declaration

```
struct card a = {"Three", "Hearts"};
```

creates variable **a** to be of type **struct card** (as defined previously) and initializes member **face** to **"Three"** and member **suit** to **"Hearts"**. If there are fewer initializers in the list than members in the structure, the remaining members are automatically initialized to **0** (or **NULL** if the member is a pointer). Structure variables declared outside a function definition (i.e., externally) are initialized to **0** or **NULL** if they are not explicitly initialized in the external declaration. Structure variables may also be initialized in assignment statements by assigning a structure variable of the same type, or by assigning values to the individual members of the structure.

10.4 Accessing Members of Structures

Two operators are used to access members of structures: The *structure member operator* (**.**)—also called the *dot operator*—and the *structure pointer operator* (**->**)—also called the *arrow operator*. The structure member operator accesses a structure member via the structure variable name. For example, to print member **suit** of structure **a** from the preceding declaration, use the statement

```
printf("%s", a.suit);
```

The structure pointer operator—consisting of a minus (**-**) sign and a greater than (**>**) sign with no intervening spaces—accesses a structure member via a pointer to the structure. Assume that the pointer **aPtr** has been declared to point to **struct card**, and that the address of structure **a** has been assigned to **aPtr**. To print member **suit** of structure **a** with pointer **aPtr**, use the statement

```
printf("%s", aPtr->suit);
```

The expression **aPtr->suit** is equivalent to **(*aPtr).suit** which dereferences the pointer and accesses the member **suit** using the structure member operator. The parentheses are needed here because the structure member operator (**.**) has a higher precedence than the pointer dereferencing operator (*****). The structure pointer operator and structure member operator, along with parentheses and brackets (**[]**) used for array subscripting, have the highest operator precedence and associate from left to right.

Good Programming Practice 10.3

Avoid using the same names for members of structures of different types. This is allowed, but it may cause confusion.

Good Programming Practice 10.4

Do not put spaces around the **->** *and* **.** *operators. This helps emphasize that the expressions the operators are contained in are essentially single variable names.*

Common Programming Error 10.4

Inserting space between the - and > components of the structure pointer operator (or inserting spaces between the components of any other multiple keystroke operator except ?:).

Common Programming Error 10.5

Attempting to refer to a member of a structure by using only the member's name.

Common Programming Error 10.6

Not using parentheses when referring to a structure member using a pointer and the structure member operator (e.g., `*aPtr.suit`, is a syntax error).

The program of Fig 10.2 demonstrates the use of the structure member and structure pointer operators. Using the structure member operator, the members of structure **a** are assigned the values **"Ace"** and **"Spades"** respectively. Pointer **aPtr** is assigned the address of structure **a**. A **printf** statement prints the members of structure variable **a** using the structure member operator with variable name **a**, the structure pointer operator with pointer **aPtr**, and the structure member operator with dereferenced pointer **aPtr**.

```c
/* Using the structure member and
   structure pointer operators */
#include <stdio.h>

struct card {
   char *face;
   char *suit;
};

main()
{
   struct card a;
   struct card *aPtr;

   a.face = "Ace";
   a.suit = "Spades";
   aPtr = &a;
   printf("%s%s%s\n%s%s%s\n%s%s%s\n",
          a.face, " of ", a.suit,
          aPtr->face, " of ", aPtr->suit,
          (*aPtr).face, " of ", (*aPtr).suit);
   return 0;
}
```

```
Ace of Spades
Ace of Spades
Ace of Spades
```

Fig. 10.2   Using the structure member operator and the structure pointer operator.

10.5 Using Structures with Functions

Structures may be passed to functions by passing individual structure members, by passing an entire structure, or by passing a pointer to a structure. When structures or individual structure members are passed to a function, they are passed call by value. Therefore, the members of a caller's structure cannot be modified by the called function.

To pass a structure call by reference, pass the address of the structure variable. Arrays of structures—like all other arrays—are automatically passed call by reference.

In Chapter 6, we stated that an array could be passed call by value by using a structure. To pass an array call by value, create a structure with the array as a member. Since structures are passed call by value, the array is passed call by value.

Common Programming Error 10.7

Assuming that structures, like arrays, are automatically passed call by reference and trying to modify the caller's structure values in the called function.

Performance Tip 10.1

Passing structures call by reference is more efficient than passing structures call by value (which requires the entire structure to be copied).

10.6 Typedef

The keyword **typedef** provides a mechanism for creating synonyms (or aliases) for previously defined data types. Names for structure types are often defined with **typedef** to create shorter type names. For example, the statement

```
typedef struct card Card;
```

defines the new type name **Card** as a synonym for type **struct card**. C programmers often use **typedef** to define a structure type so a structure tag is not required. For example, the following definition

```
typedef struct {
    char *face;
    char *suit;
} Card;
```

creates the structure type **Card** without the need for a separate **typedef** statement.

Good Programming Practice 10.5

Capitalize typedef names to emphasize that these names are synonyms for other type names.

Card can now be used to declare variables of type **struct card**. The declaration

```
Card deck[52];
```

declares an array of 52 **Card** structures (i.e., variables of type **struct card**). Creating a new name with **typedef** does not create a new type; **typedef** simply creates a new type name which may be used as an alias for an existing type name. A meaningful name helps make the program self documenting. For example, when we read the previous declaration, we know "**deck** is an array of 52 **Card**s."

Often, **typedef** is used to create synonyms for the basic data types. For example, a program requiring 4-byte integers may use type **int** on one system and type **long** on another. Programs designed for portability often use **typedef** to create an alias for 4-byte integers such as **Integer**. The alias **Integer** can be changed once in the program to make the program work on both systems.

Portability Tip 10.2

Use typedef *to help make a program more portable.*

10.7 Example: High-Performance Card Shuffling and Dealing Simulation

The program in Fig. 10.3 is based on the card shuffling and dealing simulation discussed in Chapter 7. The program represents the deck of cards as an array of structures. The program uses high-performance shuffling and dealing algorithms. The output for the high-performance card shuffling and dealing program is shown in Fig. 10.4.

In the program, function **fillDeck** initializes the **Card** array in order with Ace through King of each suit. The **Card** array is passed to function **shuffle** where the high-performance shuffling algorithm is implemented. Function **shuffle** takes an array of 52 **Card** structures as an argument. The function loops through the 52 cards (array subscripts 0 to 51) using a **for** structure. For each card, a number between 0 and 51 is picked randomly. Next, the current **Card** structure and the randomly selected **Card** structure are swapped in the array. A total of 52 swaps are made in a single pass of the entire array, and the array of **Card** structures is shuffled! This algorithm can not suffer from indefinite postponement like the shuffling algorithm presented in Chapter 7. Since the **Card** structures were swapped in place in the array, the high-performance dealing algorithm implemented in function **deal** requires only one pass of the array to deal the shuffled cards.

Common Programming Error 10.8

Forgetting to include the array subscript when referring to individual structures in an array of structures.

10.8 Unions

A *union* is a derived data type—like a structure—whose members share the same storage space. For different situations in a program, some variables may not be relevant, but other variables are—so a union shares the space instead of wasting storage on variables that are not being used. The members of a union can be of any type. The number of bytes used to store a union must be at least enough to hold the largest member. In most cases, unions contain two or more data types. Only one member, and thus one data type, can be referenced at a time. It is the programmer's responsibility to ensure that the data in a union is referenced with the proper data type.

```
/* The card shuffling and dealing program using structures */
#include <stdio.h>
#include <stdlib.h>
#include <time.h>

struct card {
   char *face;
   char *suit;
};

typedef struct card Card;

void fillDeck(Card *, char *[], char *[]);
void shuffle(Card *);
void deal(Card *);

main()
{
   Card deck[52];
   char *face[] = {"Ace", "Deuce", "Three", "Four", "Five",
                   "Six", "Seven", "Eight", "Nine", "Ten",
                   "Jack", "Queen", "King"};
   char *suit[] = {"Hearts", "Diamonds", "Clubs", "Spades"};

   srand(time(NULL));

   fillDeck(deck, face, suit);
   shuffle(deck);
   deal(deck);
   return 0;
}

void fillDeck(Card *wDeck, char *wFace[], char *wSuit[])
{
   int i;

   for (i = 0; i < 52; i++) {
      wDeck[i].face = wFace[i % 13];
      wDeck[i].suit = wSuit[i / 13];
   }
}

void shuffle(Card *wDeck)
{
   int i, j;
   Card temp;

   for (i = 0; i < 52; i++) {
      j = rand() % 52;
      temp = wDeck[i];
      wDeck[i] = wDeck[j];
      wDeck[j] = temp;
   }
}
```

Fig. 10.3   High-performance card shuffling and dealing simulation (part 1 of 2).

```
void deal(Card *wDeck)
{
   int i;

   for (i = 0; i < 52; i++)
      printf("%5s of %-8s%c", wDeck[i].face, wDeck[i].suit,
             (i + 1) % 2 ? '\t' : '\n');
}
```

Fig. 10.3 High-performance card shuffling and dealing simulation (part 2 of 2).

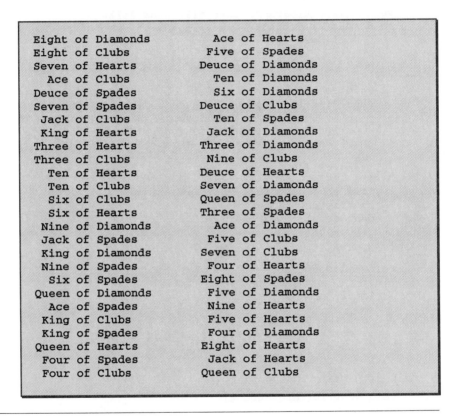

```
  Eight of Diamonds        Ace of Hearts
  Eight of Clubs          Five of Spades
  Seven of Hearts        Deuce of Diamonds
    Ace of Clubs           Ten of Diamonds
  Deuce of Spades          Six of Diamonds
  Seven of Spades        Deuce of Clubs
   Jack of Clubs           Ten of Spades
   King of Hearts         Jack of Diamonds
  Three of Hearts        Three of Diamonds
  Three of Clubs          Nine of Clubs
    Ten of Hearts        Deuce of Hearts
    Ten of Clubs         Seven of Diamonds
    Six of Clubs         Queen of Spades
    Six of Hearts        Three of Spades
   Nine of Diamonds        Ace of Diamonds
   Jack of Spades         Five of Clubs
   King of Diamonds      Seven of Clubs
   Nine of Spades         Four of Hearts
    Six of Spades        Eight of Spades
  Queen of Diamonds       Five of Diamonds
    Ace of Spades         Nine of Hearts
   King of Clubs          Five of Hearts
   King of Spades         Four of Diamonds
  Queen of Hearts        Eight of Hearts
   Four of Spades         Jack of Hearts
   Four of Clubs         Queen of Clubs
```

Fig. 10.4 Output for the high-performance card shuffling and dealing simulation.

Common Programming Error 10.9

Referencing with the wrong type, data stored in a union with a different type, is a logic error.

Portability Tip 10.3

If data is stored in a union as one type and referenced as another type, the results are implementation dependent.

A union is declared with the **union** keyword in the same format as a structure. The **union** declaration

```
union number {
    int x;
    float y;
};
```

indicates that **number** is a **union** type with members **int x** and **float y**. The union definition normally precedes **main** in a program so the definition can be used to declare variables in all the program's functions.

Software Engineering Observation 10.1

As with a **struct** *declaration, a* **union** *declaration simply creates a new type. Placing a* **union** *or* **struct** *declaration outside any function does not create a global variable.*

The operations that can be performed on a union are: Assigning a union to another union of the same type, taking the address (**&**) of a union, and accessing union members using the structure member operator and the structure pointer operator. Unions may not be compared for the same reasons that structures cannot be compared.

In a declaration, a union may be initialized only with a value of the same type as the first union member. For example, with the preceding union, the declaration

```
union number value = {10};
```

is a valid initialization of union variable **value** because the union is initialized with an **int**, but the following declaration would be invalid:

```
union number value = {1.43};
```

Common Programming Error 10.10

Comparing unions is a syntax error because of the different alignment requirements on various systems.

Common Programming Error 10.11

Initializing a union in a declaration with a value whose type is different from the type of the union's first member.

Portability Tip 10.4

The amount of storage required to store a union is implementation dependent.

Portability Tip 10.5

Some unions may not port easily to other computer systems. Whether a union is portable or not often depends on the storage alignment requirements for the union member data types on a given system.

Performance Tip 10.2

Unions conserve storage.

The program in Fig. 10.5 uses the variable **value** of type **union number** to display the value stored in the union as both an **int** and a **float**. The program output is implementation dependent. The program output shows that the internal representation of a **float** value can be quite different from the representation of **int**.

10.9 Bitwise Operators

All data is represented internally by computers as sequences of bits. Each bit can assume the value **0** or the value **1**. On most systems, a sequence of 8 bits forms a byte—the standard storage unit for a variable of type **char**. Other data types are stored in larger num-

```
/* An example of a union */
#include <stdio.h>

union number {
    int x;
    float y;
};

main()
{
    union number value;

    value.x = 100;
    printf("%s\n%s\n%s%d\n%s%f\n\n",
            "Put a value in the integer member",
            "and print both members.",
            "int:   ", value.x,
            "float: ", value.y);

    value.y = 100.0;
    printf("%s\n%s\n%s%d\n%s%f\n",
            "Put a value in the floating member",
            "and print both members.",
            "int:   ", value.x,
            "float: ", value.y);
    return 0;
}
```

```
Put a value in the integer member
and print both members.
int:   100
float: 0.000000

Put a value in the floating member
and print both members.
int:   17096
float: 100.000000
```

Fig. 10.5 Printing the value of a union in both member data types.

bers of bytes. The bitwise operators are used to manipulate the bits of integral operands (**char**, **short**, **int**, and **long**; both **signed** and **unsigned**). Unsigned integers are normally used with the bitwise operators.

Portability Tip 10.6

Bitwise data manipulations are machine dependent.

Note that the bitwise operator discussions in this section show the binary representations of the integer operands. For a detailed explanation of the binary (also called base 2) number system see Appendix E, "Number Systems". Also, the programs in Sections 10.9 and 10.10 were tested on an Apple Macintosh using Think C and on a PC compatible using Borland C++. Both systems use 16-bit (2-byte) integers. Because of the machine-dependent nature of bitwise manipulations, these programs may not work on your system.

The bitwise operators are: *bitwise AND (&), bitwise inclusive OR (|), bitwise exclusive OR (^), left shift (<<), right shift (>>)*, and *complement (~)*. The bitwise AND, bitwise inclusive OR, and bitwise exclusive OR operators compare their two operands bit-by-bit. The bitwise AND operator sets each bit in the result to 1 if the corresponding bit in both operands is 1. The bitwise inclusive OR operator sets each bit in the result to 1 if the corresponding bit in either (or both) operand(s) is 1. The bitwise exclusive OR operator sets each bit in the result to 1 if the corresponding bit in exactly one operand is 1. The left shift operator shifts the bits of its left operand to the left by the number of bits specified in its right operand. The right shift operator shifts the bits in its left operand to the right by the number of bits specified in its right operand. The bitwise complement operator sets all 0 bits in its operand to 1 in the result and sets all 1 bits to 0 in the result. Detailed discussions of each bitwise operator appear in the following examples. The bitwise operators are summarized in Fig. 10.6.

Operator		Description
&	bitwise AND	The bits in the result are set to 1 if the corresponding bits in the two operands are both 1.
|	bitwise inclusive OR	The bits in the result are set to 1 if at least one of the corresponding bits in the two operands is 1.
^	bitwise exclusive OR	The bits in the result are set to 1 if exactly one of the corresponding bits in the two operands is 1.
<<	left shift	Shifts the bits of the first operand left by the number of bits specified by the second operand; fill from the right with 0 bits.
>>	right shift	Shifts the bits of the first operand right by the number of bits specified by the second operand; the method of filling from the left is machine dependent.
~	one's complement	All 0 bits are set to 1 and all 1 bits are set to 0.

Fig 10.6   The bitwise operators.

When using the bitwise operators, it is useful to print values in their binary representation to illustrate the precise effects of these operators. The program of Fig. 10.7 prints an **unsigned** integer in its binary representation in groups of eight bits each. Function **displayBits** uses the bitwise AND operator to combine variable **value** with variable **displayMask**. Often, the bitwise AND operator is used with an operand called a *mask*—an integer value with specific bits set to 1. Masks are used to hide some bits in a value while selecting other bits. In function **displayBits**, mask variable **display-Mask** is assigned the value **1 << 15 (10000000 00000000)**. The left shift operator shifts the value **1** from the low order (rightmost) bit to the high order (leftmost) bit in **displayMask**, and fills in **0** bits from the right. The statement

```
putchar(value & displayMask ? '1' : '0');
```

```
/* Printing an unsigned integer in bits */
#include <stdio.h>

main()
{
   unsigned x;
   void displayBits(unsigned);

   printf("Enter an unsigned integer: ");
   scanf("%u", &x);
   displayBits(x);
   return 0;
}

void displayBits(unsigned value)
{
   unsigned c, displayMask = 1 << 15;

   printf("%7u = ", value);

   for (c = 1; c <= 16; c++) {
      putchar(value & displayMask ? '1' : '0');
      value <<= 1;

      if (c % 8 == 0)
         putchar(' ');
   }

   putchar('\n');
}
```

```
Enter an unsigned integer: 65000
  65000 = 11111101 11101000
```

Fig. 10.7   Printing an unsigned integer in bits.

determines whether a **1** or a **0** should be printed for the current leftmost bit of variable **value**. Assume variable **value** contains **65000** (**11111101 11101000**). When **value** and **displayMask** are combined using **&**, all the bits except the high order bit in variable **value** are "masked off" (hidden) because any bit "ANDed" with **0** yields **0**. If the leftmost bit is **1**, **value & displayMask** evaluates to **1**, and **1** is printed—otherwise, **0** is printed. Variable **value** is then left shifted one bit by the expression **value <<= 1** (this is equivalent to **value = value << 1**). These steps are repeated for each bit in **unsigned** variable **value**. Fig 10.8 summarizes the results of combining two bits with the bitwise AND operator.

Common Programming Error 10.12

Using the logical AND operator (&&) for the bitwise AND operator (&) and vice versa.

The program of Fig. 10.9 demonstrates the use of the bitwise AND operator, the bitwise inclusive OR operator, the bitwise exclusive OR operator, and the bitwise complement operator. The program uses function **displayBits** to print the **unsigned** integer values. The output is shown in Fig. 10.10.

In Fig. 10.9, integer variable **mask** is assigned the value **1** (**00000000 00000001**), and variable **number1** is assigned value **65535** (**11111111 11111111**). When **mask** and **number1** are combined using the bitwise AND operator (**&**) in the expression **number1 & mask**, the result is **00000000 00000001**. All the bits except the low order bit in variable **number1** are "masked off" (hidden) by "ANDing" with variable **mask**.

The bitwise inclusive OR operator is used to set specific bits to 1 in an operand. In Fig. 10.9, variable **number1** is assigned **15** (**00000000 00001111**), and variable **setBits** is assigned **241** (**00000000 11110001**). When **number1** and **setBits** are combined using the bitwise OR operator in the expression **number1 | setBits**, the result is **255** (**00000000 11111111**). Figure 10.11 summarizes the results of combining two bits with the bitwise inclusive OR operator.

Common Programming Error 10.13

Using the logical OR operator (| |) for the bitwise OR operator (|) and vice versa.

The bitwise exclusive OR operator (^) sets each bit in the result to 1 if *exactly* one of the corresponding bits in its two operands is 1. In Fig. 10.9, variables **number1** and

Bit 1	Bit 2	Bit 1 & Bit 2
0	0	0
1	0	0
0	1	0
1	1	1

Fig 10.8   Results of combining two bits with the bitwise AND operator **&**.

```
/* Using the bitwise AND, bitwise inclusive OR, bitwise
   exclusive OR, and bitwise complement operators */

#include <stdio.h>

void displayBits(unsigned);

main()
{
   unsigned number1, number2, mask, setBits;

   number1 = 65535;
   mask = 1;
   printf("The result of combining the following\n");
   displayBits(number1);
   displayBits(mask);
   printf("using the bitwise AND operator & is\n");
   displayBits(number1 & mask);

   number1 = 15;
   setBits = 241;
   printf("\nThe result of combining the following\n");
   displayBits(number1);
   displayBits(setBits);
   printf("using the bitwise inclusive OR operator | is\n");
   displayBits(number1 | setBits);

   number1 = 139;
   number2 = 199;
   printf("\nThe result of combining the following\n");
   displayBits(number1);
   displayBits(number2);
   printf("using the bitwise exclusive OR operator ^ is\n");
   displayBits(number1 ^ number2);

   number1 = 21845;
   printf("\nThe one's complement of\n");
   displayBits(number1);
   printf("is\n");
   displayBits(~number1);

   return 0;
}
```

Fig. 10.9 Using the bitwise AND, bitwise inclusive OR, bitwise exclusive OR, and bitwise complement operators (part 1 of 2).

number2 are assigned the values **139** (**00000000 10001011**) and **199** (**00000000 11000111**) respectively. When these variables are combined with the exclusive OR operator in the expression **number1 ^ number2**, the result is **00000000 01001100**. Figure 10.12 summarizes the results of combining two bits with the bitwise exclusive OR operator.

```
void displayBits(unsigned value)
{
   unsigned c, displayMask = 1 << 15;

   printf("%7u = ", value);

   for (c = 1; c <= 16; c++) {
      putchar(value & displayMask ? '1' : '0');
      value <<= 1;

      if (c % 8 == 0)
         putchar(' ');
   }

   putchar('\n');
}
```

Fig. 10.9 Using the bitwise AND, bitwise inclusive OR, bitwise exclusive OR, and bitwise complement operators (part 2 of 2).

```
The result of combining the following
   65535 = 11111111 11111111
       1 = 00000000 00000001
using the bitwise AND operator & is
       1 = 00000000 00000001

The result of combining the following
      15 = 00000000 00001111
     241 = 00000000 11110001
using the bitwise inclusive OR operator | is
     255 = 00000000 11111111

The result of combining the following
     139 = 00000000 10001011
     199 = 00000000 11000111
using the bitwise exclusive OR operator ^ is
      76 = 00000000 01001100

The one's complement of
   21845 = 01010101 01010101
is
   43690 = 10101010 10101010
```

Fig. 10.10 Output for the program of Fig. 10.9.

The *bitwise* complement operator (~) sets all **1** bits in its operand to **0** in the result and sets all **0** bits to **1** in the result—otherwise referred to as "taking the *one's comple-ment* of the value." In Fig. 10.9, variable **number1** is assigned the value **21845** (**01010101 01010101**). When the expression **~number1** is evaluated, the result is (**10101010 10101010**).

Bit 1	Bit 2	Bit 1 | Bit 2
0	0	0
1	0	1
0	1	1
1	1	1

Fig 10.11   Results of combining two bits with the bitwise inclusive OR operator |.

Bit 1	Bit 2	Bit 1 ^ Bit 2
0	0	0
1	0	1
0	1	1
1	1	0

Fig 10.12   Results of combining two bits with the bitwise exclusive OR operator ^.

The program of Fig. 10.13 demonstrates the left shift operator (`<<`) and the right shift operator (`>>`). Function `displayBits` is used to print the `unsigned` integer values.

The left shift operator (`<<`) shifts the bits of its left operand to the left by the number of bits specified in its right operand. Bits vacated to the right are replaced with 0s; 1s shifted off the left are lost. In the program of Fig. 10.13, variable `number1` is assigned the value `960` (`00000011 11000000`). The result of left shifting variable `number1` 8 bits in the expression `number1 << 8` is `49152` (`11000000 00000000`).

The right shift operator (`>>`) shifts the bits of its left operand to the right by the number of bits specified in its right operand. Performing a right shift on an `unsigned` integer causes the vacated bits at the left to be replaced by 0s; 1s shifted off the right are lost. In the program of Fig. 10.13, the result of right shifting `number1` in the expression `number1 >> 8` is `3` (`00000000 00000011`).

Common Programming Error 10.14

The result of shifting a value is undefined if the right operand is negative or if the right operand is larger than the number of bits in which the left operand is stored.

Portability Tip 10.7

Right shifting is machine dependent. Right shifting a signed integer fills the vacated bits with 0s on some machines and 1s on others.

Each bitwise operator (except the bitwise complement operator) has a corresponding assignment operator. These *bitwise assignment operators* are shown in Fig. 10.14 and are used in a similar manner to the arithmetic assignment operators introduced in Chapter 3.

```c
/* Using the bitwise shift operators */
#include <stdio.h>

void displayBits(unsigned);

main()
{
   unsigned number1 = 960;

   printf("\nThe result of left shifting\n");
   displayBits(number1);
   printf("8 bit positions using the ");
   printf("left shift operator << is\n");
   displayBits(number1 << 8);

   printf("\nThe result of right shifting\n");
   displayBits(number1);
   printf("8 bit positions using the ");
   printf("right shift operator >> is\n");
   displayBits(number1 >> 8);
   return 0;
}

void displayBits(unsigned value)
{
   unsigned c, displayMask = 1 << 15;

   printf("%7u = ", value);

   for (c = 1; c <= 16; c++) {
      putchar(value & displayMask ? '1' : '0');
      value <<= 1;

      if (c % 8 == 0)
         putchar(' ');
   }

   putchar('\n');
}
```

```
The result of left shifting
    960 = 00000011 11000000
8 bit positions using the left shift operator << is
  49152 = 11000000 00000000

The result of right shifting
    960 = 00000011 11000000
8 bit positions using the right shift operator >> is
      3 = 00000000 00000011
```

Fig. 10.13 Using the bitwise shift operators.

Bitwise assignment operators	
&=	Bitwise AND assignment operator.
|=	Bitwise inclusive OR assignment operator.
^=	Bitwise exclusive OR assignment operator.
<<=	Left shift assignment operator.
>>=	Right shift assignment operator.

Fig 10.14 The bitwise assignment operators.

Figure 10.15 shows the precedence and associativity of the various operators introduced to this point in the text. They are shown top to bottom in decreasing order of precedence.

10.10 Bit Fields

C provides the ability to specify the number of bits in which an **unsigned** or **int** member of a structure or union is stored—referred to as a *bit field*. Bit fields enable better memory utilization by storing data in the minimum number of bits required. Bit field members *must* be declared as **int** or **unsigned**.

Operator	Associativity	Type
( ) [ ] . ->	left to right	highest
+ - ++ -- ! (*type*) & * ~ sizeof	right to left	unary
* / %	left to right	multiplicative
+ -	left to right	additive
<< >>	left to right	shifting
< <= > >=	left to right	relational
== !=	left to right	equality
&	left to right	bitwise AND
^	left to right	negation
|	left to right	bitwise OR
&&	left to right	logical AND
||	left to right	logical OR
?:	right to left	conditional
= += -= *= /= %= &= |= ^= <<= >>=	right to left	assignment
,	left to right	comma

Fig. 10.15 Operator precedence and associativity.

Performance Tip 10.3

Bit fields help conserve storage.

Consider the following structure definition:

```
struct bitCard {
    unsigned face : 4;
    unsigned suit : 2;
    unsigned color : 1;
};
```

The definition contains three **unsigned** bit fields—**face**, **suit**, and **color**—used to represent a card from a deck of 52 cards. A bit field is declared by following an **unsigned** or **int** member name with a colon (**:**) and an integer constant representing the *width* of the field, i.e., the number of bits in which the member is stored. The constant representing the width must be an integer between 0 and the total number of bits used to store an **int** on your system. Our examples were tested on a computer with 2-byte (16 bit) integers.

The preceding structure definition indicates that member **face** is stored in 4 bits, member **suit** is stored in 2 bits, and member **color** is stored in 1 bit. The number of bits is based on the desired range of values for each structure member. Member **face** stores values between **0** (Ace) and **12** (King)—4 bits can store a value between 0 and 15. Member suit stores values between **0** and 3 (**0** = Diamonds, **1** = Hearts, **2** = Clubs, **3** = Spades)—2 bits can store a value between **0** and 3. Finally, member **color** stores either **0** (Red) or **1** (Black)—1 bit can store either **0** or **1**.

The program in Fig. 10.16 (output shown in Fig. 10.17) creates array **deck** containing 52 **struct bitCard** structures. Function **fillDeck** inserts the 52 cards in the **deck** array, and function **deal** prints the 52 cards. Notice that bit field members of structures are accessed exactly as any other structure member. The member **color** is included as a means of indicating the card color on a system that allows color displays.

It is possible to specify an *unnamed bit field* in which case the field is used as *padding* in the structure. For example, the structure definition

```
struct example {
    unsigned a : 13;
    unsigned   : 3;
    unsigned b : 4;
};
```

uses an unnamed 3-bit field as padding—nothing can be stored in those three bits. Member **b** (on our 2-byte word computer) is stored in another storage unit.

An *unnamed bit field with a zero width* is used to align the next bit field on a new storage unit boundary. For example, the structure definition

```
struct example {
    unsigned a : 13;
    unsigned   : 0;
    unsigned b : 4;
};
```

uses an unnamed **0**-bit field to skip the remaining bits (as many as there are) of the storage unit in which **a** is stored, and align **b** on the next storage unit boundary.

Portability Tip 10.8

Bit field manipulations are machine dependent. For example, some computers allow bit fields to cross word boundaries, whereas others do not.

Common Programming Error 10.15

Attempting to access individual bits of a bit field as if they were elements of an array. Bit fields are not "arrays of bits."

Common Programming Error 10.16

Attempting to take the address of a bit field (the & operator may not be used with bit fields because they do not have addresses).

Performance Tip 10.4

Although bit fields save space, using them can cause the compiler to generate slower-executing machine language code. This occurs because it takes extra machine language operations to access only portions of an addressable storage unit. This is one of many examples of the kinds of space-time tradeoffs that occur in computer science.

10.11 Enumeration Constants

C provides one final user-defined type called an *enumeration*. An enumeration, introduced by the keyword **enum**, is a set of integer constants represented by identifiers. These *enumeration constants* are, in effect, symbolic constants whose values can be set automatically. The values in an **enum** start with **0**, unless specified otherwise, and are incremented by **1**. For example, the enumeration

```
enum months {JAN, FEB, MAR, APR, MAY, JUN, JUL, AUG, SEP,
             OCT, NOV, DEC};
```

creates a new type, **enum months**, in which the identifiers are set automatically to the integers **0** to **11**. To number the months 1 to 12, use the following enumeration:

```
enum months {JAN = 1, FEB, MAR, APR, MAY, JUN, JUL, AUG,
             SEP, OCT, NOV, DEC};
```

Since the first value in the preceding enumeration is explicitly set to **1**, the remaining values are incremented from **1** resulting in the values **1** through **12**. The identifiers in an enumeration must be unique. The value of each enumeration constant of an enumeration can be set explicitly in the definition by assigning a value to the identifier. Multiple members of an enumeration can have the same integer value. In the program of Fig. 10.18, the enumeration variable **month** is used in a **for** structure to print the months of the year from the array **monthName**. Note that we have made **monthName[0]** the empty string **""**. Some programmers might prefer to set **monthName[0]** to a value such as ***ERROR*** to indicate that a logic error occurred.

```c
/* Example using a bit field */

#include <stdio.h>

struct bitCard {
   unsigned face : 4;
   unsigned suit : 2;
   unsigned color : 1;
};

typedef struct bitCard Card;

void fillDeck(Card *);
void deal(Card *);

main()
{
   Card deck[52];

   fillDeck(deck);
   deal(deck);

   return 0;
}

void fillDeck(Card *wDeck)
{
   int i;

   for (i = 0; i <= 51; i++) {
      wDeck[i].face = i % 13;
      wDeck[i].suit = i / 13;
      wDeck[i].color = i / 26;
   }
}

/* Function deal prints the cards in two column format */
/* Column 1 contains cards 0-25 subscripted with k1 */
/* Column 2 contains cards 26-51 subscripted with k2 */

void deal(Card *wDeck)
{
   int k1, k2;

   for (k1 = 0, k2 = k1 + 26; k1 <= 25; k1++, k2++) {
      printf("Card:%3d  Suit:%2d  Color:%2d    ",
             wDeck[k1].face, wDeck[k1].suit, wDeck[k1].color);
      printf("Card:%3d  Suit:%2d  Color:%2d\n",
             wDeck[k2].face, wDeck[k2].suit, wDeck[k2].color);
   }
}
```

Fig. 10.16 Using bit fields to store a deck of cards.

```
Card:  0  Suit:  0  Color:  0    Card:  0  Suit:  2  Color:  1
Card:  1  Suit:  0  Color:  0    Card:  1  Suit:  2  Color:  1
Card:  2  Suit:  0  Color:  0    Card:  2  Suit:  2  Color:  1
Card:  3  Suit:  0  Color:  0    Card:  3  Suit:  2  Color:  1
Card:  4  Suit:  0  Color:  0    Card:  4  Suit:  2  Color:  1
Card:  5  Suit:  0  Color:  0    Card:  5  Suit:  2  Color:  1
Card:  6  Suit:  0  Color:  0    Card:  6  Suit:  2  Color:  1
Card:  7  Suit:  0  Color:  0    Card:  7  Suit:  2  Color:  1
Card:  8  Suit:  0  Color:  0    Card:  8  Suit:  2  Color:  1
Card:  9  Suit:  0  Color:  0    Card:  9  Suit:  2  Color:  1
Card: 10  Suit:  0  Color:  0    Card: 10  Suit:  2  Color:  1
Card: 11  Suit:  0  Color:  0    Card: 11  Suit:  2  Color:  1
Card: 12  Suit:  0  Color:  0    Card: 12  Suit:  2  Color:  1
Card:  0  Suit:  1  Color:  0    Card:  0  Suit:  3  Color:  1
Card:  1  Suit:  1  Color:  0    Card:  1  Suit:  3  Color:  1
Card:  2  Suit:  1  Color:  0    Card:  2  Suit:  3  Color:  1
Card:  3  Suit:  1  Color:  0    Card:  3  Suit:  3  Color:  1
Card:  4  Suit:  1  Color:  0    Card:  4  Suit:  3  Color:  1
Card:  5  Suit:  1  Color:  0    Card:  5  Suit:  3  Color:  1
Card:  6  Suit:  1  Color:  0    Card:  6  Suit:  3  Color:  1
Card:  7  Suit:  1  Color:  0    Card:  7  Suit:  3  Color:  1
Card:  8  Suit:  1  Color:  0    Card:  8  Suit:  3  Color:  1
Card:  9  Suit:  1  Color:  0    Card:  9  Suit:  3  Color:  1
Card: 10  Suit:  1  Color:  0    Card: 10  Suit:  3  Color:  1
Card: 11  Suit:  1  Color:  0    Card: 11  Suit:  3  Color:  1
Card: 12  Suit:  1  Color:  0    Card: 12  Suit:  3  Color:  1
```

Fig. 10.17 Output of the program in Fig. 10.16.

Common Programming Error 10.17

Assigning a value to an enumeration constant after it has been defined is a syntax error.

Good Programming Practice 10.6

Use only uppercase letters in the names of enumeration constants. This makes these constants stand out in a program, and reminds the programmer that enumeration constants are not variables.

Summary

- Structures are collections of related variables, sometimes referred to as aggregates, under one name.

- Structures can contain variables of different data types.

- The keyword **struct** begins every structure definition. Within the braces of the structure definition are the structure member declarations.

- Members of the same structure must have unique names.

```
/* Using an enumeration type */
#include <stdio.h>

enum months {JAN = 1, FEB, MAR, APR, MAY, JUN,
             JUL, AUG, SEP, OCT, NOV, DEC};

main()
{
    enum months month;
    char *monthName[] = {"", "January", "February", "March",
                         "April", "May", "June", "July",
                         "August", "September", "October",
                         "November", "December"};

    for (month = JAN; month <= DEC; month++)
        printf("%2d%11s\n", month, monthName[month]);

    return 0;
}
```

```
 1    January
 2   February
 3      March
 4      April
 5        May
 6       June
 7       July
 8     August
 9  September
10    October
11   November
12   December
```

Fig. 10.18 Using an enumeration.

- A structure definition creates a new data type that can be used to declare variables.

- There are two methods for declaring structure variables. The first method is to declare the variables in a declaration as is done with variables of other data types using **struct tagName** as the type. The second method is to include the variables between the closing brace of the structure definition and the semi-colon that ends the structure definition.

- The tag name of the structure is optional. If the structure is defined without a tag name, the variables of the derived data type must be declared in the structure definition, and no other variables of the new structure type can be declared.

- A structure can be initialized with an initializer list by following the variable name in the structure declaration with an equal sign and a comma-separated list of initializers enclosed in braces. If there are fewer initializers in the list than members in the struc ture, the remaining members are automatically initialized to zero (or **NULL** if the member is a pointer).

- Entire structures may be assigned to structure variables of the same type.

- A structure variable may be initialized with a structure variable of the same type.

- The structure member operator is used when accessing a member of a structure via the structure variable name.

- The structure pointer operator—created with a minus (-) sign and a greater than (>) sign—is used when accessing a member of a structure via a pointer to the structure.

- Structures and individual members of structures are passed to functions call by value.

- To pass a structure call by reference, pass the address of the structure variable.

- An array of structures is automatically passed call by reference.

- To pass an array call by value, create a structure with the array as a member.

- Creating a new name with **typedef** does not create a new type; it creates a name that is synonymous to a type defined previously.

- A union is a derived data type whose members share the same storage space. The members can be any type.

- The storage reserved for a union is large enough to store its largest member. In most cases, unions contain two or more data types. Only one member, and thus one data type, can be referenced at a time.

- A union is declared with the **union** keyword in the same format as a structure.

- A union can be initialized only with a value of the type of its first member.

- The bitwise AND operator (**&**) takes two integral operands. A bit in the result is set to 1 if the corresponding bits in each of the operands are 1.

- Masks are used to hide some bits while preserving others.

- The bitwise inclusive OR operator (|) takes two operands. A bit in the result is set to 1 if the corresponding bit in either operand is set to 1.

- Each of the bitwise operators (except the unary bitwise complement operator) has a corresponding assignment operator.

- The bitwise exclusive OR operator (^) takes two operands. A bit in the result is set to 1 if exactly one of the corresponding bits in the two operands is set to 1.

- The left shift operator (<<) shifts the bits of its left operand left by the number of bits specified by its right operand. Bits vacated to the right are replaced with 0s.

- The right shift operator (>>) shifts the bits of its left operand right by the number of bits specified in its right operand. Performing a right shift on an unsigned integer causes bits vacated at the left to be replaced by 0s. Vacated bits in signed integers can be replaced with 0s or 1s—this is machine dependent.

- The bitwise complement operator (~) takes one operand and reverses its bits—this produces the one's complement of the operand.

- Bit fields reduce storage use by storing data in the minimum number of bits required.

- Bit field members must be declared as `int` or `unsigned`.

- A bit field is declared by following an `unsigned` or `int` member name with a colon and the width of the bit field.

- The bit field width must be an integer constant between 0 and the total number of bits used to store an `int` variable on your system

- If a bit field is specified without a name, the field is used as padding in the structure.

- An unnamed bit field with width `0` is used to align the next bit field on a new machine word boundary.

- An enumeration, designated by the keyword `enum`, is a set of integers that are represented by identifiers. The values in an `enum` start with `0` unless specified otherwise, and are always incremented by `1`.

Terminology

^ bitwise exclusive OR operator
^= bitwise exclusive OR assignment operator
~ one's complement operator
& bitwise AND operator
&= bitwise AND assignment operator
| bitwise inclusive OR operator
|= bitwise inclusive OR assignment operator
<< left shift operator
<<= left shift assignment operator
>> right shift operator
>>= right shift assignment operator
accessing members of structures
aggregates
array of structures
bit field
bitwise operators
complementing
derived type
enumeration
enumeration constant
initialization of structures
left shift
mask
masking off bits
member

member name
nested structures
one's complement
padding
pointer to a structure
programmer-defined data types
record
right shift
self-referential structure
shifting
space-time tradeoffs
`struct`
structure assignment
structure declaration
structure definition
structure initialization
structure member (dot) operator (.)
structure name
structure pointer (arrow) operator (->)
structure tag
structure type
tag name
`typedef`
`union`
unnamed bit field
width of a bit field
zero-width bit field

Common Programming Errors

10.1 Forgetting the semicolon that terminates a structure definition.

10.2 Assigning a structure of one type to a structure of a different type.

10.3 Comparing structures is a syntax error because of the different alignment requirements on various systems.

10.4 Inserting space between the − and > components of the structure pointer operator (or inserting spaces between the components of other multiple keystroke operators except **? :**).

10.5 Attempting to refer to a member of a structure by using only the member's name.

10.6 Not using parentheses when referring to a structure member using a pointer and the structure member operator (e.g., ***aptr.suit**) is a syntax error.

10.7 Assuming that structures, like arrays, are automatically passed call by reference, and trying to modify the caller's structure values in the called function.

10.8 Forgetting to include the array subscript when referring to individual structures in an array of structures.

10.9 Referencing with the wrong type data stored in a union with a different type is a logic error.

10.10 Comparing unions is a compiler error because of the different alignment requirements on various systems.

10.11 Initializing a union in a declaration with a value whose type is different from the type of the union's first member.

10.12 Using the logical AND operator (**&&**) for the bitwise AND operator (**&**) and vice versa.

10.13 Using the logical OR operator (**| |**) for the bitwise OR operator (**|**) and vice versa.

10.14 The result of shifting a value is undefined if the right operand is negative or if the right operand is larger than the number of bits in which the left operand is stored.

10.15 Attempting to access individual bits of a bit field as if they were elements of an array. Bit fields are not "arrays of bits."

10.16 Attempting to take the address of a bit field (the **&** operator may not be used with bit fields because they do not have addresses).

10.17 Assigning a value to an enumeration constant after it has been defined is a syntax error.

Good Programming Practices

10.1 Always provide a structure tag name when creating a structure type. The structure tag name is convenient for declaring new variables of the structure type later in the program.

10.2 Choosing a meaningful structure tag name helps make a program self-documenting.

10.3 Avoid using the same names for members of structures of different types. This is allowed, but it may cause confusion.

10.4 Do not put spaces around the **->** and **.** operators. This helps emphasize that the expressions the operators are contained in are essentially single variable names.

10.5 Capitalize **typedef** names to emphasize that these names are synonyms for other type names.

10.6 Use only uppercase letters in the names of enumeration constants. This makes these constants stand out in a program, and reminds the programmer that enumeration constants are not variables.

Portability Tips

10.1 Because the size of data items of a particular type is machine dependent, and because storage alignment considerations are machine dependent, so too is the representation of a structure.

10.2 Use `typedef` to help make a program more portable.

10.3 If data is stored in a union as one type and referenced as another type, the results are implementation dependent.

10.4 The amount of storage required to store a union is implementation dependent.

10.5 Some unions may not port easily to other computer systems. Whether a union is portable or not often depends on the storage alignment requirements for the union member data types on a given system.

10.6 Bitwise data manipulations are machine dependent.

10.7 Right shifting is machine dependent. Right shifting a signed integer fills the vacated bits with `0`s on some machines and `1`s on others.

10.8 Bit field manipulations are machine dependent. Fields may be assigned either left-to-right or right-to-left depending on the computer. Also, some computers allow bit fields to cross word boundaries, whereas others do not.

Performance Tips

10.1 Passing structures call by reference is more efficient than passing structures call by value (which requires the entire structure to be copied).

10.2 Unions conserve storage.

10.3 Bit fields help conserve storage.

10.4 Although bit fields save space, using them can cause the compiler to generate slower-executing machine language code. This occurs because it takes extra machine language operations to access only portions of an addressable storage unit. This is one of many examples of the kinds of space-time tradeoffs that occur in computer science.

Software Engineering Observation

10.1 As with a `struct` declaration, a `union` declaration simply creates a new type. Placing a `union` or `struct` declaration outside any function does not create a global variable.

Self-Review Exercises

10.1 Fill in the blanks in each of the following:
a) A _____ is a collection of related variables under one name.
b) A _____ is a collection of variables under one name in which the variables share the same storage.
c) The bits in the result of an expression using the _____ operator are set to 1 if the corresponding bits in each operand are set to 1. Otherwise, the bits are set to zero.
d) The variables declared in a structure definition are called its _____ .
e) The bits in the result of an expression using the _____ operator are set to 1 if at least one of the corresponding bits in either operand is set to 1. Otherwise, the bits are set to zero.
f) The keyword _____ introduces a structure declaration.
g) The keyword _____ is used to create a synonym for a previously defined data type.
h) The bits in the result of an expression using the _____ operator are set to 1 if exactly one of the corresponding bits in either operand is set to 1. Otherwise, the bits are set to zero.

i)   The bitwise AND operator **&** is often used to _____ bits, that is to select certain bits from a bit string while zeroing others.

j)   The _____ keyword is used to introduce a union definition.

k)   The name of the structure is referred to as the structure _____.

l)   A structure member is accessed with either the _____ operator or the _____ operator.

m)   The _____ and _____ operators are used to shift the bits of a value to the left or to the right, respectively.

n)   An _____ is a set of integers represented by identifiers.

10.2   State whether each of the following is true or false. If false, explain why.

a)   Structures may contain only one data type.

b)   Two unions can be compared to determine if they are equal.

c)   The tag name of a structure is optional.

d)   The members of different structures must have unique names.

e)   The keyword **typedef** is used to define new data types.

f)   Structures are always passed to functions call by reference.

g)   Structures may not be compared.

10.3   Write a single statement or a set of statements to accomplish each of the following:

a)   Define a structure called **part** containing **int** variable **partNumber**, and **char** array **partName** whose values may be as long as 25 characters.

b)   Define **Part** to be a synonym for the type **struct part**.

c)   Use **Part** to declare variable **a** to be of type **struct part**, array **b[10]** to be of type **struct part**, and variable **ptr** to be of type pointer to **struct part**.

d)   Read a part number and a part name from the keyboard into the individual members of variable **a**.

e)   Assign the member values of variable **a** to element 3 of array **b**.

f)   Assign the address of array **b** to the pointer variable **ptr**.

g)   Print the member values of element 3 of array **b** using the variable **ptr** and the structure pointer operator to refer to the members.

10.4   Find the error in each of the following:

a)   Assume that **struct card** has been defined containing two pointers to type **char**, namely **face** and **suit**. Also, the variable **c** has been declared to be of type **struct card** and the variable **cPtr** has been declared to be of type pointer to **struct card**. Variable **cPtr** has been assigned the address of **c**.

```
printf("%s\n", *cPtr->face);
```

b)   Assume that **struct card** has been defined containing two pointers to type **char**, namely **face** and **suit**. Also, the array **hearts[13]** has been declared to be of type **struct card**. The following statement should print the member **face** of element 10 of the array.

```
printf("%s\n", hearts.face);
```

c)
```
union values {
    char w;
    float x;
    double y;
} v = {1.27};
```

d) ```
struct person {
    char lastName[15];
    char firstName[15];
    int age;
}
```

e) Assume **struct person** has been defined as in part (d) but with the appropriate correction.

```
person d;
```

f) Assume variable **p** has been declared as type **struct person**, and variable **c** has been declared as type **struct card**.

```
p = c;
```

Answers to Self-Review Exercises

10.1   a) structure. b) union. c) bitwise AND (**&**). d) members. e) bitwise inclusive OR (**|**). f) **struct**. g) **typedef**. h) bitwise exclusive OR (**^**). i) mask. j) **union**. k) tag. l) structure member, structure pointer. m) left shift operator (**<<**), right shift operator (**>>**). n) enumeration.

10.2   a) False. A structure can contain many data types.
   b) False. Unions can not be compared because of the same alignment problems that are associated with structures.
   c) True.
   d) False. The members of separate structures can have the same names, but the members of the same structure must have unique names.
   e) False. The keyword **typedef** is used to define new names (synonyms) for previously defined data types.
   f) False. Structures are always passed to functions call by value.
   g) True, because of alignment problems.

10.3   a) ```
struct part {
    int partNumber;
    char partName[25];
};
```
   b) `typedef struct part Part;`
   c) `Part a, b[10], *ptr;`
   d) `scanf("%d%s", &a.partNumber, &a.partName};`
   e) `b[3] = a;`
   f) `ptr = b;`
   g) ```
printf("%d %s\n", (ptr + 3)->partNumber,
        (ptr + 3)->partName);
```

10.4   a) Error: The parentheses that should enclose ***cPtr** have been omitted causing the order of evaluation of the expression to be incorrect.
   b) Error: The array subscript has been omitted. The expression should be **hearts[10].face**.
   c) Error: A union can only be initialized with a value that has the same type as the union's first member.
   d) Error: A semicolon is required to end a structure definition.
```

e) Error: The `struct` keyword was omitted from the variable declaration.

f) Error: Variables of different structure types cannot be assigned to one another.

Exercises

10.5 Provide the definition for each of the following structures and unions:

a) Structure `inventory` containing character array `partName[30]`, integer `partNumber`, floating point `price`, integer `stock`, and integer `reorder`.

b) Union `data` containing `char c`, `short s`, `long l`, `float f`, and `double d`.

c) A structure called `address` that contains character arrays `streetAddress[25]`, `city[20]`, `state[3]`, and `zipCode[6]`.

d) Structure `student` that contains arrays `firstName[15]` and `lastName[15]`, and variable `homeAddress` of type `struct address` from part (c).

e) Structure `test` containing 16 bit fields with widths of 1 bit. The names of the bit fields are the letters `a` to `p`.

10.6 Given the following structure definitions and variable declarations,

```
struct customer {
    char lastName[15];
    char firstName[15];
    int customerNumber;

    struct {
        char phoneNumber[11];
        char address[50];
        char city[15];
        char state[3];
        char zipCode[6];
    } personal;

} customerRecord, *customerPtr;

customerPtr = &customerRecord;
```

write a separate expression that can be used to access the structure members in each of the following parts.

a) Member `lastName` of structure `customerRecord`.

b) Member `lastName` of the structure pointed to by `customerPtr`.

c) Member `firstName` of structure `customerRecord`.

d) Member `firstName` of the structure pointed to by `customerPtr`.

e) Member `customerNumber` of structure `customerRecord`.

f) Member `customerNumber` of the structure pointed to by `customerPtr`.

g) Member `phoneNumber` of member `personal` of structure `customerRecord`.

h) Member `phoneNumber` of member `personal` of the structure pointed to by `customerPtr`.

i) Member `address` of member `personal` of structure `customerRecord`.

j) Member `address` of member `personal` of the structure pointed to by `customerPtr`.

k) Member `city` of member `personal` of structure `customerRecord`.

l) Member `city` of member `personal` of the structure pointed to by `customerPtr`.

m) Member `state` of member `personal` of structure `customerRecord`.

n) Member **state** of member **personal** of the structure pointed to by **customerPtr**.

o) Member **zipCode** of member **personal** of **customerRecord**.

p) Member **zipCode** of member **personal** of the structure pointed to by **customerPtr**.

10.7   Modify the program of Fig. 10.16 to shuffle the cards using a high performance shuffle (as shown in Fig. 10.3). Print the resulting deck in two column format as in Fig. 10.4. Precede each card with its color.

10.8   Create union **integer** with members **char c**, **short s**, **int i**, and **long l**. Write a program that inputs value of type **char**, **short**, **int** and **long**, and stores the values in union variables of type **union integer**. Each union variable should be printed as a **char**, a **short**, an **int**, and a **long**. Do the values always print correctly?

10.9   Create union **floatingPoint** with members **float f**, **double d**, and **long double l**. Write a program that inputs value of type **float**, **double**, and **long double**, and stores the values in union variables of type **union floatingPoint**. Each union variable should be printed as a **float**, a **double**, and a **long double**. Do the values always print correctly?

10.10   Write a program that right shifts an integer variable 4 bits. The program should print the integer in bits before and after the shift operation. Does your system place 0s or 1s in the vacated bits.?

10.11   If your computer uses 4-byte integers, modify the program of Fig. 10.7 so that it works with 4-byte integers.

10.12   Left shifting an **unsigned** integer by 1 bit is equivalent to multiplying the value 2. Write function **power2** that takes two integer arguments **number** and **pow**, and calculates

> **number * 2^pow**

Use the shift operator to calculate the result. The program should print the values as integers and as bits.

10.13   The left shift operator can be used to pack two character values into a 2-byte unsigned integer variable. Write a program that inputs two characters from the keyboard and passes them to function **packCharacters**. To pack two characters into an **unsigned** integer variable, assign the first character to the **unsigned** variable, shift the **unsigned** variable left by 8 bit positions, and combine the **unsigned** variable with the second character using the bitwise inclusive OR operator. The program should output the characters in their bit format before and after they are packed into the **unsigned** integer to prove that the characters are in fact packed correctly in the **unsigned** variable.

10.14   Using the right shift operator, the bitwise AND operator, and a mask, write function **unpackCharacters** that takes the **unsigned** integer from Exercise 10.13 and unpacks it into two characters. To unpack two characters from an **unsigned** 2-byte integer, combine the unsigned integer with the mask **65280** (11111111 00000000) and right shift the result 8 bits. Assign the resulting value to a **char** variable. Then combine the **unsigned** integer with the mask **255** (00000000 11111111). Assign the result to another **char** variable. The program should print the **unsigned** integer in bits before it is unpacked, then print the characters in bits to confirm that they were unpacked correctly.

10.15   If your system uses 4-byte integers, rewrite the program of Exercise 10.13 to pack 4 characters.

10.16   If your system uses 4-byte integers, rewrite the function `unpackCharacters` of Exercise 10.14 to unpack 4 characters. Create the masks you need to unpack the 4 characters by left shifting the value 255 in the mask variable by 8 bits 0, 1, 2, or 3 times (depending on the byte you are unpacking).

10.17   Write a program that reverses the order of the bits in an unsigned integer value. The program should input the value from the user and call function `reverseBits` to print the bits in reverse order. Print the value in bits both before and after the bits are reversed to confirm that the bits are reversed properly.

10.18   Modify the `displayBits` function of Fig. 10.7 so it is portable between systems using 2-byte integers and systems using 4-byte integers. Hint: Use the `sizeof` operator to determine the size of an integer on a particular machine.

10.19   The following program uses function `multiple` to determine if the integer entered from the keyboard is a multiple of some integer `X`. Examine the function multiple, then determine the value of `X`.

```
/* This program determines if a value is a multiple of X */

#include <stdio.h>

int multiple(int);

main()
{
   int y;

   printf("Enter an integer between 1 and 32000: ");
   scanf("%d", &y);

   if (multiple(y))
      printf("%d is a multiple of X\n", y);
   else
      printf("%d is not a multiple of X\n", y);

   return 0;
}

int multiple(int num)
{
   int i, mask = 1, mult = 1;

   for (i = 1; i <= 10; i++, mask <<= 1)
      if ((num & mask) != 0) {
         mult = 0;
         break;
      }

   return mult;
}
```

10.20 What does the following program do?

```c
#include <stdio.h>

int mystery(unsigned);

main()
{
   unsigned x;

   printf("Enter an integer: ");
   scanf("%u", &x);
   printf("The result is %d\n", mystery(x));
   return 0;
}

int mystery(unsigned bits)
{
   unsigned i, mask = 1 << 15, total = 0;

   for (i = 1; i <= 16; i++, bits <<= 1)
      if ((bits & mask) == mask)
         ++total;

   return total % 2 == 0 ? 1 : 0;
}
```

11

File
Processing

Objectives

- To be able to create, read, write, and update files.
- To become familiar with sequential access file processing.
- To become familiar with random access file processing.

I read part of it all the way through.
Samuel Goldwyn

Hats off!
The flag is passing by.
Henry Holcomb Bennett

Consciousness ... does not appear to itself chopped up in bits....
A "river" or a "stream" are the metaphors by which it is most
naturally described.
William James

I can only assume that a "Do Not File" document is filed in a
"Do Not File" file.
Senator Frank Church
Senate Intelligence Subcommittee Hearing, 1975

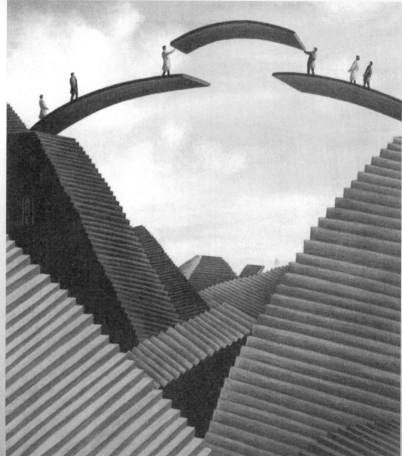

431

Outline

11.1 Introduction

Storage of data in variables and arrays is temporary; all such data is lost when a program terminates. *Files* are used for permanent retention of large amounts of data. Computers store files on secondary storage devices, especially disk storage devices. In this chapter, we explain how data files are created, updated, and processed by C programs. We consider both sequential access files and random access files.

11.2 The Data Hierarchy

Ultimately, all data items processed by a computer are reduced to combinations of zeros and ones. This occurs because it is simple and economical to build electronic devices that can assume two stable states—one of the states represents 0 and the other represents 1. It is remarkable that the impressive functions performed by computers involve only the most fundamental manipulations of 0s and 1s.

The smallest data item in a computer can assume the value 0 or the value 1. Such a data item is called a *bit* (short for *"binary digit"*—a digit that can assume one of two values). Computer circuitry performs various simple bit manipulations such as determining the value of a bit, setting the value of a bit, and reversing a bit (from 1 to 0 or from 0 to 1).

It is cumbersome for programmers to work with data in the low-level form of bits. Instead, programmers prefer to work with data in the form of *decimal digits* (i.e., 0, 1, 2,

3, 4, 5, 6, 7, 8, and 9), *letters* (i.e., A through Z, and a through z), and *special symbols* (i.e., $, @, %, &, *, (,), -, +, ", :, ?, /, and many others). Digits, letters, and special symbols are referred to as *characters*. The set of all characters that may be used to write programs and represent data items on a particular computer is called that computer's *character set*. Since computers can process only 1s and 0s, every character in a computer's character set is represented as a pattern of 1s and 0s (called a *byte*). Today, bytes are most commonly composed of eight bits. Programmers create programs and data items as characters; computers then manipulate and process these characters as patterns of bits.

Just as characters are composed of bits, *fields* are composed of characters. A field is a group of characters that conveys meaning. For example, a field consisting solely of uppercase and lowercase letters can be used to represent a person's name.

Data items processed by computers form a *data hierarchy* in which data items become larger and more complex in structure as we progress from bits, to characters (bytes), to fields, and so on.

A *record* (i.e., a **struct** in C) is composed of several fields. In a payroll system, for example, a record for a particular employee might consist of the following fields:

1. Social Security number

2. Name

3. Address

4. Hourly salary rate

5. Number of exemptions claimed

6. Year-to-date earnings

7. Amount of Federal taxes withheld, etc.

Thus, a record is a group of related fields. In the preceding example, each of the fields belongs to the same employee. Of course, a particular company may have many employees, and will have a payroll record for each employee. A *file* is a group of related records. A company's payroll file normally contains one record for each employee. Thus, a payroll file for a small company might contain only 22 records, whereas a payroll file for a large company might contain 100,000 records. It is not unusual for an organization to have hundreds or even thousands of files, with many containing millions or even billions of characters of information. With the increasing popularity of laser optical disks and multimedia technology, even trillion-byte files will soon be common. Fig. 11.1 illustrates the data hierarchy.

To facilitate the retrieval of specific records from a file, at least one field in each record is chosen as a *record key*. A record key identifies a record as belonging to a particular person or entity. For example, in the payroll record described in this section, the Social Security number would normally be chosen as the record key.

There are many ways of organizing records in a file. The most popular type of organization is called a *sequential file* in which records are typically stored in order by the record key field. In a payroll file, records are usually placed in order by Social Security number. The first employee record in the file contains the lowest Social Security number, and subsequent records contain increasingly higher Social Security numbers.

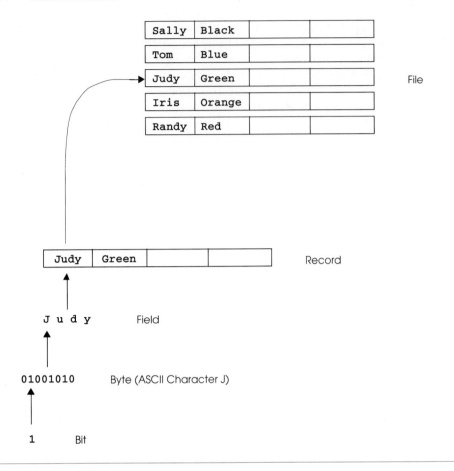

Fig. 11.1   The data hierarchy.

Most businesses utilize many different files to store data. For example, companies may have payroll files, accounts receivable files (listing money due from clients), accounts payable files (listing money due to suppliers), inventory files (listing facts about all the items handled by the business), and many other types of files. A group of related files is sometimes called a *database*. A collection of programs designed to create and manage databases is called a *database management system* (DBMS).

11.3 Files and Streams

C views each file simply as a sequential stream of bytes (Fig. 11.2). Each file ends either with an *end-of-file marker* or at a specific byte number recorded in a system maintained, administrative data structure. When a file is *opened,* a stream is associated with the file. Three files and their associated streams are automatically opened when program execution begins—the *standard input,* the *standard output,* and the *standard error.* Streams provide communication channels between files and programs. For example, the standard input stream enables a program to read data from the keyboard, and the standard output

Fig. 11.2 C's view of a file of *n* bytes.

stream enables a program to print data on the screen. Opening a file returns a pointer to a **FILE** structure (defined in **<stdio.h>**) that contains information used to process the file. This structure includes a *file descriptor*, i.e., an index into an operating system array called the *open file table*. Each array element contains a *file control block (FCB)* that the operating system uses to administer a particular file. The standard input, standard output, and standard error are manipulated using file pointers **stdin**, **stdout**, and **stderr**.

The standard library provides many functions for reading data from files and for writing data to files. Function **fgetc**, like **getchar**, reads one character from a file. Function **fgetc** receives as an argument a **FILE** pointer for the file from which a character will be read. The call **fgetc(stdin)** reads one character from **stdin**—the standard input. This call is equivalent to the call **getchar()**. Function **fputc**, like **putchar**, writes one character to a file. Function **fputc** receives as arguments a character to be written and a pointer for the file to which the character will be written. The function call **fputc('a', stdout)** writes the character **'a'** to **stdout**—the standard output. This call is equivalent to **putchar('a')**.

Several other functions used to read data from standard input and write data to standard output have similarly named file processing functions. The **fgets** and **fputs** functions, for example, can be used to read a line from a file and write a line to a file, respectively. Their counterparts for reading from standard input and writing to standard output, **gets** and **puts**, were discussed in Chapter 8. In the next several sections, we introduce the file processing equivalents of functions **scanf** and **printf**—**fscanf** and **fprintf**. Later in the chapter we discuss functions **fread** and **fwrite**.

11.4 Creating a Sequential Access File

C imposes no structure on a file. Thus, notions like a record of a file do not exist as part of the C language. Therefore, the programmer must provide any file structure to meet the requirements of each particular application. In the following example, we see how the programmer may impose a record structure on a file.

The program of Fig. 11.3 creates a simple sequential access file that might be used in an accounts receivable system to help keep track of the amounts owed by a company's credit clients. For each client, the program obtains an account number, the client's name, and the client's balance (i.e., the amount the client owes the company for goods and services received in the past). The data obtained for each client constitutes a "record" for that client. The account number is used as the record key in this application—the file will be created and maintained in account number order. This program assumes the user enters the records in account number order. In a comprehensive accounts receivable system, a sorting capability would be provided so the user could enter the records in any order. The records would then be sorted and written to the file.

```
/* Create a sequential file */
#include <stdio.h>

main()
{
    int account;
    char name[30];
    float balance;
    FILE *cfPtr;    /* cfPtr = clients.dat file pointer */

    if ((cfPtr = fopen("clients.dat", "w")) == NULL)
        printf("File could not be opened\n");
    else {
        printf("Enter the account, name, and balance.\n");
        printf("Enter EOF to end input.\n");
        printf("? ");
        scanf("%d%s%f", &account, name, &balance);

        while (!feof(stdin)) {
            fprintf(cfPtr, "%d %s %.2f\n",
                    account, name, balance);
            printf("? ");
            scanf("%d%s%f", &account, name, &balance);
        }

        fclose(cfPtr);
    }

    return 0;
}
```

```
Enter the account, name, and balance.
Enter EOF to end input.
? 100 Jones 24.98
? 200 Doe 345.67
? 300 White 0.00
? 400 Stone -42.16
? 500 Rich 224.62
?
```

Fig. 11.3   Creating a sequential file.

Now let us examine this program. The statement

```
FILE *cfPtr;
```

states that **cfptr** is a pointer to a **FILE** structure. The C program administers each file with a separate **FILE** structure. The programmer need not know the specifics of the **FILE** structure to use files. We will soon see precisely how the **FILE** structure leads indirectly to the operating system's file control block (FCB) for a file.

Portability Tip 11.1

*The **FILE** structure is operating system dependent (i.e., the members of the structure vary among systems based on how each system handles its files).*

Each open file must have a separately declared pointer of type **FILE** that is used to refer to the file. The line

```
    if ((cfPtr = fopen("clients.dat", "w")) == NULL)
```

names the file—**"clients.dat"**—to be used by the program and establishes a "line of communication" with the file. The file pointer **cfPtr** is assigned a pointer to the **FILE** structure for the file opened with **fopen**. Function **fopen** takes two arguments: a file name and a *file open mode*. The file open mode **"w"** indicates that the file is to be opened for *writing*. If a file does not exist and it is opened for writing, **fopen** creates the file. If an existing file is opened for writing, the contents of the file are discarded without warning. In the program, the **if** structure is used to determine whether the file pointer **cfPtr** is **NULL** (i.e., the file is not opened). If it is **NULL**, an error message is printed and the program ends. Otherwise, the input is processed and written to the file.

Common Programming Error 11.1

*Opening an existing file for writing (**"w"**) when, in fact, the user wants to preserve the file; the contents of the file are discarded without warning.*

Common Programming Error 11.2

Forgetting to open a file before attempting to reference it in a program.

The program prompts the user to enter the various fields for each record, or to enter end-of-file when data entry is complete. Figure 11.4 lists the key combinations for entering end-of-file for various computer systems.

The line

```
    while (!feof(stdin))
```

uses function **feof** to determine whether the *end-of-file indicator* is set for the file to which **stdin** refers. The end-of-file indicator informs the program that there is no more data to be processed. In the program of Fig. 11.3, the end-of-file indicator is set for the

Computer system	Key combination
UNIX systems	*\<return\> \<ctrl\> d*
IBM PC and compatibles	*\<ctrl\> z*
Macintosh	*\<ctrl\> d*
VAX (VMS)	*\<ctrl\> z*

Fig. 11.4 End-of-file key combinations for various popular computer systems.

standard input when the user enters the end-of-file key combination. The argument to function **feof** is a pointer to the file being tested for the end-of-file indicator (**stdin** in this case). The function returns a nonzero value (true) once the end-of-file indicator has been set; otherwise, zero is returned. The **while** structure that includes the **feof** call in this program continues executing while the end-of-file indicator is not set.

The statement

```
fprintf(cfPtr, "%d %s %.2f\n", account, name, balance);
```

writes data to the file **clients.dat**. The data may be retrieved later by a program designed to read the file (see Section 11.5). Function **fprintf** is equivalent to **printf** except that **fprintf** also receives as an argument a file pointer for the file to which the data will be written.

Common Programming Error 11.3

Using the wrong file pointer to refer to a file.

Good Programming Practice 11.1

Be sure that calls to file processing functions in a program contain the correct file pointers.

After the user enters end-of-file, the program closes the **clients.dat** file with **fclose** and terminates. Function **fclose** also receives the file pointer (rather than the file name) as an argument. If function **fclose** is not called explicitly, the operating system normally will close the file when program execution terminates. This is an example of operating system "housekeeping."

Good Programming Practice 11.2

Explicitly close each file as soon as it is known that the program will not reference the file again.

Performance Tip 11.1

Closing a file can free resources for which other users or programs may be waiting.

In the sample execution for the program of Fig. 11.3, the user enters information for five accounts, and then enters end-of-file to signal that data entry is complete. The sample execution does not show how the data records actually appear in the file. To verify that the file has been created successfully, in the next section we present a program that reads the file and prints its contents.

Figure 11.5 illustrates the relationship between **FILE** pointers, **FILE** structures, and FCBs in memory. When the file **"clients.dat"** is opened, an FCB for the file is copied into memory. The figure shows the connection between the file pointer returned by **fopen** and the FCB used by the operating system to administer the file.

Programs may process no files, one file, or several files. Each file used in a program must have a unique name and will have a different file pointer returned by **fopen**. All subsequent file processing functions after the file is opened must refer to the file with the

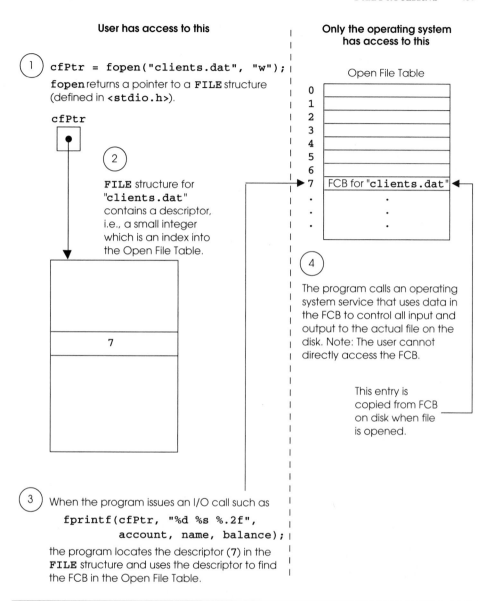

User has access to this

① `cfPtr = fopen("clients.dat", "w");`

`fopen` returns a pointer to a **FILE** structure (defined in **<stdio.h>**).

`cfPtr`

②

FILE structure for `"clients.dat"` contains a descriptor, i.e., a small integer which is an index into the Open File Table.

7

③ When the program issues an I/O call such as

`fprintf(cfPtr, "%d %s %.2f",`
`account, name, balance);`

the program locates the descriptor (**7**) in the **FILE** structure and uses the descriptor to find the FCB in the Open File Table.

Only the operating system has access to this

Open File Table

0	
1	
2	
3	
4	
5	
6	
7	FCB for "clients.dat"
·	·
·	·
·	·

④

The program calls an operating system service that uses data in the FCB to control all input and output to the actual file on the disk. Note: The user cannot directly access the FCB.

This entry is copied from FCB on disk when file is opened.

Fig. 11.5   The relationship between **FILE** pointers, **FILE** structures and FCBs.

appropriate file pointer. Files may be opened in one of several modes. To create a file, or to discard the contents of a file before writing data, open the file for writing (**"w"**). To read an existing file, open it for reading (**"r"**). To add records to the end of an existing file, open the file for appending (**"a"**). To open a file so that it may be written to and read from, open the file for updating in one of the three update modes—**"r+"**, **"w+"**, or **"a+"**. Mode **"r+"** opens a file for reading and writing. Mode **"w+"** creates a file for reading and writing. If the file already exists, the file is opened and the current contents of the file are discarded. Mode **"a+"** opens a file for reading and writing—all writing is done at the end of the file. If the file does not exist, it is created.

If an error occurs while opening a file in any mode, **fopen** returns **NULL**. Some possible errors are:

Common Programming Error 11.4

Opening a nonexistent file for reading.

Common Programming Error 11.5

Opening a file for reading or writing without having been granted the appropriate access rights to the file (this is operating-system dependent).

Common Programming Error 11.6

Opening a file for writing when no disk space is available. Figure 11.6 lists the file open modes.

Common Programming Error 11.7

*Opening a file with the incorrect file mode can lead to devastating errors. For example, opening a file in write mode (**"w"**) when it should be opened in update mode (**"r+"**) causes the contents of the file to be discarded.*

Good Programming Practice 11.3

Open a file only for reading (and not update) if the contents of the file should not be modified. This prevents unintentional modification of the file's contents. This is another example of the principle of least privilege.

11.5 Reading Data from a Sequential Access File

Data are stored in files so that the data may be retrieved for processing when needed. The previous section demonstrated how to create a file for sequential access. In this section, we discuss how to read data sequentially from a file.

Mode	Description
r	Open a file for reading.
w	Create a file for writing. If the file already exists, discard the current contents.
a	Append; open or create a file for writing at end of file.
r+	Open a file for update (reading and writing).
w+	Create a file for update. If the file already exists, discard the current contents.
a+	Append; open or create a file for update; writing is done at the end of the file.

Fig. 11.6 File open modes.

The program of Fig. 11.7 reads records from the file **"clients.dat"** created by the program of Fig. 11.3, and prints the contents of the records. The statement

```
FILE *cfPtr;
```

indicates that **cfPtr** is a pointer to a **FILE**. The line

```
if ((cfPtr = fopen("clients.dat", "r")) == NULL)
```

attempts to open the file **"clients.dat"** for reading (**"r"**), and determines whether the file is opened successfully (i.e., **fopen** does not return **NULL**). The statement

```
fscanf(cfPtr, "%d%s%f", &account, name, &balance);
```

reads a "record" from the file. Function **fscanf** is equivalent to function **scanf** except **fscanf** receives as an argument a file pointer for the file from which the data is read. After the preceding statement is executed the first time, **account** will have the value **100**, **name** will have the value **"Jones"**, and **balance** will have the value **24.98**. Each time the second **fscanf** statement is executed, another record is read from the file and **account**, **name**, and **balance** take on new values. When the end of the file is reached, the file is closed and the program terminates.

```
/* Reading and printing a sequential file */
#include <stdio.h>

main()
{
    int account;
    char name[30];
    float balance;
    FILE *cfPtr;    /* cfPtr = clients.dat file pointer */

    if ((cfPtr = fopen("clients.dat", "r")) == NULL)
        printf("File could not be opened\n");
    else {
        printf("%-10s%-13s%s\n", "Account", "Name", "Balance");
        fscanf(cfPtr, "%d%s%f", &account, name, &balance);

        while (!feof(cfPtr)) {
            printf("%-10d%-13s%7.2f\n", account, name, balance);
            fscanf(cfPtr, "%d%s%f", &account, name, &balance);
        }

        fclose(cfPtr);
    }

    return 0;
}
```

Fig. 11.7   Reading and printing a sequential file (part 1 of 2).

```
Account    Name         Balance
100        Jones         24.98
200        Doe          345.67
300        White          0.00
400        Stone        -42.16
500        Rich         224.62
```

Fig. 11.7 Reading and printing a sequential file (part 2 of 2).

To retrieve data sequentially from a file, a program normally starts reading from the beginning of the file, and reads all data consecutively until the desired data are found. It may be desirable to process the data sequentially in a file several times (from the beginning of the file) during the execution of a program. A statement such as

```
rewind(cfPtr);
```

causes a program's *file position pointer*—indicating the number of the next byte in the file to be read or written—to be repositioned to the beginning of the file (i.e., byte 0) pointed to by `cfPtr`. The file position pointer is not really a pointer. Rather it is an integer value that specifies the byte location in the file at which the next read or write is to occur. This is sometimes referred to as the *file offset*. The file position pointer is a member of the `FILE` structure associated with each file.

We now present a program (Fig. 11.8) that allows a credit manager to obtain lists of customers with zero balances (i.e., customers who do not owe any money), customers with credit balances (i.e., customers to whom the company owes money), and customers with debit balances (i.e., customers who owe the company money for goods and services received). A credit balance is a negative amount; a debit balance is a positive amount.

The program displays a menu and allows the credit manager to enter one of three options to obtain credit information. Option 1 produces a list of accounts with zero balances. Option 2 produces a list of accounts with credit balances. Option 3 produces a list of accounts with debit balances. Option 4 terminates program execution. A sample output is shown in Fig. 11.9.

Note that data in this type of sequential file cannot be modified without the risk of destroying other data in the file. For example, if the name "**White**" needed to be changed to "**Worthington**," the old name cannot simply be overwritten. The record for **White** was written to the file as

```
300 White 0.00
```

If the record is rewritten beginning at the same location in the file using the new name, the record would be

```
300 Worthington 0.00
```

The new record is larger than the original record. The characters beyond the second "**o**" in "**Worthington**" would overwrite the beginning of the next sequential record in the

```
/* Credit inquiry program */
#include <stdio.h>

main()
{
   int request, account;
   float balance;
   char name[30];
   FILE *cfPtr;

   if ((cfPtr = fopen("clients.dat", "r")) == NULL)
      printf("File could not be opened\n");
   else {
      printf("Enter request\n"
             " 1 - List accounts with zero balances\n"
             " 2 - List accounts with credit balances\n"
             " 3 - List accounts with debit balances\n"
             " 4 - End of run\n? ");
      scanf("%d", &request);

      while (request != 4) {
         fscanf(cfPtr, "%d%s%f", &account, name, &balance);

         switch (request) {
            case 1:
               printf("\nAccounts with zero balances:\n");

               while (!feof(cfPtr)) {

                  if (balance == 0)
                     printf("%-10d%-13s%7.2f\n",
                            account, name, balance);

                  fscanf(cfPtr, "%d%s%f",
                         &account, name, &balance);
               }

               break;
            case 2:
               printf("\nAccounts with credit balances:\n");

               while (!feof(cfPtr)) {

                  if (balance < 0)
                     printf("%-10d%-13s%7.2f\n",
                            account, name, balance);

                  fscanf(cfPtr, "%d%s%f",
                         &account, name, &balance);
               }

               break;
```

Fig. 11.8 Credit inquiry program (part 1 of 2).

```
            case 3:
                printf("\nAccounts with debit balances:\n");

                while (!feof(cfPtr)) {

                    if (balance > 0)
                        printf("%-10d%-13s%7.2f\n",
                                account, name, balance);

                    fscanf(cfPtr, "%d%s%f",
                            &account, name, &balance);
                }

                break;
        }

        rewind(cfPtr);
        printf("\n? ");
        scanf("%d", &request);
    }

    printf("End of run.\n");
    fclose(cfPtr);
}

return 0;
}
```

Fig. 11.8   Credit inquiry program (part 2 of 2).

```
Enter request
 1 - List accounts with zero balances
 2 - List accounts with credit balances
 3 - List accounts with debit balances
 4 - End of run
? 1

Accounts with zero balances:
300        White           0.00

? 2

Accounts with credit balances:
400        Stone         -42.16

? 3

Accounts with debit balances:
100        Jones          24.98
200        Doe           345.67
500        Rich          224.62

? 4
End of run.
```

Fig. 11.9   Sample output of the credit inquiry program of Fig. 11.8.

file. The problem here is that in the formatted input/output model using **fprintf** and **fscanf**, fields—and hence records—can vary in size. For example, 7, 14, -117, 2074, and 27383 are all **int**s stored in the same number of bytes internally, but they print on the screen or **fprintf** on the disk as different-sized fields.

Therefore, sequential access with **fprint** and **fscanf** is not usually used to update records in place. Instead, the entire file is usually rewritten. To make the preceding name change, the records before **300 White 0.00** in such a sequential access file would be copied to a new file, the new record would be written, and the records after **300 White 0.00** would be copied to the new file. This requires processing every record in the file to update one record.

11.6 Random Access Files

As we stated previously, records in a file created with the formatted output function **fprintf** are not necessarily the same length. However, individual records of a *randomly accessed file* are normally fixed in length and may be accessed directly (and thus quickly) without searching through other records. This makes randomly accessed files appropriate for airline reservation systems, banking systems, point-of-sale systems, and other kinds of *transaction processing systems* that require rapid access to specific data. There are other ways of implementing randomly accessed files, but we will limit our discussion to this straight forward approach using fixed-length records.

Because every record in a randomly accessed file normally has the same length, the exact location of a record relative to the beginning of the file can be calculated as a function of the record key. We will soon see how this facilitates immediate access to specific records, even in large files.

Figure 11.10 illustrates one way to implement a randomly accessed file. Such a file is like a freight train with many cars—some empty and some with cargo. Each car in the train is the same length.

Data can be inserted in a randomly accessed file without destroying other data in the file. Data stored previously can also be updated or deleted without rewriting the entire file. In the following sections we explain how to create a randomly accessed file, enter data, read the data both sequentially and randomly, update the data, and delete data no longer needed.

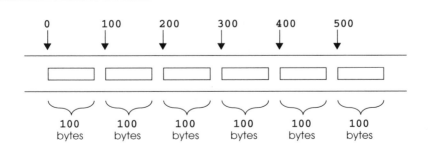

Fig. 11.10 View of a randomly accessed file with fixed-length records.

11.7 Creating a Randomly Accessed File

Function `fwrite` transfers a specified number of bytes beginning at a specified location in memory to a file. The data is written beginning at the location in the file indicated by the file position pointer. Function `fread` transfers a specified number of bytes from the location in the file specified by the file position pointer to an area in memory beginning with a specified address. Now, when writing an integer, instead of using

```
fprintf(fPtr, "%d", number);
```

which could print as few as 1 digit or as many as 11 digits (10 digits plus a sign, each of which requires 1 byte of storage) for a 4-byte integer, we can use

```
fwrite(&number, sizeof(int), 1, fPtr);
```

which always writes 4 bytes (or 2 bytes on a system with 2-byte integers) from variable **number** to the file represented by **fPtr** (we will explain the **1** argument shortly). Later, `fread` can be used to read 4 of those bytes into integer variable **number**. Although `fread` and `fwrite` read and write data such as integers in fixed-size rather than variable-size format, the data they handle is processed in computer "raw data" format (i.e., bytes of data) rather than in `printf`'s and `scanf`'s human-readable format.

The `fwrite` and `fread` functions are capable of reading and writing arrays of data to and from disk. The third argument of both `fread` and `fwrite` is the number of elements in the array that should be read from disk or written to disk. The preceding `fwrite` function call writes a single integer to disk, so the third argument is **1** (as if one element of an array is being written).

File processing programs rarely write a single field to a file. Normally, they write one **struct** at a time, as we show in the following examples.

Consider the following problem statement:

Create a credit processing system capable of storing up to 100 fixed-length records. Each record should consist of an account number that will be used as the record key, a last name, a first name, and a balance. The resulting program should be able to update an account, insert a new account record, delete an account, and list all the account records in a formatted text file for printing. Use a randomly accessed file.

The next several sections introduce the techniques necessary to create the credit processing program. The program of Fig. 11.11 shows how to open a randomly accessed file, define a record format using a **struct**, write data to the disk, and close the file. This program initializes all 100 records of the file **"credit.dat"** with empty **struct**s using function `fwrite`. Each empty **struct** contains **0** for the account number, **NULL** (represented by empty quotation marks) for the last name, **NULL** for the first name, and **0.0** for the balance. The file is initialized in this manner to create space on the disk in which the file will be stored, and to make it possible to determine if a record contains data.

Function `fwrite` writes a block (specific number of bytes) of data to a file. In our program, the statement

```
fwrite(&blankClient, sizeof(struct clientData), 1, cfPtr);
```

```
/* Creating a randomly accessed file sequentially */
#include <stdio.h>

struct clientData {
    int acctNum;
    char lastName[15];
    char firstName[10];
    float balance;
};

main()
{
    int i;
    struct clientData blankClient = {0, "", "", 0.0};
    FILE *cfPtr;

    if ((cfPtr = fopen("credit.dat", "w")) == NULL)
        printf("File could not be opened.\n");
    else {

        for (i = 1; i <= 100; i++)
            fwrite(&blankClient,
                    sizeof(struct clientData), 1, cfPtr);

        fclose (cfPtr);
    }

    return 0;
}
```

Fig. 11.11 Creating a random access file sequentially.

causes the structure **blankClient** of size **sizeof(struct clientData)** to be written to the file pointed to by **cfPtr**. The operator **sizeof** returns the size in bytes of the object contained in parentheses (in this case **struct clientData**). The **sizeof** operator is a compile-time unary operator that returns an unsigned integer. The **sizeof** operator can be used to determine the size in bytes of any data type or expression. For example, **sizeof(int)** is used to determine whether an integer is stored in 2 or 4 bytes on a particular computer.

Performance Tip 11.2

*Many programmers mistakenly think **sizeof** is a function, and that using it generates the execution-time overhead of a function call. There is no such overhead because* **sizeof** *is a compile-time operator.*

Function **fwrite** can actually be used to write several elements of an array of objects. To write several array elements, the programmer supplies a pointer to an array as the first argument in the call to **fwrite**, and specifies the number of elements to be written as the third argument in the call to **fwrite**. In the preceding statement, **fwrite** was used to write a single object that was not an array element. Writing a single object is equivalent to writing one element of an array, hence the **1** in the **fwrite** call.

11.8 Writing Data Randomly to a Randomly Accessed File

The program of Fig. 11.12 writes data to the file **"credit.dat"**. It uses the combination of **fseek** and **fwrite** to store data at specific locations in the file. Function **fseek** sets the file position pointer to a specific position in the file, then **fwrite** writes the data. A sample execution is shown in Fig. 11.13.

The statement

```
fseek(cfPtr, (accountNum - 1) * sizeof(struct clientData),
      SEEK_SET);
```

```c
/* Writing to a random access file */
#include <stdio.h>

struct clientData {
   int acctNum;
   char lastName[15];
   char firstName[10];
   float balance;
};

main()
{
   FILE *cfPtr;
   struct clientData client;

   if ((cfPtr = fopen("credit.dat", "r+")) == NULL)
      printf("File could not be opened.\n");
   else {
      printf("Enter account number"
             " (1 to 100, 0 to end input)\n? ");
      scanf("%d", &client.acctNum);

      while (client.acctNum != 0) {
         printf("Enter lastname, firstname, balance\n? ");
         scanf("%s%s%f", &client.lastName,
               &client.firstName, &client.balance);
         fseek(cfPtr, (client.acctNum - 1) *
               sizeof(struct clientData), SEEK_SET);
         fwrite(&client, sizeof(struct clientData), 1, cfPtr);
         printf("Enter account number\n? ");
         scanf("%d", &client.acctNum);
      }
   }

   fclose(cfPtr);

   return 0;
}
```

Fig. 11.12 Writing data randomly to a randomly accessed file.

```
Enter account number (1 to 100, 0 to end input)
? 37
Enter lastname, firstname, balance
? Barker Doug 0.00
Enter account number
? 29
Enter lastname, firstname, balance
? Brown Nancy -24.54
Enter account number
? 96
Enter lastname, firstname, balance
? Stone Sam 34.98
Enter account number
? 88
Enter lastname, firstname, balance
? Smith Dave 258.34
Enter account number
? 33
Enter lastname, firstname, balance
? Dunn Stacey 314.33
Enter account number
? 0
```

Fig. 11.13 Sample execution of the program in Fig. 11.12.

positions the file position pointer for the file referenced by **cfPtr** to the byte location calculated by **(accountNum - 1) * sizeof(struct clientData)**; the value of this expression is called the *offset* or the *displacement*. Because the account number is between 1 and 100 but the byte positions in the file start with **0**, 1 is subtracted from the account number when calculating the byte location of the record. Thus, for record 1, the file position pointer is set to byte 0 of the file. The symbolic constant **SEEK_SET** indicates that the file position pointer is positioned relative to the beginning of the file by the amount of the offset. As the above statement indicates, a seek for account number 1 in the file sets the file position pointer to the beginning of the file because the byte location calculated is 0. Figure 11.14 illustrates the file pointer referring to a **FILE** structure in memory. The file position pointer indicates that the next byte to be read or written is 5 bytes from the beginning of the file.

The ANSI standard shows the function prototype for **fseek** as

```
int fseek(FILE *stream, long int offset, int whence);
```

where **offset** is the number of bytes from location **whence** in the file pointed to by **stream**. The argument **whence** can have one of three values—**SEEK_SET**, **SEEK_CUR** or **SEEK_END**—indicating the location in the file from which the seek begins. **SEEK_SET** indicates that the seek starts at the beginning of the file; **SEEK_CUR** indicates that the seek starts at the current location in the file; and **SEEK_END** indicates that the seek starts at the end of the file. These three symbolic constants are defined in the **stdio.h** header file.

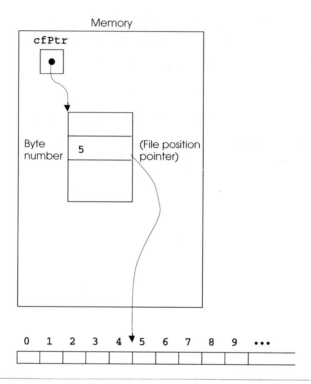

Fig. 11.14 The file position pointer indicating an offset of 5 bytes from the beginning of the file.

11.9 Reading Data Randomly from a Randomly Accessed File

Function **fread** reads a specified number of bytes from a file into memory. For example, the statement

```
fread(&client, sizeof(struct clientData), 1, cfPtr);
```

reads the number of bytes determined by **sizeof(struct clientData)** from the file referenced by **cfPtr** and stores the data in the structure **client**. The bytes are read from the location in the file specified by the file position pointer. Function **fread** can be used to read several fixed-size array elements by providing a pointer to the array in which the elements will be stored, and by indicating the number of elements to be read. The preceding statement specifies that one element should be read. To read more than one element, specify the number of elements in the third argument of the **fread** statement.

The program of Fig. 11.15 reads sequentially every record in the **"credit.dat"** file, determines whether each record contains data, and prints the formatted data for records containing data. The **feof** function determines when the end of the file is reached, and the **fread** function transfers data from the disk to the **clientData** structure **client**.

```
/* Reading a random access file sequentially */
#include <stdio.h>

struct clientData {
   int acctNum;
   char lastName[15];
   char firstName[10];
   float balance;
};

main()
{
   FILE *cfPtr;
   struct clientData client;

   if ((cfPtr = fopen("credit.dat", "r")) == NULL)
      printf("File could not be opened.\n");
   else {
      printf("%-6s%-16s%-11s%10s\n", "Acct", "Last Name",
             "First Name", "Balance");

      while (!feof(cfPtr)) {
         fread(&client, sizeof(struct clientData), 1, cfPtr);

         if (client.acctNum != 0)
            printf("%-6d%-16s%-11s%10.2f\n",
                   client.acctNum, client.lastName,
                   client.firstName, client.balance);
      }
   }

   fclose(cfPtr);

   return 0;
}
```

Acct	Last Name	First Name	Balance
29	Brown	Nancy	-24.54
33	Dunn	Stacey	314.33
37	Barker	Doug	0.00
88	Smith	Dave	258.34
96	Stone	Sam	34.98

Fig. 11.15 Reading a random access file sequentially.

11.10 Case Study: A Transaction Processing Program

We now present a substantial transaction processing program using randomly accessed files. The program maintains a bank's account information. The program updates existing accounts, adds new accounts, deletes accounts, and stores a listing of all the current accounts in a text file for printing. We assume that the program of Fig. 11.11 has been executed to create the file `credit.dat`.

The program has five options. Option 1 calls function `textFile` to store a formatted list of all the accounts in a text file called `accounts.txt` that may be printed later. The function uses `fread` and the sequential file access techniques used in the program of Fig. 11.15. After choosing option 1 the file `accounts.txt` contains:

```
Acct    Last Name       First Name      Balance
29      Brown           Nancy            -24.54
33      Dunn            Stacey           314.33
37      Barker          Doug               0.00
88      Smith           Dave             258.34
96      Stone           Sam               34.98
```

Option 2 calls the function `updateRecord` to update an account. The function will only update a record that already exists, so the function first checks to see if the record specified by the user is empty. The record is read into structure `client` with `fread`, then the member `acctNum` is compared to 0. If it is 0, the record contains no information, and a message is printed stating that the record is empty. Then, the menu choices are displayed. If the record contains information, function `updateRecord` inputs the transaction amount, calculates the new balance, and rewrites the record to the file. A typical output for option 2 is:

```
Enter account to update (1 - 100): 37
37      Barker          Doug               0.00

Enter charge (+) or payment (-): +87.99
37      Barker          Doug              87.99
```

Option 3 calls the function `newRecord` to add a new account to the file. If the user enters an account number for an existing account, `newRecord` displays an error message that the record already contains information, and the menu choices are printed again. This function uses the same process to add a new account as does the program in Fig. 11.12. A typical output for option 3 is

```
Enter new account number (1 - 100): 22
Enter lastname, firstname, balance
? Johnston Sarah 247.45
```

Option 4 calls function `deleteRecord` to delete a record from the file. Deletion is accomplished by asking the user for the account number and reinitializing the record. If the account contains no information, `deleteRecord` displays an error message that the account does not exist. Option 5 terminates program execution. The program is shown in Fig. 11.16. Note that the file `"credit.dat"` is opened for update (reading and writing) using `"r+"` mode.

```
/* This program reads a random access file sequentially, *
 * updates data already written to the file, creates new *
 * data to be placed in the file, and deletes data       *
 * already in the file.                                 */

#include <stdio.h>

struct clientData {
    int acctNum;
    char lastName[15];
    char firstName[10];
    float balance;
};

int enterChoice(void);
void textFile(FILE *);
void updateRecord(FILE *);
void newRecord(FILE *);
void deleteRecord(FILE *);

main()
{
    FILE *cfPtr;
    int choice;

    if ((cfPtr = fopen("credit.dat", "r+")) == NULL)
        printf("File could not be opened.\n");
    else {

        while ((choice = enterChoice()) != 5) {

            switch (choice) {
                case 1:
                    textFile(cfPtr);
                    break;
                case 2:
                    updateRecord(cfPtr);
                    break;
                case 3:
                    newRecord(cfPtr);
                    break;
                case 4:
                    deleteRecord(cfPtr);
                    break;
            }

        }
    }

    fclose(cfPtr);
    return 0;
}
```

Fig. 11.16 Bank account program (part 1 of 4).

```c
void textFile(FILE *readPtr)
{
   FILE *writePtr;
   struct clientData client;

   if ((writePtr = fopen("accounts.txt", "w")) == NULL)
      printf("File could not be opened.\n");
   else {
      rewind(readPtr);
      fprintf(writePtr, "%-6s%-16s%-11s%10s\n",
              "Acct", "Last Name", "First Name","Balance");

      while (!feof(readPtr)) {
         fread(&client, sizeof(struct clientData), 1, readPtr);

         if (client.acctNum != 0)
            fprintf(writePtr, "%-6d%-16s%-11s%10.2f\n",
                    client.acctNum, client.lastName,
                    client.firstName, client.balance);
      }
   }

   fclose(writePtr);
}

void updateRecord(FILE *fPtr)
{
   int account;
   float transaction;
   struct clientData client;

   printf("Enter account to update (1 - 100): ");
   scanf("%d", &account);
   fseek(fPtr, (account - 1) * sizeof(struct clientData),
         SEEK_SET);
   fread(&client, sizeof(struct clientData), 1, fPtr);

   if (client.acctNum == 0)
      printf("Acount #%d has no information.\n", account);
   else {
      printf("%-6d%-16s%-11s%10.2f\n\n",
             client.acctNum, client.lastName,
             client.firstName, client.balance);
      printf("Enter charge (+) or payment (-): ");
      scanf("%f", &transaction);
      client.balance += transaction;
      printf("%-6d%-16s%-11s%10.2f\n",
             client.acctNum, client.lastName,
             client.firstName, client.balance);
      fseek(fPtr, (account - 1) * sizeof(struct clientData),
            SEEK_SET);
      fwrite(&client, sizeof(struct clientData), 1, fPtr);
   }
}
```

Fig. 11.16 Bank account program (part 2 of 4).

```
void deleteRecord(FILE *fPtr)
{
    struct clientData client, blankClient = {0, "", "", 0};
    int accountNum;

    printf("Enter account number to delete (1 - 100): ");
    scanf("%d", &accountNum);
    fseek(fPtr, (accountNum - 1) * sizeof(struct clientData),
          SEEK_SET);
    fread(&client, sizeof(struct clientData), 1, fPtr);

    if (client.acctNum == 0)
        printf("Account %d does not exist.\n", accountNum);
    else {
        fseek(fPtr, (accountNum - 1) * sizeof(struct clientData),
              SEEK_SET);
        fwrite(&blankClient, sizeof(struct clientData), 1, fPtr);
    }
}

void newRecord(FILE *fPtr)
{
    struct clientData client;
    int accountNum;
    printf("Enter new account number (1 - 100): ");
    scanf("%d", &accountNum);
    fseek(fPtr, (accountNum - 1) * sizeof(struct clientData),
          SEEK_SET);
    fread(&client, sizeof(struct clientData), 1, fPtr);

    if (client.acctNum != 0)
        printf("Account #%d already contains information.\n",
                client.acctNum);
    else {
        printf("Enter lastname, firstname, balance\n? ");
        scanf("%s%s%f", &client.lastName, &client.firstName,
              &client.balance);
        client.acctNum = accountNum;
        fseek(fPtr, (client.acctNum - 1) *
              sizeof(struct clientData), SEEK_SET);
        fwrite(&client, sizeof(struct clientData), 1, fPtr);
    }
}
```

Fig. 11.16 Bank account program (part 3 of 4).

Summary

- All data items processed by a computer are reduced to combinations of zeros and ones.

- The smallest data item in a computer can assume the value 0 or the value 1. Such a data item is called a bit (short for "binary digit"—a digit that can assume one of two values).

```
int enterChoice(void)
{
   int menuChoice;

   printf("\nEnter your choice\n"
          "1 - store a formatted text file of acounts called\n"
          "    \"accounts.txt\" for printing\n"
          "2 - update an account\n"
          "3 - add a new account\n"
          "4 - delete an account\n"
          "5 - end program\n? ");
   scanf("%d", &menuChoice);
   return menuChoice;
}
```

Fig. 11.16 Bank account program (part 4 of 4).

- Digits, letters, and special symbols are referred to as characters. The set of all characters that may be used to write programs and represent data items on a particular computer is called that computer's character set. Every character in the computer's character set is represented as a pattern of eight 1s and 0s (called a byte).

- A field is a group of characters that conveys meaning.

- A record is a group of related fields.

- At least one field in each record is normally chosen as a record key. The record key identifies a record as belonging to a particular person or entity.

- The most popular type of organization for records in a file is called a sequential access file in which records are accessed consecutively until the desired data are located.

- A group of related files is sometimes called a database. A collection of programs designed to create and manage databases is called a database management system (DBMS).

- C views each file simply as a sequential stream of bytes.

- C automatically opens three files and their associated streams—standard input, standard output, and standard error—when program execution begins.

- The file pointers assigned to the standard input, standard output, and standard error are **stdin**, **stdout**, and **stderr**, respectively.

- Function **fgetc** reads a character from a specified file.

- Function **fputc** writes a character to a specified file.

- Function **fgets** reads a line from a specified file.

- Function **fputs** writes a line to a specified file.

- **FILE** is a structure type defined in the **stdio.h** header file. The programmer need not know the specifics of this structure to use files. As a file is opened, a pointer to the file's **FILE** structure is returned.

- Function **fopen** takes two arguments—a file name and a file open mode—and opens the file. If the file exists, the contents of the file are discarded without warning. If the file does not exist and the file is being opened for writing, **fopen** creates the file.

- Function **feof** determines whether the end-of-file indicator for a file has been set.

- Function **fprintf** is equivalent to **printf** except **fprintf** receives as an argument a pointer to the file to which the data will be written.

- Function **fclose** closes the file pointed to by its argument.

- To create a file, or to discard the contents of a file before writing data, open the file for writing (**"w"**). To read an existing file, open it for reading (**"r"**). To add records to the end of an existing file, open the file for appending (**"a"**). To open a file so that it may be written to and read from, open the file for updating in one of the three updating modes—**"r+"**, **"w+"**, or **"a+"**. Mode **"r+"** simply opens the file for reading and writing. Mode **"w+"** creates the file if it does not exist, and discards the current contents of the file if it does exist. Mode **"a+"** creates the file if it does not exist, and writing is done at the end of the file.

- Function **fscanf** is equivalent to **scanf** except **fscanf** receives as an argument a pointer to the file (normally other than **stdin**) from which the data will be read.

- Function **rewind** causes the program to reposition the file position pointer for the specified file to the beginning of the file.

- Random access file processing is used to access a record directly.

- To facilitate random access, data is stored in fixed-length records. Since every record is the same length, the computer can quickly calculate (as a function of the record key) the exact location of a record in relation to the beginning of the file.

- Data can be added easily to a random access file without destroying other data in the file. Data stored previously in a file with fixed-length records can also be changed and deleted without rewriting the entire file.

- Function **fwrite** writes a block (specific number of bytes) of data to a file.

- The compile-time operator **sizeof** returns the size in bytes of its operand.

- Function **fseek** sets the file position pointer to a specific position in a file based on the starting location of the seek in the file. The seek can start from one of three locations—**SEEK_SET** starts from the beginning of the file, **SEEK_CUR** starts from the current position in the file, and **SEEK_END** starts from the end of the file.

- Function **fread** reads a block (specific number of bytes) of data from a file.

Terminology

a file open mode	alpha order
a+ file open mode	binary digit
alphabetic field	bit
alphanumeric field	byte

character	**fscanf**
character field	**fseek**
character set	**fwrite**
close a file	integer number
data hierarchy	leading spaces
database	letter
database management system	numeric field
decimal digit	offset
displacement	open a file
double-precision number	**r** file open mode
end-of-file	random access
end-of-file indicator	random access file
fclose	record
feof	record key
fgetc	record number parameter
fgets	**rewind**
field	**r+** file open mode
file	**SEEK_CUR**
file buffer	**SEEK_END**
file name	**SEEK_SET**
file open mode	sequential access file
file pointer	single-precision number
file position pointer	**stderr** (standard error)
FILE structure	**stdin** (standard input)
fopen	**stdout** (standard output)
formatted input/output	stream
fprintf	trailing spaces
fputc	**w** file open mode
fputs	**w+** file open mode
fread	zeros and ones

Common Programming Errors

11.1 Opening an existing file for writing (**"w"**) when, in fact, the user wants to preserve the file; the contents of the file are discarded without warning.

11.2 Forgetting to open a file before attempting to reference it in a program.

11.3 Using the wrong file pointer to refer to a file.

11.4 Opening a nonexistent file for reading.

11.5 Opening a file for reading or writing without having been granted the appropriate access rights to the file (this is operating-system dependent).

11.6 Opening a file for writing when no disk space is available. Figure 11.6 lists the file open modes.

11.7 Opening a file with the incorrect file mode can lead to devastating errors. For example, opening a file in write mode (**"w"**) when it should be opened in update mode (**"r+"**) causes the contents of the file to be discarded.

Good Programming Practices

11.1 Be sure that calls to file processing functions in a program contain the correct file pointers.

11.2 Explicitly close each file as soon as it is known that the program will not reference the file again.

11.3 Open a file only for reading (and not update) if the contents of the file should not be modified. This prevents unintentional modification of the file's contents. This is another example of the principle of least privilege.

Performance Tips

11.1 Closing a file can free resources for which other users or programs may be waiting.

11.2 Many programmers mistakenly think `sizeof` is a function, and that using it generates the execution-time overhead of a function call. There is no such overhead because `sizeof` is a compile-time operator.

Portability Tip

11.1 The `FILE` structure is operating system dependent (i.e., the members of the structure vary among systems based on how each system handles its files).

Self-Review Exercises

11.1 Fill in the blanks in each of the following:

a) Ultimately, all data items processed by a computer are reduced to combinations of _____ and _____.

b) The smallest data item a computer can process is called a _____.

c) A _____ is a group of related records.

d) Digits, letters, and special symbols are referred to as _____.

e) A group of related files is called a _____.

f) The _____ function closes a file.

g) The _____ statement reads data from a file in a manner similar to how `scanf` reads from `stdin`.

h) The _____ function reads a character from a specified file.

i) The _____ function reads a line from a specified file.

j) The _____ function opens a file.

k) The _____ function is normally used when reading data from a file in random access applications.

l) The _____ function repositions the file position pointer to a specific location in the file.

11.2 State which of the following are true and which are false (for those that are false, explain why):

a) Function `fscanf` cannot be used to read data from the standard input.

b) The programmer must explicitly use `fopen` to open the standard input, standard output, and standard error streams.

c) A program must explicitly call function `fclose` to close a file.

d) If the file position pointer points to a location in a sequential file other than the beginning of the file, the file must be closed and reopened to read from the beginning of the file.

e) Function `fprintf` can write to the standard output.

f) Data in sequential access files is always updated without overwriting other data.

g) It is not necessary to search through all the records in a randomly accessed file to find a specific record.

h) Records in randomly accessed files are not of uniform length.

i) Function `fseek` may only seek relative to the beginning of a file.

11.3 Write a single statement to accomplish each of the following. Assume that each of these statements applies to the same program.

a) Write a statement that opens file `"oldmast.dat"` for reading and assigns the returned file pointer to `ofPtr`.

b) Write a statement that opens file `"trans.dat"` for reading and assigns the returned file pointer to `tfPtr`.

c) Write a statement that opens file `"newmast.dat"` for writing (and creation) and assigns the returned file pointer to `nfPtr`.

d) Write a statement that reads a record from the file `"oldmast.dat"`. The record consists of integer `accountNum`, string `name`, and floating point `currentBalance`.

e) Write a statement that reads a record from the file `"trans.dat"`. The record consists of integer `accountNum` and floating point `dollarAmount`.

f) Write a statement that writes a record to the file `"newmast.dat"`. The record consists of integer `accountNum`, string `name`, and floating point `currentBalance`.

11.4 Find the error in each of the following program segments. Explain how the error can be corrected.

a) The file referred to by `fPtr` (`"payables.dat"`) has not been opened.
`fprintf(fPtr, "%d%s%d\n", account, company, amount);`

b) `open("receive.dat", "r+");`

c) The following statement should read a record from the file `"payables.dat"`. File pointer `payPtr` refers to this file, and file pointer `recPtr` refers to the file `"receive.dat"`.
`fscanf(recPtr, "%d%s%d\n", &account, company, &amount);`

d) The file `"tools.dat"` should be opened to add data to the file without discarding the current data.
`if ((tfPtr = fopen("tools.dat", "w")) != NULL)`

e) The file `"courses.dat"` should be opened for appending without modifying the current contents of the file.
`if ((cfPtr = fopen("courses.dat", "w+")) != NULL)`

Answers to Self-Review Exercises

11.1 a) 1s, 0s. b) Bit. c) File. d) Characters. e) Database. f) `fclose`. g) `fscanf`. h) `getc` or `fgetc`. i) `fgets`. j) `fopen`. k) `fread`. l) `fseek`.

11.2
a) False. Function `fscanf` can be used to read from the standard input by including the pointer to the standard input stream, `stdin`, in the call to `fscanf`.

b) False. These three streams are opened automatically by C when program execution begins.

c) False. The files will be closed when program execution terminates, but all files should be explicitly closed with `fclose`.

d) False. Function `rewind` can be used to reposition the file position pointer to the beginning of the file.

e) True.

f) False. In most cases, sequential file records are not of uniform length. Therefore, it is possible that updating a record will cause other data to be overwritten.

g) True.

h) False. Records in a random access file are normally of uniform length.

i) False. It is possible to seek from the beginning of the file, from the end of the file, and from the current location in the file according to the file position pointer.

11.3   a) `ofPtr = fopen("oldmast.dat", "r");`

b) `tfPtr = fopen("trans.dat", "r");`

c) `nfPtr = fopen("newmast.dat", "w");`

d) `fscanf(ofPtr, "%d%s%f", &accountNum, name, &currentBalance);`

e) `fscanf(tfPtr, "%d%f", &accountNum, &dollarAmount);`

f) `fprintf(nfPtr, "%d %s %.2f", accountNum, name, currentBalance);`

11.4   a) Error: The file `"payables.dat"` has not been opened before the reference to its file pointer.

Correction: Use `fopen` to open `"payables.dat"` for writing, appending, or updating.

b) Error: The function `open` is not an ANSI C function.

Correction: Use function `fopen`.

c) Error: The `fscanf` statement uses the incorrect file pointer to refer to file `"payables.dat"`.

Correction: Use file pointer `payPtr` to refer to `"payables.dat"`.

d) Error: The contents of the file are discarded because the file is opened for writing (`"w"`).

Correction: To add data to the file, either open the file for updating (`"r+"`) or open the file for appending (`"a"`).

e) Error: File `"courses.dat"` is opened for updating in `"w+"` mode which discards the current contents of the file.

Correction: Open the file `"a"` mode.

Exercises

11.5   Fill in the blanks in each of the following:

a) Computers store large amounts of data on secondary storage devices as _____.

b) A _____ is composed of several fields.

c) A field that may contain digits, letters, and blanks is called an _____ field.

d) To facilitate the retrieval of specific records from a file, one field in each record is chosen as a _____.

e) The vast majority of information stored in computer systems is stored in _____ files.

f) A group of related characters that conveys meaning is called a _____.

g) The file pointers for the three files that are opened automatically by C when program execution begins are named _____, _____, and _____.

h) The _____ function writes a character to a specified file.

i) The _____ function writes a line to a specified file.

j) The _____ function is generally used to write data to a randomly accessed file.

k) The _____ function repositions the file position pointer to the beginning of the file.

11.6   State which of the following are true and which are false (for those that are false, explain why):

a) The impressive functions performed by computers essentially involve the manipulation of zeros and ones.

b) People prefer to manipulate bits instead of characters and fields because bits are more compact.

c) People specify programs and data items as characters; computers then manipulate and process these characters as groups of zeros and ones.

d) A person's zip code is an example of a numeric field.

e) A person's street address is generally considered to be an alphabetic field in computer applications.

f) Data items processed by a computer form a data hierarchy in which data items become larger and more complex as we progress from fields to characters to bits, etc.

g) A record key identifies a record as belonging to a particular field.

h) Most organizations store all their information in a single file to facilitate computer processing.

i) Files are always referred to by name in C programs.

j) When a program creates a file, the file is automatically retained by the computer for future reference.

11.7   Exercise 11.3 asked the reader to write a series of single statements. Actually, these statements form the core of an important type of file processing program, namely, a file-matching program. In commercial data processing, it is common to have several files in each system. In an accounts receivable system, for example, there is generally a master file containing detailed information about each customer such as the customer's name, address, telephone number, outstanding balance, credit limit, discount terms, contract arrangements, and possibly a condensed history of recent purchases and cash payments.

As transactions occur (i.e., sales are made and cash payments arrive in the mail), they are entered into a file. At the end of each business period (i.e., a month for some companies, a week for others, and a day in some cases) the file of transactions (called **"trans.dat"** in Exercise 11.3 is applied to the master file (called **"oldmast.dat"** in Exercise 11.3), thus updating each account's record of purchases and payments. After each of these updating runs, the master file is rewritten as a new file (**"newmast.dat"**), which is then used at the end of the next business period to begin the updating process again.

File-matching programs must deal with certain problems that do not exist in single-file programs. For example, a match does not always occur. A customer on the master file may not have made any purchases or cash payments in the current business period, and therefore no record for this customer will appear on the transaction file. Similarly, a customer who did make some purchases or cash payments may have just moved to this community, and the company may not have had a chance to create a master record for this customer.

Use the statements written in Exercise 11.3 as a basis for writing a complete file-matching accounts receivable program. Use the account number on each file as the record key for matching purposes. Assume that each file is a sequential file with records stored in increasing account number order.

When a match occurs (i.e., records with the same account number appear on both the master file and the transaction file), add the dollar amount on the transaction file to the current balance on the master file, and write the **"newmast.dat"** record. (Assume that purchases are indicated by positive amounts on the transaction file, and that payments are indicated by negative amounts.) When there is a master record for a particular account but no corresponding transaction record, merely write the master record to **"newmast.dat"**. When there is a transaction record but no corresponding master record, print the message **"Unmatched transaction record for account number …"** (fill in the account number from the transaction record).

11.8   After writing the program of Exercise 11.7, write a simple program to create some test data for checking out the program of Exercise 11.7. Use the following sample account data:

Master File: Account number	Name	Balance
100	Alan Jones	348.17
300	Mary Smith	27.19
500	Sam Sharp	0.00
700	Suzy Green	-14.22

Transaction File: Account number	Dollar amount
100	27.14
300	62.11
400	100.56
900	82.17

11.9   Run the program of Exercise 11.7 using the files of test data created in Exercise 11.8. Use the listing program of Section 11.7 to print a new master file. Check the results carefully.

11.10   It is possible (actually common) to have several transaction records with the same record key. This occurs because a particular customer might make several purchases and cash payments during a business period. Rewrite your accounts receivable file-matching program of Exercise 11.7 to provide for the possibility of handling several transaction records with the same record key. Modify the test data of Exercise 11.8 to include the following additional transaction records:

Account number	Dollar amount
300	83.89
700	80.78
700	1.53

11.11   Write statements that accomplish each of the following. Assume that the structure

```
struct person {
   char lastName[15];
   char firstName[15];
   char age[2];
};
```

has been defined, and that the file is already open for writing.

a) Initialize the file `"nameage.dat"` so that there are 100 records with `lastName` = `"unassigned"`, `firstname` = `""`, and `age` = `"0"`.
b) Input `10` last names, first names, and ages, and write them to the file.
c) Update a record; if there is no information in the record, tell the user `"No info"`.
d) Delete a record that has information by reinitializing that particular record.

11.12   You are the owner of a hardware store and need to keep an inventory that can tell you what tools you have, how many you have, and the cost of each one. Write a program that initializes the file `"hardware.dat"` to 100 empty records, lets you input the data concerning each tool, enables you to list all your tools, lets you delete a record for a tool that you no longer have, and lets you update *any* information in the file. The tool identification number should be the record number. Use the following information to start your file:

Record #	Tool name	Quantity	Cost
3	Electric sander	7	57.98
17	Hammer	76	11.99
24	Jig saw	21	11.00
39	Lawn mower	3	79.50
56	Power saw	18	99.99
68	Screwdriver	106	6.99
77	Sledge hammer	11	21.50
83	Wrench	34	7.50

11.13   *Telephone Number Word Generator.* Standard telephone keypads contain the digits 0 through 9. The numbers 2 through 9 each have three letters associated with them, as is indicated by the following table:

Digit	Letter
2	A B C
3	D E F
4	G H I
5	J K L
6	M N O
7	P R S
8	T U V
9	W X Y

Many people find it difficult to memorize phone numbers, so they use the correspondence between digits and letters to develop seven-letter words that correspond to their phone numbers. For example, a person whose telephone number is 686-2377 might use the correspondence indicated in the above table to develop the seven-letter word "NUMBERS."

Businesses frequently attempt to get telephone numbers that are easy for their clients to remember. If a business can advertise a simple word for its customers to dial, then no doubt the business will receive a few more calls.

Each seven-letter word corresponds to exactly one seven-digit telephone number. The restaurant wishing to increase its take-home business could surely do so with the number 825-3688 (i.e., "TAKEOUT").

Each seven-digit phone number corresponds to many separate seven-letter words. Unfortunately, most of these represent unrecognizable juxtapositions of letters. It is possible, however, that the owner of a barber shop would be pleased to know that the shop's telephone number, 424-7288, corresponds to "HAIRCUT." The owner of a liquor store would, no doubt, be delighted to find that the store's telephone number, 233-7226, corresponds to "BEERCAN." A veterinarian with the phone number 738-2273 would be pleased to know that the number corresponds to the letters "PETCARE."

Write a C program that, given a seven-digit number, writes to a file every possible seven-letter word corresponding to that number. There are 2187 (3 to the seventh power) such words. Avoid phone numbers with the digits 0 and 1.

11.14 If you have a computerized dictionary available, modify the program you wrote in Exercise 11.13 to look up the words in the dictionary. Some seven-letter combinations created by this program consist of two or more words (the phone number 843-2677 produces "THEBOSS").

11.15 Modify the example of Fig. 8.14 to use functions **fgetc** and **fputs** rather than **getchar** and **puts**. The program should give the user the option to read from the standard input and write to the standard output, or to read from a specified file and write to a specified file. If the user chooses the second option, have the user enter the file names for the input and output files.

11.16 Write a program that uses the **sizeof** operator to determine the sizes in bytes of the various data types on your computer system. Write the results to the file **"datasize.dat"** so you may print the results later. The format for the results in the file should be:

Data type	Size
char	1
unsigned char	1
short int	2
unsigned short int	2
int	4
unsigned int	4
long int	4
unsigned long int	4
float	4
double	8
long double	16

Note: The type sizes on your computer may not be the same as the ones listed above.

11.17 In Exercise 7.19, you wrote a software simulation of a computer that used a special machine language called Simpletron Machine Language (SML). In the simulation, each time you wanted to run an SML program, you entered the program into the simulator from the keyboard. If you made a mistake while typing the SML program, the simulator was restarted and the SML code was reentered. It would be nice to be able to read the SML program from a file rather than type it each time. This would reduce time and mistakes in preparing to run SML programs.

    a)   Modify the simulator you wrote in Exercise 7.19 to read SML programs from a file specified by the user at the keyboard.

    b)   After the Simpletron executes, it outputs the contents of its registers and memory on the screen. It would be nice to capture the output in a file, so modify the simulator to write its output to a file in addition to displaying the output on the screen.

12

Data Structures

Objectives

- To be able to allocate and free memory dynamically for data objects.
- To be able to form linked data structures using pointers, self-referential structures, and recursion.
- To be able to create and manipulate linked lists, queues, stacks, and binary trees.
- To understand various important applications of linked data structures.

Much that I bound, I could not free;
Much that I freed returned to me.
Lee Wilson Dodd

'Will you walk a little faster?' said a whiting to a snail,
'There's a porpoise close behind us, and he's
treading on my tail.'
Lewis Carroll

There is always room at the top.
Daniel Webster

Push on — keep moving.
Thomas Morton

I think that I shall never see
A poem as lovely as a tree.
Joyce Kilmer

467

Outline

12.1 Introduction

We have studied fixed-size *data structures* such as single-subscripted arrays, double-subscripted arrays, and **struct**s. This chapter introduces *dynamic data structures* with sizes that grow and shrink at execution time. *Linked lists* are collections of data items "lined up in a row"—insertions and deletions are made anywhere in a linked list. *Stacks* are important in compilers and operating systems—insertions and deletions are made only at one end of a stack—its *top*. *Queues* represent waiting lines; insertions are made at the back (also referred to as the *tail*) of a queue, and deletions are made from the front (also referred to as the head) of a queue. *Binary trees* facilitate high-speed searching and sorting of data, efficient elimination of duplicate data items, representing file system directories, and compiling expressions into machine language. Each of these data structures has many other interesting applications.

We will discuss each of the major types of data structures and implement programs that create and manipulate these data structures. In the next part of the book—the introduction to C++ and object-oriented programming in Chapters 15 through 21—we will study data abstraction. This technique will enable us to build these data structures in a dramatically different manner designed for producing software that is much easier to maintain and especially easier to reuse.

This is a challenging chapter. The programs are substantial and they incorporate most of what you have learned in the earlier chapters. The programs are especially heavy on pointer manipulation, a subject many people consider to be among the most difficult topics in C. The chapter is loaded with highly practical programs that you will be able to use in more advanced courses; the chapter includes a rich collection of exercises that emphasize practical applications of the data structures.

We sincerely hope that you will attempt the major project described in the special section entitled "Building Your Own Compiler." You have been using a compiler to translate your C programs to machine language so that you could execute your programs on your computer. In this project, you will actually build your own compiler. It will read a file of statements written in a simple, yet powerful, high-level language similar to early versions of the popular language BASIC. Your compiler will translate these statements into a file of Simpletron Machine Language instructions. SML is the language you learned in the Chapter 7 special section, "Building Your Own Computer." Your Simpletron Simulator program will then execute the SML program produced by your compiler! This project will give you a wonderful opportunity to exercise most of what you have learned in this course. The special section carefully walks you through the specifications of the high-level language, and describes the algorithms you will need to convert each type of high-level language statement into machine language instructions. If you enjoy being challenged, you might attempt the many enhancements to both the compiler and the Simpletron Simulator suggested in the Exercises.

12.2 Self-Referential Structures

A *self-referential structure* contains a pointer member that points to a structure of the same structure type. For example, the definition

```
struct node {
   int data;
   struct node *nextPtr;
};
```

defines a type, **struct node**. A structure of type **struct node** has two members— integer member **data** and pointer member **nextPtr**. Member **nextPtr** points to a structure of type **struct node**—a structure of the same type as the one being declared here, hence the term "self-referential structure." Member **nextPtr** is referred to as a *link*—i.e., **nextPtr** can be used to "tie" a structure of type **struct node** to another structure of the same type. Self-referential structures can be linked together to form useful data structures such as lists, queues, stacks, and trees. Figure 12.1 illustrates two self-referential structures linked together to form a list. Note that a slash—representing a **NULL** pointer—is placed in the link member of the second self-referential structure to indicate that the link does not point to another structure. The slash is only for illustration purposes; it does not correspond to the backslash character in C. A **NULL** pointer normally indicates the end of a data structure just as the **NULL** character indicates the end of a string.

Common Programming Error 12.1

*Not setting the link in the last node of a list to **NULL**.*

Fig. 12.1 Two self-referential structures linked together.

12.3 Dynamic Memory Allocation

Creating and maintaining dynamic data structures requires *dynamic memory allocation*—
the ability for a program to obtain more memory space at execution time to hold new
nodes, and to release space no longer needed. The limit for dynamic memory allocation
can be as large as the amount of available physical memory in the computer or the
amount of available virtual memory in a virtual memory system. Often, the limits are
much smaller because available memory must be shared among many users.

Functions **malloc** and **free**, and operator **sizeof**, are essential to dynamic
memory allocation. Function **malloc** takes as an argument the number of bytes to be allocated, and returns a pointer of type **void *** *(pointer to void)* to the allocated memory.
A **void *** pointer may be assigned to a variable of any pointer type. Function **malloc** is
normally used with the **sizeof** operator. For example, the statement

```
newPtr = malloc(sizeof(struct node));
```

evaluates **sizeof(struct node)** to determine the size in bytes of a structure of type
struct node, allocates a new area in memory of **sizeof(struct node)** bytes, and
stores a pointer to the allocated memory in variable **newPtr**. If no memory is available,
malloc returns a **NULL** pointer.

The **free** function deallocates memory—i.e., the memory is returned to the system
so that the memory can be reallocated in the future. To free memory dynamically allocated by the preceding **malloc** call, use the statement

```
free(newPtr);
```

The following sections discuss lists, stacks, queues, and trees. Each of these data
structures is created and maintained with dynamic memory allocation and self-referential
structures.

Portability Tip 12.1

*A structure's size is not necessarily the sum of the sizes of its members. This is so because
of various machine-dependent boundary alignment requirements (see Chapter 10).*

Common Programming Error 12.2

Assuming that the size of a structure is simply the sum of the sizes of its members.

Good Programming Practice 12.1

*Use the **sizeof** operator to determine the size of a structure.*

Good Programming Practice 12.2

*When using **malloc**, test for a **NULL** pointer return value. Print an error message if the
requested memory is not allocated.*

Common Programming Error 12.3

*Not returning dynamically allocated memory when it is no longer needed can cause the
system to run out of memory prematurely. This is sometimes called a "memory leak."*

Good Programming Practice 12.3

When memory that was dynamically allocated is no longer needed, use **free** *to return the memory to the system immediately.*

Common Programming Error 12.4

Freeing memory not allocated dynamically with **malloc**.

Common Programming Error 12.5

Referring to memory that has been freed.

12.4 Linked Lists

A *linked list* is a linear collection of self-referential structures, called *nodes,* connected by pointer *links*—hence, the term "linked" list. A linked list is accessed via a pointer to the first node of the list. Subsequent nodes are accessed via the link pointer member stored in each node. By convention, the link pointer in the last node of a list is set to **NULL** to mark the end of the list. Data are stored in a linked list dynamically—each node is created as necessary. A node can contain data of any type including other **struct**s. Stacks and queues are also linear data structures, and, as we will see, are constrained versions of linked lists. Trees are nonlinear data structures.

Lists of data can be stored in arrays, but linked lists provide several advantages. A linked list is appropriate when the number of data elements to be represented in the data structure at once is unpredictable. Linked lists are dynamic, so the length of a list can increase or decrease as necessary. The size of an array, however cannot be altered, because array memory is allocated at compile time. Arrays can become full. Linked lists become full when the system has insufficient memory to satisfy dynamic storage allocation requests.

Performance Tip 12.1

An array can be declared to contain more elements than the number of data items expected, but this can waste memory. Linked lists can provide better memory utilization in these situations.

Linked lists can be maintained in sorted order by inserting each new element at the proper point in the list.

Performance Tip 12.2

Insertion and deletion in a sorted array can be time consuming—all the elements following the inserted or deleted element must be shifted appropriately.

Performance Tip 12.3

The elements of an array are stored contiguously in memory. This allows immediate access to any array element because the address of any element can be calculated directly based on its position relative to the beginning of the array. Linked lists do not afford such immediate access to their elements.

Linked list nodes are normally not stored contiguously in memory. Logically, however, the nodes of a linked list appear to be contiguous. Figure 12.2 illustrates a linked list with several nodes.

Performance Tip 12.4

Using dynamic memory allocation (instead of arrays) for data structures that grow and shrink at execution time can save memory. Keep in mind, however, that the pointers take up space, and that dynamic memory allocation incurs the overhead of function calls.

The program of Fig. 12.3 (output shown in Fig 12.4) manipulates a list of characters. The program provides two options: 1) insert a character in the list in alphabetical order (function **insert**), and 2) delete a character from the list (function **delete**). This is a large and complex program. A detailed discussion of the program follows. Exercise 12.20 asks the student to implement a recursive function that prints a list backwards. Exercise 12.21 asks the student to implement a recursive function that searches a linked list for a particular data item.

The two primary functions of linked lists are **insert** and **delete**. Function **isEmpty** is called a *predicate function*—it does not alter the list in any way; rather it determines if the list is empty (i.e., the pointer to the first node of the list is **NULL**). If the list is empty, **1** is returned; otherwise, **0** is returned. Function **printList** prints the list.

Characters are inserted in the list in alphabetical order. Function **insert** receives the *address* of the list and a character to be inserted. The address of the list is necessary when a value is to be inserted at the start of the list. Providing the address of the list enables the list (i.e., the pointer to the first node of the list) to be modified via a call by reference. Since the list itself is a pointer (to its first element), passing the address of the list creates a *pointer to a pointer* (i.e., *double indirection*). This is a complex notion and requires careful programming. The steps for inserting a character in the list are as follows (see Fig. 12.5):

1) Create a node by calling **malloc**, assigning to **newPtr** the address of the allocated memory, assigning the character to be inserted to **newPtr->data**, and assigning **NULL** to **newPtr->nextPtr**.

2) Initialize **previousPtr** to **NULL**, and **currentPtr** to ***sPtr** (the pointer to the start of the list). Pointers **previousPtr** and **currentPtr** are used to store the locations of the node preceding the insertion point and the node after the insertion point.

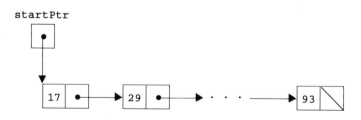

Fig. 12.2 A graphical representation of a linked list.

```
/* Operating and maintaining a list */
#include <stdio.h>
#include <stdlib.h>

struct listNode {  /* self-referential structure */
   char data;
   struct listNode *nextPtr;
};

typedef struct listNode LISTNODE;
typedef LISTNODE *LISTNODEPTR;

void insert(LISTNODEPTR *, char);
char delete(LISTNODEPTR *, char);
int isEmpty(LISTNODEPTR);
void printList(LISTNODEPTR);
void instructions(void);

main()
{
   LISTNODEPTR startPtr = NULL;
   int choice;
   char item;

   instructions();  /* display the menu */
   printf("? ");
   scanf("%d", &choice);

   while (choice != 3) {

      switch (choice) {
         case 1:
            printf("Enter a character: ");
            scanf("\n%c", &item);
            insert(&startPtr, item);
            printList(startPtr);
            break;
         case 2:
            if (!isEmpty(startPtr)) {
               printf("Enter character to be deleted: ");
               scanf("\n%c", &item);

               if (delete(&startPtr, item)) {
                  printf("%c deleted.\n", item);
                  printList(startPtr);
               }
               else
                  printf("%c not found.\n\n", item);
            }
            else
               printf("List is empty.\n\n");

            break;
```

Fig. 12.3   Inserting and deleting nodes in a list (part 1 of 3).

```
                     default:
                         printf("Invalid choice.\n\n");
                         instructions();
                         break;
                }

            printf("? ");
            scanf("%d", &choice);
        }

        printf("End of run.\n");
        return 0;
    }

    /* Print the instructions */
    void instructions(void)
    {
        printf("Enter your choice:\n"
                "   1 to insert an element into the list.\n"
                "   2 to delete an element from the list.\n"
                "   3 to end.\n");
    }

    /* Insert a new value into the list in sorted order */
    void insert(LISTNODEPTR *sPtr, char value)
    {
        LISTNODEPTR newPtr, previousPtr, currentPtr;

        newPtr = malloc(sizeof(LISTNODE));

        if (newPtr != NULL) {    /* is space available */
            newPtr->data = value;
            newPtr->nextPtr = NULL;

            previousPtr = NULL;
            currentPtr = *sPtr;

            while (currentPtr != NULL && value > currentPtr->data) {
                previousPtr = currentPtr;          /* walk to ...  */
                currentPtr = currentPtr->nextPtr;  /* ... next node */
            }

            if (previousPtr == NULL) {
                newPtr->nextPtr = *sPtr;
                *sPtr = newPtr;
            }
            else {
                previousPtr->nextPtr = newPtr;
                newPtr->nextPtr = currentPtr;
            }
        }
        else
            printf("%c not inserted. No memory available.\n", value);
    }
```

Fig. 12.3   Inserting and deleting nodes in a list (part 2 of 3).

```c
/* Delete a list element */
char delete(LISTNODEPTR *sPtr, char value)
{
    LISTNODEPTR previousPtr, currentPtr, tempPtr;

    if (value == (*sPtr)->data) {
        tempPtr = *sPtr;
        *sPtr = (*sPtr)->nextPtr;   /* de-thread the node */
        free(tempPtr);              /* free the de-threaded node */
        return value;
    }
    else {
        previousPtr = *sPtr;
        currentPtr = (*sPtr)->nextPtr;

        while (currentPtr != NULL && currentPtr->data != value) {
            previousPtr = currentPtr;          /* walk to ...    */
            currentPtr = currentPtr->nextPtr;  /* ... next node */
        }

        if (currentPtr != NULL) {
            tempPtr = currentPtr;
            previousPtr->nextPtr = currentPtr->nextPtr;
            free(tempPtr);
            return value;
        }
    }

    return '\0';
}

/* Return 1 if the list is empty, 0 otherwise */
int isEmpty(LISTNODEPTR sPtr)
{
    return sPtr == NULL;
}

/* Print the list */
void printList(LISTNODEPTR currentPtr)
{
    if (currentPtr == NULL)
        printf("List is empty.\n\n");
    else {
        printf("The list is:\n");

        while (currentPtr != NULL) {
            printf("%c --> ", currentPtr->data);
            currentPtr = currentPtr->nextPtr;
        }

        printf("NULL\n\n");
    }
}
```

Fig. 12.3   Inserting and deleting nodes in a list (part 3 of 3).

```
Enter your choice:
   1 to insert an element into the list.
   2 to delete an element from the list.
   3 to end.
? 1
Enter a character: B
The list is:
B --> NULL

? 1
Enter a character: A
The list is:
A --> B --> NULL

? 1
Enter a character: C
The list is:
A --> B --> C --> NULL

? 2
Enter character to be deleted: D
D not found.

? 2
Enter character to be deleted: B
B deleted.
The list is:
A --> C --> NULL

? 2
Enter character to be deleted: C
C deleted.
The list is:
A --> NULL

? 2
Enter character to be deleted: A
A deleted.
List is empty.

? 4
Invalid choice.

Enter your choice:
   1 to insert an element into the list.
   2 to delete an element from the list.
   3 to end.
? 3
End of run.
```

Fig. 12.4 Sample output for the program of Fig. 12.3.

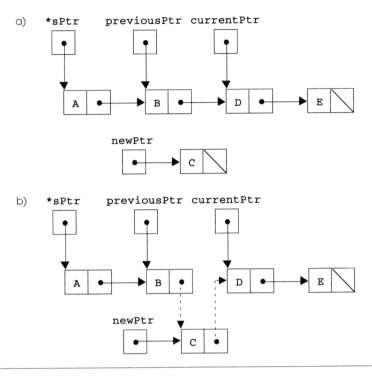

Fig. 12.5 Inserting a node in order in a list.

3) While **currentPtr** is not **NULL** and the value to be inserted is greater than **currentPtr->data**, assign **currentPtr** to **previousPtr** and advance **currentPtr** to the next node in the list. This locates the insertion point for the value in the list.

4) If **previousPtr** is NULL, the new node is inserted as the first node in the list. Assign ***sPtr** to **newPtr->nextPtr** (the new node link points to the former first node), and assign **newPtr** to ***sPtr** (***sPtr** points to the new node). If **previousPtr** is not NULL, the new node is inserted in place. Assign **newPtr** to **previousPtr->nextPtr** (the previous node points to the new node), and assign **currentPtr** to **newPtr->nextPtr** (the new node link points to the current node).

Good Programming Practice 12.4

Assign NULL to the link member of a new node. Pointers should be initialized before they are used.

Figure 12.5 illustrates the insertion of a node containing the character **'C'** into an ordered list. Part a) of the figure shows the list and the new node before the insertion. Part b) of the figure shows the result of inserting the new node. The reassigned pointers are dotted arrows.

Function **delete** receives the address of the pointer to the start of the list and a character to be deleted. The steps for deleting a character from the list are as follows:

1) If the character to be deleted matches the character in the first node of the list, assign ***sPtr** to **tempPtr** (**tempPtr** will be used to **free** the unneeded memory), assign **(*sPtr)->nextPtr** to ***sPtr** (***sPtr** now points to the second node in the list), **free** the memory pointed to by **tempPtr**, and return the character that was deleted.

2) Otherwise, initialize **previousPtr** with ***sPtr** and initialize **currentPtr** with **(*sPtr)->nextPtr**.

3) While **currentPtr** is not **NULL** and the value to be deleted is not equal to **currentPtr->data**, assign **currentPtr** to **previousPtr**, and assign **currentPtr->nextPtr** to **currentPtr**. This locates the character to be deleted if it is contained in the list.

4) If **currentPtr** is not **NULL**, assign **currentPtr** to **tempPtr**, assign **currentPtr->nextPtr** to **previousPtr->nextPtr**, free the node pointed to by **tempPtr**, and return the character that was deleted from the list. If **currentPtr** is **NULL**, return the **NULL** character (**'\0'**) to signify that the character to be deleted was not found in the list.

Figure 12.6 illustrates the deletion of a node from a linked list. Part a) of the figure shows the linked list after the preceding insert operation. Part b) shows the reassignment of the link element of **previousPtr** and the assignment of **currentPtr** to **tempPtr**. Pointer **tempPtr** is used to free the memory allocated to store **'C'**.

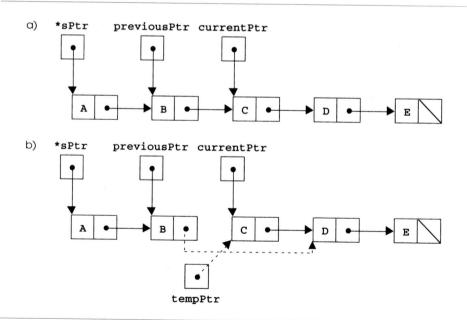

Fig. 12.6   Deleting a node from a list.

Function `printList` receives a pointer to the start of the list as an argument, and refers to the pointer as `currentPtr`. The function first determines if the list is empty. If so, `printList` prints `"The list is empty."` and terminates. Otherwise, it prints the data in the list. While `currentPtr` is not `NULL`, `currentPtr->data` is printed by the function, and `currentPtr->nextPtr` is assigned to `currentPtr`. Note that if the link in the last node of the list is not `NULL`, the printing algorithm will try to print past the end of the list, and an error will occur. The printing algorithm is identical for linked lists, stacks, and queues.

12.5 Stacks

A *stack* is a constrained version of a linked list. New nodes can be added to a stack and removed from a stack only at the top. For this reason, a stack is referred to as a *last-in, first-out (LIFO)* data structure. A stack is referenced via a pointer to the top element of the stack. The link member in the last node of the stack is set to `NULL` to indicate the bottom of the stack.

Figure 12.7 illustrates a stack with several nodes. Note that stacks and linked lists are represented identically. The difference between stacks and linked lists is that insertions and deletions may occur anywhere in a linked list, but only at the top of a stack.

Common Programming Error 12.6

Not setting the link in the bottom node of a stack to NULL.

The primary functions used to manipulate a stack are **push** and **pop**. Function **push** creates a new node and places it on top of the stack. Function **pop** removes a node from the top of the stack, frees the memory that was allocated to the popped node, and returns the popped value.

The program of Fig. 12.8 (output shown in Fig. 12.9) implements a simple stack of integers. The program provides three options: 1) push a value onto the stack (function **push**), 2) pop a value off the stack (function **pop**), and 3) terminate the program.

Function **push** places a new node at the top of the stack. The function consists of three steps:

1) Create a new node by calling `malloc`, assign the location of the allocated memory to `newPtr`, assign to `newPtr->data` the value to be placed on the stack, and assign `NULL` to `newPtr->nextPtr`.

2) Assign `*topPtr` (the stack top pointer) to `newPtr->nextPtr`—the link member of `newPtr` now points to the previous top node.

3) Assign `newPtr` to `*topPtr`—`*topPtr` now points to the new stack top.

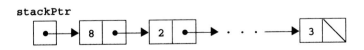

Fig. 12.7 Graphical representation of a stack.

```c
/* dynamic stack program */
#include <stdio.h>
#include <stdlib.h>

struct stackNode {   /* self-referential structure */
    int data;
    struct stackNode *nextPtr;
};

typedef struct stackNode STACKNODE;
typedef STACKNODE *STACKNODEPTR;

void push(STACKNODEPTR *, int);
int pop(STACKNODEPTR *);
int isEmpty(STACKNODEPTR);
void printStack(STACKNODEPTR);
void instructions(void);

main()
{
    STACKNODEPTR stackPtr = NULL;   /* points to the stack top */
    int choice, value;

    instructions();
    printf("? ");
    scanf("%d", &choice);

    while (choice != 3) {

        switch (choice) {
            case 1:        /* push value onto stack */
                printf("Enter an integer: ");
                scanf("%d", &value);
                push(&stackPtr, value);
                printStack(stackPtr);
                break;
            case 2:        /* pop value off stack */
                if (!isEmpty(stackPtr))
                    printf("The popped value is %d.\n",
                           pop(&stackPtr));

                printStack(stackPtr);
                break;
            default:
                printf("Invalid choice.\n\n");
                instructions();
                break;
        }

        printf("? ");
        scanf("%d", &choice);
    }

    printf("End of run.\n");
    return 0;
}
```

Fig. 12.8   A simple stack program (part 1 of 3).

```c
/* Print the instructions */
void instructions(void)
{
   printf("Enter choice:\n"
          "1 to push a value on the stack\n"
          "2 to pop a value off the stack\n"
          "3 to end program\n");
}

/* Insert a node at the stack top */
void push(STACKNODEPTR *topPtr, int info)
{
   STACKNODEPTR newPtr;

   newPtr = malloc(sizeof(STACKNODE));
   if (newPtr != NULL) {
      newPtr->data = info;
      newPtr->nextPtr = *topPtr;
      *topPtr = newPtr;
   }
   else
      printf("%d not inserted. No memory available.\n", info);
}

/* Remove a node from the stack top */
int pop(STACKNODEPTR *topPtr)
{
   STACKNODEPTR tempPtr;
   int popValue;

   tempPtr = *topPtr;
   popValue = (*topPtr)->data;
   *topPtr = (*topPtr)->nextPtr;
   free(tempPtr);
   return popValue;
}

/* Print the stack */
void printStack(STACKNODEPTR currentPtr)
{
   if (currentPtr == NULL)
      printf("The stack is empty.\n\n");
   else {
      printf("The stack is:\n");

      while (currentPtr != NULL) {
         printf("%d --> ", currentPtr->data);
         currentPtr = currentPtr->nextPtr;
      }

      printf("NULL\n\n");
   }
}
```

Fig. 12.8 A simple stack program (part 2 of 3).

```
/* Is the stack empty? */
int isEmpty(STACKNODEPTR topPtr)
{
   return topPtr == NULL;
}
```

Fig. 12.8 A simple stack program (part 3 of 3).

```
Enter choice:
1 to push a value on the stack
2 to pop a value off the stack
3 to end program
? 1
Enter an integer: 5
The stack is:
5 --> NULL

? 1
Enter an integer: 6
The stack is:
6 --> 5 --> NULL

? 1
Enter an integer: 4
The stack is:
4 --> 6 --> 5 --> NULL

? 2
The popped value is 4.
The stack is:
6 --> 5 --> NULL

? 2
The popped value is 6.
The stack is:
5 --> NULL

? 2
The popped value is 5.
The stack is empty.

? 2
The stack is empty.

? 4
Invalid choice.

Enter choice:
1 to push a value on the stack
2 to pop a value off the stack
3 to end program
? 3
End of run.
```

Fig. 12.9 Sample output from the program of Fig. 12.8.

Manipulations involving `*topPtr` change the value of **stackPtr** in **main**. Figure 12.10 illustrates function **push**. Part a) of the figure shows the stack and the new node before the **push** operation. The dotted arrows in part b) illustrate steps 2 and 3 of the **push** operation that enable the node containing **12** to become the new stack top.

Function **pop** removes a node from the top of the stack. Note that **main** determines if the stack is empty before calling **pop**. The **pop** operation consists of five steps:

1) Assign `*topPtr` to `tempPtr` (`tempPtr` will be used to free the unneeded memory).

2) Assign `(*topPtr)->data` to `popValue` (save the value stored in the top node).

3) Assign `(*topPtr)->nextPtr` to `*topPtr` (assign `*topPtr` the address of the new top node).

4) Free the memory pointed to by `tempPtr`.

5) Return `popValue` to the caller (**main** in the program of Fig. 12.8).

Figure 12.11 illustrates function **pop**. Part a) shows the stack after the previous **push** operation. Part b) shows `tempPtr` pointing to the first node of the stack and `topPtr` pointing to the second node of the stack. Function **free** is used to free the memory pointed to by `tempPtr`.

Stacks have many interesting applications. For example, whenever a function call is made, the called function must know how to return to its caller, so the return address is pushed onto a stack. If a series of function calls occurs, the successive return values are pushed onto the stack in last-in, first-out order so that each function can return to its caller. Stacks support recursive function calls in the same manner as conventional nonrecursive calls.

Stacks contain the space created for automatic variables on each invocation of a function. When the function returns to its caller, the space for that function's automatic variables is popped off the stack, and these variables no longer are known to the program.

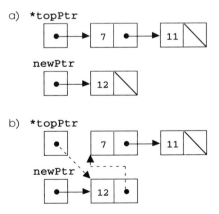

Fig. 12.10 The **push** operation.

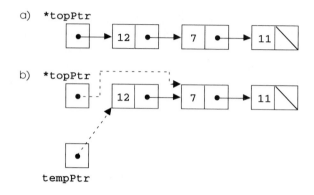

Fig. 12.11 The **pop** operation.

Stacks are used by compilers in the process of evaluating expressions and generating machine language code. The Exercises explore several applications of stacks.

12.6 Queues

Another common data structure is the *queue*. A queue is similar to a checkout line in a grocery store—the first person in line is serviced first, and other customers enter the line only at the end and wait to be serviced. Queue nodes are removed only from the *head* of the queue, and are inserted only at the *tail* of the queue. For this reason, a queue is referred to as a *first-in, first-out (FIFO)* data structure. The insert and remove operations are known as *enqueue* and *dequeue*.

Queues have many applications in computer systems. Most computers have only a single processor, so only one user at a time may be serviced. Entries for the other users are placed in a queue. Each entry gradually advances to the front of the queue as users receive service. The entry at the front of the queue is the next to receive service.

Queues are also used to support print spooling. A multiuser environment may have only a single printer. Many users may be generating outputs to be printed. If the printer is busy, other outputs may still be generated. These are "spooled" to disk where they wait in a queue until the printer becomes available.

Information packets also wait in queues in computer networks. Each time a packet arrives at a network node, it must be routed to the next node on the network along the path to the packet's final destination. The routing node routes one packet at a time, so additional packets are enqueued until the router can route them. Figure 12.12 illustrates a queue with several nodes. Note the pointers to the head of the queue and the tail of the queue.

Common Programming Error 12.7

*Not setting the link in the last node of a queue to **NULL**.*

The program of Fig. 12.13 (output in Fig. 12.14) performs queue manipulations. The program provides several options: insert a node in the queue (function **enqueue**), remove a node from the queue (function **dequeue**), and terminate the program.

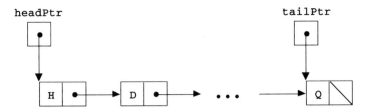

Fig. 12.12 A graphical representation of a queue.

```
/* Operating and maintaining a queue */

#include <stdio.h>
#include <stdlib.h>

struct queueNode {   /* self-referential structure */
   char data;
   struct queueNode *nextPtr;
};

typedef struct queueNode QUEUENODE;
typedef QUEUENODE *QUEUENODEPTR;

/* function prototypes */
void printQueue(QUEUENODEPTR);
int isEmpty(QUEUENODEPTR);
char dequeue(QUEUENODEPTR *, QUEUENODEPTR *);
void enqueue(QUEUENODEPTR *, QUEUENODEPTR *, char);
void instructions(void);

main()
{
   QUEUENODEPTR headPtr = NULL, tailPtr = NULL;
   int choice;
   char item;

   instructions();
   printf("? ");
   scanf("%d", &choice);

   while (choice != 3) {

      switch(choice) {

         case 1:
            printf("Enter a character: ");
            scanf("\n%c", &item);
            enqueue(&headPtr, &tailPtr, item);
            printQueue(headPtr);
            break;
```

Fig. 12.13 Processing a queue (part 1 of 3).

```
                case 2:
                    if (!isEmpty(headPtr)) {
                        item = dequeue(&headPtr, &tailPtr);
                        printf("%c has been dequeued.\n", item);
                    }

                    printQueue(headPtr);
                    break;

                default:
                    printf("Invalid choice.\n\n");
                    instructions();
                    break;
            }

        printf("? ");
        scanf("%d", &choice);
    }

    printf("End of run.\n");
    return 0;
}

void instructions(void)
{
    printf ("Enter your choice:"
            "   1 to add an item to the queue"
            "   2 to remove an item from the queue"
            "   3 to end");
}

void enqueue(QUEUENODEPTR *headPtr, QUEUENODEPTR *tailPtr,
             char value)
{
    QUEUENODEPTR newPtr;

    newPtr = malloc(sizeof(QUEUENODE));

    if (newPtr != NULL) {
        newPtr->data = value;
        newPtr->nextPtr = NULL;

        if (isEmpty(*headPtr))
            *headPtr = newPtr;
        else
            (*tailPtr)->nextPtr = newPtr;

        *tailPtr = newPtr;
    }
    else
        printf("%c not inserted. No memory available.\n", value);
}
```

Fig. 12.13 Processing a queue (part 2 of 3).

```c
char dequeue(QUEUENODEPTR *headPtr, QUEUENODEPTR *tailPtr)
{
    char value;
    QUEUENODEPTR tempPtr;

    value = (*headPtr)->data;
    tempPtr = *headPtr;
    *headPtr = (*headPtr)->nextPtr;

    if (*headPtr == NULL)
        *tailPtr = NULL;

    free(tempPtr);
    return value;
}

int isEmpty(QUEUENODEPTR headPtr)
{
    return headPtr == NULL;
}

void printQueue(QUEUENODEPTR currentPtr)
{
    if (currentPtr == NULL)
        printf("Queue is empty.\n\n");
    else {
        printf("The queue is:\n");

        while (currentPtr != NULL) {
            printf("%c --> ", currentPtr->data);
            currentPtr = currentPtr->nextPtr;
        }

        printf("NULL\n\n");
    }
}
```

Fig. 12.13 Processing a queue (part 3 of 3).

Function **enqueue** receives three arguments from **main**: the address of the pointer to the head of the queue, the address of the pointer to the tail of the queue, and the value to be inserted in the queue. The function consists of three steps:

1) To create a new node: Call **malloc**, assign the allocated memory location to **newPtr**, assign the value to be inserted in the queue to **newPtr->data**, and assign **NULL** to **newPtr->nextPtr**.

2) If the queue is empty, assign **newPtr** to ***headPtr**; otherwise, assign pointer **newPtr** to **(*tailPtr)->nextPtr**.

3) Assign **newPtr** to ***tailPtr**.

Figure 12.15 illustrates an **enqueue** operation. Part a) of the figure shows the queue and the new node before the operation. The dotted arrows in part b) illustrate steps 2 and 3 of function **enqueue** that enable a new node to be added to the end of a queue that is not empty.

```
Enter your choice:
   1 to add an item to the queue
   2 to remove an item from the queue
   3 to end
? 1
Enter a character: A
The queue is:
A --> NULL

? 1
Enter a character: B
The queue is:
A --> B --> NULL

? 1
Enter a character: C
The queue is:
A --> B --> C --> NULL

? 2
A has been dequeued.
The queue is:
B --> C --> NULL

? 2
B has been dequeued.
The queue is:
C --> NULL

? 2
C has been dequeued.
Queue is empty.

? 2
Queue is empty.

? 4
Invalid choice.

Enter your choice:
   1 to add an item to the queue
   2 to remove an item from the queue
   3 to end
? 3
End of run.
```

Fig. 12.14 Sample output from the program in Fig. 12.13.

Function **dequeue** receives the address of the pointer to the head of the queue and the address of the pointer to the head of the queue as arguments, and removes the first node from the queue. The **dequeue** operation consists of six steps:

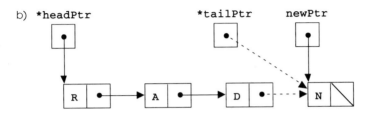

Fig. 12.15 A graphical representation of the **enqueue** operation.

1) Assign **(*headPtr)->data** to **value** (save the data).

2) Assign ***headPtr** to **tempPtr** (**tempPtr** is used to **free** the unneeded memory).

3) Assign **(*headPtr)->nextPtr** to ***headPtr** (***headPtr** now points to the new first node in the queue).

4) If ***headPtr** is **NULL**, assign **NULL** to ***tailPtr**.

5) Free the memory pointed to by **tempPtr**.

6) Return **value** to the caller (function **dequeue** is called from **main** in the program of Fig. 12.13).

Figure 12.16 illustrates function **dequeue**. Part a) shows the queue after the preceding **enqueue** operation. Part b) shows **tempPtr** pointing to the dequeued node, and **headPtr** pointing to the new first node of the queue. Function **free** is used to reclaim the memory pointed to by **tempPtr**.

12.7 Trees

Linked lists, stacks, and queues are *linear data structures*. A tree is a nonlinear, two-dimensional data structure with special properties. Tree nodes contain two or more links. This section discusses *binary trees* (Fig. 12.17)—trees whose nodes all contain two links (none, one, or both of which may be **NULL**). The *root node* is the first node in a tree. Each link in the root node refers to a *child*. The *left child* is the first node in the *left subtree*, and the *right child* is the first node in the *right subtree*. The children of a node are called *siblings*. A node with no children is called a *leaf node*. Computer scientists normally draw trees from the root node down—exactly the opposite of trees in nature.

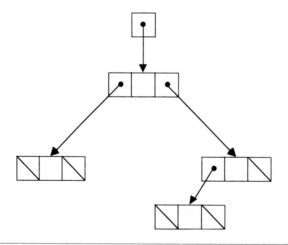

Fig. 12.16 A graphical representation of the **dequeue** operation.

Fig. 12.17 A graphical representation of a binary tree.

In this section, a special binary tree called a *binary search tree* is created. A binary search tree (with no duplicate node values) has the characteristic that the values in any left subtree are less than the value in its parent node, and the values in any right subtree are greater than the value in its parent node. Figure 12.18 illustrates a binary search tree with 12 values. Note that the shape of the binary search tree that corresponds to a set of data can vary, depending on the order in which the values are inserted into the tree.

Common Programming Error 12.8

Not setting to NULL the links in leaf nodes of a tree.

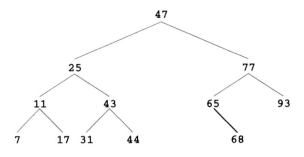

Fig. 12.18 A binary search tree.

The program of Fig. 12.19 (output shown in Fig. 12.20) creates a binary search tree and traverses it three ways—*inorder, preorder,* and *postorder.* The program generates 10 random numbers and inserts each in the tree, except that duplicate values are discarded.

The functions used in Fig. 12.19 to create a binary search tree and traverse the tree are recursive. Function **insertNode** receives the address of the tree and an integer to be stored in the tree as arguments. *A node can only be inserted as a leaf node in a binary search tree.* The steps for inserting a node in a binary search tree are as follows:

1) If ***treePtr** is **NULL**, create a new node. Call **malloc**, assign the allocated memory to ***treePtr**, assign to **(*treePtr)->data** the integer to be stored, assign to **(*treePtr)->leftPtr** and **(*treePtr)->rightPtr** the value **NULL**, and return control to the caller (either **main** or a previous call to **insertNode**).

2) If the value of ***treePtr** is not **NULL** and the value to be inserted is less than **(*treePtr)->data**, function **insertNode** is called with the address of **(*treePtr)->leftPtr**. Otherwise, function **insertNode** is called with the address of **(*treePtr)->rightPtr**. The recursive steps continue until a **NULL** pointer is found, then step 1) is executed to insert the new node.

Functions **inOrder**, **preOrder**, and **postOrder** each receive a tree (i.e., the pointer to the root node of the tree) and traverse the tree.

The steps for an **inOrder** traversal are:

1) Traverse the left subtree **inOrder**.

2) Process the value in the node.

3) Traverse the right subtree **inOrder**.

The value in a node is not processed until the values in its left subtree are processed. The **inOrder** traversal of the tree in Fig. 12.21 is:

        6 13 17 27 33 42 48

Note that the **inOrder** traversal of a binary search tree prints the node values in ascending order. The process of creating a binary search tree actually sorts the data—and thus this process is called the *binary tree sort.*

```c
/* Create a binary tree and traverse it
   preorder, inorder, and postorder */
#include <stdio.h>
#include <stdlib.h>
#include <time.h>

struct treeNode {
   struct treeNode *leftPtr;
   int data;
   struct treeNode *rightPtr;
};

typedef struct treeNode TREENODE;
typedef TREENODE *TREENODEPTR;

void insertNode(TREENODEPTR *, int);
void inOrder(TREENODEPTR);
void preOrder(TREENODEPTR);
void postOrder(TREENODEPTR);

main()
{
   int i, item;
   TREENODEPTR rootPtr = NULL;

   srand(time(NULL));

   /* attempt to insert 10 random values between 0 and 14
      in the tree */
   printf("The numbers being placed in the tree are:\n");

   for (i = 1; i <= 10; i++) {
      item = rand() % 15;
      printf("%3d", item);
      insertNode(&rootPtr, item);
   }

   /* traverse the tree preOrder */
   printf("\n\nThe preOrder traversal is:\n");
   preOrder(rootPtr);

   /* traverse the tree inOrder */
   printf("\n\nThe inOrder traversal is:\n");
   inOrder(rootPtr);

   /* traverse the tree postOrder */
   printf("\n\nThe postOrder traversal is:\n");
   postOrder(rootPtr);

   return 0;
}
```

Fig. 12.19 Creating and traversing a binary tree (part 1 of 2).

```c
void insertNode(TREENODEPTR *treePtr, int value)
{
   if (*treePtr == NULL) {    /* *treePtr is NULL */
      *treePtr = malloc(sizeof(TREENODE));

      if (*treePtr != NULL) {
         (*treePtr)->data = value;
         (*treePtr)->leftPtr = NULL;
         (*treePtr)->rightPtr = NULL;
      }
      else
         printf("%d not inserted. No memory available.\n",
                value);

   }
   else
      if (value < (*treePtr)->data)
         insertNode(&((*treePtr)->leftPtr), value);
      else
         if (value > (*treePtr)->data)
            insertNode(&((*treePtr)->rightPtr), value);
         else
            printf("dup");
}

void inOrder(TREENODEPTR treePtr)
{
   if (treePtr != NULL) {
      inOrder(treePtr->leftPtr);
      printf("%3d", treePtr->data);
      inOrder(treePtr->rightPtr);
   }
}

void preOrder(TREENODEPTR treePtr)
{
   if (treePtr != NULL) {
      printf("%3d", treePtr->data);
      preOrder(treePtr->leftPtr);
      preOrder(treePtr->rightPtr);
   }
}

void postOrder(TREENODEPTR treePtr)
{
   if (treePtr != NULL) {
      postOrder(treePtr->leftPtr);
      postOrder(treePtr->rightPtr);
      printf("%3d", treePtr->data);
   }
}
```

Fig. 12.19 Creating and traversing a binary tree (part 2 of 2).

```
The numbers being placed in the tree are:
   7  8  0  6 14  1  0dup 13   0dup  7dup

The preOrder traversal is:
   7  0  6  1  8 14 13

The inOrder traversal is:
   0  1  6  7  8 13 14

The postOrder traversal is:
   1  6  0 13 14  8  7
```

Fig. 12.20 Sample output from the program of Fig. 12.19.

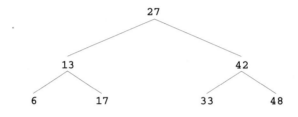

Fig. 12.21 A binary search tree.

The steps for a **preOrder** traversal are:

1) Process the value in the node.

2) Traverse the left subtree **preOrder**.

3) Traverse the right subtree **preOrder**.

The value in each node is processed as the node is visited. After the value in a given node is processed, the values in the left subtree are processed, then the values in the right subtree are processed. The **preOrder** traversal of the tree in Fig. 12.21 is:

```
27 13 6 17 42 33 48
```

The steps for a **postOrder** traversal are:

1) Traverse the left subtree **postOrder**.

2) Traverse the right subtree **postOrder**.

3) Process the value in the node.

The value in each node is not printed until the values of its children are printed. The **postOrder** traversal of the tree in Fig. 12.21 is:

```
6 17 13 33 48 42 27
```

The binary search tree facilitates duplicate elimination. As the tree is being created, an attempt to insert a duplicate value will be recognized because a duplicate will follow the same "go left" or "go right" decisions on each comparison as the original value did. Thus, the duplicate will eventually be compared with a node containing the same value. The duplicate value may simply be discarded at this point.

Searching a binary tree for a value that matches a key value is also fast. If the tree is tightly packed, then each level contains about twice as many elements as the previous level. So a binary search tree with n elements would have a maximum of $\log_2 n$ levels, and thus a maximum of $\log_2 n$ comparisons would have to be made either to find a match or to determine that no match exists. This means, for example, that when searching a (tightly packed) 1000-element binary search tree, no more than 10 comparisons need to be made because $2^{10} > 1000$. When searching a (tightly packed) 1,000,000 element binary search tree, no more than 20 comparisons need to be made because $2^{20} > 1,000,000$.

In the Exercises, algorithms are presented for several other binary tree operations such as deleting an item from a binary tree, printing a binary tree in a two-dimensional tree format, and performing a level order traversal of a binary tree. The level order traversal of a binary tree visits the nodes of the tree row-by-row starting at the root node level. On each level of the tree, the nodes are visited from left to right. Other binary tree exercises include allowing a binary search tree to contain duplicate values, inserting string values in a binary tree, and determining how many levels are contained in a binary tree.

Summary

- Self-referential structures contain members called links that point to structures of the same structure type.

- Self-referential structures enable many structures to be linked together in stacks, queues, lists, and trees.

- Dynamic memory allocation reserves a block of bytes in memory to store a data object during program execution.

- Function **malloc** takes the number of bytes to be allocated as an argument, and returns a **void** pointer to the allocated memory. Function **malloc** is usually used with the **sizeof** operator. The **sizeof** operator determines the size in bytes of the structure for which memory is being allocated.

- The **free** function deallocates memory.

- A linked list is a collection of data stored in a group of connected self-referential structures.

- A linked list is a dynamic data structure—the length of the list can increase or decrease as necessary.

- Linked lists can continue to grow while memory is available.

- Linked lists provide a mechanism for simple insertion and deletion of data by reassigning pointers.

- Stacks and queues are specialized versions of a linked list.

- New nodes are added to a stack and removed from a stack only at the top. For this reason, a stack is referred to as a last-in, first-out (LIFO) data structure.

- The link member in the last node of the stack is set to **NULL** to indicate the bottom of the stack.

- The two primary operations used to manipulate a stack are **push** and **pop**. The **push** operation creates a new node and places it on the top of the stack. The **pop** operation removes a node from the top of the stack, frees the memory that was allocated to the popped node, and returns the popped value.

- In a queue data structure, nodes are removed from the head and added to the tail. For this reason, a queue is referred to as a first-in, first-out (FIFO) data structure. The add and remove operations are known as **enqueue** and **dequeue**.

- Trees are more complex data structures than linked lists, queues, and stacks. Trees are two-dimensional data structures requiring two or more links per node.

- Binary trees contain two links per node.

- The root node is the first node in the tree.

- Each of the pointers in the root node refers to a child. The left child is the first node in the left subtree, and the right child is the first node in the right subtree. The children of a node are called siblings. If a node does not have any children it is called a leaf node.

- A binary search tree has the characteristic that the value in the left child of a node is less than the parent node value, and the value in the right child of a node is greater than or equal to the parent node value. If it can be determined that there are no duplicate data values, the value in the right child is simply greater than the parent node value.

- An inorder traversal of a binary tree traverses the left subtree inorder, processes the value in the node, and traverses the right subtree inorder. The value in a node is not processed until the values in its left subtree are processed.

- A preorder traversal processes the value in the node, traverses the left subtree preorder, and traverses the right subtree preorder. The value in each node is processed as the node is encountered.

- A postorder traversal traverses the left subtree postorder, traverses the right subtree postorder, and processes the value in the node. The value in each node is not processed until the values in both its subtrees are processed.

Terminology

binary search tree	deleting a node
binary tree	**dequeue**
binary tree sort	double indirection
child node	dynamic data structures
children	dynamic memory allocation

enqueue
FIFO (first-in, first-out)
`free`
head of a queue
inorder traversal
inserting a node
leaf node
left child
left subtree
LIFO (last-in, first-out)
linear data structure
linked list
`malloc` (allocate memory)
node
nonlinear data structure
`NULL` pointer
parent node
pointer to a pointer
`pop`

postorder traversal
predicate function
preorder traversal
`push`
queue
right child
right subtree
root node
self-referential structure
siblings
`sizeof`
stack
subtree
tail of a queue
top
traversal
tree
visit a node

Common Programming Errors

12.1   Not setting the link in the last node of a list to `NULL`.
12.2   Assuming that the size of a structure is simply the sum of the sizes of its members.
12.3   Not returning dynamically allocated memory when it is no longer needed can cause the system to run out of memory prematurely. This is sometimes called a "memory leak."
12.4   Freeing memory not allocated dynamically with `malloc`.
12.5   Referring to memory that has been freed.
12.6   Not setting the link in the bottom node of a stack to `NULL`.
12.7   Not setting the link in the last node of a queue to `NULL`.
12.8   Not setting to `NULL` the links in leaf nodes of a tree.

Good Programming Practices

12.1   Use the `sizeof` operator to determine the size of a structure.
12.2   When using `malloc`, test for a `NULL` pointer return value. Print an error message if the requested memory is not allocated.
12.3   When memory that was dynamically allocated is no longer needed, use `free` to return the memory to the system immediately.
12.4   Assign `NULL` to the link member of a new node. Pointers should be initialized before they are used.

Performance Tips

12.1   An array can be declared to contain more elements than the number of data items expected, but this can waste memory. Linked lists can provide better memory utilization in these situations.
12.2   Insertion and deletion in a sorted array can be time consuming—all the elements following the inserted or deleted element must be shifted appropriately.

12.3   The elements of an array are stored contiguously in memory. This allows immediate access to any array element because the address of any element can be calculated directly based on its position relative to the beginning of the array. Linked lists do not afford such immediate access to their elements.

12.4   Using dynamic memory allocation (instead of arrays) for data structures that grow and shrink at execution time can save memory. Keep in mind, however, that the pointers take up space, and that dynamic memory allocation incurs the overhead of function calls.

Portability Tip

12.1   A structure's size is not necessarily the sum of the sizes of its members. This is so because of various machine-dependent boundary alignment requirements (see Chapter 10).

Self-Review Exercises

12.1   Fill in the blanks in each of the following:
   a) A self-_____ structure is used to form dynamic data structures.
   b) Function _____ is used to dynamically allocate memory.
   c) A _____ is a specialized version of a linked list in which nodes can be inserted and deleted only from the start of the list.
   d) Functions that do not alter a linked list, but simply look at the list are referred to as _____.
   e) A queue is referred to as a _____ data structure because the first nodes inserted are the first nodes removed.
   f) The pointer to the next node in a linked list is referred to as a _____.
   g) Function _____ is used to reclaim dynamically allocated memory.
   h) A _____ is a specialized version of a linked list in which nodes can be inserted only at the start of the list and deleted only from the end of the list.
   i) A _____ is a nonlinear, two-dimensional data structure that contains nodes with two or more links.
   j) A stack is referred to as a _____ data structure because the last node inserted is the first node removed.
   k) The nodes of a _____ tree contain two link members.
   l) The first node of a tree is the _____ node.
   m) Each link in a tree node points to a _____ or _____ of that node.
   n) A tree node that has no children is called a _____ node.
   o) The three traversal algorithms for a binary tree are _____, _____, and _____.

12.2   What are the differences between a linked list and a stack?

12.3   What are the differences between a stack and a queue?

12.4   Write a statement or set of statements to accomplish each of the following. Assume that all the manipulations occur in **main** (therefore, no addresses of pointer variables are needed), and assume the following definitions:

```
struct gradeNode {
    char lastName[20];
    float grade;
    struct gradeNode *nextPtr;
};
```

```
typedef struct gradeNode GRADENODE;
typedef GRADENODE *GRADENODEPTR;
```

a) Create a pointer to the start of the list called **startPtr**. The list is empty.

b) Create a new node of type **GRADENODE** that is pointed to by pointer **newPtr** of type **GRADENODEPTR**. Assign the string **"Jones"** to member **lastName** and the value **91.5** to member **grade** (use **strcpy**). Provide any necessary declarations and statements.

c) Assume that the list pointed to by **startPtr** currently consists of 2 nodes—one containing **"Jones"** and one containing **"Smith"**. The nodes are in alphabetical order. Provide the statements necessary to insert in order nodes containing the following data for **lastName** and **grade**:

```
"Adams"      85.0
"Thompson"   73.5
"Pritchard"  66.5
```

Use pointers **previousPtr**, **currentPtr**, and **newPtr** to perform the insertions. State what **previousPtr** and **currentPtr** point to before each insertion. Assume that **newPtr** always points to the new node, and that the new node has already been assigned the data.

d) Write a **while** loop that prints the data in each node of the list. Use pointer **currentPtr** to move along the list.

e) Write a **while** loop that deletes all the nodes in the list and frees the memory associated with each node. Use pointer **currentPtr** and pointer **tempPtr** to walk along the list and free memory, respectively.

12.5   Manually provide the inorder, preorder, and postorder traversals of the binary search tree of Fig. 12.22.

Answers to Self-Review Exercises

12.1   a) referential. b) **malloc**. c) stack. d) predicates. e) FIFO. f) link. g) **free**. h) queue. i) tree. j) LIFO. k) binary. l) root. m) child or subtree. n) leaf. o) inorder, preorder, postorder.

12.2   It is possible to insert a node anywhere in a linked list, and remove a node from anywhere in a linked list. However, nodes in a stack may only be inserted at the top of the stack and removed from the top of a stack.

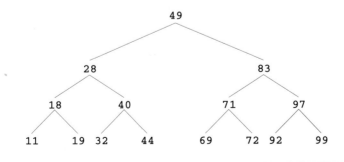

Fig. 12.22 A 15-node binary search tree.

12.3   A queue has pointers to both its head and its tail so that nodes may be inserted at the tail and deleted from the head. A stack has a single pointer to the top of the stack where both insertion and deletion of nodes is performed.

12.4   a)   `GRADENODEPTR startPtr = NULL;`

              b)   `GRADENODEPTR newPtr;`
                    `newPtr = malloc(sizeof(GRADENODE));`
                    `strcpy(newPtr->lastName, "Jones");`
                    `newPtr->grade = 91.5;`
                    `newPtr->nextPtr = NULL;`

              c)   To insert `"Adams"`:
                    `previousPtr` is NULL, `currentPtr` points to the first element in the list.
                    `newPtr->nextPtr = currentPtr;`
                    `startPtr = newPtr;`

                    To insert `"Thompson"`:
                    `previousPtr` points to the last element in the list (containing `"Smith"`)
                    `currentPtr` is NULL.
                    `newPtr->nextPtr = currentPtr;`
                    `previousPtr->nextPtr = newPtr;`

                    To insert `"Pritchard"`:
                    `previousPtr` points to the node containing `"Jones"`
                    `currentPtr` points to the node containing `"Smith"`.
                    `newPtr->nextPtr = currentPtr;`
                    `previousPtr->nextPtr = newPtr;`

              d)

```
currentPtr = startPtr;
while (currentPtr != NULL) {
    printf("Lastname = %s\nGrade = %6.2f\n",
            currentPtr->lastName, currentPtr->grade);
    currentPtr = currentPtr->nextPtr;
}
```

              e)

```
currentPtr = startPtr;
while (currentPtr != NULL) {
    tempPtr = currentPtr;
    currentPtr = currentPtr->nextPtr;
    free(tempPtr);
}
startPtr = NULL;
```

12.5   The inorder traversal is:

         `11 18 19 28 32 40 44 49 69 71 72 83 92 97 99`

The preorder traversal is:

         `49 28 18 11 19 40 32 44 83 71 69 72 97 92 99`

The postorder traversal is:

         `11 19 18 32 44 40 28 69 72 71 92 99 97 83 49`

Exercises

12.6   Write a program that concatenates two linked lists of characters. The program should include function `concatenate` that takes pointers to both lists as arguments and concatenates the second list to the first list.

12.7   Write a program that merges two ordered lists of integers into a single ordered list of integers. Function **merge** should receive pointers to the first node of each of the lists to be merged, and should return a pointer to the first node of the merged list.

12.8   Write a program that inserts 25 random integers from 0 to 100 in order in a linked list. The program should calculate the sum of the elements, and the floating-point average of the elements.

12.9   Write a program that creates a linked list of 10 characters, then creates a copy of the list in reverse order.

12.10   Write a program that inputs a line of text and uses a stack to print the line reversed.

12.11   Write a program that uses a stack to determine if a string is a palindrome (i.e., the string is spelled identically backward and forward). The program should ignore spaces and punctuation.

12.12   Stacks are used by compilers to help in the process of evaluating expressions and generating machine language code. In this and the next exercise, we investigate how compilers evaluate arithmetic expressions consisting only of constants, operators, and parentheses.

Humans generally write expressions like **3 + 4** and **7 / 9** in which the operator (**+** or **/** here) is written between its operands—this is called *infix notation*. Computers "prefer" *postfix notation* in which the operator is written to the right of its two operands. The preceding infix expressions would appear in postfix notation as **3 4 +** and **7 9 /**, respectively.

To evaluate a complex infix expression, a compiler would first convert the expression to postfix notation, and then evaluate the postfix version of the expression. Each of these algorithms requires only a single left-to-right pass of the expression. Each algorithm uses a stack in support of its operation, and in each the stack is used for a different purpose.

In this exercise, you will write a C version of the infix-to-postfix conversion algorithm. In the next exercise, you will write a C version of the postfix expression evaluation algorithm.

Write a program that converts an ordinary infix arithmetic expression (assume a valid expression is entered) with single digit integers such as

       (6 + 2) * 5 - 8 / 4

to a postfix expression. The postfix version of the preceding infix expression is

       6 2 + 5 * 8 4 / -

The program should read the expression into character array **infix**, and use modified versions of the stack functions implemented in this chapter to help create the postfix expression in character array **postfix**. The algorithm for creating a postfix expression is as follows:

  1) Push a left parenthesis **' ('** on the stack.
  2) Append a right parenthesis **') '** to the end of **infix**.
  3) While the stack is not empty, read **infix** from left to right and do the following:
      If the current character in **infix** is a digit, copy it to the next element of **postfix**.
      If the current character in **infix** is a left parenthesis, push it on the stack.
      If the current character in **infix** is an operator,
           Pop operators (if there are any) at the top of the stack while they have equal or
              higher precedence than the current operator, and insert the popped
              operators in **postfix**.
      Push the current character in **infix** on the stack.
      If the current character in **infix** is a right parenthesis
           Pop operators from the top of the stack and insert them in **postfix** until a left
              parenthesis is at the top of the stack.
           Pop (and discard) the left parenthesis from the stack.

The following arithmetic operations are allowed in an expression:

+	addition
–	subtraction
*	multiplication
/	division
^	exponentiation
%	modulus

The stack should be maintained with the following declarations:

```
struct stackNode {
   char data;
   struct stackNode *nextPtr;
};

typedef struct stackNode STACKNODE;
typedef STACKNODE *STACKNODEPTR;
```

The program should consist of **main** and eight other functions with the following function headers:

void convertToPostfix(char infix[], char postfix[])
  Convert the infix expression to postfix notation.

int isOperator(char c)
  Determine if **c** is an operator.

int precedence(char operator1, char operator2)
  Determine if the precedence of **operator1** is less than, equal to, or greater than the precedence of **operator2**. The function returns -1, 0, and 1, respectively.

void push(STACKNODEPTR *topPtr, char value)
  Push a value on the stack.

char pop(STACKNODEPTR *topPtr)
  Pop a value off the stack.

char stackTop(STACKNODEPTR topPtr)
  Return the top value of the stack without popping the stack.

int isEmpty(STACKNODEPTR topPtr)
  Determine if the stack is empty.

void printStack(STACKNODEPTR topPtr)
  Print the stack.

12.13   Write a program that evaluates a postfix expression (assume it is valid) such as

        6 2 + 5 * 8 4 / -

The program should read a postfix expression consisting of digits and operators into a character array. Using modified versions of the stack functions implemented earlier in this chapter, the program should scan the expression and evaluate it. The algorithm is as follows:

1) Append the **NULL** character (**'\0'**) to the end of the postfix expression. When the **NULL** character is encountered, no further processing is necessary.

2) While **'\0'** has not been encountered, read the expression from left to right.
   If the current character is a digit,
       push its integer value on the stack (the integer value of a digit character is its value in the computer's character set minus the value of **'0'** in the computer's character set).
   Otherwise, if the current character is an operator,
       Pop the two top elements of the stack into variables **x** and **y**.
       Calculate **y operator x**.
       Push the result of the calculation on the stack.

3) When the **NULL** character is encountered in the expression, pop the top value of the stack. This is the result of the postfix expression.

Note: In 2) above, if the operator is ' **/** ', the top of the stack is **2**, and the next element in the stack is **8**, then pop **2** into **x**, pop **8** into **y**, evaluate **8 / 2**, and push the result, **4**, back on the stack. This note also applies to operator ' **-** '. The arithmetic operations allowed in an expression are:

+	addition
-	subtraction
*	multiplication
/	division
^	exponentiation
%	modulus

The stack should be maintained with the following declarations:

```
struct stackNode {
   int data;
   struct stackNode *nextPtr;
};

typedef struct stackNode STACKNODE;
typedef STACKNODE *STACKNODEPTR;
```

The program should consist of **main** and six other functions with the following function headers:

int evaluatePostfixExpression(char *expr)
Evaluate the postfix expression.

int calculate(int op1, int op2, char operator)
Evaluate the expression **op1 operator op2.**

void push(STACKNODEPTR *topPtr, int value)
Push a value on the stack.

int pop(STACKNODEPTR *topPtr)
Pop a value off the stack.

int isEmpty(STACKNODEPTR topPtr)
Determine if the stack is empty.

void printStack(STACKNODEPTR topPtr)
Print the stack.

12.14   Modify tne postfix evaluator program of Exercise 12.13 so that it can process integer operands larger than 9.

12.15   *(Supermarket simulation)* Write a program that simulates a check-out line at a supermarket. The line is a queue. Customers arrive in random integer intervals of 1 to 4 minutes. Also, each customer is serviced in random integer intervals of 1 to 4 minutes. Obviously, the rates need to be balanced. If the average arrival rate is larger than the average service rate, the queue will grow infinitely. Even with balanced rates, randomness can still cause long lines. Run the supermarket simulation for a 12-hour day (720 minutes) using the following algorithm:

1) Choose a random integer between 1 and 4 to determine the minute at which the first customer arrives.

2) At the first customer's arrival time:
Determine customer's service time (random integer from 1 to 4);
Begin servicing the customer;
Schedule the arrival time of the next customer (random integer 1 to 4 added to the current time).

3) For each minute of the day:
   If the next customer arrives,
      Enqueue the customer;
      Schedule the arrival time of the next customer;
      If service was completed for the last customer;
         Say so
         Dequeue next customer to be serviced
         Determine customer's service completion time (random integer from 1 to 4 added to the current time).

Now run your simulation for 720 minutes and answer each of the following:

a) What is the maximum number of customers in the queue at any time?
b) What is the longest wait any one customer experienced?
c) What happens if the arrival interval is changed from 1 to 4 minutes to 1 to 3 minutes?

12.16 Modify the program of Fig. 12.19 to allow the binary tree to contain duplicate values.

12.17 Write a program based on the program of Fig. 12.19 that inputs a line of text, tokenizes the sentence into separate words, inserts the words in a binary search tree, and prints the inorder, preorder, and postorder traversals of the tree.

Hint: Read the line of text into an array. Use **strtok** to tokenize the text. When a token is found, create a new node for the tree, assign the pointer returned by **strtok** to member **string** of the new node, and insert the node in the tree.

12.18 In this chapter, we saw that duplicate elimination is straightforward when creating a binary search tree. Describe how you would perform duplicate elimination using only a single subscripted array. Compare the performance of array-based duplicate elimination with the performance of binary-search-tree-based duplicate elimination.

12.19 Write a function **depth** that receives a binary tree and determines how many levels it has.

12.20 (*Recursively print a list backwards*) Write a function **printListBackwards** that recursively outputs the items in a list in reverse order. Use your function in a test program that creates a sorted list of integers and prints the list in reverse order.

12.21 (*Recursively search a list*) Write a function **searchList** that recursively searches a linked list for a specified value. The function should return a pointer to the value if it is found; otherwise, **NULL** should be returned. Use your function in a test program that creates a list of integers. The program should prompt the user for a value to locate in the list.

12.22 (*Binary tree delete*) In this exercise, we discuss deleting items from binary search trees. The deletion algorithm is not as straightforward as the insertion algorithm. There are three cases that are encountered when deleting an item—the item is contained in a leaf node (i.e., it has no children), the item is contained in a node that has one child, or the item is contained in a node that has two children.

If the item to be deleted is contained in a leaf node, the node is deleted and the pointer in the parent node is set to **NULL**.

If the item to be deleted is contained in a node with one child, the pointer in the parent node is set to point to the child node and the node containing the data item is deleted. This causes the child node to take the place of the deleted node in the tree.

The last case is the most difficult. When a node with two children is deleted, another node in the tree must take its place. However, the pointer in the parent node cannot simply be assigned to point to one of the children of the node to be deleted. In most cases, the resulting binary search tree would not adhere to the following characteristic of binary search trees: *The values in any left sub tree are less than the value in the parent node, and the values in any right subtree are greater than the value in the parent node.*

Which node is used as a *replacement node* to maintain this characteristic? Either the node containing the largest value in the tree less than the value in the node being deleted, or the node containing the smallest value in the tree greater than the value in the node being deleted. Let us consider the node with the smaller value. In a binary search tree, the largest value less than a parent's value is located in the left subtree of the parent node and is guaranteed to be contained in the rightmost node of the subtree. This node is located by walking down the left subtree to the right until the pointer to the right child of the current node is **NULL**. We are now pointing to the replacement node which is either a leaf node or a node with one child to its left. If the replacement node is a leaf node, the steps to perform the deletion are as follows:

1) Store the pointer to the node to be deleted in a temporary pointer variable (this pointer is used to free the dynamically allocated memory)
2) Set the pointer in the parent of the node being deleted to point to the replacement node
3) Set the pointer in the parent of the replacement node to **NULL**
4) Set the pointer to the right subtree in the replacement node to point to the right subtree of the node to be deleted
5) Delete the node to which the temporary pointer variable points.

The deletion steps for a replacement node with a left child are similar to those for a replacement node with no children, but the algorithm also must move the child in to the replacement node's position in the tree. If the replacement node is a node with a left child, the steps to perform the deletion are as follows:

1) Store the pointer to the node to be deleted in a temporary pointer variable
2) Set the pointer in the parent of the node being deleted to point to the replacement node
3) Set the pointer in the parent of the replacement node to point to the left child of the replacement node
4) Set the pointer to the right subtree in the replacement node to point to the right subtree of the node to be deleted
5) Delete the node to which the temporary pointer variable points.

Write function **deleteNode** which takes as its arguments a pointer to the root node of the tree and the value to be deleted. The function should locate in the tree the node containing the value to be deleted and use the algorithms discussed here to delete the node. If the value is not found in the tree, the function should print a message that indicates whether or not the value is deleted. Modify the program of Fig. 12.19 to use this function. After deleting an item, call the **inOrder**, **preOrder**, and **postOrder** traversal functions to confirm that the delete operation was performed correctly.

12.23   (*Binary tree search*) Write function **binaryTreeSearch** that attempts to locate a specified value in a binary search tree. The function should take as arguments a pointer to the root node of the binary tree and a search key to be located. If the node containing the search key is found, the function should return a pointer to that node; otherwise, the function should return a **NULL** pointer.

12.24   (*Level order binary tree traversal*) The program of Fig. 12.19 illustrated three recursive methods of traversing a binary tree—inorder traversal, preorder traversal, and postorder traversal. This exercise presents the *level order traversal* of a binary tree in which the node values are printed level-by-level starting at the root node level. The nodes on each level are printed from left to right. The level order traversal is not a recursive algorithm. It uses the queue data structure to control the output of the nodes. The algorithm is as follows:

1) Insert the root node in the queue
2) While there are nodes left in the queue,

    Get the next node in the queue

    Print the node's value

    If the pointer to the left child of the node is not **NULL**

        Insert the left child node in the queue

    If the pointer to the right child of the node is not **NULL**

        Insert the right child node in the queue.

Write function **levelOrder** to perform a level order traversal of a binary tree. The function should take as an argument a pointer to the root node of the binary tree. Modify the program of Fig 12.19 to use this function. Compare the output from this function to the outputs of the other traversal algorithms to see that it worked correctly. (Note: You will also need to modify and incorporate the queue processing functions of Fig. 12.13 in this program.)

12.25 (*Printing trees*) Write a recursive function **outputTree** to display a binary tree on the screen. The function should output the tree row-by-row with the top of the tree at the left of the screen and the bottom of the tree toward the right of the screen. Each row is output vertically. For example, the binary tree illustrated in Fig. 12.22 is output as follows:

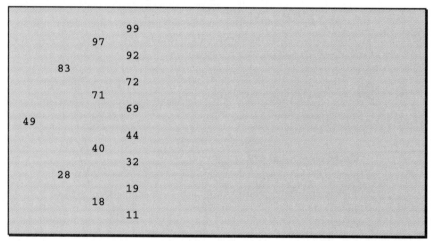

Note the rightmost leaf node appears at the top of the output in the rightmost column and the root node appears at the left of the output. Each column of output starts five spaces to the right of the previous column. Function **outputTree** should receive as arguments a pointer to the root node of the tree and an integer **totalSpaces** representing the number of spaces preceding the value to be output (this variable should start at zero so the root node is output at the left of the screen). The function uses a modified inorder traversal to output the tree—it starts at the rightmost node in the tree and works back to the left. The algorithm is as follows:

While the pointer to the current node is not **NULL**

    Recursively call **outputTree** with the right subtree of the current node and **totalSpaces** + 5

    Use a **for** structure to count from 1 to **totalSpaces** and output spaces

    Output the value in the current node

    Set the pointer to the current node to point to the left subtree of the current node

    Increment **totalSpaces** by 5.

Special Section: Building Your Own Compiler

In Exercises 7.18 and 7.19, we introduced Simpletron Machine Language (SML) and created the Simpletron computer simulator to execute programs written in SML. In this section, we build a compiler that converts programs written in a high-level programming language to SML. This section "ties" together the entire programming process. We will write programs in this new high-level language, compile the programs on the compiler we build, and run the programs on the simulator we built in Exercise 7.19.

12.26   (*The Simple Language*) Before we begin building the compiler, we discuss a simple, yet powerful, high-level language similar to early versions of the popular language BASIC. We call the language *Simple*. Every Simple *statement* consists of a *line number* and a Simple *instruction*. Line numbers must appear in ascending order. Each instruction begins with one of the following Simple *commands*: `rem`, `input`, `let`, `print`, `goto`, `if/goto`, or `end` (see Fig. 12.23). All commands except `end` can be used repeatedly. Simple evaluates only integer expressions using the +, -, *, and / operators. These operators have the same precedence as in C. Parentheses can be used to change the order of evaluation of an expression.

Our Simple compiler recognizes only lowercase letters. All characters in a Simple file should be lowercase (uppercase letters result in a syntax error unless they appear in a `rem` statement in which case they are ignored). A *variable name* is a single letter. Simple does not allow descriptive variable names, so variables should be explained in remarks to indicate their use in the program. Simple uses only integer variables. Simple does not have variable declarations—merely mentioning a variable name in a program causes the variable to be declared and initialized to zero automatically. The syntax of Simple does not allow string manipulation (reading a string, writing a string, comparing strings, etc.). If a string is encountered in a Simple program (after a command

Command	Example statement	Description
rem	50 rem this is a remark	Any text following the command **rem** is for documentation purposes only and is ignored by the compiler.
input	30 input x	Display a question mark to prompt the user to enter an integer. Read that integer from the keyboard and store the integer in **x**.
let	80 let u = 4 * (j - 56)	Assign **u** the value of **4 * (j - 56)**. Note that an arbitrarily complex expression can appear to the right of the equal sign.
print	10 print w	Display the value of **w**.
goto	70 goto 45	Transfer program control to line **45**.
if/goto	35 if i == z goto 80	Compare **i** and **z** for equality and transfer program control to line **80** if the condition is true; otherwise, continue execution with the next statement.
end	99 end	Terminate program execution.

Fig. 12.23 Simple commands.

other than **rem**), the compiler generates a syntax error. Our compiler will assume that Simple programs are entered correctly. Exercise 12.29 asks the student to modify the compiler to perform syntax error checking.

Simple uses the conditional **if/goto** statement and the unconditional **goto** statement to alter the flow of control during program execution. If the condition in the **if/goto** statement is true, control is transferred to a specific line of the program. The following relational and equality operators are valid in an **if/goto** statement: <, >, <=, >=, ==, or !=. The precedence of these operators is the same as in C.

Let us now consider several Simple programs that demonstrate Simple's features. The first program (Fig. 12.24) reads two integers from the keyboard, stores the values in variables **a** and **b**, and computes and prints their sum (stored in variable **c**).

The program of Fig. 12.25 determines and prints the larger of two integers. The integers are input from the keyboard and stored in **s** and **t**. The **if/goto** statement tests the condition **s >= t**. If the condition is true, control is transferred to line **90** and **s** is output; otherwise, **t** is output and control is transferred to the **end** statement in line **99** where the program terminates.

```
10 rem    determine and print the sum of two integers
15 rem
20 rem    input the two integers
30 input a
40 input b
45 rem
50 rem    add integers and store result in c
60 let c = a + b
65 rem
70 rem    print the result
80 print c
90 rem    terminate program execution
99 end
```

Fig. 12.24 Determine the sum of two integers.

```
10 rem    determine the larger of two integers
20 input s
30 input t
32 rem
35 rem    test if s >= t
40 if s >= t goto 90
45 rem
50 rem    t is greater than s, so print t
60 print t
70 goto 99
75 rem
80 rem    s is greater than or equal to t, so print s
90 print s
99 end
```

Fig. 12.25 Find the larger of two integers.

Simple does not provide a repetition structure (such as C's **for**, **while**, or **do/while**). However, Simple can simulate each of C's repetition structures using the **if/goto** and **goto** statements. Figure 12.26 uses a sentinel-controlled loop to calculate the squares of several integers. Each integer is input from the keyboard and stored in variable **j**. If the value entered is the sentinel **-9999**, control is transferred to line **99** where the program terminates. Otherwise, **k** is assigned the square of **j**, **k** is output to the screen, and control is passed to line **20** where the next integer is input.

Using the sample programs of Fig. 12.24, Fig. 12.25, and Fig. 12.26 as your guide, write a Simple program to accomplish each of the following:

    a) Input three integers, determine their average, and print the result.

    b) Use a sentinel-controlled loop to input 10 integers and compute and print their sum.

    c) Use a counter-controlled loop to input 7 integers, some positive and some negative, and compute and print their average.

    d) Input a series of integers and determine and print the largest. The first integer input indicates how many numbers should be processed.

    e) Input 10 integers and print the smallest.

    f) Calculate and print the sum of the even integers from 2 to 30.

    g) Calculate and print the product of the odd integers from 1 to 9.

12.27   *(Building A Compiler; Prerequisite: Complete Exercises 7.18, 7.19, 12.12, 12.13, and 12.26)* Now that the Simple language has been presented (Exercise 12.26), we discuss how to build our Simple compiler. First, we consider the process by which a Simple program is converted to SML and executed by the Simpletron simulator (see Fig. 12.27). A file containing a Simple program is read by the compiler and converted to SML code. The SML code is output to a file on disk, in which SML instructions appear one per line. The SML file is then loaded into the Simpletron simulator, and the results are sent to a file on disk and to the screen. Note that the Simpletron program developed in Exercise 7.19 took its input from the keyboard. It must be modified to read from a file so it can run the programs produced by our compiler.

The compiler performs two *passes* of the Simple program to convert it to SML. The first pass constructs a *symbol table* in which every *line number*, *variable name* and *constant* of the Simple program is stored with its type and corresponding location in the final SML code (the symbol table is discussed in detail below). The first pass also produces the corresponding SML instruction(s) for each Simple statement. As we will see, if the Simple program contains statements that

```
10 rem    calculate the squares of several integers
20 input j
23 rem
25 rem    test for sentinel value
30 if j == -9999 goto 99
33 rem
35 rem    calculate square of j and assign result to k
40 let k = j * j
50 print k
53 rem
55 rem    loop to get next j
60 goto 20
99 end
```

Fig. 12.26 Calculate the squares of several integers.

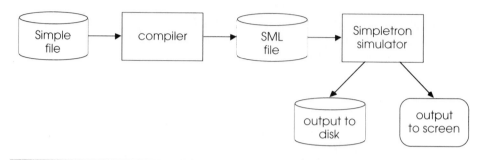

Fig. 12.27 Writing, compiling, and executing a Simple language program.

transfer control to a line later in the program, the first pass results in an SML program containing some incomplete instructions. The second pass of the compiler locates and completes the unfinished instructions, and outputs the SML program to a file.

First Pass

The compiler begins by reading one statement of the Simple program into memory. The line must be separated into its individual *tokens* (i.e., "pieces" of a statement) for processing and compilation (standard library function **strtok** can be used to facilitate this task). Recall that every statement begins with a line number followed by a command. As the compiler breaks a statement into tokens, if the token is a line number, a variable, or a constant, it is placed in the symbol table. A line number is placed in the symbol table only if it is the first token in a statement. The **symbolTable** is an array of **tableEntry** structures representing each symbol in the program. There is no restriction on the number of symbols that can appear in the program. Therefore, the **symbolTable** for a particular program could be large. Make the **symbolTable** a 100-element array for now. You can increase or decrease its size once the program is working.

    The **tableEntry** structure definition is as follows:

```
struct tableEntry {
    int symbol;
    char type;       /* 'C', 'L', or 'V' */
    int location;    /* 00 to 99 */
}
```

Each **tableEntry** structure contains three members. Member **symbol** is an integer containing the ASCII representation of a variable (remember that variable names are single characters), a line number, or a constant. Member **type** is one of the following characters indicating the symbol's type: **'C'** for constant, **'L'** for line number, or **'V'** for variable. Member **location** contains the Simpletron memory location (**00** to **99**) to which the symbol refers. Simpletron memory is an array of 100 integers in which SML instructions and data are stored. For a line number, the location is the element in the Simpletron memory array at which the SML instructions for the Simple statement begin. For a variable or constant, the location is the element in the Simpletron memory array in which the variable or constant is stored. Variables and constants are allocated from the end of Simpletron's memory backwards. The first variable or constant is stored in location at **99**, the next in location at **98**, etc.

    The symbol table plays an integral part in converting Simple programs to SML. We learned in Chapter 7 that an SML instruction is a four-digit integer comprised of two parts—the *operation code* and the *operand*. The operation code is determined by commands in Simple. For example, the simple command **input** corresponds to SML operation code **10** (read), and the

Simple command **print** corresponds to SML operation code **11**(write). The operand is a memory location containing the data on which the operation code performs its task (e.g., operation code **10** reads a value from the keyboard and stores it in the memory location specified by the operand). The compiler searches **symbolTable** to determine the Simpletron memory location for each symbol so the corresponding location can be used to complete the SML instructions.

The compilation of each Simple statement is based on its command. For example, after the line number in a **rem** statement is inserted in the symbol table, the remainder of the statement is ignored by the compiler, because a remark is for documentation purposes only. The **input**, **print**, **goto** and **end** statements correspond to the SML *read*, *write*, *branch* (to a specific location) and *halt* instructions. Statements containing these Simple commands are converted directly to SML (note that a **goto** statement may contain an unresolved reference if the specified line number refers to a statement further into the Simple program file; this is sometimes called a forward reference).

When a **goto** statement is compiled with an unresolved reference, the SML instruction must be *flagged* to indicate that the second pass of the compiler must complete the instruction. The flags are stored in 100-element array **flags** of type **int** in which each element is initialized to **-1**. If the memory location to which a line number in the Simple program refers is not yet known (i.e., it is not in the symbol table), the line number is stored in array **flags** in the element with the same subscript as the incomplete instruction. The operand of the incomplete instruction is set to **00** temporarily. For example, an unconditional branch instruction (making a forward reference) is left as **+4000** until the second pass of the compiler. The second pass of the compiler will be described shortly.

Compilation of **if/goto** and **let** statements is more complicated than other statements—they are the only statements that produce more than one SML instruction. For an **if/goto** statement, the compiler produces code to test the condition and to branch to another line if necessary. The result of the branch could be an unresolved reference. Each of the relational and equality operators can be simulated using SML's *branch zero* and *branch negative* instructions (or possibly a combination of both).

For a **let** statement, the compiler produces code to evaluate an arbitrarily complex arithmetic expression consisting of integer variables and/or constants. Expressions should separate each operand and operator with spaces. Exercises 12.12 and 12.13 presented the infix-to-postfix conversion algorithm and the postfix evaluation algorithm used by compilers to evaluate expressions. Before proceeding with your compiler, you should complete each of these exercises. When a compiler encounters an expression, it converts the expression from infix notation to postfix notation, then evaluates the postfix expression.

How is it that the compiler produces the machine language to evaluate an expression containing variables? The postfix evaluation algorithm contains a "hook" that allows our compiler to generate SML instructions rather than actually evaluating the expression. To enable this "hook" in the compiler, the postfix evaluation algorithm must be modified to search the symbol table for each symbol it encounters (and possibly insert it), determine the symbol's corresponding memory location, and *push the memory location on the stack instead of the symbol.* When an operator is encountered in the postfix expression, the two memory locations at the top of the stack are popped and machine language for effecting the operation is produced using the memory locations as operands. The result of each subexpression is stored in a temporary location in memory and pushed back onto the stack so the evaluation of the postfix expression can continue. When postfix evaluation is complete, the memory location containing the result is the only location left on the stack. This is popped and SML instructions are generated to assign the result to the variable at the left of the **let** statement.

Second Pass

The second pass of the compiler performs two tasks: resolve any unresolved references and output the SML code to a file. Resolution of references occurs as follows:

1) Search the **flags** array for an unresolved reference (i.e., an element with a value other than **-1**).
2) Locate the structure in array **symbolTable** containing the symbol stored in the **flags** array (be sure that the type of the symbol is **'L'** for line number).
3) Insert the memory location from structure member **location** into the instruction with the unresolved reference (remember that an instruction containing an unresolved reference has operand **00**).
4) Repeat steps 1, 2, and 3 until the end of the **flags** array is reached.

After the resolution process is complete, the entire array containing the SML code is output to a disk file with one SML instruction per line. This file can be read by the Simpletron for execution (after the simulator is modified to read its input from a file).

A Complete Example

The following example illustrates a complete conversion of a Simple program to SML as it will be performed by the Simple compiler. Consider a Simple program that inputs an integer and sums the values from 1 to that integer. The program and the SML instructions produced by the first pass are illustrated in Fig. 12.28. The symbol table constructed by the first pass is shown in Fig. 12.29.

Most Simple statements convert directly to single SML instructions. The exceptions in this program are remarks, the **if/goto** statement in line **20**, and the **let** statements. Remarks do not translate into machine language. However, the line number for a remark is placed in the symbol table in case the line number is referenced in a **goto** statement or an **if/goto** statement. Line **20** of the program specifies that if the condition **y == x** is true, program control is transferred to line **60**. Because line **60** appears later in the program, the first pass of the compiler has not as yet placed **60** in the symbol table (line numbers are placed in the symbol table only when they appear as the first token in a statement). Therefore, it is not possible at this time to determine the operand of the SML *branch zero* instruction at location **03** in the array of SML instructions. The compiler places **60** in location **03** of the **flags** array to indicate that the second pass completes this instruction.

We must keep track of the next instruction location in the SML array because there is not a one-to-one correspondence between Simple statements and SML instructions. For example, the **if/goto** statement of line **20** compiles into three SML instructions. Each time an instruction is produced, we must increment the *instruction counter* to the next location in the SML array. Note that the size of Simpletron's memory could present a problem for Simple programs with many statements, variables and constants. It is conceivable that the compiler will run out of memory. To test for this case, your program should contain a *data counter* to keep track of the location at which the next variable or constant will be stored in the SML array. If the value of the instruction counter is larger than the value of the data counter, the SML array is full. In this case, the compilation process should terminate and the compiler should print an error message indicating that it ran out of memory during compilation.

A Step-by-Step View of the Compilation Process

Let us now walk through the compilation process for the Simple program in Fig. 12.28. The compiler reads the first line of the program

        5 rem sum 1 to x

into memory. The first token in the statement (the line number) is determined using **strtok** (see Chapter 8 for a discussion of C's string manipulation functions). The token returned by **strtok** is

Simple program	SML location and instruction		Description
5 rem sum 1 to x		*none*	**rem** ignored
10 input x	00	+1099	read **x** into location 99
15 rem check y == x		*none*	**rem** ignored
20 if y == x goto 60	01	+2098	load **y** (98) into accumulator
	02	+3199	sub **x** (99) from accumulator
	03	+4200	*branch zero to unresolved location*
25 rem increment y		*none*	**rem** ignored
30 let y = y + 1	04	+2098	load **y** into accumulator
	05	+3097	add 1 (97) to accumulator
	06	+2196	store in temporary location 96
	07	+2096	load from temporary location 96
	08	+2198	store accumulator in **y**
35 rem add y to total		*none*	**rem** ignored
40 let t = t + y	09	+2095	load **t** (95) into accumulator
	10	+3098	add **y** to accumulator
	11	+2194	store in temporary location 94
	12	+2094	load from temporary location 94
	13	+2195	store accumulator in **t**
45 rem loop y		*none*	**rem** ignored
50 goto 20	14	+4001	branch to location 01
55 rem output result		*none*	**rem** ignored
60 print t	15	+1195	output **t** to screen
99 end	16	+4300	terminate execution

Fig. 12.28   SML instructions produced after the compiler's first pass.

converted to an integer using **atoi** so the symbol 5 can be located in the symbol table. If the symbol is not found, it is inserted in the symbol table. Since we are at the beginning of the program and this is the first line, no symbols are in the table yet. So, 5 is inserted into the symbol table as type **L** (line number) and assigned the first location in SML array (00). Although this line is a remark, a space in the symbol table is still allocated for the line number (in case it is referenced by a **goto** or an **if/goto**). No SML instruction is generated for a **rem** statement, so the instruction counter is not incremented.

The statement

```
10 input x
```

is tokenized next. The line number **10** is placed in the symbol table as type **L** and assigned the first location in the SML array (00 because a remark began the program so the instruction counter is currently 00). The command **input** indicates that the next token is a variable (only a variable can appear in an **input** statement). Because **input** corresponds directly to an SML operation code, the compiler simply has to determine the location of **x** in the SML array. Symbol **x** is not found in

Symbol	Type	Location
5	L	00
10	L	00
'x'	V	99
15	L	01
20	L	01
'y'	V	98
25	L	04
30	L	04
1	C	97
35	L	09
40	L	09
't'	V	95
45	L	14
50	L	14
55	L	15
60	L	15
99	L	16

Fig. 12.29 Symbol table for program of Fig. 12.28.

the symbol table. So, it is inserted into the symbol table as the ASCII representation of **x**, given type **V**, and assigned location **99** in the SML array (data storage begins at **99** and is allocated backwards). SML code can now be generated for this statement. Operation code **10** (the SML read operation code) is multiplied by 100, and the location of **x** (as determined in the symbol table) is added to complete the instruction. The instruction is then stored in the SML array at location **00**. The instruction counter is incremented by 1 because a single SML instruction was produced.

The statement

```
15 rem    check y == x
```

is tokenized next. The symbol table is searched for line number **15** (which is not found). The line number is inserted as type **L** and assigned the next location in the array, **01** (remember that **rem** statements do not produce code, so the instruction counter is not incremented).

The statement

```
20 if y == x goto 60
```

is tokenized next. Line number **20** is inserted in the symbol table and given type **L** with the next location in the SML array **01**. The command **if** indicates that a condition is to be evaluated. The variable **y** is not found in the symbol table, so it is inserted and given the type **V** and the SML location **98**. Next, SML instructions are generated to evaluate the condition. Since there is no direct equivalent in SML for the **if/goto**, it must be simulated by performing a calculation using **x** and **y** and branching based on the result. If **y** is equal to **x**, the result of subtracting **x** from **y** is zero, so the *branch zero* instruction can be used with the result of the calculation to simulate the **if/goto** statement. The first step requires that **y** be loaded (from SML location **98**) into the accumulator. This produces the instruction **01 +2098**. Next, **x** is subtracted from the accumulator. This produces the instruction **02 +3199**. The value in the accumulator may be zero, positive, or negative.

Since the operator is ==, we want to *branch zero*. First, the symbol table is searched for the branch location (60 in this case), which is not found. So, 60 is placed in the `flags` array at location 03, and the instruction 03 +4200 is generated (we cannot add the branch location because we have not assigned a location to line 60 in the SML array yet). The instruction counter is incremented to 04.

The compiler proceeds to the statement

```
25 rem    increment y
```

The line number 25 is inserted in the symbol table as type L and assigned SML location 04. The instruction counter is not incremented.

When the statement

```
30 let y = y + 1
```

is tokenized, the line number 30 is inserted in the symbol table as type L and assigned SML location 04. Command `let` indicates that the line is an assignment statement. First, all the symbols on the line are inserted in the symbol table (if they are not already there). The integer 1 is added to the symbol table as type C and assigned SML location 97. Next, the right side of the assignment is converted from infix to postfix notation. Then the postfix expression (y 1 +) is evaluated. Symbol y is located in the symbol table and its corresponding memory location is pushed onto the stack. Symbol 1 is also located in the symbol table and its corresponding memory location is pushed onto the stack. When the operator + is encountered, the postfix evaluator pops the stack into the right operand of the operator and pops the stack again into the left operand of the operator, then produces the SML instructions

```
04 +2098    (load y)
05 +3097    (add 1)
```

The result of the expression is stored in a temporary location in memory (96) with instruction

```
06 +2196    (store temporary)
```

and the temporary location is pushed on the stack. Now that the expression has been evaluated, the result must be stored in y (i.e., the variable on the left side of =). So, the temporary location is loaded into the accumulator and the accumulator is stored in y with the instructions

```
07 +2096    (load temporary)
08 +2198    (store y)
```

The reader will immediately notice that SML instructions appear to be redundant. We will discuss this issue shortly.

When the statement

```
35 rem    add y to total
```

is tokenized, line number 35 is inserted in the symbol table as type L and assigned location 09.

The statement

```
40 let t = t + y
```

is similar to line 30. The variable t is inserted in the symbol table as type V and assigned SML location 95. The instructions follow the same logic and format as line 30, and the instructions 09 +2095, 10 +3098, 11 +2194, 12 +2094, and 13 +2195 are generated. Note that the result of t + y is assigned to temporary location 94 before being assigned to t (95). Once again, the reader will note that the instructions in memory locations 11 and 12 appear to be redundant. Again, we will discuss this shortly.

The statement

```
45 rem    loop y
```

is a remark, so line **45** is added to the symbol table as type **L** and assigned SML location **14**.

The statement

```
50 goto 20
```

transfers control to line **20**. Line number **50** is inserted in the symbol table as type **L** and assigned SML location **14**. The equivalent of **goto** in SML is the *unconditional branch* (**40**) instruction that transfers control to a specific SML location. The compiler searches the symbol table for line **20** and finds that it corresponds to SML location **01**. The operation code (**40**) is multiplied by 100 and location **01** is added to it to produce the instruction **14 +4001**.

The statement

```
55 rem    output result
```

is a remark, so line **55** is inserted in the symbol table as type **L** and assigned SML location **15**.

The statement

```
60 print t
```

is an output statement. Line number **60** is inserted in the symbol table as type **L** and assigned SML location **15**. The equivalent of **print** in SML is operation code **11** (*write*). The location of **t** is determined from the symbol table and added to the result of the operation code multiplied by 100.

The statement

```
99 end
```

is the final line of the program. Line number **99** is stored in the symbol table as type **L** and assigned SML location **16**. The **end** command produces the SML instruction **+4300** (**43** is *halt* in SML) which is written as the final instruction in the SML memory array.

This completes the first pass of the compiler. We now consider the second pass. The **flags** array is searched for values other than **-1**. Location **03** contains **60**, so the compiler knows that instruction **03** is incomplete. The compiler completes the instruction by searching the symbol table for **60**, determining its location, and adding the location to the incomplete instruction. In this case, the search determines that line **60** corresponds to SML location **15**, so the completed instruction **03 +4215** is produced replacing **03 +4200**. The Simple program has now been compiled successfully.

To build the compiler, you will have to perform each of the following tasks:

a) Modify the Simpletron simulator program you wrote in Exercise 7.19 to take its input from a file specified by the user (see Chapter 11). Also, the simulator should output its results to a disk file in the same format as the screen output.

b) Modify the infix-to-postfix evaluation algorithm of Exercise 12.12 to process multi-digit integer operands and single-letter variable name operands. Hint: Standard library function **strtok** can be used to locate each constant and variable in an expression, and constants can be converted from strings to integers using standard library function **atoi**. (Note: The data representation of the postfix expression must be altered to support variable names and integer constants.)

c) Modify the postfix evaluation algorithm to process multi-digit integer operands and variable name operands. Also, the algorithm should now implement the "hook" discussed above so that SML instructions are produced rather than directly evaluating the expression. Hint: Standard library function **strtok** can be used to locate each constant and variable in an expression, and constants can be converted from strings to integers using standard library function **atoi**. (Note: The data representation of the postfix expression must be altered to support variable names and integer constants.)

    d) Build the compiler. Incorporate parts (b) and (c) for evaluating expressions in `let` statements. Your program should contain a function that performs the first pass of the compiler and a function that performs the second pass of the compiler. Both functions can call other functions to accomplish their tasks.

12.28 (*Optimizing the Simple Compiler*) When a program is compiled and converted into SML, a set of instructions is generated. Certain combinations of instructions often repeat themselves, usually in triplets called *productions*. A production normally consists of three instructions such as *load*, *add*, and *store*. For example, Fig. 12.30 illustrates five of the SML instructions that were produced in the compilation of the program in Fig. 12.28. The first three instructions are the production that adds `1` to `y`. Note that instructions `06` and `07` store the accumulator value in temporary location `96`, then load the value back into the accumulator so instruction `08` can store the value in location `98`. Often a production is followed by a load instruction for the same location that was just stored. This code can be *optimized* by eliminating the store instruction and the subsequent load instruction that operate on the same memory location. This optimization would enable the Simpletron to execute the program faster because there are fewer instructions in this version. Figure 12.31 illustrates the optimized SML for the program of Fig. 12.28. Note that there are four fewer instructions in the optimized code—a memory-space savings of 25%.

    Modify the compiler to provide an option for optimizing the Simpletron Machine Language code it produces. Manually compare the non-optimized code with the optimized code, and calculate the percentage reduction.

12.29 (*Modifications to the Simple compiler*) Perform the following modifications to the Simple compiler. Some of these modifications may also require modifications to the Simpletron Simulator program written in Exercise 7.19.

    a) Allow the modulus operator (`%`) to be used in `let` statements. Simpletron Machine Language must be modified to include a modulus instruction.

    b) Allow exponentiation in a `let` statement using `^` as the exponentiation operator. Simpletron Machine Language must be modified to include an exponentiation instruction.

    c) Allow the compiler to recognize uppercase and lowercase letters in Simple statements (e.g., `'A'` is equivalent to `'a'`). No modifications to the Simpletron Simulator are required.

    d) Allow `input` statements to read values for multiple variables such as `input x, y`. No modifications to the Simpletron Simulator are required.

    e) Allow the compiler to output multiple values in a single `print` statement such as `print a, b, c`. No modifications to the Simpletron Simulator are required.

    f) Add syntax checking capabilities to the compiler so error messages are output when syntax errors are encountered in a Simple program. No modifications to the Simpletron Simulator are required.

    g) Allow arrays of integers. No modifications to the Simpletron Simulator are required.

```
04  +2098    (load)
05  +3097    (add)
06  +2196    (store)

07  +2096    (load)
08  +2198    (store)
```

Fig. 12.30 Unoptimized code from the program of Fig. 12.28.

Simple program	SML location and instruction		Description
5 rem sum 1 to x		*none*	**rem** ignored
10 input x	00	+1099	read **x** into location **99**
15 rem check y == x		*none*	**rem** ignored
20 if y == x goto 60	01	+2098	load **y** (**98**) into accumulator
	02	+3199	sub **x** (**99**) from accumulator
	03	+4211	branch to location **11** if zero
25 rem increment y		*none*	**rem** ignored
30 let y = y + 1	04	+2098	load **y** into accumulator
	05	+3097	add **1** (**97**) to accumulator
	06	+2198	store accumulator in **y** (**98**)
35 rem add y to total		*none*	**rem** ignored
40 let t = t + y	07	+2096	load **t** from location (**96**)
	08	+3098	add **y** (**98**) accumulator
	09	+2196	store accumulator in **t** (**96**)
45 rem loop y		*none*	**rem** ignored
50 goto 20	10	+4001	branch to location **01**
55 rem output result		*none*	**rem** ignored
60 print t	11	+1196	output **t** (**96**) to screen
99 end	12	+4300	terminate execution

Fig. 12.31   Optimized code for the program of Fig. 12.28.

i) Allow subroutines specified by the Simple commands **gosub** and **return**. Command **gosub** passes program control to a subroutine and command **return** passes control back to the statement after the **gosub**. This is similar to a function call in C. The same subroutine can be called from many **gosub**s distributed throughout a program. No modifications to the Simpletron Simulator are required.

j) Allow repetition structures of the form

```
for x = 2 to 10 step 2
    Simple statements
next
```

This **for** statement loops from **2** to **10** with an increment of **2**. The **next** line marks the end of the body of the **for** line. No modifications to the Simpletron Simulator are required.

k) Allow repetition structures of the form

```
for x = 2 to 10
    Simple statements
next
```

This **for** statement loops from **2** to **10** with a default increment of **1**. No modifications to the Simpletron Simulator are required.

l) Allow the compiler to process string input and output. This requires the Simpletron Simulator to be modified to process and store string values. Hint: Each Simpletron word can be divided into two groups, each holding a two-digit integer. Each two-digit integer represents the ASCII decimal equivalent of a character. Add a machine language instruction that will print a string beginning at a certain Simpletron memory location. The first half of the word at that location is a count of the number of characters in the string (i.e., the length of the string). Each succeeding half word contains one ASCII character expressed as two decimal digits. The machine language instruction checks the length and prints the string by translating each two-digit number into its equivalent character .

m) Allow the compiler to process floating point values in addition to integers. The Simpletron Simulator must also be modified to process floating point values.

12.30   (*A Simple interpreter*) An interpreter is a program that reads a high-level language program statement, determines the operation to be performed by the statement, and executes the operation immediately. The program is not converted into machine language first. Interpreters execute slowly because each statement encountered in the program must first be deciphered. If statements are contained in a loop, the statements are deciphered each time they are encountered in the loop. Early versions of the BASIC programming language were implemented as interpreters.

Write an interpreter for the Simple language discussed in Exercise 12.26. The program should use the infix-to-postfix converter developed in Exercise 12.12 and the postfix evaluator developed in Exercise 12.13 to evaluate expressions in a `let` statement. The same restrictions placed on the Simple language in Exercise 12.26 should be adhered to in this program. Test the interpreter with the Simple programs written in Exercise 12.26. Compare the results of running these programs in the interpreter with the results of compiling the Simple programs and running them in the Simpletron simulator built in Exercise 7.19.

13

The Preprocessor

Objectives

- To be able to use **# include** for developing large programs.
- To be able to use **# define** to create macros and macros with arguments.
- To understand conditional compilation.
- To be able to display error messages during conditional compilation.
- To be able to use assertions to test if the values of expressions are correct.

Hold thou the good; define it well.
Alfred, Lord Tennyson

I have found you an argument; but I am not obliged to find you an understanding.
Samuel Johnson

A good symbol is the best argument, and is a missionary to persuade thousands.
Ralph Waldo Emerson

Conditions are fundamentally sound.
Herbert Hoover (December 1929)

The partisan, when he is engaged in a dispute, cares nothing about the rights of the question, but is anxious only to convince his hearers of his own assertions.
Plato

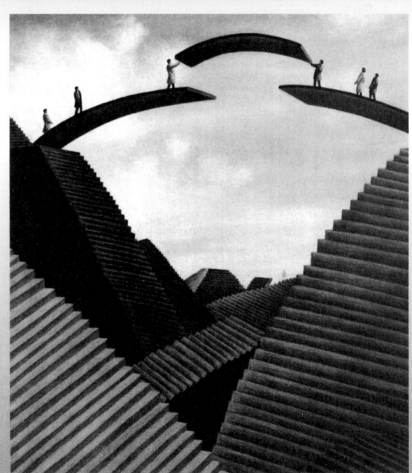

Outline

13.1 Introduction

This chapter introduces the *C preprocessor*. Preprocessing occurs before a program is compiled. Some possible actions are: inclusion of other files in the file being compiled, definition of *symbolic constants* and *macros, conditional compilation* of program code, and *conditional execution of preprocessor directives.* All preprocessor directives begin with **#**, and only whitespace characters may appear before a preprocessor directive on a line.

13.2 The #include Preprocessor Directive

The *#include preprocessor directive* has been used throughout this text. The **#include** directive causes a copy of a specified file to be included in place of the directive. The two forms of the **#include** directive are:

```
#include <filename>
#include "filename"
```

The difference between these is the location the preprocessor searches for the file to be included. If the file name is enclosed in quotes, the preprocessor searches in the same directory as the file being compiled for the file to be included. This method is normally used to include programmer-defined header files. If the file name is enclosed in angle brackets (**<** and **>**)—used for *standard library header files*—the search is performed in an implementation-dependent manner, normally through predesignated directories.

The **#include** directive is normally used to include standard library header files such as **stdio.h** and **stdlib.h** (see Fig. 5.6). The **#include** directive is also used with programs consisting of several source files that are to be compiled together. A *header file* containing declarations common to the separate program files is often created and included in the file. Examples of such declarations are structure and union declarations, enumerations, and function prototypes.

In UNIX, program files are compiled using the *cc command*. For example, to compile and link **main.c** and **square.c** enter the command

```
cc main.c square.c
```

at the UNIX prompt. This produces the executable file **a.out**. See the reference manuals for your compiler for more information on compiling, linking, and executing programs.

13.3 The #define Preprocessor Directive: Symbolic Constants

The *#define directive* creates *symbolic constants*—constants represented as symbols—and *macros*—operations defined as symbols. The **#define** directive format is

> **#define** *identifier replacement-text*

When this line appears in a file, all subsequent occurrences of *identifier* will be replaced by *replacement-text* automatically before the program is compiled. For example,

> **#define PI 3.14159**

replaces all subsequent occurrences of the symbolic constant **PI** with the numeric constant **3.14159**. Symbolic constants enable the programmer to create a name for a constant and use the name throughout the program. If the constant needs to be modified throughout the program, it can be modified once in the **#define** directive—and when the program is recompiled, all occurrences of the constant in the program will be modified automatically. Note: *Everything to the right of the symbolic constant name replaces the symbolic constant.* For example, **#define PI = 3.14159** causes the preprocessor to replace every occurrence of **PI** with **= 3.14159**. This is the cause of many subtle logic and syntax errors. Redefining a symbolic constant with a new value is also an error.

> *Good Programming Practice 13.1*
> ─────────────────────────────────
> *Using meaningful names for symbolic constants helps make programs more self-documenting.*

13.4 The #define Preprocessor Directive: Macros

A *macro* is an operation defined in a **#define** preprocessor directive. As with symbolic constants, the *macro-identifier* is replaced in the program with the *replacement-text* before the program is compiled. Macros may be defined with or without *arguments*. A macro without arguments is processed like a symbolic constant. In a macro with arguments, the arguments are substituted in the replacement text, then the macro is *expanded*—i.e., the replacement-text replaces the identifier and argument list in the program.

Consider the following macro definition with one argument for the area of a circle:

```
#define CIRCLE_AREA(x) ( PI * (x) * (x) )
```

Wherever **CIRCLE_AREA(x)** appears in the file, the value of **x** is substituted for **x** in the replacement text, the symbolic constant **PI** is replaced by its value (defined previously), and the macro is expanded in the program. For example, the statement

```
area = CIRCLE_AREA(4);
```

is expanded to

```
area = ( 3.14159 * (4) * (4) );
```

Since the expression consists only of constants, at compile time, the value of the expression is evaluated and assigned to variable **area**. The parentheses around each **x** in the replacement text force the proper order of evaluation when the macro argument is an expression. For example, the statement

```
area = CIRCLE_AREA(c + 2);
```

is expanded to

```
area = ( 3.14159 * (c + 2) * (c + 2) );
```

which evaluates correctly because the parentheses force the proper order of evaluation. If the parentheses are omitted, the macro expansion is

```
area = 3.14159 * c + 2 * c + 2;
```

which evaluates incorrectly as

```
area = (3.14159 * c) + (2 * c) + 2;
```

because of the rules of operator precedence.

Common Programming Error 13.1

Forgetting to enclose macro arguments in parentheses in the replacement text.

Macro **CIRCLE_AREA** could be defined as a function. Function **circleArea**

```
double circleArea(double x)
{
   return 3.14159 * x * x;
}
```

performs the same calculation as macro **CIRCLE_AREA**, but the overhead of a function call is associated with function **circleArea**. The advantages of macro **CIRCLE_AREA** are that macros insert code directly in the program—avoiding function overhead—and the program remains readable because the **CIRCLE_AREA** calculation is defined separately and named meaningfully. A disadvantage is that its argument is evaluated twice.

Performance Tip 13.1

Macros can sometimes be used to replace a function call with inline code prior to execution time. This eliminates the overhead of a function call.

The following is a macro definition with 2 arguments for the area of a rectangle:

```
#define RECTANGLE_AREA(x, y)   ( (x) * (y) )
```

Wherever **RECTANGLE_AREA(x, y)** appears in the program, the values of **x** and **y** are substituted in the macro replacement text, and the macro is expanded in place of the macro name. For example, the statement

```
rectArea = RECTANGLE_AREA(a + 4, b + 7);
```

is expanded to

```
rectArea = ( (a + 4) * (b + 7) );
```

The value of the expression is evaluated and assigned to variable **rectArea**.

The replacement text for a macro or symbolic constant is normally any text on the line after the identifier in the **#define** directive. If the replacement text for a macro or symbolic constant is longer than the remainder of the line, a backslash (\) must be placed at the end of the line indicating that the replacement text continues on the next line.

Symbolic constants and macros can be discarded using the *#undef preprocessor directive*. Directive **#undef** "undefines" a symbolic constant or macro name. The *scope* of a symbolic constant or macro is from its definition until it is undefined with **#undef**, or until the end of the file. Once undefined, a name can be redefined with **#define**.

Functions in the standard library sometimes are defined as macros based on other library functions. A macro commonly defined in the **stdio.h** header file is

```
#define getchar() getc(stdin)
```

The macro definition of **getchar** uses function **getc** to get one character from the standard input stream. Function **putchar** of the **stdio.h** header, and the character handling functions of the **ctype.h** header often are implemented as macros as well. Note that expressions with side effects (i.e., variable values are modified) should not be passed to a macro because macro arguments may be evaluated more than once.

13.5 Conditional Compilation

Conditional compilation enables the programmer to control the execution of preprocessor directives, and the compilation of program code. Each of the conditional preprocessor directives evaluates a constant integer expression. Cast expressions, **sizeof** expressions, and enumeration constants cannot be evaluated in preprocessor directives.

The conditional preprocessor construct is much like the **if** selection structure. Consider the following preprocessor code:

```
#if !defined(NULL)
    #define NULL 0
#endif
```

These directives determine if **NULL** is defined. The expression **defined(NULL)** evaluates to **1** if **NULL** is defined; 0 otherwise. If the result is **0**, **!defined(NULL)** evaluates to **1**, and **NULL** is defined. Otherwise, the **#define** directive is skipped. Every **#if** construct ends with **#endif**. Directives *#ifdef* and *#ifndef* are shorthand for **#if defined**(*name*) and **#if !defined**(*name*). A multiple-part conditional preprocessor construct may be tested using the **#elif** (the equivalent of **else if** in an **if** structure) and the **#else** (the equivalent of **else** in an **if** structure) directives.

During program development, programmers often find it helpful to "comment out" large portions of code to prevent it from being compiled. If the code contains comments, **/*** and ***/** cannot be used to accomplish this task. Instead, the programmer can use the following preprocessor construct

```
#if 0
    code prevented from compiling
#endif
```

To enable the code to be compiled, the **0** in the preceding construct is replaced by **1**.

Conditional compilation is commonly used as a debugging aid. Many C implementations provide *debuggers*. However, debuggers often are difficult to use and understand, so they are rarely used by students in a first programming course. Instead, **printf** statements are used to print variable values and to confirm the flow of control. These **printf** statements can be enclosed in conditional preprocessor directives so the statements are only compiled while the debugging process is not completed. For example,

```
#ifdef DEBUG
    printf("Variable x = %d\n", x);
#endif
```

causes a **printf** statement to be compiled in the program if the symbolic constant **DE-BUG** has been defined (**#define DEBUG**) before directive **#ifdef DEBUG**. When debugging is completed, the **#define** directive is removed from the source file, and the **printf** statements inserted for debugging purposes are ignored during compilation. In larger programs, it may be desirable to define several different symbolic constants that control the conditional compilation in separate sections of the source file.

> ### Common Programming Error 13.2
>
> *Inserting conditionally compiled* **printf** *statements for debugging purposes in locations where C currently expects a single statement. In this case, the conditionally compiled statement should be enclosed in a compound statement. Thus, when the program is compiled with debugging statements, the flow of control of the program is not altered.*

13.6 The #error and #pragma Preprocessor Directives

The *#error directive*

```
#error tokens
```

prints an implementation-dependent message including the *tokens* specified in the directive. The tokens are sequences of characters separated by spaces. For example,

```
#error 1 - Out of range error
```

contains 6 tokens. In Borland C++ for PCs, for example, when a **#error** directive is processed, the tokens in the directive are displayed as an error message, preprocessing stops, and the program does not compile.

The **#pragma** *directive*

```
#pragma tokens
```

causes an implementation-defined action. A pragma not recognized by the implementation is ignored. Borland C++, for example, recognizes several pragmas that enable the programmer to take full advantage of the Borland C++ implementation. For more information on **#error** and **#pragma**, see the documentation for your C implementation.

13.7 The # and ## Operators

The # and ## preprocessor operators are available only in ANSI C. The # operator causes a replacement text token to be converted to a string surrounded by quotes. Consider the following macro definition:

```
#define HELLO(x) printf("Hello, " #x "\n");
```

When **HELLO(John)** appears in a program file, it is expanded to

```
printf("Hello, " "John" "\n");
```

The string **"John"** replaces **#x** in the replacement text. Strings separated by white space are concatenated during preprocessing, so the above statement is equivalent to

```
printf("Hello, John\n");
```

Note that the **#** operator must be used in a macro with arguments because the operand of **#** refers to an argument of the macro.

The **##** operator concatenates two tokens. Consider the following macro definition:

```
#define TOKENCONCAT(x, y)  x ## y
```

When **TOKENCONCAT** appears in the program, its arguments are concatenated and used to replace the macro. For example, **TOKENCONCAT(O, K)** is replaced by **OK** in the program. The **##** operator must have two operands.

13.8 Line Numbers

The **#line** *preprocessor directive* causes the subsequent source code lines to be renumbered starting with the specified constant integer value. The directive

```
#line 100
```

starts line numbering from **100** beginning with the next source code line. A file name can be included in the **#line** directive. The directive

```
#line 100 "file1.c"
```

indicates that lines are numbered from **100** beginning with the next source code line, and that the name of the file for the purpose of any compiler messages is **"file1.c"**. The directive normally is used to help make the messages produced by syntax errors and compiler warnings more meaningful. The line numbers do not appear in the source file.

13.9 Predefined Symbolic Constants

There are five *predefined symbolic constants* (Fig. 13.1). The indentifiers for each of the predefined symbolic constants begin and end with *two* underscores. These identifiers and the **defined** identifier (used in Section 13.5) cannot be used in **#define** or **#undef** directives.

13.10 Assertions

The *assert macro*—defined in the **assert.h** header file—tests the value of an expression. If the value of the expression is **0** (false), then **assert** prints an error message and calls function *abort* (of the general utilities library—**stdlib.h**) to terminate program execution. This is a useful debugging tool for testing if a variable has a correct value. For example, suppose variable **x** should never be larger than **10** in a program. An assertion may be used to test the value of **x** and print an error message if the value of **x** is incorrect. The statement would be:

```
assert(x <= 10);
```

If **x** is greater than **10** when the preceding statement is encountered in a program, an error message containing the line number and file name is printed, and the program terminates. The programmer may then concentrate on this area of the code to find the error. If the symbolic constant **NDEBUG** is defined, subsequent assertions will be ignored. Thus, when assertions are no longer needed, the line

Symbolic constant	Explanation
__LINE__	The line number of the current source code line (an integer constant).
__FILE__	The presumed name of the source file (a string).
__DATE__	The date the source file is compiled (a string of the form **"Mmm dd yyyy"** such as **"Jan 19 1991"**).
__TIME__	The time the source file is compiled (a string literal of the form **"hh:mm:ss"**).
__STDC__	The integer constant 1. This is intended to indicate that the implementation is ANSI compliant.

Fig. 13.1   The predefined symbolic constants.

```
#define NDEBUG
```

is inserted in the program file rather than deleting each assertion manually.

Summary

- All preprocessor directives begin with **#**.

- Only whitespace characters may appear before a preprocessor directive on a line.

- The **#include** directive includes a copy of the specified file. If the file name is enclosed in quotes, the preprocessor begins searching in the same directory as the file being compiled for the file to be included. If the file name is enclosed in angle brackets (**<** and **>**), the search is performed in an implementation-defined manner.

- The **#define** preprocessor directive is used to create symbolic constants and macros.

- A symbolic constant is a name for a constant.

- A macro is an operation defined in a **#define** preprocessor directive. Macros may be defined with or without arguments.

- The replacement text for a macro or symbolic constant is any text remaining on the line after the identifier in the **#define** directive. If the replacement text for a macro or symbolic constant is longer than the remainder of the line, a backslash (****) is placed at the end of the line indicating that the replacement text continues on the next line.

- Symbolic constants and macros can be discarded using the **#undef** preprocessor directive. Directive **#undef** "undefines" the symbolic constant or macro name.

- The scope of a symbolic constant or macro is from its definition until it is undefined with **#undef**, or until the end of the file.

- Conditional compilation enables the programmer to control the execution of preprocessor directives and the compilation of program code.

- The conditional preprocessor directives evaluate constant integer expressions. Cast expressions, **sizeof** expressions, and enumeration constants cannot be evaluated in preprocessor directives.

- Every **#if** construct ends with **#endif**.

- Directives **#ifdef** and **#ifndef** are provided as shorthand for **#if defined**(*name*) and **#if !defined**(*name*).

- A multiple-part conditional preprocessor construct may be tested using the **#elif** (the equivalent of **else if** in an **if** structure) and the **#else** (the equivalent of **else** in an **if** structure) directives.

- The **#error** directive prints an implementation-dependent message that includes the tokens specified in the directive.

- The **#pragma** directive causes an implementation-defined action. If the pragma is not recognized by the implementation, the pragma is ignored.

- The **#** operator causes a replacement text token to be converted to a string surrounded by quotes. The **#** operator must be used in a macro with arguments because the operand of **#** must be an argument of the macro.

- The **##** operator concatenates two tokens. The **##** operator must have two operands.

- The **#line** preprocessor directive causes the subsequent source code lines to be renumbered starting with the specified constant integer value.

- There are five predefined symbolic constants. Constant **__LINE__** is the line number of the current source code line (an integer). Constant **__FILE__** is the presumed name of the file (a string). Constant **__DATE__** is the date the source file is compiled (a string). Constant **__TIME__** is the time the source file is compiled (a string). Constant **__STDC__** is **1**; it is intended to indicate that the implementation is ANSI compliant. Note that each of the predefined symbolic constants begins and ends with two underbars.

- The **assert** macro—defined in the **assert.h** header file—tests the value of an expression. If the value of the expression is **0** (false), then **assert** prints an error message and calls function **abort** to terminate program execution.

Terminology

#define	assert
#elif	assert.h
#else	C preprocessor
#endif	cc command in UNIX
#error	concatenation preprocessor operator ##
#if	conditional compilation
#ifdef	conditional execution of preprocessor direc-
#ifndef	tives
#include <filename>	convert-to-string preprocessor operator #
#include "filename"	debugger
#line	expand a macro
#pragma	header file
#undef	macro
\ (backslash) continuation character	macro with arguments
__DATE__	predefined symbolic constants
__FILE__	preprocessing directive
__LINE__	replacement text
__STDC__	scope of a symbolic constant or macro
__TIME__	standard library header files
a.out in UNIX	stdio.h
abort	stdlib.h
argument	symbolic constant

Common Programming Errors

13.1   Forgetting to enclose macro arguments in parentheses in the replacement text.

13.2   Inserting conditionally compiled `printf` statements for debugging purposes in locations where C currently expects a single statement. In this case, the conditionally compiled statement should be enclosed in a compound statement. Thus, when the program is compiled with debugging statements the flow of control of the program is not altered.

Good Programming Practice

13.1   Using meaningful names for symbolic constants helps make programs more self-documenting.

Performance Tip

13.1   Macros can sometimes be used to replace a function call with inline code prior to execution time. This eliminates the overhead of a function call.

Self-Review Exercises

13.1   Fill in the blanks in each of the following:
   a) Every preprocessor directive must begin with _____.
   b) The conditional compilation construct may be extended to test for multiple cases by using the _____ and the _____ directives.
   c) The _____ directive creates macros and symbolic constants.
   d) Only _____ characters may appear before a preprocessor directive on a line.
   e) The _____ directive discards symbolic constant and macro names.
   f) The _____ and _____ directives are provided as shorthand notation for `#if defined(`*name*`)` and `#if !defined(`*name*`)`.
   g) _____ enables the programmer to control the execution of preprocessor directives, and the compilation of program code.
   h) The _____ macro prints a message and terminates program execution if the value of the expression the macro evaluates is 0.
   i) The _____ directive inserts a file in another file.
   j) The _____ operator concatenates its two arguments.
   k) The _____ operator converts its operand to a string.
   l) The character _____ indicates that the replacement text for a symbolic constant or macro continues on the next line.
   m)   The _____ directive causes the source code lines to be numbered from the indicated value beginning with the next source code line.

13.2   Write a program to print the values of the predefined symbolic constants listed in Fig. 13.1.

13.3   Write a preprocessor directive to accomplish each of the following:
   a) Define symbolic constant `YES` to have the value `1`.
   b) Define symbolic constant `NO` to have the value `0`.
   c) Include the header file `common.h`. The header is found in the same directory as the file being compiled.
   d) Renumber the remaining lines in the file beginning with line number `3000`.
   e) If symbolic constant `TRUE` is defined, undefine it, and redefine it as `1`. Do not use `#ifdef`.
   f) If symbolic constant `TRUE` is defined, undefine it, and redefine it as `1`. Use the `#ifdef` preprocessor directive.

g) If symbolic constant **TRUE** is not equal to **0**, define symbolic constant **FALSE** as **0**. Otherwise define **FALSE** as **1**.

h) Define macro **SQUARE_VOLUME** that computes the volume of a square. The macro takes one argument.

Answers to Self-Review Exercises

13.1   a) **#**. b) **#elif**, **#else**. c) **#define**. d) whitespace. e) **#undef**. f) **#ifdef**, **#ifndef**. g) Conditional compilation. h) **assert**. i) **#include**. j) **##**. k) **#**. l) ****. m) **#line**.

13.2
```
/* Print the values of the predefined macros */
#include <stdio.h>
main()
{
    printf("__LINE__  = %d\n", __LINE__);
    printf("__FILE__  = %s\n", __FILE__);
    printf("__DATE__  = %s\n", __DATE__);
    printf("__TIME__  = %s\n", __TIME__);
    printf("__STDC__  = %d\n", __STDC__);
}
```

```
__LINE__  = 5
__FILE__  = macros.c
__DATE__  = Sep 08 1993
__TIME__  = 10:23:47
__STDC__  = 1
```

13.3
a) `#define YES 1`
b) `#define NO 0`
c) `#include "common.h"`
d) `#line 3000`
e)
```
#if defined(TRUE)
    #undef TRUE
    #define TRUE 1
#endif
```
f)
```
#ifdef TRUE
    #undef TRUE
    #define TRUE 1
#endif
```
g)
```
#if TRUE
    #define FALSE 0
#else
    #define FALSE 1
#endif
```
h) `#define SQUARE_VOLUME(x)  (x) * (x) * (x)`

Exercises

13.4   Write a program that defines a macro with one argument to compute the volume of a sphere. The program should compute the volume for spheres of radius 1 to 10, and print the results in tabular format. The formula for the volume of a sphere is:

$$(4/3) \ * \ \pi \ * \ r^3$$

where π is **3.14159**.

13.5   Write a program that produces the following output:

```
The sum of x and y is 13
```

The program should define macro **SUM** with two arguments, **x** and **y**, and use **SUM** to produce the output.

13.6   Write a program that uses macro **MINIMUM2** to determine the smallest of two numeric values. Input the values from the keyboard.

13.7   Write a program that uses macro **MINIMUM3** to determine the smallest of three numeric values. Macro **MINIMUM3** should use macro **MINIMUM2** defined in Exercise 13.6 to determine the smallest number. Input the values from the keyboard.

13.8   Write a program that uses macro **PRINT** to print a string value.

13.9   Write a program that uses macro **PRINTARRAY** to print an array of integers. The macro should receive the array and the number of elements in the array as arguments.

13.10   Write a program that uses macro **SUMARRAY** to sum the values in a numeric array. The macro should receive the array and the number of elements in the array as arguments.

14

Advanced Topics

Objectives

- To be able to redirect keyboard input to come from a file.
- To be able to redirect screen output to be placed in a file.
- To be able to write functions that use variable-length argument lists.
- To be able to process command-line arguments.
- To be able to assign specific types to numeric constants.
- To be able to use temporary files.
- To be able to process unexpected events within a program.
- To be able to allocate memory dynamically for arrays.
- To be able to change the size of memory that was dynamically allocated previously.

We'll use a signal I have tried and found far-reaching and easy to yell. Waa-hoo!
Zane Grey

Use it up, wear it out;
Make it do, or do without.
Anonymous

It is quite a three-pipe problem.
Sir Arthur Conan Doyle

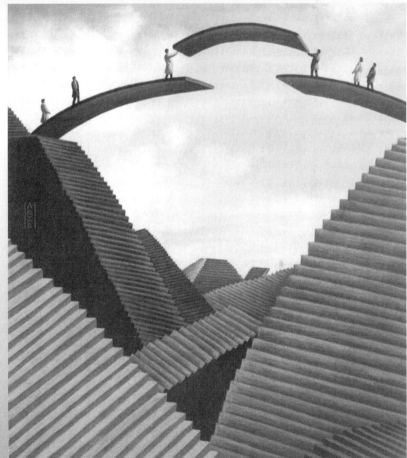

535

Outline

14.1 Introduction

This chapter presents several advanced topics not ordinarily covered in introductory courses. Many of the capabilities discussed here are specific to particular operating systems, especially UNIX and/or DOS.

14.2 Redirecting Input/Output on UNIX and DOS Systems

Normally the input to a program is from the keyboard (standard input), and the output from a program is displayed on the screen (standard output). On most computer systems—UNIX and DOS systems in particular—it is possible to *redirect* inputs to come from a file rather than the keyboard, and redirect outputs to be placed in a file rather than on the screen. Both forms of redirection can be accomplished without using the file processing capabilities of the standard library.

There are several ways to redirect input and output from the UNIX command line. Consider the executable file **sum.** that inputs integers one at a time and keeps a running total of the values until the end-of-file indicator is set, then prints the result. Normally the user inputs integers from the keyboard and enters the end-of-file key combination to indicate that no further values will be input. With input redirection, the input can be stored in a file. For example, if the data is stored in file **input**, the command line

```
$ sum < input
```

causes program **sum** to be executed; the *redirect input symbol (<)* indicates that the data in file **input** is to be used as input by the program. Redirecting input on a DOS system is performed identically.

Note that **$** is the UNIX command line prompt (some UNIX systems use a **%** prompt). Students often find it difficult to understand that redirection is an operating system function, not another C feature.

The second method of redirecting input is *piping*. A *pipe (|)* causes the output of one program to be redirected as the input to another program. Suppose program **random** outputs a series of random integers; the output of **random** can be "piped" directly to program **sum** using the UNIX command line

```
$ random | sum
```

This causes the sum of the integers produced by **random** to be calculated. Piping can be performed in UNIX and DOS.

Program output can be redirected to a file by using the *redirect output symbol (>)* (the same symbol is used for UNIX and DOS). For example, to redirect the output of program **random** to file **out**, use

```
$ random > out
```

Finally, program output can be appended to the end of an existing file by using the *append output symbol (>>)* (the same symbol is used for UNIX and DOS). For example, to append the output from program **random** to file **out** created in the preceding command line, use the command line

```
$ random >> out
```

14.3 Variable-Length Argument Lists

It is possible to create functions that receive an unspecified number of arguments. Most of the programs in the text have used the standard library function **printf** which, as you know, takes a variable number of arguments. As a minimum, **printf** must receive a string as its first argument, but **printf** can receive any number of additional arguments. The function prototype for **printf** is

```
int printf(const char *format, ...);
```

The ellipsis (**...**) in the function prototype indicates that the function receives a variable number of arguments of any type. Note that the ellipsis must always be placed at the end of the parameter list.

The macros and definitions of the *variable arguments header **stdarg.h*** (Fig. 14.1) provide the capabilities necessary to build functions with variable length argument lists. The program of Fig. 14.2 demonstrates function **average** that receives a variable number of arguments. The first argument of **average** is always the number of values to be averaged.

Identifier	Explanation
va_list	A type suitable for holding information needed by macros **va_start**, **va_arg**, and **va_end**. To access the arguments in a variable-length argument list, an object of type **va_list** must be declared.
va_start	A macro that is invoked before the arguments of a variable-length argument list can be accessed. The macro initializes the object declared with **va_list** for use by the **va_arg** and **va_end** macros.
va_arg	A macro that expands to an expression of the value and type of the next argument in the variable-length argument list. Each invocation of **va_arg** modifies the object declared with **va_list** so that the object points to the next argument in the list.
va_end	A macro that facilitates a normal return from a function whose variable-length argument list was referred to by the **va_start** macro.

Fig. 14.1 The type and the macros defined in header **stdarg.h**.

Function **average** uses all the definitions and macros of header **stdarg.h**. Object **ap**, of type **va_list**, is used by macros **va_start**, **va_arg**, and **va_end** to process the variable-length argument list of function **average**. The function begins by invoking macro **va_start** to initialize object **ap** for use in **va_arg** and **va_end**. The macro receives two arguments—object **ap** and the identifier of the rightmost argument in the argument list before the ellipsis—**i** in this case (**va_start** uses **i** here to determine where the variable-length argument list begins). Next function **average** repeatedly adds the arguments in the variable-length argument list to variable **total**. The value to be added to **total** is retrieved from the argument list by invoking macro **va_arg**. Macro **va_arg** receives two arguments—object **ap**, and the type of the value expected in the argument list—**double** in this case. The macro returns the value of the argument. Function **average** invokes macro **va_end** with object **ap** as an argument to facilitate a normal return to **main** from **average**. Finally, the average is calculated and returned to **main**.

Common Programming Error 14.1

Placing an ellipsis in the middle of a function parameter list. An ellipsis may only be placed at the end of the parameter list.

The reader may question how the **printf** function and the **scanf** function know what type to use in each **va_arg** macro. The answer is that **printf** and **scanf** scan the format conversion specifiers in the format control string to determine the type of the next argument to be processed.

```
/* Using variable-length argument lists */

#include <stdio.h>
#include <stdarg.h>

double average(int, ...);

main()
{
    double w = 37.5, x = 22.5, y = 1.7, z = 10.2;

    printf("%s%.1f\n%s%.1f\n%s%.1f\n%s%.1f\n\n",
           "w = ", w, "x = ", x, "y = ", y, "z = ", z);
    printf("%s%.3f\n%s%.3f\n%s%.3f\n",
           "The average of w and x is ",
           average(2, w, x),
           "The average of w, x, and y is ",
           average(3, w, x, y),
           "The average of w, x, y, and z is ",
           average(4, w, x, y, z));

    return 0;
}


double average(int i, ...)
{
    double total = 0;
    int j;
    va_list ap;

    va_start(ap, i);

    for (j = 1; j <= i; j++)
        total += va_arg(ap, double);

    va_end(ap);
    return total / i;
}
```

```
w = 37.5
x = 22.5
y = 1.7
z = 10.2

The average of w and x is 30.000
The average of w, x, and y is 20.567
The average of w, x, y, and z is 17.975
```

Fig. 14.2   Using variable-length argument lists.

14.4 Using Command-Line Arguments

On many systems—DOS and UNIX in particular—it is possible to pass arguments to **main** from a command line by including parameters **int argc** and **char *argv[]** in the parameter list of **main**. Parameter **argc** receives the number of command-line arguments. Parameter **argv** is an array of strings in which the actual command-line arguments are stored. Common uses of command-line arguments include printing the arguments, passing options to a program, and passing filenames to a program.

The program of Fig. 14.3 copies a file into another file one character at a time. The executable file for the program is called **copy**. A typical command line for the **copy** program on a UNIX system is

```
$ copy input output
```

This command line indicates that file **input** is to be copied to file **output**. When the program is executed, if **argc** is not **3** (**copy** counts as one of the arguments), the program prints an error message and terminates. Otherwise, array **argv** contains the strings **"copy"**, **"input"**, and **"output"**. The second and third arguments on the command line are used as file names by the program. The files are opened using function **fopen**. If both files are opened successfully, characters are read from file **input** and written to file **output** until the end-of-file indicator for file **input** is set. Then the program terminates. The result is an exact copy of file **input**. Note that not all computer systems support command-line arguments as easily as UNIX and DOS. Macintosh and VMS systems, for example, require special settings for processing command-line arguments. See the manuals for your system for more information on command-line arguments.

14.5 Notes on Compiling Multiple-Source-File Programs

As stated earlier in the text it is possible to build programs that consist of multiple source files (see Chapter 16, "Classes"). There are several considerations when creating programs in multiple files. For example, the definition of a function must be entirely contained in one file—it can not span two or more files.

In Chapter 5, we introduced the concepts of storage class and scope. We learned that variables declared outside any function definition are of storage class static by default and are referred to as global variables. Global variables are accessible to any function defined in the same file after the variable is declared. Global variables also are accessible to functions in other files, however, the global variables must be declared in each file in which they are used. For example, if we define global integer variable **flag** in one file, and refer to it in a second file, the second file must contain the declaration

```
extern int flag;
```

prior to the variable's use in that file. In the preceding declaration, the storage class specifier **extern** indicates to the compiler that variable **flag** is defined either later in the same file or in a different file. The compiler informs the linker that unresolved references to variable **flag** appear in the file (the compiler does not know where the **flag** is defined, so it lets the linker attempt to find **flag**). If the linker can not locate a definition of

```
/* Using command-line arguments */
#include <stdio.h>

main(int argc, char *argv[])
{
    FILE *inFilePtr, *outFilePtr;
    int c;

    if (argc != 3)
        printf("Usage: copy infile outfile\n");
    else
        if ((inFilePtr = fopen(argv[1], "r")) != NULL)

            if ((outFilePtr = fopen(argv[2], "w")) != NULL)

                while ((c = fgetc(inFilePtr)) != EOF)
                    fputc(c, outFilePtr);

            else
                printf("File \"%s\" could not be opened\n", argv[2]);

        else
            printf("File \"%s\" could not be opened\n", argv[1]);

    return 0;
}
```

Fig. 14.3 Using command-line arguments.

flag, a linker error is generated, and no executable file is produced. If a proper global definition is located, the linker resolves the references by indicating where **flag** is located.

Performance Tip 14.1

Global variables increase performance because they can be accessed directly by any function—the overhead of passing data to functions is eliminated.

Software Engineering Observation 14.1

Global variables should be avoided unless application performance is critical because they violate the principle of least privilege.

Just as **extern** declarations can be used to declare global variables to other program files, function prototypes can extend the scope of a function beyond the file in which it is defined (the **extern** specifier is not required in a function prototype). This is accomplished by including the function prototype in each file in which the function is invoked, and compiling the files together (see Section 13.2). Function prototypes indicate to the compiler that the specified function is defined either later in the same file or in a different file. Again, the compiler does not attempt to resolve references to such a function—that task is left to the linker. If the linker can not locate a proper function definition, an error is generated.

As an example of using function prototypes to extend the scope of a function, consider any program containing the preprocessor directive **#include <stdio.h>**. This directive includes in a file the function prototypes for functions such as **printf** and **scanf**. Other functions in the file can use **printf** and **scanf** to accomplish their tasks. The **printf** and **scanf** functions are defined for us separately. We do not need to know where they are defined. We are simply reusing the code in our programs. The linker resolves our references to these functions automatically. This process enables us to use the functions in the standard library.

Software Engineering Observation 14.2

Creating programs in multiple source files facilitates software reusability and good software engineering. Functions may be common to many applications. In such instances, those functions should be stored in their own source files, and each source file should have a corresponding header file containing function prototypes. This enables programmers of different applications to reuse the same code by including the proper header file, and compiling their application with the corresponding source file.

Portability Tip 14.1

Some systems do not support global variable names or function names of more than 6 characters. This should be considered when writing programs that will be ported to multiple platforms.

It is possible to restrict the scope of a global variable or function to the file in which it is defined. The storage class specifier **static**, when applied to a global variable or a function, prevents it from being used by any function that is not defined in the same file. This is referred to as *internal linkage*. Global variables and functions that are not preceded by **static** in their definitions have *external linkage*—they can be accessed in other files if those files contain proper declarations and/or function prototypes.

The global variable declaration

```
static float pi = 3.14159;
```

creates variable **pi** of type **float**, initializes it to **3.14159**, and indicates that **pi** is known only to functions in the file in which it is defined.

The **static** specifier is commonly used with utility functions that are called only by functions in a particular file. If a function is not required outside a particular file, the principle of least privilege should be enforced by using **static**. If a function is defined before it is used in a file, **static** should be applied to the function definition. Otherwise, **static** should be applied to the function prototype.

When building large programs in multiple source files, compiling the program becomes tedious if small changes are made to one file, and the entire program must be recompiled. Many systems provide special utilities that recompile only the modified program file. On UNIX systems the utility is called *make*. Utility **make** reads a file called *makefile* that contains instructions for compiling and linking the program. Systems such as Borland C++ and Microsoft C/C++ 7.0 for PCs provide **make** utilities as well. For more information on **make** utilities, see the manual for your particular system.

14.6 Program Termination with Exit and Atexit

The general utilities library (**stdlib.h**) provides methods of terminating program execution other than a conventional return from function **main**. Function *exit* forces a program to terminate as if it executed normally. The function often is used to terminate a program when an error is detected in the input, or if a file to be processed by the program cannot be opened. Function *atexit* *registers* a function in the program to be called upon successful termination of the program—i.e., either when the program terminates by reaching the end of **main**, or when **exit** is invoked.

Function **atexit** takes a pointer to a function (i.e., the function name) as an argument. Functions called at program termination cannot have arguments, and cannot return a value. Up to 32 functions may be registered for execution at program termination.

Function **exit** takes one argument. The argument is normally the symbolic constant *EXIT_SUCCESS* or the symbolic constant *EXIT_FAILURE*. If **exit** is called with **EXIT_SUCCESS**, the implementation-defined value for successful termination is returned to the calling environment. If **exit** is called with **EXIT_FAILURE**, the implementation-defined value for unsuccessful termination is returned. When function **exit** is invoked, any functions previously registered with **atexit** are invoked in the reverse order of their registration, all streams associated with the program are flushed and closed, and control returns to the host environment. The program of Fig. 14.4 tests functions **exit** and **atexit**. The program prompts the user to determine whether the program should be terminated with **exit** or by reaching the end of **main**. Note that function **print** is executed at program termination in each case.

14.7 The Volatile Type Qualifier

In Chapters 6 and 7, we introduced the **const** type qualifier. ANSI C also provides the **volatile** type qualifier. The ANSI standard (An90) indicates that when **volatile** is used to qualify a type, the nature of the access to an object of that type is implementation dependent. Kernighan and Ritchie (Ke88) indicate that the **volatile** qualifier is used to suppress various kinds of optimizations.

14.8 Suffixes for Integer and Floating-Point Constants

C provides integer and floating point suffixes for specifying the types of integer and floating-point constants. The integer suffixes are: u or U for an **unsigned** integer, 1 or L for a **long** integer, and u1 or UL for an **unsigned long** integer. The following constants are of type **unsigned**, **long**, and **unsigned long** respectively:

```
174u
8358L
28373ul
```

If an integer constant is not suffixed, its type is determined by the first type capable of storing a value of that size (first **int**, then **long int**, then **unsigned long int**).

The floating-point suffixes are: f or F for a **float**, and 1 or L for a **long double**. The following constants are of type **float** and **long double** respectively:

```c
/* Using the exit and atexit functions */

#include <stdio.h>
#include <stdlib.h>

void print(void);

main()
{
    int answer;

    atexit(print);          /* register function print */
    printf("Enter 1 to terminate program with function exit\n"
           "Enter 2 to terminate program normally\n");
    scanf("%d", &answer);

    if (answer == 1) {
        printf("\nTerminating program with function exit\n");
        exit(EXIT_SUCCESS);
    }

    printf("\nTerminating program by reaching the end of main\n");
    return 0;
}

void print(void)
{
    printf("Executing function print at program termination\n"
           "Program terminated\n");
}
```

```
Enter 1 to terminate program with function exit
Enter 2 to terminate program normally
: 1

Terminating program with function exit
Executing function print at program termination
Program terminated
```

```
Enter 1 to terminate program with function exit
Enter 2 to terminate program normally
: 2

Terminating program by reaching the end of main
Executing function print at program termination
Program terminated
```

Fig. 14.4   Using functions **exit** and **atexit**.

```
3.14159L
1.28f
```

A floating-point constant that is not suffixed is automatically of type **double**.

14.9 More on Files

Chapter 11 introduced capabilities for processing text files with sequential access and random access. C also provides capabilities for processing binary files, but some computer systems do not support binary files. If binary files are not supported, and a file is opened in a binary file mode (Fig. 14.5), the file will be processed as a text file. Binary files should be used instead of text files only in situations where rigid speed, storage, and/or compatibility conditions demand binary files. Otherwise, text files are always preferred for their inherent portability, and for the ability to use other standard tools to examine and manipulate the file data.

Performance Tip 14.2

Consider using binary files instead of text files in applications that demand high performance.

Mode	Description
rb	Open a binary file for reading.
wb	Create a binary file for writing. If the file already exists, discard the current contents.
ab	Append; open or create a binary file for writing at end-of-file.
rb+	Open a binary file for update (reading and writing).
wb+	Create a binary file for update. If the file already exists, discard the current contents.
ab+	Append; open or create a binary file for update; all writing is done at the end of the file.

Fig. 14.5   Binary file open modes.

Portability Tip 14.2

Use text files when writing portable programs.

In addition to the file processing functions discussed in Chapter 11, the standard library also provides function **tmpfile** that opens a temporary file in mode **"wb+"**. Although this is a binary file mode, some systems process temporary files as text files. A temporary file exists until it is closed with **fclose**, or until the program terminates.

The program of Fig. 14.6 changes the tabs in a file to spaces. The program prompts the user to enter the name of a file to be modified. If the file entered by the user and the temporary file are opened successfully, the program reads characters from the file to be modified, and writes them to the temporary file. If the character read is a tab (`'\t'`), it is replaced by a space and written to the temporary file. When the end of the file being modified is reached, the file pointers for each file are repositioned to the start of each file with **rewind**. Next, the temporary file is copied into the original file one character at a time. The program prints the original file as it copies characters into the temporary file, and prints the new file as it copies characters from the temporary file to the original file to confirm the characters being written.

```c
/* Using temporary files */
#include <stdio.h>

main()
{
    FILE *filePtr, *tempFilePtr;
    int c;
    char fileName[30];

    printf("This program changes tabs to spaces.\n"
           "Enter a file to be modified: ");
    scanf("%s", fileName);

    if ( ( filePtr = fopen(fileName, "r+") ) != NULL)

        if ( ( tempFilePtr = tmpfile() ) != NULL) {
            printf("\nThe file before modification is:\n");

            while ( ( c = getc(filePtr) ) != EOF) {
                putchar(c);
                putc(c == '\t' ? ' ': c, tempFilePtr);
            }

            rewind(tempFilePtr);
            rewind(filePtr);
            printf("\n\nThe file after modification is:\n");

            while ( ( c = getc(tempFilePtr) ) != EOF) {
                putchar(c);
                putc(c, filePtr);
            }

        }
        else
            printf("Unable to open temporary file\n");

    else
        printf("Unable to open %s\n", fileName);

    return 0;
}
```

Fig. 14.6   Using temporary files (part 1 of 2).

```
This program changes tabs to spaces.
Enter a file to be modified: data

The file before modification is:
0         1         2         3         4
          5         6         7         8         9

The file after modification is:
0 1 2 3 4
  5 6 7 8 9
```

Fig. 14.6   Using temporary files (part 2 of 2).

14.10 Signal Handling

An unexpected event, or *signal*, can cause a program to terminate prematurely. Some unexpected events include *interrupts* (typing **<ctrl> c** on a UNIX or DOS system), *illegal instructions, segmentation violations, termination orders from the operating system,* and *floating-point exceptions* (division by zero or multiplying large floating-point values). The *signal handling library* provides the capability to *trap* unexpected events with function **signal**. Function **signal** receives two arguments—an integer signal number and a pointer to the signal handling function. Signals can be generated by function *raise* which takes an integer signal number as an argument. Fig. 14.7 summarizes the standard signals defined in header file **signal.h**. The program of Fig. 14.8 demonstrates functions **signal** and **raise**.

    The program of Fig. 14.8 uses function **signal** to trap an interactive signal (**SIGINT**). The program begins by calling **signal** with **SIGINT** and a pointer to function **signal_handler** (remember that the name of a function is a pointer to the beginning of the function). When a signal of type **SIGINT** is generated, control is passed to

Signal	Explanation
SIGABRT	Abnormal termination of the program (such as a call to function **abort**).
SIGFPE	An erroneous arithmetic operation, such as a divide by zero or an operation resulting in overflow.
SIGILL	Detection of an illegal instruction.
SIGINT	Receipt of an interactive attention signal.
SIGSEGV	An invalid access to storage.
SIGTERM	A termination request set to the program.

Fig. 14.7   The signals defined in header **signal.h**.

function **signal_handler**, a message is printed, and the user is given the option to continue normal execution of the program. If the user wishes to continue execution, the signal handler is reinitialized by calling **signal** again (some systems require the signal handler to be reinitialized), and control returns to the point in the program at which the signal was detected. In this program, function **raise** is used to simulate an interactive signal. A random number between **1** and **50** is chosen. If the number is **25**, then **raise** is called to generate the signal. Normally, interactive signals are initiated outside the program. For example, typing **<ctrl> c** during program execution on a UNIX or DOS system generates an interactive signal that terminates program execution. Signal handling can be used to trap the interactive signal and prevent the program from being terminated.

14.11 Dynamic Memory Allocation: Functions Calloc and Realloc

Chapter 12, "Data Structures," introduced the notion of dynamically allocating memory using the **malloc** function. As we stated in Chapter 12, arrays are better than linked lists for rapid sorting, searching, and data access. However, arrays are normally *static data structures*. The general utilities library (**stdlib.h**) provides two other functions for dynamic memory allocation—**calloc** and **realloc**. These functions can be used to create and modify *dynamic arrays*. As shown in Chapter 7, "Pointers," a pointer to an array can be subscripted like an array. Thus, a pointer to a contiguous portion of memory created by **calloc** can be manipulated as an array. Function **calloc** dynamically allocates memory for an array. The prototype for **calloc** is

```
void *calloc(size_t nmemb, size_t size);
```

It receives two arguments—the number of elements (**nmemb**) and the size of each element (**size**)—and initializes the elements of the array to zero. The function returns a pointer to the allocated memory, or a **NULL** pointer if the memory is not allocated.

Function **realloc** changes the size of an object allocated by a previous call to **malloc**, **calloc**, or **realloc**. The original object's contents are not modified provided that the amount of memory allocated is larger than the amount allocated previously. Otherwise, the contents are unchanged up to the size of the new object. The prototype for **realloc** is

```
void *realloc(void *ptr, size_t size);
```

Function **realloc** takes two arguments—a pointer to the original object (**ptr**) and the new size of the object (**size**). If **ptr** is **NULL**, **realloc** works identically to **malloc**. If **size** is **0** and **ptr** is not **NULL**, the memory for the object is freed. Otherwise, if **ptr** is not **NULL** and size is greater than zero, **realloc** tries to allocate a new block of memory for the object. If the new space can not be allocated, the object pointed to by **ptr** is unchanged. Function **realloc** returns either a pointer to the reallocated memory, or a **NULL** pointer.

14.12 The Unconditional Branch: Goto

Throughout the text we have stressed the importance of using structured programming techniques to build reliable software that is easy to debug, maintain, and modify. In some

```c
/* Using signal handling */

#include <stdio.h>
#include <signal.h>
#include <stdlib.h>
#include <time.h>

void signal_handler(int);

main()
{
   int i, x;

   signal(SIGINT, signal_handler);
   srand(clock());

   for (i = 1; i <= 100; i++) {
      x = 1 + rand() % 50;

      if (x == 25)
         raise(SIGINT);

      printf("%4d", i);

      if (i % 10 == 0)
         printf("\n");
   }

   return 0;
}

void signal_handler(int signalValue)
{
   int response;

   printf("%s%d%s\n%s",
          "\nInterrupt signal (", signalValue, ") received.",
          "Do you wish to continue (1 = yes or 2 = no)? ");

   scanf("%d", &response);

   while (response != 1 && response != 2) {
      printf("(1 = yes or 2 = no)? ");
      scanf("%d", &response);
   }

   if (response == 1)
      signal(SIGINT, signal_handler);
   else
      exit(EXIT_SUCCESS);
}
```

Fig. 14.8 Using signal handling (part 1 of 2).

```
    1    2    3    4    5    6    7    8    9   10
   11   12   13   14   15   16   17   18   19   20
   21   22   23   24   25   26   27   28   29   30
   31   32   33   34   35   36   37   38   39   40
   41   42   43   44   45   46   47   48   49   50
   51   52   53   54   55   56   57   58   59   60
   61   62   63   64   65   66   67   68   69   70
   71   72   73   74   75   76   77   78   79   80
   81   82   83   84   85   86   87   88
Interrupt signal (4) received.
Do you wish to continue (1 = yes or 2 = no)? 1
   89   90
   91   92   93   94   95   96   97   98   99  100
```

Fig. 14.8   Using signal handling (part 2 of 2).

cases, performance is more important than strict adherence to structured programming techniques. In these cases, some unstructured programming techniques may be used. For example, we can use **break** to terminate execution of a repetition structure before the loop continuation condition becomes false. This saves unnecessary repetitions of the loop if the task is completed before loop termination.

Another instance of unstructured programming is the *goto statement*—an unconditional branch. The result of the **goto** statement is a change in the flow of control of the program to the first statement after the *label* specified in the **goto** statement. A label is an identifier followed by a colon. A label must appear in the same function as the **goto** statement that refers to it. The program of Fig. 14.9 uses **goto** statements to loop ten times and print the counter value each time. After initializing **count** to **1**, the program tests **count** to determine whether it is greater than **10** (the label **start** is skipped because labels do not perform any action). If so, control is transferred from the **goto** to the first statement after the label **end**. Otherwise, **count** is printed and incremented, and control is transferred from the **goto** to the first statement after the label **start**.

In Chapter 3, we stated that only three control structures are required to write any program—sequence, selection, and repetition. When the rules of structured programming are followed, it is possible to create deeply-nested control structures from which it is difficult to efficiently escape. Some programmers use **goto** statements in such situations as a quick exit from a deeply-nested structure. This eliminates the need to test multiple conditions to escape from a control structure.

Performance Tip 14.3

The goto statement can be used to exit deeply-nested control structures efficiently.

Software Engineering Observation 14.3

*The **goto** statement should be used only in performance-oriented applications. The **goto** statement is unstructured and can lead to programs that are more difficult to debug, maintain, and modify.*

```
/* Using goto */
#include <stdio.h>

main()
{
    int count = 1;

    start:                          /* label */
        if (count > 10)
            goto end;

        printf("%d  ", count);
        ++count;
        goto start;

    end:                            /* label */
        putchar('\n');

    return 0;
}
```

```
1  2  3  4  5  6  7  8  9  10
```

Fig. 14.9 Using `goto`.

Summary

- On many computer systems—UNIX and DOS systems in particular—it is possible to redirect input to a program and output from a program.

- Input is redirected from the UNIX and DOS command lines using the redirect input symbol (<) or using a pipe (|).

- Output is redirected from the UNIX and DOS command lines using the redirect output symbol (>) or the append output symbol (>>). The redirect output symbol simply stores the program output in a file, and the append output symbol appends the output to the end of a file.

- The macros and definitions of the variable arguments header **stdarg.h** provide the capabilities necessary to build functions with variable-length argument lists.

- An ellipsis (**. . .**) in a function prototype indicates a variable number of arguments.

- Type **va_list** is suitable for holding information needed by macros **va_start**, **va_arg**, and **va_end**. To access the arguments in a variable-length argument list, an object of type **va_list** must be declared.

- Macro **va_start** is invoked before the arguments of a variable-length argument list can be accessed. The macro initializes the object declared with **va_list** for use by the **va_arg** and **va_end** macros.

- Macro **va_arg** expands to an expression of the value and type of the next argument in the variable length argument list. Each invocation of **va_arg** modifies the object declared with **va_list** so that the object points to the next argument in the list.

- Macro **va_end** facilitates a normal return from a function whose variable argument list was referred to by the **va_start** macro.

- On many systems—DOS and UNIX in particular—it is possible to pass arguments to **main** from the command line by including the parameters **int argc** and **char *argv[]** in the parameter list of **main**. Parameter **argc** receives the number of command-line arguments. Parameter **argv** is an array of strings in which the actual command-line arguments are stored.

- The definition of a function must be entirely contained in one file—it can not span two or more files.

- Global variables must be declared in each file in which they are used.

- Function prototypes can extend the scope of a function beyond the file in which it is defined (the **extern** specifier is not required in a function prototype). This is accomplished by including the function prototype in each file in which the function is invoked and compiling the files together.

- The storage class specifier **static**, when applied to a global variable or a function, prevents it from being used by any function that is not defined in the same file. This is referred to as internal linkage. Global variables and functions that are not preceded by **static** in their definitions have external linkage—they can be accessed in other files if those files contain proper declarations and/or function prototypes.

- The **static** specifier is commonly used with utility functions that are called only by functions in a particular file. If a function is not required outside a particular file, the principle of least privilege should be enforced by using **static**.

- When building large programs in multiple source files, compiling the program becomes tedious if small changes are made to one file, and the entire program must be recompiled. Many systems provide special utilities that recompile only the modified program file. On UNIX systems the utility is called **make**. Utility **make** reads a file called **makefile** that contains instructions for compiling and linking the program.

- Function **exit** forces a program to terminate as if it executed normally.

- Function **atexit** registers a function in a program to be called upon normal termination of the program—i.e., either when the program terminates by reaching the end of **main** or when **exit** is invoked.

- Function **atexit** takes a pointer to a function (i.e., the function name) as an argument. Functions called at program termination cannot have arguments, and cannot return a value. Up to 32 functions may be registered for execution at program termination.

- Function **exit** takes one argument. The argument is normally the symbolic constant **EXIT_SUCCESS** or the symbolic constant **EXIT_FAILURE**. If **exit** is called with

EXIT_SUCCESS, the implementation-defined value for successful termination is returned to the calling environment. If **exit** is called with **EXIT_FAILURE**, the implementation-defined value for unsuccessful termination is returned.

- When function **exit** is invoked, any functions registered with **atexit** are invoked in the reverse order of their registration, all streams associated with the program are flushed and closed, and control returns to the host environment.

- The ANSI standard (An90) indicates that when **volatile** is used to qualify a type, the nature of the access to an object of that type is implementation dependent. Kernighan and Ritchie (Ke88) indicate that the **volatile** qualifier is used to suppress various kinds of optimizations.

- C provides integer and floating-point suffixes for specifying the types of integer and floating-point constants. The integer suffixes are: **u** or **U** for an **unsigned** integer, **l** or **L** for a **long** integer, and **ul** or **UL** for an **unsigned long** integer. If an integer constant is not suffixed, its type is determined by the first type capable of storing a value of that size (first **int**, then **long int**, then **unsigned long int**). The floating-point suffixes are: **f** or **F** for a **float**, and **l** or **L** for a **long double**. A floating-point constant that is not suffixed is of type **double**.

- C also provides capabilities for processing binary files, but some computer systems do not support binary files. If binary files are not supported, and a file is opened in a binary file mode, the file will be processed as a text file.

- Function **tmpfile** opens a temporary file in mode **"wb+"**. Although this is a binary file mode, some systems process temporary files as text files. A temporary file exists until it is closed with **fclose** or until the program terminates.

- The signal handling library provides the capability to trap unexpected events with function **signal**. Function **signal** receives two arguments—an integer signal number and a pointer to the signal handling function.

- Signals can also be generated with function **raise** and an integer argument.

- The general utilities library (**stdlib.h**) provides two functions for dynamic memory allocation—**calloc** and **realloc**. These functions can be used to create dynamic arrays.

- Function **calloc** receives two arguments—the number of elements (**nmemb**) and the size of each element (**size**)—and initializes the elements of the array to zero. The function returns either a pointer to the allocated memory, or a **NULL** pointer if the memory is not allocated.

- Function **realloc** changes the size of an object allocated by a previous call to **malloc**, **calloc**, or **realloc**. The original object's contents are not modified provided that the amount of memory allocated is larger than the amount allocated previously.

- Function **realloc** takes two arguments—a pointer to the original object (**ptr**) and the new size of the object (**size**). If **ptr** is **NULL**, **realloc** works identically to **malloc**. If **size** is **0** and the pointer received is not **NULL**, the memory for the ob ject is freed. Otherwise, if **ptr** is not **NULL** and size is greater than zero, **realloc** tries to allocate a new block of memory for the object. If the new space cannot be allocated, the object pointed to by **ptr** is unchanged. Function **realloc** returns either a pointer to the reallocated memory, or a **NULL** pointer.

- The result of the **goto** statement is a change in the flow of control of the program. Program execution continues at the first statement after the label specified in the **goto** statement.

- A label is an identifier followed by a colon. A label must appear in the same function as the **goto** statement that refers to it.

Terminology

append output symbol **>>**	**makefile**
argc	pipe **|**
argv	piping
atexit	**raise**
calloc	**realloc**
command-line arguments	redirect input symbol **<**
const	redirect output symbol **>**
dynamic arrays	segmentation violation
event	**signal**
exit	signal handling library
external linkage	**signal.h**
extern storage class specifier	**static** storage class specifier
EXIT_FAILURE	**stdarg.h**
EXIT_SUCCESS	temporary file
float suffix (**f** or **F**)	**tmpfile**
floating-point exception	trap
goto statement	**unsigned** integer suffix (**u** or **U**)
I/O redirection	**unsigned long** integer suffix (**ul** or **UL**)
illegal instruction	**va_arg**
internal linkage	**va_end**
interrupt	**va_list**
long double suffix (**l** or **L**)	**va_start**
long integer suffix (**l** or **L**)	variable-length argument list
make	**volatile**

Common Programming Error

14.1   Placing an ellipsis in the middle of a function parameter list. An ellipsis may only be placed at the end of the parameter list.

Portability Tips

14.1   Some systems do not support global variable names or function names of more than 6 characters. This should be considered when writing programs that will be ported to multiple platforms.

14.2   Use text files when writing portable programs.

Performance Tips

14.1   Global variables increase performance because they can be accessed directly by any function—the overhead of passing data to functions is eliminated.

14.2   Consider using binary files instead of text files in applications that demand high performance.

14.3   The `goto` statement can be used to exit deeply-nested control structures efficiently.

Software Engineering Observations

14.1   Global variables should be avoided unless application performance is critical because they violate the principle of least privilege.

14.2   Creating programs in multiple source files facilitates software reusability and good software engineering. Functions may be common to many applications. In such instances, those functions should be stored in their own source files, and each source file should have a corresponding header file containing function prototypes. This enables programmers of different applications to reuse the same code by including the proper header file, and compiling their application with the corresponding source file.

14.3   The `goto` statement should be used only in performance-oriented applications. The `goto` statement is unstructured and can lead to programs that are more difficult to debug, maintain, and modify.

Self-Review Exercises

14.1   Fill in the blanks in each of the following:

a) The _____ symbol is used to redirect input data from the keyboard to come from a file.

b) The _____ symbol is used to redirect the screen output to be placed in a file.

c) The _____ symbol is used to append the output of a program to the end of a file.

d) A _____ is used to direct the output of one program to be the input of another program.

e) An _____ in the parameter list of a function indicates that the function can receive a variable number of arguments.

f) Macro _____ must be invoked before the arguments in a variable-length argument list can be accessed.

g) Macro _____ is used to access the individual arguments of a variable-length argument list.

h) Macro _____ facilitates a normal return from a function whose variable argument list was referred to by macro `va_start`.

i) Argument _____ of `main` receives the number of arguments in a command line.

j) Argument _____ of `main` stores command-line arguments as a character strings.

k) The UNIX utility _____ reads a file called _____ that contains instructions for compiling and linking a program consisting of multiple source files. The utility only recompiles a file if the file has been modified since it was last compiled.

l) Function _____ forces a program to terminate execution.

m) Function _____ registers a function to be called upon normal termination of the program.

n) Type qualifier _____ indicates that an object should not be modified after it is initialized.

o) An integer or floating-point _____ can be appended to an integer or floating-point constant to specify the exact type of the constant.

p) Function _____ opens a temporary file that exists until it is closed or program execution terminates.

q) Function _____ can be used to trap unexpected events.

r) Function _____ generates a signal from within a program.

s) Function _____ dynamically allocates memory for an array and initializes the elements to zero.

t) Function _____ changes the size of a block of memory dynamically allocated previously.

Answers to Self-Review Exercises

14.1 a) redirect input (`<`). b) redirect output (`>`). c) append output (`>>`). d) pipe (`|`). e) ellipsis (`...`). f) `va_start`. g) `va_arg`. h) `va_end`. i) `argc`. j) `argv`. k) `make`, `makefile`. l) `exit`. m) `atexit`. n) `const`. o) suffix. p) `tmpfile`. q) `signal`. r) `raise`. s) `calloc`. t) `realloc`.

Exercises

14.2 Write a program that calculates the product of a series of integers that are passed to function `product` using a variable-length argument list. Test your function with several calls each with a different number of arguments.

14.3 Write a program that prints the command-line arguments of the program.

14.4 Write a program that sorts an array of integers into ascending order or descending order. The program should use command-line arguments to pass either argument `-a` for ascending order or `-d` for descending order. (Note: This is the standard format for passing options to a program in UNIX.)

14.5 Write a program that places a space between each character in a file. The program should first write the contents of the file being modified into a temporary file with spaces between each character, then copy the file back to the original file. This operation should overwrite the original contents of the file.

14.6 Read the manuals for your system to determine what signals are supported by the signal handling library (`signal.h`). Write a program that contains signal handlers for the standard signals `SIGABRT` and `SIGINT`. The program should test the trapping of these signals by calling function `abort` to generate a signal of type `SIGABRT`, and by typing `<ctrl> c` to generate a signal of type `SIGINT`.

14.7 Write a program that dynamically allocates an array of integers. The size of the array should be input from the keyboard. The elements of the array should be assigned values input from the keyboard. Print the values of the array. Next, reallocate the memory for the array to 1/2 of the current number of elements. Print the values remaining in the array to confirm that they match the first half of the values in the original array.

14.8 Write a program that takes two command-line arguments that are file names, reads the characters from the first file one at a time, and writes the characters in reverse order to the second file.

14.9 Write a program that uses `goto` statements to simulate a nested looping structure that prints a square of asterisks as follows:

```
*****
*   *
*   *
*   *
*****
```

The program should use only the following three `printf` statements:

```
printf("*");
printf(" ");
printf("\n");
```

15

C++ as a "Better C"

Objectives

- To become familiar with the C++ enhancements to C.
- To appreciate why C provides a foundation for further study of programming in general and C++ in particular.

*All the better to see
you with my dear.*
The Big Bad Wolf to Little Red Riding Hood

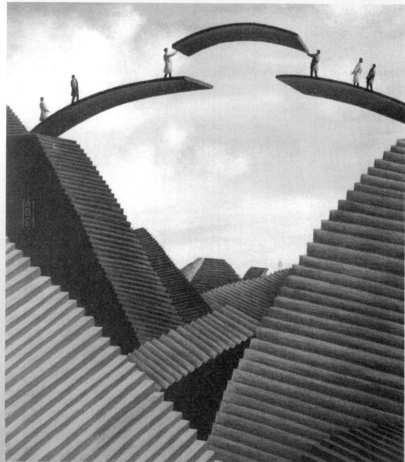

559

Outline

15.1 Introduction

Welcome to C++! C++ improves on many of C's features and provides *object-oriented programming (OOP)* capabilities that hold great promise for increasing software productivity, quality, and reusability. The remainder of this chapter discusses many of C++'s enhancements to C.

C's designers and early implementers never anticipated that the language would become such a phenomenon (the same holds true for the UNIX operating system). When a programming language becomes as entrenched as C, new requirements demand that the language evolve rather than simply be displaced by a new language.

C++ was developed by Bjarne Stroustrup at Bell Laboratories (St86), and was originally called "C with classes." The name C++ includes C's increment operator (++) to indicate that C++ is an enhanced version of C.

C++ is a superset of C, so programmers can use a C++ compiler to compile existing C programs, and then gradually evolve these programs to C++. Already, some leading software vendors offer C++ compilers and do not offer separate C products.

No ANSI standard exists yet, although an ANSI committee is developing a proposal. Many people believe that most major C programming environments will convert to C++ by the mid-1990s.

15.2 C++ Single-Line Comments

Programmers frequently insert a small comment at the end of a line of code. C requires that a comment be delimited by /* and */. C++ allows you to begin a comment with // and use the remainder of the line for comment text; the end of the line automatically terminates the comment. This form of comment saves some keystrokes, but is only applicable for comments that do not continue to the next line.

For example, the C comment

```
/* This is a single-line comment. */
```

requires both the /* and */ delimiters, even for a single-line comment. The C++ single-line version of this is

```
// This is a single-line comment.
```

For multiple-line comments such as

```
/* This is one way to   */
/* write neat multiple- */
/* line comments.       */
```

the C++ notation may appear to be more concise as in

```
// This is one way to
// write neat multiple-
// line comments.
```

But remember that C comments may span multiple lines, so only a single pair (rather than the three pairs we have used) of comment delimiters is actually needed as in

```
/* This is one way to
   write neat multiple-
   line comments.       */
```

Since C++ is a superset of C, both comment forms are acceptable in a C++ program.

Common Programming Error 15.1

*Forgetting to close a C-style comment with */.*

Good Programming Practice 15.1

*Using C++-style // comments avoids the unterminated comment errors that occur by forgetting to close C-style comments with */.*

This seemingly simple error can lead to deeply subtle errors, some of which can slip past the compiler undetected. The effect of omitting the `*/` is that the compiler assumes the comment has not ended yet, so the compiler assumes the comment continues across all subsequent lines until either another comment's `*/` or the end of the program file is reached. This could result in the compiler ignoring a key portion of a program.

15.3 C++ Stream Input/Output

C++ provides an alternative to `printf` and `scanf` function calls for handling input/output of the standard data types and strings. For example, the simple dialog

```
printf("Enter new tag: ");
scanf("%d", &tag);
printf("The new tag is: %d\n", tag);
```

is written in C++ as

```
cout << "Enter new tag: ";
cin >> tag;
cout << "The new tag is: " << tag << '\n';
```

The first statement uses the *standard output stream* `cout` and the operator `<<` (the *stream insertion operator*, pronounced *"put to"*). The statement is read

The string **"Enter new tag"** *is put to the output stream* **cout**.

Note that the stream insertion operator is also the bitwise left shift operator. The second statement uses the *standard input stream* `cin` and the operator `>>` (the *stream extraction operator*, pronounced *"get from"*). This statement is read

Get a value for tag from the input stream **cin**.

Note that the stream extraction operator is also the bitwise right shift operator when the left argument is an integer type. The stream insertion and extraction operators, unlike `printf` and `scanf`, do not require format strings and conversion specifiers to indicate the data types being output or input. C++ has many instances like this in which it automatically "knows" what types to use. Also note that, when used with the stream extraction operator, variable `tag` is not preceded by the address operator `&` required by `scanf`.

C++ programs must include the header file *iostream.h* to use stream input/output. The program of Fig. 15.1 prompts for variables `myAge` and `friendsAge` and determines whether you are older than, younger than, or the same age as your friend. Note the placement of the age declarations just before the ages are referenced in the input statements. Chapter 21, "Stream Input/Output," provides a detailed description of C++'s Stream I/O features.

Good Programming Practice 15.2

Using C++-style stream-oriented input/output makes programs more readable (and less error prone) than their counterparts in C written with `printf` *and* `scanf` *function calls.*

```
// Simple stream input/output
#include <iostream.h>

main()
{
    cout << "Enter your age: ";
    int myAge;
    cin >> myAge;

    cout << "Enter your friend's age: ";
    int friendsAge;
    cin >> friendsAge;

    if (myAge > friendsAge)
        cout << "You are older.\n";
    else
        if (myAge < friendsAge)
            cout << "You are younger.\n";
        else
            cout << "You and your friend are the same age.\n";

    return 0;
}
```

```
Enter your age: 23
Enter your friend's age: 20
You are older.
```

```
Enter your age: 20
Enter your friend's age: 23
You are younger.
```

```
Enter your age: 20
Enter your friend's age: 20
You and your friend are the same age.
```

Fig. 15.1   Stream I/O with the stream insertion and the stream extraction
operators.

15.4 Declarations in C++

In C, all declarations must appear before any executable statements in a block. In C++,
declarations can be placed anywhere an executable statement can appear provided the
declarations precede the use of what is being declared. For example,

```
cout << "Enter two integers: ";
int x, y;
cin >> x >> y;
cout << "The sum of " << x << " and " << y
     << " is " << x + y << '\n';
```

declares variables **x** and **y** after the executable **cout** statement but before they are used in the subsequent **cin** statement. Also, variables can be declared in the initialization section of a **for** structure—such variables remain in scope until the end of the block in which the **for** structure is defined. For example,

```
for (int i = 0; i <= 5; i++)
   cout << i << '\n';
```

declares variable **i** to be an integer and initializes it to **0** in the **for** structure.

The scope of a local C++ variable begins with its declaration and extends to the enclosing right brace (**}**). Therefore, statements preceding a variable declaration can not reference the variable even if the statements are in the same block. Variable declarations can not be placed in the condition of a **while**, **do/while**, **for**, or **if** structure.

Good Programming Practice 15.3

Placing a variable's declaration close to its first use can make programs more readable.

Common Programming Error 15.2

Declaring a variable after it is referenced in a statement.

15.5 Creating New Data Types in C++

C++ provides the ability to create user-defined types using the **enum** keyword, **struct** keyword, **union** keyword, and the new **class** keyword. As in C, C++ enumerations are declared with **enum**. However, unlike C, an enumeration in C++ becomes a new type when it is declared. Keyword **enum** is not required to declare variables of the new type. The same is true of **struct**s, **union**s and **class**es. For example, the declarations

```
enum Boolean {FALSE, TRUE};

struct Name {
   char first[10];
   char last[10];
};

union Number {
   int i;
   float f;
};
```

create three user-defined data types with tag names **Boolean**, **Name**, and **Number**. The tag names can be used to declare variables as follows:

```
Boolean done = FALSE;
Name student;
Number x;
```

These declarations create the **Boolean** variable **done** (initialized to **FALSE**), the **Name** variable **student**, and the **Number** variable **x**.

As in C, enumerations are valued beginning at zero by default and each subsequent element is incremented by one. Thus, the **Boolean** enumeration assigns the value **0** to **FALSE** and **1** to **TRUE**. Any element in an enumeration can be assigned an integer value. Subsequent elements that are not specifically assigned a value automatically receive the previous element's value incremented by one.

15.6 Function Prototypes and Type Checking

Function prototypes enable the C compiler to type check the accuracy of function invocations. In ANSI C, function prototypes are optional. In C++, function prototypes are required for all functions. A function defined in a file before any call to the function does not require a separate function prototype. In this case, the function header acts as the function prototype. C++ also requires all function parameters to be declared in the parentheses of the function definition and prototype. For example, a function **square** that takes an integer argument and returns an integer has the prototype:

```
int square(int);
```

Functions that do not return a value are declared with return type **void**.

Common Programming Error 15.3

*An attempt to return a value from a **void** function or to use the result of a **void** function invocation.*

To specify an empty parameter list in C, the **void** keyword is placed in parentheses. If nothing is placed in the parentheses of a C function prototype, all argument checking is turned off for that function and nothing is assumed about the number of arguments and types of arguments to the function. Any function call for that function can pass whatever arguments it wants to without the compiler reporting any errors.

In C++, an empty parameter list is specified by writing either **void** or nothing at all in parentheses. The declaration

```
void print();
```

specifies that function **print** takes no arguments and does not return a value. Fig. 15.2 demonstrates both C++ ways of declaring and using functions that take no arguments.

Portability Tip 15.1

The meaning of an empty function parameter list in C++ is dramatically different than in C. In C, it means all argument checking is disabled. In C++, it means that the function takes no arguments. Thus, C programs using this feature may perform differently when compiled in C++.

Common Programming Error 15.4

C++ programs do not compile unless function prototypes are provided for every function, or each function is defined before it is used.

```
// Functions that take no arguments
#include <iostream.h>

void f1();
void f2(void);

main()
{
    f1();
    f2();

    return 0;
}

void f1()
{
    cout << "Function f1 takes no arguments\n";
}

void f2(void)
{
    cout << "Function f2 also takes no arguments\n";
}
```

```
Function f1 takes no arguments
Function f2 also takes no arguments
```

Fig. 15.2 Two ways to declare and use functions that take no arguments.

15.7 Inline Functions

Implementing a program as a set of functions is good from a software engineering standpoint, but function calls involve execution-time overhead. C++ provides *inline functions* to help reduce function-call overhead—especially for small functions. The qualifier **inline** before a function's return type in the function definition "advises" the compiler to generate a copy the function's code in place (when appropriate) to avoid a function call. The tradeoff is that multiple copies of the function code are inserted in the program rather than having a single copy of the function to which control is passed each time the function is called. The compiler can ignore the **inline** qualifier and typically does so for all but the smallest functions.

Software Engineering Observation 15.1

*Any change to an **inline** function requires all clients of the function to be recompiled. This may be significant in some program development and maintenance situations.*

Inline functions provide advantages over preprocessor macros (see Chapter 13) that expand code in line. One advantage is that **inline** functions are just like any other C++ function. Therefore, proper type checking is performed on calls to **inline** functions;

preprocessor macros do not support type checking. Another advantage is that `inline` functions eliminate the unexpected side effects associated with improper use of preprocessor macros. Finally, `inline` functions can be debugged with a debugger program. The debugger does not recognize preprocessor macros as special units because they are simply text substitutions performed by the preprocessor before program compilation. A debugger can help locate logic errors resulting from macro substitutions, but can not attribute those errors to specific macros.

Good Programming Practice 15.4

The `inline` qualifier should be used only with small, frequently used functions.

Performance Tip 15.1

Using `inline` functions can reduce execution time, but can increase program size.

The program of Fig. 15.3 uses `inline` function `cube` to calculate the volume of a cube of side `s`. The keyword `const` in the parameter list of function cube tells the compiler that the function does not modify variable `s`. The `const` keyword is discussed in further detail in Section 15.9.

Preprocessor macros are operations defined in a `#define` preprocessor directive. A macro consists of a name (macro identifier) and replacement text. Macros can be defined with or without an argument list. Macros without arguments are processed like symbolic constants—the replacement text is substituted for the macro identifier in the program. Macros with arguments substitute the arguments in the replacement text, then expand the macro in the program.

```
// Using an inline function to calculate
// the volume of a cube
#include <iostream.h>

inline float cube(const float s) { return s * s * s; }

main()
{
   cout << "Enter the side length of your cube:   ";

   float side;

   cin >> side;
   cout << "Volume of cube with side "
        << side << " is " << cube(side) << '\n';

   return 0;
}
```

```
Enter the side length of your cube:   3.5
Volume of cube with side 3.5 is 42.875
```

Fig. 15.3   Using an inline function to calculate the volume of a cube.

Consider the following one-argument macro for calculating the area of a square:

```
#define VALIDSQUARE(x)     (x) * (x)
```

The preprocessor locates each occurrence of **VALIDSQUARE(x)** in the program, substitutes **x** (either a value or an expression) in the replacement text, and expands the macro in the program. For example,

```
cout << VALIDSQUARE(7);
```

is expanded to

```
cout << (7) * (7);
```

The parentheses in the replacement text force the proper order of evaluation of the macro operation. For example,

```
cout << VALIDSQUARE(2 + 3);
```

is expanded to

```
cout << (2 + 3) * (2 + 3);
```

which evaluates properly to **5 * 5 = 25**. The preprocessor does not evaluate expressions provided as arguments to a macro; it simply replaces each occurrence of the argument name in the replacement text with a copy of the entire expression. Therefore, parentheses are necessary to ensure arguments are evaluated correctly.

Consider a corresponding macro without parentheses in the replacement text:

```
#define INVALIDSQUARE(x)     x * x
```

If we provide 2 + 3 as the argument, the macro is expanded as follows:

```
2 + 3 * 2 + 3
```

This expression is evaluated improperly as **2 + 6 + 3 = 11** because multiplication has a higher precedence than addition.

C++ provides inline functions to eliminate the problems associated with macros, to remove the overhead associated with function calls, and to provide argument checking for functions. Inline function arguments are evaluated before they are "passed" to the function. Therefore, parentheses are not needed around each occurrence of each argument in an inline function body.

The inline function

```
inline int square(int x) { return x * x; }
```

calculates the square of its integer argument **x**. The call **square(2 + 3)** evaluates the argument **2 + 3 = 5** and substitutes its value in the function body. The program of Fig. 15.4 demonstrates the macros **VALIDSQUARE** and **INVALIDSQUARE** and the inline function **square**.

```cpp
// Comparing call by value, call by reference with
// pointers, and call by reference with references
#include <iostream.h>

int squareByValue(int);
void squareByPointer(int *);
void squareByReference(int &);

main()
{
   int x = 2, y = 3, z = 4;

   cout << "x = " << x << " before squareByValue\n"
        << "Value returned by squareByValue: "
        << squareByValue(x)
        << "\nx = " << x << " after squareByValue\n\n";

   cout << "y = " << y << " before squareByPointer\n";
   squareByPointer(&y);
   cout << "y = " << y << " after squareByPointer\n\n";

   cout << "z = " << z << " before squareByReference\n";
   squareByReference(z);
   cout << "z = " << z << " after squareByReference\n";

   return 0;
}

int squareByValue(int a)
{
   return a *= a;    // caller's argument not modified
}

void squareByPointer(int *bPtr)
{
   *bPtr *= *bPtr;   // caller's argument modified
}

void squareByReference(int &cRef)
{
   cRef *= cRef;     // caller's argument modified
}
```

```
x = 2 before squareByValue
Value returned by squareByValue: 4
x = 2 after squareByValue

y = 3 before squareByPointer
y = 9 after squareByPointer

z = 4 before squareByReference
z = 16 after squareByReference
```

Fig. 15.6 An example of call by reference.

```
int &count
```

in a function header may be pronounced "`count` is a reference to `int`." In the function call, simply mention the variable by name and it is automatically passed by reference. Then, mentioning the variable by its local name in the body of the function actually refers to the original variable in the calling function, and the original variable can be modified directly by the called function.

Figure 15.6 compares call by value, call by reference with pointers, and call by reference with reference parameters. The arguments in the calls to `squareByValue` and `squareByReference` are identical. It is impossible to tell if either function modifies its arguments without checking the function prototypes or function definitions. For this reason, some C++ programmers prefer that modifiable arguments be passed to functions by using pointers, and non-modifiable arguments be passed to functions by using references to constants. References to constants provide the efficiency of pointer passing and prevent modification of the calling program's arguments. To specify a reference to a constant, place the `const` qualifier before the type specifier in the parameter declaration (Section 15.9 discusses `const` in detail). Note the placement of `*` and `&` in the parameter lists of the two functions. Some C++ programmers prefer to write `int* bPtr` rather than `int *bPtr`, and `int& cRef` rather than `int &cRef`.

Good Programming Practice 15.5

Use pointers to pass arguments that may be modified by the called function, and use references to constants to pass large arguments that will not be modified.

Common Programming Error 15.6

Because reference parameters are mentioned only by name in the body of the called function, the programmer might inadvertently treat reference parameters as call by value parameters. This can cause unexpected side effects if the original copies of the variables are changed by the calling function.

Performance Tip 15.2

For large objects, use a `const` reference parameter to simulate the appearance and security of call by value, but to avoid the overhead of passing a copy of the large object.

References can also be used as aliases for other variables within a function. For example, the code

```
int count = 1;      // declare integer variable count
int &c = count;     // create c as an alias for count

++c;                // increment count (using its alias)
```

increments variable `count` using its alias `c`. Reference variables must be initialized in their declarations (see Fig. 15.7 and Fig. 15.8), and cannot be reassigned as aliases to other variables. Once a reference is declared as an alias for another variable, all operations supposedly performed on the alias (i.e., the reference) are actually performed on the original variable itself. The alias is simply another name for the original variable—no

C++ keywords				

C and C++

auto	break	case	char	const
continue	default	do	double	else
enum	extern	float	for	goto
if	int	long	register	return
short	signed	sizeof	static	struct
switch	typedef	union	unsigned	void
volatile	while			

C++ only

asm	Implementation-defined means of using assembly language through C++ (see the manuals for your system).
catch	Handle an exception generated by a **throw**.
class	Define a new class. Objects of this class may be created.
delete	Destroy a memory object created with **new**.
friend	Declare a function or class to be a "friend" of another class. Friends may access all the data members and member functions of a class.
inline	Advise the compiler that a particular function should be generated inline as opposed to requiring a function call.
new	Dynamically allocate a memory object "on the free store"—extra memory available to the program at execution time. Automatically determine the object's size.
operator	Declare an "overloaded" operator.
private	A class member accessible to member functions and **friend** functions of the **private** member's class.
protected	An extended form of **private** access; **protected** members may also be accessed by member functions of derived classes and friends of derived classes.
public	A class member accessible to any function.
template	Declare how to construct a class or function using a variety of types.
this	A pointer implicitly declared in every non-**static** member function of a class. It points to the object for which this member function has been invoked.
throw	Transfer control to an exception handler or terminate program execution if an appropriate handler cannot be located.
try	Creates a block containing a set of statements that may generate exceptions, and enables exception handling for any exceptions generated.
virtual	Declare a virtual function.

Fig. 15.5 The C++ keywords.

```
// Examples of valid macros, invalid macros
// and inline functions
#include <iostream.h>

#define VALIDSQUARE(x)     (x) * (x)
#define INVALIDSQUARE(x)   x * x

inline int square(int x) { return x * x; }

main()
{
   cout << "  VALIDSQUARE(2 + 3) = "
        << VALIDSQUARE(2 + 3)
        << "\nINVALIDSQUARE(2 + 3) = "
        << INVALIDSQUARE(2 + 3)
        << "\n        square(2 + 3) = "
        << square(2 + 3) << '\n';

   return 0;
}
```

```
   VALIDSQUARE(2 + 3) = 25
 INVALIDSQUARE(2 + 3) = 11
        square(2 + 3) = 25
```

Fig. 15.4   Preprocessor macros and inline functions.

Figure 15.5 contains a complete list of C++ keywords. The figure shows keywords common to C and C++ and then highlights the keywords unique to C++. Each of the new C++ keywords is explained in detail later in the book.

Common Programming Error 15.5

C++ is an evolving language and some features may not be available on your compiler. Using unimplemented features will cause syntax errors.

15.8 Reference Parameters

In C, all function calls are call by value. Call by reference is simulated in C by passing a pointer to an object and then accessing the object by dereferencing the pointer in the called function. Remember that array names in C are already (constant) pointers so arrays are automatically passed simulated call by reference. Other programming languages offer direct forms of call by reference—such as **var** parameters in Pascal. C++ corrects this weakness of C by offering *reference parameters.*

A reference parameter is an alias for its corresponding argument. To indicate that a function parameter is passed by reference, simply follow the parameter's type in the function prototype by an ampersand (**&**) (exactly as you would follow a parameter's type by ***** to indicate that a parameter is a pointer to a variable). Use the same convention when listing the parameter's type in the function header. For example, the declaration space is reserved for the alias. References cannot be dereferenced using the pointer indirection operator (*). References cannot be used to perform "reference arithmetic" (as is possible when we use pointers in pointer arithmetic to point to other array elements). Other invalid operations on references include pointing to references, taking the address of references, and comparing references (actually each of these operations does not cause a syntax error; rather each operation actually occurs on the variable for which the reference is an alias).

Functions can return pointers or references, but this can be dangerous. When returning a pointer or a reference to a variable declared in the called function, the variable should be declared **static** within that function. Otherwise the pointer or reference refers to an automatic variable that is discarded when the function terminates; such a variable is said to be "undefined" and the program's behavior would be unpredictable.

Common Programming Error 15.7

Not initializing a reference variable when it is declared.

Common Programming Error 15.8

Attempting to reassign a previously declared reference to be an alias to another variable.

Common Programming Error 15.9

Attempting to dereference a reference variable using the pointer indirection operator (remember that a reference is an alias for a variable, and is not a pointer to a variable).

```cpp
// References must be initialized
#include <iostream.h>

main()
{
    int x = 3, &y;    // Error: y must be initialized

    cout << "x = " << x << '\n'
         << "y = " << y << '\n';
    y = 7;
    cout << "x = " << x << '\n'
         << "y = " << y << '\n';

    return 0;
}
```

```
Compiling FIG15_7.CPP:
Error FIG15_7.CPP 6: Reference variable 'y' must be
    initialized
```

Fig. 15.7   Attempting to use an uninitialized reference.

```
// References must be initialized
#include <iostream.h>

main()
{
   int x = 3, &y = x;   // y is now an alias for x

   cout << "x = " << x << '\n'
        << "y = " << y << '\n';
   y = 7;
   cout << "x = " << x << '\n'
        << "y = " << y << '\n';

   return 0;
}
```

```
x = 3
y = 3
x = 7
y = 7
```

Fig. 15.8   Using an initialized reference.

Common Programming Error 15.10

Returning a pointer or reference to an automatic variable in a called function.

15.9 The Const Qualifier

Section 15.7 illustrated the use of the **const** qualifier in the parameter list of a function to specify that an argument passed to the function is not modifiable in that function. The **const** qualifier can also be used to declare so-called *"constant variables"* (instead of declaring symbolic constants in the preprocessor with **#define**) as in

```
const float PI = 3.14159;
```

This declaration creates "constant variable" **PI** and initializes it to **3.14159**. The variable must be initialized with a constant expression when it is declared, and cannot be modified thereafter (Fig. 15.9 and Fig. 15.10). "Constant variables" are also called *named constants* or *read-only variables*. Note that the term "constant variable" is an oxymoron, i.e., a contradiction in terms like "jumbo shrimp" or "freezer burn." (Please send us your favorite oxymorons via our email address listed in the Preface. Thanks!)

Constant variables can be placed anywhere a constant expression is expected. For example, the following array declaration uses a **const** variable to specify the array size:

```
const int arraySize = 100;
int array[arraySize];
```

```
// A const object must be initialized
main()
{
    const int x;   // Error: x must be initialized

    x = 7;         // Error: cannot modify a const variable

    return 0;
}
```

```
Compiling FIG15_9.CPP:
Error FIG15_9.CPP 4: Constant variable 'x' must be
    initialized
Error FIG15_9.CPP 6: Cannot modify a const object
```

Fig. 15.9   A **const** object must be initialized.

```
// Using a properly initialized constant variable
#include <iostream.h>

main()
{
    const int x = 7;   // initialized constant variable

    cout << "The value of constant variable x is: "
         << x << '\n';

    return 0;
}
```

```
The value of constant variable x is: 7
```

Fig. 15.10   Correctly initializing and using a constant variable.

Constant variables also can be placed in header files.

Common Programming Error 15.11

*Using **const** variables in array declarations and placing **const** variables in header files (that are included in multiple source files of the same program) are each illegal in C, but legal in C++.*

Good Programming Practice 15.6

*An advantage of using **const** variables rather than symbolic constants is that **const** variables are visible with a symbolic debugger; **#define** symbolic constants are not.*

There are other common uses of the **const** qualifier. For example, a constant pointer can be declared:

```
int *const iPtr = &integer;
```

This declares **iPtr** to be a constant pointer to an integer. The value pointed to by **iptr** can be changed, but **iPtr** cannot be assigned to point to a different memory location.

A pointer to a constant object can be declared as follows:

```
const int *iPtr = &integer;
```

This declares **iPtr** to be a pointer an integer constant. The value **iPtr** refers to cannot be changed using **iPtr**, but **iPtr** can be assigned to point to a different memory location. Thus, **iPtr** is a pointer through which a value can be read but not modified (in effect, a "read-only" pointer). The compiler protects data referenced by read-only pointers by preventing such pointers from being assigned to pointers that are not read-only.

Common Programming Error 15.12

*Initializing a **const** variable with a non-**const** expression such as a variable that is not declared **const**.*

Common Programming Error 15.13

Attempting to modify a constant variable.

Common Programming Error 15.14

Attempting to modify a constant pointer.

15.10 Dynamic Memory Allocation with New and Delete

The C++ *new* and *delete* operators enable programs to perform dynamic memory allocation. In ANSI C, dynamic memory allocation is normally performed with standard library functions **malloc** and **free**. Consider the declaration

```
typeName *ptr;
```

where **typeName** is any type (such as **int**, **float**, **char**, etc.). In ANSI C, the following statement dynamically allocates a **typeName** object, returns a **void** pointer to the object, and assigns that pointer to **ptr**:

```
ptr = malloc(sizeof(typeName));
```

Dynamic memory allocation in C requires a function call to **malloc** and an explicit reference to the **sizeof** operator (or an explicit mention of the number of bytes needed). The memory is allocated on the *heap* (the extra memory available to the program at execution time). Also, with pre-ANSI C implementations, the pointer returned by **malloc** must be cast to the appropriate pointer type with the cast (**typeName ***).

In C++, the statement

```
ptr = new typeName;
```

allocates memory for an object of type **typeName** from the program's *free store* (C++'s term for the extra memory available to the program at execution time). The **new** operator automatically creates an object of the proper size, and returns a pointer of the correct type. If memory can not be allocated by **new**, a null pointer is returned (C++ programmers use the value **0** rather than **NULL** to represent a null pointer).

To free the space for this object in C++ the following statement is used:

```
delete ptr;
```

In C, function **free** is invoked with argument **ptr** to deallocate memory. Operator **delete** can be used only to deallocate memory that was allocated by operator **new**. Applying **delete** to a previously deallocated pointer may lead to unexpected errors during program execution. Applying **delete** to a null pointer has no effect on program execution.

Common Programming Error 15.15

Deallocating memory with **delete** *that was not originally allocated with the* **new** *operator.*

C++ allows an *initializer* for a newly allocated object. For example,

```
float *thingPtr = new float (3.14159);
```

initializes a newly allocated **float** object to **3.14159**.

Arrays also can be created dynamically with **new**. The following statement dynamically allocates a single-subscripted array of 100 integers and assigns the pointer returned by **new** to integer pointer **arrayPtr**:

```
int *arrayPtr;
arrayPtr = new int[100];   // creates array dynamically
```

To deallocate the memory that was dynamically allocated for **arrayPtr** by **new**, use the statement

```
delete [] arrayPtr;
```

We discuss dynamic memory allocation of **class** objects in Chapter 16. We will see that the **new** and **delete** operators perform other tasks (such as automatically calling the constructor and destructor functions of a **class**) that make using **new** and **delete** more powerful and more appropriate than using **malloc** and **free**. For now, be sure to use brackets with **delete** when deallocating arrays of objects.

Common Programming Error 15.16

Using **delete** *without brackets (* **[** *and* **]** *) when deleting dynamically allocated arrays of objects (this is a problem only with arrays containing elements of user-defined types).*

15.11 Default Arguments

Function calls may commonly pass a particular value of an argument. The programmer can specify that such an argument is a *default argument,* and the programmer can provide a default value for that argument. When a default argument is omitted in a function call, the default value of that argument is automatically passed in the call.

Default arguments must be the rightmost (trailing) arguments in a function's parameter list. When calling a function with two or more default arguments, if an omitted argument is not the rightmost argument in the argument list, all arguments to the right of that argument must also be omitted. Default arguments should be specified with the first occurrence of the function name—typically in the prototype in a header file. Default arguments also can be used with `inline` functions.

Figure 15.11 demonstrates the use of default arguments in calculating the volume of a box. All three arguments have been given default values of `1`. The first call to `inline` function `boxVolume` specifies no arguments, and thus uses all three default values. The second call passes a `length` argument, and thus uses default values for the `width` and `height` arguments. The third call passes arguments for `length` and `width`, and thus uses a default value for the `height` argument. The last call passes arguments for `length`, `width`, and `height` thus using no default values.

Good Programming Practice 15.7

Using default arguments can simplify writing function calls. However, some programmers feel that specifying all arguments explicitly is clearer.

Common Programming Error 15.17

Specifying and attempting to use a default argument that is not a rightmost (trailing) argument (while not simultaneously defaulting all the rightmost arguments).

15.12 Unary Scope Resolution Operator

It is possible to declare local and global variables of the same name. In C, while the local variable is in scope, all references to that variable name pertain the local variable—the global variable is not visible within the local variable's scope. C++ provides the *unary scope resolution operator (::)* to access a global variable when a local variable of the same name is in scope. The unary scope resolution operator can not be used to access a variable of the same name in an outer block. A global variable may be accessed directly without the unary scope resolution operator if the name of the global variable is not the same as the name of a local variable in scope. In Chapter 16, we discuss the use of the *binary scope resolution operator* with classes.

Figure 15.12 demonstrates the unary scope resolution operator with local and global variables of the same name. To emphasize that the local and global versions of variable `value` are distinct, the program declares one of the variables `float` and the other `int`.

Common Programming Error 15.18

Attempting to access a non-global variable in an outer block using the unary scope resolution operator.

```
// Using default arguments
#include <iostream.h>

// Calculate the volume of a box
inline int boxVolume(int length = 1, int width = 1,
                     int height = 1)
   { return length * width * height; }

main()
{
    cout << "The default box volume is: "
         << boxVolume()
         << "\n\nThe volume of a box with length 10,\n"
         << "width 1 and height 1 is: "
         << boxVolume(10)
         << "\n\nThe volume of a box with length 10,\n"
         << "width 5 and height 1 is: "
         << boxVolume(10, 5)
         << "\n\nThe volume of a box with length 10,\n"
         << "width 5 and height 2 is: "
         << boxVolume(10, 5, 2)
         << '\n';

    return 0;
}
```

```
The default box volume is: 1

The volume of a box with length 10,
width 1 and height 1 is: 10

The volume of a box with length 10,
width 5 and height 1 is: 50

The volume of a box with length 10,
width 5 and height 2 is: 100
```

Fig. 15.11 Using default arguments.

Good Programming Practice 15.8

Avoid using variables of the same name for different purposes in a program. Although this is allowed in various circumstances, it can be confusing.

15.13 Function Overloading

In C, it is a syntax error to declare two functions of the same name in the same program. C++ enables several functions of the same name to be defined as long as these functions name different sets of parameters (at least as far as their types are concerned). This capa-

```
// Using the unary scope resolution operator
#include <iostream.h>

float value = 1.2345;

main()
{
    int value = 7;

    cout << "Local value = " << value
         << "\nGlobal value = " << ::value << '\n';

    return 0;
}
```

```
Local value = 7
Global value = 1.2345
```

Fig. 15.12 Using the unary scope resolution operator.

bility is called *function overloading*. When an overloaded function is called, the C++ compiler automatically selects the proper function by examining the number, types, and order of the arguments in the call. Function overloading is commonly used to create several functions of the same name that perform similar tasks on different data types.

Good Programming Practice 15.9

Overloading functions that perform closely related tasks can make programs more readable and understandable.

Figure 15.13 uses overloaded function **square** to calculate the square of an **int** and the square of a **double**. In Chapter 17, we discuss how to overload operators to define how they should operate on objects of user-defined data types. Section 15.15 introduces template functions for performing identical tasks on many different data types. Chapter 20 discusses template functions and template classes in detail.

Overloaded functions are distinguished by their *signature*—a combination of the function's name and its parameter types. The compiler specially encodes each function identifier (sometimes referred to as *name mangling* or *name decoration*) with the number and types of its parameters to enable t*ype-safe linkage*. Type-safe linkage ensures that the proper overloaded function is called, and that the arguments conform properly to the parameters. Linkage errors are detected and reported by the compiler. The program of Fig. 15.14 was compiled on the Borland C++ compiler. The encoded function names produced in assembly language by Borland C++ are shown in the output window. Each mangled name begins with **@** followed by the function name. The encoded parameter list begins with **$q**. In the parameter list for function **nothing2**, **z c** represents a **char**, **i** represents an **int**, **pf** represents a **float ***, and **pd** represents a **double ***. In the parameter list for function **nothing1**, **i** represents an **int**, **f** represents a **float**, **zc**

```
// Using overloaded functions
#include <iostream.h>

int square(int x) { return x * x; }

double square(double y) { return y * y; }

main()
{
    cout << "The square of integer 7 is "
         << square(7)
         << "\nThe square of double 7.5 is "
         << square(7.5) << '\n';

    return 0;
}
```

```
The square of integer 7 is 49
The square of double 7.5 is 56.25
```

Fig. 15.13 Using overloaded functions.

represents a **char**, and **pi** represents an **int ***. The two **square** functions are distinguished by their parameter lists; one specifies d for double and the other specifies i for **int**. The return types of the four functions are not specified in the encoded names. Note that encoding of function names is compiler specific. Therefore, a function compiled with Borland C++ may not have the same mangled name when using other compilers.

Overloaded functions can have different return types, but must have different parameter lists.

Common Programming Error 15.19

Creating overloaded functions with identical parameter lists and different return types causes a syntax error.

The compiler uses only the parameter lists to distinguish between functions of the same name. Overloaded functions need not have the same number of parameters. Programmers should use caution when overloading functions with default parameters as this may cause ambiguity.

Common Programming Error 15.20

A function with default arguments omitted might be called identically to another overloaded function; this is a syntax error.

Software Engineering Observation 15.2

Overloading helps eliminate C's use of #define macros to perform tasks on multiple data types, and employs C++'s strong type-checking features that are not available when using macros.

```
// Name mangling
int square(int x) { return x * x; }

double square(double y) { return y * y; }

void nothing1(int a, float b, char c, int *d) {}

char *nothing2(char a, int b, float *c, double *d) { return 0; }

main()
{
   return 0;
}
```

```
public   _main
public   @nothing2$qzcipfpd
public   @nothing1$qifzcpi
public   @square$qd
public   @square$qi
```

Fig. 15.14 Name mangling to enable type-safe linkage.

15.14 Linkage Specifications

It is possible from a C++ program to call functions written and compiled with a C compiler. As stated in Section 15.13, C++ specially encodes function names for type-safe linkage. C, however, does not encode its function names. Thus, a function compiled in C will not be recognized when an attempt is made to link C code with C++ code because the C++ code expects a specially encoded function name. C++ enables the programmer to provide *linkage specifications* to inform the compiler that a function was compiled on a C compiler, and to prevent the name of the function from being encoded by the C++ compiler. Linkage specifications are useful when large libraries of specialized functions have been developed, and the user either does not have access to the source code for recompilation into C++, or time to convert the library functions from C to C++.

To inform the compiler that one or several functions have been compiled in C, write the function prototypes as follows:

```
extern "C" function prototype    // single function

extern "C"            // multiple functions
{
   function prototypes
}
```

These declarations inform the compiler that the specified functions are not compiled in C++, so name encoding should not be performed on the functions listed in the linkage specification. These functions can then be linked properly with the program. C++ envi ronments normally include the standard C libraries and do not require the programmer to use linkage specifications for those functions.

15.15 Function Templates

Overloaded functions are normally used to perform similar operations on different types of data. If the operations are identical for each type, this may be performed more compactly and conveniently using *function templates*, a capability introduced in recent versions of C++. The programmer writes a single function template definition. Based on the argument types provided in calls to this function, C++ automatically generates separate object-code functions to handle each type of call appropriately. In C, this task can be performed using macros created with **#define**. However, macros present the possibility for serious side effects and do not enable the compiler to perform type checking. Function templates provide a compact solution like macros, but enable full type-checking.

All function template definitions begin with keyword **template** followed by a list of formal parameters to the function template enclosed in angle brackets (**<** and **>**). Every formal parameter is preceded by the **class** keyword. The formal parameters are used like built-in types or user-defined types to specify the types of the arguments to the function, to specify the return type of the function, and to declare variables within the function. The function definition follows and is defined like any other function.

The following function template is also used in the complete program in Fig. 15.15.

```
template <class T>
void printArray(T *array, const int count)
{
    for (int i = 0; i < count; i++)
        cout << array[i] << " ";

    cout << '\n';
}
```

This template function declares a single formal parameter **T** as the type of the array to be printed by function **printArray**. When the compiler detects a **printArray** invocation in the program source code, the type of **printArray**'s first argument is substituted for **T** throughout the template definition, and C++ creates a complete function template for printing an array of a specified data type. Then, the newly created function is compiled. In Fig. 15.15, three functions are instantiated—one expects an **int** array, one expects a **float** array, and one expects a **char** array. The instantiation for type **int** is:

```
void printArray(int *array, const int count)
{
    for (int i = 0; i < count; i++)
        cout << array[i] << " ";

    cout << '\n';
}
```

Every formal parameter in the template definition must appear in the function's parameter list at least once. The name of a formal parameter can be used only once in the formal parameter list of the template definition. Formal parameter names among template functions need not be unique.

Figure 15.15 illustrates the use of the **printArray** template function.

Common Programming Error 15.21

Not placing keyword ***class*** *before every formal parameter of a function template.*

Common Programming Error 15.22

Not using every formal parameter of a function template in the function signature.

```
// Using template functions
#include <iostream.h>

template <class T>
void printArray(T *array, const int count)
{
    for (int i = 0; i < count; i++)
        cout << array[i] << " ";

    cout << '\n';
}

main()
{
    const int aCount = 5, bCount = 7, cCount = 6;
    int a[aCount] = {1, 2, 3, 4, 5};
    float b[bCount] = {1.1, 2.2, 3.3, 4.4, 5.5, 6.6, 7.7};
    char c[cCount] = "HELLO";   // 6th position for null

    cout << "Array a contains:\n";
    printArray(a, aCount);   // integer version

    cout << "Array b contains:\n";
    printArray(b, bCount);   // float version

    cout << "Array c contains:\n";
    printArray(c, cCount);   // character version

    return 0;
}
```

```
Array a contains:
1 2 3 4 5
Array b contains:
1.1 2.2 3.3 4.4 5.5 6.6 7.7
Array c contains:
H E L L O
```

Fig. 15.15 Using template functions.

Summary

- C++ is a superset of C, so programmers can use a C++ compiler to compile their existing C programs, and then gradually evolve these programs to C++.

- C requires that a comment be delimited by /* and */. C++ allows a comment to begin with // and terminate at the end of the line.

- C++ allows declarations to appear anywhere that an executable statement can appear. Variable declarations may also appear in the initialization section of a **for** structure.

- C++ provides an alternative to the **printf** and **scanf** functions for handling input/output of the standard data types and strings. The output stream **cout**, and the operator **<<** (the stream insertion operator, pronounced "put to") enable data to be output. The input stream **cin** and the operator **>>** (the stream extraction operator, pronounced "get from") enable data to be input.

- C++ enables the programmer to create user-defined data types with the keywords, **enum**, **struct**, **union**, and **class**. The tag name of the enumeration, structure, union, or class can then be used to define variables of the new type.

- Programs do not compile unless a function prototype is provided for every function or a function is defined before it is used (in which case a separate function prototype is not required).

- A function that does not return a value is declared with a **void** return type. If an attempt is made either to return a value from the function or to use the result of the function invocation in the calling function, the compiler generates an error.

- In C++, an empty parameter list is specified with empty parentheses or **void** in parentheses. In C, an empty parameter list turns off the argument checking for the function.

- Inline functions eliminate function-call overhead. The programmer uses the keyword **inline** to advise the compiler to generate function code in line (when possible) to minimize function calls. The compiler may choose to ignore the **inline** advice.

- C++ offers a direct form of call by reference using reference parameters. To indicate that a function parameter is passed by reference, follow the parameter's type in the function prototype by an **&**. In the function call, mention the variable by name and it will be passed call by reference. In the called function, mentioning the variable by its local name actually refers to the original variable in the calling function. Thus, the original variable can be modified directly by the called function.

- Reference parameters can also be created for local use as aliases for other variables within a function. Reference variables must be initialized in their declarations, and they cannot be reassigned as aliases to other variables. Once a reference variable is declared as an alias for another variable, all operations supposedly performed on the alias are actually performed on the variable.

- The **const** qualifier also can create "constant variables." A constant variable must be initialized with a constant expression when the variable is declared, and cannot be modified thereafter. Constant variables are often called named constants or read-only variables. Constant variables can be placed anywhere a constant expression is expected. Other common uses of the **const** qualifier include constant pointers, pointers to constants, and constant references.

- The **new** and **delete** operators in C++ provide a nicer means of performing dynamic memory allocation than with **malloc** and **free** function calls in C. The **new** operator takes a type as an operand, automatically creates an object of the proper size, and returns a pointer of the correct type. The **delete** operator takes a pointer to an object allocated with **new** and frees the memory.

- C++ allows the programmer to specify default arguments and their default values. If a default argument is omitted in a call to a function, the default value of that argument is used. Default arguments must be the rightmost (trailing) arguments in a function's parameter list. Default arguments should be specified with the first occurrence of the function name.

- The *unary scope resolution operator (::)* enables a program to access a global variable when a local variable of the same name is in scope.

- It is possible to define several functions with the same name but with different parameter types. This is called function overloading. When an overloaded function is called, the compiler automatically selects the proper function by examining the number and types of arguments in the call.

- Overloaded functions can have different return values, and must have different parameter lists. Two functions differing only by return type will result in a compilation error.

- In some instances, it is necessary to call functions written and compiled with a C compiler (for example, a company's specialized library functions that have not been converted to C++ and recompiled). C++ processes the names of its functions differently from C. Therefore, a function compiled in C will not be recognized when an attempt is made to link C code with C++ code. C++ provides linkage specifications to inform the compiler that a function was compiled on a C compiler, and prevents the name of the function from being processed like a C++ function.

- Function templates enable the creation of functions that perform the same operations on different types of data, but the function template is defined only once.

Terminology

ampersand (**&**) suffix	**delete** operator
asm	dynamic objects
catch	free store
cin (input stream)	**friend**
const	function overloading
constant variable	"get from" operator (**>>**)
cout (output stream)	initializer
class	**inline** member function
default function arguments	**<iostream.h>**

iostream library
linkage specifications
named constant
new operator
operator keyword
overloading
"put to" operator (**<<**)
read-only variable
reference parameter
reference types
signature

single-line comment (**//**)
stream extraction operator (**>>**)
stream insertion operator (**<<**)
template
template function
this
throw
try
type-safe linkage
unary scope resolution operator (**::**)
virtual

Common Programming Errors

15.1 Forgetting to close a C-style comment with ***/**.

15.2 Declaring a variable after it is referenced in a statement.

15.3 An attempt to return a value from a **void** function or to use the result of a **void** function invocation.

15.4 C++ programs do not compile unless function prototypes are provided for every function, or each function is defined before it is used.

15.5 C++ is an evolving language and some features may not be available on your compiler. Using unimplemented features will cause syntax errors.

15.6 Because reference parameters are mentioned only by name in the body of the called function, the programmer might inadvertently treat reference parameters as call-by-value parameters. This can cause unexpected side effects if the original copies of the variables are changed by the calling function.

15.7 Not initializing a reference variable when it is declared.

15.8 Attempting to reassign a previously declared reference to be an alias to another variable.

15.9 Attempting to dereference a reference variable using the pointer indirection operator (remember that a reference is an alias for a variable, and is not a pointer to a variable).

15.10 Returning a pointer or reference to an automatic variable in a called function.

15.11 Using **const** variables in array declarations and placing **const** variables in header files (that are included in multiple source files of the same program) are each illegal in C, but legal in C++.

15.12 Initializing a **const** variable with a non-**const** expression such as a variable that is not declared **const**.

15.13 Attempting to modify a constant variable.

15.14 Attempting to modify a constant pointer.

15.15 Deallocating memory with **delete** that was not originally allocated with operator **new**.

15.16 Using **delete** without brackets (**[** and **]**) when deleting dynamically allocated arrays of objects (this is a problem only with arrays containing elements of user-defined types).

15.17 Specifying and attempting to use a default argument that is not a rightmost (trailing) argument (while not simultaneously defaulting all the rightmost arguments).

15.18 Attempting to access a non-global variable in an outer block using the unary scope resolution operator.

15.19 Creating overloaded functions with identical parameter lists and different return types causes a syntax error.

15.20 A function with default arguments omitted might be called identically to another overloaded function; this is a syntax error.

15.21   Not placing keyword **class** before every formal parameter of a function template.
15.22   Not using every formal parameter of a function template in the function signature.

Good Programming Practices

15.1   Using C++-style **//** comments avoids the unterminated comment errors that occur by forgetting to close C-style comments with ***/**.
15.2   Using C++-style stream-oriented input/output makes programs more readable (and less error prone) than their counterparts in C written with **printf** and **scanf** function calls.
15.3   Placing a variable's declaration close to its first use can make programs more readable.
15.4   The **inline** qualifier should be used only with small, frequently used functions.
15.5   Use pointers to pass arguments that may be modified by the called function, and use references to constants to pass large arguments that will not be modified.
15.6   An advantage of using **const** variables rather than symbolic constants is that **const** variables are visible with a symbolic debugger; **#define** symbolic constants are not.
15.7   Using default arguments can simplify writing function calls. However, some programmers feel that specifying all arguments explicitly is clearer.
15.8   Avoid using variables of the same name for different purposes in a program. Although this is allowed in various circumstances, it can be confusing.
15.9   Overloading functions that perform closely related tasks can make programs more readable and understandable.

Performance Tips

15.1   Using **inline** functions can reduce execution time, but can increase program size.
15.2   For large objects, use a **const** reference parameter to simulate the appearance and security of call-by-value, but to avoid the overhead of passing a copy of the large object.

Portability Tip

15.1   The meaning of an empty function parameter list in C++ is dramatically different than in C. In C, it means all argument checking is disabled. In C++, it means that the function takes no arguments. Thus, C programs using this feature may perform differently when compiled in C++.

Software Engineering Observations

15.1   Any change to an **inline** function requires all clients of the function to be recompiled. This may be significant in some program development and maintenance situations.
15.2   Overloading helps eliminate C's use of **#define** macros to perform tasks on multiple data types, and employs C++'s strong type-checking features that are not available when using macros.

Self-Review Exercises

15.1   Fill in the blanks in each of the following:
  a) In C++, it is possible to have various functions with the same name that each operate on different types and/or numbers of arguments. This is called function _____.

b) The _____ enables access to a global variable with the same name as a variable in the current scope.
c) Operator _____ dynamically allocates a new object.
d) In C, suppose **a** and **b** are integer variables and we form the sum **a + b**. Now suppose **c** and **d** are floating-point variables and we form the sum **c + d**. The two **+** operators here are clearly being used for different purposes. This is an example of a property that C++ has, and that C has as well, called function _____.
e) The two stream objects we discussed that are predefined in C++ are _____ and _____.
f) The keywords _____, _____, _____, and _____ are used to create new data types in C++.
g) The _____ qualifier is used to declare read-only variables.
h) C++ provides _____ to enable functions compiled with a C compiler to be linked properly with a C++ program.
i) _____ functions enable a single function to be defined to perform a task on many different data types.

15.2 (True/False) When writing a block-style comment that requires many lines of text, it is more concise to use the C++ comment delimiter **//** than the regular C delimiters **/*** and ***/**.

15.3 In C++, why would a function prototype contain a parameter type declaration such as **float&**?

15.4 (True/False) All calls in C++ are performed call by value.

15.5 Explain why the operators **<<** and **>>** are overloaded in C++.

15.6 Write C++ program segments to accomplish each of the following:
a) Write the string "**Welcome to C!**" to the standard output stream **cout**.
b) Read the value of variable **age** from the standard input stream **cin**.

15.7 Write a complete C++ program that uses stream input/output and an **inline** function **sphereVolume** to prompt the user for the radius of a sphere, and to calculate and print the volume of that sphere using the assignment **volume = (4/3) PI * pow(radius, 3)**.

15.8 What would happen in C if you declared the same function twice with different argument types? What would happen in C++?

Answers to Self-Review Exercises

15.1 a) overloading. b) unary scope resolution operator (**::**). c) **new**. d) overloading. e) **cin, cout**. f) **enum, struct, union, class**. g) **const**. h) linkage specifications. i) template.

15.2 False. The regular C-style delimiters each only need to be written once, whereas the C++ **//** delimiter needs to appear on the beginning of each new line.

15.3 Because the programmer is declaring a reference parameter of type "reference to" **float** to get access through call by reference to the original argument variable.

15.4 False. C++ allows direct call-by-reference via the use of reference parameters in addition to the use of pointers.

15.5 The operator **>>** is both the right-shift operator and the stream extraction operator depending on its context. The operator **<<** is both the left-shift operator and the stream insertion operator depending on its context.

15.6 a) **cout << "Welcome to C!";**
       b) **cin >> age;**

15.7
```
// Inline function that calculates the volume of a sphere
#include <iostream.h>

const float PI = 3.14159;

inline float sphereVolume(const float r) {return
                          4.0 / 3.0 * PI * r * r * r;}

main()
{
   float radius;

   cout << "Enter the length of the radius of your sphere: ";
   cin >> radius;
   cout << "Volume of sphere with radius " << radius <<
           "is " << sphereVolume(radius) << '\n';
   return 0;
}
```

15.8   In C you would get a compilation error indicating that two functions had been given the same name. In C++ this is an example of function overloading—which is allowed—and there would be no error.

Exercises

15.9   Suppose an organization currently emphasizes C programming and wishes to convert to an object-oriented programming environment in C++. What strategy is appropriate for evolving from C environments to C++ environments?

15.10   Write C++-style stream-oriented statements to accomplish each of the following:
   a) Display "**HELLO**" on the screen.
   b) Input a value for **float** variable **temperature** from the keyboard.

15.11   Compare and contrast **printf/scanf**-style input/output with C++-style stream-oriented input/output.

15.12   In the chapter, we mentioned that there are many areas in which C++ automatically "knows" what types to use. List as many of these as you can.

15.13   Write a C++ program that uses stream-oriented input/output to prompt for seven integers, and determine and print their maximum.

15.14   Write a complete C++ program that uses stream input/output and an **inline** function **circleArea** to prompt the user for the radius of a circle, and to calculate and print the area of that circle.

15.15   Write a complete C++ program with the three alternate functions specified below that each simply add 1 to the variable **count** defined in **main**. Then compare and contrast the three alternate approaches. These three functions are
   a) Function **add1CallByValue** that passes a copy of **count** call by value, adds 1 to the copy, and returns the new value.
   b) Function **add1ByPointer** that passes access to variable **count** via simulated call by reference using pointers, and uses the dereferencing operator * to add 1 to the original copy of **count** in **main**.
   c) Function **add1ByReference** that passes **count** with true call by reference via a reference parameter, and adds 1 to the original copy of **count** through its alias (i.e., the reference parameter).

15.16   What is the purpose of the unary scope resolution operator?

15.17   Compare and contrast dynamic memory allocation with the C++ operators **new** and **delete**, with dynamic memory allocation with the C Standard Library functions **malloc** and **free**.

15.18   List the various features of C++ we presented in this chapter that represent the set of non-object-oriented enhancements to C.

15.19   Write a program that uses a function template called **min** to determine the smaller of two arguments. Test the program using integer, character, and floating-point number pairs.

15.20   Write a program that uses a function template called **max** to determine the larger of three arguments. Test the program using integer, character, and floating-point number pairs.

15.21   Determine if the following program segments contain errors. For each error, explain how it can be corrected. Note: For a particular program segment, it is possible that no errors are present in the segment.

a)
```
main()
{
    cout << x;
    int x = 7;
    return 0;
}
```

b)
```
template <class A>
int sum(int num1, int num2, int num3)
{
    return num1 + num2 + num3;
}
```

c)
```
/* This is a comment
```

d)
```
void printResults(int x, int y)
{
    cout << "The sum is " << x + y << '\n';
    return x + y;
}
```

e)
```
char *s = "character string";
delete s;
```

f)
```
float &ref;
*ref = 7;
```

g)
```
int x;
const int y = x;
```

h)
```
template <A>
A product(A num1, A num2, A num3)
{
    return num1 * num2 * num3;
}
```

i)
```
const double pi = 3.14159;
pi = 3;
```

j)
```
// This is a comment
```

k)
```
char *s = new char[10];
delete s;
```

l)
```
double cube(int);
int cube(int);
```

16

Classes and Data Abstraction

Objectives

- To understand the software engineering concepts of encapsulation and data hiding.
- To understand the notions of data abstraction and abstract data types (ADTs).
- To be able to create C ++ ADTs, namely classes.
- To understand how to create, use and destroy class objects.
- To be able to control access to object data members and member functions.
- To begin to appreciate the value of object orientation.

My object all sublime
I shall achieve in time.
W. S. Gilbert

Is it a world to hide virtues in?
William Shakespeare
Twelfth-Night

Your public servants serve you right.
Adlai Stevenson

Private faces in public places
Are wiser and nicer
Than public faces in private places.
W. H. Auden

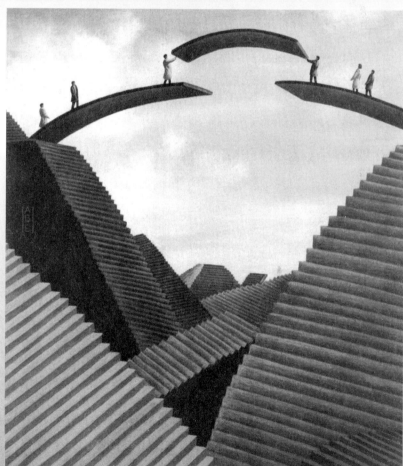

Outline

16.1 Introduction

Now we begin our introduction to object orientation. We will see that object-orientation is
a natural way of thinking about the world and of writing computer programs. Why, then,
did we not begin with object orientation on page one of this book? Why are we deferring
object-oriented programming in C++ until Chapter 16? The answer is that the objects we
will build will be composed in part of structured program pieces, so we needed to estab-
lish a basis in structured programming first.

   In our early chapters, we concentrated on the "conventional" methodology of structured programming. In this chapter, we introduce basic concepts (i.e., "object think") and
terminology (i.e., "object speak") of object-oriented programming. In subsequent chapters, we consider more substantial issues and attack challenging problems with the tech

niques of *object-oriented design (OOD):* We analyze typical problem statements that require systems to be built, determine what objects are needed to implement the systems, determine what attributes the objects will need to have, determine what behaviors these objects will need to exhibit, and specify how the objects will need to interact with one another to accomplish overall system goals.

We begin by introducing some of the key terminology of object orientation. Look around you in the real world. Everywhere you look you see them—*objects*! People, animals, plants, cars, planes, buildings, lawnmowers, computers and the like. Humans think in terms of objects. We have the marvelous ability of *abstraction* that enables us to view a screen image as objects such as people, planes, trees and mountains rather than as individual dots of color. We can, if we wish, think in terms of beaches rather than grains of sand, forests rather than trees, and houses rather than bricks.

We might be inclined to divide objects into two categories—animate objects and inanimate objects. Animate objects are "alive" in some sense. They move around and do things. Inanimate objects, like towels, seem not to do much at all. They just kind of "sit around." All these objects, however, do have some things in common. They all have *attributes* like size, shape, color, weight, and the like. And they all exhibit various *behaviors,* e.g., a ball rolls, bounces, inflates, and deflates; a baby cries, sleeps, crawls, walks, and blinks; a car accelerates, brakes, turns, etc.

Humans learn about objects by studying their attributes and observing their behaviors. Different objects can have many of the same attributes and exhibit similar behaviors. Comparisons can be made, for example, between babies and adults, and between humans and chimpanzees. Cars, trucks, little red wagons and roller skates have much in common.

Object-oriented programming (OOP) models real-world objects with software counterparts. It takes advantage of *class* relationships where objects of a certain class—such as a class of vehicles—have the same characteristics. It takes advantage of *inheritance* relationships, and even *multiple inheritance* relationships where newly created classes of objects are derived by inheriting characteristics of existing classes, yet contain unique characteristics of their own. Babies have many characteristics of their parents, yet short parents occasionally have tall children.

Object-oriented programming gives us a more natural and intuitive way to view the programming process, namely by *modeling* real-world objects, their attributes, and their behaviors. OOP also models communication between objects. Just as people send *messages* to one another (e.g., a sergeant commanding troops to stand at attention), objects also communicate via messages.

OOP *encapsulates* data (attributes) and functions (behavior) into packages called *objects;* the data and functions of an object are intimately tied together. Objects have the property of *information hiding.* This means that although objects may know how to communicate with one another across well-defined *interfaces,* objects normally are not allowed to know how other objects are implemented—implementation details are hidden within the objects themselves. Surely it is possible to drive a car effectively without knowing the details of how engines, transmissions and exhaust systems work internally. We will see why information hiding is so crucial to good software engineering.

In C and other *procedural programming languages,* programming tends to be *action-oriented,* whereas in C++ programming tends to be *object-oriented.* In C, the unit of pro gramming is the *function*. In C++, the unit of programming is the *class* from which objects are eventually *instantiated* (i.e., created).

C programmers concentrate on writing functions. Groups of actions that perform some common task are formed into functions, and functions are grouped to form programs. Data is certainly important in C, but the view is that data exists primarily in support of the actions that functions perform. The *verbs* in a system specification help the C programmer determine the set of functions that will work together to implement the system.

C++ programmers concentrate on creating their own *user-defined types* called *classes*. Each class contains data as well as the set of functions that manipulate the data. The data components of a class are called *data members*. The function components of a class are called *member functions*. Just as an instance of a built-in type such as **int** is called a *variable*, an instance of a user-defined type (i.e., a class) is called an *object*. The focus of attention in C++ is on objects rather than functions. The *nouns* in a system specification help the C++ programmer determine the set of classes from which objects will be created that will work together to implement the system.

Classes in C++ are a natural evolution of the C notion of **struct**. Before proceeding with the specifics of developing classes in C++, we review structures, and we build a user-defined type based on a structure. The weaknesses we expose in this approach will help motivate the notion of a class.

16.2 Structure Definitions

Consider the following structure definition:

```
struct Time {
    int hour;      // 0-23
    int minute;    // 0-59
    int second;    // 0-59
};
```

Let us review the terminology of structures (see Chapter 10 and Chapter 12). The keyword **struct** introduces the structure definition. The identifier **Time** is the *structure tag*. The structure tag names the structure definition, and is used to declare variables of the *structure type*. In this example, the structure type name is **Time** (as opposed to the longer type name **struct Time** required in C). The names declared in the braces of the structure definition are the structure's *members*. Members of the same structure must have unique names, but two different structures may contain members of the same name without conflict. Each structure definition must end with a semicolon. The preceding explanation is valid for classes also as we will soon see.

The definition of **Time** contains three members of type **int**—hour, **minute**, and **second**. Structure members can be any type. A structure cannot, however, contain an instance of itself. For example, a member of type **Time** cannot be declared in the structure definition for **Time**. A pointer to a **Time** structure, however, can be included. A structure containing a member that is a pointer to the same structure type is referred to as a *self-referential structure*. Self-referential structures are useful for forming linked data structures (see Chapter 12).

The preceding structure definition does not reserve any space in memory; rather, the definition creates a new data type that is used to declare variables. Structure variables are declared, like variables of other types. The declaration

```
Time timeObject, timeArray[10], *timePtr;
```

declares **timeObject** to be a variable of type **Time**, **timeArray** to be an array with 10 elements of type **Time**, and **timePtr** to be a pointer to a **Time** object.

16.3 Accessing Members of Structures

Members of a structure (or of a class) are accessed using the *member access operators*— the *dot operator* (**.**) and the *arrow operator* (**->**). The dot operator accesses a structure (or class) member via the variable name for the object or via a reference to the object. For example, to print member **hour** of structure **timeObject** use the statement

```
cout << timeObject.hour;
```

The arrow operator—consisting of a minus (**-**) sign and a greater than (**>**) sign with no intervening spaces—accesses a structure (or class) member via a pointer to the object. Assume that the pointer **timePtr** has been declared to point to a **Time** object, and that the address of structure **timeObject** has been assigned to **timePtr**. To print member **hour** of structure **timeObject** with pointer **timePtr**, use the statement

```
cout << timePtr->hour;
```

The expression **timePtr->hour** is equivalent to **(*timePtr).hour** which dereferences the pointer and accesses the member **hour** using the dot operator. The parentheses are needed here because the dot operator (**.**) has a higher precedence than the pointer dereferencing operator (*****). The arrow operator and structure member operator, along with parentheses and brackets (**[]**), have the highest operator precedence (of the operators discussed so far) and associate from left to right.

16.4 Implementing a User-Defined Type Time With a Struct

Figure 16.1 creates the user-defined structure type **Time** with three integer members: **hour**, **minute**, and **second**. The program defines a single **Time** structure called **dinnerTime** and uses the dot operator to initialize the structure members with the values **18** for **hour**, **30** for **minute**, and **0** for **second**. The program then prints the time in military format and standard format. Note that the print functions receive references to constant **Time** structures. This causes **Time** structures to be passed to the print functions by reference—thus eliminating the copying overhead associated with passing structures to functions by value—and also prevents the **Time** structure from being modified by the print functions. In Chapter 17, we discuss **const** objects and **const** member functions.

Performance Tip 16.1

Structures ordinarily pass call by value. To avoid the overhead of copying a structure, pass the structure call by reference.

```cpp
// FIG16_1.CPP
// Create a structure, set its members, and print it.
#include <iostream.h>

struct Time {       // structure definition
   int hour;        // 0-23
   int minute;      // 0-59
   int second;      // 0-59
};

void printMilitary(const Time &);   // prototype
void printStandard(const Time &);   // prototype

main()
{
   Time dinnerTime;     // variable of new type Time

   // set members to valid values
   dinnerTime.hour = 18;
   dinnerTime.minute = 30;
   dinnerTime.second = 0;

   cout << "Dinner will be held at ";
   printMilitary(dinnerTime);
   cout << " military time,\nwhich is ";
   printStandard(dinnerTime);
   cout << " standard time." << endl;

   // set members to invalid values
   dinnerTime.hour = 29;
   dinnerTime.minute = 73;
   dinnerTime.second = 103;

   cout << "\nTime with invalid values: ";
   printMilitary(dinnerTime);
   cout << endl;
   return 0;
}

// Print the time in military format
void printMilitary(const Time &t)
{
   cout << (t.hour < 10 ? "0" : "") << t.hour << ":"
        << (t.minute < 10 ? "0" : "") << t.minute << ":"
        << (t.second < 10 ? "0" : "") << t.second;
}

// Print the time in standard format
void printStandard(const Time &t)
{
   cout << ((t.hour == 0 || t.hour == 12) ? 12 : t.hour % 12)
        << ":" << (t.minute < 10 ? "0" : "") << t.minute
        << ":" << (t.second < 10 ? "0" : "") << t.second
        << (t.hour < 12 ? " AM" : " PM");
}
```

Fig. 16.1 Create a structure, set its members, and print it (part 1 of 2).

```
Dinner will be held at 18:30:00 military time,
which is 6:30:00 PM standard time.

Time with invalid values: 29:73:103
```

Fig. 16.1   Create a structure, set its members, and print it (part 2 of 2).

Performance Tip 16.2

To avoid the overhead of call by value yet still gain the benefit that the caller's original data is protected from modification, pass large-size arguments as **const** *references.*

There are drawbacks to creating new data types with structures in this manner. Since initialization is not specifically required, it is possible to have uninitialized data and the consequent problems. Even if the data is initialized, it may not be initialized correctly. Invalid values can be assigned to the members of a structure (as we did in Fig. 16.1) because the program has direct access to the data. The program assigned bad values to all three members of the **Time** object **dinnerTime**. If the implementation of the **struct** is changed, all the programs that use the **struct** must be changed. This is because the programmer is directly manipulating the data type. There is no "interface" to it to ensure that the programmer uses the data type correctly and to ensure that the data remains in a consistent state.

Software Engineering Observation 16.1

It is important to write programs that are understandable and easy to maintain. Change is the rule rather than the exception. Programmers should anticipate that their code will be modified. As we will see, classes facilitate program modifiability.

There are other problems associated with C-style structures. They cannot be printed as a unit, rather their members must be printed and formatted one at a time. A function could be written to print the members of a structure in some appropriate format. Chapter 18, "Operator Overloading," illustrates how to overload the **<<** operator to enable objects of a structure or class type to be printed easily. Structures may not be compared in their entirety; they must be compared member by member. Chapter 18, also illustrates how to overload equality operators and relational operators to compare objects of structure and class types.

The following section reimplements our **Time** structure as a class and demonstrates some of the advantages to creating abstract data types with classes. We will see that classes and structures can be used almost identically in C++. The difference between the two is in the default accessibility associated with the members of each. This will be explained shortly.

16.5 Implementing a Time Abstract Data Type with a Class

Classes enable the programmer to model objects that have *attributes* (represented as *data members*) and *behaviors* or *operations* (represented as *member functions*). Types contain

ing data members and member functions are normally defined in C++ using the keyword
`class`.

Member functions are sometimes called *methods* in other object-oriented programming languages, and are invoked in response to *messages* sent to an object. A message corresponds to a member-function call.

Once a class has been defined, the class name can be used to declare objects of that class. Figure 16.2 contains a simple definition for class `Time`.

Our `Time` class definition begins with the keyword `class`. The *body* of the class definition is delineated with left and right braces (`{` and `}`). The class definition terminates with a semicolon. Our `Time` class definition and our `Time` structure definition each contain the three integer members `hour`, `minute`, and `second`.

Common Programming Error 16.1

Forgetting the semicolon at the end of a class definition.

The remaining parts of the class definition are new. The labels `public:` and `private:` are called *member access specifiers.* Any data member or member function declared after member access specifier `public:` (and before the next member access specifier) is accessible wherever the program has access to an object of class `Time`. Any data member or member function declared after member access specifier `private:` (and up to the next member access specifier) is accessible only to member functions of the class. Member access specifiers always end with a colon (`:`) and can appear multiple times in a class definition.

Good Programming Practice 16.1

Use each member access specifier only once in a class definition for clarity and readability. Place public members first where they are easy to locate.

The class definition contains prototypes for the following four member functions after the `public:` member access specifier—`Time`, `setTime`, `printMilitary`, and `printStandard`. These are the *public member functions,* or *public services* or *interface* of the class. These functions will be used by *clients* (users) of the class to manipulate the data of the class.

```
class Time {
public:
   Time();
   void setTime(int, int, int);
   void printMilitary();
   void printStandard();
private:
   int hour;      // 0 - 23
   int minute;    // 0 - 59
   int second;    // 0 - 59
};
```

Fig. 16.2   Simple definition of **class Time**.

A member function with the same name as the class is called a *constructor* function of that class. A constructor is a special member function that initializes the data members of a class object. A class's constructor function is called automatically when an object of that class is created.

The three integer members appear after the `private:` member access specifier. This indicates that these data members of the class are only accessible to member functions—and as we will see in the next chapter, friends—of the class. Thus, the data members can only be accessed by the four functions whose prototypes appear in the class definition (or by friends of the class). Data members are normally listed in the `private:` portion of a class and member functions are normally listed in the `public:` portion. It is possible to have `private:` member functions and `public:` data as we will see later.

Once the class has been defined, it can be used as a type in declarations as follows:

```
Time sunset,                // object of type Time
     arrayOfTimes[5],       // array of Time objects
     *pointerToTime,        // pointer to a Time object
     &dinnerTime = sunset;  // reference to a Time object
```

The class name becomes a new type specifier. There may be many objects of a class, just as there may be many variables of type `int`. The programmer can create new class types as needed. This is one of many reasons why C++ is an *extensible language.*

Figure 16.3 uses the **Time** class. The program instantiates a single object of class **Time** called **t**. When the object is instantiated, the **Time** constructor is called automatically and explicitly initializes each private data member to **0**. The time is then printed in military and standard formats to confirm that the members have been initialized properly. The time is then set using the **setTime** member function and the time is printed again in both formats. Then member function **setTime** attempts to set the data members to invalid values, and the time is again printed in both formats.

```
// FIG16_3.CPP
// Time class.
#include <iostream.h>

// Time abstract data type (ADT) definition
class Time {
public:
   Time();                           // default constructor
   void setTime(int, int, int);      // set hour, minute and second
   void printMilitary();             // print military time format
   void printStandard();             // print standard time format

private:
   int hour;      // 0 - 23
   int minute;    // 0 - 59
   int second;    // 0 - 59
};
```

Fig. 16.3   Abstract data type Time implementation as a class (part 1 of 3)

```
// Time constructor initializes each data member to zero.
// Ensures all Time objects start in a consistent state.
Time::Time() { hour = minute = second = 0; }

// Set a new Time value using military time. Perform validity
// checks on the data values. Set invalid values to zero.
void Time::setTime(int h, int m, int s)
{
   hour = (h >= 0 && h < 24) ? h : 0;
   minute = (m >= 0 && m < 60) ? m : 0;
   second = (s >= 0 && s < 60) ? s : 0;
}

// Print Time in military format
void Time::printMilitary()
{
   cout << (hour < 10 ? "0" : "") << hour << ":"
        << (minute < 10 ? "0" : "") << minute << ":"
        << (second < 10 ? "0" : "") << second;
}

// Print time in standard format
void Time::printStandard()
{
   cout << ((hour == 0 || hour == 12) ? 12 : hour % 12)
        << ":" << (minute < 10 ? "0" : "") << minute
        << ":" << (second < 10 ? "0" : "") << second
        << (hour < 12 ? " AM" : " PM");
}

// Driver to test simple class Time
main()
{
   Time t;   // instantiate object t of class Time

   cout << "The initial military time is ";
   t.printMilitary();
   cout << "\nThe initial standard time is ";
   t.printStandard();

   t.setTime(13, 27, 6);
   cout << "\n\nMilitary time after setTime is ";
   t.printMilitary();
   cout << "\nStandard time after setTime is ";
   t.printStandard();

   t.setTime(99, 99, 99);   // attempt invalid settings
   cout << "\n\nAfter attempting invalid settings:\n"
        << "Military time: ";
   t.printMilitary();
   cout << "\nStandard time: ";
   t.printStandard();
   cout << endl;
   return 0;
}
```

Fig. 16.3   Abstract data type Time implementation as a class (part 2 of 3).

```
The initial military time is 00:00:00
The initial standard time is 12:00:00 AM

Military time after setTime is 13:27:06
Standard time after setTime is 1:27:06 PM

After attempting invalid settings:
Military time: 00:00:00
Standard time: 12:00:00 AM
```

Fig. 16.3   Abstract data type Time implementation as a class (part 3 of 3).

Again, note that the data members **hour**, **minute**, and **second** are preceded by the **private:** label. Private data members of a class are normally not accessible outside the class. (Again, we will see in Chapter 17 that friends of a class may access the class's private members.) The philosophy here is that the actual data representation used within the class is of no concern to the class's clients. In this sense, the implementation of a class is said to be *hidden* from its clients. Such *information hiding* promotes program modifiability and simplifies the client's perception of a class.

Software Engineering Observation 16.2

Clients of a class use the class without knowing the internal details of how the class is implemented. If the class implementation is changed (to improve performance, for example) the class's clients need not change. This makes it much easier to modify systems.

In this program, the **Time** constructor simply initializes the data members to 0 (i.e., the military time equivalent of 12 AM). This ensures that the object is in a consistent state when it is created. Invalid values can not be stored in the data members because the constructor is automatically called when the **Time** object is created and all subsequent attempts to modify the data members are scrutinized by the **setTime** function.

Software Engineering Observation 16.3

Member functions are usually only a few lines of code because no logic is required to determine if the data members are valid.

Note that the data members of a class can not be initialized where they are declared in the class body. These data members should be initialized by the class's constructor, or they can be assigned values by "set" functions.

Common Programming Error 16.2

Attempting to explicitly initialize a data member of a class.

The function with the same name as the class but preceded with a *tilde character (~)* is called the *destructor* of that class. The destructor does termination housekeeping on each class object before the memory for the object is reclaimed by the system. This example does not include a destructor. We will discuss constructors and destructors in more detail later in this chapter and in Chapter 17.

Note that the functions the class provides to the outside world are preceded by the `public:` label. Public functions implement the capabilities the class provides to its clients. The public functions of a class are called the class's *interface* or *public interface*.

Software Engineering Observation 16.4

Clients have access to a class's interface but should not have access to a class's implementation.

The class definition contains declarations of the class's data members and the class's member functions. The member function declarations are the function prototypes we discussed in earlier chapters. Member functions can be defined inside a class, but it is a good programming practice to define the functions outside the class definition.

Good Programming Practice 16.2

Define all but the smallest member functions outside the class definition. This helps separate the interface from the implementation of the class.

Note the use of the *binary scope resolution operator (::)* in each member function definition following the class definition in Fig. 16.3. Once a class is defined and its member functions are declared, the member functions must be defined. Each class member function can be defined directly in the class body (rather than including the function prototype of the class), or the function can be defined after the class body. When a member function is defined after its corresponding class definition, the function name is preceded by the class name and the binary scope resolution operator (::). Because different classes can have the same member names, the scope resolution operator "ties" the member name to the class name to uniquely address the member functions of a particular class.

Even though a member function declared in a class definition may be defined outside that class definition, that member function is still within that *class's scope,* i.e., its name is known only to other members of the class unless referred to via an object of the class, a reference to an object of the class, or a pointer to an object of the class. We will say more about class scope shortly.

It is possible to define member functions in the body of the class definition. Functions of more than one or two lines are normally defined outside the class definition—this helps separate the class interface from the class implementation. If a member function is defined in a class definition, the member function is automatically inlined. Member functions defined outside a class definition may be made inline by explicitly using the keyword `inline`. Remember that the compiler reserves the right not to inline any function.

Software Engineering Observation 16.5

Declaring member functions inside a class definition and defining those member functions outside that class definition separates the interface of a class from its implementation. This promotes good software engineering.

Performance Tip 16.3

Defining a small member function inside the class definition automatically inlines the member function (if the compiler chooses to do so). This can improve performance, but it does not promote the best software engineering.

It is interesting that the **printMilitary** and **printStandard** member functions take no arguments. This is because member functions implicitly know that they are to print the data members of the particular **Time** object for which they are invoked. This makes member function calls more concise than conventional function calls in procedural programming.

Software Engineering Observation 16.6

Using an object-oriented programming approach can often simplify function calls by reducing the number of parameters to be passed. This benefit of object-oriented programming derives from the fact that encapsulation of data members and member functions within an object gives the member functions the right to access the data members.

Classes simplify programming because the client (or user of the class object) need only be concerned with the operations encapsulated or embedded in the object. Such operations are usually designed to be client-oriented rather than implementation-oriented. Clients need not be concerned with a class's implementation. Interfaces do change, but less frequently than implementations. When an implementation changes, implementation-dependent code must change accordingly. By hiding the implementation we eliminate the possibility of other program parts becoming dependent on the details of the class implementation.

Often, classes do not have to be created "from scratch." Rather, they may be *derived* from other classes that provide operations the new classes can use. Or classes can include objects of other classes as members. Such *software reuse* can greatly enhance programmer productivity. Deriving new classes from existing classes is called *inheritance* and is discussed in detail in Chapter 19. Including classes as members of other classes is called *composition* and is discussed in Chapter 17.

16.6 Class Scope and Accessing Class Members

Variable names and function names declared in a class definition, and a class's data members and member functions, belong to that *class's scope*. Nonmember functions are defined at *file scope*.

Within a class's scope, class members are immediately accessible by all of that class's member functions and can be referenced simply by name. Outside a class's scope, class members are referenced through either an object name, a reference to an object, or a pointer to an object.

Member functions of a class can be overloaded, but only by functions in that class's scope. To overload a member function, simply provide in the class definition a prototype for each version of the overloaded function, and provide a separate function definition for each version of the function.

Common Programming Error 16.3

Attempting to overload a member function with a function not in that class's scope.

Member functions have *function scope* within a class. If a member function defines a variable with the same name as a variable with class scope, the class-scope variable is hidden by the function-scope variable within the function scope. Such a hidden variable can be accessed via the scope resolution operator by preceding the operator with the class name. Hidden global variables can be accessed with the unary scope resolution operator (see Chapter 15).

The operators used to access class members are identical to the operators used to access structure members. The *dot member selection operator (.)* is combined with an object's name or with a reference to an object to access the object's members. The *arrow member selection operator (->)* is combined with a pointer to an object to access that object's members.

The program of Fig. 16.4 uses a simple class called `Count` with public data member `x` of type `int`, and public member function `print` to illustrate accessing the members of a class with the member selection operators. The program instantiates three variables of type `Count`—`counter`, `counterRef` (a reference to a `Count` object), and `counterPtr` (a pointer to a `Count` object). Variable `counterRef` is declared to reference `counter`, and variable `counterPtr` is declared to point to `counter`. It is important to note that data member `x` has been made public here simply to demonstrate how public members are accessed. As we have stated, data is typically made private as we will do in all subsequent examples.

16.7 Separating Interface from Implementation

One of the most fundamental principles of good software engineering is to separate interface from implementation. This makes it easier to modify programs. As far as clients of a class are concerned, changes in the class's implementation do not affect the client as long as the class's interface is unchanged.

Software Engineering Observation 16.7

Place the class declaration in a header file to be included by any client that wants to use the class. This forms the class's public interface. Place the definitions of the class member functions in a source file. This forms the implementation of the class.

Software Engineering Observation 16.8

Clients of a class do not need to see the class's source code in order to use the class. The clients do, however, need to be able to link to the class's object code.

This encourages independent software vendors (ISVs) to provide class libraries for sale or license. The ISVs provide in their products only the header files and the object modules. No proprietary information is revealed—as would be the case if source code were provided. The C++ user community benefits by having more ISV-produced class libraries available.

Actually, things are not quite this rosy. Header files do contain some portion of the implementation and hints about the implementation. Inline member functions, for example, need to be in a header file, so that when the compiler compiles a client, the client can include the inline function definition in place. Private members are listed in the class declaration in the header file, so these members are visible to clients even though the clients may not access them.

```
// FIG16_4.CPP
// Demonstrating the class member access operators . and ->
//
// Caution: In future examples we will use private data.
#include <iostream.h>

// Simple class Count
class Count {
public:
    int x;
    void print() { cout << x << '\n'; }
};

main()
{
    Count counter,                    // create counter object
            *counterPtr = &counter,  // pointer to counter
            &counterRef = counter;   // reference to counter

    cout << "Assign 7 to x and print using the object's name: ";
    counter.x = 7;          // assign 7 to data member x
    counter.print();        // call member function print

    cout << "Assign 8 to x and print using a reference: ";
    counterRef.x = 8;       // assign 8 to data member x
    counterRef.print();     // call member function print

    cout << "Assign 10 to x and print using a pointer: ";
    counterPtr->x = 10;     // assign 10 to data member x
    counterPtr->print();    // call member function print
    return 0;
}
```

```
Assign 7 to x and print using the object's name: 7
Assign 8 to x and print using a reference: 8
Assign 10 to x and print using a pointer: 10
```

Fig. 16.4 Accessing an object's data members and member functions through the object's name, through a reference, and through a pointer to the object.

Software Engineering Observation 16.9

Information important to the interface to a class should be included in the header file. Information that will be used only internally in the class and will not be needed by clients of the class should be included in the unpublished source file. This is yet another example of the principle of least privilege.

Figure 16.5 splits the program of Fig. 16.3 into multiple files. When building a C++ program, each class definition is normally placed in a *header file*, and that class's member function definitions are placed in *source-code files* of the same base name. The header files are included (via `#include`) in each file in which the class is used, and the member function definitions source file is compiled and linked with the file containing the main program. See your compiler's documentation to determine how to compile and link programs consisting of multiple source files.

Figure 16.5 consists of the header file `time1.h` in which class `Time` is declared, the file `time1.cpp` in which the member functions of class `Time` are defined, and the file `fig16_5.cpp` in which function `main` is defined. The output for this program is identical to the output of Fig. 16.3.

Note that the class declaration is enclosed in the following preprocessor code (see Chapter 13):

```
// prevent multiple inclusions of header file
#ifndef TIME1_H
#define TIME1_H
   ...
#endif
```

When we build larger programs, other definitions and declarations will also be placed in header files. The preceding preprocessor directives prevent the code between `#ifndef` and `#endif` from being included if the name `TIME1_H` has been defined. If the header has not been included previously in a file, the name `TIME1_H` is defined by the `#define` directive and the header file statements are included. If the header has been included previously, `TIME1_H` is defined already and the header file is not included again. Note: The convention we use for the symbolic constant name in the preprocessor directives is simply the header file name with the underscore character replacing the period.

> ### Good Programming Practice 16.3
> *Use `#ifndef`, `#define` and `#endif` preprocessor directives to prevent header files from being included more than once in a program.*

> ### Good Programming Practice 16.4
> *Use the name of the header file with the period replaced by an underscore in the `#ifndef` and `#define` preprocessor directives of a header file.*

16.8 Controlling Access to Members

The labels `public:` and `private:` (and `protected:` as we will see in Chapter 19, "Inheritance") are used to control access to a class's data members and member functions. The default access mode for classes is `private:` so all members after the class header and before the first label are private. After each label, the mode that was invoked by that label applies until the next label or until the terminating right brace (`}`) of the class definition. The labels `public:`, `private:`, and `protected:` may be repeated, but such usage is rare and can be confusing.

Private class members can be accessed only by members (and friends) of that class. The public members of a class may be accessed by any function in the program.

```
// TIME1.H
// Declaration of the Time class.
// Member functions are defined in TIME1.CPP

// prevent multiple inclusions of header file
#ifndef TIME1_H
#define TIME1_H

// Time abstract data type definition
class Time {
public:
   Time();                        // default constructor
   void setTime(int, int, int);   // set hour, minute and second
   void printMilitary();          // print military time format
   void printStandard();          // print standard time format
private:
   int hour;      // 0 - 23
   int minute;    // 0 - 59
   int second;    // 0 - 59
};

#endif
```

Fig. 16.5 **Time** class header file (part 1 of 4).

```
// TIME1.CPP
// Member function definitions for Time class.
#include <iostream.h>
#include "time1.h"

// Time constructor initializes each data member to zero.
// Ensures all Time objects start in a consistent state.
Time::Time() { hour = minute = second = 0; }

// Set a new Time value using military time.
// Perform validity checks on the data values.
// Set invalid values to zero (consistent state).
void Time::setTime(int h, int m, int s)
{
   hour = (h >= 0 && h < 24) ? h : 0;
   minute = (m >= 0 && m < 60) ? m : 0;
   second = (s >= 0 && s < 60) ? s : 0;
}

// Print Time in military format
void Time::printMilitary()
{
   cout << (hour < 10 ? "0" : "") << hour << ":"
        << (minute < 10 ? "0" : "") << minute << ":"
        << (second < 10 ? "0" : "") << second;
}
```

Fig. 16.5 **Time** class member function definitions source file (part 2 of 4).

```
// Print time in standard format
void Time::printStandard()
{
    cout << ((hour == 0 || hour == 12) ? 12 : hour % 12)
         << ":" << (minute < 10 ? "0" : "") << minute
         << ":" << (second < 10 ? "0" : "") << second
         << (hour < 12 ? " AM" : " PM");
}
```

Fig. 16.5 **Time** class member function definitions source file (part 3 of 4).

```
// FIG16_5.CPP
// Driver for Time1 class
// NOTE: Compile with TIME1.CPP
#include <iostream.h>
#include "time1.h"

// Driver to test simple class Time
main()
{
    Time t;   // instantiate object t of class time

    cout << "The initial military time is ";
    t.printMilitary();
    cout << "\nThe initial standard time is ";
    t.printStandard();

    t.setTime(13, 27, 6);
    cout << "\n\nMilitary time after setTime is ";
    t.printMilitary();
    cout << "\nStandard time after setTime is ";
    t.printStandard();

    t.setTime(99, 99, 99);   // attempt invalid settings
    cout << "\n\nAfter attempting invalid settings:\n"
         << "Military time: ";
    t.printMilitary();
    cout << "\nStandard time: ";
    t.printStandard();
    cout << endl;
    return 0;
}
```

```
The initial military time is 00:00:00
The initial standard time is 12:00:00 AM

Military time after setTime is 13:27:06
Standard time after setTime is 1:27:06 PM

After attempting invalid settings:
Military time: 00:00:00
Standard time: 12:00:00 AM
```

Fig. 16.5 Driver program for **Time** class (part 4 of 4).

The primary purpose of public members is to present to the class's clients a view of the *services* the class provides. This set of services forms the *public interface* of the class. Clients of the class need not be concerned with how the class accomplishes its tasks. The private members of a class as well as the definitions of its public member functions are not accessible to the clients of a class. These components form the *implementation* of the class.

Software Engineering Observation 16.10

C++ encourages programs to be implementation independent. When the implementation of a class used by implementation-independent code changes, that code need not be modified, but it may need to be recompiled.

Common Programming Error 16.4

An attempt by a function which is not a member of a particular class (or a friend of that class) to access a private member of that class.

Figure 16.6 demonstrates that private class members are only accessible through the public class interface using public member functions. When this program is compiled, the compiler generates two errors stating that the private member specified in each statement is not accessible. Figure 16.6 includes **time1.h** and is compiled with **time1.cpp** from Fig. 16.5.

```
// FIG16_6.CPP
// Demonstrate errors resulting from attempts
// to access private class members.
#include <iostream.h>
#include "time1.h"

main()
{
    Time t;

    // Error: 'Time::hour' is not accessible
    t.hour = 7;

    // Error: 'Time::minute' is not accessible
    cout << "minute = " << t.minute;

    return 0;
}
```

```
Compiling FIG16_6.CPP:
Error FIG16_6.CPP 12: 'Time::hour' is not accessible
Error FIG16_6.CPP 15: 'Time::minute' is not accessible
```

Fig. 16.6   Erroneous attempt to access private members of a class.

Good Programming Practice 16.5

If you choose to list the private members first in a class declaration, explicitly use the `private:` *label despite the fact that* `private:` *is assumed by default. This improves program clarity. Our preference is to list the* `public:` *members of a class first.*

Good Programming Practice 16.6

Despite the fact that the `public:` *and* `private:` *labels may be repeated and intermixed, list all the public members of a class first in one group and then list all the private members in another group. This focuses the client's attention on the class's public interface, rather than on the class's implementation.*

Software Engineering Observation 16.11

Keep all the data members of a class private. Provide public member functions to set the values of private data members and to get the values of private data members. This architecture helps hide the implementation of a class from its clients, which reduces bugs and improves program modifiability.

A client of a class may be a member function of another class, or it may be a global function.

The default access for members of a class is private. Access to members of a class may be explicitly set to protected or public. The default access for **struct** members and union members is **public**. Access to members of a **struct** may be explicitly set to **public** or **private** (or, as we will see in Chapter 19, **protected**). The member access specifiers may not be used explicitly with a **union**.

Software Engineering Observation 16.12

Class designers use private, protected, and public members to enforce the notion of information hiding and the principle of least privilege.

Note that the members of a class are private by default, so it is never necessary to use the `private:` member access specifier explicitly. Many programmers prefer, however, to list the interface to a class first (i.e., the class's public members); then the private members are listed, thus requiring the explicit use of the `private:` member access specifier in the class definition.

Good Programming Practice 16.7

Using the member access specifiers `public:`, `protected:`, *and* `private:` *only once each in any class definition avoids confusion.*

Just because class data is **private** does not necessarily mean that clients can not effect changes to that data. The data can be changed by member functions or friends of that class. As we will see, these functions should be designed to ensure the integrity of the data.

Access to a class's private data can be carefully controlled by the use of member functions, called *access functions.* For example, to allow clients to read the value of private data, the class can provide a *"get" function.* To enable clients to modify private data, the class can provide a *"set" function.* Such modification would seem to violate the notion of private data. But a *set* member function can provide data validation capabilities (such as range checking) to ensure that the value is set properly. A *get* function need not expose the data in "raw" format; rather the *get* function can edit the data and limit the view of the data the client will see.

Software Engineering Observation 16.13

Making the data members of a class private and the member functions of the class public facilitates debugging because problems with data manipulations are localized to either the class's member functions or the friends of the class.

16.9 Access Functions and Utility Functions

Not all member functions need be made public to serve as part of the interface of a class. Some member functions remain private and serve as *utility functions* to the other functions of the class.

Software Engineering Observation 16.14

Member functions tend to fall into a number of different categories: functions that read and return the value of private data members, functions that set the value of private data members, functions that implement the features of the class, and functions that perform various mechanical chores for the class such as initializing class objects, assigning class objects, converting between classes and built-in types or between classes and other classes, and handling memory for class objects.

Access functions can read or display data. Another common use for access functions is to test the truth or falsity of conditions—such functions are often called *predicate functions.* An example of a predicate function would be an `isEmpty` function for any container class such as a linked list, a stack or a queue. A program would test `isEmpty` before attempting to read another item from the container object. An `isFull` predicate function might test a container class object to determine if it has no additional room.

Figure 16.7 demonstrates the notion of a *utility function.* A utility function is not part of a class's interface. Rather, it is a private member function that supports the operation of the class's public member functions. Utility functions are not intended to be used by clients of a class.

Class `SalesPerson` has an array of 12 monthly sales figures initialized by the constructor to zero and set to user-supplied values by function `setSales`. Public member function `printAnnualSales` prints the total sales for the last 12 months. Utility function `totalAnnualSales` totals the 12 monthly sales figures for the benefit of `printAnnualSales`. Member function `printAnnualSales` edits the sales figures into dollar amount format. Each of the C++ formatting capabilities used here is explained in depth in Chapter 21. For now, we provide only a brief explanation. The call

```
setprecision(2)
```

indicates that two digits of "precision" are to print to the right of the decimal point, exactly as we need for dollar amounts such as 23.47. This call is referred to as a "param eterized stream manipulator." A program that uses these kinds of calls must also contain the preprocessor directive

```
#include <iomanip.h>
```

The line

```
setiosflags(ios::fixed | ios::showpoint);
```

causes the sales figure to be displayed in so-called fixed-point format (as opposed to scientific notation). The **showpoint** option forces the decimal point and trailing zeros to appear even if the number is a whole dollar amount such as 47.00. In C++, such a number would print simply as 47 if the **showpoint** option were not set.

16.10 Initializing Class Objects: Constructors

After objects are created, their members can be initialized by *constructor* functions. A constructor is a class member function with the same name as the class. The programmer provides the constructor which is then invoked automatically each time an object of that class is created. *Data members of a class can not be initialized in the class definition.* Rather, data members must either be initialized in a constructor of the class, or their values may be set later after the object is created. Constructors can not specify return types nor return values. Constructors may be overloaded to provide a variety of means for initializing objects of a class.

Common Programming Error 16.5

Attempting to explicitly initialize a data member of a class in the class definition.

```
// SALESP.H
// SalesPerson class definition
// Member functions defined in SALESP.CPP

#ifndef SALESP_H
#define SALESP_H

class SalesPerson {
public:
    SalesPerson();              // constructor
    void setSales();            // user supplies sales figures
    void printAnnualSales();

private:
    double sales[13];           // 12 monthly sales figures
    double totalAnnualSales();  // utility function
};

#endif
```

Fig. 16.7   Using a utility function (part 1 of 3).

```cpp
// SALESP.CPP
// Member functions for class SalesPerson
#include <iostream.h>
#include <iomanip.h>
#include "salesp.h"

// Constructor function initializes array
SalesPerson::SalesPerson()
{
    for (int i = 0; i <= 12; i++)
        sales[i] = 0.0;
}

// Function to set the 12 monthly sales figures
void SalesPerson::setSales()
{
    for (int i = 1; i <= 12; i++) {
        cout << "Enter sales amount for month "
             << i << ": ";
        cin >> sales[i];
    }
}

// Private utility function to total annual sales
double SalesPerson::totalAnnualSales()
{
    double total = 0.0;

    for (int i = 1; i <= 12; i++)
        total += sales[i];

    return total;
}

// Print the total annual sales
void SalesPerson::printAnnualSales()
{
    cout << setprecision(2)
         << setiosflags(ios::fixed | ios::showpoint)
         << "\nThe total annual sales are: $"
         << totalAnnualSales() << endl;
}
```

Fig. 16.7   Using a utility function (part 2 of 3).

Common Programming Error 16.6

Attempting to declare a return type for a constructor, and/or attempting to return a value from a constructor.

Good Programming Practice 16.8

When appropriate (almost always), provide a constructor to ensure that every object is properly initialized with meaningful values.

```
// FIG16_7.CPP
// Demonstrating a utility function
// Compile with SALESP.CPP
#include "salesp.h"

main()
{
    SalesPerson s;          // create SalesPerson object s

    s.setSales();
    s.printAnnualSales();

    return 0;
}
```

```
Enter sales amount for month 1: 5314.76
Enter sales amount for month 2: 4292.38
Enter sales amount for month 3: 4589.83
Enter sales amount for month 4: 5534.03
Enter sales amount for month 5: 4376.34
Enter sales amount for month 6: 5698.45
Enter sales amount for month 7: 4439.22
Enter sales amount for month 8: 5893.57
Enter sales amount for month 9: 4909.67
Enter sales amount for month 10: 5123.45
Enter sales amount for month 11: 4024.97
Enter sales amount for month 12: 5923.92

Total annual sales: $60120.59
```

Fig. 16.7   Using a utility function (part 3 of 3).

Good Programming Practice 16.9

Every member function (and friend) that modifies the private data members of an object should ensure that the data remains in a consistent state.

When an object of a class is declared, *initializers* can be provided in parentheses to the right of the object name and before the semicolon. These initializers are passed as arguments to the class's constructor. We will soon see several examples of these *constructor calls.*

16.11 Using Default Arguments with Constructors

The constructor from **time1.cpp** (Fig. 16.5) initialized **hour, minute,** and **second** to **0** (i.e., 12 midnight in military time). Constructors can contain default arguments. Figure 16.8 redefines the **Time** constructor function to include default arguments of zero for each variable. By providing default arguments to the constructor, even if no values are provided in a constructor call, the object is still guaranteed to be in a consistent state due to the default arguments. A programmer-supplied constructor that defaults all its arguments is also a default constructor (it can be invoked with no arguments). The constructor uses the same kind of validation code as **setTime** to ensure that the value supplied for **hour** is in the range 0 to 23, and that the values for **minute** and **second** are each in the range 0 to 59. If a value is out of range, it is set to zero (this is an example of ensuring that a data member remains in a consistent state). The constructor could call **setTime** directly, but this would create the overhead of an additional function call. The program of Fig. 16.8 initializes five **Time** objects—one with all three arguments defaulted in the constructor call, one with one argument specified, one with two arguments specified, one with three arguments specified, and one with three invalid arguments specified. The contents of each object's data members after instantiation and initialization are displayed.

If no constructor is defined for a class, the compiler creates a *default constructor.* Such a constructor does not perform any initialization, so when the object is created, it is not guaranteed to be in a consistent state.

Good Programming Practice 16.10

Always provide a constructor that performs appropriate initialization for its class.

16.12 Using Destructors

A *destructor* is a special member function of a class. The name of the destructor for a class is the *tilde (~)* character followed by the name of the class. This naming convention has intuitive appeal, because the tilde operator is the bitwise complement operator, and, in a sense, the destructor is the complement of the constructor.

```
// TIME2.H
// Declaration of the Time class.
// Member functions defined in TIME2.CPP

// prevent multiple inclusions of header file
#ifndef TIME2_H
#define TIME2_H

class Time {
public:
   Time(int = 0, int = 0, int = 0);  // default constructor
   void setTime(int, int, int);
   void printMilitary();
   void printStandard();
private:
   int hour;
   int minute;
   int second;
};

#endif
```

Fig. 16.8 Using a constructor with default arguments (part 1 of 4).

```
// TIME2.CPP
// Member function definitions for Time class.
#include "time2.h"
#include <iostream.h>

// Constructor function to initialize private data.
// Default values are 0 (see class definition).
Time::Time(int hr, int min, int sec)
{
   hour = (hr >= 0 && hr < 24) ? hr : 0;
   minute = (min >= 0 && min < 60) ? min : 0;
   second = (sec >= 0 && sec < 60) ? sec : 0;
}

// Set values of hour, minute, and second.
// Invalid values are set to 0.
void Time::setTime(int h, int m, int s)
{
   hour = (h >= 0 && h < 24) ? h : 0;
   minute = (m >= 0 && m < 60) ? m : 0;
   second = (s >= 0 && s < 60) ? s : 0;
}

// Display time in military format: HH:MM:SS
void Time::printMilitary()
{
   cout << (hour < 10 ? "0" : "") << hour << ":"
        << (minute < 10 ? "0" : "") << minute << ":"
        << (second < 10 ? "0" : "") << second;
}

// Display time in standard format: HH:MM:SS AM (or PM)
void Time::printStandard()
{
   cout << ((hour == 0 || hour == 12) ? 12 : hour % 12)
        << ":" << (minute < 10 ? "0" : "") << minute
        << ":" << (second < 10 ? "0" : "") << second
        << (hour < 12 ? " AM" : " PM");
}
```

Fig. 16.8   Using a constructor with default arguments (part 2 of 4).

A class's destructor is called automatically when an object of a class leaves scope. The destructor itself does not actually destroy the object, rather it performs *termination housekeeping* before the system reclaims the object's memory space so that it may be used to hold new objects.

A destructor receives no parameters and returns no value. A class may have only one destructor—destructor overloading is not allowed.

Common Programming Error 16.7

Attempting to pass arguments to a destructor, to return values from a destructor, or to overload a destructor.

```
// FIG16_8.CPP
// Demonstrating a default constructor
// function for class Time.
#include <iostream.h>
#include "time2.h"

main()
{
    Time t1, t2(2), t3(21, 34), t4(12, 25, 42),
        t5(27, 74, 99);

    cout << "Constructed with:\n"
        << "all arguments defaulted:\n    ";
    t1.printMilitary();
    cout << "\n    ";
    t1.printStandard();

    cout << "\nhour specified; minute and second defaulted:\n    ";
    t2.printMilitary();
    cout << "\n    ";
    t2.printStandard();

    cout << "\nhour and minute specified; second defaulted:\n    ";
    t3.printMilitary();
    cout << "\n    ";
    t3.printStandard();

    cout << "\nhour, minute, and second specified:\n    ";
    t4.printMilitary();
    cout << "\n    ";
    t4.printStandard();

    cout << "\nall invalid values specified:\n    ";
    t5.printMilitary();
    cout << "\n    ";
    t5.printStandard();
    cout << endl;

    return 0;
}
```

Fig. 16.8   Using a constructor with default arguments (part 3 of 4).

Notice that we have not provided destructors for the classes we have presented so far. Actually, destructors are rarely used with simple classes. In Chapter 18, we will see that destructors are appropriate for classes whose objects contain dynamically allocated storage (for arrays and strings, for example).

16.13 When Destructors and Constructors are Called

Normally, constructors and destructors are called automatically. The order in which these function calls are made depends on the order in which objects enter and leave scope. Gen-

```
Constructed with:
all arguments defaulted:
    00:00:00
    12:00:00 AM
hour specified; minute and second defaulted:
    02:00:00
    2:00:00 AM
hour and minute specified; second defaulted:
    21:34:00
    9:34:00 PM
hour, minute, and second specified:
    12:25:42
    12:25:42 PM
all invalid values specified:
    00:00:00
    12:00:00 AM
```

Fig. 16.8   Using a constructor with default arguments (part 4 of 4).

erally, destructor calls are made in the reverse order of the constructor calls. However, the storage duration of objects can alter the order in which the destructors are called.

Constructors are called for objects declared in global scope when the program begins execution. The corresponding destructors are called at program termination.

Constructors are called for automatic local objects when the objects are declared. The corresponding destructors are called when the objects leave scope (i.e., the block in which they are declared is exited). Note that constructors and destructors for automatic local objects could be called many times as the objects enter and leave scope.

Constructors are called for static local objects once when the objects are declared. Corresponding destructors are called at program termination.

The program of Fig. 16.9 demonstrates the order in which constructors and destructors are called for objects of type **CreateAndDestroy** in several scopes. The program declares **first** in global scope. Its constructor is called as the program begins execution and its destructor is called at program termination after all other objects are destroyed.

Function **main** declares three objects. Objects **second** and **fourth** are local automatic objects, and object **third** is a static local object. The constructors for each of these objects are called when each object is declared. The destructors for objects **fourth** and **second** are called in that order when the end of **main** is reached. Because object **third** is static, it exists from the point at which it is declared until program termination. The destructor for object **third** is called before the destructor for **first**, but after all other objects are destroyed.

Function **create** declares three objects. Objects **fifth** and **seventh** are local automatic objects, and object **sixth** is a static local object. The destructors for objects **seventh** and **fifth** are called in that order when the end of **create** is reached. Because object **sixth** is static, it exists from the point at which it is declared to program termination. The destructor for object **sixth** is called before the destructors for **third** and **first**, but after all other objects are destroyed.

```
// CREATE.H
// Definition of class CreateAndDestroy.
// Member functions defined in CREATE.CPP.

#ifndef CREATE_H
#define CREATE_H

class CreateAndDestroy {
public:
   CreateAndDestroy(int);   // constructor
   ~CreateAndDestroy();     // destructor
private:
   int data;
};

#endif
```

Fig. 16.9 Demonstrating the order in which constructors and destructors are called (part 1 of 3).

```
// CREATE.CPP
// Member function definitions for class CreateAndDestroy
#include <iostream.h>
#include "create.h"

CreateAndDestroy::CreateAndDestroy(int value)
{
   data = value;
   cout << "Object " << data << "   constructor";
}

CreateAndDestroy::~CreateAndDestroy()
   { cout << "Object " << data << "   destructor " << endl; }
```

Fig. 16.9 Demonstrating the order in which constructors and destructors are called (part 2 of 3).

16.14 Using Data Members and Member Functions

Private data members can be manipulated only by member functions (and friends) of the class. A typical manipulation might be the adjustment of a customer's bank balance (e.g., a private data member of a class **BankAccount**) by a member function **computeInterest**.

Classes often provide public member functions to allow clients of the class to set (i.e., write) or get (i.e., read) the values of private data members. These functions need not be called "set" and "get" specifically, but they often are. More specifically, a member function that sets data member **interestRate** would typically be named **setInterestRate**, and a member function that gets the **interestRate** would typically be called **getInterestRate**. Get functions are also commonly called "query" functions.

```
// FIG16_9.CPP
// Demonstrating the order in which constructors and
// destructors are called.
#include <iostream.h>
#include "create.h"

void create(void);   // prototype

CreateAndDestroy first(1);  // global object

main()
{
    cout << "    (global created before main)\n";

    CreateAndDestroy second(2);        // local object
    cout << "    (local automatic in main)\n";

    static CreateAndDestroy third(3);  // local object
    cout << "    (local static in main)\n";

    create();  // call function to create objects

    CreateAndDestroy fourth(4);        // local object
    cout << "    (local automatic in main)\n";
    return 0;
}

// Function to create objects
void create(void)
{
    CreateAndDestroy fifth(5);
    cout << "    (local automatic in create)\n";

    static CreateAndDestroy sixth(6);
    cout << "    (local static in create)\n";

    CreateAndDestroy seventh(7);
    cout << "    (local automatic in create)\n";
}
```

```
Object 1    constructor    (global created before main)
Object 2    constructor    (local automatic in main)
Object 3    constructor    (local static in main)
Object 5    constructor    (local automatic in create)
Object 6    constructor    (local static in create)
Object 7    constructor    (local automatic in create)
Object 7    destructor
Object 5    destructor
Object 4    constructor    (local automatic in main)
Object 4    destructor
Object 2    destructor
Object 6    destructor
Object 3    destructor
Object 1    destructor
```

Fig. 16.9   Demonstrating the order in which constructors and destructors are called (part 3 of 3).

It would seem that providing both set and get capabilities would be essentially the same as making the data members public. This is yet another subtlety of C++ that makes the language so desirable for software engineering. If a data member is public, then the data member may be read or written at will by any function in the program. If a data member is private, a public "get" function would certainly seem to allow other functions to read the data at will but the get function could control the formatting and display of the data. A public "set" function could—and most likely would—carefully scrutinize any attempt to modify the value of the data member. This would ensure that the new value is appropriate for that data item. For example, an attempt to set the day of the month to 37 would be rejected, an attempt to set a person's weight to a negative value would be rejected, an attempt to set a numeric quantity to an alphabetic value would be rejected, an attempt to set a grade on an exam to 185 (when the proper range is zero to 100) would be rejected, and so on.

Software Engineering Observation 16.15

Making data members private and controlling access, especially write access, to those data members through public member functions helps ensure data integrity.

The benefits of data integrity are not automatic simply because data members are made private—the programmer must provide the validity checking. C++ does, however, provide a framework in which programmers can design better programs in a convenient manner.

Good Programming Practice 16.11

Member functions that set the values of private data should verify that the intended new values are proper; if they are not, the set functions should place the private data members into an appropriate consistent state.

Figure 16.10 extends our **Time** class to include get and set functions for the **hour**, **minute**, and **second** private data members. The set functions strictly control the setting of the data members. Attempts to set any data member to an incorrect value cause the data member to be set to zero (thus leaving the data member in a consistent state). Each get function simply returns the appropriate data member's value. The program first uses the set functions to set the private data members of **Time** object **t** to valid values, then uses the get functions to retrieve the values for output. Next the set functions attempt to set the **hour** and **second** members to invalid values and the **minute** member to a valid value, and then the get functions retrieve the values for output. The output confirms that the invalid values cause the data members to be set to zero. Finally, the program sets the time to **11:58:00** and increments the minute value by 3 with a call to function **incrementMinutes**. Function **incrementMinutes** is a nonmember function that uses the get and set member functions to increment the **minute** member properly. Although this works, it incurs the performance burden of issuing multiple function calls. In the next chapter, we discuss the notion of friend functions as a means of eliminating this performance burden.

The availability of set functions in a class provides some flexibility in designing constructors.

```
// TIME3.H
// Declaration of the Time class.
// Member functions defined in TIME3.CPP

// prevent multiple inclusions of header file
#ifndef TIME3_H
#define TIME3_H

class Time {
public:
   Time(int = 0, int = 0, int = 0);   // constructor

   // set functions
   void setTime(int, int, int);   // set hour, minute, second
   void setHour(int);      // set hour
   void setMinute(int);    // set minute
   void setSecond(int);    // set second

   // get functions
   int getHour();          // return hour
   int getMinute();        // return minute
   int getSecond();        // return second

   void printMilitary();   // output military time
   void printStandard();   // output standard time
private:
   int hour;               // 0 - 23
   int minute;             // 0 - 59
   int second;             // 0 - 59
};

#endif
```

Fig. 16.10 Declaration of the **Time** class (part 1 of 5).

Common Programming Error 16.8

A constructor can call other member functions of the class such as set or get functions, but because the constructor is initializing the object, the data members may not yet be in a consistent state. Using data members before they have been properly initialized can cause errors.

Set functions are certainly important from a software engineering standpoint because they can perform validity checking. Set and get functions have another important software engineering advantage.

Software Engineering Observation 16.16

Accessing private data through set and get member functions not only protects the data members from receiving invalid values, but it also insulates clients of the class from the representation of the data members. Thus, if the representation of the data changes for some reason (typically to reduce the amount of storage required or to improve performance), only the member functions need to change—the clients need not change as long as the interface provided by the member functions remains the same. The clients may, however, need to be recompiled.

```
// TIME3.CPP
// Member function definitions for Time class.

#include "time3.h"
#include <iostream.h>

// Constructor function to initialize private data.
// Default values are 0 (see class definition).
Time::Time(int hr, int min, int sec)
{
   hour = (hr >= 0 && hr < 24) ? hr : 0;
   minute = (min >= 0 && min < 60) ? min : 0;
   second = (sec >= 0 && sec < 60) ? sec : 0;
}

// Set the values of hour, minute, and second.
void Time::setTime(int h, int m, int s)
{
   hour = (h >= 0 && h < 24) ? h : 0;
   minute = (m >= 0 && m < 60) ? m : 0;
   second = (s >= 0 && s < 60) ? s : 0;
}

// Set the hour value
void Time::setHour(int h)
   { hour = (h >= 0 && h < 24) ? h : 0; }

// Set the minute value
void Time::setMinute(int m)
   { minute = (m >= 0 && m < 60) ? m : 0; }

// Set the second value
void Time::setSecond(int s)
   { second = (s >= 0 && s < 60) ? s : 0; }

// Get the hour value
int Time::getHour() { return hour; }

// Get the minute value
int Time::getMinute() { return minute; }

// Get the second value
int Time::getSecond() { return second; }

// Display military format time: HH:MM:SS
void Time::printMilitary()
{
   cout << (hour < 10 ? "0" : "") << hour << ":"
        << (minute < 10 ? "0" : "") << minute << ":"
        << (second < 10 ? "0" : "") << second;
}
```

Fig. 16.10 Member function definitions for **Time** class (part 2 of 5).

```
// Display standard format time: HH:MM:SS AM (or PM)
void Time::printStandard()
{
    cout << ((hour == 0 || hour == 12) ? 12 : hour % 12) << ":"
         << (minute < 10 ? "0" : "") << minute << ":"
         << (second < 10 ? "0" : "") << second
         << (hour < 12 ? " AM" : " PM");
}
```

Fig. 16.10 Member function definitions for **Time** class (part 3 of 5).

```
// FIG16_10.CPP
// Demonstrating the Time class set and get functions
#include <iostream.h>
#include "time3.h"

void incrementMinutes(Time &, const int);

main()
{
    Time t;

    t.setHour(17);
    t.setMinute(34);
    t.setSecond(25);

    cout << "Result of setting all valid values:\n  Hour: "
         << t.getHour()
         << "  Minute: " << t.getMinute()
         << "  Second: " << t.getSecond() << "\n\n";

    t.setHour(234);        // invalid hour set to 0
    t.setMinute(43);
    t.setSecond(6373);     // invalid second set to 0

    cout << "Result of attempting to set invalid hour and"
         << " second:\n  Hour: " << t.getHour()
         << "  Minute: " << t.getMinute()
         << "  Second: " << t.getSecond() << "\n\n";

    t.setTime(11, 58, 0);
    incrementMinutes(t, 3);
    return 0;
}
```

Fig. 16.10 Using set and get functions (part 4 of 5).

16.15 A Subtle Trap: Returning a Reference to Private Data Member

A reference to an object is an alias for the object itself and hence may be used on the left side of an assignment statement. In this context, the reference makes a perfectly accept-

```
    void incrementMinutes(Time &tt, const int count)
    {
        cout << "Incrementing minute " << count
             << " times:\nStart time: ";
        tt.printStandard();

        for (int i = 1; i <= count; i++) {
            tt.setMinute((tt.getMinute() + 1) % 60);

            if (tt.getMinute() == 0)
                tt.setHour((tt.getHour() + 1) % 24);

            cout << "\nminute + 1: ";
            tt.printStandard();
        }

        cout << endl;
    }
```

```
    Result of setting all valid values:
      Hour: 17  Minute: 34  Second: 25

    Result of attempting to set invalid hour and second:
      Hour: 0  Minute: 43  Second: 0

    Incrementing minute 3 times:
    Start time: 11:58:00 AM
    minute + 1: 11:59:00 AM
    minute + 1: 12:00:00 PM
    minute + 1: 12:01:00 PM
```

Fig. 16.10 Using set and get functions (part 5 of 5).

able *lvalue* that can receive a value. One way to use this capability (unfortunately!) is to have a public member function of a class return a reference to a private data member of that class.

Figure 16.11 uses a simplified version of the **Time** class to demonstrate returning a reference to a private data member. Such a return actually makes a call to function **badSetHour** an alias for the private data member **hour**! The function call can be used in any way the private data member can be used, including as an *lvalue* in an assignment statement!

Good Programming Practice 16.12

*Never have a public member function return a non-**const** reference (or a pointer) to a private data member. Returning such a reference violates the encapsulation of the class.*

The program begins by declaring **Time** object **t** and reference **hourRef** that is assigned the reference returned by the call **t.badSetHour(20)**. The program displays the value of the alias **hourRef**. Next, the alias is used to set the value of **hour** to 30 (an invalid value) and the value is displayed again. Finally, the function call itself is used as an *lvalue* and assigned the value 74 (another invalid value), and the value is displayed.

```
// TIME4.H
// Declaration of the Time class.
// Member functions defined in TIME4.CPP

// prevent multiple inclusions of header file
#ifndef TIME4_H
#define TIME4_H

class Time {
public:
   Time(int = 0, int = 0, int = 0);
   void setTime(int, int, int);
   int getHour();
   int &badSetHour(int);   // DANGEROUS reference return
private:
   int hour;
   int minute;
   int second;
};

#endif
```

Fig. 16.11 Returning a reference to a private data member (part 1 of 3) .

```
// TIME4.CPP
// Member function definitions for Time class.
#include "time4.h"
#include <iostream.h>

// Constructor function to initialize private data.
// Calls member function setTime to set variables.
// Default values are 0 (see class definition).
Time::Time(int hr, int min, int sec)
   { setTime(hr, min, sec); }

// Set the values of hour, minute, and second.
void Time::setTime(int h, int m, int s)
{
   hour = (h >= 0 && h < 24) ? h : 0;
   minute = (m >= 0 && m < 60) ? m : 0;
   second = (s >= 0 && s < 60) ? s : 0;
}

// Get the hour value
int Time::getHour() { return hour; }

// BAD PROGRAMMING PRACTICE:
// Returning a reference to a private data member.
int &Time::badSetHour(int hh)
{
   hour = (hh >= 0 && hh < 24) ? hh : 0;

   return hour;   // DANGEROUS reference return
}
```

Fig. 16.11 Returning a reference to a private data member (part 2 of 3).

- Drawbacks to creating new data types with C-style `struct`s are the possibility of having uninitialized data; improper initialization; all programs using a C-style `struct` must be changed if the `struct` implementation changes; and no protection is provided to ensure that data is kept in a consistent state with proper data values.

- Classes enable the programmer to model objects with attributes and behaviors. Class types can be defined in C++ using the keywords `class` and `struct`, but keyword `class` is normally used for this purpose.

- The class name can be used to declare objects of that class.

- Class definitions begin with the keyword `class`. The body of the class definition is delineated with braces (`{` and `}`). Class definitions terminate with a semicolon.

- Any data member or member function declared after `public:` in a class is visible to any function with access to an object of the class.

- Any data member or member function declared after `private:` is only visible to friends and other members of the class.

- Member access specifiers always end with a colon (`:`) and can appear multiple times in a class definition.

- Private data are not accessible from outside the class.

- The implementation of a class is said to be hidden from its clients or "encapsulated."

- A constructor is a special member function with the same name as the class that is used to initialize the members of a class object. Constructors are called when an object of their class is instantiated.

- The function with the same name as the class but preceded with a tilde character (~) is called a destructor.

- The set of public member functions of a class is called the class's interface or public interface.

- When a member function is defined outside the class definition, the function name is preceded by the class name and the binary scope resolution operator (`::`).

- Member functions defined using the scope resolution operator outside a class definition are within that class's scope.

- Member functions defined in a class definition are automatically inlined. The compiler reserves the right not to inline any function.

- Calling member functions is more concise than calling functions in procedural programming because member functions assume that names not declared are members of the class in which the member function is defined.

- Within a class's scope, class members may be referenced simply by their names. Outside a class's scope, class members are referenced through either an object name, a reference to an object, or a pointer to an object.

- Member selection operators `.` and `->` are used to access class members.

Objects may be passed as function arguments and may be returned from functions. Such passing and returning is performed call by value by default—a copy of the object is passed or returned (we present several examples in Chapter 18, "Operator Overloading."

> *Performance Tip 16.4*
>
> *Passing an object call by value is good from a security standpoint because the called function has no access to the original object, but call by value can degrade performance when making a copy of a large object. An object can be passed call by reference by passing either a pointer or a reference to the object. Call by reference offers good performance but is weaker from a security standpoint because the called function is given access to the original object. Call-by-**const**-reference is a safe alternative.*

16.17 Software Reusability

People who write object-oriented programs concentrate on implementing useful classes. There is a tremendous opportunity to capture and catalog classes so that they can be accessed by large segments of the programming community. Many *class libraries* exist and others are being developed worldwide. There are efforts to make these libraries broadly accessible. Software could then be constructed from existing, well-defined, carefully tested, well-documented, portable, widely available components. This kind of *software reusability* can speed the development of powerful, high-quality software. *Rapid applications development (RAD)* becomes possible.

Significant problems must be solved, however, before the full potential of software reusability can be realized. We need cataloging schemes, licensing schemes, protection mechanisms to ensure that master copies of classes are not corrupted, description schemes so that designers of new systems can determine if existing objects meet their needs, browsing mechanisms to determine what classes are available and how closely they meet software developer requirements, and the like. Many interesting research and development problems need to be solved. These problems *will* be solved because the potential value of their solutions is enormous.

Summary

- Structures are aggregate data types built using objects of other types.

- The keyword **struct** introduces the structure definition. The body of a structure is delineated by braces (**{** and **}**). The definition of every structure must end with a semicolon.

- A structure tag name can be used to declare variables of a structure type.

- Structure definitions do not reserve space in memory; they create new data types that are used to declare variables.

- Members of a structure or a class are accessed using the member access operators—the dot operator (**.**) and the arrow operator (**->**). The dot operator accesses a structure member via the object's variable name or a reference to the object. The arrow operator accesses a structure member via a pointer to the object.

```
// FIG16_12.CPP
// Demonstrating that class objects can be assigned
// to each other using default memberwise copy
#include <iostream.h>

// Simple Date class
class Date {
public:
   Date(int = 1, int = 1, int = 1990);  // default constructor
   void print();
private:
   int month;
   int day;
   int year;
};

// Simple Date constructor with no range checking
Date::Date(int m, int d, int y)
{
   month = m;
   day = d;
   year = y;
}

// Print the Date in the form mm-dd-yyyy
void Date::print()
{ cout << month << '-' << day << '-' << year; }

main()
{
   Date d1(7, 4, 1993), d2;  // d2 defaults to 1/1/90

   cout << "d1 = ";
   d1.print();
   cout << "\nd2 = ";
   d2.print();

   d2 = d1;     // assignment by default memberwise copy
   cout << "\n\nAfter default memberwise copy, d2 = ";
   d2.print();
   cout << endl;

   return 0;
}
```

```
d1 = 7-4-1993
d2 = 1-1-1990

After default memberwise copy, d2 = 7-4-1993
```

Fig. 16.12 Assigning one object to another with default memberwise copy.

```
// FIG16_11.CPP
// Demonstrating a public member function that
// returns a reference to a private data member.
// Time class has been trimmed for this example.

#include <iostream.h>
#include "time4.h"

main()
{
    Time t;
    int &hourRef = t.badSetHour(20);

    cout << "Hour before modification: "
         << hourRef << '\n';
    hourRef = 30;  // modification with invalid value
    cout << "Hour after modification: "
         << t.getHour() << '\n';

    // Dangerous: Function call that returns
    // a reference can be used as an lvalue.
    t.badSetHour(12) = 74;
    cout << "\n********************************\n"
         << "BAD PROGRAMMING PRACTICE!!!!!!!!!\n"
         << "badSetHour as an lvalue, Hour: "
         << t.getHour()
         << "\n********************************\n";

    return 0;
}
```

```
Hour before modification: 20
Hour after modification: 30

********************************
BAD PROGRAMMING PRACTICE!!!!!!!!!
badSetHour as an lvalue, Hour: 74
********************************
```

Fig. 16.11 Returning a reference to a private data member (part 3 of 3).

16.16 Assignment by Default Memberwise Copy

The assignment operator (=) is used to assign an object to another object of the same type. Such assignment is normally performed by *memberwise copy*—each member of one object is copied individually to the same member in another object (see Fig. 16.12). (Note: Memberwise copy can cause serious problems when used with a class whose data members contain dynamically allocated storage; in Chapter 18, "Operator Overloading," we will discuss these problems and show how to deal with them.)

- A fundamental principle of good software engineering is to separate interface from implementation for ease of program modifiability.

- Class definitions are normally placed in header files and member function definitions are normally placed in source-code files of the same base name.

- The default access mode for classes is `private:` so all members after the class header and before the first label are considered to be private.

- Public class members present a view of the services the class provides.

- Access to a class's private data can be carefully controlled by the use of member functions called access functions. If a class wants to allow clients to read private data, the class can provide a "get" function. To enable clients to modify private data, the class can provide a "set" function.

- Data members of a class are normally made private and member functions of a class are normally made public. Some member functions remain private and serve as utility functions to the other functions of the class.

- Data members of a class can not be initialized in a class definition. They must be initialized in a constructor, or their values may be set later after their object is created.

- Constructors can be overloaded.

- Once a class object is properly initialized, all member functions that manipulate the object should ensure that the object remains in a consistent state.

- When an object of a class is declared, initializers can be provided. These initializers are passed to the class's constructor.

- Constructors can specify default arguments.

- Constructors may not specify return types, nor may they attempt to return values.

- If no constructor is defined for a class, the compiler creates a default constructor. A default constructor supplied by the compiler does not perform any initialization, so when the object is created, it is not guaranteed to be in a consistent state.

- A class's destructor is called automatically when an object of a class leaves scope. The destructor itself does not actually destroy the object, but it does perform termination housekeeping before the system reclaims the object's storage.

- Destructors do not receive parameters and do not return values. A class may have only one destructor.

- The assignment operator (=) is used to assign an object to another object of the same type. Such assignment is normally performed by memberwise copy—each member of one object is copied individually to the same member in another object.

Terminology

& address operator	**::** scope resolution operator
& reference operator	abstract data type (ADT)

access function
assignment operator (=)
attribute
behavior
class
class member selector operator (.)
class declaration
class definition
class scope
class tag name
client of a class
consistent state for a data member
constructor
data abstraction
data hiding
data member
data type
default constructor
destructor
dynamic objects
encapsulation
enter scope
extensibility
file scope
forward declaration of a class
get function
global object
header file
implementation of a class
information hiding
initialize a class object
inline member function
instance of a class
instantiate an object of a class

interface to a class
leave scope
member access control
member access specifiers
member function
member initializer
memberwise copy
message
method
nonmember function
nonstatic local object
object
object-oriented programming (OOP)
predicate function
principle of least privilege
private:
procedural programming
protected:
public interface of a class
public:
query function
rapid applications development (RAD)
reusable code
scope resolution operator (: :)
services of a class
set function
software reusability
source-code file
static local object
termination housekeeping
tilde (~) in destructor name
user-defined type
utility function

Common Programming Errors

16.1   Forgetting the semicolon at the end of a class definition.

16.2   Attempting to explicitly initialize a data member of a class.

16.3   Attempting to overload a member function with a function not in that class's scope.

16.4   An attempt by a function which is not a member of a particular class (or a friend of that class) to access a private member of that class.

16.5   Attempting to explicitly initialize a data member of a class in the class definition.

16.6   Attempting to declare a return type for a constructor, and/or attempting to return a value from a constructor.

16.7   Attempting to pass arguments to a destructor, to return values from a destructor, or to overload a destructor.

16.8   A constructor can call other member functions of the class such as set or get functions, but because the constructor is initializing the object, the data members may not yet be in a consistent state. Using data members before they have been properly initialized can cause errors.

Good Programming Practices

16.1   Use each member access specifier only once in a class definition for clarity and readability. Place public members first where they are easy to locate.

16.2   Define all but the smallest member functions outside the class declaration. This helps separate the interface from the implementation of the class.

16.3   Use `#ifndef`, `#define` and `#endif` preprocessor directives to prevent header files from being included more than once in a program.

16.4   Use the name of the header file with the period replaced by an underscore in the `#ifndef` and `#define` preprocessor directives of a header file.

16.5   If you choose to list the private members first in a class declaration, explicitly use the `private:` member access specifier despite the fact that `private:` is assumed by default. This improves program clarity. Our preference is to list the `public:` members of a class first.

16.6   Despite the fact that the `public:` and `private:` member access specifiers may be repeated and intermixed, list all the public members of a class first in one group and then list all the private members in another group. This focuses the client's attention on the class's public interface, rather than on the class's implementation.

16.7   Using the member access specifiers `public:`, `protected:`, and `private:` only once each in any class definition avoids confusion.

16.8   When appropriate (almost always), provide a constructor to ensure that every object is properly initialized with meaningful values.

16.9   Every member function (and friend) that modifies the private data members of an object should ensure that the data remains in a consistent state.

16.10   Always provide a constructor that performs appropriate initialization for its class.

16.11   Member functions that set the values of private data should verify that the intended new values are proper; if they are not, the set functions should place the private data members into an appropriate consistent state.

16.12   Never have a public member function return a non-`const` reference (or a pointer) to a private data member. Returning such a reference violates the encapsulation of the class.

Performance Tips

16.1   Structures ordinarily pass call by value. To avoid the overhead of copying a structure, pass the structure call by reference.

16.2   To avoid the overhead of call by value yet still gain the benefit that the caller's original data is protected from modification, pass large-size arguments as `const` references.

16.3   Defining a small member function inside the class definition automatically inlines the member function (if the compiler chooses to do so). This can improve performance, but it does not promote the best software engineering.

16.4   Passing an object call by value is good from a security standpoint because the called function has no access to the original object, but call by value can degrade performance when making a copy of a large object. An object can be passed call by reference by passing either a pointer or a reference to the object. Call by reference offers good performance but is weaker from a security standpoint because the called function is given access to the original object. Call-by-**const**-reference is a safe alternative.

Software Engineering Observations

16.1 It is important to write programs that are understandable and easy to maintain. Change is the rule rather than the exception. Programmers should anticipate that their code will be modified. As we will see, classes facilitate program modifiability.

16.2 Clients of a class use the class without knowing the internal details of how the class is implemented. If the class implementation is changed (to improve performance, for example) the class's clients need not change. This makes it much easier to modify systems.

16.3 Member functions are usually only a few lines of code because no logic is required to determine if the data members are valid.

16.4 Clients have access to a class's interface but should not have access to a class's implementation.

16.5 Declaring member functions inside a class definition and defining those member functions outside that class definition separates the interface of a class from its implementation. This promotes good software engineering.

16.6 Using an object-oriented programming approach can often simplify function calls by reducing the number of parameters to be passed. This benefit of object-oriented programming derives from the fact that encapsulation of data members and member functions within an object gives the member functions the right to access the data members.

16.7 Place the class declaration in a header file to be included by any client that wants to use the class. This forms the class's public interface. Place the definitions of the class member functions in a source file. This forms the implementation of the class.

16.8 Clients of a class do not need to see the class's source code in order to use the class. The clients do, however, need to be able to link to the class's object code.

16.9 Information important to the interface to a class should be included in the header file. Information that will be used only internally in the class and will not be needed by clients of the class should be included in the unpublished source file. This is yet another example of the principle of least privilege.

16.10 C++ encourages programs to be implementation independent. When the implementation of a class used by implementation-independent code changes, that code need not be modified, but it may need to be recompiled.

16.11 Keep all the data members of a class private. Provide public member functions to set the values of private data members and to get the values of private data members. This architecture helps hide the implementation of a class from its clients, which reduces bugs and improves program modifiability.

16.12 Class designers use private, protected, and public members to enforce the notion of information hiding and the principle of least privilege.

16.13 Making the data members of a class private and the member functions of the class public facilitates debugging because problems with data manipulations are localized to either the class's member functions or the friends of the class.

16.14 Member functions tend to fall into a number of different categories: functions that read and return the value of private data members, functions that set the value of private data members, functions that implement the features of the class, and functions that perform various mechanical chores for the class such as initializing class objects, assigning class objects, converting between classes and built-in types or between classes and other classes, and handling memory for class objects.

16.15   Making data members private and controlling access, especially write access, to those data members through public member functions helps ensure data integrity.

16.16   Accessing private data through set and get member functions not only protects the data members from receiving invalid values, but it also insulates clients of the class from the representation of the data members. Thus, if the representation of the data changes for some reason (typically to reduce the amount of storage required or to improve performance), only the member functions need to change—the clients need not change as long as the interface provided by the member functions remains the same. The clients may, however, need to be recompiled.

Self-Review Exercises

16.1   Fill in the blanks in each of the following:

a)   The keyword _____ introduces a structure definition.

b)   Class members are accessed via the _____ operator in conjunction with an object of the class or via the _____ operator in conjunction with a point to an object of the class.

c)   Members of a class specified as _____ are accessible only to member functions of the class and friends of the class.

d)   A _____ is a special member function used to initialize the data members of a class.

e)   The default access for members of a class is _____ .

f)   A _____ function is used to assign values to private data members of a class.

g)   _____ can be used to assign an object of a class to another object of the same class.

h)   Member functions of a class are normally made _____ and data members of a class are normally made _____ .

i)   A _____ function is used to retrieve values of private data of a class.

j)   The set of public member functions of a class is referred to as the class's _____ .

k)   A class implementation is said to be hidden from its clients or _____ .

l)   The keywords _____ and _____ can be used to introduce a class definition.

m)   Members of a class specified as _____ are accessible anywhere an object of the class is in scope.

16.2   Find the error(s) in each of the following and explain how to correct it.

a)   Assume the following prototype is declared in class **Time**.

```
void ~Time(int);
```

b)   The following is a partial definition of class **Time**.

```
class Time {
public:
    // function prototypes
private:
    int hour = 0;
    int minute = 0;
    int second = 0;
};
```

c)   Assume the following prototype is declared in class **Employee**.

```
int Employee(const char *, const char *);
```

Answers to Self-Review Exercises

16.1 a) `struct`. b) dot (`.`), arrow (`->`). c) `private`. d) constructor. e) `private`. f) set.
g) Default memberwise copy. h) `private, public`. i) get. j) interface. k) encapsulated.
l) `public`. m) `class, struct`.

16.2 a) Error: Destructors are not allowed to return values or take arguments.
Correction: Remove the return type **void** and the parameter **int** from the declaration.
b) Error: Members can not be explicitly initialized in the class definition.
Correction: Remove the explicit initialization from the class definition and initialize the data members in a constructor.
c) Error: Constructors are not allowed to return values.
Correction: Remove the return type **int** from the declaration.

Exercises

16.3 What is the purpose of the scope resolution operator?

16.4 Compare and contrast the notions of **struct** and **class** in C++.

16.5 Provide a constructor that is capable of using the current time from the **time()** function—declared in the C Standard Library header **time.h**—to initialize an object of the **Time** class.

16.6 Create a class called **Complex** for performing arithmetic with complex numbers. Write a driver program to test your class.

Complex numbers have the form

    realPart + imaginaryPart * i

where i is

$$\sqrt{-1}$$

Use floating point variables to represent the private data of the class. Provide a constructor function that enables an object of this class to be initialized when it is declared. The constructor should contain default values in case no initializers are provided. Provide public member functions for each of the following:
a) Addition of two **Complex** numbers: The real parts are added together and the imaginary parts are added together.
b) Subtraction of two **Complex** numbers: The real part of the right operand is subtracted from the real part of the left operand and the imaginary part of the right operand is subtracted from the imaginary part of the left operand.
c) Printing **Complex** numbers in the form **(a, b)** where **a** is the real part and **b** is the imaginary part.

16.7 Create a class called **RationalNumber** for performing arithmetic with fractions. Write a driver program to test your class.

Use integer variables to represent the private data of the class—the numerator and the denominator. Provide a constructor function that enables an object of this class to be initialized when it is declared. The constructor should contain default values in case no initializers are provided and should store the fraction in reduced form (i.e., the fraction

$$\frac{2}{4}$$

would be stored in the object as 1 in the numerator and 2 in the denominator). Provide public member functions for each of the following:

    a) Addition of two **Rational** numbers. The result should be stored in reduced form.

    b) Subtraction of two **Rational** numbers. The result should be stored in reduced form.

    c) Multiplication of two **Rational** numbers. The result should be stored in reduced form.

    d) Division of two **Rational** numbers. The result should be stored in reduced form.

    e) Printing **Rational** numbers in the form **a/b** where **a** is the numerator and **b** is the denominator.

    f) Printing **Rational** numbers in floating point format.

16.8   Modify the **Time** class of Fig. 16.10 to include a **tick** member function that increments the time stored in a **Time** object by one second. The **Time** object should always remain in a consistent state. Write a driver program that tests the **tick** member function in a loop that prints the time in standard format during each iteration of the loop to illustrate that the **tick** member function works correctly. Be sure to test the following cases:

    a) Incrementing into the next minute.

    b) Incrementing into the next hour.

    c) Incrementing into the next day (i.e., 11:59:59 PM to 12:00:00 AM).

16.9   Modify the **Date** class of Fig. 16.12 to perform error checking on the initializer values for data members **month**, **day**, and **year**. Also, provide a member function **nextDay** to increment the day by one. The **Date** object should always remain in a consistent state. Write a driver program that tests the **nextDay** function in a loop that prints the date during each iteration of the loop to illustrate that the **nextDay** function works correctly. Be sure to test the following cases:

    a) Incrementing into the next month.

    b) Incrementing into the next year.

16.10   Combine the modified **Time** class of Exercise 16.8 and the modified **Date** class of Exercise 16.9 into one class called **DateAndTime** (in Chapter 19 we will discuss inheritance which will enable us to accomplish this task quickly without modifying the existing class definitions). Modify the **tick** function to call the **nextDay** function if the time is incremented into the next day. Modify function **printStandard** and **PrintMilitary** to output the date in addition to the time. Write a driver program to test the new class **DateAndTime**. Specifically test incrementing the time into the next day.

17

Classes: Part II

Objectives

- To be able to create and destroy objects dynamically.
- To be able to specify constant objects and constant member functions.
- To understand the purpose of friend functions and friend classes.
- To understand how to use static data members and member functions.
- To understand various types of container classes.
- To be able to develop iterator classes that walk through the elements of container classes.
- To understand the use of the this pointer
- To be able to create and use template classes.

But what, to serve our private ends,
Forbids the cheating of our friends?
Charles Churchill

Instead of this absurd division into sexes they ought to class
people as static and dynamic.
Evelyn Waugh

This above all: to thine own self be true.
William Shakespeare
Hamlet

Have no friends not equal to yourself.
Confucius

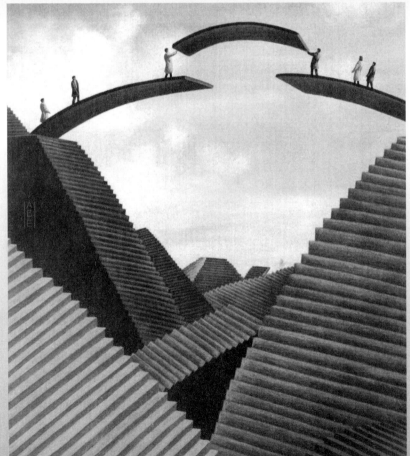

Outline

17.1 Introduction

In this chapter we continue our study of classes and data abstraction. We discuss many more advanced topics and lay the groundwork for the discussion of classes and operator overloading in Chapter 18. The discussion in Chapters 16 through 18 encourages programmers to use objects. Then, Chapters 19 and 20 introduce inheritance and polymorphism—the techniques of truly object-oriented programming.

17.2 Constant Objects and Const Member Functions

We have repeatedly emphasized the *principle of least privilege* as one of the most fundamental principles of good software engineering. Let us see one way in which this principle applies to objects.

Some objects need to be modifiable and some do not. The programmer may use the keyword **const** to specify that an object is not modifiable, and that any attempt to modify the object is an error. For example,

```
const Time noon(12, 0, 0);
```

declares a **const** object **noon** of class **Time** and initializes it to 12 o'clock.

Software Engineering Observation 17.1

Declaring an object as **const** *helps enforce the principle of least privilege. Accidental attempts to modify the object are caught at compile time rather than causing execution-time errors.*

C++ compilers respect **const** declarations so rigidly that the compilers totally disallow any member function calls for **const** objects (some compilers provide only a warning). This is harsh because clients of the object will probably want to use various "get" member functions with the object. To provide for this, the programmer may declare **const** member functions; only these can operate on **const** objects. Of course, **const** member functions can not modify the object.

Common Programming Error 17.1

Defining as **const** *a member function that modifies a data member of an object.*

Common Programming Error 17.2

Defining as **const** *a member function that calls a non-***const** *member function.*

Common Programming Error 17.3

*Calling a non-***const** *member function for a* **const** *object.*

Common Programming Error 17.4

Attempting to modify a **const** *object.*

A function is specified as **const** *both* in its declaration and in its definition by inserting the keyword **const** after the function's parameter list, and, in the case of the function definition, before the left brace that begins the function body. For example, the member function

```
int getValue() const {return privateDataMember};
```

which simply returns the value of one of the object's data members, is declared to be **const**. If a **const** member function is defined outside the class's definition, the member function's declaration and definition must each include **const**.

Software Engineering Observation 17.2

A **const** *member function can be overloaded with a non-***const** *version. The choice of which overloaded member function to use is automatically made by the compiler based on whether the object has been declared* **const** *or not.*

An interesting problem arises here for constructors and destructors, each of which certainly modifies objects. The **const** declaration is not required for constructors and destructors of **const** objects. A constructor must be allowed to modify an object so that the object can be initialized properly. A destructor must be able to perform its termination housekeeping chores before an object is destroyed.

The program of Fig. 17.1 instantiates a constant object of class **Time** and attempts to modify the object with non-constant member functions **setHour**, **setMinute**, and **setSecond**. The warnings generated by the Borland C++ compiler are shown in the output window. The compiler was set so that it would not compile if any warning messages were produced.

Good Programming Practice 17.1

Declare as **const** *all member functions that are intended to be used with* **const** *objects.*

A **const** object can not be modified by assignment so it must be initialized. When a member object is **const**, a *member initializer* must be used to provide the constructor with the initial values for the object. Figure 17.2 demonstrates the uses of the member initializer syntax to initialize **const** data member **increment** of class **Increment**. The constructor for **Increment** is modified as follows:

```
// TIME5.H
// Declaration of the class Time.
// Member functions defined in TIME5.CPP

#ifndef TIME5_H
#define TIME5_H

class Time {
public:
   Time(int = 0, int = 0, int = 0);  // default constructor

   // set functions
   void setTime(int, int, int);  // set time
   void setHour(int);      // set hour
   void setMinute(int);    // set minute
   void setSecond(int);    // set second

   // get functions (normally declared const)
   int getHour() const;    // return hour
   int getMinute() const;  // return minute
   int getSecond() const;  // return second

   // print functions (normally declared const)
   void printMilitary() const;  // print military time
   void printStandard() const;  // print standard time
private:
   int hour;              // 0 - 23
   int minute;            // 0 - 59
   int second;            // 0 - 59
};

#endif
```

Fig. 17.1   Using a **Time** class with **const** objects and **const** member functions (part 1 of 4).

```
// TIME5.CPP
// Member function definitions for Time class.
#include "time5.h"
#include <iostream.h>

// Constructor function to initialize private data.
// Default values are 0 (see class definition).
Time::Time(int hr, int min, int sec)
{
    hour = (hr >= 0 && hr < 24) ? hr : 0;
    minute = (min >= 0 && min < 60) ? min : 0;
    second = (sec >= 0 && sec < 60) ? sec : 0;
}

// Set the values of hour, minute, and second.
void Time::setTime(int h, int m, int s)
{
    hour = (h >= 0 && h < 24) ? h : 0;
    minute = (m >= 0 && m < 60) ? m : 0;
    second = (s >= 0 && s < 60) ? s : 0;
}

// Set the hour value
void Time::setHour(int h)
    { hour = (h >= 0 && h < 24) ? h : 0; }

// Set the minute value
void Time::setMinute(int m)
    { minute = (m >= 0 && m < 60) ? m : 0; }

// Set the second value
void Time::setSecond(int s)
    { second = (s >= 0 && s < 60) ? s : 0; }

// Get the hour value
int Time::getHour() const { return hour; }

// Get the minute value
int Time::getMinute() const { return minute; }

// Get the second value
int Time::getSecond() const { return second; }

// Display military format time: HH:MM:SS
void Time::printMilitary() const
{
    cout << (hour < 10 ? "0" : "") << hour << ":"
         << (minute < 10 ? "0" : "") << minute << ":"
         << (second < 10 ? "0" : "") << second;
}
```

Fig. 17.1 Using a **Time** class with **const** objects and **const** member functions (part 2 of 4).

```
// Display standard format time: HH:MM:SS AM (or PM)
void Time::printStandard() const
{
   cout << ((hour == 0 || hour == 12) ? 12 : hour % 12) << ":"
        << (minute < 10 ? "0" : "") << minute << ":"
        << (second < 10 ? "0" : "") << second
        << (hour < 12 ? " AM" : " PM");
}
```

Fig. 17.1　Using a **Time** class with **const** objects and **const** member functions (part 3 of 4).

```
// FIG17_1.CPP
// Attempting to access a const object with
// non-const member functions.
#include <iostream.h>
#include "time5.h"

main()
{
   const Time t(19, 33, 52);   // constant object

   t.setHour(12);      // ERROR: non-const member function
   t.setMinute(20);    // ERROR: non-const member function
   t.setSecond(39);    // ERROR: non-const member function

   return 0;
}
```

```
Compiling FIG17_1.CPP:
Warning FIG17_1.CPP: Non-const function
   Time::setHour(int) called for const object
Warning FIG17_1.CPP: Non-const function
   Time::setMinute(int) called for const object
Warning FIG17_1.CPP: Non-const function
   Time::setSecond(int) called for const object
```

Fig. 17.1　Using a **Time** class with **const** objects and **const** member functions (part 4 of 4).

```
Increment::Increment(int c, int i)
   : increment(i)
{ count = c; }
```

The notation **: increment(i)** causes increment to be initialized to the value i. If multiple member initializers are needed, simply include them in a comma-separated list after the colon.

```
// FIG17_2.CPP
// Using a member initializer to initialize a
// constant of a built-in data type.

#include <iostream.h>

class Increment {
public:
   Increment(int c = 0, int i = 1);
   void addIncrement() { count += increment; }
   void print() const;
private:
   int count;
   const int increment;        // const data member
};

// Constructor for class Increment
Increment::Increment(int c, int i)
   : increment(i)    // Member initializer
{ count = c; }

// Print the data
void Increment::print() const
{
   cout << "count = " << count
        << ", increment = " << increment << endl;
}

main()
{
   Increment value(10, 5);

   cout << "Before incrementing: ";
   value.print();

   for (int j = 1; j <= 3; j++) {
      value.addIncrement();
      cout << "After increment " << j << ": ";
      value.print();
   }

   return 0;
}
```

```
Before incrementing: count = 10, increment = 5
After increment 1: count = 15, increment = 5
After increment 2: count = 20, increment = 5
After increment 3: count = 25, increment = 5
```

Fig. 17.2   Using a member initializer to initialize a constant of a built-in data type.

Figure 17.3 illustrates the compiler errors for a program that attempts to initialize **increment** with an assignment statement rather than with a member initializer.

Common Programming Error 17.5

Not providing a member initializer for a **const** *member object.*

Software Engineering Observation 17.3

Both **const** *objects and* **const** *"variables" need to be initialized with member initializer syntax. Assignments are not allowed.*

17.3 Composition: Classes as Members of Other Classes

An **AlarmClock** class object needs to know when it is supposed to sound its alarm, so why not include a **Time** object as a member of the **AlarmClock** object? Such a capability is called *composition*. A class can have other classes as members.

Software Engineering Observation 17.4

One form of software reusability is composition in which a class has objects of other classes as members.

When an object enters scope, its constructor is called automatically, so we need to specify how arguments are passed to member-object constructors. Member objects are constructed before their enclosing class objects are.

Software Engineering Observation 17.5

If an object has several member objects, the member objects are constructed in the order in which they are defined. However, do not write code that depends on member object constructors executing in a specific order.

Figure 17.4 uses class **Employee** and class **Date** to demonstrate objects as members of other objects. Class **Employee** contains private data members **lastName**, **firstName**, **birthDate**, and **hireDate**. Members **birthDate** and **hireDate** are objects of class **Date** which contains private data members **month**, **day** and **year**. The program instantiates an **Employee** object, and initializes and displays its data members. Note the syntax of the function header in the **Employee** constructor definition:

```
Employee::Employee(char *fname, char *lname,
                   int bmonth, int bday, int byear,
                   int hmonth, int hday, int hyear)
    : birthDate(bmonth, bday, byear),
      hireDate(hmonth, hday, hyear)
```

The constructor takes eight arguments (**fname**, **lname**, **bmonth**, **bday**, **byear**, **hmonth**, **hday**, and **hyear**). The colon in the header separates the member initializers from the parameter list. The member initializers specify the **Employee** arguments passed to the constructors of the member objects. Thus, **bmonth**, **bday**, and **byear** are passed to the **birthDate** constructor, and **hmonth**, **hday**, and **hyear** are passed to the **hireDate** constructor. Multiple member initializers are separated by commas.

```
// FIG17_3.CPP
// Attempting to initialize a constant of
// a built-in data type with an assignment.
#include <iostream.h>

class Increment {
public:
   Increment(int c = 0, int i = 1);
   void addIncrement() { count += increment; }
   void print() const;
private:
   int count;
   const int increment;
};

// Constructor for class Increment
Increment::Increment(int c, int i)
{                  // Constant member 'increment' is not initialized
   count = c;
   increment = i;   // ERROR: Cannot modify a const object
}

// Print the data
void Increment::print() const
{
   cout << "count = " << count
        << ", increment = " << increment << '\n';
}

main()
{
   Increment value(10, 5);

   cout << "Before incrementing: ";
   value.print();

   for (int j = 1; j <= 3; j++) {
      value.addIncrement();
      cout << "After increment " << j << ": ";
      value.print();
   }

   return 0;
}
```

```
Compiling FIG17_3.CPP:
Warning FIG17_3.CPP 18: Constant member 'increment' is
   not initialized
Error FIG17_3.CPP 20: Cannot modify a const object
Warning FIG17_3.CPP 21: Parameter 'i' is never used
```

Fig. 17.3 Erroneous attempt to initialize a constant of a built-in data type by assignment.

```
// DATE1.H
// Declaration of the Date class.
// Member functions defined in DATE1.CPP
#ifndef DATE1_H
#define DATE1_H

class Date {
public:
   Date(int = 1, int = 1, int = 1900);  // default constructor
   void print() const;  // print date in month/day/year format

private:
   int month;  // 1-12
   int day;    // 1-31 based on month
   int year;   // any year

   // utility function to test proper day for month and year
   int checkDay(int);
};

#endif
```

Fig. 17.4   Using member-object initializers (part 1 of 5).

A member object does not need to be initialized through a member initializer. If a member initializer is not provided, the member object's default constructor will be called automatically. Values, if any, established by the default constructor can then be overridden by set functions.

Common Programming Error 17.6

Not providing a default constructor for a member object when no member initializer is provided for that member object. The compiler generates an error.

Performance Tip 17.1

Initialize member objects explicitly through member initializers. This eliminates the overhead of doubly initializing member objects—once when the member object's default constructor is called and again when set functions are used to initialize the member object.

17.4 Friend Functions and Friend Classes

A *friend function* of a class is defined outside that class's scope, yet has the right to access **private** (and as we will see in Chapter 19, "Inheritance," **protected**) members of the class. A function or an entire class may be declared to be a **friend** of another class.

To declare a function as a **friend** of a class, precede the function prototype in the class definition with the keyword **friend**. To declare class **ClassTwo** as a friend of class **ClassOne** place a declaration of the form

```
friend ClassTwo;
```

as a member of class **ClassOne**.

```
// DATE1.CPP
// Member function definitions for Date class.

#include <iostream.h>
#include "date1.h"


// Constructor: Confirm proper value for month;
// call utility function checkDay to confirm proper
// value for day.
Date::Date(int mn, int dy, int yr)
{
   month = (mn > 0 && mn <= 12) ? mn : 1;  // validate
   year = yr;                       // could also check
   day = checkDay(dy);                      // validate

   cout << "Date object constructor for date ";
   print();
   cout << endl;
}

// Utility function to confirm proper day value
// based on month and year.
int Date::checkDay(int testDay)
{
   static int daysPerMonth[13] = {0, 31, 28, 31, 30,
                                  31, 30, 31, 31, 30,
                                  31, 30, 31};

   if (month != 2) {

      if (testDay > 0 && testDay <= daysPerMonth[month])
         return testDay;

   }
   else {  // February: Check for possible leap year
      int days = (year % 400 == 0 ||
                  (year % 4 == 0 && year % 100 != 0) ? 29 : 28);

      if (testDay > 0 && testDay <= days)
         return testDay;
   }

   cout << "Day " << testDay << " invalid. Set to day 1.\n";
   return 1;  // leave object in consistent state if bad value
}


// Print Date object in form  month/day/year
void Date::print() const
   { cout << month << '/' << day << '/' << year; }
```

Fig. 17.4 Using member-object initializers (part 2 of 5).

```
// EMPLY1.H
// Declaration of the Employee class.
// Member functions defined in EMPLY1.CPP
#ifndef EMPLY1_H
#define EMPLY1_H

#include "date1.h"

class Employee {
public:
   Employee(char *, char *, int, int, int, int, int, int);
   void print() const;
private:
   char lastName[25];
   char firstName[25];
   Date birthDate;
   Date hireDate;
};

#endif
```

Fig. 17.4   Using member-object initializers (part 3 of 5).

```
// EMPLY1.CPP
// Member function definitions for Employee class.
#include <iostream.h>
#include <string.h>
#include "emply1.h"
#include "date1.h"

Employee::Employee(char *fname, char *lname,
                   int bmonth, int bday, int byear,
                   int hmonth, int hday, int hyear)
   : birthDate(bmonth, bday, byear),
     hireDate(hmonth, hday, hyear)
{
   strncpy(firstName, fname, 24);
   firstName[24] = '\0';
   strncpy(lastName, lname, 24);
   lastName[24] = '\0';
   cout << "Employee object constructor: "
        << firstName << ' ' << lastName << endl;
}

void Employee::print() const
{
   cout << lastName << ", " << firstName << "\nHired: ";
   hireDate.print();
   cout << "  Birthday: ";
   birthDate.print();
   cout << endl;
}
```

Fig. 17.4   Using member-object initializers (part 4 of 5).

```
// FIG17_4.CPP
// Demonstrating an object with a member object.
#include <iostream.h>
#include "emply1.h"

main()
{
    Employee e("Bob", "Jones", 7, 24, 49, 3, 12, 88);

    cout << endl;
    e.print();

    cout << "\nTest Date constructor with invalid values:\n";
    Date d(14, 35, 94);   // invalid Date values

    return 0;
}
```

```
Date object constructor for date 7/24/49
Date object constructor for date 3/12/88
Employee object constructor: Bob Jones

Jones, Bob
Hired: 3/12/88   Birthday: 7/24/49

Test Date constructor with invalid values:
Day 35 invalid. Set to day 1.
Date object constructor for date 1/1/94
```

Fig. 17.4   Using member-object initializers (part 5 of 5).

Software Engineering Observation 17.6

Member access notions of `private`, `protected`, *and* `public` *are not relevant to friendship declarations, so friendship declarations can be placed anywhere in the class definition.*

Good Programming Practice 17.2

Place all friendship declarations first in the class immediately after the class header and do not precede them with any member-access specifier.

Friendship is granted, not taken, i.e., for class B to be a friend of class A, class A must declare that class B is its friend. Also, friendship is neither symmetric nor transitive, i.e., if class A is a friend of class B, and class B is a friend of class C, you can not infer that class B is a friend of class A, class C is a friend of class B, or class A is a friend of class C.

Software Engineering Observation 17.7

Some people in the OOP community feel that "friendship" corrupts information hiding and weakens the value of the object-oriented design approach.

The program of Fig. 17.5 demonstrates the declaration and use of friend function **setX** for setting the private data member **x** of class **count**. Note that the **friend** declaration appears first (by convention) in the class declaration, even before public member functions are declared. The program of Fig. 17.6 demonstrates the messages produced by the compiler when non-friend function **cannotSetX** is called to modify private data member **x**.

It is possible to specify overloaded functions as friends of a class. Each overloaded function intended to be a friend must be explicitly declared in the class definition as a friend of the class.

```
// FIG17_5.CPP
// Friends can access private members of a class.
#include <iostream.h>

// Modified Count class
class Count {
    friend void setX(Count &, int);   // friend declaration
public:
    Count() { x = 0; }                    // constructor
    void print() const { cout << x << endl; }   // output
private:
    int x;   // data member
};

// Can modify private data of Count because
// setX is declared as a friend function of Count
void setX(Count &c, int val)
{
    c.x = val;   // legal: setX is a friend of Count
}

main()
{
    Count object;

    cout << "object.x after instantiation: ";
    object.print();
    cout << "object.x after call to setX friend function: ";
    setX(object, 8);   // set x with a friend
    object.print();

    return 0;
}
```

```
object.x after instantiation: 0
object.x after call to setX friend function: 8
```

Fig. 17.5   Friends can access private members of a class.

```
// FIG17_6.CPP
// Non-friend/non-member functions cannot access
// private data of a class.
#include <iostream.h>

// Modified Count class
class Count {
public:
    Count() { x = 0; }                          // constructor
    void print() const { cout << x << '\n'; }   // output
private:
    int x;   // data member
};

// Function tries to modify private data of Count,
// but cannot because it is not a friend of Count.
void cannotSetX(Count &c, int val)
{
    c.x = val;   // ERROR: 'Count::x' is not accessible
}

main()
{
    Count object;

    cannotSetX(object, 3); // cannotSetX is not a friend

    return 0;
}
```

```
Compiling FIG17_6.CPP:
Error FIG17_6.CPP 17: 'Count::x' is not accessible
Warning FIG17_6.CPP 18: Parameter 'c' is never used
Warning FIG17_6.CPP 18: Parameter 'val' is never used
```

Fig. 17.6   Non-friend/non-member functions cannot access private members of a class.

17.5 Using the This Pointer

When a member function references another member of a class for a specific object of that class, how does C++ ensure that the proper object is referenced? The answer is that each object maintains a pointer to itself—called the *this pointer*—that is an implicit argument in all references to members within that object. The **this** pointer may also be used explicitly. Each object can determine its own address by using the **this** keyword.

The **this** pointer is implicitly used to reference both the data members and member functions of an object. The type of the **this** pointer depends on the type of the object and whether the member function in which **this** is used is declared **const**. In a non-constant member function of class **Employee** the **this** pointer has type **Employee * const** (a constant pointer to an **Employee** object). In a constant member function of class **Employee** the **this** pointer has type **Employee const * const** (a constant pointer to a constant **Employee** object).

For now, we show a simple example of using the **this** pointer explicitly; later we show some substantial and subtle examples of using **this**. Every member function has access to the **this** pointer to the object for which the member is being invoked.

Performance Tip 17.2

For reasons of economy of storage, only one copy of each member function exists per class, and this member function is invoked by every object of that class. Each object, on the other hand, has its own copy of the class's data members.

Figure 17.7 demonstrates the explicit use of the **this** pointer to enable a member function of class **Test** to print the private data **x** of a **Test** object. The program uses both the arrow operator (`->`) off the **this** pointer and the dot operator (`.`) off the dereferenced **this** pointer.

```
// FIG17_7.CPP
// Using the this pointer to refer to object members.
#include <iostream.h>

class Test {
public:
   Test(int = 0);
   void print() const;
private:
   int x;
};

Test::Test(int a) { x = a; }     // constructor

void Test::print() const
{
   cout << "       x = " << x
        << "\n  this->x = " << this->x
        << "\n(*this).x = " << (*this).x << '\n';
}

main()
{
   Test a(12);

   a.print();

   return 0;
}
```

```
        x = 12
  this->x = 12
(*this).x = 12
```

Fig. 17.7 Using the **this** pointer.

Note the parentheses around ***this** when used with the dot member selection operator (**.**). The parentheses are needed because the dot operator has higher precedence than the ***** operator. Without the parentheses, the expression

```
*this.x
```

would be evaluated as if it were parenthesized as follows:

```
*(this.x)
```

The C++ compiler would treat this expression as a syntax error because the member selection operator cannot be used with a pointer.

Common Programming Error 17.7

Attempting to use the member selection operator (.) with a pointer to an object (the member selection operator may only be used with an object or with a reference to an object).

One interesting use of the **this** pointer is to prevent an object from being assigned to itself. As we will see in Chapter 18, "Operator Overloading," self-assignment can cause serious errors when the objects contain pointers to storage allocated dynamically with operator **new**.

Figure 17.8 illustrates returning a reference to a **Time** object to enable member function calls of class **Time** to be concatenated. Each of the **Time** member functions **setTime, setHour, setMinute**, and **setSecond** returns ***this** with a return type of **Time &**.

Why does the technique of returning ***this** as a reference work? The dot operator (**.**) associates from left to right, so the expression

```
t.setHour(18).setMinute(30).setSecond(22);
```

first evaluates t.**setHour(18)** then returns a reference to object **t** as the value of this function call. The remaining expression is then interpreted as

```
t.setMinute(30).setSecond(22);
```

The **t.setMinute(30)** call executes and returns the equivalent of **t**. The remaining expression is interpreted as

```
t.setSecond(22);
```

Note the calls

```
t.setTime(20, 20, 20).printStandard();
```

also use the concatenation feature. These calls must appear in this order in this expression because **printStandard** as defined in the class does not return a reference to **t**. Placing the call to **printStandard** in the preceding statement before the call to **setTime** results in a syntax error.

```
// TIME6.H
// Declaration of class Time.
// Member functions defined in TIME6.CPP

#ifndef TIME6_H
#define TIME6_H

class Time {
public:
   Time(int = 0, int = 0, int = 0);  // default constructor

   // set functions
   Time &setTime(int, int, int);  // set hour, minute, second
   Time &setHour(int);     // set hour
   Time &setMinute(int);   // set minute
   Time &setSecond(int);   // set second

   // get functions (normally declared const)
   int getHour() const;    // return hour
   int getMinute() const;  // return minute
   int getSecond() const;  // return second

   // print functions (normally declared const)
   void printMilitary() const;  // print military time
   void printStandard() const;  // print standard time
private:
   int hour;              // 0 - 23
   int minute;            // 0 - 59
   int second;            // 0 - 59
};

#endif
```

Fig. 17.8   Chaining member function calls (part 1 of 4).

```
// TIME6.CPP
// Member function definitions for Time class.

#include "time6.h"
#include <iostream.h>

// Constructor function to initialize private data.
// Default values are 0 (see class definition).
Time::Time(int hr, int min, int sec)
{
   hour = (hr >= 0 && hr < 24) ? hr : 0;
   minute = (min >= 0 && min < 60) ? min : 0;
   second = (sec >= 0 && sec < 60) ? sec : 0;
}
```

Fig. 17.8   Chaining member function calls (part 2 of 4).

```cpp
// Set the values of hour, minute, and second.
Time &Time::setTime(int h, int m, int s)
{
    hour = (h >= 0 && h < 24) ? h : 0;
    minute = (m >= 0 && m < 60) ? m : 0;
    second = (s >= 0 && s < 60) ? s : 0;
    return *this;    // enables chaining
}

// Set the hour value
Time &Time::setHour(int h)
{
    hour = (h >= 0 && h < 24) ? h : 0;
    return *this;    // enables chaining
}

// Set the minute value
Time &Time::setMinute(int m)
{
    minute = (m >= 0 && m < 60) ? m : 0;
    return *this;    // enables chaining
}

// Set the second value
Time &Time::setSecond(int s)
{
    second = (s >= 0 && s < 60) ? s : 0;
    return *this;    // enables chaining
}

// Get the hour value
int Time::getHour() const { return hour; }

// Get the minute value
int Time::getMinute() const { return minute; }

// Get the second value
int Time::getSecond() const { return second; }

// Display military format time: HH:MM:SS
void Time::printMilitary() const
{
    cout << (hour < 10 ? "0" : "") << hour << ":"
         << (minute < 10 ? "0" : "") << minute << ":"
         << (second < 10 ? "0" : "") << second;
}

// Display standard format time: HH:MM:SS AM (or PM)
void Time::printStandard() const
{
    cout << ((hour == 0 || hour == 12) ? 12 : hour % 12) << ":"
         << (minute < 10 ? "0" : "") << minute << ":"
         << (second < 10 ? "0" : "") << second
         << (hour < 12 ? " AM" : " PM");
}
```

Fig. 17.8 Chaining member function calls (part 3 of 4).

```
// FIG17_8.CPP
// Chaining member function calls together
// with the this pointer
#include <iostream.h>
#include "time6.h"

main()
{
    Time t;

    t.setHour(18).setMinute(30).setSecond(22);
    cout << "Military time: ";
    t.printMilitary();
    cout << "\nStandard time: ";
    t.printStandard();

    cout << "\n\nNew standard time: ";
    t.setTime(20, 20, 20).printStandard();
    cout << endl;

    return 0;
}
```

```
Military time: 18:30:22
Standard time: 6:30:22 PM

New standard time: 8:20:20 PM
```

Fig. 17.8   Chaining member function calls (part 4 of 4).

17.6 Dynamic Memory Allocation with Operators New and Delete

The *new* and *delete* operators provide a nicer means of performing dynamic memory allocation than with **malloc** and **free** function calls in C. Consider the following code

        TypeName *typeNamePtr;

In ANSI C, to dynamically create an object of type **TypeName**, you would say

        typeNamePtr = malloc(sizeof(TypeName));

This requires a function call to **malloc** and an explicit reference to the **sizeof** operator. In versions of C prior to ANSI C, you would also have to cast the pointer returned by **malloc** with the cast **(TypeName *)**. Function **malloc** does not provide any method of initializing the block of memory allocated. In C++, you simply write

        typeNamePtr = new TypeName;

The **new** operator automatically creates an object of the proper size, calls the constructor for the object (if one is available) and returns a pointer of the correct type. If **new** is unable to find space, it returns a **0** pointer. To free the space for this object in C++ use the **delete** operator as follows:

```
delete typeNamePtr;
```

C++ allows you to provide an *initializer* for a newly created object as in:

```
float *thingPtr = new float (3.14159);
```

which initializes a newly created **float** object to **3.14159**.

An array can be created and assigned to **int * chessBoardPtr** as follows:

```
chessBoardPtr = new int[8][8];
```

This array can be deleted with the statement

```
delete [] chessBoardPtr;
```

As we will see, using **new** and **delete** instead of **malloc** and **free** offers other benefits as well. In particular, **new** automatically invokes the constructor, and **delete** automatically invokes the class's destructor.

Common Programming Error 17.8

Mixing **new**-*and*-**delete**-*style dynamic memory allocation with* **malloc**-*and*-**free**-*style dynamic memory allocation: Space created by* **malloc** *can not be freed by* **delete**; *objects created by* **new**, *can not be deleted by* **free**.

Good Programming Practice 17.3

Although C++ programs can contain storage created by **malloc** *and deleted by* **free**, *and objects created by* **new** *and deleted by* **delete**, *it is best to use only* **new** *and* **delete**.

17.7 Static Class Members

Normally, each object of a class has its own copy of all the data members of the class. Sometimes this is wasteful. In certain cases only one copy of a particular data member should be shared by all members of a class. A static data member is used for these and other reasons. A static data member represents "class-wide" information. The declaration of a static member begins with the keyword **static**.

Performance Tip 17.3

Use static data members to save storage when only a single copy of the data will suffice.

Although static data members may seem like global variables, static data members have class scope. Static members can be public, private or protected. Static data members must be initialized at file scope. Public static class members can be accessed through any object of that class, or they can be accessed through the class name using the binary scope resolution operator. Private and protected static class members must be accessed through public member functions of the class. Static class members exist even when no objects of that class exist. To access a public static class member when no objects of the class exist, simply prefix the class name and the binary scope resolution operator to the data member.

To access a private or protected static class member when no objects of the class exist, a public static member function must be provided and the function must be called by prefixing its name with the class name and binary scope resolution operator.

The program of Fig. 17.9 demonstrates the use of a private **static** data member and a public **static** member function. The data member **count** is initialized to zero at file scope with the statement

```
int Employee::count = 0;
```

Data member **count** maintains a count of the number of objects of class **Employee** that have been instantiated. When objects of class **Employee** exist, member **count** can be referenced through any member function of an **Employee** object—in this example, **count** is referenced by both the constructor and the destructor. When no objects of class **Employee** exist, member **count** can still be referenced, but only through a call to static member function **getCount** as follows:

```
Employee::getCount()
```

In this example, function **getCount** is used to determine the number of **Employee** objects currently instantiated. Note that when there are no objects instantiated, the preceding function call is issued. However, when there are objects instantiated function **getCount** can be called through one of the objects as in

```
e1Ptr->getCount()
```

```
// EMPLOY1.H
// An employee class
#ifndef EMPLOY1_H
#define EMPLOY1_H

class Employee {
public:
   Employee(const char*, const char*);  // constructor
   ~Employee();                // destructor
   char *getFirstName() const;  // return first name
   char *getLastName() const;   // return last name

   // static member function
   static int getCount();  // return # objects instantiated
private:
   char *firstName;
   char *lastName;

   // static data member
   static int count;  // number of objects instantiated
};

#endif
```

Fig 17.9   Using a static data member to maintain a count of the number of objects of a class (part 1 of 5).

```
// EMPLOY1.CPP
// Member functions definitions for class Employee
#include <iostream.h>
#include <string.h>
#include <assert.h>
#include "employ1.h"

// Initialize the static data member
int Employee::count = 0;

// Define the static member function that
// returns the number of employee objects instantiated.
int Employee::getCount() { return count; }

// Constructor dynamically allocates space for the
// first and last name and uses strcpy to copy
// the first and last names into the object
Employee::Employee(const char *first, const char *last)
{
    firstName = new char[ strlen(first) + 1 ];
    assert(firstName != 0);    // ensure memory allocated
    strcpy(firstName, first);

    lastName = new char[ strlen(last) + 1 ];
    assert(lastName != 0);     // ensure memory allocated
    strcpy(lastName, last);

    ++count;   // increment static count of employees
    cout << "Employee constructor for " << firstName
         << ' ' << lastName << " called.\n";
}

// Destructor deallocates dynamically allocated memory
Employee::~Employee()
{
    cout << "~Employee() called for " << firstName
         << ' ' << lastName << endl;
    delete [] firstName;   // recapture memory
    delete [] lastName;    // recapture memory
    --count;   // decrement static count of employees
}

// Return first name of employee
char *Employee::getFirstName() const
{
    char *tempPtr = new char[strlen(firstName) + 1];
    assert(tempPtr != 0);    // ensure memory allocated
    strcpy(tempPtr, firstName);
    return tempPtr;
}
```

Fig. 17.9 Using a static data member to maintain a count of the number of objects of a class (part 2 of 5).

```
// Return last name of employee
char *Employee::getLastName() const
{
    char *tempPtr = new char[strlen(lastName) + 1];
    assert(tempPtr != 0);    // ensure memory allocated
    strcpy(tempPtr, lastName);
    return tempPtr;
}
```

Fig. 17.9   Using a static data member to maintain a count of the number of objects of a class (part 3 of 5).

```
// FIG17_9.CPP
// Driver to test the employee class
#include <iostream.h>
#include "employ1.h"

main()
{
    cout << "Number of employees before instantiation is "
         << Employee::getCount() << endl;    // use class name

    Employee *e1Ptr = new Employee("Susan", "Baker");
    Employee *e2Ptr = new Employee("Robert", "Jones");

    cout << "Number of employees after instantiation is "
         << e1Ptr->getCount() << endl;

    cout << "\nEmployee 1: "
         << e1Ptr->getFirstName()
         << " " << e1Ptr->getLastName()
         << "\nEmployee 2: "
         << e2Ptr->getFirstName()
         << " " << e2Ptr->getLastName() << "\n\n";

    delete e1Ptr;    // recapture memory
    delete e2Ptr;    // recapture memory

    cout << "Number of employees after deletion is "
         << Employee::getCount() << endl;

    return 0;
}
```

Fig. 17.9   Using a static data member to maintain a count of the number of objects of a class (part 4 of 5).

A member function may be declared **static** if it does not access non-static class members. Unlike nonstatic member functions, a static member function has no **this** pointer because static data members and static member functions exist independently of any objects of a class.

```
Number of employees before instantiation is 0
Employee constructor for Susan Baker called.
Employee constructor for Robert Jones called.
Number of employees after instantiation is 2

Employee 1: Susan Baker
Employee 2: Robert Jones

~Employee() called for Susan Baker
~Employee() called for Robert Jones
Number of employees after deletion is 0
```

Fig. 17.9 Using a static data member to maintain a count of the number of objects of a class (part 5 of 5).

Common Programming Error 17.9

*Referring to the **this** pointer within a static member function.*

Common Programming Error 17.10

*Declaring a static member function **const**.*

Software Engineering Observation 17.8

Static data members and static member functions exist and can be used even if no objects of that class have been instantiated.

17.8 Data Abstraction and Information Hiding

Classes normally hide their implementation details from clients (i.e., users) of the classes. This is called information hiding. Thus, for example, the programmer may create a stack class and hide from its users the implementation of the stack. Stacks can easily be implemented with arrays or linked lists. A client of a stack class need not know how the stack is implemented. What the user really cares about is that when data items are placed in the stack, the data items will be recalled in last-in, first-out (LIFO) order. This concept is referred to as *data abstraction,* and C++ classes define *abstract data types (ADTs).* Although users may know the details of how a class is implemented, users may not write code that depends on these details. This means that a particular class (such as one that implements a stack and its operations of **push** and **pop**) can be replaced with another version without affecting the rest of the system, as long as the public interface to that class does not change.

The job of a high-level language is to create a view convenient for programmers to use. There is no single accepted standard view—that is one reason why there are so many programming languages. Object-oriented programming in C++ presents yet another view.

Most programming languages emphasize actions. In these languages, data exists in support of the actions programs need to take. Data is "less interesting" than actions, any way. Data is "crude." There are only a few built-in data types, and it is difficult for programmers to create their own new data types.

This view changes with C++ and the object-oriented style of programming. C++ elevates the importance of data. The primary activity in C++ is creating new data types (i.e., classes) and expressing the interactions among objects of those data types.

To move in this direction, the programming-languages community needed to formalize some notions about data. The formalization we consider is the notion of abstract data type (ADT). ADTs receive as much attention today as structured programming did over the last two decades. ADTs do not replace structured programming. Rather, they provide an additional formalization that can further improve the program development process.

What is an abstract data type? Consider the built-in type `int`. What comes to mind is the notion of an integer in mathematics, but `int` on a computer is not precisely what an integer is in mathematics. In particular, computer `int`s are normally quite limited in size. For example, `int` on a 32-bit machine may be limited to the range -2 billion to +2 billion. If the result of a calculation falls outside this range, an error occurs and the machine responds in some machine-dependent manner. Mathematical integers do not have this problem. So the notion of a computer `int` is really only an approximation to the notion of a real-world integer. The same is true with `float`.

Even `char` is such an approximation. Values of type `char` are normally 8-bit patterns that look nothing like the characters they are supposed to represent such as a capital `Z`, a lowercase `z`, a dollar sign (`$`), a digit (e.g., `5`), and so on. Values of type `char` on most computers are quite limited compared to the range of real-world characters. The 7-bit ASCII character set provides for 127 different character values. This is completely inadequate for representing languages such as Japanese and Chinese that require thousands of characters.

The point is that even the built-in data types provided with programming languages like C++ are really only approximations or models of real-world concepts and behaviors. We have taken `int` for granted until this point, but now the reader has a new perspective to consider. Types like `int`, `float`, `char` and others are all examples of so-called *abstract data types*. They are essentially ways of representing real-world notions to some satisfactory level of precision within a computer system.

An abstract data type actually captures two notions, namely a data representation and the operations that are allowed on that data. For example, the notion of `int` defines addition, subtraction, multiplication, division, and modulus operations in C++, but division by zero is undefined; and these allowed operations perform in a manner sensitive to machine parameters such as the fixed-word size of the underlying computer system. In C++, the programmer uses classes to implement abstract data types.

17.8.1 Array Abstract Data Type

We discussed arrays in Chapter 6. An array is not much more than a pointer. This primitive capability is acceptable for performing array operations if the programmer is cautious. There are many operations that would be nice to perform with arrays, but that are not built into C++. With C++, the programmer can develop an array ADT that is preferable to "raw" arrays. The array class can provide many nice new capabilities such as

- Subscript range checking.

- An arbitrary range of subscripts.

- Array assignment.

- Array comparison.

- Array input/output.

- Arrays know their sizes.

The weakness here is that we are creating a customized, nonstandard data type which is not likely to be available in precisely this form across most C++ implementations. The use of C++ and object-oriented programming is increasing rapidly. It is crucial that the programming profession work towards the large-scale standardization and distribution of class libraries to realize the full potential of object orientation.

C++ has a small set of built-in types. ADTs extend the base programming language.

Software Engineering Observation 17.9

The programmer is able to create new types through the use of the class mechanism. These new types may be designed to be used as conveniently as the built-in types. Thus, C++ is an extensible language. Although the language is easy to extend with these new types, the base language itself is not changeable.

New ADTs created in C++ environments can be proprietary to an individual, to small groups, or to companies. ADTs can also be placed in standard class libraries intended for wide distribution. This does not necessarily promote standards although de facto standards are likely to emerge. The full value of C++ will be realized only when substantial and standardized class libraries become widely available. A formal process needs to be put in place to encourage the development of standardized libraries. In the United States, such standardization often happens through ANSI, the American National Standards Institute. ANSI is currently evolving a standard version of C++. Regardless of how these libraries ultimately appear, the reader who learns C++ and object-oriented programming will be ready to take advantage of the new kinds of rapid, component-oriented software development made possible with libraries of ADTs.

17.8.2 Example: String Abstract Data Type

C++ is an intentionally sparse language that provides programmers with only the raw capabilities needed to build a broad range of systems. The language's designers did not want to create performance burdens. They intended that C++ be appropriate for systems programming which demands that programs execute efficiently. Certainly, it would have been possible to include a string type among C++'s built-in types, but the designers instead opted to include the mechanism for creating and implementing such ADTs through classes. We will develop our own string ADT in Chapter 18.

17.8.3 Example: Queue Abstract Data Type

Each of us stands in line from time to time. A waiting line is also called a *queue.* We wait in line at the supermarket checkout counter, we wait in line to get gasoline, we wait in line to board a bus, we wait in line to pay a toll on the highway, and students know all too well about waiting in line during registration to get the courses they want. Computer systems use many waiting lines internally, so we need to write programs that simulate what queues are and do.

A queue is a nice example of an abstract data type. A queue offers well-understood behavior to its clients. Clients put things in a queue one at a time—using an *enqueue* operation, and the clients get those things back one at a time on demand—using a *dequeue* operation. Conceptually, a queue can become infinitely long. A real queue, of course, is finite. Items are returned from a queue in *first-in, first-out (FIFO)* order.

The queue hides an internal data representation that somehow keeps track of the items currently waiting in line, and it offers a set of operations to its clients, namely *enqueue* and *dequeue.* The clients are not concerned about the implementation of the queue. Clients merely want the queue to operate "as advertised." When a client enqueues a new item, the queue should accept that item and place it internally in some kind of first-in, first-out data structure. When the client wants the next item from the front of the queue, the queue should remove the item from its internal representation and should deliver the item to the outside world in FIFO order, i.e., the item that has been in the queue the longest should be the next one returned by the next *dequeue* operation.

The queue ADT guarantees the integrity of its internal data structure. Clients may not manipulate this data structure directly. Only the queue ADT has access to its internal data. Clients may cause only allowable operations to be performed on the data representation; operations not provided in the ADT's public interface are rejected by the ADT in some appropriate manner. This could mean issuing an error message, terminating execution, or simply ignoring the operation request.

17.9 Container Classes and Iterators

Among the most popular types of classes are *container classes* (also called *collection classes*), i.e., classes designed to hold collections of objects. Container classes commonly provide services such as insertion, deletion, searching, sorting, testing an item for membership in the class, and the like. Arrays and linked lists are examples of container classes.

It is common to associate *iterator objects*—or more simply *iterators*—with collection class. An iterator is an object that returns the next item of a collection. Once an iterator for a class has been written, obtaining the next element from the class can be expressed simply. Iterators are written as friends of the classes through which they iterate. Just as a book being shared by several people could have several bookmarks in it at once, a container class can have several iterators operating on it at once.

17.10 Template Classes

In Chapter 15, we discussed template functions and how they encourage software reusability. We close this chapter with a discussion of *template classes.*

It is possible to understand what a stack is independent of the type of the items being placed in the stack. But when it comes to actually programming a stack, a data type must be provided. This creates a wonderful opportunity for software reusability. What we need is a means of describing the notion of a stack generically and instantiating classes that are copies of this generic class, but are type specific. This is the capability provided by template classes in C++.

Software Engineering Observation 17.10

Template classes encourage software reusability.

Template classes became available with AT&T's Version 3 C++ compiler, so they are a relatively recent addition to the language.

Template classes are often called *parameterized types* because they require one or more type parameters to specify how to customize the generic template specification.

The programmer who wishes to use template classes simply writes one generic template class definition. Each time the programmer needs a new class, the programmer uses a concise, simple notation and the compiler writes the source code for the class the programmer specifies. One template stack class, for example, could thus become the basis for creating many stack classes (such as "stack of `float`," "stack of `int`," "stack of `char`," etc.) used in a program.

Note the definition of the template stack class in Fig. 17.10. It looks like a conventional class definition except that it is preceded with the header

```
template <class T>
```

to indicate that this is a template class definition that receives one type parameter `T` indicating the type of the stack class the programmer wants to create. The type of element to be stored on this stack is mentioned only generically as `T` throughout the stack class header and member function definitions.

```
// TSTACK1.H
// Simple template class Stack

#ifndef TSTACK1_H
#define TSTACK1_H

template <class T>
class Stack {
public:
   Stack(int = 10);        // Constructor with default size 10
   ~Stack() { delete [] stackPtr; } // Destructor
   int push(const T&);     // Push an element onto the stack
   int pop(T&);            // Pop an element off the stack
   int isEmpty() const { return top == -1; } // 1 if empty
   int isFull() const { return top == size - 1; } // 1 if full
private:
   int size;               // # of elements in the stack
   int top;                // location of the top element
   T *stackPtr;            // pointer to the stack
};
```

Fig. 17.10 Definition of template class **Stack** (part 1 of 4).

```
// Constructor with default size 10
template <class T>
Stack<T>::Stack(int s)
{
   size = s;
   top = -1;   // Empty stack
   stackPtr = new T[size];
}

// Push an element onto the stack
// return 1 if successful, 0 otherwise
template <class T>
int Stack<T>::push(const T &item)
{
   if (!isFull()) {
      stackPtr[++top] = item;
      return 1;   // push successful
   }
   return 0;      // push unsuccessful
}

// Pop an element off the stack
template <class T>
int Stack<T>::pop(T &popValue)
{
   if (!isEmpty()) {
      popValue = stackPtr[top--];
      return 1;   // pop successful
   }
   return 0;      // pop unsuccessful
}

#endif
```

Fig. 17.10 Definition of template class **Stack** (part 2 of 4).

Now let us consider the test driver (function **main**) for the template stack class. The driver begins by instantiating object **floatStack** of size 5. This object is declared to be of class **Stack<float>**. The compiler associates type **float** with parameterized type **T** in the template to produce the source code for a stack class of type **float**.

The driver then successively pushes the **float** values 1.1, 2.2, 3.3, 4.4 and 5.5 on **floatStack**. The push loop terminates when the driver attempts to push a sixth value on **floatStack** (which is already full because it was created with 5 elements).

The driver now pops the five values off the stack (in LIFO order). The driver attempts to pop a sixth value, but **floatStack** is empty, so the pop loop terminates.

Next, the driver instantiates an integer stack with the declaration

```
Stack<int> intStack;
```

Because no size is specified, the size defaults to 10 as specified in the default constructor. Once again, the driver loops pushing values on **intStack** until it is full, and then loops popping values off **intStack** until it is empty.

```
// FIG17_10.CPP
// Test driver for Stack template

#include <iostream.h>
#include "tstack1.h"

main()
{
    Stack<float> floatStack(5);
    float f = 1.1;
    cout << "Pushing elements onto floatStack\n";

    while (floatStack.push(f)) { // success (1 returned)
        cout << f << ' ';
        f += 1.1;
    }

    cout << "\nStack is full. Cannot push " << f
         << "\n\nPopping elements from floatStack" << endl;

    while (floatStack.pop(f))  // success (1 returned)
        cout << f << ' ';

    cout << "\nStack is empty. Cannot pop" << endl;

    Stack<int> intStack;
    int i = 1;
    cout << "\nPushing elements onto intStack\n";

    while (intStack.push(i)) { // success (1 returned)
        cout << i << ' ';
        i++;
    }

    cout << "\nStack is full. Cannot push " << i
         << "\n\nPopping elements from intStack" << endl;

    while (intStack.pop(i))  // success (1 returned)
        cout << i << ' ';

    cout << "\nStack is empty. Cannot pop" << endl;
    return 0;
}
```

Fig. 17.10 Driver for template class **Stack** (part 3 of 4).

The member function definitions outside the template class header each begin with the header

```
template <class T>
```

Then each definition looks like a conventional definition except that the type of stack element is always listed generically as parameterized type **T**. The binary scope resolution

```
Pushing elements onto floatStack
1.1 2.2 3.3 4.4 5.5
Stack is full. Cannot push 6.6

Popping elements from floatStack
5.5 4.4 3.3 2.2 1.1
Stack is empty. Cannot pop

Pushing elements onto intStack
1 2 3 4 5 6 7 8 9 10
Stack is full. Cannot push 11

Popping elements from intStack
10 9 8 7 6 5 4 3 2 1
Stack is empty. Cannot pop
```

Fig. 17.10 Driver for template class **Stack** (part 4 of 4).

operator is used as always to tie each member function definition to the proper class's scope. In this case, the class name is **Stack<T>**. When **floatStack** is instantiated to be of type **Stack<float>**, the **Stack** constructor creates an array of elements of type **T** to represent the stack. The type **float** is substituted for **T** and the statement

```
stackPtr = new T[size];
```

is generated by the compiler in the **Stack<float>** version as

```
stackPtr = new float[size];
```

Parameterized types (i.e., templates) can take more than one parameter as in

```
template <class T, class S, class R>
```

Each parameter must be preceded by keyword **class**.

Summary

- The keyword **const** can be used to specify that an object is not modifiable and that any attempt to modify it is an error.
- The C++ compiler disallows non-**const** member function calls for a **const** object.
- **const** member functions can not modify an object.
- A function is specified as **const** both in its declaration and its definition.
- A **const** member function may be overloaded with a non-**const** version. The choice of which overloaded member function to use is automatically made by the compiler based on whether the object has been declared **const** or not.
- A **const** object must be initialized.

- Member initializers must be provided to the constructor when a class contains `const` member objects.

- Classes can be composed of objects of other classes.

- Member objects are constructed before their enclosing class objects are.

- If a member initializer is not provided for a member object, the member object's default constructor is called.

- A friend function of a class is a function defined outside that class and has the right to access `private` and `protected` members of the class.

- Friendship declarations can be placed anywhere in the class definition.

- Each overloaded function intended to be a friend must be explicitly declared as a friend of the class.

- Each object maintains a pointer to itself—called the `this` pointer—that becomes an implicit argument in all references to members within that object. The `this` pointer is implicitly used to reference both the member functions and data members of an object.

- Each object can determine its own address by using the `this` keyword.

- The `this` pointer may be used explicitly, but it is most often used implicitly.

- The `new` operator automatically creates an object of the proper size, and returns a pointer of the correct type. To free the space for this object in C++ you use the `delete` operator.

- A static data member represents "class-wide" information. The declaration of a static member begins with the keyword `static`.

- Static data members have class scope.

- Static members of a class can be accessed through an object of that class, or they can be accessed through the class name using the scope resolution operator.

- A member function may be declared static if it does not access non-static class members. Unlike nonstatic member functions, a static member function has no `this` pointer. This is because static data members and static member functions exist independently of any objects of a class.

- Template classes provide a means of describing the notion of a class generically and instantiating classes that are copies of this generic class, but are type specific.

- Template classes are often called parameterized types because they require one or more type parameters to specify how to customize the generic template specification.

- Template class definitions begin with the line

```
template <class T>
```

on the line before the class definition. There can be more than one parameterized type. If so, they are separated by commas and each type is preceded by keyword `class`.

- A template class is instantiated by specifying the type of the class following the class name as follows:

```
ClassName<type> objectName;
```

The compiler substitutes `type` throughout the class definition and member function definitions for the parameterized type of the class.

Terminology

binary scope resolution operator (`::`)	iterator
chaining member function calls	member selection operator (`.`)
class scope	member access specifiers
composition	member initializer
`const` member function	member object
`const` object	member object constructor
constructor	nested class
container classes	`new` operator
default constructor	parameterized type
default destructor	pointer member selector operator (`->`)
`delete` operator	pointer to member
`delete[]` operator	principle of least privilege
destructor	static data member
dynamic objects	static member function
extensibility	template class
`friend` class	`this` pointer
`friend` function	

Common Programming Errors

17.1 Defining as `const` a member function that modifies a data member of an object.

17.2 Defining as `const` a member function that calls a non-`const` member function.

17.3 Calling a non-`const` member function for a `const` object.

17.4 Attempting to modify a `const` object.

17.5 Not providing a member initializer for a `const` member object.

17.6 Not providing a default constructor for a member object when no member initializer is provided for that member object. The compiler generates an error.

17.7 Attempting to use the member selection operator (`.`) with a pointer to an object (the member selection operator may only be used with a member object or with a reference to an object).

17.8 Mixing `new`-and-`delete`-style dynamic memory allocation with `malloc`-and-`free`-style dynamic memory allocation: Space created by `malloc` can not be freed by `delete`; objects created by `new`, can not be deleted by `free`.

17.9 Referring to the `this` pointer within a static member function.

17.10 Declaring a static member function `const`.

Good Programming Practices

17.1 Declare as `const` all member functions that are intended to be used with `const` objects.

17.2   Place all friendship declarations first in the class immediately after the class header and do not precede them with any member-access specifier.

17.3   Although C++ programs can contain storage created by `malloc` and deleted by `free`, and objects created by `new` and deleted by `delete`, it is best to use only `new` and `delete`.

Performance Tips

17.1   Initialize member objects explicitly through member initializers. This eliminates the overhead of doubly initializing member objects—once when the member object's default constructor is called and again when set functions are used to initialize the member object.

17.2   For reasons of economy of storage, only one copy of each member function exists per class, and this member function is invoked by every object of that class. Each object, on the other hand, has its own copy of the class's data members.

17.3   Use static data members to save storage when only a single copy of the data will suffice.

Software Engineering Observations

17.1   Declaring objects `const` helps enforce the principle of least privilege. Accidental attempts to modify the object are caught at compile time rather than causing execution-time errors.

17.2   A `const` member function can be overloaded with a non-`const` version. The choice of which overloaded member function to use is made by the compiler based on whether the object has been declared `const` or not.

17.3   Both `const` objects and `const` "variables" need to be initialized with member initializer syntax. Assignments are not allowed.

17.4   One form of software reusability is composition in which a class has objects of other classes as members.

17.6   If an object has several member objects, the member objects are constructed in the order in which they are defined. However, do not write code that depends on member object constructors executing in a specific order.

17.7   Member access specifiers `private`, `protected`, and `public` are not relevant to friendship declarations, so such declarations can be placed anywhere in the class definition.

17.8   Some people in the OOP community feel that "friendship" corrupts information hiding and weakens the value of the object-oriented design approach.

17.9   Static data members and static member functions exist and can be used even if no objects of that class have been instantiated.

17.8   The programmer is able to create new types through the use of the class mechanism. These new types may be designed to be used as conveniently as the built-in types. Thus, C++ is an extensible language. Although the language is easy to extend with these new types, the base language itself is not changeable.

17.10 Template classes encourage software reusability.

Self-Review Exercises

17.1   Fill in the blanks in each of the following:

  a)   _____ syntax is used to initialize constant members of a class.

  b)   A _____ must be declared in a class to have access to that class's `private` data members.

d) A constant object must be _____; it can not be modified after it is created.

e) A _____ data member represents class-wide information.

f) Every object maintains a pointer to itself called the _____ pointer.

g) _____ provide a means of describing the notion of a class generically.

h) The keyword _____ specifies that an object or variable is not modifiable.

i) If a member initializer is not provided for a member object of a class, the object's _____ is called.

j) A member function can be **static** if it does not access _____ class members.

k) Friend functions can access the _____ and _____ members of a class.

l) Template classes are sometimes referred to as _____ types.

m) Member objects are constructed _____ their enclosing class object.

n) The _____ operator reclaims memory previously allocated by **new**.

17.2 Find the error(s) in each of the following and explain how to correct it.

a)
```
char *string;
string = new char[20];
free(string);
```

b)
```
class Example {
public:
    Example(int y = 10) { data = y; }
    int getIncrementedData() const { return ++data; }
    static int getCount()
    {
        cout << "Data is " << data << endl;
        return count;
    }
private:
    int data;
    static int count;
};
```

Answers to Self-Review Exercises

17.1   a) Member initializer. b) **friend**. c) **new**, pointer. d) initialized. e) **static**. f) **this**. g) Template classes. h) **const**. i) default constructor. j) non-**static**. k) **private**, **protected**. l) parameterized. m) before. n) **delete**.

17.2   a) Error: Memory dynamically allocated by **new** is deleted by the C standard library function **free**.
Correction: Use C++'s **delete** operator to reclaim the memory. C-style dynamic memory allocation should not be mixed with C++'s **new** and **delete** operators.

b) Error: The class definition for **Example** has two errors. The first occurs in function **getIncrementedData**. The function is declared **const**, but it modifies the object.
Correction: To correct the first error, remove the **const** keyword from the definition of **getIncrementedData**.

Error: The second error occurs in function **getCount**. This function is declared **static**, so it is not allowed to access any non-**static** member of the class.
Correction: To correct the second error, remove the output line from the definition of **getCount**.

Exercises

17.3   Compare and contrast dynamic memory allocation with the C++ operators **new** and **delete**, with dynamic memory allocation with the C Standard Library functions **malloc** and **free**.

17.4   Explain the notion of friendship in C++. Explain the negative aspects of friendship as described in the text.

17.5   Can a correct **Time** class definition include both of the following constructors?

```
Time (int h = 0, int m = 0, int s = 0);
Time();
```

17.6   What happens when a return type, even **void**, is specified for a constructor or destructor?

17.7   Create a **Date** class with the following capabilities:
a)   Output the date in multiple formats such as

```
DDD YYYY
MM/DD/YY
June 14, 1992
```

b)   Use overloaded constructors to create **Date** objects initialized with dates of the formats in part (a).
c)   Create a **Date** constructor that reads the system date using the standard library functions of the **time.h** header and sets the **Date** members.

In Chapter 18, we will be able to create operators for testing the equality of two dates and for comparing dates to determine if one date is prior to another or after another.

17.8   Using the list processing program of Fig. 12.3 as your guide, build a **List** class. The class should provide the same capabilities as the example. Write a driver program to thoroughly test the class.

17.9   Using the queue processing program of Fig. 12.13 as your guide, build a **Queue** class. The class should provide the same capabilities as the example. Write a driver program to thoroughly test the class.

17.10   Using the **List** class developed in Exercise 17.8 as a starting point, create a template **List** class that is capable of instantiating **List** objects to hold many different data types. Write a driver program to thoroughly test the template class.

17.11   Using the **Queue** class developed in Exercise 17.9 as a starting point, create a template **Queue** class that is capable of instantiating **Queue** objects to hold many different data types. Write a driver program to thoroughly test the template class.

18

Operator Overloading

Objectives

- To understand how to redefine operators to work with new types.
- To understand how to convert objects from one class to another class.
- To learn when to, and when not to, overload operators.
- To study several interesting classes that use over-loaded operators.

The whole difference between construction and creation is exactly this: that a thing constructed can only be loved after it is constructed; but a thing created is loved before it exists.
Gilbert Keith Chesterton
Preface to Dickens, Pickwick Papers

The die is cast.
Julius Caesar

Our doctor would never really operate unless it was necessary. He was just that way. If he didn't need the money, he wouldn't lay a hand on you.
Herb Shriner

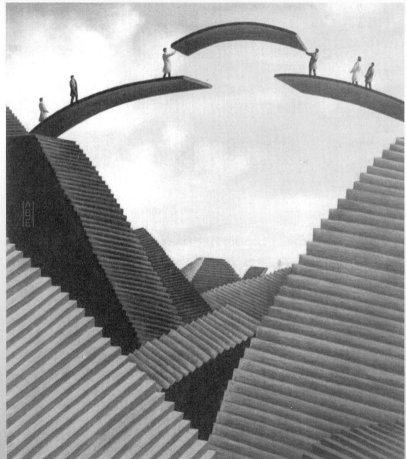

Outline

18.1 Introduction

In Chapters 16 and 17 we introduced the basics of C++ classes and the notion of abstract data types (ADTs). Manipulations on class objects (i.e., instances of ADTs) were accomplished by sending messages (in the form of member function calls) to the objects. This function-call notation is cumbersome for certain kinds of classes, especially mathematical classes. For these kinds of classes it would be nice to use C++'s rich set of built-in operators to specify object manipulations. In this chapter, we show how to enable C++'s operators to work with class objects. This process is called operator overloading. It is straightforward and natural to extend C++ with these new capabilities.

The operator `<<` is used for multiple purposes in C++—as the stream insertion operator and as the left-shift operator. This is an example of *operator overloading*. Similarly, `>>` is also overloaded; it is used both as the stream extraction operator and as the right-shift operator. Both of these operators are overloaded in the C++ class library. The C++ language itself overloads `+` and `-`. These operators perform differently depending on their context in integer arithmetic, floating-point arithmetic, and pointer arithmetic.

More generally, C++ enables the programmer to overload most operators to be sensitive to the context in which they are used. The compiler generates the appropriate code based on the manner in which the operator is used. Some operators are overloaded frequently, especially the assignment operator and various arithmetic operators such as **+** and **-**. The job performed by overloaded operators can also be performed by explicit function calls, but operator notation is usually easier to read.

We will discuss when to use operator overloading and when not to. We show how to overload operators, and we present many complete programs using overloaded operators.

18.2 Fundamentals of Operator Overloading

C++ programming is a type-sensitive and type-focused process. Programmers can use built-in types and can define new types. The built-in types can be used with C++'s rich collection of operators. Operators provide programmers with a concise notation for expressing manipulations of objects of built-in types.

Programmers can use operators with user-defined types as well. Although C++ does not allow new operators to be created, it does allow existing operators to be overloaded so that when these operators are used with class objects, the operators have meaning appropriate to the new types. This is one of C++'s most powerful features. Operator overloading contributes to C++'s extensibility, surely one of the language's most appealing attributes.

Good Programming Practice 18.1

Use operator overloading when it makes a program clearer than accomplishing the same operations with explicit function calls.

Good Programming Practice 18.2

Avoid excessive or inconsistent use of operator overloading as this can make a program cryptic and difficult to read.

Although operator overloading may sound like an exotic capability, most programmers implicitly use overloaded operators regularly. For example, the plus operator (**+**) operates quite differently on integers, floats, and doubles. But plus nevertheless works fine with variables of type **int**, **float**, **double**, and a number of other built-in types because the plus operator (**+**) has been overloaded in the C++ language itself.

Operators are overloaded by writing a function definition (with a header and body) as you normally would, except that the function name now becomes the keyword **operator** followed by the symbol for the operator being overloaded. For example, the function name **operator+** would be used to overload the addition operator.

To use an operator on class objects, that operator *must* be overloaded—with two exceptions. The assignment operator (**=**) may be used with every class without overloading. The default behavior when no overloaded assignment operator is provided is a *memberwise copy* of the data members of the class. We will soon see that such default memberwise copy is dangerous for classes with members that point to dynamically allocated storage; we will typically overload the assignment operator for such classes. The address operator (**&**) may also be used with objects of any class without overloading; it simply returns the address of the object in memory. The address operator can also be overloaded.

Overloading is most appropriate for mathematical classes. These often require that a substantial set of operators be overloaded to ensure consistency with the way these math ematical classes are handled in the real world. For example, it would be unusual to overload only addition for a complex number class, because other arithmetic operators are also commonly used with complex numbers.

C++ is an operator-rich language. C++ programmers understand the meaning and context of each operator. So when it comes to overloading operators for new classes, programmers are likely to make reasonable choices.

The point of operator overloading is to provide the same concise expressions for user-defined types that C++ provides with its rich collection of operators for built-in types. Operator overloading is not automatic, however; the programmer must write operator overloading functions to perform the desired operations. Sometimes these functions are best made member functions; sometimes they are best as friend functions; and occasionally they can be made nonmember, nonfriend functions.

A misuse of overloading would be to overload the + operator to perform subtraction-like operations or to overload the / operator to perform multiplication-like operations. Such use overloading can make a program confusing.

Good Programming Practice 18.3

Overload operators to perform the same function or closely similar functions on class objects as the operators perform on objects of built-in types.

Good Programming Practice 18.4

Before writing C++ programs with overloaded operators, consult the C++ manuals for your compiler to become aware of various restrictions and requirements unique to particular operators.

18.3 Restrictions on Operator Overloading

Most of C++'s operators can be overloaded. These are shown in Fig. 18.1. Figure 18.2 shows the operators that can not be overloaded.

The precedence of an operator can not be changed by overloading. This can lead to awkward situations in which an operator is overloaded in a manner for which its fixed precedence is inappropriate. However, parentheses can be used to force the order of evaluation of overloaded operators in an expression.

Operators that can be overloaded

+	–	*	/	%	^	&	|
~	!	=	<	>	+=	-=	*=
/=	%=	^=	&=	|=	<<	>>	>>=
<<=	==	!=	<=	>=	&&	||	++
--	->*	,	->	[]	()	new	delete

Fig. 18.1 Operators that can be overloaded.

Operators that cannot be overloaded				
.	.*	::	?:	sizeof

Fig. 18.2   Operators that cannot be overloaded.

The associativity of an operator can not be changed by overloading. Default arguments can not be used to overload an operator.

It is not possible to change the number of operands an operator takes: Overloaded unary operators remain as unary operators; overloaded binary operators remain as binary operators. C++'s only ternary operator (**?:**) can not be overloaded. Operators **&**, *****, **+** and **–** each have unary and binary versions; these unary and binary versions can be overloaded separately.

It is not possible to create new operators; only existing operators may be overloaded. This prevents the programmer from using popular notations like the ****** operator used in BASIC for exponentiation

Common Programming Error 18.1

Attempting to create new operators.

The meaning of how an operator works on objects of built-in types can not be changed by operator overloading. The programmer can not, for example, change the meaning of how **+** adds two integers. Operator overloading works only with objects of user-defined types or with a mixture of an object of a user-defined type and an object of a built-in type.

Common Programming Error 18.2

Attempting to modify how an operator works with objects of built-in types.

Software Engineering Observation 18.1

At least one argument of an operator function must be a class object or a reference to a class object. This prevents programmers from changing how operators work on objects of built-in types.

When overloading **( )**, **[ ]**, **->**, or **=** the operator overloading function must be declared as a class member. For the other operators, the operator overloading functions can be friends.

Overloading an assignment operator and an addition operator to allow statements such as

```
object2 = object2 + object1;
```

does not imply that the **+=** operator is also automatically overloaded to allow statements such as

```
object2 += object1;
```

However, such behavior can be achieved by explicitly overloading the `+=` operator for that class.

18.4 Operator Functions as Class Members vs. as Friend Functions

Operator functions can be member functions or nonmember functions; nonmember functions are normally friends. The member functions use the `this` pointer implicitly to obtain one of their class object arguments. That class argument must be explicitly listed in a nonmember function call.

Whether an operator function is implemented as a member function or as a nonmember function, the operator is still used the same way in expressions. So which implementation is best?

When an operator function is implemented as a member function, the leftmost (or only) operand must be a class object (or a reference to a class object) of the operator's class. If the left operand must be an object of a different class or a built-in type, this operator function must be implemented as a nonmember function exactly as shown in Section 18.5 when overloading `<<` and `>>` as the stream insertion and stream extraction operators, respectively. An operator function implemented as a nonmember function needs to be a friend if that function must access private or protected members of that class directly.

The overloaded `<<` operator must have a left operand of type `ostream &` (such as `cout` in the expression `cout << classObject`), so it must be a nonmember function. Similarly, the overloaded `>>` operator must have a left operand of type `istream &` (such as `cin` in the expression `cin >> classObject`), so it, too, must be a nonmember function. Also, each of these overloaded operator functions requires access to the private data members of the class object being output or input, so these overloaded operator functions are ordinarily made friend functions of the class for performance reasons.

Operator member functions are called only when the left operand of a binary operator is specifically an object of that class, or when the single operand of a unary operator is an object of that class.

Another reason why one might choose a nonmember function to overload an operator is to enable the operator to be commutative. For example, suppose we have an object, `number`, of type `long int`, and an object `bigInteger1`, of class `HugeInteger` (a class in which integers may be arbitrarily large rather than being limited by the machine word size of the underlying hardware; class `HugeInteger` is developed in the chapter exercises). The addition operator (**+**) produces a temporary **HugeInteger** object as the sum of a **HugeInteger** and a **long int** (as in the expression **bigInteger1 + number**), or as the sum of a **long int** and a **HugeInteger** (as in the expression **number + bigInteger1**). Thus, we require the addition operator to be commutative (exactly as it is normally). The problem is that the class object must appear on the left of the addition if the operator is to be overloaded as a member function. So, we overload the operator as a friend to allow the **HugeInteger** to appear on the right of the addition. The **operator+** function that deals with the **HugeInteger** on the left can still be a member function.

18.5 Overloading Stream-Insertion and Stream-Extraction Operators

C++ is able to input and output the standard data types using the stream-extraction operator **>>** and stream-insertion operator **<<**. These operators are overloaded (in the class libraries provided with C++ compilers) to process each standard data type including strings and memory addresses. The stream-insertion and stream-extraction operators also can be overloaded to perform input and output for user-defined types. Figure 18.3 demonstrates overloading the stream-extraction and stream-insertion operators to handle data of a user-defined telephone number class called **PhoneNumber**. This program assumes telephone numbers are input correctly. We leave it to the exercises to provide error-checking.

The stream-extraction operator function (**operator>>**) takes an **istream** reference (**input**) and a reference (**num**) to a user-defined type (**PhoneNumber**) as arguments, and returns an **istream** reference. In Fig. 18.3, operator function **operator>>** is used to input phone numbers of the form

```
(800) 555-1212
```

into objects of class **PhoneNumber**. When the compiler sees the expression

```
cin >> phone
```

in **main**, the compiler generates the function call

```
operator>>(cin, phone);
```

When this call is executed, parameter **input** becomes an alias for **cin** and parameter **num** becomes an alias for **phone**. The operator function uses **istream** member function **getline** to read as strings the three parts of the telephone number into the **areaCode**, **exchange**, and **line** members of the referenced **PhoneNumber** object (**num** in the operator function and **phone** in **main**). Function **getline** is explained in detail in Chapter 21. The parentheses, space, and dash characters are skipped by calling **istream** member function **ignore** which discards the specified number of characters in the input stream (one character by default). Function **operator>>** returns **istream** reference **input** (i.e., **cin**). This enables input operations on **PhoneNumber** objects to be *concatenated* with input operations on other **PhoneNumber** objects or on objects of other data types. For example, two **PhoneNumber** objects could be input as follows:

```
cin >> phone1 >> phone2;
```

```
// FIG18_3.CPP
// Overloading the stream-insertion and
// stream-extraction operators.
#include <iostream.h>

class PhoneNumber {
    friend ostream &operator<<(ostream &, const PhoneNumber &);
    friend istream &operator>>(istream &, PhoneNumber &);
private:
    char areaCode[4];   // 3-digit area code and null
    char exchange[4];   // 3-digit exchange and null
    char line[5];       // 4-digit line and null
};

// Overloaded stream insertion operator (cannot be
// a member function).
ostream &operator<<(ostream &output, const PhoneNumber &num)
{
    output << "(" << num.areaCode << ") "
           << num.exchange << "-" << num.line;

    return output;      // enables cout << a << b << c;
}

// overloaded stream extraction operator
istream &operator>>(istream &input, PhoneNumber &num)
{
    input.ignore();                     // skip (
    input.getline(num.areaCode, 4); // input area code
    input.ignore(2);                    // skip ) and space
    input.getline(num.exchange, 4); // input exchange
    input.ignore();                     // skip dash (-)
    input.getline(num.line, 5);     // input line

    return input;       // enables cin >> a >> b >> c;
}

main()
{
    PhoneNumber phone; // create object phone

    cout << "Enter a phone number in the "
         << "form (123) 456-7890:\n";

    // cin >> phone invokes operator>> function by
    // issuing the call operator>>(cin, phone).
    cin >> phone;

    // cout << phone invokes operator<< function by
    // issuing the call operator<<(cout, phone).
    cout << "The phone number entered was:\n"
         << phone << endl;
    return 0;
}
```

Fig. 18.3   User-defined stream-insertion and stream-extraction operators (part 1 of 2).

```
Enter a phone number in the form (123) 456-7890:
(800) 555-1212
The phone number entered was:
(800) 555-1212
```

Fig. 18.3   User-defined stream-insertion and stream-extraction operators (part 2 of 2).

First, the expression **cin >> phone1** would execute by making the call

```
operator>>(cin, phone1);
```

This call would then return **cin** as the value of **cin >> phone1** so the remaining portion of the expression would be interpreted simply as **cin >> phone2**.

The stream-insertion operator takes an **ostream** reference (**output**) and a reference (**num**) to a user-defined type (**PhoneNumber**) as arguments, and returns an **ostream** reference. Function **operator<<** displays objects of type **PhoneNumber**. When the compiler sees the expression

```
cout << phone
```

in **main**, the compiler generates the function call

```
operator<<(cout, phone);
```

Function **operator<<** displays the parts of the telephone number as strings because they are stored in string format (**istream** member function **getline** stores a null character after it completes its input).

Note that the functions **operator>>** and **operator<<** are declared in **class PhoneNumber** as nonmember, friend functions. These operators must be nonmembers because the object of class **PhoneNumber** appears in each case as the right operand of the operator; the class operand must appear on the left in order to overload the operator as a member function. Overloaded input and output operators must be declared as friends if they must access non-public class members directly.

Software Engineering Observation 18.2

New input/output capabilities for user-defined types can be added to C++ without modifying the declarations or private data members for either the **ostream** *class or the* **istream** *class. This promotes the extensibility of the C++ programming language—one of C++'s most attractive aspects.*

18.6 Overloading Unary Operators

A unary operator for a class can be overloaded as a nonstatic member function with no arguments, or as a nonmember function with one argument; that argument must be either an object of the class or a reference to an object of the class.

Later in this chapter, we will overload unary operator **!** to test if a string is empty. When overloading a unary operator such as **!** as a nonstatic member function with no arguments, if **s** is a class object, when the compiler sees the expression **!s** the compiler generates the call **s.operator!()**. The operand **s** is the class object **s** for which the member function **operator!** is being invoked:

```
class String {
public:
    int operator!() const;
    ...
};
```

A unary operator such as **!** may be overloaded as a nonmember function with one argument two different ways—either with an argument that is an object, or with an argument that is a reference to an object. If **s** is a class object, then **!s** is treated as if the call **operator!(s)** had been written.

```
class String {
    friend int operator!(const String &);
    ...
};
```

Good Programming Practice 18.5

When overloading unary operators, it is preferable to make the operator functions class members instead of nonmember friend functions. This is a tidier solution. Friend functions and friend classes should be avoided unless they are absolutely necessary. The use of friends violates the encapsulation of a class.

18.7 Overloading Binary Operators

A binary operator can be overloaded as a nonstatic member function with one argument, or as a nonmember function with two arguments (one of those arguments must be either a class object or a reference to a class object).

Later in this chapter, we will overload **+=** to indicate concatenation of two string objects. When overloading binary operator **+=** as a nonstatic member function of a **String** class with one argument, if **y** and **z** are class objects, then **y += z** is treated as if **y.operator+=(z)** had been written.

```
class String {
public:
    String &operator+=(const String &);
    ...
};
```

Binary operator **+=** may be overloaded as a nonmember function with two arguments—one of which must be a class object or a reference to a class object. If **y** and **z** are class objects, then **y += z** is treated as if the call **operator+=(y, z)** had been written in the program.

```
class String {
   friend String &operator+=(String &, const String &);
   ...
};
```

18.8 Case Study: An Array Class

Arrray notation in C and C++ is just an alternative to pointers, so arrays have much potential for errors. For example, a program can easily "walk off" an array because C and C++ do not check whether subscripts fall outside the range of an array. Arrays of size n must number their elements 0, ..., $n − 1$; alternate subscript ranges are not allowed. An entire array cannot be input or output at once; each array element must be read or written individually. Two arrays cannot be compared with equality operators or relational operators. When an array is passed to a general-purpose function designed to handle arrays of any size, the size of the array must be passed as an additional argument. One array cannot be assigned to another with the assignment operator(s). These and other capabilities certainly seem like "naturals" for dealing with arrays, but C and C++ do not provide such capabilities. However, C++ does provide the means to implement such array capabilities through the mechanisms of operator overloading.

In this example, we develop an array class that performs range checking to ensure that subscripts remain within the bounds of the array. The class allows one array object to be assigned to another with the assignment operator. Objects of the array class automatically know their size so the size does not need to be passed as an argument when passing an array to a function. Entire arrays can be input or output with the stream-extraction and stream-insertion operators, respectively. Array comparisons can be made with the equality operators == and !=. Our array class uses a static member to keep track of the number of array objects that have been instantiated in the program. This example will sharpen your appreciation of data abstraction. You will probably want to suggest many enhancements to this array class. Class development is an interesting and intellectually challenging activity.

The program of Fig. 18.4 demonstrates class **Array** and its overloaded operators. First we walk through the driver program in **main**. Then we consider the class definition and each of the class's member function and friend function definitions. The program instantiates two objects of class **Array**—**integers1** with seven elements and **integers2** with default size ten elements (the default value specified by the **Array** constructor). Static data member **arrayCount** of class **Array** contains the number of **Array** objects instantiated during program execution. Static member function **getArrayCount** returns this value. Member function **getSize** returns the size of the **integers1** array. The program outputs the size of array **integers1**, then outputs the array itself using the overloaded stream-insertion operator to confirm that the array elements were initialized correctly by the constructor. Next, the size of array **integers2** is output, then the array is output using the overloaded stream-insertion operator.

The user is prompted to input 17 integers. The overloaded stream-extraction operator is used to read these values into both arrays with the statement

```
cin >> integers1 >> integers2;
```

The first seven values are stored in `integers1` and the remaining values are stored in `integers2`. The two arrays are output with the stream-insertion operator to confirm that the input was performed correctly.

Next the program tests the overloaded inequality operator by evaluating the condition

```
integers1 != integers2
```

and the program reports that the arrays are indeed not equal.

The program instantiates a third array called `integers3` and initializes it with array `integers1`. The program outputs the size of array `integers3`, then outputs the array itself using the overloaded stream-insertion operator to confirm that the array elements were initialized correctly by the constructor.

Next the program tests the overloaded assignment operator (=) with the expression `integers1 = integers2`. Both arrays are then printed to confirm that the assignment was correct. It is interesting to note that `integers1` originally held 7 integers and needed to be resized to hold a copy of the 10 elements in `integers2`. As we will see, the overloaded assignment operator performs this resizing in a manner transparent to the invoker of the operator.

Next the program uses the overloaded equality operator (==) to see that objects `integers1` and `integers2` are indeed identical after the assignment.

The program then uses the overloaded subscript operator to reference element `integers1[5]`—an in-range element of `integers1`. This subscripted name is then used as an *rvalue* to print the value in `integers1[5]`, and the name is then used as an *lvalue* on the left side of an assignment statement to receive a new value, 1000, for `integers1[5]`. Note that `operator[]` provides the reference and assigns the value.

The program then attempts to assign the value 1000 to `integers1[15]`—an out-of-range element. The program catches this error and terminates abnormally.

Interestingly, the array subscript operator `[]` is not restricted for use only with arrays; it can be used to select elements from other kinds of container classes such as linked lists, strings, dictionaries, and so on. Also, subscripts no longer have to be integers; characters or strings could be used, for example.

Now that we have seen how this program operates, let us walk through the class header and the member function definitions. The lines

```
int *ptr;               // pointer to first element of array
int size;               // size of the array
static int arrayCount;  // # of Arrays instantiated
```

represent the private data members of the class. The array consists of a pointer, `ptr`, (to the appropriate type, in this case `int`), a `size` member indicating the number of elements in the array, and static member `arrayCount` indicating the number of array objects that have been instantiated.

The lines

```
friend ostream &operator<<(ostream &, const Array &);
friend istream &operator>>(istream &, Array &);
```

declare the overloaded stream-insertion operator and the overloaded stream-extraction operator to be friends of class `Array`. When the compiler sees an expression like

```
cout << arrayObject
```

it invokes the **operator<<** function by generating the call

```
operator<<(cout, arrayObject)
```

When the compiler sees an expression like

```
cin >> arrayObject
```

it invokes the **operator>>** function by generating the call

```
operator>>(cin, arrayObject)
```

We note again that these operator functions cannot be members of class **Array** because the **Array** object is always mentioned on the right side of the stream-insertion operator and the stream-extraction operator. Function **operator<<** prints the number of elements indicated by the **size** from the array stored at **ptr**. Function **operator>>** inputs directly into the array pointed to by **ptr**. Each of these operator functions returns an appropriate reference to enable concatenated calls.

The line

```
Array(int arraySize = 10);            // default constructor
```

declares the default constructor for the class and specifies that the array size defaults to 10 elements. When the compiler sees a declaration like

```
Array integers1(7);
```

or the equivalent form

```
Array integers1 = 7;
```

it invokes the default constructor. The default constructor member function **Array** increments **arrayCount**, copies the argument into the **size** data member, uses **new** to obtain the space to hold the internal representation of this array and assigns the pointer returned by **new** to data member **ptr**, uses **assert** to test that **new** was successful, then uses a **for** loop to initialize all the elements of the array to zero. It would be perfectly reasonable to have an **Array** class that does not initialize its members if, for example, these members were to be read at some later time.

The line

```
Array(const Array &);                     // copy constructor
```

is a *copy constructor*. It initializes an **Array** object by making a copy of an existing **Array** object. Such copying must be done carefully to avoid the pitfall of having both **Array** objects pointing to the same dynamically allocated storage, exactly the problem that would occur with default memberwise copy. Copy constructors are invoked whenever a copy of an object is needed such as in call by value, when returning an object from a called function, or when initializing an object to be a copy of another object of the same class. The copy constructor is called in a declaration when an object of class **Array** is instantiated and initialized with another object of class **Array** as in the following declaration:

```
Array integers3(integers1);
```

or the equivalent declaration

```
Array integers3 = integers1;
```

The copy constructor member function **Array** increments **arrayCount**, copies the **size** of the array used for initialization into the **size** data member, uses **new** to obtain the space to hold the internal representation of this array and assigns the pointer returned by **new** to data member **ptr**, uses **assert** to test that **new** was successful, then uses a **for** loop to copy all the elements of the initializer array into this array. It is important to note that if the copy constructor simply copied the **ptr** in the source object to the target object's **ptr**, then both objects would point to the same dynamically allocated storage. The first destructor to execute would then delete the dynamically allocated storage and the other object's **ptr** would then be undefined, a situation likely to cause a serious run-time error.

Good Programming Practice 18.6

A destructor, the assignment operator, and a copy constructor for a class are usually provided as a group.

The line

```
~Array();                              // destructor
```

declares the destructor for the class. The destructor is invoked automatically when the life of an object of class **Array** is terminated. The destructor decrements **arrayCount** then uses **delete** to reclaim the dynamic storage created by **new** in the constructor.
The line

```
int getSize() const;                   // return size
```

declares a function that reads the size of the array.
The line

```
const Array &operator=(const Array &);     // assign arrays
```

declares the overloaded assignment operator function for the class. When the compiler sees an expression like

```
integers1 = integers2;
```

it invokes the **operator=** function by generating the call

```
integers1.operator=(integers2)
```

The **operator=** member function tests for self assignment. If a self assignment is being attempted, the assignment is skipped (i.e., the object already is itself). If it this not a self assignment, then the member function uses **delete** to reclaim the space originally allo-cated in the target array, copies the **size** of the source array to the **size** of the target ar ray, uses **new** to allocate that amount of space for the target array and places the pointer returned by **new** into the array's **ptr** member, uses **assert** to verify that **new** succeeded, then uses a **for** loop to copy the array elements from the source array to the target array. Regardless of whether this is a self assignment or not, the member function then returns the current object (i.e., ***this**) as a constant reference; this enables concatenated **Array** assignments such as **x = y = z**. If the test for self assignment were omitted, the member function would begin by deleting the target array's space. Because this is also the source array in a self assignment, the array would have been destroyed.

Common Programming Error 18.4

Not testing for and avoiding self assignment when overloading the assignment operator for a class that includes a pointer to dynamic storage.

Common Programming Error 18.5

Not providing an overloaded assignment operator and a copy constructor for a class when objects of that class contain pointers to dynamically allocated storage.

Software Engineering Observation 18.3

It is possible to prevent one class object from being assigned to another. This is done by defining the assignment operator as a private member of the class.

The line

```
int operator==(const Array &) const; // compare equal
```

declares the overloaded equality operator (**==**) for the class. When the compiler sees the expression

```
integers1 == integers2
```

in **main**, the compiler invokes the **operator==** member function by generating the call

```
integers1.operator==(integers2)
```

The **operator==** member function immediately returns 0 (false) if the **size** members of the arrays are different. Otherwise, the member function compares each pair of elements. If they are all the same, 1 (true) is returned. The first pair of elements to differ causes 0 to be returned immediately.

The line

```
int operator!=(const Array &) const; // compare !equal
```

declares the overloaded inequality operator (**!=**) for the class. The **operator!=** member function is invoked and operates similarly to the overloaded equality operator function.

The line

```
int &operator[](int);                          // subscript operator
```

declares the overloaded subscript operator for the class. When the compiler sees the expression

```
integers1[5]
```

in **main**, the compiler invokes the overloaded **operator[]** member function by generating the call

```
integers1.operator[](5)
```

The **operator[]** member function tests if the subscript is in range, and if it is not, the program terminates abnormally. If the subscript is in range, the appropriate element of the array is returned as a reference so that it may be used as an *lvalue* (for example, on the left side of an assignment statement).

The line

```
static int getArrayCount();           // return count of Arrays
```

declares static member function **getArrayCount** that returns the value of static data member **arrayCount**, even if no objects of class **Array** exist.

```
// ARRAY1.H
// Simple class Array (for integers)
#ifndef ARRAY1_H
#define ARRAY1_H

#include <iostream.h>

class Array {
   friend ostream &operator<<(ostream &, const Array &);
   friend istream &operator>>(istream &, Array &);
public:
   Array(int = 10);                     // default constructor
   Array(const Array &);                // copy constructor
   ~Array();                            // destructor
   int getSize() const;                 // return size
   const Array &operator=(const Array &);  // assign arrays
   int operator==(const Array &) const; // compare equal
   int operator!=(const Array &) const; // compare !equal
   int &operator[](int);                // subscript operator
   static int getArrayCount();          // return count of
                                        // arrays instantiated
private:
   int *ptr; // pointer to first element of array
   int size; // size of the array
   static int arrayCount;  // # of Arrays instantiated
};

#endif
```

Fig. 18.4 Definition of class **Array** (part 1 of 7).

```
// ARRAY1.CPP
// Member function definitions for class Array
#include <iostream.h>
#include <stdlib.h>
#include <assert.h>
#include "array1.h"

// Initialize static data member at file scope
int Array::arrayCount = 0;    // no objects yet

// Return the number of Array objects instantiated
int Array::getArrayCount() { return arrayCount; }

// Default constructor for class Array
Array::Array(int arraySize)
{
   ++arrayCount;              // count one more object
   size = arraySize;         // default size is 10
   ptr = new int[size];      // create space for array
   assert(ptr != 0);  // terminate if memory not allocated

   for (int i = 0; i < size; i++)
      ptr[i] = 0;            // initialize array
}

// Copy constructor for class Array
Array::Array(const Array &init)
{
   ++arrayCount;              // count one more object
   size = init.size;         // size this object
   ptr = new int[size];      // create space for array
   assert(ptr != 0);  // terminate if memory not allocated

   for (int i = 0; i < size; i++)
      ptr[i] = init.ptr[i];  // copy init into object
}

// Destructor for class Array
Array::~Array()
{
   --arrayCount;              // one fewer objects
   delete [] ptr;            // reclaim space for array
}

// Get the size of the array
int Array::getSize() const { return size; }

// Overloaded subscript operator
int &Array::operator[](int subscript)
{
   // check for subscript out of range error
   assert(0 <= subscript && subscript < size);

   return ptr[subscript];    // reference return creates lvalue
}
```

Fig. 18.4 Member function definitions for class **Array** (part 2 of 7).

```
// Determine if two arrays are equal and
// return 1 if true, 0 if false.
int Array::operator==(const Array &right) const
{
   if (size != right.size)
      return 0;     // arrays of different sizes

   for (int i = 0; i < size; i++)
      if (ptr[i] != right.ptr[i])
         return 0; // arrays are not equal

   return 1;        // arrays are equal
}

// Determine if two arrays are not equal and
// return 1 if true, 0 if false.
int Array::operator!=(const Array &right) const
{
   if (size != right.size)
      return 1;     // arrays of different sizes

   for (int i = 0; i < size; i++)
      if (ptr[i] != right.ptr[i])
         return 1;       // arrays are not equal

   return 0;        // arrays are equal
}

// Overloaded assignment operator
const Array &Array::operator=(const Array &right)
{
   if (&right != this) {    // check for self-assignment
      delete [] ptr;        // reclaim space
      size = right.size;    // resize this object
      ptr = new int[size];  // create space for array copy
      assert(ptr != 0);     // terminate if memory not allocated

      for (int i = 0; i < size; i++)
         ptr[i] = right.ptr[i];  // copy array into object
   }

   return *this;    // enables x = y = z;
}

// Overloaded input operator for class Array;
// inputs values for entire array.
istream &operator>>(istream &input, Array &a)
{
   for (int i = 0; i < a.size; i++)
      input >> a.ptr[i];

   return input;    // enables cin >> x >> y;
}
```

Fig. 18.4   Member function definitions for class **Array** (part 3 of 7).

```
// Overloaded output operator for class Array
ostream &operator<<(ostream &output, const Array &a)
{
   for (int i = 0; i < a.size; i++) {
      output << a.ptr[i] << ' ';

      if ((i + 1) % 10 == 0)
         output << endl;
   }

   if (i % 10 != 0)
      output << endl;

   return output;     // enables cout << x << y;
}
```

Fig. 18.4 Member function definitions for class **Array** (part 4 of 7).

```
// FIG18_4.CPP
// Driver for simple class Array
#include <iostream.h>
#include "array1.h"

main()
{
   // no objects yet
   cout << "# of arrays instantiated = "
        << Array::getArrayCount() << '\n';

   // create two arrays and print Array count
   Array integers1(7), integers2;
   cout << "# of arrays instantiated = "
        << Array::getArrayCount();

   // print integers1 size and contents
   cout << "\n\nSize of array integers1 is "
        << integers1.getSize()
        << "\nArray after initialization:\n"
        << integers1;

   // print integers2 size and contents
   cout << "\nSize of array integers2 is "
        << integers2.getSize()
        << "\nArray after initialization:\n"
        << integers2;

   // input and print integers1 and integers2
   cout << "\nInput 17 integers:\n";
   cin >> integers1 >> integers2;
   cout << "After input, the arrays contain:\n"
        << "integers1: " << integers1
        << "integers2: " << integers2;
```

Fig. 18.4 Driver for class **Array** (part 5 of 7).

```
// create array integers3 using integers1 as an
// initializer; print size and contents
Array integers3(integers1);

cout << "\nSize of array integers3 is "
     << integers3.getSize()
     << "\nArray after initialization:\n"
     << integers3;

// use overloaded inequality (!=) operator
cout << "\nEvaluating: integers1 != integers2\n";
if (integers1 != integers2)
   cout << "They are not equal\n\n";

// use overloaded assignment (=) operator
cout << "Assigning integers2 to integers1:\n";
integers1 = integers2;
cout << "integers1: " << integers1
     << "integers2: " << integers2;

// use overloaded equality (==) operator
cout << "\nEvaluating: integers1 == integers2\n";
if (integers1 == integers2)
   cout << "They are equal\n\n";

// use overloaded subscript operator to create rvalue
cout << "integers1[5] is " << integers1[5] << endl;

// use overloaded subscript operator to create lvalue
cout << "Assigning 1000 to integers1[5]\n";
integers1[5] = 1000;
cout << "integers1: " << integers1;

// attempt to use out of range subscript
cout << "\nAttempt to assign 1000 to integers1[15]\n";
integers1[15] = 1000;   // ERROR: out of range

return 0;
}
```

Fig. 18.4   Driver for class **Array** (part 6 of 7).

18.9 Converting Between Types

Most programs process information of a variety of types. Sometimes all the operations "stay within a type." For example, adding an integer to an integer produces an integer (as long as the result is not too large to be represented as an integer). But, it is often necessary to convert data of one type to data of another type. This can happen in assignments, in calculations, in passing values to functions, and in returning values from functions. The compiler knows how to perform conversions among built-in types. Programmers can force conversions among built-in types by casting.

```
# of arrays instantiated = 0
# of arrays instantiated = 2

Size of array integers1 is 7
Array after initialization:
0 0 0 0 0 0 0

Size of array integers2 is 10
Array after initialization:
0 0 0 0 0 0 0 0 0 0

Input 17 integers:
1 2 3 4 5 6 7 8 9 10 11 12 13 14 15 16 17
After input, the arrays contain:
integers1: 1 2 3 4 5 6 7
integers2: 8 9 10 11 12 13 14 15 16 17

Size of array integers3 is 7
Array after initialization:
1 2 3 4 5 6 7

Evaluating: integers1 != integers2
They are not equal

Assigning integers2 to integers1:
integers1: 8 9 10 11 12 13 14 15 16 17
integers2: 8 9 10 11 12 13 14 15 16 17

Evaluating: integers1 == integers2
They are equal

integers1[5] is 13
Assigning 1000 to integers1[5]
integers1: 8 9 10 11 12 1000 14 15 16 17

Attempt to assign 1000 to integers1[15]
Assertion failed: 0 <= subscript && subscript < size,
    file ARRAY1.CPP, line 98
Abnormal program termination
```

Fig. 18.4   Output from driver for class **Array** (part 7 of 7).

But what about user-defined types? The compiler can not automatically know how to convert among user-defined types and built-in types. The programmer must explicitly specify how such conversions are to occur. Such conversions can be performed with *conversion constructors,* i.e., single-argument constructors, that simply turn objects of other types into objects of a particular class. We will use a conversion constructor later in this chapter to convert ordinary **char *** strings into C++ **String** objects.

A *conversion operator* (also called a *cast operator*) can be used to convert an object of one class into an object of another class or into an object of a built-in type. Such a con version operator must be a nonstatic member function; this kind of conversion operator can not be a friend function.

The function prototype

```
operator char *() const;
```

declares an overloaded cast operator function for creating a temporary **char *** object out of an object of a user-defined type. An overloaded cast operator function does not specify a return type—the return type is the type to which the object is being converted. If **s** is a class object, when the compiler sees the expression **(char *) s** the compiler generates the call **s.operator char *()**. The operand **s** is the class object **s** for which the member function **operator char *** is being invoked.

Overloaded cast operator functions can be defined for converting objects of user-defined types into built-in types or into objects of other user-defined types. The function prototypes

```
operator int() const;
operator otherClass() const;
```

declare overloaded cast operator functions for converting an object of a user-defined type into an integer and for converting an object of a user-defined type into an object of user-defined type **otherClass**.

One of the wonderful features of cast operators and conversion constructors is that, when necessary, the compiler can call these functions automatically to create temporary objects. For example, if an object **s** of a user-defined **String** class appears in a program at a location where an ordinary **char *** is expected, such as

```
cout << s;
```

the compiler calls the overloaded cast operator function **operator char *** to convert the object into a **char *** and uses the resulting **char *** in the expression.

18.10 Case Study: A String Class

As a capstone exercise to our study of overloading we will build a class that handles the creation and manipulation of strings. Neither C nor C++ has a built-in string data type. But C++ enables us to add our own string type as a class, and—through the mechanisms of overloading—provides a collection of operators for conveniently manipulating strings. The various parts of Fig. 18.5 include a class header, member function definitions, and a driver program to test our new class **String**.

First, we will present the header for class **String**. We discuss the private data used for representing **String** objects. Then we walk through the class's public interface, discussing each of the services the class provides.

Next, we will walk through the driver program in **main**. We will discuss the coding style we "aspire to," i.e., the kinds of operator-intensive expressions we would like to be able to write with objects of our new **String** class and with the class's collection of overloaded operators.

Then we discuss the member function definitions for class **String**. For each of the overloaded operators, we show the code in the driver program that invokes the overloaded operator function, and we explain how the overloaded operator function works.

We begin with the internal representation of a **String**. The lines

```
private:
    char *sPtr;             // pointer to start of string
    int length;             // string length
```

declare the private data members of the class. A **String** object has a pointer to its dynamically allocated storage representing the character string and has a length field which represents the number of characters in the string not including the null character at the end of the character string.

Now we walk through of the **String** class header file in Fig. 18.5. The lines

```
friend ostream &operator<<(ostream &, const String &);
friend istream &operator>>(istream &, String &);
```

declare the overloaded stream-insertion operator function **operator<<** and the overloaded stream-extraction operator function **operator>>** as friends of the class. The implementation of these is straightforward.

The line

```
String(const char * = ""); // conversion constructor
```

declares a *conversion constructor*. This constructor takes a **char *** argument (that defaults to the empty string) and instantiates a **String** object that includes that same character string. Any single argument constructor can be thought of as a conversion constructor. As we will see, such constructors are helpful when we are doing assignments of character strings to **String** objects. The conversion constructor converts the conventional string into a **String** object that is then assigned to the target **String** object. The availability of this conversion constructor means that it is not necessary to supply an overloaded assignment operator for specifically assigning character strings to **String** objects. The compiler automatically invokes the conversion constructor to create a temporary **String** object containing the character string. Then, the overloaded assignment operator is invoked to assign the temporary **String** object to another **String** object. Note that when C++ uses a conversion constructor in this manner it can only apply a single constructor to try to match the needs of the overloaded assignment operator. It is not possible to match an overloaded operator's needs by performing a series of implicit, user-defined conversions. The **String** conversion constructor could be invoked in a declaration such as **String s1("happy")**. The conversion constructor member function calculates the length of the character string and assigns this to private data member **length**, uses **new** to assign a sufficient amount of space to private data member **sPtr**, uses **assert** to test that **new** succeeded and, if it did, uses **strcpy** to copy the character string into the object.

The line

```
String(const String &);    // copy constructor
```

is a copy constructor. It initializes a **String** object by making a copy of an existing **String** object. Such copying must be done carefully to avoid the pitfall of having both **String** objects pointing to the same dynamically allocated storage, exactly the problem that would occur with default memberwise copy. The copy constructor operates similarly to the conversion constructor except that it simply copies the **length** member from the source **String** object to the target **String** object. Note that the copy constructor creates new space for the target object's internal character string. If it simply copied the **sPtr** in the source object to the target object's **sPtr**, then both objects would point to the same dynamically allocated storage. The first destructor to execute would then delete the dynamically allocated storage and the other object's **sPtr** would then be undefined, a situation likely to cause a serious run-time error.

The line

```
~String();                                    // destructor
```

declares the destructor for class **String**. The destructor uses **delete** to reclaim the dynamic storage obtained by **new** in the constructors to provide the space for the character string.

The line

```
const String &operator=(const String &);     // assignment
```

declares the overloaded assignment operator. When the compiler sees an expression like **string1 = string2**, the compiler generates the function call

```
string1.operator=(string2);
```

The overloaded assignment operator function **operator=** tests for self-assignment, exactly as the copy constructor did. If this is a self-assignment, the function simply returns because the object is already itself. If this test were omitted, the function would immediately delete the space in the target object and thus lose the character string. Assuming that it is not a self-assignment, the function does delete the space, copies the length field of the source object to the target object, creates new space for the target object, uses **assert** to determine that **new** succeeded, and then uses **strcpy** to copy the character string from the source object to the target object. Whether or not this is a self-assignment, ***this** is returned to enable concatenated assignments.

The line

```
String &operator+=(const String &);     // concatenation
```

declares the overloaded string concatenation operator. When the compiler sees the expression **s1 += s2** in **main**, the function call **s1.operator+=(s2)** is generated by the compiler. Function **operator+=** creates a temporary pointer to hold the current object's character string pointer until the character string's memory can be deleted, calculates the combined length of the concatenated string, uses **new** to reserve space for the string, uses **assert** to test that **new** succeeded, uses **strcpy** to copy the original string into the newly allocated space, uses **strcat** to concatenate the source object's character string to the newly allocated space, uses **delete** to reclaim the space occupied by this object's original character string, and returns ***this** as a **String &** to enable concatenation of **+=** operators.

Do we need a second overloaded concatenation operator to allow concatenation of a **String** and a **char ***? No. The **const char *** conversion constructor converts a conventional string into a **String** object which then matches the existing overloaded concatenation operator. C++ can perform such conversions only one level deep to facilitate a match. C++ can also perform an implicit compiler-defined conversion between built-in types before it performs the conversion between a built-in type and a class.

Performance Tip 18.2

Having the overloaded += concatenation operator that takes a single argument of type **const char *** *operates more efficiently than having to do the implicit conversion first then the concatenation. Implicit conversions requires less code and cause fewer errors.*

The line

```
int operator!() const;                    // is String empty?
```

declares the overloaded negation operator. This operator is commonly used with string classes to test if a string is empty. For example, when the compiler sees the expression **!string1**, it generates the function call

```
string1.operator!()
```

This function simply returns the result of testing if **length** is equal to zero.

The lines

```
int operator==(const String &) const;  // test s1 == s2
int operator!=(const String &) const;  // test s1 != s2
int operator<(const String &)  const;  // test s1 < s2
int operator>(const String &)  const;  // test s1 > s2
int operator>=(const String &) const;  // test s1 >= s2
int operator<=(const String &) const;  // test s1 <= s2
```

declare the overloaded equality operators and the overloaded relational operators for the **String** class. These are all similar, so let us discuss one example, namely overloading the **>=** operator. When the compiler sees the expression **string1 >= string2**, the compiler generates the function call

```
string1.operator>=(string2)
```

which returns 1 (true) if **string1** is greater than or equal to **string2**. Each of these operators uses **strcmp** to compare the character strings in the **String** objects.

The line

```
char &operator[](int);        // return char reference
```

declares the overloaded subscript operator. When the compiler sees an expression like **string1[0]**, the compiler generates the function call **string1.operator[](0)**.

Function `operator[]` first uses `assert` to perform a range check on the subscript; if the subscript is out of range, the program will print an error message and terminate abnormally. If the subscript is within range, `operator[]` returns as a `char &` the appropriate character of the `String` object; this `char &` may be used as an *lvalue* to modify the designated character of the `String` object.

The line

```
String &operator()(int, int); // return a substring
```

declares the *overloaded function call operator*. In string classes, it is common to overload this operator to select a substring from a `String` object. The two integer parameters specify the start location and the length of the substring being selected from the `String`. If the start location is out of range or the substring length is negative, an error message is generated. By convention, if the substring length is 0, then the substring is selected all the

```
// STRING2.H
// Definition of a String class
#ifndef STRING1_H
#define STRING1_H

#include <iostream.h>

class String {
   friend ostream &operator<<(ostream &, const String &);
   friend istream &operator>>(istream &, String &);
public:
   String(const char * = ""); // conversion constructor
   String(const String &);    // copy constructor
   ~String();                 // destructor
   const String &operator=(const String &);  // assignment
   String &operator+=(const String &);    // concatenation
   int operator!() const;                 // is String empty?
   int operator==(const String &) const;  // test s1 == s2
   int operator!=(const String &) const;  // test s1 != s2
   int operator<(const String &)  const;  // test s1 < s2
   int operator>(const String &)  const;  // test s1 > s2
   int operator>=(const String &) const;  // test s1 >= s2
   int operator<=(const String &) const;  // test s1 <= s2
   char &operator[](int);         // return char reference
   String &operator()(int, int); // return a substring
   int getLength() const;         // return string length
private:
   char *sPtr;                 // pointer to start of string
   int length;                 // string length
};

#endif
```

Fig. 18.5   Definition of a basic `String` class (part 1 of 8).

way to the end of the **String** object. For example, suppose **string1** is a **String** object containing the character string **"AEIOU"**. When the compiler sees the expression **string1(2, 2)**, it generates the function call **string1.operator()(2,2)**. When this call executes, it produces a temporary **String** object containing the string **"IO"** and returns a reference to this object. Overloading the function call operator **()** is powerful because functions can take arbitrarily long and complex parameter lists. So we can use this capability for many interesting purposes. Another use of the function call operator is an alternate array subscripting notation: Instead of using C's awkward double square bracket notation for double arrays such as in **a[b][c]**, for example, some programmers prefer to overload the function call operator to enable the notation **a(b, c)**. The overloaded function call operator can only be a nonstatic member function. This operator is used only when the "function name" is an object of class **String**.

The line

```
    int getLength() const;        // return string length
```

declares a function that returns the length of the **String** object. Note that this function obtain the length by returning the value of the private data of class **String**.

At this point, the reader should now step through the code in **main**, examine the output window, and check each use of an overloaded operator.

```
// STRING2.CPP
// Member function definitions for class String

#include <iostream.h>
#include <string.h>
#include <assert.h>
#include "string2.h"

// Conversion constructor: Convert char * to String
String::String(const char *s)
{
    cout << "Conversion constructor: " << s << endl;
    length = strlen(s);            // compute length
    sPtr = new char[length + 1]; // allocate storage
    assert(sPtr != 0);  // terminate if memory not allocated
    strcpy(sPtr, s);               // copy literal to object
}

// Copy constructor
String::String(const String &copy)
{
    cout << "Copy constructor: " << copy.sPtr << endl;
    length = copy.length;          // copy length
    sPtr = new char[length + 1]; // allocate storage
    assert(sPtr != 0);             // ensure memory allocated
    strcpy(sPtr, copy.sPtr);       // copy string
}
```

Fig. 18.5   Member function definitions for class **String** (part 2 of 8).

```
// Destructor
String::~String()
{
   cout << "Destructor: " << sPtr << endl;
   delete [] sPtr;                    // reclaim string
}

// Overloaded = operator; avoids self assignment
const String &String::operator=(const String &right)
{
   cout << "operator= called" << endl;

   if (&right != this) {              // avoid self assignment
      delete [] sPtr;                 // prevents memory leak
      length = right.length;          // new String length
      sPtr = new char[length + 1];    // allocate memory
      assert(sPtr != 0);              // ensure memory allocated
      strcpy(sPtr, right.sPtr);       // copy string
   }
   else
      cout << "Attempted assignment of a String to itself\n";

   return *this;    // enables concatenated assignments
}

// Concatenate right operand to this object and
// store in this object.
String &String::operator+=(const String &right)
{
   char *tempPtr = sPtr;              // hold to be able to delete
   length += right.length;           // new String length
   sPtr = new char[length + 1];      // create space
   assert(sPtr != 0);     // terminate if memory not allocated
   strcpy(sPtr, tempPtr);            // left part of new String
   strcat(sPtr, right.sPtr);         // right part of new String
   delete [] tempPtr;                // reclaim old space
   return *this;                     // enables concatenated calls
}

// Is this String empty?
int String::operator!() const { return length == 0; }

// Is this String equal to right String?
int String::operator==(const String &right) const
{ return strcmp(sPtr, right.sPtr) == 0; }

// Is this String not equal to right String?
int String::operator!=(const String &right) const
{ return strcmp(sPtr, right.sPtr) != 0; }

// Is this String less than right String?
int String::operator<(const String &right) const
{ return strcmp(sPtr, right.sPtr) < 0; }
```

Fig. 18.5   Member function definitions for class **String** (part 3 of 8).

```
// Is this String greater than right String?
int String::operator>(const String &right) const
{ return strcmp(sPtr, right.sPtr) > 0; }

// Is this String greater than or equal to right String?
int String::operator>=(const String &right) const
{ return strcmp(sPtr, right.sPtr) >= 0; }

// Is this String less than or equal to right String?
int String::operator<=(const String &right) const
{ return strcmp(sPtr, right.sPtr) <= 0; }

// Return a reference to a character in a String.
char &String::operator[](int subscript)
{
   // First test for subscript out of range
   assert(subscript >= 0 && subscript < length);

   return sPtr[subscript];   // creates lvalue
}

// Return a substring beginning at index and
// of length subLength as a reference to a String object.
String &String::operator()(int index, int subLength)
{
   // ensure index is in range and substring length >= 0
   assert(index >= 0 && index < length && subLength >= 0);

   String *subPtr = new String;   // empty String
   assert(subPtr != 0);      // ensure new String allocated

   // determine length of substring
   int size;

   if ((subLength == 0) || (index + subLength > length))
      size = length - index + 1;
   else
      size = subLength + 1;

   // allocate memory for substring
   delete subPtr->sPtr;
   subPtr->length = size;
   subPtr->sPtr = new char[size];
   assert(subPtr->sPtr != 0);   // ensure space allocated

   // copy substring into new String
   for (int i = index, j = 0; i < index + size - 1; i++, j++)
      subPtr->sPtr[j] = sPtr[i];

   subPtr->sPtr[j] = '\0';   // terminate the new String
   return *subPtr;           // return new String
}
```

Fig. 18.5   Member function definitions for class **String** (part 4 of 8).

```
// Return string length
int String::getLength() const { return length; }

// Overloaded output operator
ostream &operator<<(ostream &output, const String &s)
{
   output << s.sPtr;
   return output;    // enables concatenation
}

// Overloaded input operator
istream &operator>>(istream &input, String &s)
{
   static char temp[100];    // buffer to store input

   input >> temp;
   s = temp;              // use String class assignment operator
   return input;          // enables concatenation
}
```

Fig. 18.5 Member function definitions for class **String** (part 5 of 8).

```
// FIG18_5.CPP
// Driver for class String
#include <iostream.h>
#include "string2.h"

main()
{
   String s1("happy"), s2(" birthday"), s3;

   // test overloaded equality and relational operators
   cout << "s1 is \"" << s1 << "\"; s2 is \"" << s2
        << "\"; s3 is empty\n"
        << "The results of comparing s2 and s1:"
        << "\ns2 == s1 yields " << (s2 == s1)
        << "\ns2 != s1 yields " << (s2 != s1)
        << "\ns2 >  s1 yields " << (s2 > s1)
        << "\ns2 <  s1 yields " << (s2 < s1)
        << "\ns2 >= s1 yields " << (s2 >= s1)
        << "\ns2 <= s1 yields " << (s2 <= s1) << "\n\n";

   // test overloaded String empty (!) operator
   cout << "Testing !s3:\n";
   if (!s3) {
      cout << "s3 is empty; assigning s1 to s3;\n";
      s3 = s1;              // test overloaded assignment
      cout << "s3 is \"" << s3 << "\"\n\n";
   }
```

Fig. 18.5 Driver for testing class **String** (part 6 of 8).

```
    // test overloaded String concatenation operator
    cout << "s1 += s2 yields s1 = ";
    s1 += s2;                      // test overloaded concatenation
    cout << s1 << "\n\n";

    // test conversion constructor
    cout << "s1 += \" to you\" yields\n";
    s1 += " to you";               // test conversion constructor
    cout << "s1 = " << s1 << "\n\n";

    // test overloaded function call operator () for substring
    cout << "The substring of s1 starting at\n"
         << "location 0 for 14 characters, s1(0, 14), is: "
         << s1(0, 14) << "\n\n";

    // test substring "to-end-of-String" option
    cout << "The substring of s1 starting at\n"
         << "location 15, s1(15, 0), is: "
         << s1(15, 0) << "\n\n";   // 0 means "to end of string"

    // test copy constructor
    String *s4Ptr = new String(s1);
    cout << "*s4Ptr = " << *s4Ptr << "\n\n";

    // test assignment (=) operator with self-assignment
    cout << "assigning *s4Ptr to *s4Ptr\n";
    *s4Ptr = *s4Ptr;               // test overloaded self-assignment
    cout << "*s4Ptr = " << *s4Ptr << endl;

    // test destructor
    delete s4Ptr;

    // test using subscript operator to create lvalue
    s1[0] = 'H';
    s1[6] = 'B';
    cout << "\ns1 after s1[0] = 'H' and s1[6] = 'B' is: "
         << s1 << "\n\n";

    // test subscript out of range
    cout << "Attempt to assign 'd' to s1[30] yields:\n";
    s1[30] = 'd';       // ERROR: subscript out of range

    return 0;
}
```

Fig. 18.5   Driver for testing class `String` (part 7 of 8).

18.11 Overloading ++ and --

All four increment and decrement operators—preincrement, postincrement, predecrement, and postdecrement—can be overloaded. We will see how the compiler indicates that the prefix version or the postfix version of an increment or decrement operator is being used.

```
Conversion constructor: happy
Conversion constructor:  birthday
Conversion constructor:
s1 is "happy"; s2 is " birthday"; s3 is empty
The results of comparing s2 and s1:
s2 == s1 yields 0
s2 != s1 yields 1
s2 >  s1 yields 0
s2 <  s1 yields 1
s2 >= s1 yields 0
s2 <= s1 yields 1

Testing !s3:
s3 is empty; assigning s1 to s3;
operator= called
s3 is "happy"

s1 += s2 yields s1 = happy birthday

s1 += " to you" yields
Conversion constructor:  to you
Destructor:  to you
s1 = happy birthday to you

Conversion constructor:
The substring of s1 starting at
location 0 for 14 characters, s1(0, 14), is: happy birthday

Conversion constructor:
The substring of s1 starting at
location 15, s1(15, 0), is: to you

Copy constructor: happy birthday to you
*s4Ptr = happy birthday to you

assigning *s4Ptr to *s4Ptr
operator= called
Attempted assignment of a String to itself
*s4Ptr = happy birthday to you
Destructor: happy birthday to you

s1 after s1[0] = 'H' and s1[6] = 'B' is: Happy Birthday to you

Attempt to assign 'd' to s1[30] yields:
Assertion failed: subscript >= 0 && subscript < length,
   file STRING2.CPP, line 98
Abnormal program termination
```

Fig. 18.5   Output from driver for testing class `String` (part 8 of 8).

To overload the increment operator to allow both preincrement and postincrement usage, each overloaded operator function must have a distinct signature so the compiler will be able to determine which version of `++` is intended. The prefix versions are overloaded exactly as any other prefix unary operator would be.

Suppose, for example, that we want to add 1 to the day in **Date** object **d1**. When the compiler sees the preincrementing expression

```
++d1
```

the compiler generates the member function call

```
d1.operator++()
```

whose prototype would be

```
Date operator++();
```

If the preincrementing is implemented as a nonmember function, when the compiler sees the expression

```
++d1
```

the compiler generates the function call

```
operator++(d1)
```

whose prototype would be declared in the **Date** class as

```
friend Date operator++(Date &);
```

Overloading the postincrementing operator presents a bit of a challenge because the compiler must be able to distinguish between the signatures of the overloaded preincrement and postincrement operator functions. The convention that has been adopted in C++ is that when the compiler sees the postincrementing expression

```
d1++
```

it will generate the member function call

```
d1.operator++(0)
```

whose prototype would be

```
Date operator++(int)
```

The 0 is strictly a dummy value so that the argument list of **operator++** used for postincrementing is distinguishable from the argument list of **operator++** used for preincrementing.

If the postincrementing is implemented as a nonmember function, when the compiler sees the expression

```
d1++
```

the compiler generates the function call

```
operator++(d1, 0)
```

whose prototype would be

```
friend Date operator++(Date &, int);
```

Once again, the **0 int** agrument is used by the compiler so that the argument list of **operator++** used for postincrementing is distinguishable from the argument list for preincrementing.

Everything we have said in this section for overloading preincrement and postincrement operators applies to overloading predecrement and postdecrement operators. In the next section, we examine a **Date** class that uses overloaded preincrement and postincrement operators.

18.12 Case Study: A Date Class

Figure 18.6 illustrates a **Date** class. The class uses overloaded preincrement and postincrement operators to add 1 to the day in a **Date** object.

The class provides the following member functions: an overloaded stream-insertion operator, a default constructor, a **setDate** function, an overloaded preincrement operator function, an overloaded postincrement operator function, and an overloaded addition assignment operator (**+=**).

The driver program in **main** creates the date objects **d1** which is initialized to January 1, 1990; **d2** which is initialized to December 27, 1992; and **d3** which is initialized to an invalid date. The **Date** constructor calls **setDate** to validate the month, day, and year specified. If the month is invalid it is set to 1. An invalid year is set to 1900. An invalid day is set to 1.

The driver program outputs each of the constructed **Date** objects using the overloaded stream-insertion operator. The overloaded operator **+=** is used to add 7 days to **d2**. Then the **setDate** function is used to set **d3** to February 28, 1992. Next, a new **Date** object, **d4**, is set to March 18, 1969. Then **d4** is incremented by 1 with the overloaded preincrement operator. The date is printed before and after the preincrementing to confirm that it worked correctly. Finally, **d4** is incremented with the overloaded postincrement operator. The date is printed before and after the postincrementing to confirm that it worked correctly.

Overloading the preincrementing operator is straightforward. The program calls utility function **helpIncrement** to do the actual incrementing. This function must deal with wraparounds or carries that occur when we attempt to increment a day of the month which is already at its maximum value. These carries require that the month be incremented. If the month is already 12, then the year must also be incremented.

The overloaded preincrement operator returns an incremented *copy* of the current object. This occurs because the current object, ***this**, is returned as a **Date**. This actually invokes the copy constructor.

Overloading the postincrement operator is a bit trickier. To emulate the effect of the postincrement, we must return an unincremented copy of the **Date** object. On entry to **operator++**, we save the current object (***this**) in **temp**. Then we call **helpIncrement** to increment the object. Then we return the unincremented copy of the object in **temp**.

```
// DATE1.H
// Definition of class Date
#ifndef DATE1_H
#define DATE1_H
#include <iostream.h>

class Date {
   friend ostream &operator<<(ostream &, const Date &);
public:
   Date(int m = 1, int d = 1, int y = 1900);  // def. constructor
   void setDate(int, int, int);  // set the date
   Date operator++();            // preincrement
   Date operator++(int);         // postincrement
   Date &operator+=(int);        // add days, modify object
private:
   int month;
   int day;
   int year;
   static int days[];      // array of days per month
   void helpIncrement();   // utility function
};

#endif
```

Fig. 18.6 Definition of class **Date** (part 1 of 6).

```
// DATE1.CPP
// Member function definitions for Date class
#include <iostream.h>
#include "date1.h"

// Initialize static member at file scope;
// one class-wide copy.
int Date::days[] = {0, 31, 28, 31, 30, 31, 30,
                    31, 31, 30, 31, 30, 31};

// Date constructor
Date::Date(int m, int d, int y) { setDate(m, d, y); }

// Set the date
void Date::setDate(int mm, int dd, int yy)
{
   month = (mm >= 1 && mm <= 12) ? mm : 1;
   year = (yy >= 1900 && yy <= 2100) ? yy : 1900;

   // test for a leap year
   if (month == 2 && year % 4 == 0 && (year % 400 == 0 ||
                                       year % 100 != 0))
      day = (dd >= 1 && dd <= 29) ? dd : 1;
   else
      day = (dd >= 1 && dd <= days[month]) ? dd : 1;
}
```

Fig. 18.6 Member function definition for class **Date** (part 2 of 6).

```cpp
// Preincrement operator overloaded as a member function.

Date Date::operator++()
{
   helpIncrement();
   return *this;  // value return; not a reference return
}

// Postincrement operator overloaded as a member function.
// Note that the dummy integer parameter does not have a
// parameter name.

Date Date::operator++(int)
{
   Date temp = *this;
   helpIncrement();

   // return non-incremented, saved, temporary object
   return temp;    // value return; not a reference return
}

// Add a specific number of days to a date

Date &Date::operator+=(int additionalDays)
{
   for (int i = 1; i <= additionalDays; i++)
      helpIncrement();

   return *this;    // enables concatenation
}

// Function to help increment the date

void Date::helpIncrement()
{
   // test for a leap year first
   if (month == 2 && day < 29 && year % 4 == 0 &&
      (year % 400 == 0 || year % 100 != 0))
      ++day;
   else if (day < Date::days[month])  // not last day of month
      ++day;
   else if (month < 12) {  // last day of month < December
      ++month;
      day = 1;
   }
   else {                     // December 31
      month = 1;
      day = 1;
      ++year;
   }
}
```

Fig. 18.6   Member function definition for class **Date** (part 3 of 6).

```
// Overloaded output operator
ostream &operator<<(ostream &output, const Date &d)
{
    static char *monthName[13] = {"", "January",
        "February", "March", "April", "May", "June",
        "July", "August", "September", "October",
        "November", "December"};

    output << monthName[d.month] << ' '
           << d.day << ", " << d.year;

    return output;    // enables concatenation
}
```

Fig. 18.6   Member function definition for class **Date** (part 4 of 6).

```
// FIG18_6.CPP
// Driver for class Date
#include <iostream.h>
#include "date1.h"

main()
{
    Date d1, d2(12, 27, 1992), d3(0, 99, 8045);
    cout << "d1 is " << d1
         << "\nd2 is " << d2
         << "\nd3 is " << d3;

    cout << "\n\nd2 += 7 is " << (d2 += 7) << "\n\n";

    d3.setDate(2, 28, 1992);
    cout << "  d3 is " << d3;
    cout << "\n++d3 is " << ++d3 << "\n\n";

    Date d4(3, 18, 1969);

    cout << "Testing the preincrement operator:\n"
         << "  d4 is " << d4
         << "\n++d4 is " << ++d4
         << "\n  d4 is " << d4;

    cout << "\n\nTesting the postincrement operator:\n"
         << "  d4 is " << d4
         << "\nd4++ is " << d4++
         << "\n  d4 is " << d4 << endl;

    return 0;
}
```

Fig.18.6   Driver for class **Date** (part 5 of 6).

```
d1 is January 1, 1900
d2 is December 27, 1992
d3 is January 1, 1900

d2 += 7 is January 3, 1993

  d3 is February 28, 1992
++d3 is February 29, 1992

Testing the preincrement operator:
  d4 is March 18, 1969
++d4 is March 19, 1969
  d4 is March 19, 1969

Testing the postincrement operator:
  d4 is March 19, 1969
d4++ is March 19, 1969
  d4 is March 20, 1969
```

Fig.18.6   Output from driver for class **Date** (part 6 of 6).

Summary

- The operator **<<** is used for multiple purposes in C++—as the stream-insertion operator and as the left-shift operator. This is an example of operator overloading. Similarly, **>>** is also overloaded; it is used both as the stream-extraction operator and as the right-shift operator.

- More generally, C++ enables the programmer to overload most operators to be sensitive to the context in which they are used. The compiler generates the appropriate code based on the manner in which the operator is used.

- Operator overloading contributes to C++'s extensibility.

- Operators are overloaded by writing a function definition (with a header and body). The function name becomes the keyword **operator** followed by the symbol for the operator being overloaded.

- To use an operator on class objects, that operator *must* be overloaded—with two exceptions. The assignment operator (**=**) may be used with every class to perform a default memberwise copy without overloading. The address operator (**&**) may also be used with objects of any class without overloading; it simply returns the address of the object in memory.

- The point of operator overloading is to provide the same concise expressions for user-defined types that C++ provides with its rich collection of operators that work on built-in types.

- Most of C++'s operators can be overloaded.

- The precedence and associativity of an operator can not be changed by overloading.

- Default arguments can not be used to overload an operator.

- It is not possible to change the number of operands an operator takes: Overloaded unary operators remain as unary operators; overloaded binary operators remain as binary operators.

- It is not possible to create symbols for new operators; only existing operators may be overloaded.

- The meaning of how an operator works on objects of built-in types cannot be changed by overloading.

- When overloading (), [], ->, or =, the operator overloading function must be declared as a class member.

- Operator functions can be member functions or nonmember functions.

- When an operator function is implemented as a member function, the leftmost operand must be a class object (or a reference to a class object) of the operator's class.

- If the left operand must be an object of a different class, this operator function must be implemented as a nonmember function.

- Operator member functions are called only when the left operand of a binary operator is specifically an object of that class, or when the single operand of a unary operator is an object of that class.

- One might choose a nonmember function to overload an operator in order to enable the operator to be commutative.

- A unary operator can be overloaded as a nonstatic member function with no arguments or as a nonmember function with one argument; that argument must be either an object of a user-defined type or a reference to an object of a user-defined type.

- A binary operator can be overloaded as a nonstatic member function with one argument, or as a nonmember function with two arguments (one of those arguments must be either a class object or a reference to a class object).

- The array subscript operator [] is not restricted for use only with arrays; it can be used to select elements from other kinds of container classes such as linked lists, strings, dictionaries, and so on. Also, subscripts no longer have to be integers; characters or strings could be used, for example.

- A copy constructor is used to initialize an object with another object of the same class. Copy constructors are also invoked whenever a copy of an object is needed, such as in call by value, and when returning a value from a called function.

- The compiler does not automatically know how to convert between user-defined types and built-in types. The programmer must explicitly specify how such conversions are to occur. Such conversions can be performed with conversion constructors (i.e., single-argument constructors) that simply turn objects of other types into objects of a particular class.

- A conversion operator (or cast) can be used to convert an object of one class into an object of another class or into an object of a built-in type. Such a conversion operator must be a nonstatic member function; this kind of conversion operator can not be a friend function.

- A conversion constructor is a single argument constructor used to convert the argument into an object of the constructor's class. The compiler can call such a constructor implicitly.

- The assignment operator is the most frequently overloaded operator. It is normally used to assign an object to another object of the same class, but through the use of conversion constructors it can also be used to assign between classes.

- If an overloaded assignment operator is not defined, assignment is still allowed, but it defaults to a memberwise copy of each data member. In some cases this is acceptable. For objects that contain pointers to dynamically allocated storage, memberwise copy results in two different objects pointing to the same dynamically allocated storage. When the destructor for either of these objects is called, the dynamically allocated storage is released. If the other object then refers to that storage, the result is undefined.

- To overload the increment operator to allow both preincrement and postincrement usage, each overloaded operator function must have a distinct signature so the compiler will be able to determine which version of ++ is intended. The prefix versions are overloaded exactly as any other prefix unary operator. Providing a unique signature to the postincrement operator function is achieved by providing a second argument—which must be of type **int**. Actually, the user does not supply a value for this special integer argument. It is there simply to help the compiler distinguish between prefix and postfix versions of increment and decrement operators.

Terminology

built-in type	member function overloaded operator
class **Array**	nonoverloadable operators
class **Date**	**operator** keyword
class **String**	operator overloading
concatenated function calls	operators as functions
conversion ambiguity resolution	overloadable operators
conversion constructor	overloaded == operator
conversion function	overloaded != operator
conversion operator	overloaded < operator
conversions between classes of different	overloaded <= operator
types	overloaded > operator
conversions between built-in types and	overloaded >= operator
classes	overloaded assignment (=) operator
copy constructor	overloaded [] operator
explicit type conversions (with casts)	overloading
friend function overloaded operator	overloading a binary operator
function overloading	overloading a unary operator
implicit type conversions	postfix operator overloading

prefix operator overloading   user-defined type
user-defined conversion

Common Programming Errors

18.1   Attempting to create new operators.

18.2   Attempting to modify how an operator works with objects of built-in types.

18.3   Assuming that overloading an operator (such as **+**) automatically overloads related operators (such as **+=**). Operators can be overloaded only explicitly; there is no implicit overloading.

18.4   Not testing for and avoiding self assignment when overloading the assignment operator for
a class that includes a pointer to dynamic storage.

18.5   Not providing an overloaded assignment operator and a copy constructor for a class when
objects of that class contain pointers to dynamically allocated storage.

Good Programming Practices

18.1   Use operator overloading when it makes a program clearer than accomplishing the same
operations with explicit function calls.

18.2   Avoid excessive or inconsistent use of operator overloading as this can make a program
cryptic and difficult to read.

18.3   Overload operators to perform the same function or closely similar functions on class objects as the operators perform on objects of built-in types.

18.4   Before writing C++ programs with overloaded operators, consult the C++ manuals for your
compiler to become aware of various restrictions and requirements unique to particular operators.

18.5   When overloading unary operators, it is preferable to make the operator functions class
members instead of nonmember friend functions. This is a tidier solution. Friend functions
and classes should be avoided unless they are absolutely necessary. The use of friends violates the encapsulation of a class.

18.6   A destructor, the assignment operator, and a copy constructor for a class are usually
provided as a group.

Performance Tips

18.1   It is possible to overload an operator as a nonmember, nonfriend function, but such a
function needing access to a class's private or protected data would need to use set or get
functions provided in that class's public interface. The overhead of calling these functions
could cause poor performance.

18.2   Having the overloaded **+=** concatenation operator that takes a single argument of type
const char * operates more efficiently than having to do the implicit conversion first
then the concatenation. Implicit conversions requires less code and cause fewer errors.

Software Engineering Observations

18.1   At least one argument of an operator function must be a class object or a reference to a
class object. This prevents programmers from changing the meaning of how operators
work on objects of built-in types.

18.2   New input/output capabilities for user-defined types can be added to C++ without modifying the declarations or private data members for either the **ostream** class or the

istream class. This promotes the extensibility of the C++ programming language—one of C++'s most attractive aspects.

18.3   It is possible to prevent one class object from being assigned to another. This is done by defining the assignment operator as a private member of the class.

Self-Review Exercises

18.1   Fill in the blanks in each of the following:

a) Suppose **a** and **b** are integer variables and we form the sum **a + b**. Now suppose **c** and **d** are floating-point variables and we form the sum **c + d**. The two + operators here are clearly being used for different purposes. This is an example of _____.

b) The keyword _____ introduces an overloaded operator function definition.

c) To use operators on class objects, they must be overloaded with the exception of the operators _____ and _____.

d) The _____ and _____ of an operator can not be changed by overloading.

18.2   Explain the multiple meanings of the operators **< <** and **> >** in C++.

18.3   In what context might the name **operator/** be used in C++?

18.4   (True/False) In C++, only existing operators can be overloaded.

18.5   How does the precedence of an overloaded operator in C++ compare with the precedence of the original operator?

Answers to Self-Review Exercises

18.1   a) operator overloading. b) **operator**. c) assignement (=), address(**&**). d) precedence, associativity.

18.2   The operator **> >** is both the right-shift operator and the stream-extraction operator depending on its context. The operator **< <** is both the left-shift operator and the stream-insertion operator depending on its context.

18.3   For operator overloading: It would be the name of a function that would provide a new version of the **/** operator.

18.4   True.

18.5   Identical.

Exercises

18.6   Give as many examples as you can of operator overloading implicit in C. Give as many examples as you can of operator overloading implicit in C++. Give a reasonable example of a situation in which you might want to overload an operator explicitly in C++.

18.7   The C++ operators that can not be overloaded are _____, _____, _____, _____, and _____.

18.8   String concatenation requires two operands—the two strings that are to be concatenated. In the text we showed how to implement an overloaded concatenation operator that concatenates the second **String** object to the right of the first **String** object, thus modifying the first **String** object. In some applications, it is desirable to produce a concatenated **String** object without modifying the two **String** arguments. Implement **operator+** to allow operations such as

```
string1 = string2 + string3;
```

18.9   *(Ultimate operator overloading exercise)* To appreciate the care that should go into select-ing operators for overloading, list each of C++'s overloadable operators and for each list a possible meaning (or several, if appropriate) for each of several classes you have studied in this course. We suggest you try:

a)   Array
b)   Stack
c)   String

After doing this, comment on what operators seem to have meaning for a wide variety of classes. What operators seem to be of little value for overloading? What operators seem ambiguous?

18.10   Now work the process described in the previous problem in reverse. List each of C++'s overloadable operators. For each, list what you feel is perhaps the "ultimate operation" the operator should be used to represent. If there are several excellent operations, list them all.

18.11   *(Project)* C++ is an evolving language, and new languages are always being developed. What additional operators would you recommend adding to C++ or to a future language like C++ that would support both procedural programming and object-oriented programming? Write a careful justification. You might consider sending your suggestions to the ANSI C++ Committee.

18.12   One nice example of overloading the function call operator `()` is to allow the more com-mon form of double array subscripting. Instead of saying

```
chessBoard[row][column]
```

for an array of objects, overload the function call operator to allow the alternate form

```
chessBoard(row, column)
```

18.13   Overload the subscript operator to return a given member of a linked list.

18.14   Overload the subscript operator to return the largest element of a collection, the second largest, the third largest, etc.

18.15   Consider class `Complex` shown in Fig. 18.7. The class enables operations on so-called *complex numbers*. These are numbers of the form `realPart + imaginaryPart * i` where *i* has the value:

$$\sqrt{-1}$$

a)   Modify the class to enable input and output of complex numbers through the over-loaded `>>` and `<<` operators, respectively (you should remove the print function from the class).
b)   Overload the multiplication operator to enable multiplication of two complex numbers as in algebra.
c)   Overload the `==` and `!=` operators to allow comparisons of complex numbers.

18.16   A machine with 32-bit integers can represent integers in the range of approximately −2 bil-lion to +2 billion. This fixed-size restriction is rarely troublesome. But there are many applications in which we would like to be able to use a much wider range of integers. This is what C++ was built to do, namely create powerful new data types. Consider class `HugeInt` of Fig. 18.8. Study the class carefully, then

a)   Describe precisely how it operates.
b)   What restrictions does the class have?
c)   Modify the class to be able to process arbitrarily large integers. (Hint: Use a linked list to represent a `HugeInt`.)
d)   Overload the `*` multiplication operator.
e)   Overload the `/` division operator.
f)   Overload all the relational and equality operators.

```
// COMPLEX1.H
// Definition of class Complex
#ifndef COMPLEX1_H
#define COMPLEX1_H

class Complex {
public:
   Complex(double = 0.0, double = 0.0);      // constructor
   Complex operator+(const Complex &) const; // addition
   Complex operator-(const Complex &) const; // subtraction
   Complex &operator=(const Complex &);      // assignment
   void print() const;                       // output
private:
   double real;        // real part
   double imaginary;   // imaginary part
};

#endif
```

Fig. 18.7   Definition of class **Complex** (part 1 of 5).

```
// COMPLEX1.CPP
// Member function definitions for class Complex
#include <iostream.h>
#include "complex1.h"

// Constructor
Complex::Complex(double r, double i)
{
   real = r;
   imaginary = i;
}

// Overloaded addition operator
Complex Complex::operator+(const Complex &operand2) const
{
   Complex sum;
   sum.real = real + operand2.real;
   sum.imaginary = imaginary + operand2.imaginary;
   return sum;
}

// Overloaded subtraction operator
Complex Complex::operator-(const Complex &operand2) const
{
   Complex diff;
   diff.real = real - operand2.real;
   diff.imaginary = imaginary - operand2.imaginary;
   return diff;
}
```

Fig. 18.7   Member function definitions for class **Complex** (part 2 of 5).

```
// Overloaded = operator
Complex& Complex::operator=(const Complex &right)
{
   real = right.real;
   imaginary = right.imaginary;
   return *this;    // enables concatenation
}

// Display a Complex object in the form: (a, b)
void Complex::print() const
   { cout << '(' << real << ", " << imaginary << ')'; }
```

Fig. 18.7 Member function definitions for class **Complex** (part 3 of 5).

```
// FIG18_7.CPP
// Driver for class Complex
#include <iostream.h>
#include "complex1.h"

main()
{
   Complex x, y(4.3, 8.2), z(3.3, 1.1);

   cout << "x: ";
   x.print();
   cout << "\ny: ";
   y.print();
   cout << "\nz: ";
   z.print();

   x = y + z;
   cout << "\n\nx = y + z:\n";
   x.print();
   cout << " = ";
   y.print();
   cout << " + ";
   z.print();

   x = y - z;
   cout << "\n\nx = y - z:\n";
   x.print();
   cout << " = ";
   y.print();
   cout << " - ";
   z.print();
   cout << '\n';

   return 0;
}
```

Fig. 18.7 Driver for class **Complex** (part 4 of 5).

```
x:  (0, 0)
y:  (4.3, 8.2)
z:  (3.3, 1.1)

x = y + z:
(7.6, 9.3) = (4.3, 8.2) + (3.3, 1.1)

x = y - z:
(1, 7.1) = (4.3, 8.2) - (3.3, 1.1)
```

Fig. 18.7   Output from driver for class **Complex** (part 5 of 5).

```
// HUGEINT1.H
// Definition of the HugeInt class
#ifndef HUGEINT1_H
#define HUGEINT1_H

#include <iostream.h>

class HugeInt {
   friend ostream &operator<<(ostream &, HugeInt &);
public:
   HugeInt(long = 0);              // conversion constructor
   HugeInt(const char *);          // conversion constructor
   HugeInt operator+(HugeInt &);   // addition
private:
   short integer[30];
};

#endif
```

Fig. 18.8   A user-defined huge integer class (part 1 of 4).

```
// HUGEINT1.CPP
// Member and friend function definitions for class HugeInt
#include <string.h>
#include "hugeint1.h"

// Conversion constructor
HugeInt::HugeInt(long val)
{
   for (int i = 0; i <= 29; i++)
      integer[i] = 0;   // initialize array to zero

   for (i = 29; val != 0 && i >= 0; i--) {
      integer[i] = val % 10;
      val /= 10;
   }
}
```

Fig. 18.8   A user-defined huge integer class (part 2 of 4).

```
HugeInt::HugeInt(const char *string)
{
    int i, j;

    for (i = 0; i <= 29; i++)
        integer[i] = 0;

    for (i = 30 - strlen(string), j = 0; i <= 29; i++, j++)
        integer[i] = string[j] - '0';
}

// Addition
HugeInt HugeInt::operator+(HugeInt &op2)
{
    HugeInt temp;
    int carry = 0;

    for (int i = 29; i >= 0; i--) {
        temp.integer[i] = integer[i] + op2.integer[i] + carry;

        if (temp.integer[i] > 9) {
            temp.integer[i] %= 10;
            carry = 1;
        }
        else
            carry = 0;
    }

    return temp;
}

ostream& operator<<(ostream &output, HugeInt &num)
{
    for (int i = 0; (num.integer[i] == 0) && (i <= 29); i++)
        ; // skip leading zeros

    if (i == 30)
        output << 0;
    else
        for ( ; i <= 29; i++)
            output << num.integer[i];

    return output;
}
```

Fig. 18.8   A user-defined huge integer class (part 3 of 4).

18.17 Create a class `rationalNumber` (fractions) with the following capabilities:
   a) Create a constructor that prevents a 0 denominator in a fraction, reduces or simplifies fractions that are not in reduced form, and avoids negative denominators.
   b) Overload the addition, subtraction, multiplication and division operators for this class.
   c) Overload the relational and equality operators for this class.

```
// FIG18_8.CPP
// Test driver for HugeInt class
#include <iostream.h>
#include "hugeint1.h"

main()
{
   HugeInt n1(7654321), n2(7891234),
           n3("9999999999999999999999999999"),
           n4("1"), n5;

   cout << "n1 is " << n1 << "\nn2 is " << n2
        << "\nn3 is " << n3 << "\nn4 is " << n4
        << "\nn5 is " << n5 << "\n\n";

   n5 = n1 + n2;
   cout << n1 << " + " << n2 << " = " << n5 << "\n\n";

   cout << n3 << " + " << n4 << "\n= " << (n3 + n4) << "\n\n";

   n5 = n1 + 9;
   cout << n1 << " + " << 9 << " = " << n5 << "\n\n";

   n5 = n2 + "10000";
   cout << n2 << " + " << "10000" << " = " << n5 << "\n\n";

   return 0;
}
```

```
n1 is 7654321
n2 is 7891234
n3 is 9999999999999999999999999999
n4 is 1
n5 is 0

7654321 + 7891234 = 15545555

9999999999999999999999999999 + 1
= 10000000000000000000000000000

7654321 + 9 = 7654330

7891234 + 10000 = 7901234
```

Fig. 18.8   A user-defined huge integer class (part 4 of 4).

18.18   The `sizeof` operator on a `String` object only returns the size of the `String` object data members; it does not include the length of the `String` space allocated by `new`. Overload operator `sizeof` to return the size of a `String` object including the dynamically allocated memory.

18.19   Study the C string handling library functions and implement each of the functions as part of the **String** class. Then, use these functions to perform text manipulations.

18.20   Develop class **Polynomial**. The internal representation of a **Polynomial** is a linked list of terms. Each term contains a coefficient and an exponent. The term

$$2x^4$$

has a coefficient of 2 and an exponent of 4. Develop a full class containing proper constructor and destructor functions as well as *set* and *get* functions. The class should also provide the following overloaded operator capabilities:

    a)   Overload the addition operator (**+**) to add two **Polynomials**.
    b)   Overload the subtraction operator (**-**) to subtract two **Polynomials**.
    c)   Overload the assignment operator to assign one **Polynomial** to another.
    d)   Overload the multiplication operator (*****) to multiply two **Polynomials**.
    e)   Overload the addition assignment operator (**+=**), the subtraction assignment operator (**-=**), the multiplication assignment operator (***=**).

19

Inheritance

Objectives
- To be able to create new classes by inheriting from existing classes.
- To understand how inheritance promotes software reuseability.
- To understand the notions of base classes and derived classes.
- To be able to use multiple inheritance to derive a class from several base classes.

Say not you know another entirely, till you have divided an inheritance with him.
Johann Kasper Lavater

This method is to define as the number of a class the class of all classes similar to the given class.
Bertrand Russell

A deck of cards was built like the purest of hierarchies, with every card a master to those below it, a lackey to those above it.
Ely Culbertson

Good as it is to inherit a library, it is better to collect one.
Augustine Birrell

Save base authority from others' books.
William Shakespeare
Love's Labour's Lost

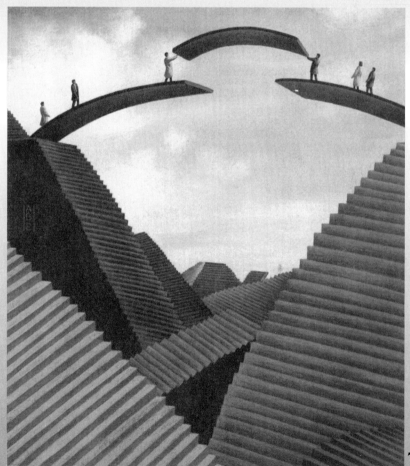

Outline

19.1 Introduction

In this and the next chapter we discuss two of the most important capabilities object-oriented programming provides—*inheritance* and *polymorphism.* Inheritance is a form of *software reusability* in which new classes are created from existing classes by absorbing their attributes and behaviors and embellishing these with capabilities the new classes require. Software reusability saves time in program development, encourages the reuse of proven and debugged high-quality software, and reduces problems after a system becomes functional. These are exciting possibilities. Polymorphism enables us to write programs in a general fashion to process a wide variety of existing and yet-to-be-specified related classes. Inheritance and polymorphism are effective techniques for dealing with software complexity.

When creating a new class, instead of writing completely new data members and member functions, the programmer can designate that the new class is to *inherit* the data members and member functions of a previously defined *base class.* The new class is re ferred to as a *derived class.* Each derived class itself becomes a candidate to be a base class for some future derived class. With *single inheritance,* a class is derived from only one base class. With *multiple inheritance,* a derived class inherits from multiple (possibly unrelated) base classes. A derived class normally adds data members and member functions of its own, so a derived class is generally larger than its base class. A derived class is more specific than its base class and represents a smaller group of objects. With single inheritance, the derived class starts out essentially the same as the base class. The real strength of inheritance comes from the ability to define in the derived class additions, replacements, or refinements to the features inherited from the base class.

Every object of a derived class is also an object of that derived class's base class. However, the converse is not true—base-class objects are not objects of that base class's derived classes. We will take advantage of this "derived-class-object-is-a-base-class-object" relationship to perform some interesting manipulations. For example, we can thread a wide variety of different objects related through inheritance into a linked list of base-class objects. This allows a variety of objects to be processed in a general way. As we will see in this and the next chapter, this is a key thrust of object-oriented programming.

We add a new form of member access control in this chapter, namely protected access. Derived classes and their friends receive favored treatment over other functions in accessing protected base-class members.

Experience in building software systems indicates that large portions of the code deal with closely related special cases. It becomes difficult in such systems to see the "big picture" because the designer and the programmer become preoccupied with the special cases. Object-oriented programming provides several ways of "seeing the forest through the trees"—a process sometimes called *abstraction.*

If a program is loaded with closely related special cases, then it is common to see `switch` statements that distinguish among the special cases and provide the processing logic to deal with each case individually. In Chapter 20, we show how to use inheritance and polymorphism to replace `switch` logic with simpler logic.

We distinguish between *"is a" relationships* and *"has a" relationships.* "Is a" is inheritance. In an "is a" relationship, an object of a derived-class type may also be treated as an object of the base-class type. "Has a" is composition (see Fig. 17.4). In a "has a" relationship, a class object has one or more objects of other classes as members.

A derived class can not access the private members of its base class; allowing this would violate the encapsulation of the base class. A derived class can, however, access the public and protected members of its base class. Base-class members that should not be accessible to a derived class via inheritance are declared private in the base class. A derived class can access private members of the base class only through access functions provided in the base class's public interface.

One problem with inheritance is that a derived class can inherit public member functions that it does not need to have or should expressly not have. When a base-class member is inappropriate for a derived class, that member can be redefined in the derived class with an appropriate implementation.

Most exciting is the notion that new classes can inherit from existing *class libraries.* Organizations develop their own class libraries and can take advantage of other libraries available worldwide. The view is that someday software will be constructed from *stan dardized reusable components* exactly as hardware is often constructed today. This will help to meet the challenges of developing the ever more powerful software we will need in the future.

19.2 Base Classes and Derived Classes

Often an object of one class really "is an" object of another class as well. A rectangle certainly *is a* quadrilateral (as is a square, a parallelogram, and a trapezoid). Thus, class **Rectangle** can be said to *inherit* from class **Quadrilateral**. In this context, class **Quadrilateral** is called a *base class* and class **Rectangle** is called a *derived class*. A rectangle *is a* specific type of quadrilateral, but it is incorrect to claim that a quadrilateral *is a* rectangle. Figure 19.1 shows several simple inheritance examples.

Other object-oriented programming languages such as Smalltalk use different terminology: In inheritance, the base class is called the *superclass* and the derived class is called the *subclass*. Because inheritance normally produces derived classes that are larger than base classes, the terms superclass and subclass seem inappropriate; we will avoid these terms.

Inheritance forms tree-like hierarchical structures. A base class exists in a hierarchical relationship with its derived classes. A class can certainly exist by itself, but it is when a class is used with the mechanism of inheritance that the class becomes either a base class that supplies attributes and behaviors to other classes, or the class becomes a derived class that inherits those attributes and behaviors.

Let us develop a simple inheritance hierarchy. A typical university community has thousands of people who are community members. These people consist of employees and students. Employees are either faculty members or staff members. Faculty members are either administrators (such as deans and department chairpersons) or teaching faculty. This yields the inheritance hierarchy shown in Fig. 19.2.

Base class	Derived classes
Student	CommuterStudent ResidentStudent
Shape	Circle Triangle Rectangle
Loan	CarLoan HomeImprovementLoan MortgageLoan
Employee	FacultyMember StaffMember
Account	CheckingAccount SavingsAccount

Fig. 19.1 Some simple inheritance examples.

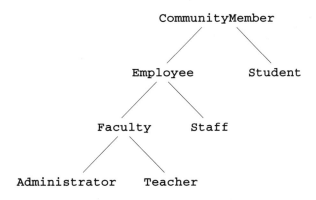

Fig. 19.2 An inheritance hierarchy for university community members.

Another substantial inheritance hierarchy is the **Shape** hierarchy of Fig. 19.3. A common observation among students studying object-oriented programming for the first time is that there are abundant examples of hierarchies in the real world. It is just that these students have never been asked to categorize the real world in this manner, so it takes some adjustment in their thinking.

To specify that class **CommissionWorker** is derived from class **Employee**, class **CommissionWorker** would typically be defined as follows

```
class CommissionWorker : public Employee {
   ...
};
```

This is called *public inheritance* and is the type the reader is most likely to use. We will also discuss *private inheritance* and *protected inheritance*. With public inheritance, the public and protected members of the base class are inherited as public and protected members of the derived class, respectively.

It is possible to treat base-class objects and derived-class objects similarly. Commonality is expressed in the attributes and behaviors of the base class. Objects of any publicly derived class from a common base class can all be treated as objects of that base class.

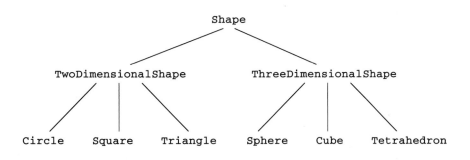

Fig. 19.3 A portion of a **Shape** class hierarchy.

We will consider many examples in which we can take advantage of this relationship with an ease of programming not available in non-object-oriented languages such as C.

19.3 Protected Members

Public members of a base class are accessible by all functions in the program. Private members of a base class are accessible only by member functions and friends of the base class.

Protected access serves as an intermediate level of protection between public access and private access. Protected members of a base class may be accessed only by members and friends of the base class and by members and friends of derived classes.

Derived-class members can refer to public and protected members of the base class simply by using the member names. There is no need to use the scope-resolution operator. The current object is assumed.

19.4 Casting Base-Class Pointers to Derived-Class Pointers

An object of a publicly derived class can also be treated as an object of its corresponding base class. This makes possible some interesting manipulations. For example, despite the fact that objects of a variety of classes derived from a particular base class may be quite different from one another, we can still create a linked list of them—again, as long as we treat them as base-class objects. But the reverse is not true: A base-class object is not also automatically a derived-class object.

Common Programming Error 19.1
***
Treating a base-class object as a derived-class object can cause errors.

The programmer may, however, use an explicit cast to convert a base-class pointer to a derived-class pointer. But be careful—if such a pointer is to be dereferenced, then it should first be made to point to an object of the derived-class type.

Common Programming Error 19.2
***
Explicitly casting a base-class pointer that points to a base-class object into a derived-class pointer and then referring to derived-class members that do not exist in that object.

Our first example is shown in Fig. 19.4, parts 1 through 5. Parts 1 and 2 show the **Point** class definition and **Point** member function definitions. Parts 3 and 4 show the **Circle** class definition and **Circle** member function definition. Part 5 shows a driver program in which we demonstrate assigning derived-class pointers to base-class pointers and casting base-class pointers to derived-class pointers.

Let us first examine the **Point** class definition (Fig. 19.4, part 1). The public interface to **Point** contains member functions **setPoint**, **getX**, and **getY**. The data members **x** and **y** of **Point** are specified as **protected**. This prevents users of **Point** objects from directly accessing the data, but enables classes derived from **Point** to access the inherited data members directly. If the data were specified as **private**, the public member functions of **Point** would be used to access the data. Note that the **Point** overloaded stream insertion operator function (Fig. 19.4, part 2) is able to reference variables **x** and **y** directly because these are protected members of class **Point**. Note also that it is necessary to reference **x** and **y** through objects as in **p.x** and **p.y**. This is because the overloaded stream insertion operator function is not a member function of the class **Circle**, but is a friend of the class.

```
// POINT.H
// Definition of class Point
#ifndef POINT_H
#define POINT_H

class Point {
    friend ostream &operator<<(ostream &, const Point &);
public:
    Point(float = 0, float = 0);      // default constructor
    void setPoint(float, float);      // set coordinates
    float getX() const { return x; }  // get x coordinate
    float getY() const { return y; }  // get y coordinate
protected:           // accessible by derived classes
    float x, y;      // x and y coordinates of the Point
};

#endif
```

Fig. 19.4   Definition of class **Point** (part 1 of 5).

```
// POINT.CPP
// Member functions for class Point
#include <iostream.h>
#include "point.h"

// Constructor for class Point
Point::Point(float a, float b)
{
    x = a;
    y = b;
}

// Set x and y coordinates of Point
void Point::setPoint(float a, float b)
{
    x = a;
    y = b;
}

// Output Point (with overloaded stream insertion operator)
ostream &operator<<(ostream &output, const Point &p)
{
    output << '[' << p.x << ", " << p.y << ']';

    return output;    // enables concatenated calls
}
```

Fig. 19.4   Member function definitions for class **Point** (part 2 of 5).

```
// CIRCLE.H
// Definition of class Circle
#ifndef CIRCLE_H
#define CIRCLE_H

#include <iostream.h>
#include <iomanip.h>
#include "point.h"

class Circle : public Point {  // Circle inherits from Point
   friend ostream &operator<<(ostream &, const Circle &);
public:
   // default constructor
   Circle(float r = 0.0, float x = 0, float y = 0);

   void setRadius(float);     // set radius
   float getRadius() const;   // return radius
   float area() const;        // calculate area
protected:
   float radius;
};

#endif
```

Fig. 19.4 Definition of class **Circle** (part 3 of 5).

```
// CIRCLE.CPP
// Member function definitions for class Circle
#include "circle.h"

// Constructor for Circle calls constructor for Point
// with a member initializer then initializes radius.
Circle::Circle(float r, float a, float b)
   : Point(a, b)        // call base-class constructor
{ radius = r; }

// Set radius of Circle
void Circle::setRadius(float r) { radius = r; }

// Get radius of Circle
float Circle::getRadius() const { return radius; }

// Calculate area of Circle
float Circle::area() const
{ return 3.14159 * radius * radius; }

// Output a Circle in the form:
// Center = [x, y]; Radius = #.##
ostream &operator<<(ostream &output, const Circle &c)
{
   output << "Center = [" << c.x << ", " << c.y
          << "]; Radius = " << setiosflags(ios::showpoint)
          << setprecision(2) << c.radius;

   return output;    // enables concatenated calls
}
```

Fig. 19.4 Member function definition for class **Circle** (part 4 of 5).

```
// FIG19_4.CPP
// Casting base-class pointers to derived-class pointers

#include <iostream.h>
#include <iomanip.h>
#include "point.h"
#include "circle.h"

main()
{
    Point *pointPtr, p(3.5, 5.3);
    Circle *circlePtr, c(2.7, 1.2, 8.9);

    cout << "Point p: " << p << "\nCircle c: " << c << endl;

    // Treat a Circle as a Circle (with some casting)
    pointPtr = &c;     // assign address of Circle to pointPtr
    circlePtr = (Circle *) pointPtr;   // cast base to derived
    cout << "\nArea of c (via circlePtr): "
         << circlePtr->area() << endl;

    // DANGEROUS: Treat a Point as a Circle
    pointPtr = &p;     // assign address of Point to pointPtr
    circlePtr = (Circle *) pointPtr;   // cast base to derived
    cout << "\nRadius of object circlePtr points to: "
         << circlePtr->getRadius() << endl;

    return 0;
}
```

```
Point p: [3.5, 5.3]
Circle c: Center = [1.2, 8.9]; Radius = 2.70

Area of c (via circlePtr): 22.90

Radius of object circlePtr points to: 4.02e-38
```

Fig. 19.4 Casting base-class pointers to derived-class pointers (part 5 of 5).

Class **Circle** (Fig. 19.4, part 3) inherits from class **Point** with public inheritance. This is specified in the first line of the class definition

```
class Circle : public Point {   // Circle inherits from Point
```

The colon (:) in the header of the class definition indicates inheritance. The keyword **public** indicates the type of inheritance (see Section 19.7). All the members of class **Point** are inherited into class **Circle**. This means that the public interface to **Circle** includes the **Point** public member functions as well as the **Circle** member functions **area**, **setRadius**, and **getRadius**.

The **Circle** constructor (Fig. 19.4, part 4) must invoke the **Point** constructor to initialize the base-class portion of a **Circle** object. This is accomplished with the member initializer syntax introduced in Chapter 17 as follows

```
Circle::Circle(float r, float a, float b)
    : Point(a, b)          // call base-class constructor
```

The second line of the constructor function header invokes the **Point** constructor by name. Values **a** and **b** are passed from the **Circle** constructor to the **Point** constructor to initialize the base-class members **x** and **y**. Note that the **Circle** overloaded stream insertion operator function is able to reference variables **x** and **y** directly because these are protected members of base class **Point**. Note also that it is necessary to reference **x** and **y** through objects as in **c.x** and **c.y**. This is because the overloaded stream insertion operator function is not a member of the class **Circle**, but is a friend of the class.

The driver program (Fig. 19.4, part 5) creates **pointPtr** as a pointer to a **Point** object and instantiates **Point** object **p**, then creates **circlePtr** as a pointer to a **Circle** object and instantiates **Circle** object **c**. The **Point** and **Circle** objects are output using their overloaded stream insertion operators to show that they were initialized correctly. Next, the driver demonstrates assigning a derived-class pointer (the address of object **c**) to base-class pointer **pointPtr** and casting **pointPtr** back to a **Circle ***. The result of the cast operation is assigned to **circlePtr**. The area of **Circle** object **c** is output via **circlePtr**. This results in a valid area value because the pointers are always pointing to a **Circle** object. It is always valid to assign a derived-class pointer to a base-class pointer because a derived-class object *is a* base-class object. The base-class pointer "sees" only the base-class part of the derived-class object. The compiler performs an implicit conversion of the derived-class pointer to a base-class pointer. A base-class pointer can not be assigned directly to a derived-class pointer because this is an inherently dangerous assignment—derived-class pointers expect to be pointing to derived class-objects. The compiler does not perform an implicit conversion in this case. Using an explicit cast informs the compiler that the programmer knows this type of pointer conversion is dangerous—the programmer assumes responsibility for using the pointer appropriately.

Next, the driver demonstrates assigning a base-class pointer (the address of object **p**) to base-class pointer **pointPtr** and casting **pointPtr** back to a **Circle ***. The result of the cast operation is assigned to **circlePtr**. The radius of the object pointed to by **circlePtr** (**Point** object **p**) is output via **circlePtr**. This results in a invalid value because the pointers are always pointing to a **Point** object. A **Point** object does not have a **radius** member. Therefore, the program outputs whatever value happens to be in memory at the location that **circlePtr** expects the **radius** data member to be.

19.5 Using Member Functions

When a derived class is formed from a base class, the derived-class member functions may need to access certain base-class members.

Software Engineering Observation 19.1

A derived class cannot directly access private members of its base class.

This is a crucial aspect of software engineering in C++. If a derived class could access the base class's private members, this would violate the encapsulation of the base class. Hiding private members is a huge help in testing, debugging and correctly modifying systems. If a derived class could access its base class's private members, it would then be possible for classes derived from that derived class to access that data as well, and so on. This would propagate access to what is supposed to be private data, and the benefits of encapsulation would be lost throughout the class hierarchy.

19.6 Redefining Base-Class Members in a Derived Class

A derived class can redefine a base-class member function. When that function is mentioned by name in the derived class, the derived-class version is automatically selected. The scope-resolution operator may be used to access the base-class version from the derived class.

> ### *Common Programming Error 19.3*
>
> *When a base-class member function is redefined in a derived class, it is common to have the derived-class version call the base-class version and do some additional work. Not using the scope resolution operator to reference the base class's member function causes infinite recursion because the derived class member function actually calls itself.*

> ### *Good Programming Practice 19.1*
>
> *When inheriting capabilities that are not needed in the derived class, mask those capabilities by redefining the functions.*

> ### *Software Engineering Observation 19.2*
>
> *A redefinition of a base-class member function in a derived class need not have the same signature as the base-class member function.*

Consider a simplified class **Employee**. It stores the employee's **firstName** and **lastName**. This information is common to all employees including those in classes derived from class **Employee**. From class **Employee** now derive classes **Hourly-Worker**, **PieceWorker**, **Boss**, and **CommissionWorker**. The **HourlyWorker** gets paid by the hour with "time-and-a-half" for overtime hours in excess of 40 hours per week. The **PieceWorker** gets paid a fixed rate per item produced—for simplicity, assume this person makes only one type of item, so the private data members are number of items produced and rate per item. The **Boss** gets a fixed wage per week. The **CommissionWorker** gets a small fixed weekly base salary plus a fixed percentage of that person's gross sales for the week. For simplicity, we study only class **Employee** and derived class **HourlyWorker**.

Our next example is shown in Fig. 19.5, parts 1 through 5. Parts 1 and 2 show the **Employee** class definition and **Employee** member function definitions. Parts 3 and 4 show the **HourlyWorker** class definition and **HourlyWorker** member function definition. Part 5 shows a driver program for the **Employee/HourlyWorker** inheritance hierarchy that simply instantiates an **HourlyWorker** object, initializes it, and calls **HourlyWorker** member function **print** to output the object's data.

```
// EMPLOY.H
// Definition of class Employee
#ifndef EMPLOY_H
#define EMPLOY_H

class Employee {
public:
   Employee(const char*, const char*);  // constructor
   void print() const;  // output first and last name
   ~Employee();          // destructor
private:
   char *firstName;      // dynamically allocated string
   char *lastName;       // dynamically allocated string
};

#endif
```

Fig. 19.5 Definition of class **Employee** (part 1 of 5).

```
// EMPLOY.CPP
// Member function definitions for class Employee
#include <string.h>
#include <iostream.h>
#include <assert.h>
#include "employ.h"

// Constructor dynamically allocates space for the
// first and last name and uses strcpy to copy
// the first and last names into the object.
Employee::Employee(const char *first, const char *last)
{
   firstName = new char[ strlen(first) + 1 ];
   assert(firstName != 0); // terminate if memory not allocated
   strcpy(firstName, first);

   lastName = new char[ strlen(last) + 1 ];
   assert(lastName != 0);  // terminate if memory not allocated
   strcpy(lastName, last);
}

// Output employee name
void Employee::print() const
{ cout << firstName << ' ' << lastName; }

// Destructor deallocates dynamically allocated memory
Employee::~Employee()
{
   delete [] firstName;   // reclaim dynamic memory
   delete [] lastName;    // reclaim dynamic memory
}
```

Fig. 19.5 Member function definitions for class **Employee** (part 2 of 5).

```
// HOURLY.H
// Definition of class HourlyWorker
#ifndef HOURLY_H
#define HOURLY_H

#include "employ.h"

class HourlyWorker : public Employee {
public:
   HourlyWorker(const char*, const char*, float, float);
   float getPay() const;   // calculate and return salary
   void print() const;     // redefined base-class print
private:
   float wage;             // wage per hour
   float hours;            // hours worked for week
};

#endif
```

Fig. 19.5   Definition of class **HourlyWorker** (part 3 of 5).

```
// HOURLY_B.CPP
// Member function definitions for class HourlyWorker
#include <iostream.h>
#include <iomanip.h>
#include "hourly.h"

// Constructor for class HourlyWorker
HourlyWorker::HourlyWorker(const char *first, const char *last,
                           float initHours, float initWage)
   : Employee(first, last)    // call base-class constructor
{
   hours = initHours;
   wage = initWage;
}

// Get the HourlyWorker's pay
float HourlyWorker::getPay() const { return wage * hours; }

// Print the HourlyWorker's name and pay
void HourlyWorker::print() const
{
   cout << "HourlyWorker::print()\n\n";

   Employee::print();    // call base-class print function

   cout << " is an hourly worker with pay of"
        << " $" << setiosflags(ios::showpoint)
        << setprecision(2) << getPay() << endl;
}
```

Fig. 19.5   Member function definitions for class **HourlyWorker** (part 4 of 5).

```
// FIG19_5.CPP
// Redefining a base-class member function in a
// derived class.
#include <iostream.h>
#include "hourly.h"

main()
{
    HourlyWorker h("Bob", "Smith", 40.0, 7.50);
    h.print();
    return 0;
}
```

```
HourlyWorker::print()

Bob Smith is an hourly worker with pay of $300.00
```

Fig. 19.5   Redefining a base-class member function in a derived class (part 5 of 5).

The **Employee** class definition (Fig. 19.5, part 1) consists of two private **char *** data members—**firstName** and **lastName**—and three member functions—a constructor, a destructor, and **print**. The constructor function (Fig. 19.5, part 2) receives two strings and dynamically allocates character arrays to store the strings. Note that the **assert** macro (discussed in Chapter 14, "Advanced Topics") is used to determine if memory was allocated to **firstName** and **lastName**. If not, the program terminates with an error message indicating the condition tested, the line number on which the condition appears, and the file in which the condition is located. Because the data of **Employee** are **private**, the only access to the data is through member function **print** which simply outputs the first name and last name of the employee. The destructor function returns the dynamically allocated memory to the system.

Class **HourlyWorker** (Fig. 19.5, part 3) inherits from class **Employee** with public inheritance. Again, this is specified in the first line of the class definition as follows

```
class HourlyWorker : public Employee
```

The public interface to **HourlyWorker** includes the **Employee print** function and **HourlyWorker** member functions **getPay** and **print**. Note that class **Hourly-Worker** defines its own **print** function. Therefore, class **HourlyWorker** has access to two **print** functions. Class **HourlyWorker** also contains private data members **wage** and **hours** for calculating the employee's weekly salary.

The **HourlyWorker** constructor (Fig. 19.5, part 4) uses member initializer syntax to pass the strings **first** and **last** to the **Employee** constructor so the base-class members can be initialized, then initializes members **wage** and **hours**. Member function **getPay** calculates the salary of the **HourlyWorker**.

HourlyWorker member function **print** is an example of a base-class member function being redefined in a derived class. Often base-class member functions are rede fined in a derived-class to provide more functionality. The redefined functions sometimes call the base-class version of the function to perform part of the new task. In this example, the derived-class `print` function calls the base-class `print` function to output the employee's name (the base-class `print` is the only function with access to the private data of the base class). The derived-class `print` function also outputs the employee's pay. Note how the base class version of the print function is called

```
Employee::print();
```

Because the base-class function and derived-class function have the same name, the base-class function must be preceded by its class name and the scope resolution operator. Otherwise, the derived-class version of the function is called which results in infinite recursion (the `HourlyWorker print` function calls itself).

19.7 Public, Protected, and Private Base Classes

When deriving a class from a base class, the base class may be inherited as either **public**, **protected**, or **private**. Protected inheritance and private inheritance are rare and each should be used only with great care; we use only public inheritance in the examples in this book.

When deriving a class from a public base class, public members of the base class become public members of the derived class, and protected members of the base class become protected members of the derived class. Private members of a base class are never directly accessible from a derived class.

When deriving a class from a protected base class, public and protected members of the base class become protected members of the derived class.

When deriving a class from a private base class, public and protected members of the base class become private members of the derived class.

19.8 Direct Base Classes and Indirect Base Classes

A base class may be a *direct base class* of a derived class, or a base class may be an *indirect base class* of a derived class. A direct base class of a derived class is explicitly listed in that derived class's header when that derived class is declared. An indirect base class is not explicitly listed in the derived class's header; rather the indirect base class is inherited from several levels up the class hierarchy.

19.9 Using Constructors and Destructors in Derived Classes

Because a derived class inherits its base class's members, when an object of a derived class is instantiated, the base class's constructor must be called to initialize the base-class members of the derived-class object. The derived class's constructor can call the base class's constructor implicitly, or a *base-class initializer* (which uses the member-initializer syntax we have seen) can be provided in the derived-class constructor to call the base-class constructor explicitly.

Base-class constructors and base-class assignment operators are not inherited by derived classes. Derived-class constructors and assignment operators, however, can call base-class constructors and assignment operators.

A derived-class constructor always calls the constructor for its base class first to initialize the derived class's base-class members. If the derived-class constructor is omitted, the derived class's default constructor calls the base-class constructor. Destructors are called in the reverse order of constructor calls, so a derived-class destructor is called before its base-class destructor.

Software Engineering Observation 19.3

When an object of a derived class is created, first the base-class constructor executes, then the constructors for the derived class's member objects execute, then the derived class's constructor executes. Destructors are called in the reverse of the order in which their corresponding constructors are called.

The C++ standard specifies that the order in which member objects are constructed is the order in which those objects are declared within the class definition. The order in which the member initializers are listed does not affect construction. In inheritance, base-class constructors are called in the order in which inheritance is specified in the derived-class definition. The order in which the base-class constructors are specified in the derived-class constructor does not affect construction.

Common Programming Error 19.4

Writing a program that depends on member objects being constructed in a particular order can produce subtle errors.

The program of Fig. 19.6 demonstrates the order in which base-class and derived-class constructors and destructors are called. The program consists of five parts. Parts 1 and 2 show a simple **Point** class containing a constructor, a destructor, and protected data members **x** and **y**. The constructor and destructor both print the **Point** object for which they are invoked. Parts 3 and 4 show a simple **Circle** class derived from **Point** with public inheritance containing a constructor, and destructor, and private data member **radius**. The constructor and destructor both print the **Circle** object for which they are invoked. The **Circle** constructor also invokes the **Point** constructor using member initializer syntax and passes the values **a** and **b** so the base-class data members can be initialized.

Part 5 shows a driver program for this **Point/Circle** hierarchy. The program begins by instantiating a **Point** object in its own scope inside **main**. The object goes in and out of scope immediately, so the **Point** constructor and destructor are both called. The program then instantiates **Circle** object **circle1**. This invokes the **Point** constructor to perform output with values passed from the **Circle** constructor, then performs the output specified in the **Circle** constructor. **Circle** object **circle2** is instantiated next. Again, the **Point** and **Circle** constructors are both called. Note that the body of the **Point** constructor is performed before the body of the **Circle** constructor. The end of **main** is reached, so the destructors must be called for the **circle1** and **circle2** objects. Destructors are called in the reverse order of their corresponding constructors. Therefore, the **Circle** destructor and **Point** destructor are called in that order for object **circle2**, then the **Circle** destructor and **Point** destructor are called in that order for object **circle1**.

```
// POINT2.H
// Definition of class Point
#ifndef POINT2_H
#define POINT2_H

class Point {
public:
   Point(float = 0.0, float = 0.0);  // default constructor
   ~Point();    // destructor
protected:       // accessible by derived classes
   float x, y;  // x and y coordinates of Point
};

#endif
```

Fig. 19.6 Definition of class **Point** (part 1 of 5).

```
// POINT2.CPP
// Member function definitions for class Point
#include <iostream.h>
#include "point2.h"

// Constructor for class Point
Point::Point(float a, float b)
{
   x = a;
   y = b;

   cout << "Point  constructor: "
        << '[' << x << ", " << y << ']' << endl;
}

// Destructor for class Point
Point::~Point()
{
   cout << "Point  destructor:   "
        << '[' << x << ", " << y << ']' << endl;
}
```

Fig. 19.6 Member function definitions for class **Point** (part 2 of 5).

19.10 Implicit Derived-Class Object to Base-Class Object Conversion

Despite the fact that a derived-class object also "is a" base-class object, the derived-class type and the base-class type are different. Derived-class objects can be treated as base-class objects. This kind of assignment makes sense because the derived class has members corresponding to each of the base-class members—remember that the derived class normally has more members than the base class has. Assignment in the other direction is not allowed because assigning a base-class object to a derived-class object would leave

```
// CIRCLE2.H
// Definition of class Circle
#ifndef CIRCLE2_H
#define CIRCLE2_H

#include "point2.h"
#include <iomanip.h>

class Circle : public Point {
public:
   // default constructor
   Circle(float r = 0.0, float x = 0, float y = 0);

   ~Circle();       // destructor
private:
   float radius;    // radius of Circle
};

#endif
```

Fig. 19.6   Definition of class `Circle` (part 3 of 5).

```
// CIRCLE2.CPP
// Member function definitions for class Circle
#include "circle2.h"

// Constructor for Circle calls constructor for Point
Circle::Circle(float r, float a, float b)
   : Point(a, b)    // call base-class constructor
{
   radius = r;

   cout << "Circle constructor: radius is "
        << radius << " [" << a << ", " << b << ']' << endl;
}

// Destructor for class Circle
Circle::~Circle()
{
   cout << "Circle destructor:  radius is "
        << radius << " [" << x << ", " << y << ']' << endl;
}
```

Fig. 19.6   Member function definitions for class `Circle` (part 4 of 5).

the additional derived-class members undefined. Although such assignment is not "naturally" allowed, it could be made legitimate by providing a properly overloaded assignment operator and/or conversion constructor.

Common Programming Error 19.5

Assigning a derived-class object to an object of a corresponding base class, and then attempting to reference derived-class-only members in the new base-class object.

```
// FIG19_6.CPP
// Demonstrate when base-class and derived-class
// constructors and destructors are called.
#include <iostream.h>
#include "point2.h"
#include "circle2.h"

main()
{
    // Show constructor and destructor calls for Point
    {
        Point p(1.1, 2.2);
    }

    cout << endl;
    Circle circle1(4.5, 7.2, 2.9);
    cout << endl;
    Circle circle2(10, 5, 5);
    cout << endl;
    return 0;
}
```

```
Point  constructor:  [1.1, 2.2]
Point  destructor:   [1.1, 2.2]

Point  constructor:  [7.2, 2.9]
Circle constructor:  radius is 4.5 [7.2, 2.9]

Point  constructor:  [5, 5]
Circle constructor:  radius is 10 [5, 5]

Circle destructor:   radius is 10 [5, 5]
Point  destructor:   [5, 5]
Circle destructor:   radius is 4.5 [7.2, 2.9]
Point  destructor:   [7.2, 2.9]
```

Fig. 19.6   Order in which base-class and derived-class constructors and destructors are called (part 5 of 5).

A pointer to a derived-class object may be implicitly converted into a pointer to a base-class object because a derived-class object is a base-class object.

There are four possible ways to mix and match base-class pointers and derived-class pointers with base-class objects and derived-class objects:

1. Referring to a base-class object with a base-class pointer is straightforward.

2. Referring to a derived-class object with a derived-class pointer is straightforward.

3. Referring to a derived-class object with a base-class pointer is safe because the derived-class object is an object of its base class as well. The program can only

refer to base-class members. If the program refers to derived-class-only members through the base-class pointer, the compiler will report a syntax error.

4. Referring to a base-class object with a derived-class pointer is a syntax error. The derived-class pointer must first be cast to a base-class pointer.

Common Programming Error 19.6

Casting a base-class pointer to a derived-class pointer can cause errors if that pointer is then used to reference a base-class object that does not have the desired derived-class members.

As convenient as it may be to treat derived-class objects as base-class objects, and to do this by manipulating all these objects with base-class pointers, there is a problem. In a payroll system, for example, we would like to be able to walk through a linked list of employees and calculate the weekly pay for each person. But using base-class pointers enables the program to call only the base-class payroll calculation routine (if indeed there is such a routine in the base class). We need a way to invoke the proper payroll calculation routine for each object, whether it is a base-class object or a derived-class object, and to do this simply by using the base-class pointer. The solution is to use virtual functions and polymorphism as discussed in Chapter 20.

19.11 Software Engineering with Inheritance

We can use inheritance to *customize* existing software. We inherit the attributes and behaviors of an existing class, then add or subtract attributes and behaviors to customize the class to meet our needs. This is done in C++ without the derived class having access to the base class's source code, but the derived class does need to be able to link to the base class's object code. This powerful capability is attractive to independent software vendors (ISVs). The ISVs can develop proprietary classes for sale or license and make these classes available to users in object-code format. Users can then derive new classes from these library classes rapidly and without accessing the ISVs' proprietary source code. All the ISVs need to supply with the object code are the header files.

It can be difficult for students to appreciate the problems faced by designers and implementers on large-scale software projects. People experienced on such projects will invariably state that a key to improving the software development process is encouraging software reuse. Object-oriented programming in general, and C++ in particular, encourage software reuse.

It is the availability of substantial and useful class libraries that delivers the maximum benefits of software reuse through inheritance. As interest in C++ grows, interest in class libraries will increase. Just as shrink-wrapped software produced by independent software vendors became an explosive growth industry with the arrival of the personal computer, so, too, will the creation and sale of class libraries. Application designers will build their applications with these libraries, and library designers will be rewarded by having their libraries wrapped with the applications. Libraries currently being shipped with C++ compilers tend to be rather general-purpose and limited in scope. What we see coming is a massive worldwide commitment to the development of class libraries for a huge variety of applications arenas.

Software Engineering Observation 19.4

Creating a derived class does not affect its base class's source code or object code; the integrity of a base class is preserved by inheritance.

A base class specifies commonality. All classes derived from a base class inherit the capabilities of that base class. In the object-oriented design process, the designer looks for commonality and factors it out to form desirable base classes. Derived classes are then customized beyond the capabilities inherited from the base class.

Just as the designer of non-object-oriented systems seeks to avoid unnecessary proliferation of functions, the designer of object-oriented systems should avoid unnecessary proliferation of classes. Such a proliferation of classes creates management problems and can hinder software reusability simply because it is more difficult for a potential reuser of a class to locate that class in a huge collection. The tradeoff is to create fewer classes, each providing substantial additional functionality. Such classes might be a bit too rich for certain reusers; they can mask the excessive functionality, thus "toning down" the classes to meet their needs.

Performance Tip 19.1

If classes produced through inheritance are larger than they need to be, memory and processing resources may be wasted.

Note that reading a set of derived-class declarations can be confusing because inherited members are not shown. But inherited members are nevertheless present in the derived classes.

Software Engineering Observation 19.5

In an object-oriented system, classes are often closely related. "Factor out" common attributes and behavior and place these in a base class. Then use inheritance to form derived classes.

Software Engineering Observation 19.6

A derived class contains the attributes and behaviors of its base class. A derived class can also contain additional attributes and behaviors. With inheritance, the base class can be compiled independently of the derived class. Only the derived class's incremental attributes and behaviors need to be compiled to be able to combine these with the base class to form the derived class.

Software Engineering Observation 19.7

Modifications to a base class do not require derived classes to change as long as the public interface to the base class remains unchanged. Derived classes may, however, need to be recompiled.

19.12 Composition Vs. Inheritance

We have discussed *is a* relationships which are supported by inheritance. We have also discussed *has a* relationships (and seen examples in preceding chapters) in which an ob ject may have other objects as members—such relationships create new classes by *composition* of existing classes. For example, given the classes **Employee, BirthDate,** and **TelephoneNumber,** it is improper to say that an **Employee** *is a* **BirthDate** or that an **Employee** *is a* **TelephoneNumber**. But it is certainly appropriate to say that an **Employee** *has a* **BirthDate** and that an **Employee** *has a* **TelephoneNumber**.

Remember that the order in which member objects are constructed is specified as the order in which those object are declared. Base-class constructors are called in the order in which inheritance is specified in the derived class.

Software Engineering Observation 19.8

Modifications to a member class do not require its enclosing composed class to change as long as the public interface to the member class remains unchanged. Note that the composite class may, however, need to be recompiled.

19.13 "Uses A" and "Knows A" Relationships

Inheritance and composition each encourage software reuse by creating new classes that have much in common with existing classes. There are other ways to utilize the services of classes. Although a person object is not a car, and a person object does not contain a car, a person object certainly *uses a* car. A function uses an object simply by issuing a function call to a member function of that object.

An object can be *aware of* another object. Knowledge networks frequently have such relationships. One object can contain a pointer or a reference to another object to be aware of that object. In this case, one object is said to have a *knows a* relationship with the other object.

19.14 Case Study: Point, Circle, Cylinder

Now let us consider the capstone exercise for this chapter. We consider a point, circle, cylinder hierarchy. First we develop and use class **Point** (Fig. 19.7). Then we present an example in which we derive class **Circle** from class **Point** (Fig. 19.8). Finally, we present an example in which we derive class **Cylinder** from class **Circle** (Fig. 19.9).

Figure 19.7 shows class **Point**. Part 1 of Fig. 19.7 shows the class **Point** definition. Note that the data members of **Point** are protected. Thus, when we derive class **Circle** from class **Point**, the member functions of class **Circle** will be able to directly reference coordinates **x** and **y** rather than having to use access functions. This may result in better performance.

Figure 19.7, part 2, shows the member function definitions for class **Point**. Figure 19.7, part 3, shows a driver program for class **Point**. Note that **main** must use the access functions **getX** and **getY** to read the values of protected data members **x** and **y**; remember that protected data members are accessible only to members and friends of their class and members and friends of their derived classes.

Our next example is shown in Fig. 19.8, parts 1 through 3. The **Point** class definition and the member function definitions from Fig. 19.7 are reused here. Parts 1 through 3 show the **Circle** class definition, **Circle** member function definitions, and a driver program, respectively. Note that class **Circle** inherits from class **Point** with public

```
// POINT2.H
// Definition of class Point
#ifndef POINT2_H
#define POINT2_H

class Point {
    friend ostream &operator<<(ostream &, const Point &);
public:
    Point(float = 0, float = 0);        // default constructor
    void setPoint(float, float);        // set coordinates
    float getX() const { return x; }    // get x coordinate
    float getY() const { return y; }    // get y coordinate
protected:            // accessible to derived classes
    float x, y;       // coordinates of the point
};

#endif
```

Fig. 19.7 Definition of class **Point** (part 1 of 3).

```
// POINT2.CPP
// Member functions for class Point
#include <iostream.h>
#include "point2.h"

// Constructor for class Point
Point::Point(float a, float b)
{
    x = a;
    y = b;
}

// Set the x and y coordinates
void Point::setPoint(float a, float b)
{
    x = a;
    y = b;
}

// Output the Point
ostream &operator<<(ostream &output, const Point &p)
{
    output << '[' << p.x << ", " << p.y << ']';

    return output;              // enables concatenation
}
```

Fig. 19.7 Member functions for class **Point** (part 2 of 3).

inheritance. This means that the public interface to **Circle** includes the **Point** member functions as well as the **Circle** member functions **setRadius**, **getRadius**, and **area**. Note that the **Circle** overloaded stream insertion operator function is able to ref-

```
// FIG19_7.CPP
// Driver for class Point
#include <iostream.h>
#include "point2.h"

main()
{
    Point p(7.2, 11.5);    // instantiate Point object p

    // protected data of Point inaccessible to main
    cout << "X coordinate is " << p.getX()
         << "\nY coordinate is " << p.getY();

    p.setPoint(10, 10);
    cout << "\n\nThe new location of p is " << p << endl;

    return 0;
}
```

```
X coordinate is 7.2
Y coordinate is 11.5

The new location of p is [10, 10]
```

Fig. 19.7   Driver for class `Point` (part 3 of 3).

erence variables **x** and **y** directly because these are protected members of base class
Point. Note also that it is necessary to reference **x** and **y** through objects, as in **c.x** and
c.y. This is because the overloaded stream insertion operator function is not a member
function of the class **Circle**, but is a friend of the class. The driver program instantiates
an object of class **Circle** then uses *get* functions to obtain the information about the
Circle object. Again, **main** is neither a member function nor a friend of class **Circle**
so it cannot directly reference the protected data of class **Circle**. The driver program
then uses *set* functions **setRadius** and **setPoint** to reset the radius and coordinates
of the center of the circle. Finally, the driver does something especially interesting. It initializes reference variable **pRef** of type "reference to **Point** object" (**Point &**) to
Circle object **c**. The driver then prints **pRef** which, despite the fact that it is initialized
with a **Circle** object, "thinks" it is a **Point** object, so the **Circle** object actually
prints as a **Point** object.

Our last example is shown in Fig. 19.9, parts 1 through 3. The **Point** class and
Circle class definitions, and their member function definitions from Fig. 19.7 and Fig.
19.8 are reused here. Parts 1 through 3 show the **Cylinder** class definition, **Cylinder**
member function definitions, and a driver program, respectively. Note that class **Cylinder** inherits from class **Circle** with public inheritance. This means that the public interface to **Cylinder** includes the **Circle** member functions as well as the **Cylinder**
member functions **setHeight**, **getHeight**, **area** (redefined from **Circle**) and
volume. Note that the **Cylinder** overloaded stream insertion operator function is able

```
// CIRCLE2.H
// Definition of class Circle
#ifndef CIRCLE2_H
#define CIRCLE2_H

#include "point2.h"

class Circle : public Point {
   friend ostream &operator<<(ostream &, const Circle &);
public:
   // default constructor
   Circle(float r = 0.0, float x = 0, float y = 0);
   void setRadius(float);       // set radius
   float getRadius() const;     // return radius
   float area() const;          // calculate area
protected:            // accessible to derived classes
   float radius;      // radius of the Circle
};

#endif
```

Fig. 19.8 Definition of class `Circle` (part 1 of 3).

```
// CIRCLE2.CPP
// Member function definitions for class Circle
#include <iostream.h>
#include <iomanip.h>
#include "circle2.h"

// Constructor for Circle calls constructor for Point
// with a member initializer and initializes radius
Circle::Circle(float r, float a, float b)
   : Point(a, b)        // call base-class constructor
{ radius = r; }

// Set radius
void Circle::setRadius(float r) { radius = r; }

// Get radius
float Circle::getRadius() const { return radius; }

// Calculate area of Circle
float Circle::area() const
   { return 3.14159 * radius * radius; }

// Output a circle in the form:
// Center = [x, y]; Radius = #.##
ostream &operator<<(ostream &output, const Circle &c)
{
   output << "Center = [" << c.x << ", " << c.y
          << "]; Radius = " << setiosflags(ios::showpoint)
          << setprecision(2) << c.radius;

   return output;    //  enables concatenated calls
}
```

Fig. 19.8 Member function definitions for class `Circle` (part 2 of 3).

```
// FIG19_8.CPP
// Driver for class Circle
#include <iostream.h>
#include "point2.h"
#include "circle2.h"

main()
{
    Circle c(2.5, 3.7, 4.3);

    cout << "X coordinate is " << c.getX()
         << "\nY coordinate is " << c.getY()
         << "\nRadius is " << c.getRadius();

    c.setRadius(4.25);
    c.setPoint(2, 2);
    cout << "\n\nThe new location and radius of c are\n"
         << c << "\nArea " << c.area() << endl;

    Point &pRef = c;
    cout << "\nCircle printed as a Point is: "
         << pRef << endl;

    return 0;
}
```

```
X coordinate is 3.7
Y coordinate is 4.3
Radius is 2.5

The new location and radius of c are
Center = [2, 2]; Radius = 4.25
Area: 56.74

Circle printed as a Point is: [2.00, 2.00]
```

Fig. 19.8 Driver for class `Circle` (part 3 of 3).

to reference variables **x**, **y**, and **radius** directly because these are protected members of base class **Circle** (**x** and **y** were inherited by **Circle** from **Point**). Note also that it is necessary to reference **x**, **y**, and **radius** through objects, as in **c.x**, **c.y**, and **c.radius**. This is because the overloaded stream insertion operator function is not a member function of the class **Cylinder**, but is a friend of the class. The driver program instantiates an object of class **Cylinder** then uses *get* functions to obtain the information about the **Cylinder** object. Again, **main** is neither a member function nor a friend of class **Cylinder** so it cannot directly reference the protected data of class **Cylinder**. The driver program then uses *set* functions **setHeight**, **setRadius**, and **setPoint** to reset the height, radius, and coordinates of the cylinder. Finally, the driver does something especially interesting. It initializes reference variable **pRef** of type "reference to **Point** object" (**Point &**) to **Cylinder** object **cyl**. It then prints **pRef** which, despite the fact that it is initialized with a **Cylinder** object, "thinks" it is a **Point** object, so the **Cylinder** object actually prints as a **Point** object. The driver then initializes reference variable **cRef** of type "reference to **Circle** object" (**Circle &**) to **Cylinder** object **cyl**. It then prints **cRef** which, despite the fact that it is initialized with a **Cylinder** object, "thinks" it is a **Circle** object, so the **Cylinder** object actually prints as a **Circle** object. The area of the **Circle** is also output.

This example nicely demonstrates public inheritance and defining and referencing protected data members. The reader should now be confident with the basics of inheritance. In the next chapter, we show how to program with inheritance hierarchies in a general manner using polymorphism. Data abstraction, inheritance, and polymorphism are the crux of object-oriented programming.

19.15 Multiple Inheritance

So far in this chapter, we have discussed single inheritance in which each class is derived from exactly one base class. A class may be derived from more than one base class; such derivation is called *multiple inheritance*. Multiple inheritance means that a derived class inherits the members of several base classes. This powerful capability encourages interesting forms of software reuse, but can cause a variety of ambiguity problems.

Good Programming Practice 19.2

Multiple inheritance is a powerful capability when used properly. Multiple inheritance should be used when an "is a" relationship exists between a new type and two or more existing types (i.e., type A "is a" type B and "is a" type C).

```
// CYLINDR2.H
// Definition of class Cylinder
#ifndef CYLINDR2_H
#define CYLINDR2_H
#include "circle2.h"

class Cylinder : public Circle {
   friend ostream& operator<<(ostream&, const Cylinder&);
public:
   // default constructor
   Cylinder(float h = 0.0, float r = 0.0,
            float x = 0.0, float y = 0.0);
   void setHeight(float);    // set height
   float getHeight() const;  // return height
   float area() const;       // calculate and return area
   float volume() const;     // calculate and return volume
protected:
   float height;             // height of the Cylinder
};

#endif
```

Fig. 19.9 Definition of class **Cylinder** (part 1 of 3).

```
// CYLINDR2.CPP
// Member and friend function definitions for class Cylinder
#include <iostream.h>
#include <iomanip.h>
#include "cylindr2.h"

// Cylinder constructor calls Circle constructor
Cylinder::Cylinder(float h, float r, float x, float y)
    : Circle(r, x, y)    // call base-class constructor
{ height = h; }

// Set height of Cylinder
void Cylinder::setHeight(float h) { height = h; }

// Get height of Cylinder
float Cylinder::getHeight() const { return height; }

// Calculate area of Cylinder (i.e., surface area)
float Cylinder::area() const
{
    return 2 * Circle::area() +
           2 * 3.14159 * radius * height;
}

// Calculate volume of Cylinder
float Cylinder::volume() const
    { return Circle::area() * height; }

// Output Cylinder dimensions
ostream& operator<<(ostream &output, const Cylinder& c)
{
    output << "Center = [" << c.x << ", " << c.y
           << "]; Radius = " << setiosflags(ios::showpoint)
           << setprecision(2) << c.radius
           << "; Height = " << c.height;

    return output;    // enables concatenated calls
}
```

Fig. 19.9   Member function and friend function definitions for class `Cylinder` (part 2 of 3).

Consider the multiple inheritance example in Fig. 19.10. Class **Base1** contains one protected data member—**int value**. **Base1** contains a constructor that sets **value** and public member function **getData** that reads **value**.

Class **Base2** is similar to class **Base1** except that its protected data is **char letter**. **Base2** also has a public member function **getData**, but this function reads the value of **char letter**.

Class **Derived** is inherited from both class **Base1** and class **Base2** through multiple inheritance. **Derived** has private data member **float real** and has public member function **getReal** that reads the value of **float real**.

```
// FIG19_9.CPP
// Driver for class Cylinder
#include <iostream.h>
#include <iomanip.h>
#include "point2.h"
#include "circle2.h"
#include "cylindr2.h"

main()
{
    // create Cylinder object
    Cylinder cyl(5.7, 2.5, 1.2, 2.3);

    // use get functions to display the Cylinder
    cout << "X coordinate is " << cyl.getX()
         << "\nYcoordinate is " << cyl.getY()
         << "\nRadius is " << cyl.getRadius()
         << "\nHeight is " << cyl.getHeight();

    // use set functions to change the Cylinder's attributes
    cyl.setHeight(10);
    cyl.setRadius(4.25);
    cyl.setPoint(2, 2);
    cout << "\n\nThe new location, radius, "
         << "and height of cyl are:\n" << cyl << endl << "Area: "
         << cyl.area() << "   Volume: " << cyl.volume();

    // display the Cylinder as a Point
    Point &pRef = cyl;   // pRef "thinks" it is a Point
    cout << "\n\nCylinder printed as a Point is: " << pRef;

    // display the Cylinder as a Circle
    Circle &cRef = cyl;  // cRef "thinks" it is a Circle
    cout << "\n\nCylinder printed as a Circle is:\n" << cRef
         << "\nArea: " << cRef.area() << endl;
    return 0;
}
```

```
X coordinate is 1.2
Y coordinate is 2.3
Radius is 2.5
Height is 5.7

The new location, radius, and height of cyl are:
Center = [2, 2]; Radius = 4.25; Height = 10.00
Area: 380.53    Volume: 567.45

Cylinder printed as a Point is: [2.00, 2.00]

Cylinder printed as a Circle is:
Center = [2.00, 2.00]; Radius = 4.25
Area: 56.74
```

Fig. 19.9 Driver for class **Cylinder** (part 3 of 3).

```
// BASE1.H
// Definition of class Base1
#ifndef BASE1_H
#define BASE1_H

class Base1 {
public:
   Base1(int x) { value = x; }
   int getData() const { return value; }
protected:        // accessible to derived classes
   int value;     // inherited by derived class
};

#endif
```

Fig. 19.10 Definition of class **Base1** (part 1 of 6).

```
// BASE2.H
// Definition of class Base2
#ifndef BASE2_H
#define BASE2_H

class Base2 {
public:
   Base2(char c) { letter = c; }
   char getData() const { return letter; }
protected:        // accessible to derived classes
   char letter;   // inherited by derived class
};

#endif
```

Fig. 19.10 Definition of class **Base2** (part 2 of 6).

Note how straightforward it is to indicate multiple inheritance by following the colon (:) after **class Derived** with a comma-separated list of public base classes. Note also that constructor **Derived** calls base-class constructors for each of its base classes, **Base1** and **Base2**, through the member-initializer syntax.

The overloaded stream insertion operator for **Derived** uses dot notation off the derived object **d** to print **value**, **letter**, and **real**. This operator function is a friend of **Derived**, so **operator<<** can directly access private data member **real** of **Derived**. Also, because this operator is a friend of a derived class, it can access the protected members **value** and **letter** of **Base1** and **Base2**, respectively.

Now let us examine the driver program in **main**. We create object **b1** of class **Base1** and initialize it to **int** value **10**. We create object **b2** of class **Base2** and initialize it to **char** value **'Z'**. Then, we create object **d** of class **Derived** and initialize it to contain **int** value 7, **char** value **'A'**, and **float** value 3.5.

The contents of each of the base-class objects is printed using static binding. Even though there are two **getData** functions, the calls are not ambiguous because they refer directly to the object **b1** version of **getData** and the object **b2** version of **getData**.

```
// DERIVED.H
// Definition of class Derived which inherits
// multiple base classes (Base1 and Base2).
#ifndef DERIVED_H
#define DERIVED_H

#include <iostream.h>
#include "base1.h"
#include "base2.h"

// multiple inheritance
class Derived : public Base1, public Base2 {
   friend ostream &operator<<(ostream &, const Derived &);
public:
   Derived(int, char, float);
   float getReal() const;
private:
   float real;    // derived class's private data
};

#endif
```

Fig. 19.10 Definition of class `Derived` (part 3 of 6).

```
// DERIVED.CPP
// Member function definitions for class Derived
#include "derived.h"

// Constructor for Derived calls constructors for
// class Base1 and class Base2.
Derived::Derived(int i, char c, float f)
   : Base1(i), Base2(c)  // call both base-class constructors
{ real = f; }

// Return the value of real
float Derived::getReal() const { return real; }

// Display all the data members of Derived
ostream &operator<<(ostream &output, const Derived &d)
{
   output << "    Integer: " << d.value
          << "\n  Character: " << d.letter
          << "\nReal number: " << d.real;

   return output;    // enables concatenated calls
}
```

Fig. 19.10 Member function definitions for class `Derived` (part 4 of 6).

Next we print the contents of `Derived` object **d** with static binding. But we do have an ambiguity problem because this object contains two `getData` functions, one inherited from `Base1` and one inherited from `Base2`. This problem is easy to solve by using

```
// FIG19_10.CPP
// Driver for multiple inheritance example
#include <iostream.h>
#include "base1.h"
#include "base2.h"
#include "derived.h"

main()
{
    Base1 b1(10), *base1Ptr;    // create base-class object
    Base2 b2('Z'), *base2Ptr;   // create other base-class object
    Derived d(7, 'A', 3.5);     // create derived-class object

    // print data members of base class objects
    cout << "Object b1 contains integer "
         << b1.getData()
         << "\nObject b2 contains character "
         << b2.getData()
         << "\nObject d contains:\n" << d;

    // print data members of derived class object
    // scope resolution operator resolves getData ambiguity
    cout << "\n\nData members of Derived can be"
         << " accessed individually:\n"
         << "    Integer: " << d.Base1::getData()
         << "\n  Character: " << d.Base2::getData()
         << "\nReal number: " << d.getReal() << "\n\n";

    cout << "Derived can be treated as an "
         << "object of either base class:\n";

    // treat Derived as a Base1 object
    base1Ptr = &d;
    cout << "base1Ptr->getData() yields "
         << base1Ptr->getData();

    // treat Derived as a Base2 object
    base2Ptr = &d;
    cout << "\nbase2Ptr->getData() yields "
         << base2Ptr->getData() << endl;

    return 0;
}
```

Fig. 19.10 Driver for the multiple inheritance example (part 5 of 6).

the binary scope resolution operator as in **d.Base1::getData()** to print the **int** in
value and **d.Base2::getData()** to print the **char** in **letter**. The **float** value
in **real** is printed without ambiguity with the call **d.getReal()**.

Next we demonstrate that the *is a* relationships of single inheritance also apply to
multiple inheritance. We assign the address of derived object **d** to base-class pointer
base1Ptr, and we print **int value** by invoking **Base1** member function **getData**

```
Object b1 contains integer 10
Object b2 contains character Z
Object d contains:
     Integer: 7
   Character: A
Real number: 3.5

Data members of Derived can be accessed individually:
     Integer: 7
   Character: A
Real number: 3.5

Derived can be treated as an object of either base class:
base1Ptr->getData() yields 7
base2Ptr->getData() yields A
```

Fig. 19.10 Driver for the multiple inheritance example (part 6 of 6).

off **base1Ptr**. We then assign the address of derived object **d** to base-class pointer **base2Ptr** and we print **char letter** by invoking **Base2** member function **get-Data** off **base2Ptr**.

This example showed the mechanics of multiple inheritance and introduced a simple ambiguity problem. Multiple inheritance is a complex topic dealt with in more detail in C++ texts such as our *C++ How to Program* (Prentice-Hall, 1994).

Summary

- One of the keys to the power of object-oriented programming is achieving software reusability through inheritance.

- The programmer can designate that the new class is to inherit the data members and member functions of a previously defined base class. In this case, the new class is referred to as a derived class.

- With single inheritance, a class is derived from only one base class. With multiple inheritance, a derived class inherits from multiple (possibly unrelated) base classes.

- A derived class normally adds data members and member functions of its own, so a derived class generally has a larger definition than its base class. A derived class is more specific than its base class and normally represents fewer objects.

- A derived class can not access the private members of its base class; allowing this would violate the encapsulation of the base class. A derived class can, however, access the public and protected members of its base class.

- A derived-class constructor always calls the constructor for its base class first to create and initialize the derived class's base-class members.

- Destructors are called in the reverse order of constructor calls, so a derived-class destructor is called before its base-class destructor.

- Inheritance enables software reusability which saves time in development and encourages the use of previously proven and debugged high-quality software.

- Inheritance can be accomplished from existing class libraries.

- Someday software for the most part will be constructed from standardized reusable components exactly as much hardware is constructed today.

- The implementor of a derived class does not need to have access to the source code of a base class, but does need to know the interface to the base class and to be able to link the base class's object code.

- An object of a derived class can be treated as an object of its corresponding public base class. However, the reverse is not true.

- A base class exists in a hierarchical relationship with its derived classes.

- A class can exist by itself. When that class is used with the mechanism of inheritance, it becomes either a base class that supplies attributes and behaviors to other classes, or the class becomes a derived class that inherits those attributes and behaviors.

- An inheritance hierarchy can be arbitrarily deep within the physical limitations of a particular system.

- Hierarchies are useful tools for understanding and managing complexity. With software becoming increasingly complex, C++ provides mechanisms for supporting hierarchical structures through inheritance and polymorphism.

- An explicit cast can be used to convert a base-class pointer to a derived-class pointer. If such a pointer is to be dereferenced, then it should first be made to point to an object of the derived class type.

- Protected access serves as an intermediate level of protection between public access and private access. Protected members of a base class may be accessed by members and friends of the base class and by members and friends of derived classes; no other functions can access the protected members of a base class.

- Protected members are used to extend privileges to derived classes while denying those privileges to non-class, non-friend functions.

- Multiple inheritance produces graph-like hierarchies. These graphs have no cycles because all the arrows point in the same direction. Such a graph is called a directed acyclic graph (DAG).

- When deriving a class from a base class, the base class may be declared as either **public**, **protected**, or **private**.

- When deriving a class from a **public** base class, **public** members of the base class become **public** members of the derived class, and **protected** members of the base class become **protected** members of the derived class.

- When deriving a class from a **protected** base class, **public** and **protected** members of the base class become **protected** members of the derived class.

- When deriving a class from a `private` base class, `public` and `protected` members of the base class become `private` members of the derived class.

- A base class may be either a direct base class of a derived class or an indirect base class of a derived class. A direct base class is explicitly listed when the derived class is declared. An indirect base class is not explicitly listed; rather it is inherited from several levels up the class hierarchy tree structure.

- When a base-class member is inappropriate for a derived class, we may simply redefine that member in the derived class.

- It is important to distinguish between "is a" relationships and "has a" relationships. In a "has a" relationship, a class object has an object of another class as a member. In an "is a" relationship, an object of a derived-class type may also be treated as an object of the base-class type. "Is a" is inheritance. "Has a" is composition.

- A derived class object can be assigned to a base class object. This kind of assignment makes sense because the derived class has members corresponding to each of the base class members.

- A pointer to a derived-class object may be implicitly converted into a pointer for a base-class object.

- It is possible to convert a base-class pointer to a derived-class pointer by using an explicit cast. The target should be a derived class object.

- A base class specifies commonality. All classes derived from a base class inherit the capabilities of that base class. In the object-oriented design process, the designer looks for commonality and factors it out to form desirable base classes. Derived classes are then customized beyond the capabilities inherited from the base class.

- Reading a set of derived-class declarations can be confusing because not all the members of the derived class are present in these declarations. In particular, inherited members are not listed in the derived-class declarations, but these members are indeed present in the derived classes.

- "Has a" relationships are examples of creating new classes by composition of existing classes.

- Member object constructors are called in the order in which the objects are declared. In inheritance, base-class constructors are called in the order in which inheritance is specified and before the derived-class constructor.

- For a derived-class object, first the base-class constructor is called, then the derived-class constructor is called.

- When the derived-class object goes out of scope, the destructors are called in the reverse order of the constructors—first the derived-class destructor is called, then the base-class destructor is called.

- A class may be derived from more than one base class; such derivation is called multiple inheritance.

- Indicate multiple inheritance by following the colon (:) inheritance indicator with a comma-separated list of base classes.

- The derived-class constructor calls base-class constructors for each of its base classes through the member-initializer syntax.

Terminology

abstraction	inheritance
ambiguity in multiple inheritance	*is a* relationship
base class	*knows a* relationship
base class default constructor	member access control
base-class constructor	member class
base-class destructor	member object
base-class initializer	multiple inheritance
base-class pointer	object-oriented programming (OOP)
class hierarchy	pointer to a base-class object
class libraries	pointer to a derived-class object
client of a class	private base class
composition	private inheritance
customize software	protected base class
derived class	protected derivation
derived-class constructor	**protected** keyword
derived-class destructor	protected member of a class
derived-class pointer	public base class
direct base class	public inheritance
directed acyclic graph (DAG)	redefine a base-class member
friends of a base class	single inheritance
friends of a derived class	software reusability
has a relationship	standardized software components
hierarchical relationship	subclass
indirect base class	superclass
infinite recursion error	*uses a* relationship

Common Programming Errors

19.1   Treating a base-class object as a derived-class object can cause errors.

19.2   Explicitly casting a base-class pointer that points to a base-class object into a derived-class pointer and then referring to derived-class members that do not exist in that object.

19.3   When a base-class member function is redefined in a derived class, it is common to have the derived-class version call the base-class version and do some additional work. Not using the scope resolution operator to reference the base class's member function causes infinite recursion because the derived class member function actually calls itself.

19.4   Writing a program that depends on member objects being constructed in a particular order can produce subtle errors.

19.5   Assigning a derived-class object to an object of a corresponding base class, and then attempting to reference derived-class-only members in the new base-class object.

19.6   Casting a base-class pointer to a derived-class pointer can cause errors if that pointer is then used to reference a base-class object that does not have the desired derived-class members.

Good Programming Practices

19.1   When inheriting capabilities that are not needed in the derived class, mask those capabilities by redefining the functions.

19.2   Multiple inheritance is a powerful capability when used properly. Multiple inheritance should be used when an "is a" relationship exists between a new type and two or more existing types (i.e., type A "is a" type B and "is a" type C) .

Performance Tip

19.1   If classes produced through inheritance are larger than they need to be, memory and processing resources may be wasted..

Software Engineering Observations

19.1   A derived class cannot directly access private members of its base class.

19.2   A redefinition of a base-class member function in a derived class need not have the same signature as the base-class member function.

19.3   When an object of a derived class is created, first the base-class constructor executes, then the constructors for the derived class's member objects execute, then the derived class's constructor executes. Destructors are called in the reverse of the order in which their corresponding constructors are called.

19.4   Creating a derived class does not affect its base class's source code or object code; the integrity of a base class is preserved by inheritance.

19.5   In an object-oriented system, classes are often closely related. "Factor out" common attributes and behavior and place these in a base class. Then use inheritance to form derived classes.

19.6   A derived class contains the attributes and behaviors of its base class. A derived class can also contain additional attributes and behaviors. With inheritance, the base class can be compiled independently of the derived class. Only the derived class's incremental attributes and behaviors need to be compiled to be able to combine these with the base class to form the derived class.

19.7   Modifications to a base class do not require derived classes to change as long as the public interface to the base class remains unchanged. Derived classes may, however, need to be recompiled.

19.8   Modifications to a member class do not require its enclosing composed class to change as long as the public interface to the member class remains unchanged. Note that the composite class may, however, need to be recompiled.

Self-Review Exercises

19.1   Fill in the blanks in each of the following:
    a) If the class **Alpha** inherits from the class **Beta**, class **Alpha** is called the _____ class and class **Beta** is called the _____ class.

b) C++ provides for _____ which allows a derived class to inherit from many base classes, even if these base classes are unrelated.

c) Inheritance enables _____ which saves time in development, and encourages using previously proven and high-quality software.

d) An object of a _____ class can be treated as an object of its corresponding _____ class.

e) To convert a base-class pointer to a derived class pointer, a _____ must be used because the compiler considers this a dangerous operation.

f) The three member access specifiers are _____, _____, and _____.

g) When deriving a class from a base class with **public** inheritance, **public** members of the base class become _____ members of the derived class, and **protected** members of the base class become _____ members of the derived class.

h) When deriving a class from a base class with **protected** inheritance, **public** members of the base class become _____ members of the derived class, and **protected** members of the base class become _____ members of the derived class.

i) A "has a" relationship between classes represents _____ and an "is a" relationship between classes represents _____ .

19.1 a) derived, base. b) multiple inheritance. c) software reusability. d) derived, base. e) cast. f) **public**, **protected**, **private**. g) **public**, **protected**. h) **protected**, **protected**. i) composition, inheritance.

Exercises

19.2 Consider the class **Bicycle**. Given your knowledge of some common components of bicycles, show a class hierarchy in which the class **Bicycle** inherits from other classes, which, in turn, inherit from yet other classes. Discuss the instantiation of various objects of class **Bicycle**. Discuss inheritance from class **Bicycle** for other closely related derived classes.

19.3 Briefly define each of the following terms: inheritance, multiple inheritance, base class, and derived class.

19.4 Discuss why converting a base-class pointer to a derived-class pointer is considered dangerous by the compiler.

19.5 Write down all the shapes you can think of—both two-dimensional and three-dimensional—and form those shapes into a shape hierarchy. Your hierarchy should have base class **Shape** from which class **TwoDimensionalShape** and class **ThreeDimensionalShape** are derived. Once you have developed the hierarchy, define each of the classes in the hierarchy. We will use this hierarchy in the exercises of Chapter 20 to process all shapes as objects of base-class **Shape**. This is a technique called polymorphism.

19.6 A popular kind of class is called a collection class or a container class. Such a class holds items of other classes. Some popular kinds of collection classes are arrays, stacks, queues, linked lists, trees, character strings, sets, bags, dictionaries, tables, etc. A collection class typically provides services such as insert an element, delete and element, search for an element, combine two collections, determine the intersection of two collections (i.e., the elements they have in common), print a collection, find the largest element in the collection, find the smallest element in the collection find the sum of the elements in the collection, etc.

a) Make a list of all the collection class types you can think of (including the ones we mentioned).

b) Arrange these collection classes into a class hierarchy. You might want to distinguish between ordered collections and unordered collections.

c) Implement as many of these classes as you can using inheritance to minimize the amount of new code you must write to create each new class.

d) Write a driver program that tests each of the classes in your inheritance hierarchy.

20

Virtual Functions and Polymorphism

Objectives

- To understand the notion of polymorphism.
- To understand how to declare and use virtual functions to effect polymorphism.
- To understand the distinction between abstract classes and concrete classes.
- To learn how to declare pure virtual functions to create abstract classes.
- To appreciate how polymorphism makes systems extensible and maintainable.

O! Thou hast damnable iteration, and art indeed able to corrupt a saint.
William Shakespeare
Henry IV, Part I, 1, ii

General propositions do not decide concrete cases.
Oliver Wendell Holmes

A philosopher of imposing stature doesn't think in a vacuum. Even his most abstract ideas are, to some extent, conditioned by what is or is not known in the time when he lives.
Alfred North Whitehead

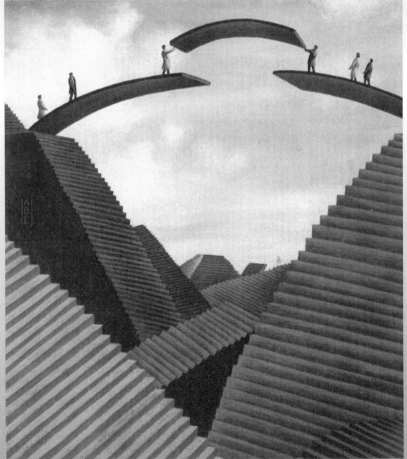

Outline

20.1 Introduction

With *virtual functions* and *polymorphism,* it becomes possible to design and implement systems that are more easily *extensible.* Programs can be written to process objects of existing classes and of classes that do not exist when the program is under development. If these classes are to be derived from base classes the program knows about, the program can provide a general framework for manipulating objects of the base classes, and objects of the derived classes will fit this framework nicely. Indeed, complete products called application frameworks are built on this principle.

20.2 Type Fields and Switch Statements

One means of dealing with objects of many different types is to use a `switch` statement to take the appropriate action on each object based on that object's type. There are many problems with using `switch` logic. The programmer might forget to make such a type test when one is warranted. The programmer may forget to test all possible cases in a `switch`. If a switch-based system is modified, the programmer might forget to insert the new cases in existing `switch` statements. Every modification to the `switch` statements to handle new types demands that every `switch` statement in the system be modified; tracking these down can be time consuming and error prone.

As we will see, virtual functions and polymorphic programming can eliminate the need for `switch` logic. The programmer can use the virtual function mechanism to perform the equivalent logic automatically, thus avoiding the kinds of errors typically associated with `switch` logic.

Software Engineering Observation 20.1

An interesting consequence of using virtual functions and polymorphism is that programs take on a simplified appearance. They contain less branching logic in favor of simpler sequential code. This simplification facilitates testing, debugging, and program maintenance.

20.3 Virtual Functions

Suppose a set of shape classes such as `Circle`, `Triangle`, `Rectangle`, `Square`, etc. are all derived from base class `Shape`. In object-oriented programming, each of these classes might be endowed with the ability to draw itself. Although each class has its own `draw` function, the `draw` function for each shape is quite different. When drawing a shape, whatever that shape may be, it would be nice to be able to treat all these shapes generically as objects of the base class `Shape`. Then to draw any shape, we could simply call function `draw` of base class `Shape` and let the program determine dynamically (i.e., at execution time) which derived class `draw` function to use.

To enable this kind of behavior, we declare `draw` in the base class as a *virtual function*, and then we *redefine* `draw` in each of the derived classes to draw the appropriate shape. A virtual function is declared by preceding the function's prototype with the keyword `virtual` in the base class.

Software Engineering Observation 20.2

Once a function has been declared virtual, it remains virtual all the way down the inheritance hierarchy from that point.

Good Programming Practice 20.1

Even though certain functions are implicitly virtual because of a declaration made higher in the class hierarchy, some programmers prefer to explicitly declare these virtual functions at every level of the hierarchy to promote program clarity.

Software Engineering Observation 20.3

When a derived class chooses not to define a virtual function, the derived class simply inherits its immediate base class's virtual function.

If function `draw` in the base class has been declared `virtual`, and if we then use a base-class pointer to point to the derived-class object and invoke the `draw` function using this pointer, the program will choose the correct derived class's `draw` function dynamically (i.e., at execution time). This is called *dynamic binding* (see Figs. 20.1 and 20.2).

Software Engineering Observation 20.4

Redefined virtual functions must have the same return type and signature as the base virtual function.

Common Programming Error 20.1

Redefining in a derived class a base-class virtual function and not ensuring that the derived function has the same return type and signature as the base class's version is a syntax error.

If a virtual function is called by referencing a specific object by name and using the dot member selection operator, the reference is resolved at compile time (this is called *static binding*), and the virtual function that is called is the one defined for (or inherited by) the class of that particular object.

Overloading does not use dynamic binding. Rather, overloading is resolved at compile time by selecting the function definition with a signature that matches the function call (possibly using implicit type casting to effect the match). This is static binding.

20.4 Abstract Base Classes and Concrete Classes

When we think of a class as a type, we assume that objects of that type will be instantiated. There are many situations, however, in which it is useful to define classes for which the programmer never intends to instantiate any objects. Such classes are called *abstract classes*. Because these are used in inheritance situations as base classes, we will normally refer to them as *abstract base classes*. No objects of an abstract base class can be instantiated.

The sole purpose of an abstract class is to provide an appropriate base class from which classes may inherit interface and/or implementation. Classes from which objects can be instantiated are called *concrete classes*.

We could have an abstract base class **TwoDimensionalObject** and derive concrete classes such as **Square**, **Circle**, **Triangle**, etc. We could also have an abstract base class **ThreeDimensionalObject** and derive concrete classes such as **Cube**, **Sphere**, **Cylinder**, **Pyramid**, etc. These abstract base classes are too generic to define real objects; we need to be more specific before we can think of instantiating objects. That is what concrete classes do; they provide the specifics that make it reasonable to instantiate objects.

A class with virtual functions is made abstract by declaring one or more of its virtual functions to be pure. A *pure virtual function* is one with an *initializer of = 0* in its declaration as in

```
virtual float earnings() const = 0;    // pure virtual
```

Software Engineering Observation 20.5

If a class is derived from a class with a pure virtual function, and if no definition is supplied for that pure virtual function in the derived class, then that virtual function remains pure in the derived class. Consequently, the derived class is also an abstract class.

Common Programming Error 20.2

Attempting to instantiate an object of an abstract class (i.e., a class that contains one or more pure virtual functions) is a syntax error.

A hierarchy does not need to contain any abstract classes, but as we will see, many good object-oriented systems have class hierarchies headed by an abstract base class. In some cases, abstract classes constitute the top few levels of the hierarchy. A good example of this is a shape hierarchy. The hierarchy could be headed by abstract base class **Shape**. On the next level down, we can have two more abstract base classes, namely

TwoDimensionalShape and **ThreeDimensionalShape**. The next level down would start defining concrete classes for two-dimensional shapes such as circles and squares, and concrete classes for three-dimensional shapes such as spheres and cubes.

20.5 Polymorphism

C++ enables *polymorphism*—the ability for objects of different classes related by inheritance to respond differently to the same member function call. If, for example, class **Rectangle** is derived from class **Quadrilateral**, then a **Rectangle** object *is a* more specific version of a **Quadrilateral** object. An operation (such as calculating the perimeter or the area) that can be performed on an object of class **Quadrilateral** can also be performed on an object of class **Rectangle**.

Polymorphism is implemented via virtual functions. When a request is made through a base-class pointer (or reference) to use a virtual function, C++ chooses the correct redefined function in the appropriate derived class associated with the object.

Sometimes a nonvirtual member function is defined in a base class and redefined in a derived class. If such a member function is called through a base-class pointer, the base-class version is used. If the member function is called through a derived-class pointer, the derived-class version is used. This is nonpolymorphic behavior.

Through the use of virtual functions and polymorphism, one member function call can cause different actions to occur depending on the type of the object receiving the call. This gives the programmer tremendous expressive capability. We will see examples of the power of polymorphism and virtual functions in the next several sections.

Software Engineering Observation 20.6

With virtual functions and polymorphism, the programmer can deal in generalities and let the execution-time environment concern itself with the specifics. The programmer can command a wide variety of objects to behave in manners appropriate to those objects without even knowing the types of those objects.

Software Engineering Observation 20.7

Polymorphism promotes extensibility: Software written to invoke polymorphic behavior is written independently of the types of the objects to which messages are sent. Thus, new types of objects that can respond to existing messages can be added into such a system without modifying the base system. Except for client code that instantiates new objects, programs need not be recompiled.

Software Engineering Observation 20.8

An abstract class defines an interface for the various members of a class hierarchy. The abstract class contains pure virtual functions that will be defined in the derived classes. All functions in the hierarchy can use this same interface through polymorphism.

Although we cannot instantiate objects of abstract base classes, we *can* declare pointers to abstract base classes. Such pointers can then be used to enable polymorphic manipulations of derived-class objects when such objects are instantiated from concrete classes.

Let us consider applications of polymorphism and virtual functions. A screen manager needs to display a variety of objects, including new types of objects that will be added to the system even after the screen manager is written. The system may need to display various shapes (i.e., the base class is **Shape**) such as squares, circles, triangles, rectangles, and the like (each of these shape classes is derived from the base class **Shape**). The screen manager uses base-class pointers to manage all the objects to be displayed. To draw any object (regardless of the level at which that object appears in the inheritance hierarchy), the screen manager uses a base-class pointer to the object and simply sends a **draw** message to the object. Function **draw** has been declared pure virtual in base class **Shape** and has been redefined in each of the derived classes. Each object knows how to draw itself. The screen manager does not have to worry about these details; it simply tells each object to draw itself.

Polymorphism is particularly effective for implementing layered software systems. In operating systems, for example, each type of physical device may operate quite differently from the others. Regardless of this, commands to *read* or *write* data from and to devices can have a certain uniformity. The *write* message sent to a device-driver object needs to be interpreted specifically in the context of that device driver and how that device driver manipulates devices of a specific type. But the *write* call itself is really no different from the *write* to any other device—simply place some number of bytes from memory onto that device. An object-oriented operating system might use an abstract base class to provide an interface appropriate for all device drivers. Then, through inheritance from that abstract base class, derived classes are formed that all operate similarly. The capabilities (i.e., the public interface) offered by the device drivers are provided as pure virtual functions in the abstract base class. The implementations of these virtual functions are provided in the derived classes that correspond to the specific types of device drivers.

In Chapter 17, we introduced the concept of iterators. It is common to define an *iterator class* that will walk through all the objects in a collection. If you want to print a list of objects in a linked list, for example, an iterator object can be instantiated that will return the next element of the linked list each time the iterator is called. Iterators are commonly used in polymorphic programming to walk through a linked list of objects from various levels of a hierarchy. The pointers in such a list would all be base-class pointers.

20.6 Case Study: A Payroll System Using Polymorphism

Let us use virtual functions and polymorphism to perform payroll calculations based on the type of an employee (Fig. 20.1). We use a base class **Employee**. The derived classes of **Employee** are **Boss** who gets paid a fixed weekly salary regardless of the number of hours worked, **CommissionWorker** who gets a flat base salary plus a percentage of sales, **PieceworkWorker** who gets paid by the number of items produced, and **HourlyWorker** who gets paid by the hour and receives overtime pay.

An **earnings** function call certainly applies generically to all employees. But the way each person's earnings are calculated depends on the class of the employee, and these classes are all derived from the base class **Employee**. So **earnings** is declared **virtual** in base class **Employee** and appropriate implementations of **earnings** are provided for each of the derived classes. Then, to calculate any employee's earnings, the program simply uses a base-class pointer to that employee's object and invokes the **earnings** function. In a real payroll system, the various employee objects might be stored in a linked list in which each of the pointers is of type **Employee ***. The program would then simply walk through the linked list one node at a time using the **Employee *** pointers to invoke the **earnings** function of each object.

Let us consider the **Employee** class (Fig. 20.1, parts 1 and 2). The public member functions include a constructor that takes the first name and last name as arguments; a destructor that reclaims dynamically allocated memory; a *get* function that returns the first name; a *get* function that returns the last name; and finally, two pure virtual functions—**earnings** and **print**. Why are these functions pure virtual? The answer is that it does not make sense to provide implementations of these functions in the **Employee** class. By making these functions pure virtual we are indicating that we will provide implementations in derived classes, but not in the base class itself. We cannot calculate the earnings for a generic employee—we must first know what kind of employee it is—nor can we print the type of employee for a generic employee.

Class **Boss** (Fig. 20.1, parts 3 and 4) is derived from **Employee** with public inheritance. The public member functions include a constructor that takes a first name, a last name, and a weekly salary as arguments and passes the first name and last name to the **Employee** constructor to initialize the **firstName** and **lastName** members of the base-class part of the derived-class object; a *set* function to assign a new value to private data member **weeklySalary**; a virtual **earnings** function defining how to calculate a **Boss**'s earnings; and a virtual **print** function that outputs the type of the employee followed by the employee's name.

```
// EMPLOY2.H
// Abstract base class Employee
#ifndef EMPLOY2_H
#define EMPLOY2_H

class Employee {
public:
   Employee(const char *, const char *);
   ~Employee();
   const char *getFirstName() const;
   const char *getLastName() const;

   // Pure virtual functions make
   // Employee an abstract base class.
   virtual float earnings() const = 0; // pure virtual
   virtual void print() const = 0;      // pure virtual
private:
   char *firstName;
   char *lastName;
};

#endif
```

Fig. 20.1 Abstract base class **Employee** (part 1 of 12).

```
// EMPLOY2.CPP
// Member function definitions for
// abstract base class Employee.
//
// Note: No definitions given for pure virtual functions.
#include <iostream.h>
#include <string.h>
#include <assert.h>
#include "employ2.h"

// Constructor dynamically allocates space for the
// first and last name and uses strcpy to copy
// the first and last names into the object.
Employee::Employee(const char *first, const char *last)
{
   firstName = new char[ strlen(first) + 1 ];
   assert(firstName != 0);      // test that new worked
   strcpy(firstName, first);

   lastName = new char[ strlen(last) + 1 ];
   assert(lastName != 0);       // test that new worked
   strcpy(lastName, last);
}

// Destructor deallocates dynamically allocated memory
Employee::~Employee()
{
   delete [] firstName;
   delete [] lastName;
}

// Return a pointer to the first name
const char *Employee::getFirstName() const
{
   // Const prevents caller from modifying private data.
   // Caller should copy returned string before destructor
   // deletes dynamic storage to prevent undefined pointer.

   return firstName;    // caller must delete memory
}

// Return a pointer to the last name
const char *Employee::getLastName() const
{
   // Const prevents caller from modifying private data.
   // Caller should copy returned string before destructor
   // deletes dynamic storage to prevent undefined pointer.

   return lastName;    // caller must delete memory
}
```

Fig. 20.1   Member function definitions for abstract base class **Employee** (part 2 of 12).

```
// BOSS1.H
// Boss class derived from Employee
#ifndef BOSS1_H
#define BOSS1_H
#include "employ2.h"

class Boss : public Employee {
public:
   Boss(const char *, const char *, float = 0.0);
   void setWeeklySalary(float);
   virtual float earnings() const;
   virtual void print() const;
private:
   float weeklySalary;
};

#endif
```

Fig. 20.1 Class **Boss** derived from abstract base class **Employee** (part 3 of 12).

```
// BOSS1.CPP
// Member function definitions for class Boss
#include <iostream.h>
#include "boss1.h"

// Constructor function for class Boss
Boss::Boss(const char *first, const char *last, float s)
   : Employee(first, last)  // call base-class constructor
{ weeklySalary = s > 0 ? s : 0; }

// Set the Boss's salary
void Boss::setWeeklySalary(float s)
{ weeklySalary = s > 0 ? s : 0; }

// Get the Boss's pay
float Boss::earnings() const { return weeklySalary; }

// Print the Boss's name
void Boss::print() const
{
   cout << "\n             Boss: " << getFirstName()
        << ' ' << getLastName();
}
```

Fig. 20.1 Member function definitions for class **Boss** (part 4 of 12).

Class **CommissionWorker** (Fig. 20.1, parts 5 and 6) is derived from **Employee** with public inheritance. The public member functions include a constructor that takes a first name, a last name, a salary, a commission, and a quantity of items sold as arguments and passes the first name and last name to the **Employee** constructor to initialize the **firstName** and **lastName** members of the base-class part of the derived-class object; *set* functions to assign new values to private data members **salary**, **commission**, and

```
// COMMIS1.H
// CommissionWorker class derived from Employee
#ifndef COMMIS1_H
#define COMMIS1_H
#include "employ2.h"

class CommissionWorker : public Employee {
public:
   CommissionWorker(const char *, const char *,
                    float = 0.0, float = 0.0, int = 0);
   void setSalary(float);
   void setCommission(float);
   void setQuantity(int);
   virtual float earnings() const;
   virtual void print() const;
private:
   float salary;      // base salary per week
   float commission;  // amount per item sold
   int quantity;      // total items sold for week
};

#endif
```

Fig. 20.1   Class `CommissionWorker` derived from abstract base class `Employee` (part 5 of 12).

`quantity`; a virtual `earnings` function defining how to calculate a `Commission-Worker`'s earnings; and a virtual `print` function that outputs the type of the employee followed by the employee's name.

Class `PieceWorker` (Fig. 20.1, parts 7 and 8) is derived from `Employee` with public inheritance. The public member functions include a constructor that takes a first name, a last name, a wage per piece, and a quantity of items produced as arguments and passes the first name and last name to the `Employee` constructor to initialize the `firstName` and `lastName` members of the base-class part of the derived-class object; *set* functions to assign new values to private data members `wagePerPiece` and `quantity`; a virtual `earnings` function defining how to calculate a `PieceWorker`'s earnings; and a virtual `print` function that outputs the type of the employee followed by the employee's name.

Class `HourlyWorker` (Fig. 20.1, parts 9 and 10) is derived from `Employee` with public inheritance. The public member functions include a constructor that takes a first name, a last name, a wage, and the number of hours worked as arguments and passes the first name and last name to the `Employee` constructor to initialize the `firstName` and `lastName` members of the base-class part of the derived-class object; *set* functions to assign new values to private data members `wage` and `hours`; a virtual `earnings` function defining how to calculate an `HourlyWorker`'s earnings; and a virtual `print` function that outputs the type of the employee followed by the employee's name.

The driver program (Fig. 20.1, parts 11 and 12) begins by declaring base-class pointer, `ptr`, of type `Employee *`. Each of the subsequent three code segments in `main` is similar, so we discuss only the first segment which deals with a `Boss` object. The line

```
// COMMIS1.CPP
// Member function definitions for class CommissionWorker
#include <iostream.h>
#include "commis1.h"

// Constructor for class CommissionWorker
CommissionWorker::CommissionWorker(const char *first,
   const char *last, float s, float c, int q)
   : Employee(first, last)  // call base-class constructor
{
   salary = s > 0 ? s : 0;
   commission = c > 0 ? c : 0;
   quantity = q > 0 ? q : 0;
}

// Set CommissionWorker's weekly base salary
void CommissionWorker::setSalary(float s)
{ salary = s > 0 ? s : 0; }

// Set CommissionWorker's commission
void CommissionWorker::setCommission(float c)
{ commission = c > 0 ? c : 0; }

// Set CommissionWorker's quantity sold
void CommissionWorker::setQuantity(int q)
{ quantity = q > 0 ? q : 0; }

// Determine CommissionWorker's earnings
float CommissionWorker::earnings() const
{ return salary + commission * quantity; }

// Print the CommissionWorker's name
void CommissionWorker::print() const
{
   cout << "\nCommission worker: " << getFirstName()
        << ' ' << getLastName();
}
```

Fig. 20.1 Member function definitions for class **CommissionWorker**
(part 6 of 12).

```
Boss b("John", "Smith", 800.00);
```

instantiates derived-class object **b** of class **Boss** and provides various constructor arguments including a first name, a last name, and a fixed weekly salary. The line

```
ptr = &b;  // base-class pointer to derived-class object
```

places in base-class pointer **ptr** the address of derived class object **b**. This is precisely what we must do to effect polymorphic behavior. The line

```
ptr->print();                              // dynamic binding
```

invokes the **print** member function of the object pointed to by **ptr**. Because **print** has been declared to be a virtual function in the base class, the system invokes the derived

```
// PIECE1.H
// PieceWorker class derived from Employee
#ifndef PIECE1_H
#define PIECE1_H
#include "employ2.h"

class PieceWorker : public Employee {
public:
   PieceWorker(const char *, const char *,
               float = 0.0, int = 0 );
   void setWage(float);
   void setQuantity(int);
   virtual float earnings() const;
   virtual void print() const;

private:
   float wagePerPiece; // wage for each piece output
   int quantity;       // output for week
};

#endif
```

Fig. 20.1   Class **PieceWorker** derived from abstract base class **Employee** (part 7 of 12).

class object's **print** function—again, precisely what we call polymorphic behavior. This function call is an example of dynamic binding—the function is invoked through a base-class pointer, so the decision as to what function to invoke is deferred until execution time. The line

```
cout << " earned $" << ptr->earnings(); // dynamic binding
```

invokes the **earnings** member function of the object pointed to by **ptr**. Because **earnings** has been declared to be a virtual function in the base class, the system invokes the derived-class object's **earnings** function. This is also an example of dynamic binding. The line

```
b.print();                              // static binding
```

explicitly invokes the **Boss** version of member function **print** by using the dot member selection operator off the specific **Boss** object **b**. This is an example of static binding because the type of the object for which the function is called is known at compile time. This call is included for comparison purposes to illustrate that the correct **print** function is invoked using dynamic binding. The line

```
cout << " earned $" << b.earnings();    // static binding
```

explicitly invokes the **Boss** version of member function **earnings** by using the dot member selection operator off the specific **Boss** object **b**. This is also an example of static binding. This call is included for comparison purposes to illustrate that the correct **earnings** function is invoked using dynamic binding.

```
// PIECE1.CPP
// Member function definitions for class PieceWorker

#include <iostream.h>
#include "piece1.h"

// Constructor for class PieceWorker
PieceWorker::PieceWorker(const char *first, const char *last,
                         float w, int q)
   : Employee(first, last)  // call base-class constructor
{
   wagePerPiece = w > 0 ? w : 0;
   quantity = q > 0 ? q : 0;
}

// Set the wage
void PieceWorker::setWage(float w)
{ wagePerPiece = w > 0 ? w : 0; }

// Set the number of items output
void PieceWorker::setQuantity(int q)
{ quantity = q > 0 ? q : 0; }

// Determine the PieceWorker's earnings
float PieceWorker::earnings() const
{ return quantity * wagePerPiece; }

// Print the PieceWorker's name
void PieceWorker::print() const
{
   cout << "\n   Piece worker: " << getFirstName()
        << ' ' << getLastName();
}
```

Fig. 20.1   Member function definitions for class **PieceWorker** (part 8 of 12).

20.7 New Classes and Dynamic Binding

Polymorphism and virtual functions could certainly work nicely in a world in which all possible classes were known in advance. But they also work when new kinds of classes are regularly added to systems.

New classes are accommodated by dynamic binding (also called *late binding*). The type of an object need not be known at compile time for a virtual function call to be compiled. At execution time, the virtual function call is matched with the member function of the called object.

A screen manager program can now handle new display objects as they are added to the system without being recompiled. The **draw** function call remains the same. The new objects themselves contain the actual drawing capabilities. This makes it easy to add new capabilities to systems with minimal impact. It also promotes software reuse.

```
// HOURLY1.H
// Definition of class HourlyWorker
#ifndef HOURLY1_H
#define HOURLY1_H
#include "employ2.h"

class HourlyWorker : public Employee {
public:
   HourlyWorker(const char *, const char *,
                float = 0.0, float = 0.0);
   void setWage(float);
   void setHours(float);
   virtual float earnings() const;
   virtual void print() const;
private:
   float wage;    // wage per hour
   float hours;   // hours worked for week
};

#endif
```

Fig. 20.1 Class `HourlyWorker` derived from abstract base class `Employee` (part 9 of 12).

```
// HOURLY1.CPP
// Member function definitions for class HourlyWorker
#include <iostream.h>
#include "hourly1.h"

// Constructor for class HourlyWorker
HourlyWorker::HourlyWorker(const char *first, const char *last,
                           float w, float h)
   : Employee(first, last)    // call base-class constructor
{
   wage = w > 0 ? w : 0;
   hours = h >= 0 && h < 168 ? h : 0;
}

// Set the wage
void HourlyWorker::setWage(float w) { wage = w > 0 ? w : 0; }

// Set the hours worked
void HourlyWorker::setHours(float h)
{ hours = h >= 0 && h < 168 ? h : 0; }

// Get the HourlyWorker's pay
float HourlyWorker::earnings() const { return wage * hours; }

// Print the HourlyWorker's name
void HourlyWorker::print() const
{
   cout << "\n   Hourly worker: " << getFirstName()
        << ' ' << getLastName();
}
```

Fig. 20.1 Member function definitions for class `HourlyWorker` (part 10 of 12).

```
// FIG20_1.CPP
// Driver for Employee hierarchy

#include <iostream.h>
#include <iomanip.h>
#include "employ2.h"
#include "boss1.h"
#include "commis1.h"
#include "piece1.h"
#include "hourly1.h"

main()
{
    // set output formatting
    cout << setiosflags(ios::showpoint) << setprecision(2);

    Employee *ptr;   // base-class pointer

    Boss b("John", "Smith", 800.00);
    ptr = &b;   // base-class pointer to derived-class object
    ptr->print();                               // dynamic binding
    cout << " earned $" << ptr->earnings(); // dynamic binding
    b.print();                                  // static binding
    cout << " earned $" << b.earnings();    // static binding

    CommissionWorker c("Sue", "Jones", 200.0, 3.0, 150);
    ptr = &c;   // base-class pointer to derived-class object
    ptr->print();                               // dynamic binding
    cout << " earned $" << ptr->earnings(); // dynamic binding
    c.print();                                  // static binding
    cout << " earned $" << c.earnings();    // static binding

    PieceWorker p("Bob", "Lewis", 2.5, 200);
    ptr = &p;   // base-class pointer to derived-class object
    ptr->print();                               // dynamic binding
    cout << " earned $" << ptr->earnings(); // dynamic binding
    p.print();                                  // static binding
    cout << " earned $" << p.earnings();    // static binding

    HourlyWorker h("Karen", "Price", 13.75, 40);
    ptr = &h;   // base-class pointer to derived-class object
    ptr->print();                               // dynamic binding
    cout << " earned $" << ptr->earnings(); // dynamic binding
    h.print();                                  // static binding
    cout << " earned $" << h.earnings();    // static binding

    cout << endl;

    return 0;
}
```

Fig. 20.1   Employee class derivation hierarchy that uses an abstract base class
(part 11 of 12).

```
                    Boss: John Smith earned $800.00
                    Boss: John Smith earned $800.00
        Commission worker: Sue Jones earned $650.00
        Commission worker: Sue Jones earned $650.00
             Piece worker: Bob Lewis earned $500.00
             Piece worker: Bob Lewis earned $500.00
            Hourly worker: Karen Price earned $550.00
            Hourly worker: Karen Price earned $550.00
```

Fig. 20.1　Employee class derivation hierarchy that uses an abstract base class (part 12 of 12).

Dynamic binding enables independent software vendors (ISVs) to distribute software without revealing proprietary secrets. Software distributions can consist of only header files and object files. No source code needs to be revealed. Software developers can then use inheritance to derive new classes from those provided by the ISVs. The software that works with the classes the ISVs provide will continue to work with the derived classes and will use (via dynamic binding) the redefined virtual functions provided in these classes.

Dynamic binding requires that at execution time, the call to a virtual member function be routed to the virtual function version appropriate for the class. A *virtual function table* called the *vtable* is implemented as an array containing function pointers. Each class that contains virtual functions has a *vtable*. For each virtual function in the class, the *vtable* has an entry containing a function pointer to the version of the virtual function to use for an object of that class. The virtual function to use for a particular class could be the function defined in that class, or it could be a function inherited either directly or indirectly from a base class higher in the hierarchy.

When a base class provides a member function and declares it **virtual**, derived classes can redefine the virtual function, but they do not have to redefine it. Thus a derived class can use a base class's version of a virtual member function, and this would be indicated in the *vtable*.

Each object of a class with virtual functions contains a pointer to the *vtable* for that class. This pointer is not accessible to the programmer. The appropriate function pointer in the *vtable* is obtained and dereferenced to complete the call at execution time. This *vtable* lookup and pointer dereferencing requires nominal execution time overhead.

Performance Tip 20.1

Polymorphism as implemented with virtual functions and dynamic binding is efficient. Programmers may use these capabilities with nominal impact on system performance.

Performance Tip 20.2

Virtual functions and dynamic binding enable polymorphic programming as opposed to **switch** *logic programming. C++ optimizing compilers normally generate code that runs at least as efficiently as hand-coded* **switch**-*based logic.*

20.8 Virtual Destructors

A problem can occur when using polymorphism to process dynamically allocated objects of a class hierarchy. If each object is destroyed explicitly by applying the **delete** operator to a base-class pointer to the object, the base-class destructor function is called on the object. This occurs regardless of the type of the object to which the base-class pointer is pointing and regardless of the fact that each class's destructor has a different name.

There is a simple solution to this problem—declare the base-class destructor virtual. This will automatically make all derived-class destructors virtual even though they do not have the same name as the base-class destructor. Now, if an object in the hierarchy is destroyed explicitly by applying the **delete** operator to a base-class pointer to a derived-class object, the destructor for the appropriate class is called.

Good Programming Practice 20.2

If a class has virtual functions, provide a virtual destructor even if one is not required for the class. Classes derived from this class may contain destructors that must be called properly.

Common Programming Error 20.3

Declaring a constructor as a virtual function. Constructors cannot be virtual.

20.9 Case Study: Inheriting Interface and Implementation

Our next example (Fig. 20.2) re-examines the point, circle, cylinder hierarchy from the previous chapter except that we now head the hierarchy with abstract base class **Shape**. **Shape** has a pure virtual function—**printShapeName**—so **Shape** is an abstract base class. **Shape** contains two other virtual functions, namely **area** and **volume**, each of which has an implementation that returns a value of zero. **Point** inherits these implementations from **Shape**. This makes sense because both the area and volume of a point are zero. **Circle** inherits the **volume** function from **Point**, but **Circle** provides its own implementation for the **area** function. **Cylinder** provides its own implementations for both the **area** function and the **volume** function.

Note that although **Shape** is an abstract base class, it still contains implementations of certain member functions, and these implementations are inheritable. The **Shape** class provides an inheritable interface in the form of three virtual functions that all members of the hierarchy will contain. The **Shape** class also provides some implementations that derived classes in the first few levels of the hierarchy will use.

This case study emphasizes that a class can inherit interface and/or implementation from a base class. Hierarchies designed for implementation inheritance tend to have their functionality high in the hierarchy. Hierarchies designed for interface inheritance tend to have their functionality lower in the hierarchy.

Base class **Shape** (Fig. 20.2, part 1) consists of three public virtual functions and does not contain any data. Function **printShapeName** is pure virtual, so it is redefined in each of the derived classes. Functions **area** and **volume** are defined to return **0.0**. These functions are redefined in derived classes when it is appropriate for those classes to have a different **area** calculation and/or a different **volume** calculation.

```
// SHAPE.H
// Definition of abstract base class Shape
#ifndef SHAPE_H
#define SHAPE_H

class Shape {
public:
   virtual float area() const { return 0.0; }
   virtual float volume() const { return 0.0; }
   virtual void printShapeName() const = 0; // pure virtual
};

#endif
```

Fig. 20.2   Definition of abstract base class **Shape** (part 1 of 9).

Class **Point** (Fig. 20.2, parts 2 and 3) is derived from **Shape** with public inheritance. A **Point** does not have area or volume, so the base-class member functions **area** and **volume** are not redefined here—they are inherited as defined in **Shape**. Function **printShapeName** is an implementation of a virtual function that was defined as pure virtual in the base class. Other member functions include a *set* function to assign new **x** and **y** coordinates to a **Point** and *get* functions to return the **x** and **y** coordinates of a **Point**.

Class **Circle** (Fig. 20.2, parts 4 and 5) is derived from **Point** with public inheritance. A **Circle** does not have volume, so base-class member function **volume** is not redefined here—it is inherited from **Shape** (and subsequently into **Point**). A **Circle** has area, so the **area** function is redefined in this class. Function **printShapeName**

```
// POINT1.H
// Definition of class Point
#ifndef POINT1_H
#define POINT1_H
#include <iostream.h>
#include "shape.h"

class Point : public Shape {
   friend ostream &operator<<(ostream &, const Point &);
public:
   Point(float = 0, float = 0);  // default constructor
   void setPoint(float, float);
   float getX() const { return x; }
   float getY() const { return y; }
   virtual void printShapeName() const { cout << "Point: "; }
private:
   float x, y;    // x and y coordinates of Point
};

#endif
```

Fig. 20.2   Definition of class **Point** (part 2 of 9).

```
// POINT1.CPP
// Member function definitions for class Point
#include <iostream.h>
#include "point1.h"

Point::Point(float a, float b)
{
   x = a;
   y = b;
}

void Point::setPoint(float a, float b)
{
   x = a;
   y = b;
}

ostream &operator<<(ostream &output, const Point &p)
{
   output << '[' << p.x << ", " << p.y << ']';

   return output;   // enables concatenated calls
}
```

Fig. 20.2   Member function definitions for class **Point** (part 3 of 9).

```
// CIRCLE1.H
// Definition of class Circle
#ifndef CIRCLE1_H
#define CIRCLE1_H
#include "point1.h"

class Circle : public Point {
   friend ostream &operator<<(ostream &, const Circle &);
public:
   // default constructor
   Circle(float r = 0.0, float x = 0.0, float y = 0.0);

   void setRadius(float);
   float getRadius() const;
   virtual float area() const;
   virtual void printShapeName() const { cout << "Circle: "; }
private:
   float radius;   // radius of Circle
};

#endif
```

Fig. 20.2   Definition of class **Circle** (part 4 of 9).

is an implementation of a virtual function that was defined as pure virtual in the base class. If this function is not redefined here, the **Point** version of the function would be

```
// CIRCLE1.CPP
// Member function definitions for class Circle
#include <iostream.h>
#include <iomanip.h>
#include "circle1.h"

// Constructor for Circle call constructor for Point
Circle::Circle(float r, float a, float b)
   : Point(a, b)  // call base-class constructor
{ radius = r > 0 ? r : 0; }

// Set radius
void Circle::setRadius(float r) { radius = r > 0 ? r : 0; }

// Get radius
float Circle::getRadius() const { return radius; }

// Calculate area of a Circle
float Circle::area() const { return 3.14159 * radius * radius; }

// Output a circle in the form: Center=[x, y]; Radius=#.##
ostream &operator<<(ostream &output, const Circle &c)
{
    output << '[' << c.getX() << ", " << c.getY()
           << "]; Radius = " << setiosflags(ios::showpoint)
           << setprecision(2) << c.radius;

    return output;    // enables concatenated calls
}
```

Fig. 20.2 Member function definitions for class `Circle` (part 5 of 9).

inherited. Other member functions include a *set* function to assign a new **radius** to a **Circle** and a *get* function to return **radius** of a **Circle**.

Class **Cylinder** (Fig. 20.2, parts 6 and 7) is derived from **Circle** with public inheritance. A **Cylinder** has area and volume, so the **area** and **volume** functions are both redefined in this class. Function **printShapeName** is an implementation of a virtual function that was defined as pure virtual in the base class. If this function is not redefined here, the **Circle** version of the function would be inherited. Other member functions include a *set* function to assign a new **radius** to a **Circle** and a *get* function to return **radius** of a **Circle**.

The driver program (Fig. 20.2, parts 8 and 9) begins by instantiating **Point** object **point**, **Circle** object **circle**, and **Cylinder** object **cylinder**. Function **printShapeName** is invoked for each object and each object is output with its overloaded stream insertion operator to illustrate the objects are initialized correctly. Next, pointer **ptr** of type **Shape *** is declared. This pointer is used to point to each of the derived-class objects. First the address of **point** is assigned to **ptr** and the following calls

```
ptr->printShapeName()
ptr->area()
ptr->volume()
```

```
// CYLINDER.H
// Definition of class Cylinder
#ifndef CYLINDER_H
#define CYLINDER_H
#include "circle1.h"

class Cylinder : public Circle {
    friend ostream &operator<<(ostream &, const Cylinder &);
public:
    // default constructor
    Cylinder(float h = 0.0, float r = 0.0,
             float x = 0.0, float y = 0.0);

    void setHeight(float);
    virtual float area() const;
    virtual float volume() const;
    virtual void printShapeName() const { cout << "Cylinder: "; }
private:
    float height;    // height of Cylinder
};

#endif
```

Fig. 20.2   Definition of class **Cylinder** (part 6 of 9).

are made to invoke these functions on the object to which **ptr** is pointing. The output illustrates that the functions are invoked properly for **point**—**"Point: "** is output and
the area and volume are both **0.00**. Next, **ptr** is assigned the address of object **circle**
and the same functions are invoked. The output illustrates that the functions are invoked
properly for object **circle**—**"Circle: "** is output, the area of **circle** is calculated,
and the volume is **0.00**. Finally, **ptr** is assigned the address of object **cylinder** and
the same functions are invoked. The output illustrates that the functions are invoked
properly for object **cylinder**—**"Cylinder: "** is output, the area of **cylinder** is
calculated, and the volume of **cylinder** is calculated. All the **printShapeName**,
area, and **volume** function calls are resolved at run-time with dynamic binding.

Summary

- With virtual functions and polymorphism, it becomes possible to design and implement systems that are more easily extensible. Programs can be written to process objects of types that may not exist when the program is under development.

- Virtual functions and polymorphic programming can eliminate the need for **switch**
  logic. The programmer can use the virtual function mechanism to perform the equivalent logic automatically, thus avoiding the kinds of errors typically associated with
  switch logic. Client code making decisions about object types and representations
  indicates poor class design.

- A virtual function is declared by preceding the function's prototype with the keyword
  virtual in the base class.

```
// CYLINDR1.CPP
// Member function definitions for class Cylinder
#include <iostream.h>
#include <iomanip.h>
#include "cylindr1.h"

Cylinder::Cylinder(float h, float r, float x, float y)
    : Circle(r, x, y)  // call base-class constructor
{ height = h > 0 ? h : 0; }

void Cylinder::setHeight(float h)
{ height = h > 0 ? h : 0; }

float Cylinder::area() const
{
    // surface area of Cylinder
    return 2 * Circle::area() +
           2 * 3.14159 * Circle::getRadius() * height;
}

float Cylinder::volume() const
{
    float r = Circle::getRadius();
    return 3.14159 * r * r * height;
}

ostream &operator<<(ostream &output, const Cylinder& c)
{
    output << '[' << c.getX() << ", " << c.getY()
           << "]; Radius = " << setiosflags(ios::showpoint)
           << setprecision(2) << c.getRadius()
           << "; Height = " << c.height;

    return output;    // enables concatenated calls
}
```

Fig. 20.2   Member function definitions for class **Cylinder** (part 7 of 9).

- Derived classes can provide their own implementations of a base class virtual function if they want to, but if they do not, then the base class's implementation is used.

- If a virtual function is called by referencing a specific object by name and using the dot member selection operator, the reference is resolved at compile time (this is called *static binding*), and the virtual function that is called is the one defined for (or inherited by) the class of that particular object.

- There are many situations, however, in which it is useful to define classes for which the programmer never intends to instantiate any objects. Such classes are called abstract classes. Because these are used in inheritance situations as base classes, we will normally refer to them as abstract base classes. No objects of an abstract class may be instantiated.

```cpp
// FIG20_2.CPP
// Driver for point, circle, cylinder hierarchy
#include <iostream.h>
#include <iomanip.h>
#include "shape.h"
#include "point1.h"
#include "circle1.h"
#include "cylindr1.h"

main()
{
    // create some shape objects
    Point point(7, 11);
    Circle circle(3.5, 22, 8);
    Cylinder cylinder(10, 3.3, 10, 10);

    point.printShapeName();      // static binding
    cout << point << endl;

    circle.printShapeName();     // static binding
    cout << circle << endl;

    cylinder.printShapeName();   // static binding
    cout << cylinder << "\n\n";

    cout << setiosflags(ios::showpoint) << setprecision(2);
    Shape *ptr;                  // create base-class pointer

    // aim base-class pointer at derived-class Point object
    ptr = &point;
    ptr->printShapeName();       // dynamic binding
    cout << "x = " << point.getX() << "; y = " << point.getY()
         << "\nArea = " << ptr->area()
         << "\nVolume = " << ptr->volume() << "\n\n";

    // aim base-class pointer at derived-class Circle object
    ptr = &circle;
    ptr->printShapeName();       // dynamic binding
    cout << "x = " << circle.getX() << "; y = " << circle.getY()
         << "\nArea = " << ptr->area()
         << "\nVolume = " << ptr->volume() << "\n\n";

    // aim base-class pointer at derived-class Cylinder object
    ptr = &cylinder;
    ptr->printShapeName();       // dynamic binding
    cout << "x = " << cylinder.getX()
         << "; y = " << cylinder.getY()
         << "\nArea = " << ptr->area()
         << "\nVolume = " << ptr->volume() << endl;

    return 0;
}
```

Fig. 20.2 Driver for point, circle, cylinder hierarchy (part 8 of 9).

```
Point: [7, 11]
Circle: [22, 8]; Radius = 3.50
Cylinder: [10, 10]; Radius = 3.30; Height = 10.00

Point: x = 7.00; y = 11.00
Area = 0.00
Volume = 0.00

Circle: x = 22.00; y = 8.00
Area = 38.48
Volume = 0.00

Cylinder: x = 10.00; y = 10.00
Area = 275.77
Volume = 342.12
```

Fig. 20.2   Driver for point, circle, cylinder hierarchy (part 9 of 9).

- Classes from which objects can be instantiated are called concrete classes.

- A class with virtual functions may be made abstract by declaring one or more of its virtual functions to be pure. A pure virtual function is one with an initializer of = 0 in its declaration.

- If a class is derived from a class with a pure virtual function without supplying a definition for that pure virtual function in the derived class, then that virtual function remains pure in the derived class. Consequently, the derived class is also an abstract class.

- C++ enables polymorphism—the ability for objects of different classes related by inheritance to respond differently to the same member function call.

- Polymorphism is implemented via virtual functions.

- When a request is made through a base-class pointer to use a virtual function, C++ chooses the correct redefined function in the appropriate derived class associated with the object.

- Through the use of virtual functions and polymorphism, one member function call can cause different actions to occur depending on the type of the object receiving the call.

- Although we cannot instantiate objects of abstract base classes, we *can* declare pointers to abstract base classes. Such pointers can then be used to enable polymorphic manipulations of derived-class objects when such objects are instantiated from concrete classes.

- New kinds of classes are regularly added to systems. New classes are accommodated by dynamic binding (also called late binding). The type of an object need not be known at compile time for a virtual function call to be compiled. At execution time, the virtual function call is matched with the member function of the called object.

- Dynamic binding enables independent software vendors (ISVs) to distribute software without revealing proprietary secrets. Software distributions can consist of only header files and object files. No source code needs to be revealed. Software developers can then use inheritance to derive new classes from those provided by the ISVs. The software that works with the classes the ISVs provide will continue to work with the derived classes and will use (via dynamic binding) the redefined virtual functions provided in these classes.

- Dynamic binding requires that at execution time, the call to a virtual member function be routed to the virtual function version appropriate for the class. A virtual function table called the vtable is implemented as an array containing function pointers. Each class that contains virtual functions has a vtable. For each virtual function in the class, the vtable has an entry containing a function pointer to the version of the virtual function to use for an object of that class. The virtual function to use for a particular class could be the function defined in that class, or it could be a function inherited either directly or indirectly from a base class higher in the hierarchy.

- When a base class provides a member function and declares it **virtual**, derived classes can redefine the virtual function, but they do not have to redefine it. Thus a derived class can use a base class's version of a virtual member function, and this would be indicated in the vtable.

- Each object of a class with virtual functions contains a pointer to the vtable for that class. This pointer is not accessible to the programmer. The appropriate function pointer in the vtable is obtained and dereferenced to complete the call at execution time. This vtable lookup and pointer dereferencing require nominal execution time overhead, usually less than the best possible client code.

- Declare the base-class destructor virtual if the class contains virtual functions. This makes all derived-class destructors virtual even though they do not have the same name as the base-class destructor. If an object in the hierarchy is destroyed explicitly by applying the **delete** operator to a base-class pointer to a derived-class object, the destructor for the appropriate class is called.

Terminology

abstract base class
abstract class
base-class **virtual** function
class hierarchy
convert derived-class object to base-class
    object
convert derived-class pointer to base-class
    pointer
derived class
derived-class constructor
direct base class
dynamic binding

early binding
eliminating **switch** statements
explicit pointer conversion
extensibility
implicit pointer conversion
indirect base class
inheritance
late binding
object-oriented programming (OOP)
pointer to a base class
pointer to a derived class
pointer to an abstract class

polymorphism
pure virtual function (=0)
redefined virtual function
reference to a base class
reference to a derived class
reference to an abstract class

software reusability
static binding
`switch` logic
virtual destructor
virtual function
`virtual` keyword

Common Programming Errors

20.1   Redefining in a derived class a base-class virtual function and not ensuring that the derived function has the same return type and signature as the base class's version is a syntax error.

20.2   Attempting to instantiate an object of an abstract class (i.e., a class that contains one or more pure virtual functions) is a syntax error.

20.3   Declaring a constructor as a virtual function. Constructors cannot be virtual.

Good Programming Practices

20.1   Even though certain functions are implicitly virtual because of a declaration made higher in the class hierarchy, some programmers prefer to explicitly declare these virtual functions at every level of the hierarchy to promote program clarity.

20.2   If a class has virtual functions, provide a virtual destructor even if one is not required for the class. Classes derived from this class may contain destructors that must be called properly.

Performance Tips

20.1   Polymorphism as implemented with virtual functions and dynamic binding is efficiently. Programmers may use these capabilities with nominal impact on system performance.

20.2   Virtual functions and dynamic binding enable polymorphic programming as opposed to `switch` logic programming. C++ optimizing compilers normally generate code that runs at least as efficiently as hand-coded `switch`-based logic.

Software Engineering Observations

20.1   An interesting consequence of using virtual functions and polymorphism is that programs take on a simplified appearance. They contain less branching logic in favor of simpler sequential code. This simplification facilitates testing, debugging, and program maintenance.

20.2   Once a function has been declared virtual, it remains virtual all the way down the inheritance hierarchy from that point.

20.3   When a derived class chooses not to define a virtual function, the derived class simply inherits its immediate base class's virtual function.

20.4   Redefined virtual functions must have the same return type and signature as the base virtual function.

20.5   If a class is derived from a class with a pure virtual function, and if no definition is supplied for that pure virtual function in the derived class, then that virtual function remains pure in the derived class. Consequently, the derived class is also an abstract class.

20.6   With virtual functions and polymorphism, the programmer can deal in generalities and let the execution-time environment concern itself with the specifics. The programmer can command a wide variety of objects to behave in manners appropriate to those objects with out even knowing the types of those objects. Except for client code that instantiates new objects, programs need not be recompiled.

20.7 Polymorphism promotes extensibility: Software written to invoke polymorphic behavior is written independently of the types of the objects to which messages are sent. Thus, new types of objects that can respond to existing messages can be added into such a system without modifying the base system.

20.8 An abstract class defines an interface for the various members of a class hierarchy. The abstract class contains pure virtual functions that will be defined in the derived classes. All functions in the hierarchy can use this same interface through polymorphism.

Self-Review Exercises

20.1 Fill in the blanks in each of the following:
a) Using inheritance and polymorphism helps eliminate _____ logic.
b) A pure virtual function is specified by placing _____ at the end of its prototype in the class definition.
c) If a class contains one or more pure virtual functions, it is an _____.
d) A function call resolved at compile time is referred to as _____ binding.
e) A function call resolved at run time is referred to as _____ binding.

Answers to Self-Review Exercises

20.1 a) `switch`. b) = 0. c) abstract base class. d) static. e) dynamic.

Exercises

20.2 What are virtual functions? Describe a circumstance in which virtual functions would be appropriate.

20.3 Given that constructors cannot be virtual, describe a scheme for how you might achieve a similar effect.

20.4 In Exercise 19.5, you developed a **Shape** class hierarchy and defined the classes in the hierarchy. Modify the hierarchy so that class **Shape** is an abstract base class containing the interface to the hierarchy. Derive **TwoDimensionalShape** and **ThreeDimensionalShape** from class **Shape**—these classes should also be abstract. Use a virtual **print** function to output the type and dimensions of each class. Also include virtual **area** and **volume** functions so these calculations can be performed for objects of each concrete class in the hierarchy. Write a driver program that tests the **Shape** class hierarchy.

20.5 Using the template **List** class you developed in Exercise 17.10, create a linked list of pointers to **Shape** objects (i.e., pointers to any shape in the hierarchy). Provide an overloaded stream insertion operator for the **Shape** class that simply calls the pure virtual function **print**. Use the linked list printing capability to walk the list and output each object.

21

C++ Stream Input/Output

Objectives

- To understand how to use C++ object-oriented stream input/output.
- To be able to format inputs and outputs.
- To understand the stream I/O class hierarchy.
- To understand how to input/output objects of user-defined types.
- To be able to create user-defined stream manipulators.
- To be able to determine the success or failure of input/output operations.
- To be able to tie output streams to input streams.

Consciousness... does not appear to itself chopped up in bits ...A "river" or a "stream" are the metaphors by which it is most naturally described.
William James

All the news that's fit to print.
Adolph S. Ochs

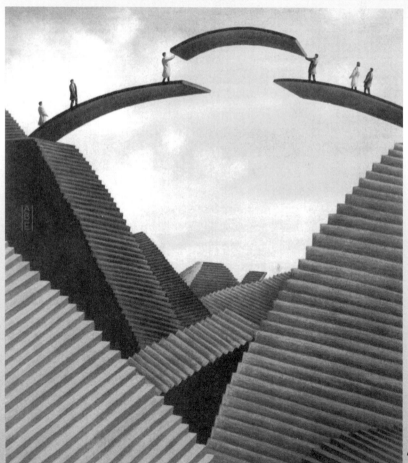

Outline

Summary • Terminology • Common Programming Errors • Good Programming Practices • Performance Tips • Software Engineering Observations • Self-Review Exercises • Answers to Self-Review Exercises • Exercises

21.1 Introduction

The C++ standard libraries provide an extensive set of input/output capabilities. This chapter discusses a range of capabilities sufficient for performing most common I/O operations, and overviews the remaining capabilities.

Many of the input/output features described here are object-oriented. The reader should find it interesting to see how such capabilities are implemented. This style of I/O also makes heavy use of other C++ features such as references, function overloading, and operator overloading.

As we will see, C++ uses *type safe I/O*. Each I/O operation is performed in a manner sensitive to the type of the data. If an I/O function has been properly defined to handle a particular data type, then that function is automatically called to handle that type of data. If there is no match between the type of the actual data and a function for handling that data type, a compiler error indication is set. Thus, improper data cannot sneak through the system (as can occur in C—a hole in C that allows for some rather subtle and often bizarre errors).

Users may specify I/O of user-defined types as well as standard types. This *extensibility* is one of the most valued features of C++.

Good Programming Practice 21.1

Use the C++ form of I/O exclusively in C++ programs, despite the fact that C-style I/O is available to C++ programmers.

Software Engineering Observation 21.1

C++ style I/O is type safe.

Software Engineering Observation 21.2

C++ enables a common treatment of I/O of predefined types and user-defined types. This kind of commonality facilitates software development in general and software reuse in particular.

21.2 Streams

C++ I/O occurs in *streams* of bytes. A stream is simply a sequence of bytes. In input operations, the bytes flow from a device (e.g., a keyboard, a disk drive, a network connection) to main memory. In output operations, bytes flow from main memory to a device (e.g., a display screen, a printer, a disk drive, a network connection).

The application associates meaning with bytes. The bytes may represent ASCII characters, internal format raw data, graphics images, digital speech, digital video, or any other kind of information an application may require.

The job of the system I/O mechanisms is to move bytes from devices to memory and vice versa in a consistent and reliable manner. Such transfers often involve mechanical motion such as the rotation of a disk or a tape, or typing keystrokes at a keyboard. The time these transfers take is normally huge compared to the time the processor takes to manipulate data internally. Thus, I/O operations require careful planning and tuning to ensure maximum performance. Issues like this are discussed in depth in operating systems textbooks (De90).

C++ provides both "low-level" and "high-level" I/O capabilities. Low-level I/O-capabilities (i.e., unformatted I/O) typically specify that some number of bytes should simply be transferred device-to-memory or memory-to-device. In such transfers, the individual byte is the item of interest. Such low-level capabilities do provide high-speed, high-volume transfers, but these capabilities are not particularly convenient for people.

People prefer a higher-level view of I/O, i.e., *formatted I/O,* in which bytes are grouped into meaningful units such as integers, floating point numbers, characters, strings, and user-defined types. These type-oriented capabilities are satisfactory for most I/O other than high-volume file processing.

Performance Tip 21.1
_____

Use unformatted I/O for the best performance in high-volume file processing.

21.2.1 Iostream Library Header Files

The C++ **iostream** library provides hundreds of I/O capabilities. Several header files contain portions of the library interface.

Most C++ programs should include the **iostream.h** header file which contains basic information required for all stream-I/O operations. The **iostream.h** header file contains the **cin**, **cout**, **cerr**, and **clog** objects which, as we will see, correspond to the standard input stream, standard output stream, and standard error stream. Both unformatted- and formatted-I/O capabilities are provided.

The **iomanip.h** header contains information useful for performing formatted I/O with so-called *parameterized stream manipulators.*

The **fstream.h** header contains information important for user-controlled file processing operations.

The **strstream.h** header contains information important for performing *in-memory formatting* (also called *in-core formatting*). This resembles file processing, but the "I/O" operations are performed to and from character arrays rather than files.

The **stdiostream.h** header contains information important for programs that mix the C and C++ styles of I/O. New programs should avoid C-style I/O, but people who need to modify existing C programs, or evolve C programs to C++, may find these capabilities useful.

Each C++ implementation generally contains other I/O-related libraries that provide system-specific capabilities such as controlling special-purpose devices for audio and video I/O.

21.2.2 Stream Input/Output Classes and Objects

The **iostream** library contains many classes for handling a wide variety of I/O operations. The **istream** class supports stream input operations. The **ostream** class supports stream output operations. The **iostream** class supports both stream input and stream output operations.

The **istream** class and the **ostream** class are each derived through single inheritance from the **ios** base class. The **iostream** class is derived through multiple inheritance from both the **istream** class and the **ostream** class. These inheritance relationships are summarized in Fig. 21.1.

Operator overloading provides a convenient notation for performing input/output. The left shift operator (<<) is overloaded to designate stream output and is referred to as the *stream-insertion operator*. The right shift operator (>>) is overloaded to designate stream input and is referred to as the *stream-extraction operator*. These operators are used with the standard stream objects **cin**, **cout**, **cerr**, and **clog**, and with user-defined stream objects.

cin is an object of the **istream** class and is said to be "tied to" (or connected to) the standard input device, normally the keyboard. The stream-extraction operator as used in the following statement causes a value for integer variable **grade** to be input from **cin** to memory.

```
cin >> grade;
```

Note that the stream extraction operation is "smart enough" to "know" what the type of the data is. Assuming that **grade** has been properly declared, no additional type information needs to be specified for use with the stream-extraction operator (as is the case, incidentally, in C-style I/O).

cout is an object of the **ostream** class and is said to be "tied to" the standard output device, normally the display screen. The stream-insertion operator as used in the following statement causes the value of integer variable **grade** to be output from memory to the standard output device.

```
cout << grade;
```

Note that the stream-insertion operator is "smart enough" to "know" the type of **grade** (assuming it has been properly declared), so no additional type information needs to be specified for use with the stream-insertion operator.

cerr is an object of the **ostream** class and is said to be "tied to" the standard error device. Outputs to object **cerr** are unbuffered. This means that each insertion to **cerr** causes its output to appear immediately; this is appropriate for promptly notifying a user of trouble.

Fig. 21.1 Portion of the stream I/O class hierarchy.

clog is an object of the **ostream** class and is also said to be "tied to" the standard error device. Outputs to **clog** are buffered.

C++ file processing uses the classes **ifstream** to perform file input operations, **ofstream** for file output operations, and **fstream** for file input/output operations. The **ifstream** class inherits from **istream**, the **ofstream** class inherits from **ostream**, and the **fstream** class inherits from **iostream**. The inheritance relationships of the I/O-related classes are summarized in Fig. 21.2. There are many more classes in the full stream-I/O class hierarchy supported at most installations, but the classes shown here provide the vast majority of the capabilities most programmers will need. See the class library reference for your C++ system for more file processing information.

21.3 Stream Output

The C++ **ostream** class provides the ability to perform formatted and unformatted output. Capabilities for output include: output of standard data types with the stream-insertion operator; output of characters with the **put** member function; unformatted output with the **write** member function (Section 21.5); output of integers in decimal, octal and hexadecimal formats (Section 21.6.1); output of floating point values with various precisions (Section 21.6.2), with forced decimal points (Section 21.7.2), in scientific notation, and in fixed notation (Section 21.7.6); output of data justified in fields of designated field widths (Section 21.7.3); output of data in fields padded with specified characters (Section 21.7.4); and output of uppercase letters in scientific notation and hexadecimal notation (Section 21.7.7).

21.3.1 Stream-Insertion Operator

Stream output may be performed with the stream-insertion operator, i.e., the overloaded **<<** operator. The **<<** operator is overloaded to output data items of built-in types, to output strings and to output pointer values. In Section 21.9, we will see how to overload **<<** to output data items of user-defined types. Figure 21.3 demonstrates output of a string.

The previous example uses a single stream insertion statement to display the output string. Multiple insertion statements may be used as in Fig. 21.4. When this program is run, it produces the same output as the previous program.

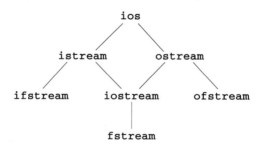

Fig. 21.2 Portion of stream-I/O class hierarchy with key file-processing classes.

```
// fig21_03.cpp
// Outputting a string using stream insertion.

#include <iostream.h>

main()
{
    cout << "Welcome to C++!\n";

    return 0;
}
```

```
Welcome to C++!
```

Fig. 21.3 Outputting a string using stream insertion.

```
// fig21_04.cpp
// Outputting a string using two stream insertions.

#include <iostream.h>

main()
{
    cout << "Welcome to ";
    cout << "C++!\n";

    return 0;
}
```

```
Welcome to C++!
```

Fig. 21.4 Outputting a string using two stream insertions.

The effect of the **\n** (newline) escape sequence is also achieved by the **endl** (end line) *stream manipulator* as in Fig. 21.5. The **endl** stream manipulator issues a newline character and, in addition, flushes the output buffer (i.e., causes the output buffer to be output immediately even if it is not full). The output buffer may also be flushed simply by

```
cout << flush;
```

Stream manipulators are discussed in detail in Section 21.6.
Expressions can be output as shown in Fig. 21.6.

Good Programming Practice 21.2

When outputting expressions, place them in parentheses to prevent operator precedence problems between the operators in the expression and the **<<** *operator.*

```
// fig21_05.cpp
// Using the endl stream manipulator.
#include <iostream.h>

main()
{
   cout << "Welcome to ";
   cout << "C++!";
   cout << endl;    // end line stream manipulator

   return 0;
}
```

```
Welcome to C++!
```

Fig. 21.5   Using the **endl** stream manipulator.

```
// fig21_06.cpp
// Outputting expression values.
#include <iostream.h>

main()
{
   cout << "47 plus 53 is ";
   cout << 47 + 53;        // expression
   cout << endl;

   return 0;
}
```

```
47 plus 53 is 100
```

Fig. 21.6   Outputting expression values.

21.3.2 Concatenating Stream Insertion/Extraction Operators

The overloaded **<<** and **>>** operators may each be used in a *concatenated form* as shown in Fig. 21.7.

The multiple stream insertions in Fig. 21.7 are executed as if they had been written:

```
(((cout << "47 plus 53 is ") << 47 + 53) << endl);
```

This is allowed because the overloaded **<<** operator returns a reference to its left-operand object, i.e., **cout**. Thus the leftmost parenthesized expression

```
(cout << "47 plus 53 is ")
```

```
// fig21_07.cpp
// Concatenating the overloaded << operator.
#include <iostream.h>

main()
{
    cout << "47 plus 53 is " << 47 + 53 << endl;

    return 0;
}
```

```
47 plus 53 is 100
```

Fig. 21.7   Concatenating the overloaded << operator.

outputs the specified character string and returns a reference to **cout**. This allows the middle parenthesized expression to be evaluated as

```
(cout << 47 + 53)
```

which outputs the integer value **100** and returns a reference to **cout**. The rightmost parenthesized expression is then evaluated as

```
cout << endl
```

which outputs a newline, flushes **cout**, and returns a reference to **cout**. This last return is not used.

21.3.3 Output of Char * Variables

In C-style I/O, it is necessary to supply type information. C++ determines data types automatically—a nice improvement over C. But sometimes this "gets in the way." For example, we know that a character string is of type **char***. Suppose we want to print the value of that pointer, i.e., the memory address of the first character of that string. But the **<<** operator has been overloaded to print data of type **char*** as a null-terminated string. The solution is to cast the pointer to **void*** (this should be done to any pointer variable the programmer wishes to output as an address). Figure 21.8 demonstrates printing a **char*** variable in both string and address formats. Note that the address prints as a hexadecimal (base 16) number. Hexadecimal numbers in C++ begin with **0x** or **0X**. We say more about controlling the bases of numbers in Sections 21.6.1, 21.7.4, 21.7.5, and 21.7.7.

21.3.4 Character Output with the Put Member Function; Concatenating Puts

The **put** member function outputs one character as in

```
cout.put('A');
```

```
// fig21_08.cpp
// Printing the address stored in a char* variable

#include <iostream.h>

main()
{
    char *string = "test";

    cout << "Value of string is: " << string
         << "\nValue of (void *)string is: "
         << (void *)string << endl;

    return 0;
}
```

```
Value of string is: test
Value of (void *)string is: 0x00aa
```

Fig. 21.8   Printing the address stored in a **char *** variable.

which displays **A** on the screen. Calls to **put** may be concatenated as in

```
cout.put('A').put('\n');
```

which outputs the letter **A** followed by a newline character. The **put** function may also be called with an ASCII-valued expression as in **cout.put(65)** which also outputs **A**.

21.4 Stream Input

Now let us consider stream input. This may be performed with the stream-extraction operator, i.e., the overloaded **>>** operator. This operator normally skips *whitespace characters* (such as blanks, tabs, and newlines) in the input stream. Later we will see how to change this behavior. The stream-extraction operator returns zero (false) when end-of-file is encountered on a stream. Each stream contains a set of *state bits* used to control the state of the stream (i.e., formatting, setting error states, etc.). Stream extraction causes the stream's **failbit** to be set for input of the wrong type, and causes the stream's **badbit** to be set if the operation fails. We will soon see how to test these bits after an I/O operation. Sections 21.7 and 21.8 discuss the stream state bits in detail.

21.4.1 Stream-Extraction Operator

To read two integers, use the **cin** object and the overloaded **>>** stream-extraction operator as in Fig. 21.9.

The relatively high precedence of the **>>** and **<<** operators can cause problems. For example, the program of Fig. 21.10 will not compile properly without the parentheses around the conditional expression. The reader should verify this.

```
// fig21_09.cpp
// Calculating the sum of two integers
// input from the keyboard with cin
// and the stream extraction operator.
#include <iostream.h>

main()
{
    int x, y;

    cout << "Enter two integers: ";
    cin >> x >> y;
    cout << "Sum of " << x << " and " << y << " is: "
         << x + y << endl;

    return 0;
}
```

```
Enter two integers: 30 92
Sum of 30 and 92 is: 122
```

Fig. 21.9 Calculating the sum of two integers input from the keyboard with `cin` and the stream extraction operator.

```
// fig21_10.cpp
// Revealing a precedence problem.
// Need parentheses around the conditional expression.
#include <iostream.h>

main()
{
    int x, y;

    cout << "Enter two integers: ";
    cin >> x >> y;
    cout << x << (x == y ? " is" : " is not")
         << " equal to " << y << endl;

    return 0;
}
```

```
Enter two integers: 7 5
7 is not equal to 5
```

```
Enter two integers: 8 8
8 is equal to 8
```

Fig. 21.10 Avoiding a precedence problem between the stream-insertion operator and the conditional operator.

Common Programming Error 21.1

Attempting to read from an ostream (or from any other output-only stream).

Common Programming Error 21.2

Attempting to write to an istream (or to any other input-only stream).

Common Programming Error 21.3

Not providing parentheses to force proper precedence when using the relatively high precedence stream-insertion operator << or stream-extraction operator >>.

One popular way to input a series of values is to use the stream extraction operation in the header of a **while** loop. The extraction returns false (zero) when end-of-file is encountered. Consider the program of Fig. 21.11 which finds the highest grade on an exam. Assume the number of grades is not known in advance and that the user will type end-of-file to indicate that all the grades have been entered. The **while** condition, **(cin >> grade)**, becomes zero (i.e., false) when the user enters end-of-file.

```
// fig21_11.cpp
// Stream extraction operator returning
// false on end-of-file.
#include <iostream.h>

main()
{
   int grade, highestGrade = -1;

   cout << "Enter grade (enter end-of-file to end): ";
   while (cin >> grade) {
      if (grade > highestGrade)
         highestGrade = grade;

      cout << "Enter grade (enter end-of-file to end): ";
   }

   cout << "\nHighest grade is: " << highestGrade
        << endl;
   return 0;
}
```

```
Enter grade (enter end-of-file to end): 67
Enter grade (enter end-of-file to end): 87
Enter grade (enter end-of-file to end): 73
Enter grade (enter end-of-file to end): 95
Enter grade (enter end-of-file to end): 34
Enter grade (enter end-of-file to end): 99
Enter grade (enter end-of-file to end): ^Z

Highest grade is: 99
```

Fig. 21.11 Stream extraction operator returning false on end-of-file.

21.4.2 Get and Getline Member Functions

The **get** member function without any arguments inputs one character from the designated stream (even if this is whitespace) and returns this character as the value of the function call. This version of **get** returns **EOF** when end-of-file on the stream is encountered. **EOF** is commonly **-1** to distinguish it from ASCII character values (this may vary between systems).

Figure 21.12 demonstrates the use of member functions **eof** and **get** on input stream **cin** and member function **put** on output stream **cout**. The program first prints the value of **cin.eof()**, i.e., **0** (false) to show that end-of-file has not occurred on **cin**. The user enters a line of text followed by end-of-file (**<ctrl>-z** followed by **<return>** on IBM PC compatible systems, **<ctrl>-d** on UNIX and Macintosh systems). The program reads each character and outputs it to **cout** using member function **put**. When the end-of-file is encountered, the **while** ends, and **cin.eof()**—now **1** (true)—is printed again to show that end-of-file has been set on **cin**. Note that this program uses the version of **istream** member function **get** that takes no arguments and returns the character being input.

```
// fig21_12.cpp
// Using member functions get, put, and eof.

#include <iostream.h>

main()
{
   int c;

   cout << "Before input, cin.eof() is "
        << cin.eof() << '\n'
        << "Enter a sentence followed by end-of-file:\n";

   while ((c = cin.get()) != EOF)
      cout.put(c);

   cout << "\nAfter input, cin.eof() is "
        << cin.eof() << endl;

   return 0;
}
```

```
Before input, cin.eof() is 0
Enter a sentence followed by end-of-file:
Testing the get and put member functions^Z
Testing the get and put member functions
After input cin.eof() is 1
```

Fig. 21.12 Using member functions **get**, **put**, and **eof**.

The **get** member function with a character argument inputs the next character from the input stream (even if this is a whitespace character). This version of **get** returns false when end-of-file is encountered; otherwise this version of **get** returns a reference to the **istream** object for which the **get** member function is being invoked.

A third version of the **get** member function takes three arguments—a character array, a size limit, and a delimiter (with default value '**\n**'). This version reads characters from the input stream. It reads up to one less than the specified maximum number of characters and terminates, or terminates as soon as the delimiter is read. A null character is inserted to terminate the input string in the character array used as a buffer by the program. The delimiter is not placed in the character array, but does remain in the input stream. Figure 21.13 compares input using **cin** with stream extraction and input with **cin.get**.

```
// fig21_13.cpp
// Contrasting input of a string with cin and cin.get.

#include <iostream.h>

const int SIZE = 80;

main()
{
    char buffer1[SIZE], buffer2[SIZE];

    cout << "Enter a sentence:\n";
    cin >> buffer1;
    cout << "\nThe string read with cin was:\n"
         << buffer1 << "\n\n";

    cin.get(buffer2, SIZE);
    cout << "The string read with cin.get was:\n"
         << buffer2 << endl;

    return 0;
}
```

```
Enter a sentence:
Contrasting string input with cin and cin.get

The string read with cin was:
Contrasting

The string read with cin.get was:
 string input with cin and cin.get
```

Fig. 21.13 Contrasting input of a string using **cin** with stream extraction and input with **cin.get**.

The **getline** member function operates like the third version of the **get** member function and inserts a null character after the line in the character array. The **getline** function removes the delimiter from the stream, but does not store it in the character array. The program of Fig. 21.14 demonstrates the use of the **getline** member function to input a line of text.

21.4.3 Other Istream Member Functions (Peek, Putback, Ignore)

The **ignore** member function skips over a designated number of characters (default is one character) or terminates upon encountering a designated delimiter (the default delimiter is **EOF**).

The **putback** member function places the previous character obtained by a **get** on an input stream back onto that stream. This function is useful for applications that scan an input stream looking for a field beginning with a specific character. When that character is input, the application puts that character back on the stream so the character can be included in the data about to be input.

The **peek** member function returns the next character from an input stream, but does not remove the character from the stream.

```
// fig21_14.cpp
// Character input with member function getline.

#include <iostream.h>

const SIZE = 80;

main()
{
    char buffer[SIZE];

    cout << "Enter a sentence:\n";
    cin.getline(buffer, SIZE);

    cout << "\nThe sentence entered is:\n"
         << buffer << endl;

    return 0;
}
```

```
Enter a sentence:
Using the getline member function

The sentence entered is:
Using the getline member function
```

Fig. 21.14 Character input with member function **getline**.

21.4.4 Type-Safe I/O

C++ offers *type-safe I/O*. The `<<` and `>>` operators are overloaded to accept data items of specific types. If unexpected data is processed, various error flags are set which the user may test to determine if an I/O operation succeeded or failed. In this manner the program "stays in control." We discuss these error flags in Section 21.8.

21.5 Unformatted I/O with Read, Gcount, and Write

Unformatted input/output is performed with the `read` and `write` member functions. Each of these inputs or outputs some number of bytes to or from a character array in memory. These bytes are not formatted in any way. They are simply input or output as raw bytes. For example, the call

```
char buffer[] = "HAPPY BIRTHDAY";
cout.write(buffer, 10);
```

outputs the first 10 bytes of `buffer`. Since a character string evaluates to the address of its first character, the call

```
cout.write("ABCDEFGHIJKLMNOPQRSTUVWXYZ", 10);
```

displays the first 10 characters of the alphabet.

The `read` member function inputs into a character array a designated number of characters. If fewer than the designated number of characters are read, `failbit` is set. We will soon see how to determine if `failbit` has been set (see Section 21.8).

Figure 21.15 demonstrates `istream` member functions `read` and `gcount` and `ostream` member function `write`. The program inputs 20 characters (from a longer input sequence) into character array `buffer` with `read`, determines the number of characters input with `gcount`, and outputs the characters in `buffer` with `write`.

21.6 Stream Manipulators

C++ provides various *stream manipulators* that perform formatting tasks. The stream manipulators provide capabilities such as setting field widths, setting precisions, setting and unsetting format flags, setting the fill character in fields, flushing streams, inserting a newline in the output stream and flushing the stream, inserting a null character in the output stream, and skipping whitespace in the input stream. These features are described in the following sections.

21.6.1 Integral Stream Base: Dec, Oct, Hex, and Setbase Stream Manipulators

Integers are normally interpreted as decimal (base 10) values. To change the base in which integers are interpreted on a stream, insert the manipulator `hex` to set the base to hexadecimal (base 16) or insert the manipulator `oct` to set the base to octal (base 8). Insert the `dec` stream manipulator to reset the stream base to decimal.

```
// fig21_15.cpp
// Unformatted I/O with the read,
// gcount and write member functions.

#include <iostream.h>

const int SIZE = 80;

main()
{
    char buffer[SIZE];

    cout << "Enter a sentence:\n";
    cin.read(buffer, 20);
    cout << "\nThe sentence entered was:\n";
    cout.write(buffer, cin.gcount());
    cout << endl;

    return 0;
}
```

```
Enter a sentence:
Using the read, write, and gcount member functions

The sentence entered was:
Using the read, writ
```

Fig. 21.15 Unformatted I/O with the **read, gcount,** and **write** member functions.

The base of a stream may also be changed by the stream manipulator **setbase** which takes one integer argument of **10**, **8**, or **16** to set the base. Because **setbase** takes an argument, it is called a *parameterized stream manipulator.* Using **setbase** or any other parameterized manipulator requires the inclusion of the **iomanip.h** header file. The stream base remains the same until it is explicitly changed. Fig. 21.16 shows the use of the **hex**, **oct**, **dec**, and **setbase** stream manipulators.

21.6.2 Floating Point Precision (Precision, Setprecision)

We can control the *precision* of floating point numbers, i.e., the number of digits to the right of the decimal point, by using either the **setprecision** stream manipulator or the **precision** member function. A call to either of these sets the precision for all subsequent output operations until the next precision-setting call. The **precision** member function with no argument returns the current precision setting. The program of Fig. 21.17 uses both the **precision** member function and the **setprecision** manipulator to print a table showing the square root of **2** with precisions varying from **0** through **9**. Note that precision **0** has special meaning. This restores the *default precision* value **6**.

```
// fig21_16.cpp
// Using hex, oct, dec and setbase stream manipulators.
#include <iostream.h>
#include <iomanip.h>

main()
{
    int n;

    cout << "Enter a decimal number: ";
    cin >> n;

    cout << n << " in hexadecimal is: "
         << hex << n << '\n'
         << dec << n << " in octal is: "
         << oct << n << '\n'
         << setbase(10) << n << " in decimal is: "
         << n << endl;

    return 0;
}
```

```
Enter a decimal number: 20
20 in hexadecimal is: 14
20 in octal is: 24
20 in decimal is: 20
```

Fig. 21.16 Using the **hex**, **oct**, **dec**, and **setbase** stream manipulators.

21.6.3 Field Width (`setw`, `width`)

The **width** member function sets the field width and returns the previous width. If values processed are smaller than the field width, *fill characters* are inserted as *padding*. A value wider than the designated width will not be truncated—the full number will be printed. The width setting applies only for the next insertion or extraction; afterward the width is implicitly set to **0**, i.e., output values will simply be as wide as they need to be. The **width** function with no argument returns the current setting.

Common Programming Error 21.4

When not providing a sufficiently wide field to handle outputs, the outputs print as wide as they need to be, possibly causing difficult-to-read or erroneous outputs.

Figure 21.18 demonstrates the use of the **width** member function on both input and output. Note that on input, a maximum of one fewer characters than the width will be read because provision is made for the null character to be placed in the input string. Remember that stream extraction terminates when nonleading whitespace is encountered. The **setw** stream manipulator may also be used to set the field width.

```
// fig21_17.cpp
// Controlling precision of floating point values
#include <iostream.h>
#include <iomanip.h>
#include <math.h>

main()
{
    double root2 = sqrt(2.0);

    cout << "Square root of 2 with precisions 0-9.\n"
         << "Precision set by the "
         << "precision member function:\n";

    for (int places = 0; places <= 9; places++) {
        cout.precision(places);
        cout << root2 << endl;
    }

    cout << "\nPrecision set by the "
         << "setprecision manipulator:\n";

    for (places = 0; places <= 9; places++)
        cout << setprecision(places) << root2 << endl;

    return 0;
}
```

```
Square root of 2 with precisions 0-9.
Precision set by the precision member function:
1.414214
1.4
1.41
1.414
1.4142
1.41421
1.414214
1.4142136
1.41421356
1.414213562

Precision set by the setprecision manipulator:
1.414214
1.4
1.41
1.414
1.4142
1.41421
1.414214
1.4142136
1.41421356
1.414213562
```

Fig. 21.17 Controlling precision of floating point values.

```
// fig21_18.cpp
// Demonstrating the width member function

#include <iostream.h>

main()
{
   int w = 4;
   char string[10];

   cout << "Enter a sentence:\n";
   cin.width(5);

   while (cin >> string) {
      cout.width(w++);
      cout << string << '\n';
      cin.width(5);
   }

   return 0;
}
```

```
Enter a sentence:
This is a test of the width member function^Z
This
   is
      a
   test
      of
      the
      widt
            h
         memb
            er
         func
            tion
```

Fig. 21.18 Demonstrating the **width** member function.

21.6.4 User-Defined Manipulators

Users may create their own stream manipulators. Figure 21.19 shows the creation and use of new stream manipulators **bell**, **ret** (carriage return), **tab**, and **endLine**. Users may also create their own parameterized stream manipulators—consult your installation's manuals for instructions on how to do this.

21.7 Stream Format States

Various *format flags* specify the kinds of formatting to be performed during stream I/O operations. The **setf**, **unsetf**, and **flags** member functions control the flag settings.

```
// fig21_19.cpp
// Testing user-defined, nonparameterized manipulators

#include <iostream.h>

// bell manipulator (using escape sequence \a)
ostream& bell(ostream& output)
{
   return output << '\a';
}

// ret manipulator (using escape sequence \r)
ostream& ret(ostream& output)
{
   return output << '\r';
}

// tab manipulator (using escape sequence \t)
ostream& tab(ostream& output)
{
   return output << '\t';
}

// endLine manipulator (using escape sequence \n
// and the flush member function)
ostream& endLine(ostream& output)
{
   return output << '\n' << flush;
}

main()
{
   cout << "Testing the tab manipulator:\n"
        << 'a' << tab << 'b' << tab << 'c' << endLine
        << "Testing the ret and bell manipulators:\n"
        << ".........";

   for (int i = 1; i <= 100; i++)
      cout << bell;

   cout << ret << "-----" << endLine;

   return 0;
}
```

```
Testing the tab manipulator:
a        b        c
Testing the ret and bell manipulators:
-----.....
```

Fig. 21.19 Testing user-defined, nonparameterized manipulators.

21.7.1 Format State Flags

The format state flags shown in Fig. 21.20 are defined as an enumeration in class **ios** and are explained in the next several sections.

These flags can be controlled by the **flags**, **setf**, and **unsetf** member functions, but many C++ programmers prefer to use stream manipulators (see Section 10.7.8). The programmer may use the bitwise-or operation, |, to combine various options into a single **int** value (see Fig. 10.23). Calling the **flags** member function for a stream and specifying these "or-ed" options sets the options on that stream and returns a value containing the prior options. This value is often saved so that **flags** may be called with this saved value to restore the previous stream options.

The **flags** function must specify a value representing the settings of all the flags. The one-argument **setf** function, on the other hand, specifies one or more "or-ed" flags and "ors" them with the existing flag settings to form a new format state.

The **setiosflags** parameterized stream manipulator performs the same functions as the **setf** member function. The **resetiosflags** stream manipulator performs the same functions as the **unsetf** member function. To use either of these stream manipulators, be sure to #include <iomanip.h>.

The **skipws** flag indicates that >> should skip whitespace on an input stream. The default behavior of >> is to skip whitespace. To change this, use the call **unsetf(ios::skipws)**. The **ws** stream manipulator may also be used to specify that whitespace should be skipped.

21.7.2 Trailing Zeros and Decimal Points (ios::showpoint)

The **showpoint** flag is set to force a floating point number to be output with its decimal point and trailing zeros. A floating point value of **79.0** will print as **79** without **showpoint** set and as **79.000000** (or as many trailing zeros as are specified by the current

```
ios::skipws

ios::left
ios::right
ios::internal

ios::dec
ios::oct
ios::hex

ios::showbase
ios::showpoint
ios::uppercase
ios::showpos

ios::scientific
ios::fixed

ios::unitbuf
ios::stdio
```

Fig. 21.20 Format state flags.

precision) with `showpoint` set. The program in Fig. 21.21 shows the use of the `setf` member function to set the `showpoint` flag to control trailing zeros and the printing of the decimal point for floating point values.

21.7.3 Justification (ios::left, ios::right, ios::internal)

The `left` and `right` flags enable fields to be left-justified with padding characters to the right, or right-justified with padding characters to the left, respectively. The character to be used for padding is specified by the `fill` member function or the `setfill` parameterized stream manipulator (see Section 10.7.4). Figure 21.22 shows the use of the `setw`, `setiosflags`, and `resetiosflags` manipulators and the `setf` and `unsetf` member functions to control the left- and right-justification of integer data in a field.

```cpp
// fig21_21.cpp
// Controlling the printing of trailing
// zeros and decimal points when using
// floating point values with float values.

#include <iostream.h>
#include <iomanip.h>
#include <math.h>

main()
{
    cout << "cout prints 9.9900 as: " << 9.9900
         << "\ncout prints 9.9000 as: " << 9.9000
         << "\ncout prints 9.0000 as: " << 9.0000
         << "\n\nAfter setting the ios::showpoint flag\n";
    cout.setf(ios::showpoint);

    cout << "cout prints 9.9900 as: " << 9.9900
         << "\ncout prints 9.9000 as: " << 9.9000
         << "\ncout prints 9.0000 as: " << 9.0000 << endl;
    return 0;
}
```

```
cout prints 9.9900 as: 9.99
cout prints 9.9000 as: 9.9
cout prints 9.0000 as: 9

After setting the ios::showpoint flag
cout prints 9.9900 as: 9.990000
cout prints 9.9000 as: 9.900000
cout prints 9.0000 as: 9.000000
```

Fig. 21.21 Controlling the printing of trailing zeros and decimal points with float values.

```
// fig21_22.cpp
// Left-justification and right-justification.

#include <iostream.h>
#include <iomanip.h>

main()
{
   int x = 12345;

   cout << "Default is right justified:\n"
        << setw(10) << x
        << "\n\nUSING MEMBER FUNCTIONS\n"
        << "Use setf to set ios::left:\n" << setw(10);

   cout.setf(ios::left, ios::adjustfield);
   cout << x << "\nUse unsetf to restore default:\n";
   cout.unsetf(ios::left);
   cout << setw(10) << x
        << "\n\nUSING PARAMETERIZED STREAM MANIPULATORS"
        << "\nUse setiosflags to set ios::left:\n"
        << setw(10) << setiosflags(ios::left) << x
        << "\nUse resetiosflags to restore default:\n"
        << setw(10) << resetiosflags(ios::left)
        << x << endl;
   return 0;
}
```

```
Default is right justified:
     12345

USING MEMBER FUNCTIONS
Use setf to set ios::left:
12345
Use unsetf to restore default:
     12345

USING PARAMETERIZED STREAM MANIPULATORS
Use setiosflags to set ios::left:
12345
Use resetiosflags to restore default:
     12345
```

Fig. 21.22 Left-justification and right-justification.

The **internal** flag indicates that a number's sign (or base when the **ios::showbase** flag is set; see Section 21.7.5) should be left-justified within a field, the number's magnitude should be right-justified, and intervening spaces should be padded with the fill character. The **left**, **right**, and **internal** flags are contained in static data member **ios::adjustfield**. The **ios::adjustfield** argument must be provided as the second argument to **setf** when setting the **left**, **right**, or **internal** justification flags. This enables **setf** to ensure that only one of the three justification flags is set (they are mutually exclusive). Figure 21.23 shows the use of the **setiosflags** and **setw** stream manipulators to specify internal spacing. Note the use of the **ios::showpos** flag to force the printing of the plus sign.

21.7.4 Padding (Fill, Setfill)

The *fill member function* specifies the fill character to be used with adjusted fields; if no value is specified, spaces are used for padding. The **fill** function returns the prior padding character. The *setfill manipulator* also sets the padding character. Figure 21.24 demonstrates the use of the **fill** member function and the **setfill** manipulator to control the setting and resetting of the fill character.

21.7.5 Integral Stream Base (ios::dec, ios::oct, ios::hex, ios::showbase)

The *ios::basefield static member* (used similarly to **ios::adjustfield** with **setf**) includes the **oct**, **hex**, and **dec** bits to specify that integers are to be treated as octal, hexadecimal, and decimal values, respectively. Stream insertions default to decimal if none of these bits is set; the default for stream extractions is to process the data in the form in which it is supplied—integers starting with **0** are treated as octal values, integers starting with **0x** or **0X** are treated as hexadecimal values, and all other integers are treated as decimal values. Once a particular base is specified for a stream, all integers on that stream are processed with that base until a new base is specified or until the end of the program.

```
// fig21_23.cpp
// Printing an integer with internal spacing and
// forcing the plus sign.

#include <iostream.h>
#include <iomanip.h>

main()
{
    cout << setiosflags(ios::internal | ios::showpos)
         << setw(10) << 123 << endl;

    return 0;
}
```

```
+        123
```

Fig. 21.23 Printing an integer with internal spacing and forcing the plus sign.

```cpp
// fig21_24.cpp
// Using the fill member function and the setfill
// manipulator to change the padding character for
// fields larger than the values being printed.

#include <iostream.h>
#include <iomanip.h>

main()
{
   int x = 10000;

   cout << x
        << " printed as int right and left justified\n"
        << "and as hex with internal justification.\n"
        << "Using the default pad character (space):\n";
   cout.setf(ios::showbase);
   cout << setw(10) << x << '\n';
   cout.setf(ios::left, ios::adjustfield);
   cout << setw(10) << x << '\n';
   cout.setf(ios::internal, ios::adjustfield);
   cout << setw(10) << hex << x << "\n\n";

   cout << "Using various padding characters:\n";
   cout.setf(ios::right, ios::adjustfield);
   cout.fill('*');
   cout << setw(10) << dec << x << '\n';
   cout.setf(ios::left, ios::adjustfield);
   cout << setw(10) << setfill('%') << x << '\n';
   cout.setf(ios::internal, ios::adjustfield);
   cout << setw(10) << setfill('^') << hex
        << x << endl;

   return 0;
}
```

```
10000 printed as int right and left justified
and as hex with internal justification.
Using the default pad character (space):
     10000
10000
0x    2710

Using various padding characters:
*****10000
10000%%%%
0x^^^^2710
```

Fig. 21.24 Using the `fill` member function and the `setfill` manipulator to change the padding character for fields larger than the values being printed.

Set the **showbase** flag to force the base of an integral value to be output. Decimal numbers are output normally, octal numbers are output with a leading **0**, and hexadecimal numbers are output with either a leading **0x** or a leading **0X** (the **uppercase** flag determines which option is chosen). Figure 21.25 demonstrates the use of the **showbase** flag to force an integer to print in decimal, octal, and hexadecimal formats.

21.7.6 Floating Point Numbers; Scientific Notation (ios::scientific, ios::fixed)

The *ios::scientific flag* and the *ios::fixed flag* are contained in the *static data member ios::floatfield* (used similarly to **ios::adjustfield** and **ios::basefield** in **setf**). These flags are used to control the output format of floating point numbers. The **scientific** flag is set to force the output of a floating point number in scientific format. The **fixed** flag forces a floating point number to display a specific number of digits (as specified by the **precision** member function) to the right of the decimal point. Without these flags set, the value of the floating point number determines the output format.

The call **cout.setf(0, ios::floatfield)** restores the system default format for outputting floating point numbers. Figure 21.26 demonstrates the display of floating point numbers in fixed and scientific formats.

```cpp
// fig21_25.cpp
// Using the ios::showbase flag

#include <iostream.h>
#include <iomanip.h>

main()
{
    int x = 100;

    cout << setiosflags(ios::showbase)
         << "Printing integers preceded by their base:\n"
         << x << '\n'
         << oct << x << '\n'
         << hex << x << endl;

    return 0;
}
```

```
Printing integers preceded by their base:
100
0144
0x64
```

Fig. 21.25 Using the **ios::showbase** flag.

```
// fig21_26.cpp
// Displaying floating point values in system default,
// scientific, and fixed formats.

#include <iostream.h>

main()
{
    double x = .001234567, y = 1.946e9;

    cout << "Displayed in default format:\n"
         << x << '\t' << y << '\n';
    cout.setf(ios::scientific, ios::floatfield);
    cout << "Displayed in scientific format:\n"
         << x << '\t' << y << '\n';
    cout.unsetf(ios::scientific);
    cout << "Displayed in default format after unsetf:\n"
         << x << '\t' << y << '\n';
    cout.setf(ios::fixed, ios::floatfield);
    cout << "Displayed in fixed format:\n"
         << x << '\t' << y << endl;

    return 0;
}
```

```
Displayed in default format:
0.001235    1.946e+09
Displayed in scientific format:
1.234567e-03   1.946e+09
Displayed in default format after unsetf:
0.001235    1.946e+09
Displayed in fixed format:
0.001235    1946000000
```

Fig. 21.26 Displaying floating point values in system default, scientific, and fixed formats.

21.7.7 Uppercase/Lowercase Control (ios::uppercase)

The `ios::uppercase` flag is set to force an uppercase **X** or **E** to be output with hexadecimal integers or with scientific notation floating point values, respectively (Fig. 21.27). When set, the `ios::uppercase` flag causes all letters in a hexadecimal value to be uppercase.

21.7.8 Setting and Resetting the Format Flags (Flags, Setiosflags, Resetiosflags)

The `flags` member function without an argument simply returns (as a `long` value) the current settings of the format flags. The `flags` member function with a `long` argument

```
// fig21_27.cpp
// Using the ios::uppercase flag
#include <iostream.h>
#include <iomanip.h>

main()
{
    cout << setiosflags(ios::uppercase)
         << "Printing uppercase letters in scientific\n"
         << "notation exponents and hexadecimal values:\n"
         << 4.345e10 << '\n'
         << hex << 123456789 << endl;

    return 0;
}
```

```
Printing uppercase letters in scientific
notation exponents and hexadecimal values:
4.345E+10
75BCD15
```

Fig. 21.27 Using the `ios::uppercase` flag.

sets the format flags as specified by the argument and returns the prior flag settings. Any format flags not specified in the argument to **flags** are reset. The program of Fig. 21.28 demonstrates the use of the **flags** member function to set a new format state and save the previous format state, then restore the original format settings.

The **setf** member function sets the format flags provided in its argument and returns the previous flag settings as a **long** value as in

```
long previousFlagSettings =
    cout.setf(ios::showpoint | ios::showpos);
```

The **setf** member function with two **long** arguments as in

```
cout.setf(ios::left, ios::adjustfield);
```

first clears the bits of **ios::adjustfield** and then sets the **ios::left** flag. This version of **setf** is used with the bit fields associated with **ios::basefield** (represented by **ios::dec**, **ios::oct**, and **ios::hex**), **ios::floatfield** (represented by **ios::scientific** and **ios::fixed**), and **ios::adjustfield** (represented by **ios::left**, **ios::right**, and **ios::internal**).

The **unsetf** member function resets the designated flags and returns the value of the flags prior to being reset.

21.8 Stream Error States

The state of a stream may be tested through bits in class **ios**—the base class for the classes **istream**, **ostream**, and **iostream** we are using for I/O.

```
// fig21_28.cpp
// Demonstrating the flags member function.
#include <iostream.h>

main()
{
    int i = 1000;
    double d = 0.0947628;

    cout << "The value of the flags variable is: "
         << cout.flags() << '\n'
         << "Print int and double in original format:\n"
         << i << '\t' << d << "\n\n";
    long originalFormat = cout.flags(ios::oct | ios::scientific);
    cout << "The value of the flags variable is: "
         << cout.flags() << '\n'
         << "Print int and double in a new format\n"
         << "specified using the flags member function:\n"
         << i << '\t' << d << "\n\n";
    cout.flags(originalFormat);
    cout << "The value of the flags variable is: "
         << cout.flags() << '\n'
         << "Print values in original format again:\n"
         << i << '\t' << d << endl;

    return 0;
}
```

```
The value of the flags variable is: 1
Print int and double in original format:
1000    0.094763

The value of the flags variable is: 4040
Print int and double in a new format
specified using the flags member function:
1750    9.47628e-02

The value of the flags variable is: 1
Print values in original format again:
1000    0.094763
```

Fig. 21.28 Demonstrating the **flags** member function.

The **eofbit** is set automatically for an input stream when end-of-file is encountered. A program can use the **eof** member function to determine if end-of-file has been encountered on a stream. The call

```
cin.eof()
```

returns true if end-of-file has been encountered on **cin**, and false otherwise.

The **failbit** is set for a stream when a format error occurs on the stream, but characters have not been lost. The **fail** member function determines if a stream operation has failed; it is normally possible to recover from such errors.

The **badbit** is set for a stream when an error occurs that results in the loss of data. The **bad** member function determines if a stream operation has failed. Such serious failures are normally nonrecoverable.

The **goodbit** is set for a stream if none of the bits **eofbit**, **failbit**, or **badbit** are set for the stream.

The **good** member function returns true if the **bad**, **fail**, and **eof** functions would all return false. I/O operations should only be performed on "good" streams.

The **rdstate** member function returns the error state of the stream. A call to **cout.rdstate**, for example, would return the state of the stream which could then be tested by a **switch** statement that examines **ios::eofbit**, **ios::badbit**, **ios::failbit**, and **ios::goodbit**. The preferred means of testing the state of a stream is to use the member functions **eof**, **bad**, **fail**, and **good**—using these functions does not require the programmer to be familiar with particular status bits.

The **clear** member function is normally used to restore a stream's state to "good" so that I/O may proceed on that stream. The default argument for **clear** is **ios::goodbit**, so the statement

```
cin.clear();
```

clears **cin** and sets **goodbit** for the stream.. The statement

```
cin.clear(ios::failbit)
```

actually sets the **failbit**. The user might want to do this when performing input on **cin** with a user-defined type and encountering a problem. The name **clear** seems inappropriate in this context, but it is correct.

The program of Fig. 21.29 illustrates the use of the **rdstate**, **eof**, **fail**, **bad**, **good**, and **clear** member functions.

The **operator!** member function returns true if either the **badbit** is set, the **failbit** is set, or both are set. The **operator void*** member function returns false if either the **badbit** is set, the **failbit** is set, or both are set. These functions are useful in file processing when a true/false condition is being tested in the condition of a selection structure or repetition structure.

21.9 I/O of User-Defined Types

C++ is able to input and output the standard data types using the stream-extraction operator **>>** and stream-insertion operator **<<**. These operators are overloaded to process each standard data type including strings and memory addresses. The programmer can overload the stream insertion and extraction operators to perform I/O for user-defined types. Figure 21.30 demonstrates overloading the stream extraction and insertion operators to handle data of a user-defined telephone number class called **PhoneNumber**. Note that this program assumes telephone numbers are input correctly. We leave it to the exercises to provide error-checking.

```cpp
// fig21_29.cpp
// Testing error states.

#include <iostream.h>

main()
{
   int x;
   cout << "Before a bad input operation:\n"
        << "cin.rdstate(): " << cin.rdstate()
        << "\n    cin.eof(): " << cin.eof()
        << "\n   cin.fail(): " << cin.fail()
        << "\n    cin.bad(): " << cin.bad()
        << "\n   cin.good(): " << cin.good()
        << "\n\nExpects an integer, but enter a character: ";
   cin >> x;

   cout << "\nAfter a bad input operation:\n"
        << "cin.rdstate(): " << cin.rdstate()
        << "\n    cin.eof(): " << cin.eof()
        << "\n   cin.fail(): " << cin.fail()
        << "\n    cin.bad(): " << cin.bad()
        << "\n   cin.good(): " << cin.good() << "\n\n";

   cin.clear();

   cout << "After cin.clear()\n"
        << "cin.fail(): " << cin.fail() << endl;

   return 0;
}
```

```
Before a bad input operation:
cin.rdstate(): 0
    cin.eof(): 0
   cin.fail(): 0
    cin.bad(): 0
   cin.good(): 1

Expects an integer, but enter a character: A

After a bad input operation:
cin.rdstate(): 2
    cin.eof(): 0
   cin.fail(): 2
    cin.bad(): 0
   cin.good(): 0

After cin.clear()
cin.fail(): 0
```

Fig. 21.29 Testing error states.

The stream-extraction operator takes an **istream** reference and a reference to a user-defined type (**PhoneNumber** in this instance) as arguments, and returns an **istream** reference. In Fig. 21.30, the overloaded stream-extraction operator is used to input phone numbers of the form

```
(800) 555-1212
```

into objects of type **PhoneNumber**. The operator function reads the three parts of a telephone number into the **areaCode**, **exchange**, and **line** members of the referenced **PhoneNumber** object (**num** in the operator function and **phone** in **main**). The parentheses, space, and dash characters are discarded by calling the **ignore istream** member function. The operator function returns the **input istream** reference. By returning the stream reference, input operations on **PhoneNumber** objects can be concatenated with input operations on other **PhoneNumber** objects or other data types. For example, two **PhoneNumber** objects could be input as follows:

```
cin >> phone1 >> phone2;
```

The stream-insertion operator takes an **ostream** reference and a reference to a user-defined type (**PhoneNumber** in this instance) as arguments, and returns an **ostream** reference. In Fig. 21.30, the overloaded stream-insertion operator displays objects of type **PhoneNumber** in the same form as they are input. The **operator** function displays the parts of the telephone number as strings because they are stored in string format (recall that **istream** member function **getline** stores a null character after it completes its input).

The overloaded **operator** functions are declared in **class PhoneNumber** as **friend** functions. Overloaded input and output operators must be declared as **friend**s to access non-public class members. Friends of a class can access the private class members.

Software Engineering Observation 21.3

New input/output capabilities for user-defined types are added to C++ without modifying the declarations or private data members for either the **ostream** *class or the* **istream** *class. This promotes the extensibility of the C++ programming language—one of C++'s most attractive aspects.*

21.10 Tying an Output Stream to an Input Stream

Interactive applications generally involve an **istream** for input and an **ostream** for output. When a prompting message appears on the screen, the user responds by entering the appropriate data. Obviously, the prompt needs to appear before the input operation proceeds. With output buffering, outputs appear only when the buffer fills, when outputs are flushed explicitly by the program or automatically at the end of the program. C++ provides the **tie** member function to synchronize, i.e., "tie together," the operation of an **istream** and an **ostream** to ensure that outputs appear before their subsequent inputs. A call such as

```cpp
// fig21_30.cpp
// User-defined insertion and extraction operators

#include <iostream.h>

class PhoneNumber {
   friend ostream& operator<<(ostream&, PhoneNumber&);
   friend istream& operator>>(istream&, PhoneNumber&);
private:
   char areaCode[4];
   char exchange[4];
   char line[5];
};

ostream& operator<<(ostream& output, PhoneNumber& num)
{
   output << "(" << num.areaCode << ") "
          << num.exchange << "-" << num.line;

   return output;
}

istream& operator>>(istream& input, PhoneNumber& num)
{
   input.ignore();                   // skip (
   input.getline(num.areaCode, 4);
   input.ignore(2);                  // skip ) and space
   input.getline(num.exchange, 4);
   input.ignore();                   // skip -
   input.getline(num.line, 5);

   return input;
}

main()
{
   PhoneNumber phone;

   cout << "Enter a phone number in the "
        << "form (123) 456-7890:\n";
   cin >> phone;
   cout << "The phone number entered was:\n"
        << phone << endl;

   return 0;
}
```

```
Enter a phone number in the form (123) 456-7890:
(800) 555-1212
The phone number entered was:
(800) 555-1212
```

Fig. 21.30 User-defined stream-insertion and stream extraction-operators.

```
cin.tie(cout);
```

ties **cout** (an **ostream**) to **cin** (an **istream**). Actually, this particular call is redundant because C++ performs this operation automatically to create a user's standard input/output environment. The user would, however, explicitly tie together other **istream/ostream** pairs. To untie an input stream, **inputStream**, from an output stream, use the call

```
inputStream.tie(0);
```

Summary

- I/O operations are performed in a manner sensitive to the type of the data.

- C++ I/O occurs in streams of bytes. A stream is simply a sequence of bytes.

- I/O mechanisms of the system move bytes from devices to memory and vice versa in an efficient and reliable manner.

- C++ provides "low-level" and "high-level" I/O capabilities. Low-level I/O-capabilities specify that some number of bytes should be transferred device-to-memory or memory-to-device. High-level I/O is performed with bytes grouped into meaningful units such as integers, floats, characters, strings, and user-defined types.

- C++ provides both unformatted I/O and formatted I/O operations. Unformatted I/O transfers are fast, but process raw data that is difficult for people to use. Formatted I/O processes data in meaningful units, but requires extra processing time that can negatively impact high-volume data transfers.

- Most C++ programs include the **iostream.h** header file that contains basic information required for all stream I/O operations.

- The **iomanip.h** header contains information for formatted input/output with parameterized stream manipulators.

- The **fstream.h** header contains information for file processing operations.

- The **strstream.h** header contains information for in-memory formatting.

- The **stdiostream.h** header contains information for programs that mix the C and C++ styles of I/O.

- The **istream** class supports stream input operations.

- The **ostream** class supports stream output operations.

- The **iostream** class supports both stream input and stream output operations.

- The **istream** class and the **ostream** class are each derived through single inheritance from the **ios** base class.

- The **iostream** class is derived through multiple inheritance from both the **istream** class and the **ostream** class.

- The left shift operator (`<<`) is overloaded to designate stream output and is referred to as the stream-insertion operator.

- The right shift operator (`>>`) is overloaded to designate stream input and is referred to as the stream-extraction operator.

- The `istream` class object `cin` is tied to the standard input device, normally the keyboard.

- The `ostream` class object `cout` is tied to the standard output device, normally the display screen.

- The `ostream` class object `cerr` is tied to the standard error device. Outputs to `cerr` are unbuffered; each insertion to `cerr` appears immediately.

- Stream manipulator `endl` issues a newline character and flushes the output buffer.

- The C++ compiler determines data types automatically for input and output.

- Addresses are displayed in hexadecimal format by default.

- To print the address in a variable of type `char*` cast the pointer to `void*`.

- Member function `put` outputs one character. Calls to `put` may be concatenated.

- Stream input is performed with the stream-extraction operator `>>`. This operator automatically skips whitespace characters in the input stream.

- The `>>` operator returns false when end-of-file is encountered on a stream.

- Stream extraction causes `failbit` to be set for improper input, and `badbit` to be set if the operation fails.

- A series of values can be input using the stream extraction operation in a `while` loop header. The extraction returns false (zero) when end-of-file is encountered.

- The `get` member function with no arguments inputs one character and returns the character; `EOF` is returned if end-of-file is encountered on the stream.

- The `get` member function with an argument of type `char` inputs one character. False is returned when end-of-file is encountered; otherwise the `istream` object for which the `get` member function is being invoked is returned.

- The `get` member function with three arguments—a character array, a size limit, and a delimiter (with default value newline)—reads characters from the input stream up to a maximum of limit – 1 characters and terminates, or terminates when the delimiter is read. The input string is terminated with a null character. The delimiter is not placed in the character array, but remains in the input stream.

- The `getline` member function operates like the three argument `get` member function. The `getline` function removes the delimiter from the input stream.

- Member function `ignore` skips the specified number of characters (default is one character) in the input stream; it terminates if the specified delimiter is encountered (the default delimiter is `EOF`).

- The **putback** member function places the previous character obtained by a **get** on a stream back onto that stream.

- The **peek** member function returns the next character from an input stream, but does not remove the character from the stream.

- C++ offers type-safe input/output. If unexpected data is processed by the **<<** and **>>** operators, various error flags are set that the user may test to determine if an I/O operation succeeded or failed.

- Unformatted I/O is performed with member functions **read** and **write**. These input or output some number of bytes to or from memory beginning at a designated memory address. They are input or output as raw bytes with no formatting.

- The **gcount** member function returns the number of characters input by the previous **read** operation on that stream.

- Member function **read** inputs a specified number of characters into a character array. **failbit** is set if fewer than the specified number of characters are read.

- To change the base in which integers output, use the manipulator **hex** to set the base to hexadecimal (base 16) or **oct** to set the base to octal (base 8). Use manipulator **dec** to reset the base to decimal. The base remains the same until explicitly changed.

- The parameterized stream manipulator **setbase** also sets the base for integer output. **setbase** takes one integer argument of **10**, **8**, or **16** to set the base.

- Floating point precision can be controlled using either the **setprecision** stream manipulator or the **precision** member function. Both set the precision for all subsequent output operations until the next precision-setting call. The **precision** member function with no argument returns the current precision value. A precision of **0** specifies the default precision value (**6**).

- Parameterized manipulators require the inclusion of the **iomanip.h** header file.

- Member function **width** sets the field width and returns the previous width. Values smaller than the field are padded with fill characters. The field width setting applies only for the next insertion or extraction; the field width is implicitly set to **0** afterward (subsequent values will be output as large as they need to be). Values larger than a field are printed in their entirety. Function **width** with no argument returns the current width setting. Manipulator **setw** also sets the width.

- For input, the **setw** stream manipulator establishes a maximum string size; if a larger string is entered, the larger line is broken into pieces no larger than the designated size.

- Users may create their own stream manipulators.

- Member functions **setf**, **unsetf**, and **flags** control the flag settings.

- The **skipws** flag indicates that **>>** should skip whitespace on an input stream. The **ws** stream manipulator also skips over leading whitespace in an input stream.

- Format flags are defined as an enumeration in class **ios**.

- Format flags are controlled by the **flags** and **setf** member functions, but many C++ programmers prefer to use stream manipulators. The bitwise-or operation, **|**, can be used to combine various options into a single **long** value. Calling the **flags** member function for a stream and specifying these "or-ed" options sets the options on that stream and returns a **long** value containing the prior options. This value is often saved so **flags** may be called with this saved value to restore the previous stream options.

- The **flags** function must specify a value representing the total settings of all the flags. The **setf** function with one argument, on the other hand, automatically "ors" the specified flags with the existing flag settings to form a new format state.

- The **showpoint** flag is set to force a floating point number to be output with a decimal point and number of significant digits specified by the precision.

- The **left** and **right** flags cause fields to be left-justified with padding characters to the right, or right-justified with padding characters to the left, respectively.

- The **internal** flag indicates that a number's sign (or base when the flag **ios::showbase** is set) should be left-justified within a field, magnitude should be right-justified, and intervening spaces should be padded with the fill character.

- **ios::adjustfield** contains the flags **left**, **right**, and **internal**.

- Member function **fill** specifies the fill character to be used with **left**, **right**, and **internal** adjusted fields (space is the default); the prior padding character is returned. Stream manipulator **setfill** also sets the fill character.

- Static member **ios::basefield** includes the **oct**, **hex**, and **dec** bits to specify that integers are to be treated as octal, hexadecimal, and decimal values, respectively. Integer output defaults to decimal if none of these bits is set; stream extractions process the data in the form in which it is supplied.

- Set the **showbase** flag to force the base of an integral value to be output.

- Static data member **ios::floatfield** contains the flags **scientific** and the **fixed**. Set the **scientific** flag to output a floating point number in scientific format. Set the **fixed** flag to output a floating point number with the precision specified by the **precision** member function.

- The call **cout.setf(0, ios::floatfield)** restores the default format for displaying floating point numbers.

- Set the **uppercase** flag to force an uppercase **X** or **E** to be output with hexadecimal integers or with scientific notation floating point values, respectively. When set, the **ios::uppercase** flag causes all letters in a hexadecimal value to be uppercase.

- Member function **flags** with no argument returns the **long** value of the current settings of the format flags. Member function **flags** with a **long** argument sets the format flags specified by the argument and returns the prior flag settings.

- Member function **setf** sets the format flags in its argument and returns the previous flag settings as a **long** value.

- Member function **setf** with two **long** arguments—a **long** bit and a **long** bit field—clears the bits of the bitfield, then sets the bit in the first argument.

- Member function **unsetf** resets the designated flags and returns the value of the flags prior to being reset.

- Parameterized stream manipulator **setiosflags** performs the same functions as member function **flags**.

- Parameterized stream manipulator **resetiosflags** performs the same functions as member function **unsetf**.

- The state of a stream may be tested through bits in class **ios**.

- The **eofbit** is set for an input stream when end-of-file is encountered during an input operation. The **eof** member function is used to determine if the **eofbit** has been set.

- The **failbit** is set for a stream when a format error occurred on the stream, but characters have not been lost. The **fail** member function determines if a stream operation has failed; it is normally possible to recover from such errors.

- The **badbit** is set for a stream when an error occurred that resulted in the loss of data. The **bad** member function determines if a stream operation has failed. Such serious failures are normally nonrecoverable.

- The **good** member function returns true if the **bad**, **fail**, and **eof** functions would all return false. I/O operations should only be performed on "good" streams.

- The **rdstate** member function returns the error state of the stream.

- Member function **clear** is normally used to restore a stream's state to "good" so that I/O may proceed on that stream.

- The user can overload the stream insertion and extraction operators to perform I/O for user-defined types.

- The overloaded stream-extraction operator takes an **istream** reference and a reference to a user-defined type as arguments, and returns an **istream** reference.

- The overloaded stream-insertion operator takes an **ostream** reference and a reference to a user-defined type as arguments, and returns an **ostream** reference.

- Often, overloaded **operator** functions are declared as **friend** functions to a class; this enables access to non-public class members.

- C++ provides the **tie** member function to synchronize **istream** and **ostream** operations to ensure that outputs appear before subsequent inputs.

Terminology

bad member function	**clear** member function
badbit	**clog**
cerr	**cout**
cin	**dec** stream manipulator

Common Programming Errors

21.1   Attempting to read from an **ostream** (or from any other output-only stream).

21.2   Attempting to write to an **istream** (or to any other input-only stream).

21.3   Not providing parentheses to force proper precedence when using the relatively high precedence stream-insertion operator **<<** or stream-extraction operator **>>**.

21.4 When not providing a sufficiently wide field to handle outputs, the outputs print as wide as they need to be, possibly causing difficult-to-read or erroneous outputs.

Good Programming Practices

21.1 Use the C++ form of I/O exclusively in C++ programs, despite the fact that C-style I/O is available to C++ programmers.

Performance Tips

21.1 Use unformatted I/O for the best performance in high-volume file processing.

Software Engineering Observations

21.1 C++ style I/O is type safe.

21.2 C++ enables a common treatment of I/O of predefined types and user-defined types. This kind of commonality facilitates software development in general and software reuse in particular.

21.3 New input/output capabilities for user-defined types are added to C++ without modifying the declarations or private data members for either the **ostream** class or the **istream** class. This promotes the extensibility of the C++ programming language—one of C++'s most attractive aspects.

Self-Review Exercises

21.1 Answer each of the following:
  a) Overloaded stream operator functions should be defined as _____ functions of a class.
  b) The format justification bits that can be set include _____, _____, and _____.
  c) Input/output in C++ occurs as _____ of bytes.
  d) Parameterized stream manipulators _____ and _____ can be used to set and reset format state flags.
  e) Most C++ programs should include the _____ header file that contains basic information required for all stream I/O operations.
  f) Member functions _____ and _____ can be used to set and reset format state flags.
  g) The _____ header file contains information for performing "in-memory" formatting.
  h) When using parameterized manipulators, the header file _____ must be included in the program.
  i) The _____ header file contains information for performing user-controlled file processing.
  j) The _____ stream manipulator inserts a newline character in the output stream and flushes the output stream.
  k) The _____ header file contains information for programs that mix C-style and C++-style I/O.
  l) The **ostream** member function _____ is used to perform unformatted output.
  m) Input operations are supported by the _____ class.

n) Outputs to the standard error stream are directed to either the _____ or the _____ stream object.

o) Output operations are supported by the _____ class.

p) The symbol for the stream-insertion operator is _____.

q) The four objects that correspond to the standard devices on the system include _____, _____, _____, and _____.

r) The symbol for the stream-extraction operator is _____.

s) The stream manipulators _____, _____, and _____ are used to specify that integers should be displayed in octal, hexadecimal, and decimal formats respectively.

t) The default precision for displaying floating point values is _____.

u) When set, the _____ flag causes positive numerical values to be displayed with a plus sign.

21.2   State whether the following are true or false. If the answer is false, explain why.

a) The stream member function **flags()** with a long argument sets the **flags** state variable to its argument and returns its previous value.

b) The stream-insertion operator << and the stream-extraction operator >> are overloaded to handle all standard data types—including strings and memory addresses—and all user-defined data types.

c) The stream member function **flags()** with no arguments resets all the flag bits in the **flags** state variable.

d) The stream-extraction operator >> can be overloaded with an operator function that takes an **istream** reference and a reference to a user-defined type as arguments and returns an **istream** reference.

e) The **ws** stream manipulator skips leading whitespace in an input stream.

f) The stream-insertion operator << can be overloaded with an operator function that takes an istream reference and a reference to a user-defined type as arguments and returns an istream reference.

g) Input with the stream-extraction operator >> always skips leading whitespace characters in the input stream.

h) The input and output features are provided as part of C++.

i) The stream member function **rdstate()** returns the state of the current stream.

j) The **cout** stream is normally connected to the display screen.

k) The stream member function **good()** returns true if the **bad()**, **fail()**, and **eof()** member functions all return false.

l) The **cin** stream is normally connected to the display screen.

m) If a nonrecoverable error occurs during a stream operation, the **bad()** member function will return true.

n) Output to **cerr** is unbuffered and output to **clog** is buffered.

o) When the **ios::showpoint** flag is set, floating point values are forced to print with the default six digits of precision—provided that the precision value has not been changed, in which case floating point values print with the specified precision.

p) The **ostream** member function **put** outputs the specified number of characters.

q) The stream manipulators **dec**, **oct**, and **hex** only affect the next integer output operation.

r) When output, memory addresses are displayed as **long** integers by default.

21.3   For each of the following, write a single statement that performs the indicated task.

a) Output the string **"Enter your name: "**.

b) Set a flag to cause the exponent in scientific notation and the letters in hexadecimal values to print in capital letters.

c) Output the address of the variable **string** of type **char ***.

d) Set a flag so that floating point values print in scientific notation.

e) Output the address of the variable **integerPtr** of type **int ***.

f) Set a flag so that when integer values are output the integer base for octal and hexadecimal values is displayed.

g) Output the value pointed to by **floatPtr** of type **float ***.

h) Use a stream member function to set the fill character to **'*'** for printing in field widths larger than the values being output. Write a separate statement to do this with a stream manipulator.

i) Output the characters **'O'** and **'K'** in one statement with **ostream** function **put**.

j) Get the next character in the input stream without extracting it from the stream.

k) Input a single character into variable **c** of type **char** using the **istream** member function **get** in two different ways.

l) Input and discard the next six characters in the input stream.

m) Use the **istream** member function **read** to input 50 characters into array **line** of type **char**.

n) Read 10 characters into character array **name**. Stop reading characters if the **'.'** delimiter is encountered. Do not remove the delimiter from the input stream. Write another statement that performs this task and removes the delimiter from the input stream.

o) Use the **istream** member function **gcount** to determine the number of characters input into character array **line** by the last call to **istream** member function **read** and output that number of characters using **ostream** member function **write**.

p) Write separate statements to flush the output stream using a member function and a stream manipulator.

q) Output the following values: **124**, **18.376**, **'Z'**, **1000000**, and **"String"**.

r) Print the current precision setting using a member function.

s) Input an integer value into **int** variable **months** and a floating point value into **float** variable **percentageRate**.

t) Print **1.92**, **1.925**, and **1.9258** with 3 digits of precision using a manipulator.

u) Print integer **100** in octal, hexadecimal, and decimal using stream manipulators.

v) Print integer **100** in decimal, octal, and hexadecimal using a single stream manipulator to change the base.

w) Print **1234** right-justified in a **10** digit field.

x) Read characters into character array **line** until the character **'z'** is encountered up to a limit of **20** characters (including a terminating null character). Do not extract the delimiter character from the stream.

y) Use integer variables **x** and **y** to specify the field width and precision used to display the **double** value **87.4573** and display the value.

21.4   Identify the error in each of the following statements and explain how to correct it.

a) `cout << "Value of x <= y is: " << x <= y;`

b) The following statement should print the integer value of **'c'**.

`cout << 'c';`

c) `cout << ""A string in quotes"";`

21.5   For each of the following, show the output.

a) `cout << "12345\n";`

```
     cout.width(5);
     cout.fill('*');
     cout << 123 << '\n' << 123;
 b)  cout << setw(10) << setfill('$') << 10000;
 c)  cout << setw(8) << setprecision(3) << 1024.987654;
 d)  cout << setiosflags(ios::showbase) << oct << 99
         << '\n' << hex << 99;
 e)  cout << 100000 << '\n'
         << setiosflags(ios::showpos) << 100000;
 f)  cout << setw(10) << setprecision(2) <<
         << setiosflags(ios::scientific) << 444.93738;
```

Answers to Self-Review Exercises

21.1   a) `friend`. b) `ios::left`, `ios::right`, and `ios::internal`. c) streams. d) `setiosflags`, `resetiosflags`. e) `iostream.h`. f) `setf`, `unsetf`. g) `strstream.h`. h) `iomanip.h`. i) `fstream.h`. j) `endl`. k) `stdiostream.h`. l) `write`. m) `istream`. n) `cerr` or `clog`. o) `ostream`. p) `<<`. q) `cin`, `cout`, `cerr`, and `clog`. r) `>>`. s) `oct`, `hex`, `dec`. t) six digits of precision. u) `ios::showpos`.

21.2   a) True.
   b) False. The stream insertion and stream abstraction operators are not overloaded for all user-defined types. The programmer of a class must specifically provide the overloaded operator functions to overload the stream operators for use with each user-defined type.
   c) False. The stream member function `flags()` with no arguments simply returns the current value of the `flags` state variable.
   d) True.
   e) True.
   f) False. To overload the stream-insertion operator `<<`, the overloaded operator function must take an `ostream` reference and a reference to a user-defined type as arguments, and return an `ostream` reference.
   g) True. Unless `ios::skipws` is off.
   h) False. The input and output features of C++ are provided as part of the C++ standard library. The C++ language does not contain capabilities for input, output, or file processing.
   i) True.
   j) True.
   k) True.
   l) False. The `cin` stream is connected to the standard input of the computer which is normally the keyboard.
   m) True.
   n) True.
   o) True.
   p) False. The `ostream` member function `put` outputs its single character argument.
   q) False. The stream manipulators `dec`, `oct`, and `hex` set the output format state for integers to the specified base until the base is specifically changed again or the program terminates.
   r) False. Memory addresses are displayed in hexadecimal format by default. To display addresses as `long` integers, the address must be cast to a `long` value.

21.3 a) `cout << "Enter your name: ";`
   b) `cout.setf(ios::uppercase);`
   c) `cout << long(string);`
   d) `cout.setf(ios::scientific, ios::floatfield);`
   e) `cout << integerPtr;`
   f) `cout << setiosflags(ios::showbase);`
   g) `cout << *floatPtr;`
   h) `cout.fill('*');`
      `cout << setfill('*');`
   i) `cout.put('O').put('K');`
   j) `cin.peek();`
   k) `c = cin.get();`
      `cin.get(c);`
   l) `cin.ignore(6);`
   m) `cin.read(line, 50);`
   n) `cin.get(name, 10, '.');`
      `cin.getline(name, 10, '.');`
   o) `cout.write(line, cin.gcount());`
   p) `cout.flush();`
      `cout << flush;`
   q) `cout << 124 << 18.376 << 'Z' << 1000000 << "String";`
   r) `cout.precision();`
   s) `cin >> months >> percentageRate;`
   t) `cout << setprecision(3) << 1.92 << '\t'`
         `<< 1.925 << '\t' << 1.9258;`
   u) `cout << oct << 100 << hex << 100 << dec << 100;`
   v) `cout << 100 << setbase(8) << 100 << setbase(16) << 100;`
   w) `cout << setw(10) << 1234;`
   x) `cin.get(line, 20, 'z');`
   y) `cout << setw(x) << setprecision(y) << 87.4573;`

21.4 a) Error: The precedence of the `<<` operator is higher than the precedence of `<=` which causes the statement to be evaluated improperly and causes an error to be issued by the compiler.
      Correction: To correct the statement, add parentheses around the expression **x <= y**. This problem will occur with any expression that uses operators of lower precedence than the `<<` operator if the expression is not placed in parentheses.
   b) Error: In C++, characters are not treated as small integers as they are in C.
      Correction: To print the numerical value for a character in the computer's character set, the character must be cast to an integer value as in the following:

      `cout << int('c');`

   c) Error: Quote characters cannot be printed in a string unless an escape sequence is used.
      Correction: Print the string in one of the following ways:

      `cout << '"' << "A string in quotes" << '"';`
      `cout << "\"A string in quotes\"";`

21.5 a) 12345

      **123

      123

b) `$$$$$10000`
c) `1024.988`
d) `0143`
   `0x63`
e) `100000`
   `+100000`
f) `   4.45e+02`

Exercises

21.6   Write a statement for each of the following:
   a) Print integer **40000** left justified in a **15**-digit field.
   b) Read a string into character array variable **state**.
   c) Print **200** with and without a sign.
   d) Print **100** in hexadecimal form preceded by **0x**.
   e) Read characters into array **s** until the character **'p'** is encountered up to a limit of 10 characters (including the terminating null character). Extract the delimiter from the input stream and discard it.
   f) Print **1.234** in a 9-digit field with preceding zeros.
   g) Read a string of the form **"characters"** from the standard input. Store the string in character array **s**. Eliminate the quotation marks from the input stream. Read a maximum of 50 characters (including the terminating null character).

21.7   Write a program to test inputting integer values in decimal, octal, and hexadecimal format. Output each integer read by the program in all three formats. Test the program with the following input data: 10, 010, 0x10.

21.8   Write a program that prints pointer values using casts to all the integer data types. Which ones print strange values? Which ones cause errors?

21.9   Write a program to test the results of printing the integer value **12345** and the floating point value **1.2345** in various size fields. What happens when the values are printed in fields containing fewer digits than the values?

21.10   Write a program that prints the value **100.453627** rounded to the nearest digit, tenth, hundredth, thousandth, and ten thousandth.

21.11   Write a program that inputs a string from the keyboard and determines the length of the string. Print the string using twice the length as the field width.

21.12   Write a program that converts integer Fahrenheit temperatures from **0** to **212** degrees to floating point Celsius temperatures with **3** digits of precision. Use the formula

```
celsius = 5.0/9.0 * (fahrenheit - 32);
```

to perform the calculation. The output should be printed in two right-justified columns, and the Celsius temperatures should be preceded by a sign for both positive and negative values.

21.13   In some programming languages, strings are entered surrounded by either single or double quotation marks. Write a program that reads the three strings **suzy**, **"suzy"**, and **'suzy'**. Are the single and double quotes ignored or read as part of the string?

21.14   In Fig. 21.30, the stream-extraction and stream-insertion operators were overloaded for input and output of objects of the **PhoneNumber** class. Rewrite the stream-extraction operator to perform the following error checking tasks on input. Note that the **operator>>** function will need to be entirely recoded.

a) Input the entire phone number into an array. Test that the proper number of characters have been entered (there should be a total of 14 characters read for a phone number of the form **(800) 555-1212**). Use the stream member function **clear** to set the **ios::fail** bit for improper input.

b) The area code and exchange in a phone number do not begin with **0** or **1**. Test the first digit of the area code and exchange portions of the phone number to be sure that neither begins with **0** or **1**. Use the stream member function **clear** to set the **ios::fail** bit for improper input.

c) The middle digit of an area code is always **0** or **1**. Test the middle digit for a value of **0** or **1**. Use the stream member function **clear** to set the **ios::fail** bit for improper input. If none of the above operations results in the **ios::fail** bit being set for improper input, copy the three parts of the telephone number into the **areaCode**, **exchange**, and **line** members of the **PhoneNumber** object In the main program, if the **ios::fail** bit has been set on the input, have the program print an error message and end rather than print the phone number.

21.15 Write a program that accomplishes each of the following:
a) Create the user-defined class **point** that contains the private integer data members **xCoordinate** and **yCoordinate**, and declares stream insertion and stream extraction overloaded operator functions as **friend**s of the class.

b) Define the stream insertion and stream-extraction operator functions. The stream-extraction operator function should determine if the data entered is valid data, and if not, it should set the **ios::fail** bit to indicate improper input. The stream-insertion operator should not be able to display the point after an input error occurred.

c) Write a **main** function that tests input and output of user-defined class **point** using the overloaded stream extraction and stream-insertion operators.

21.16 Write a program that accomplishes each of the following:
a) Create the user-defined class **complex** that contains the private integer data members **real** and **imaginary**, and declares stream insertion and stream extraction overloaded operator functions as **friend**s of the class.

b) Define the stream insertion and stream-extraction operator functions. The stream-extraction operator function should determine if the data entered is valid data, and if not, it should set the **ios::fail** bit to indicate improper input. The input should be of the form:

        3 + 8i

The values can be negative or positive, and it is possible that one of the two values is not provided. If a value is not provided, the appropriate data member should be set to **0**. The stream-insertion operator should not be able to display the point if an input error occurred. The output format should be identical to the input format shown above. For negative imaginary values, a minus sign should be printed rather than a plus sign.

c) Write a **main** function that tests input and output of user-defined class **complex** using the overloaded stream extraction and stream-insertion operators.

21.17 Write a program that uses a **for** structure to print a table of ASCII values for the characters in the ASCII characters set from **33** to **126**. The program should print the decimal value, octal value, hexadecimal value, and character value for each character. Use the stream manipulators **dec**, **oct**, and **hex** to print the integer values.

21.18 Write a program to show that the **getline** and three-argument **get** istream member functions each end the input string with a string terminating null character. Also show that **get**

leaves the delimiter character on the input stream while `getline` extracts the delimiter character and discards it. What happens to the unread characters in the stream?

21.19   Write a program that creates the user-defined manipulator `skipwhite` to skip leading whitespace characters in the input stream. The manipulator should use the `isspace` function from the `ctype.h` library to test if the character is a whitespace character. Each character should be input using the `istream` member function `get`. When a non-whitespace character is encountered, the `skipwhite` manipulator finishes its job by placing the character back on the input stream and returning an `istream` reference.

Test the user-defined manipulator by creating a `main` function in which the `ios::skipws` flag is unset so that the stream-extraction operator does not automatically skip whitespace. Then test the manipulator on the input stream by entering a character preceded by whitespace as input. Print the character that was input to confirm that a whitespace character was not input.

Bibliography

(Al93)   Allison, C., "Code Capsules: A C++ Date Class, Part 1," *The C Users Journal,* Vol. 11, No. 2, February 1993, pp. 123–131.

(An92)   Anderson, A. E., and W. J. Heinze, *C++ Programming and Fundamental Concepts,* Englewood Cliffs, NJ: Prentice Hall, 1992.

(Ba93)   Bar-David, T., *Object-Oriented Design for C++,* Englewood Cliffs, NJ: Prentice Hall, 1993.

(Be93)   Berard, E. V., Essays on Object-Oriented Software Engineering: Volume I, Englewood Cliffs, NJ: Prentice Hall, 1993.

(Br91)   Borland, *Borland C++ Programmer's Guide,* Part No. 14MN-TCP04, Scotts Valley, CA: Borland International, Inc., 1991.

(Br91a)   Borland, *Borland C++ Getting Started,* Part No. 14MN-TCP02, Scotts Valley, CA: Borland International, Inc., 1991.

(Br91b)   Borland, *Borland C++ 3.0 Programmers Guide,* Scotts Valley, CA: Borland International, Inc., 1991.

(By93)   Byron, D., "The Case for Object Technology Standards," *CASE Trends,* September 1993, pp. 22–26.

(Co93)   Computerworld, "The CW Guide to Object-Oriented Programming," *Computerworld,* June 14, 1993, pp. 107–130.

(De90)   Deitel, H. M., *Operating Systems,* Second Edition, Reading, MA: Addison-Wesley, 1990.

(El90)   Ellis, M. A. and B. Stroustrup, *The Annotated C++ Reference Manual,* Reading, MA: Addison-Wesley, 1990.

(Fl93)   Flamig, B., *Practical Data Structures in C++,* John Wiley & Sons, 1993.

(Ha93)   Hagan, T., "C++ Class Libraries for GUIs," *Open Systems Today,* February 15, 1993, pp. 54, 58.

(Ja93)   Jacobson, I., "Is Object Technology Software's Industrial Platform?" *IEEE Software Magazine,* Vol. 10, No. 1, January 1993, pp. 24–30.

(Ko93)   Kozaczynski, W., and A. Kuntzmann-Combelles, "What It Takes to Make OO Work," *IEEE Software Magazine,* Vol. 10, No. 1, January 1993, pp. 20–23.

(Li91)   Lippman, S. B., *C++ Primer* (Second Edition), Reading, MA: Addison-Wesley Publishing Company, 1991.

(Lo93)   Lorenz, M., *Object-Oriented Software Development: A Practical Guide,* Englewood Cliffs, NJ: Prentice Hall, 1993.

(Lu92)   Lucas, P. J., *The C++ Programmer's Handbook,* Englewood Cliffs, NJ: Prentice Hall, 1992.

(Ma93)   Martin, J., *Principles of Object-Oriented Analysis and Design,* Englewood Cliffs, NJ: Prentice Hall, 1993.

(Me93)   Matsche, J. J., "Object-oriented programming in Standard C," *Object Magazine,* Vol. 2, No. 5, January/February 1993, pp. 71-74.

(Mi91)   Microsoft, *Microsoft C/C++ Class Libraries Reference* (Version 7.0), Redmond, WA: Microsoft Corporation, 1991.

(Mi91a)   Microsoft, *Microsoft C/C++ C++ Language Reference* (Version 7.0), Redmond, WA: Microsoft Corporation, 1991.

(Mi91b)   Microsoft, *Microsoft C/C++ C++ Tutorial* (Version 7.0), Redmond, WA: Microsoft Corporation, 1991.

(Pi93)   Pittman, M., "Lessons Learned in Managing Object-Oriented Development," *IEEE Software Magazine,* Vol. 10, No. 1, January 1993, pp. 43–53.

(Pr93)   Prieto-Diaz, R., "Status Report: Software Reusability," *IEEE Software,* Vol. 10, No. 3, May 1993, pp. 61–66.

(Ra92)   Ranade, J., and S. Zamir, C++ *Primer for C Programmers,* New York, NY McGraw-Hill, Inc., 1992.

(Re91)   Reed, D. R., "Moving from C to C++," *Object Magazine,* Vol. 1, No. 3, September/October, 1991, pp. 46–60.

(Rl93)   Rettig, M., G. Simmons, and J. Thomson, "Extended Objects," *Communications of the ACM,* Vol. 36, No. 8, August 1993, pp. 19–24.

(Sa93)   Saks, D., "Inheritance, Part 2," *The C Users Journal,* May 1993, pp. 81–89.

(Sh91)   Shiffman, H., "C++ Object-Oriented Extensions to C," *SunWorld,* Vol. 4, No. 5, May 1991, pp. 63–70.

(Sk93)   Skelly, C., "Pointer Power in C and C++, Part 1," *The C Users Journal,* Vol. 11, No. 2, February 1993, pp. 93–98.

(Sn93)   Snyder, A., "The Essence of Objects: Concepts and Terms," *IEEE Software Magazine,* Vol. 10, No. 1, January 1993, pp. 31–42.

(St91)   Stroustrup, B., *The C++ Programming Language* (Second Edition), Reading, MA: Addison-Wesley Series in Computer Science, 1991.

(St93)   Stroustrup, B., "Why Consider Language Extensions?: Maintaining a Delicate Balance," *C++ Report,* September 1993, pp. 44–51.

(Vo93)   Voss, G., "Objects and Messages," *Windows Tech Journal,* February 1993, pp. 15–16.

(Wi93)   Wiebel, M., and S. Halladay, "Using OOP Techniques Instead of *switch* in C++," Vol. 10, No. 10, *The C Users Journal,* October 1992, pp. 105–106.

(Wl93)   Wilde, N., P. Matthews, and R. Huitt, "Maintaining Object-Oriented Software, *IEEE Software Magazine,* Vol. 10, No. 1, January 1993, pp. 75–80.

(Wt93)   Wilt, N., "Templates in C++," *The C Users Journal,* May 1993, pp. 33–51.

Appendix A*
C Syntax

In the syntax notation used, syntactic categories (nonterminals) are indicated by *italic* type, and literal words and character set members (terminals) by **bold** type. A colon (:) following a nonterminal introduces its definition. Alternative definitions are listed on separate lines, except when prefaced by the words "one of." An optional symbol is indicated by the subscript "opt," so that

> { *expression* $_{opt}$ }

indicates an optional expression enclosed in braces.

Language Syntax Summary
A.1 Lexical Grammar
A.1.1 Tokens
token:
    keyword
    identifier
    constant
    string-literal
    operator
    punctuator

preprocessing-token:
    header-name
    identifier
    pp-number
    character-constant
    string-literal
    operator

* Permissions Acknowledgement: This material has been condensed and adapted from American National Standard for Information Systems—Programming Language—C, ANSI/ISO 9899: 1990. Copies of this standard may be purchased from the American National Standards Institute at 11 West 42nd Street, New York, NY 10036.

punctuator
each non-white-space character that cannot be one of the above

A.1.2 Keywords
keyword: one of

auto	double	int	struct
break	else	long	switch
case	enum	register	typedef
char	extern	return	union
const	float	short	unsigned
continue	for	signed	void
default	goto	sizeof	volatile
do	if	static	while

A.1.3 Identifiers
identifier:
  nondigit
  identifier nondigit
  identifier digit

nondigit: one of
  _ a b c d e f g h i j k l m
  n o p q r s t u v w x y z
  A B C D E F G H I J K L M
  N O P Q R S T U V W X Y Z

digit: one of
  0 1 2 3 4 5 6 7 8 9

A.1.4 Constants
constant:
  floating-constant
  integer-constant
  enumeration-constant
  character-constant

floating-constant:
  fractional-constant exponent-part$_{opt}$ floating-suffix$_{opt}$
  digit-sequence exponent-part floating-suffix$_{opt}$

fractional-constant:
  digit-sequence$_{opt}$. digit-sequence
  digit-sequence .

exponent-part:
  e *sign$_{opt}$ digit-sequence*
  E *sign$_{opt}$ digit-sequence*

sign: one of
  + −

digit-sequence:
    digit
    digit-sequence digit

floating-suffix: one of
    `f  l  F  L`

integer-constant:
    decimal-constant integer-suffix$_{opt}$
    octal-constant integer-suffix$_{opt}$
    hexadecimal-constant integer-suffix$_{opt}$

decimal-constant:
    nonzero-digit
    decimal-constant digit

octal-constant:
    `0`
    octal-constant octal-digit

hexadecimal-constant:
    `0x` *hexadecimal-digit*
    `0X` *hexadecimal-digit*
    hexadecimal-constant hexadecimal-digit

nonzero-digit: one of
    `1  2  3  4  5  6  7  8  9`

octal-digit: one of
    `0  1  2  3  4  5  6  7`

hexadecimal-digit: one of
    `0  1  2  3  4  5  6  7  8  9`
    `a  b  c  d  e  f`
    `A  B  C  D  E  F`

integer-suffix:
    unsigned-suffix long-suffix$_{opt}$
    long-suffix unsigned-suffix$_{opt}$

unsigned-suffix: one of
    `u  U`

long-suffix: one of
    `l  L`

enumeration-constant:
    identifier

character-constant:
    'c-char-sequence'
    L*'c-char-sequence'*

c-char-sequence:
    c-char
    c-char-sequence c-char

c-char:
    any member of the source character set except the single-quote **'**, backslash ****, or new-line
        character
    escape-sequence

escape-sequence:
    simple-escape-sequence
    octal-escape-sequence
    hexadecimal-escape-sequence

simple-escape-sequence: one of
    `\' \" \? \\`
    `\a \b \f \n \r \t \v`

octal-escape-sequence:
    `\` *octal-digit*
    `\` *octal-digit octal-digit*
    `\` *octal-digit octal-digit octal-digit*

hexadecimal-escape-sequence:
    `\x` *hexadecimal-digit*
    hexadecimal-escape-sequence hexadecimal-digit

A.1.5 String Literals
string-literal:
    "s-char-sequence$_{opt}$"
    L*"s-char-sequence$_{opt}$"*

s-char-sequence:
    s-char
    s-char-sequence s-char

s-char:
    any member of the source character set except the double-quote **"**, backslash ****, or new-line
        character
    escape-sequence

A.1.6 Operators

operator: one of

```
[ ]    ( )    .       ->
++     --     &    *     +     -     ~     !     sizeof
/      %      <<   >>    <     >     <=    >=    ==  !=  ^    |    &&   ||
?      :
=      *=     /=   %=    +=    -=    <<=   >>=   &=  ^=  |=
,      #      ##
```

A.1.7 Punctuators

punctuator: one of

```
[ ]    ( )    { }    *    ,    :    =    ;    ...    #
```

A.1.8 Header Names

header-name:
  <h-char-sequence>
  "q-char-sequence"

h-char-sequence:
  h-char
  h-char-sequence h-char

h-char:
  any member of the source character set except the new-line character and >

q-char-sequence:
  q-char
  q-char-sequence q-char

q-char:
  any member of the source character set except the new-line character and "

A.1.9 Preprocessing Numbers

pp-number:
  digit
  . digit
  pp-number digit
  pp-number nondigit
  pp-number **e** *sign*
  pp-number **E** *sign*
  pp-number **.**

A.2 Phrase Structure Grammar
A.2.1 Expressions

primary-expression:
  identifier
  constant
  string-literal
  (expression)

postfix-expression:
  primary-expression
  postfix-expression [*expression*]
  postfix-expression (*argument-expression-list$_{opt}$*)
  postfix-expression **.** *identifier*
  postfix-expression **->** *identifier*
  postfix-expression **++**
  postfix-expression **--**

argument-expression-list:
  assignment-expression
  argument-expression-list **,** *assignment-expression*

unary-expression:
  postfix-expression
  ++ *unary-expression*
  -- *unary-expression*
  unary-operator cast-expression
  sizeof *unary-expression*
  sizeof (*type-name*)

unary-operator: one of
  & * + - ~ !

cast-expression:
  unary-expression
  (*type-name*) *cast-expression*

multiplicative-expression:
  cast-expression
  multiplicative-expression ***** *cast-expression*
  multiplicative-expression **/** *cast-expression*
  multiplicative-expression **%** *cast-expression*

additive-expression:
  multiplicative-expression
  additive-expression **+** *multiplicative-expression*
  additive-expression **-** *multiplicative-expression*

shift-expression:
  additive-expression
  shift-expression **<<** *additive-expression*
  shift-expression **>>** *additive-expression*

relational-expression:
  shift-expression
  relational-expression **<** *shift-expression*
  relational-expression **>** *shift-expression*

   relational-expression <= *shift-expression*
   relational-expression >= *shift-expression*

equality expression:
   relational-expression
   equality-expression == *relational-expression*
   equality-expression ! = *relational-expression*

AND-expression:
   equality-expression
   AND-expression & *equality-expression*

exclusive-OR-expression:
   AND-expression
   exclusive-OR-expression ^ *AND-expression*

inclusive-OR-expression:
   exclusive-OR-expression
   inclusive-OR-expression | *exclusive-OR-expression*

logical-AND-expression:
   inclusive-OR-expression
   logical-AND-expression && *inclusive-OR-expression*

logical-OR-expression:
   logical-AND-expression
   logical-OR-expression | | *logical-AND-expression*

conditional-expression:
   logical-OR-expression
   logical-OR-expression ? *expression* : *conditional-expression*

assignment-expression:
   conditional-expression
   unary-expression assignment-operator assignment-expression

assignment-operator: one of
   = *= /= %= += -= <<= >>= &= ^= |=

expression:
   conditional-expression
   expression , *assignment-expression*

constant-expression:
   conditional-expression

A.2.2 Declarations
declaration:
   declaration-specifiers init-declarator-list$_{opt}$;

declaration-specifiers:
    storage-class-specifier declaration-specifiers$_{opt}$
    type-specifier declaration-specifiers$_{opt}$
    type-qualifier declaration-specifiers$_{opt}$

init-declarator-list:
    init-declarator
    init-declarator-list , init-declarator

init-*declarator:*
    declarator
    declarator = initializer

storage-class-specifier:
    `typedef`
    `extern`
    `static`
    `auto`
    `register`

type-specifier:
    `void`
    `char`
    `short`
    `int`
    `long`
    `float`
    `double`
    `signed`
    `unsigned`
    struct-or-union-specifier
    enum-specifier
    typedef-name

struct-or-union-specifier:
    struct-or-union identifier$_{opt}$ **{** *struct-declaration-list* **}**
    struct-or-union identifier

struct-or-union:
    `struct`
    `union`

struct-declaration-list:
    struct-declaration
    struct-declaration-list struct-declaration

struct-declaration:
    specifier-qualifier-list struct-declarator-list **;**

specifier-qualifier-list:
    type-specifier specifier-qualifier-list$_{opt}$
    type-qualifier specifier-qualifier-list$_{opt}$

struct-declarator-list:
    struct-declarator
    struct-declarator-list , struct-declarator

struct-declarator:
    declarator
    declarator$_{opt}$: *constant-expression*

enum-specifier:
    enum *identifier$_{opt}$* { *enumerator-list* }
    enum *identifier*

enumerator-list:
    enumerator
    enumerator-list , enumerator

enumerator:
    enumeration-constant
    enumeration-constant = constant-expression

type-qualifier:
    `const`
    `volatile`

declarator:
    pointer$_{opt}$ direct-declarator

direct-declarator:
    identifier
    (*declarator*)
    direct-declarator [*constant-expression$_{opt}$*]
    direct-declarator (*parameter-type-list*)
    direct-declarator (*identifier-list$_{opt}$*)

pointer:
    * *type-qualifier-list$_{opt}$*
    * *type-qualifier-list$_{opt}$ pointer*

type-qualifier-list:
    type-qualifier
    type-qualifier-list type-qualifier

parameter-type-list:
    parameter-list
    parameter-list , ...

parameter-list:
    parameter-declaration
    parameter-list , parameter-declaration

parameter-declaration:
    declaration-specifiers declarator
    declaration-specifiers abstract-declarator$_{opt}$

identifier-list:
    identifier
    identifier-list , identifier

type-name:
    specifier-qualifier-list abstract-declarator$_{opt}$

abstract-declarator:
    pointer
    pointer$_{opt}$ direct-abstract-declarator

direct-abstract-declarator:
    (abstract-declarator)
    direct-abstract-declarator$_{opt}$ [*constant-expression$_{opt}$*]
    direct-abstract-declarator$_{opt}$ (*parameter-type-list$_{opt}$*)

typedef-name:
    identifier

initializer:
    assignment-expression
    { *initializer-list* }
    { *initializer-list ,* }

initializer-list:
    initializer
    initializer-list , initializer

A.2.3 Statements

statement:
    labeled-statement
    compound-statement
    expression-statement
    selection-statement
    iteration-statement
    jump-statement

labeled-statement:
    identifier : *statement*
    case *constant-expression* : *statement*
    default : *statement*

compound-statement:
    { *declaration-list$_{opt}$ statement-list$_{opt}$*   }

declaration-list:
    declaration
    declaration-list declaration

statement-list:
    statement
    statement-list statement

expression-statement:
    expression$_{opt}$ **;**

selection-statement:
    if (*expression*) *statement*
    if (*expression*) *statement* **else** *statement*
    switch (*expression*) *statement*

iteration-statement:
    while (*expression*) *statement*
    do *statement* **while** (*expression*) **;**
    for (*expression$_{opt}$* **;** *expression$_{opt}$* **;** *expression$_{opt}$*) *statement*

jump-statement:
    goto *identifier* **;**
    continue ;
    break ;
    return *expression$_{opt}$* **;**

A.2.4 External Definitions

translation-unit:
    external-declaration
    translation-unit external-declaration

external-declaration:
    function-definition
    declaration

function-definition:
    declaration-specifiers$_{opt}$ declarator declaration-list$_{opt}$ compound-statement

A.3 Preprocessing Directives

preprocessing-file:
    group$_{opt}$

group:
    group-part
    group group-part

group-part:
    pp-tokens$_{opt}$ new-line
    if-section
    control-line

if-section:
    if-group elif-groups$_{opt}$ else-group$_{opt}$ endif-line

if-group:
    `# if`   *constant-expression new-line group$_{opt}$*
    `# ifdef`   *identifier new-line group$_{opt}$*
    `# ifndef` *identifier new-line group$_{opt}$*

elif-groups:
    elif-group
    elif-groups elif-group

elif-group:
    `# elif`   *constant-expression new-line group$_{opt}$*

else-group:
    `# else`   *new-line group$_{opt}$*

endif-line:
    `# endif`   *new-line*

control-line:
    `# include` *pp-tokens new-line*
    `# define`   *identifier replacement-list new-line*
    `# define`   *identifier lparen identifier-list$_{opt}$) replacement-list new-line*
    `# undef`   *identifier new-line*
    `# line`   *pp-tokens new-line*
    `# error`   *pp-tokens$_{opt}$ new-line*
    `# pragma` *pp-tokens$_{opt}$ new-line*
    `#`   *new-line*

lparen:
    the left-parenthesis character without preceding white space

replacement-list:
    pp-tokens$_{opt}$

pp-tokens:
    preprocessing-token
    pp-tokens preprocessing-token

new-line:
    the new-line character

Appendix B*
Standard Library

B.1 Errors `<errno.h>`

EDOM

ERANGE

These expand to integral constant expressions with distinct nonzero values, suitable for use in `#if` preprocessing directives.

errno

A value of type `int` which is set to a positive error number by several library functions. The value of `errno` is zero at program startup, but is never set to zero by any library function. A program that uses `errno` for error checking should set it to zero before a library function call, and inspect it before a subsequent library function call. A library function can save the value of `errno` on entry and then set it to zero, as long as the original value is restored if `errno`'s value is still zero just before the return. The value of `errno` may be set to nonzero by a library function call whether or not there is an error, provided the use of `errno` is not documented in the function description in the standard.

B.2 Common Definitions `<stddef.h>`

NULL

An implementation-defined null pointer constant.

`offsetof`(*type*, *member-designator*)

Expands to an integral constant expression of type `size_t`, the value of which is the offset in bytes to the structure member (designated by *member-designator*) from the beginning of its structure type (designated by *type*). The *member-designator* shall be such that given

```
static type t;
```

---

* Permissions Acknowledgment: This material has been condensed and adapted from American National Standard for Information Systems—Programming Language—C, ANSI/ISO 9899: 1990. Copies of this standard may be purchased from the American National Standards Institute at 11 West 42nd Street, New York, NY 10036.

then the expression **&** (**t**.*member-designator*) evaluates to an address constant. (If the specified member is a bit-field, the behavior is undefined.)

ptrdiff_t

> The signed integral type of the result of subtracting two pointers.

size_t

> The unsigned integral type of the result of the **sizeof** operator.

wchar_t

> An integral type whose range of values can represent distinct codes for all members of the largest extended character set specified among the supported locales; the null character shall have the code value zero and each member of the basic character set shall have a code value equal to its value when used as the lone character in an integer character constant.

B.3 Diagnostics <assert.h>

void assert(int expression);

> Macro **assert** puts diagnostics into programs. When it is executed, if **expression** is false, the **assert** macro writes information about the particular call that failed (including the text of the argument, the name of the source file, and the source line number—the latter are respectively the values of the preprocessing macros **__FILE__** and **__LINE__**) on the standard error file in an implementation-defined format. The message written might be of the form
>
> > **Assertion failed:** *expression,* **file** *xyz,* **line** *nnn*
>
> Macro **assert** then calls function **abort**. If the preprocessor directive
>
> > **#define NDEBUG**
>
> appears in the source file where **assert.h** is included, any assertions in the file are ignored.

B.4 Character Handling <ctype.h>

The functions in this section return nonzero (true) if and only if the value of the argument c conforms to that in the description of the function.

int isalnum(int c);

> Tests for any character for which **isalpha** or **isdigit** is true.

int isalpha(int c);

> Tests for any character for which **isupper** or **islower** is true.

int iscntrl(int c);

> Tests for any control character.

int isdigit(int c);

> Tests for any decimal-digit character.

int isgraph(int c);

> Tests for any printing character except space (' ').

int islower(int c);

> Tests for any character that is a lowercase letter.

int isprint(int c);

> Tests for any printing character including space (' ').

int ispunct(int c);

> Tests for any printing character that is neither space (' ') nor a character for which **isalnum** is true.

`int isspace(int c);`

Tests for any character that is a standard white-space character. The standard white-space characters are: space (' '), form feed ('\f'), new-line ('\n'), carriage return ('\r'), horizontal tab ('\t'), and vertical tab ('\v').

`int isupper(int c);`

Tests for any character that is an uppercase letter.

`int isxdigit(int c);`

Tests for any hexadecimal-digit character.

`int tolower(int c);`

Converts an uppercase letter to the corresponding lowercase letter. If the argument is a character for which `isupper` is true and there is a corresponding character for which `islower` is true, the `tolower` function returns the corresponding character; otherwise, the argument is returned unchanged.

`int toupper(int c);`

Converts a lowercase letter to the corresponding uppercase letter. If the argument is a character for which `islower` is true and there is a corresponding character for which `isupper` is true, the `toupper` function returns the corresponding character; otherwise, the argument is returned unchanged.

B.5 Localization `<locale.h>`

`LC_ALL`
`LC_COLLATE`
`LC_CTYPE`
`LC_MONETARY`
`LC_NUMERIC`
`LC_TIME`

These expand to integral constant expressions with distinct values, suitable for use as the first argument to the `setlocale` function.

`NULL`

An implementation-defined null pointer constant.

`struct lconv`

Contains members related to the formatting of numeric values. The structure shall contain at least the following members, in any order. In the "`C`" locale, the members shall have the values specified in the comments.

```
char *decimal_point;        /* "." */
char *thousands-sep;        /* "" */
char *grouping;             /* "" */
char *int_curr_symbol;      /* "" */
char *currency_symbol;      /* "" */
char *mon_decimal_point;    /* "" */
char *mon_thousands_sep;    /* "" */
char *mon_grouping;         /* "" */
char *positive_sign;        /* "" */
char *negative_sign;        /* "" */
char int_frac_digits;       /* CHAR_MAX */
char frac_digits;           /* CHAR_MAX */
```

```
char p_cs_precedes;                /* CHAR_MAX */
char p_sep_by_space;               /* CHAR_MAX */
char n_cs_precedes;                /* CHAR_MAX */
char n_sep_by_space;               /* CHAR_MAX */
char p_sign_posn;                  /* CHAR_MAX */
char n_sign_posn;                  /* CHAR_MAX */
```

`char *setlocale(int category, const char *locale);`

Function **setlocale** selects the appropriate portion of the program's locale as specified by the **category** and **locale** arguments. Function **setlocale** may be used to change or query the program's entire current locale or portions thereof. The value **LC_ALL** for **category** names the program's entire locale; the other values for **category** name only a portion of the program's locale. **LC_COLLATE** affects the behavior of the **strcoll** and **strxfrm** functions. **LC_CTYPE** affects the behavior of the character handling functions and the multibyte functions. **LC_MONETARY** affects the monetary formatting information returned by the **localeconv** function. **LC_NUMERIC** affects the decimal-point character for the formatted input/output functions, the string conversion functions, and the nonmonetary formatting information returned by **localeconv**. **LC_TIME** affects the behavior of **strftime**.

A value of **"C"** for **locale** specifies the minimal environment for C translation; a value of **""** for **locale** specifies the implementation-defined native environment. Other implementation-defined strings may be passed to **setlocale**. At program startup, the equivalent of

`setlocale(LC_ALL, "C");`

is executed. If a pointer to a string is given for **locale** and the selection can be honored, the **setlocale** function returns a pointer to the string associated with the specified **category** for the new locale. If the selection cannot be honored, the **setlocale** function returns a null pointer and the program's locale is not changed.

A null pointer for **locale** causes the **setlocale** function to return a pointer to the string associated with the **category** for the program's current locale; the program's locale is not changed.

The pointer to string returned by the **setlocale** function is such that a subsequent call with that string value and its associated category will restore that part of the program's locale. The string pointed to shall be modified by the program, but may be overwritten by a subsequent call to the **setlocale** function.

`struct lconv *localeconv(void);`

The **localeconv** function sets the components of an object with type **struct lconv** with values appropriate for the formatting of numeric quantities (monetary and otherwise) according to the rules of the current locale.

The members of the structure with type **char *** are pointers to strings, any of which (except **decimal_point**) can point to **""**, to indicate that the value is not available in the current locale or is of zero length. The members with type **char** are nonnegative numbers, any of which can be **CHAR_MAX** to indicate that the value is not available in the current locale. The members include the following:

`char *decimal_point`

The decimal-point character used to format nonmonetary quantities.

`char *thousands_sep`

The character used to separate groups of digits before the decimal-point character in formatted nonmonetary quantities.

`char *grouping`
> A string whose elements indicate the size of each group of digits in formatted nonmonetary quantities.

`char *int_curr_symbol`
> The international currency symbol applicable to the current locale. The first three characters contain the alphabetic international currency symbol in accordance with those specified in ISO 4217:1987. The fourth character (immediately preceding the null character) is the character used to separate the international currency symbol from the monetary quantity.

`char *currency_symbol`
> The locale currency symbol applicable to the current locale.

`char *mon_decimal_point`
> The decimal-point used to format monetary quantities.

`char *mon_thousands_sep`
> The separator for groups of digits before the decimal-point in formatted monetary quantities.

`char *mon_grouping`
> A string whose elements indicate the size of each group of digits in formatted monetary quantities.

`char *positive_sign`
> The string used to indicate a nonnegative-valued formatted monetary quantity.

`char *negative_sign`
> The string used to indicate a negative-valued formatted monetary quantity.

`char int_frac_digits`
> The number of fractional digits (those after the decimal-point) to be displayed in an internationally formatted monetary quantity.

`char frac_digits`
> The number of fractional digits (those after the decimal-point) to be displayed in a formatted monetary quantity.

`char p_cs_precedes`
> Set to 1 or 0 the `currency_symbol` respectively precedes or succeeds the value for a nonnegative formatted monetary quantity.

`char p_sep_by_space`
> Set to 1 or 0 the `currency_symbol` respectively is or is not separated by a space from the value for a nonnegative formatted monetary quantity.

`char n_cs_precedes`
> Set to 1 or 0 the `currency_symbol` respectively precedes or succeeds the value for a negative formatted monetary quantity.

`char n_sep_by_space`
> Set to 1 or 0 the `currency_symbol` respectively is or is not separated by a space from the value for a negative formatted monetary quantity.

`char p_sign_posn`
> Set to a value indicating the positioning of the `positive_sign` for a nonnegative formatted monetary quantity.

`char n_sign_posn`

Set to a value indicating the positioning of the **negative_sign** for a negative formatted monetary quantity.

The elements of **grouping** and **mon_grouping** are interpreted according to the following:

> **CHAR_MAX**   No further grouping is to be performed.
>
> **0**   The previous element is to be repeatedly used for the remainder of the digits.
>
> *other*   The integer value is the number of digits that comprise the current group. The next element is examined to determine the size of the next group of digits before the current group.

The values of **p_sign_posn** and **n_sign_posn** are interpreted according to the following:

0   Parentheses surround the quantity and **currency_symbol**.

1   The sign string precedes the quantity and **currency_symbol**.

2   The sign string succeeds the quantity and **currency_symbol**.

3   The sign string immediately precedes the **currency_symbol**.

4   The sign string immediately succeeds the **currency_symbol**.

The **localeconv** function returns a pointer to the filled-in object. The structure pointed to by the return value shall not be modified by the program, but may be overwritten by a subsequent call to the **localeconv** function. In addition, calls to the **setlocale** function with categories **LC_ALL**, **LC_MONETARY**, or **LC_NUMERIC** may overwrite the contents of the structure.

B.6 Mathematics `<math.h>`

`HUGE_VAL`

A symbolic constant representing a positive **double** expression.

`double acos(double x);`

Computes the principal value of the arc cosine of **x**. A domain error occurs for arguments not in the range [-1, +1]. The **acos** function returns the arc cosine in the range [0, π] radians.

`double asin(double x);`

Computes the principal value of the arc sine of **x**. A domain error occurs for arguments not in the range [-1, +1]. The **asin** function returns the arc sine in the range [-π/2, +π/2] radians.

`double atan(double x);`

Computes the principal value of the arc tangent of **x**. The **atan** function returns the arc tangent in the range [-π/2, +π/2] radians.

`double atan2(double y, double x);`

The **atan2** function computes the principal value of the arc tangent **y/x**, using the signs of both arguments to determine the quandrant of the return value. A domain error may occur if both arguments are zero. The **atan2** function returns the arc tangent of **y/x**, in the range [-π, +π] radians.

`double cos(double x);`

Computes the cosine of **x** (measured in radians).

```
double sin(double x);
```
Computes the sine of **x** (measured in radians).

```
double tan(double x);
```
Returns the tangent of **x** (measured in radians).

```
double cosh(double x);
```
Computes the hyperbolic cosine of **x**. A range error occurs if the magnitude of **x** is too large.

```
double sinh(double x);
```
Computes the hyperbolic sine of **x**. A range error occurs if the magnitude of **x** is too large.

```
double tanh(double x);
```
The **tanh** function computes the hyperbolic tangent of **x**.

```
double exp(double x);
```
Computes the exponential function of **x**. A range error occurs if the magnitude of **x** is too large.

```
double frexp(double value, int *exp);
```
Breaks the floating-point number onto a normalized fraction and an integral power of 2. It stores the integer in the **int** object pointed to by **exp**. The **frexp** function returns the value **x**, such that **x** is a **double** with magnitude in the interval [1/2, 1] or zero, and **value** equals **x** times 2 raised to the power ***exp**. If **value** is zero, both parts of the result are zero.

```
double ldexp(double x, int exp);
```
Multiplies a floating-point number by an integral power of 2. A range error may occur. The **ldexp** function returns the value of **x** times 2 raised to the power **exp**.

```
double log(double x);
```
Computes the natural logarithm of **x**. A domain error occurs if the argument is negative. A range error may occur if the argument is zero.

```
double log10(double x);
```
Computes the base-ten logarithm of **x**. A domain error occurs if the argument is negative. A range error may occur if the argument is zero.

```
double modf(double value, double *iptr);
```
Breaks the argument **value** into integral and fractional parts, each of which has the same sign as the argument. It stores the integral part as a **double** in the object pointed to by **iptr**. The **modf** function returns the signed frantional part of **value**

```
double pow(double x, double y);
```
Computes **x** raised to the power **y**. A domain error occurs if **x** is negative and **y** is not an integral value. A domain error occurs if the result cannot be represented when **x** is zero and **y** is less than or equal to zero. A range error may occur.

```
double sqrt(double x);
```
Computes the nonnegative square root of **x**. A domain error occurs if the argument is negative.

```
double ceil(double x);
```
Computes the smallest integral value not less than **x**.

```
double fabs(double x);
```
Computes the absolute value of a floating-point number **x**.

```
double floor(double x);
```
Computes the largest integral value not greater than **x**.

```
double fmod(double x, double y);
```
Computes the floating-point remainder of **x/y**.

B.7 Nonlocal Jumps `<setjmp.h>`

`jmp_buf`

An array type suitable for holding the information needed to restore a calling environment.

```
int setjmp(jmp_buf env);
```
Saves its calling environment in argument **jmp_buf** for later use by the **longjmp** function.

If the return is from a direct invocation, the **setjmp** macro returns the value zero. If the return is from a call to the **longjmp** function, the **setjmp** macro returns a nonzero value.

An invocation of the **setjmp** macro shall appear only in one of the following contexts:

- the entire controlling expression of a selection or iteration statement;

- one operand of a relational or equality operator with the other operand an integral constant expression, with the resulting expression being the entire controlling expression of a selection or iteration statement;

- the operand of a unary **!** operator with the resulting expression being the entire controlling expression of a selection or iteration statement; or

- the entire expression of an expression statement.

```
void longjmp(jmp_buf env, int val);
```
Restores the environment saved by the most recent invocation of the **setjmp** macro in the same invocation of the program, with the corresponding **jmp_buf** argument. If there has been no such invocation, or if the function containing the invocation of the **setjmp** macro has terminated execution in the interim, the behavior is undefined.

All accessible objects have values as of the time **longjmp** was called, except that the values of objects of automatic storage duration that are local to the function containing the invocation of the corresponding **setjmp** macro that are not volatile type and have been changed between the **setjmp** invocation and **longjmp** invocation call are indeterminate.

As it bypasses the usual function call and return mechanisms, **longjmp** shall execute correctly in context of interrupts, signals, and any of their associated functions. However, if the **longjmp** function is invoked from a nested signal handler (that is, from a function invoked as a result of a signal raised during the handling of another signal), the behavior is undefined.

After **longjmp** is completed, program execution continues as if the corresponding invocation of the **setjmp** macro had just returned the value specified by **val**. The **longjmp** function cannot cause the **setjmp** macro to return the value 0; if **val** is 0, the **setjmp** macro returns the value 1.

B.8 Signal Handling `<signal.h>`

`sig_atomic_t`

The integral type of an object that can be accessed as an atomic entity, even in the presence of asynchronous interrupts.

`SIG_DFL`
`SIG_ERR`
`SIG_IGN`

These expand to constant expressions with distinct values that have type compatible with the second argument to and the return value of the **signal** function, and whose value compares unequally to the address of any declarable function; and the following, each of which expands to a positive integral constant expression that is the signal number for the specified condition:

SIGABRT   abnormal termination, such as is initiated by the **abort** function

SIGFPE   an erroneous arithmetic operation, such as zero divide or an operation resulting in overflow

SIGILL   detection of an invalid function image, such as an illegal instruction

SIGINT   receipt of an interactive attention signal

SIGSEGV   an invalid access to storage

SIGTERM   a termination request sent to the program

An implementation need not generate any of these signals, except as a result of explicit calls to the **raise** function.

```
void (*signal(int sig, void (*func)(int)))(int);
```
Chooses one of three ways in which receipt of the signal number **sig** is to be subsequently handled. If the value of **func** is **SIG_DEF**, default handling for that signal will occur. If the value of **func** is **SIG_IGN**, the signal will be ignored. Otherwise, **func** shall point to a function to be called when that signal occurs. Such a function is called a *signal handler*.

When a signal occurs, if **func** points to a function, first the equivalent of **signal(sig, SIG_DFL);** is executed or an implementation-defined blocking of the signal is performed. (If the value of **sig** is **SIGILL**, whether the reset to **SIG_DFL** occurs is implementation-defined.) Next the equivalent of **(*func) (sig);** is executed. The function **func** may terminate by executing a **return** statement or by calling the **abort**, **exit**, or **longjmp** function. If **func** executes a **return** statement and the value if **sig** was **SIGFPE** or any other implementation-defined value corresponding to a computational exception, the behavior is undefined. Otherwise, the program will resume execution at the point it was interrupted.

If the signal occurs other than as the result of calling the **abort** or **raise** function, the behavior is undefined if the signal handler calls any function in the standard library other than the **signal** function itself (with a first argument of the signal number corresponding to the signal that caused the invocation of the handler) or refers to any object with static storage duration other than by assigning a value to a static storage duration variable of type **volatile sig_atomic_t**. Furthermore, if such a call to the **signal** function results in a **SIG_ERR** return, the value of **errno** in indeterminate.

At program startup, the equivalent of

```
signal(sig, SIG_IGN);
```

may be executed for some signals selected in an implementation-defined manner; the equivalent of

```
signal(sig, SIG_DFL);
```

is executed for all other signals defined by the implementation.

If the request can be honored, the **signal** function returns the value of **func** for the most recent call to **signal** for the specified signal **sig**. Otherwise, a value of **SIG_ERR** is returned and a positive value is stored in **errno**.

```
int raise(int sig);
```
The **raise** function sends the signal **sig** to the executing program The **raise** function returns zero if successful, nonzero if unsuccessful.

B.9 Variable Arguments `<stdarg.h>`

`va_list`

> A type suitable for holding information needed by the macros **va_start**, **va_arg**, and **va_end**. If access to the varying arguments is desired, the called function shall declare an object (referred to as **ap** in this section) having type **va_list**. The object **ap** may be passed as an argument to another function; if that function invokes the **va_arg** macro with parameter **ap**, the value of **ap** in the calling function is determinate and shall be passed to the **va_end** macro prior to any further reference to **ap**.

`void va_start(va_list ap, `*parmN*`);`

> Shall be invoked before any access to the unnamed arguments. The **va_start** marco initializes **ap** for subsequent use by **va_arg** and **va_end**. The parameter *parmN* is the identifier of the rightmost parameter in the variable parameter list in the function definition (the one just before the **,...**). If the parameter *parmN* is declared with the **register** storage class, with a function or array type, or with a type that is not compatible with the type that results after application of the default argument promotions, the behavior is undefined.

type `va_arg(va_list ap, `*type*`);`

> Expands to an expression that has the type and value of the next argument in the call. The parameter **ap** shall be the same as the **va_list ap** initialized by **va_start**. Each invocation of **va_arg** modifies **ap** so that the values of successive arguments are returned in turn. The parameter *type* is a type name specified such that the type of a pointer to an object that has the specified type can be obtained simply by postfixing a ***** to *type*. If there is no next argument, or if *type* is not compatible with the type of the next argument (as promoted according to the default argument promotions), the behavior is undefined. The first invocation of the **va_arg** macro after that of the **va_start** macro returns the value of the argument after that specified by *parmN*. Successive invocations return the values of the remaining arguments in succession.

`void va_end(va_list ap);`

> Facilitates a normal return from the function whose variable argument list was referred to by the expansion of **va_start** that initialized **va_list ap**. The **va_end** macro may modify **ap** so that it is no longer usable (without an intervening invocation of **va_start**). If there is no corresponding invocation of the **va_start** macro, or if the **va_end** macro is not invoked before the return, the behavior is undefined.

B.10 Input/Output `<stdio.h>`

`_IOFBF`
`_IOLBF`
`_IONBF`

> Integral constant expressions with distinct values, suitable for use as the third argument to the **setvbuf** function.

`BUFSIZ`

> An integral constant expression, which is the size of the buffer used by the **setbuf** function.

`EOF`

> A negative integral constant expression that is returned by several functions to indicate end-of-file, that is, no more input from a stream.

`FILE`

> An object type capable of recording all the information needed to control a stream, including its file position indicator, a pointer to its associated buffer (if any), an error indicator that

records whether a read/write error has occurred, and an end-of-file indicator that records whether the end of the file has been reached.

FILENAME_MAX

An integral constant expression that is the size needed for an array of **char** large enough to hold the longest file name string that the implementation guarantees can be opened.

FOPEN_MAX

An integral constant expression that is the minimum number of files that the implementation guarantees can be open simultaneously.

fpos_t

An object type capable of recording all the information needed to specify uniquely every position within a file.

L_tmpnam

An integral constant expression that is the size needed for an array of **char** large enough to hold a temporary file name string generated by the **tmpnam** function.

NULL

An implementation-defined null pointer constant.

SEEK_CUR
SEEK_END
SEEK_SET

Integral constant expressions with distinct values, suitable for use as the third argument to the **fseek** function.

size_t

The unsigned integral type of the result of the **sizeof** operator.

stderr

Expression of type "pointer to **FILE**" that points to the **FILE** object associated with the standard error stream.

stdin

Expression of type "pointer to **FILE**" that points to the **FILE** object associated with the standard input stream.

stdout

Expression of type "pointer to **FILE**" that points to the **FILE** object associated with the standard output stream.

TMP_MAX

An integral constant expression that is the minimum number of unique file names that shall be generated by the **tmpnam** function. The value of the macro **TMP_MAX** shall be at least 25.

int remove(const char *filename);

Causes the file whose name is the string pointed to by **filename** to be no longer accessible by that name. A subsequent attempt to open that file using that name will fail, unless it is created anew. If the file is open, the behavior of the **remove** function is implementation-defined. Thr **remove** function returns zero if the operation succeeds, nonzero if it fails.

int rename(const char *old, const char *new);

Causes the file whose name is the string pointed to by **old** to be henceforth known by the name given by the string pointed to by **new**. The file named **old** is no longer accessible by that name. If a file named by the string pointed to by **new** exists prior to the call to the **re-**

name function, the behavior is implementation-defined. The **rename** function returns zero if the operation succeeds, nonzero if it fails, in which case if the file existed previously it is still known by its original name.

`FILE *tmpfile(void);`

Creates a temporary binary file that will automatically be removed when it is closed or at program termination. If the program terminates abnormally, whether an open temporary file is removed is implementation-defined. The file is opened for update with `"wb+"` mode. The `tmpfile` function returns a pointer to the stream of the file that is created. If the file cannot be created, the `tmpfile` function returns a null pointer.

`char *tmpnam(char *s);`

The `tmpnam` function generates a string that is a valid file name and that is not the same as the name of an existing file. The `tmpnam` function generates a different string each time it is called, up to `TMP_MAX` times. If it is called more than `TMP_MAX` times, the behavior is implementation-defined.

If the argument is a null pointer, the `tmpnam` function leaves its result in an internal static object and returns a pointer to that object. Subsequent calls to the `tmpnam` function may modify the same object. If the argument is not a null pointer, it is assumed to point to an array of at least `L_tmpnam char`s; the `tmpnam` function writes its result in that array and returns the argument as its value.

`int fclose(FILE *stream);`

The `fclose` function causes the stream pointed to by `stream` to be flushed and the associated file to be closed. Any unwritten buffered data for the stream are delivered to the host environment to be written to the file; any unread buffered data are discarded. The stream is disassociated from the file. If the associated buffer was automatically allocated, it is deallocated. The `fclose` function returns zero if the stream was successfully closed, or `EOF` if any errors were detected.

`int fflush(FILE *stream);`

If `stream` points to an output stream or an update stream in which the most recent operation was not input, the `fflush` function causes any unwritten data for that stream to be delivered to the host environment or to be written to the file; otherwise, the behavior is undefined.

If `stream` is a null pointer, the `fflush` function performs this flushing action on all streams for which the behavior is defined above. The `fflush` function returns `EOF` if a write error occurs, otherwise zero.

`FILE *fopen(const char *filename, const char *mode);`

The `fopen` function opens the file whose name is the string pointed to by `filename`, and associates a stream with it. The argument `mode` points to a string beginning with one of the following sequences:

`r`	open text file for reading
`w`	truncate to zero length or create text file for writing
`a`	append; open or create text file for writing at end-of-file
`rb`	open binary file for reading
`wb`	truncate to zero length or create binary file for writing
`ab`	append; open or create binary file for writing at end-of-file
`r+`	open text file for update (reading and writing)

w+	truncate to zero length or create text file for update
a+	append; open or create text file for update, writing at end-of-file
r+b or rb+	open binary file for update (reading and writing)
w+b or wb+	truncate to zero length or create binary file for update
a+b or ab+	append; open or create binary file for update, writing at end-of-file

Opening a file with read mode (`'r'` as the first character in the **mode** argument) fails if the file does not exist or cannot be read. Opening the file with append mode (`'a'` as the first character in the **mode** argument) causes all subsequent writes to the file to be forced to the then current end-of-file, regardless of intervening calls to the **fseek** function. In some implementations, opening a binary file with append mode (`'b'` as the second or third character in the above list of **mode** argument values) may initially position the file position indicator for the stream beyond the last data written, because of null character padding.

When a file is opened with update mode (`'+'` as the second or third character in the above list of **mode** argument values), both input and output may be performed on the associated stream. However, output may not be directly followed by input without an intervening call to the **fflush** function or to a file positioning function (**fseek**, **fsetpos**, or **rewind**), and input may not be directly followed by output without an intervening call to a file positioning function, unless the input operation encounters end-of-file. Opening (or creating) a text file with update mode may instead open (or create) a binary stream in some implementations.

When opened, a stream is fully buffered if and only if it can be determined not to refer to an interactive device. The error and end-of-file indicators for the stream are cleared. The **fopen** function returns a pointer to the object controlling the stream. If the open operation fails, **fopen** returns a null pointer.

```
FILE *freopen(const char *filename, const char *mode,
              FILE *stream);
```
The **freopen** function opens the file whose name is the string pointed to by **filename** and associates the stream pointed to by **stream** with it. The **mode** argument is used just as in the **fopen** function.

The **freopen** function first attempts to close any file that is associated with the specified stream. Failure to close the file successfully is ignored. The error and end-of-file indicators for the stream are cleared. The **freopen** function returns a null pointer if the open operation fails. Otherwise, **freopen** returns the value of **stream**.

```
void setbuf(FILE *stream, char *buf);
```
The **setbuf** function is equivalent to the **setvbuf** function invoked with the values **_IOFBF** for **mode** and **BUFSIZ** for **size**, or (if **buf** is a null pointer), with the value **_IONBF** for **mode**. The **setbuf** function returns no value.

```
int setvbuf(FILE *stream, char *buf, int mode, size_t size);
```
The **setvbuf** function may be used only after the stream pointed to by **stream** has been associated with an open file and before any other operation is performed on the stream. The argument **mode** determines how **stream** will be buffered, as follows: **_IOFBF** causes input/output to be fully buffered; **_IOLBF** causes input/output to be line buffered; **_IONBF** causes input/output to be unbuffered. If **buf** is not a null pointer, the array it points to may be used instead of a buffer allocated by the **setvbuf** function. The argument **size** specifies the size of the array. The contents of the array at any time are indeterminate. The **setvbuf** function returns zero on success, or nonzero if an invalid value is given for **mode** or if the request cannot be honored.

```
int fprintf(FILE *stream, const char *format, ...);
```
The **fprintf** function writes output to the stream pointed to by **stream**, under control of the string pointed to by **format** that specifies how subsequent arguments are converted for output. If there are insufficient arguments for the format, the behavior is undefined. If the format is exhausted while arguments remain, the excess arguments are evaluated (as always) but are otherwise ignored. The **fprintf** function returns when the end of the format string is encountered. See Chapter 9, "Formatted Input/Output," for a detailed description of the output conversion specifications. The **fprintf** function returns the number of characters transmitted, or a negative value if an output error occurred.

```
int fscanf(FILE *stream, const char *format, ...);
```
The **fscanf** function reads input from the stream pointed to by **stream**, under control of the string pointed to by **format** that specifies the admissible input sequences and how they are to be converted for assignment, using subsequent arguments as pointers to the objects to receive the converted input. If there are insufficient arguments for the format, the behavior is undefined. If the format is exhausted while arguments remain, the excess arguments are evaluated (as always) but are otherwise ignored. See Chapter 9, "Formatted Input/Output," for a detailed description of the input conversion specifications.

The **fscanf** function returns the value of the macro **EOF** if an input failure occurs before any conversion. Otherwise, the **fscanf** function returns the number of input items assigned, which can be fewer than provided for, or even zero, in the event of an early matching failure.

```
int printf(const char *format, ...);
```
The **printf** function is equivalent to **fprintf** with the argument **stdout** interposed before the arguments to **printf**. The **printf** function returns the number of characters transmitted, or a negative value if an output error occurred.

```
int scanf(const char *format, ...);
```
Function **scanf** is equivalent to **fscanf** with the argument **stdin** interposed before the arguments to **scanf**. Function **scanf** returns the value of the macro **EOF** if an input failure occurs before any conversion. Otherwise, **scanf** returns the number of input items assigned, which can be fewer than provided for, or even zero, in the event of an early matching failure.

```
int sprintf(char *s, const char *format, ...);
```
Function **sprintf** is equivalent to **fprintf**, except that the argument **s** specifies an array into which the generated output is to be written, rather than to a stream. A null character is written at the end of the characters written; it is not counted as part of the returned sum. The behavior of copying between objects that overlap is undefined. Function **sprintf** returns the number of characters written by the array, not counting the terminating null character.

```
int sscanf(const char *s, const char *format, ...);
```
The **sscanf** function is equivalent to **fscanf**, except that the argument **s** specifies a string from which the input is to be obtained, rather than from a stream. Reaching the end of the string is equivalent to encountering end-of-file for the **fscanf** function. If copying takes place between objects that overlap, the behavior is undefined.

The **sscanf** function returns the value of the macro **EOF** if an input failure occurs before any conversion. Otherwise, the **sscanf** function returns the number of input items assigned, which can be fewer than provided for, or even zero, in the event of an early matching failure.

```
int vfprintf(FILE *stream, const char *format, va_list arg);
```
Function **vfprintf** is equivalent to **fprintf**, with the variable argument list replaced by **arg**, which is initialized by the **va_start** macro (and possibly subsequent **va_arg** calls).

Function `vfprintf` does not invoke the `va_end` macro. The `vfprintf` function returns the number of characters transmitted, or a negative value if an output error occurred.

`int vprintf(const char *format, va_list arg);`

The `vprintf` function is equivalent to `printf`, with the variable argument list replaced by `arg`, which shall have been initialized by the `va_start` macro (and possibly subsequent `va_arg` calls). Function `vprintf` does not invoke the `va_end` macro. Function `vprintf` returns the number of characters transmitted, or a negative value if an output error occurred.

`int vsprintf(char *s, const char *format, va_list arg);`

Function `vsprintf` is equivalent to `sprintf`, with the variable argument list replaced by `arg`, which shall have been initialized by the `va_start` macro (and possibly subsequent `va_arg` calls). Function `vsprintf` does not invoke the `va_end` macro. If copying takes place between objects that overlap, the behavior is undefined. Function `vsprintf` returns the number of characters written in the array, not counting the terminating null character.

`int fgetc(FILE *stream);`

The `fgetc` function obtains the next character (if present) as an **unsigned char** converted to an `int`, from the input stream pointed to by `stream`, and advances the associated file position indicator for the stream (if defined). The `fgetc` function returns the next character from the input stream pointed to by `stream`. If the stream is at end-of-file, the end-of-file indicator for the stream is set and `fgetc` returns `EOF`. If a read error occurs, the error indicator for the stream is set and `fgetc` returns `EOF`.

`char *fgets(char *s, int n, FILE *stream);`

The `fgets` function reads at most one less than the number of characters specified by `n` from the stream pointed to by `stream` into the array pointed to by `s`. No additional characters are read after a new-line character (which is retained) or after end-of-file. A null character is written immediately after the last character read into the array.

The `fgets` function returns `s` if successful. If end-of-file is encountered and no characters have been read into the array, the contents of the array remain unchanged and a null pointer is returned. If a read error occurs during the operation, the array contents are indeterminate and a null pointer is returned.

`int fputc(int c, FILE *stream);`

The `fputc` function writes the character specified by `c` (converted to an **unsigned char**) to the output stream pointed to by `stream`, at the position indicated by the associated file position indicator for the stream (if defined), and advances the indicator appropriately. If the file cannot support positioning requests, or if the stream was opened with append mode, the character is appended to the output stream. The `fputc` function returns the character written. If a write error occurs, the error indicator for the stream is set and `fputc` returns `EOF`.

`int fputs(const char *s, FILE *stream);`

The `fputs` function writes the string pointed to by `s` to the stream pointed to by `stream`. The terminating null character is not written. The `fputs` function returns `EOF` of a write error occurs; otherwise it returns a nonnegative value.

`int getc(FILE *stream);`

Function `getc` is equivalent to `fgetc`, except that if it is implemented as a macro, it may evaluate `stream` more than once—the argument should be an expression without side effects.

Function `getc` returns the next character from the input stream pointed to by `stream`. If the stream is at end-of-file, the end-of-file indicator for the stream is set and `getc` returns `EOF`. If a read error occurs, the error indicator for the stream is set and `getc` returns `EOF`.

```
int getchar(void);
```

The **getchar** function is equivalent to **getc** with the argument **stdin**. The **getchar** function returns the next character from the input stream pointed to by **stdin**. If the stream is at end-of-file, the end-of-file indicator for the stream is set and **getchar** returns **EOF**. If a read error occurs, the error indicator for the stream is set and **getchar** returns **EOF**.

```
char *gets(char *s);
```

The **gets** function reads characters from the input stream pointed to by **stdin**, into the array pointed to by **s**, until end-of-file is encountered or a new-line character is read. Any new-line character is discarded, and a null character is written immediately after the last character read into the array. The **gets** function returns **s** if successful. If end-of-file is encountered and no characters have been read into the array, the contents of the array remain unchanged and a null pointer is returned. If a read error occurs during the operation, the array contents are indeterminate and a null pointer is returned.

```
int putc(int c, FILE *stream);
```

The **putc** function is equivalent to **fputc**, except that if it is implemented as a macro, it may evaluate **stream** more than once, so the argument should never be an expression with side effects. The **putc** function returns the character written. If a write error occurs, the error indicator for the stream is set and **putc** returns **EOF**.

```
int putchar(int c);
```

The **putchar** is equivalent to **putc** with the second argument **stdout**. The **putchar** function returns the character written. If a write error occurs, the error indicator for the stream is set and **putchar** returns **EOF**.

```
int puts(const char *s);
```

The **puts** function writes the string pointed to by **s** to the stream pointed to by **stdout**, and appends a new-line character to the output. The terminating null character is not written. The **puts** function returns **EOF** if a write error occurs; otherwise it returns a nonnegative value.

```
int ungetc(int c, FILE *stream);
```

The **ungetc** function pushes the character specified by **c** (converted to an **unsigned char**) back onto the input stream pointed to by **stream**. The pushed-back characters will be returned by subsequent reads on that stream in the reverse order of their pushing. A successful intervening call (with the stream pointed to by **stream**) to a file positioning function (**fseek**, **fsetpos**, or **rewind**) discards any pushed-back characters for the stream. The external storage corresponding to the stream is unchanged.

One character of pushback is guaranteed. If the **ungetc** function is called too many times on the same stream without an intervening read or file positioning operation on that stream, the operation may fail. If the value of c equals that of the macro **EOF**, the operation fails and the input stream is unchanged.

A successful call to the **ungetc** function clears the end-of-file indicator for the stream. The value of the file position indicator for the stream after reading or discarding all pushed-back characters shall be the same as it was before the characters were pushed back. For a text stream, the value of its file position indicator after a successful call to the **ungetc** function is unspecified until all pushed-back characters are read or discarded. For a binary stream, its file position indicator is determined by each successful call to the **ungetc** function; if its value was zero before a call, it is indeterminate after the call. The **ungetc** function returns the character pushed back after conversion, or **EOF** if the operation fails.

`size_t fread(void *ptr, size_t size, size_t nmemb, FILE *stream);`

The **fread** function reads, into the array pointed to by **ptr**, up to nmemb elements whose size is specified by **size**, from the stream pointed to by **stream**. The file position indicator for the stream (if defined) is advanced by the number of characters successfully read. If an error occurs, the resulting value of the file position indicator for the stream is indeterminate. If a partial element is read, its value is indeterminate.

The **fread** function returns the number of elements successfully read, which may be less than **nmemb** if a read error or end-of-file is encountered. If **size** or **nmemb** is zero, **fread** returns zero and the contents of the array and the state of the stream remain unchanged.

`size_t fwrite(const void *ptr, size_t size, size_t nmemb,`
`             FILE *stream);`

The **fwrite** function writes, from the array pointed to by **ptr**, up to nmemb elements whose size is specified by **size**, to the stream pointed to by **stream**. The file position indicator for the stream (if defined) is advanced by the number of characters successfully written. If an error occurs, the resulting value of the file position for the stream is indeterminate. The **fwrite** function returns the number of elements successfully written, which will be less than **nmemb** only if a write error is encountered.

`int fgetpos(FILE *stream, fpos_t *pos);`

The **fgetpos** function stores the current value of the file position indicator for the stream pointed to by **stream** in the object pointed to by **pos**. The value stored contains unspecified information usable by the **fsetpos** function for repositioning the stream to its position at the time of the call to the **fgetpos** function. If successful, the **fgetpos** function returns zero; on failure, the **fgetpos** function returns nonzero and stores an implementation-defined positive value in **errno**.

`int fseek(FILE *stream, long int offset, int whence);`

The **fseek** function sets the file position indicator for the stream pointed to by **stream**. For a binary stream, the new position, measured in characters from the beginning of the file, is obtained by adding **offset** to the position specified by **whence**. The specified position is the beginning of the file if **whence** is SEEK_SET, the current value of the file position indicator if SEEK_CUR, or end-of-file if SEEK_END. A binary stream need not meaningfully support **fseek** calls with a **whence** value of SEEK_END. For a text stream, either **offset** shall be zero, or **offset** shall be a value returned by an earlier call to the **ftell** function on the same stream and **whence** shall be SEEK_SET.

A successful call to the **fseek** function clears the end-of-file indicator for the stream and undoes any effects of the **ungetc** function on the same stream. After an **fseek** call, the next operation on an update stream may be either input or output. The **fseek** function returns nonzero only for a request that cannot be satisfied.

`int fsetpos(FILE *stream, const fpos_t *pos);`

The **fsetpos** function sets the file position indicator for the stream pointed to by **stream** according to the value of the object pointed to by **pos**, which shall be a value obtained from an earlier call to the **fgetpos** function on the same stream. A successful call to the **fsetpos** function clears the end-of-file indicator for the stream and undoes any effects of the **ungetc** function on the same stream. After an **fsetpos** call, the next operation on an update stream may be either input or output. If successful, the **fsetpos** function returns zero; on failure, the **fsetpos** function returns nonzero and stores an implementation-defined positive value in **errno**.

`long int ftell(FILE *stream);`

> Function `ftell` obtains the current value of the file position indicator for the stream pointed to by `stream`. For a binary stream, the value is the number of characters from the beginning of the file. For a text stream, its file position indicator contains unspecified information, usable by the `fseek` function for returning the file position indicator for the stream to its position at the time of the `ftell` call; the difference between two such return values is not necessarily a meaningful measure of the number of characters written or read. If successful, the `ftell` function returns the current value of the file position indicator for the stream. On failure, the `ftell` function returns `-1L` and stores an implementation-defined positive value in `errno`.

`void rewind(FILE *stream);`

> The `rewind` function sets the file position indicator for the stream pointed to by `stream` to the beginning of the file. It is equivalent to
>
> `(void)fseek(stream, 0L, SEEK_SET)`
>
> except that the error indicator for the stream is also cleared.

`void clearerr(FILE *stream);`

> The `clearerr` function clears the end-of-file and error indicators for the stream pointed to by `stream`.

`int feof(FILE *stream);`

> The `feof` function tests the end-of-file indicator for the stream pointed to by `stream`. The `feof` function returns nonzero if and only if the end-of-file indicator is set for `stream`.

`int ferror(FILE *stream);`

> The `ferror` function tests the error indicator for the stream pointed to by `stream`. The `ferror` function returns nonzero if and only if the error indicator is set for `stream`.

`void perror(const char *s);`

> The `perror` function maps the error number in the integer expression `errno` to an error message. It writes a sequence of characters to the standard error stream thus: first (if `s` is not a null pointer and the character pointed to by `s` is not the null character), the string pointed to by `s` followed by a colon (:) and a space; then an appropriate error message string followed by a new-line character. The contents of the error message strings are the same as those returned by the `strerror` function with argument `errno`, which are implementation-defined.

B.11 General Utilities `<stdlib.h>`

`EXIT_FAILURE`

`EXIT_SUCCESS`

> Integral expressions that may be used as the argument to the `exit` function to return unsuccessful or successful termination status, respectively, to the host environment.

`MB_CUR_MAX`

> A positive integer expression whose value is the maximum number of bytes in a multibyte character for the extended character set specified by the current locale (category `LC_CTYPE`), and whose value is never greater than `MB_LEN_MAX`.

`NULL`

> An implementation-defined null pointer constant.

`RAND_MAX`

> An interval constant expression, the value of which is the maximum value returned by the `rand` function. The value of the `RAND_MAX` macro shall be at least 32767.

`div_t`

A structure type that is the type of the value returned by the **div** function.

`ldiv_t`

A structure type that is the type of the value returned by the **ldiv** function.

`size_t`

The unsigned integral type of the result of the **sizeof** operator.

`wchar_t`

An integral type whose range of values can represent distinct codes for all members of the largest extended character set specified among the supported locales; the null character shall have the code value zero and each member of the basic character set shall have a code value equal to its value when used as the lone character in an integer character constant.

`double atof(const char *nptr);`

Converts the initial portion of the string pointed to by **nptr** to **double** representation. The **atof** function returns the converted value.

`int atoi(const char *nptr);`

Converts the initial portion of the string pointed to by **nptr** to **int** representation. The **atoi** function returns the converted value.

`long int atol(const char *nptr);`

Converts the initial portion of the string pointed to by **nptr** to **long** representation. The **atol** function returns the converted value.

`double strtod(const char *nptr, char **endptr);`

Converts the initial portion of the string pointed to by **nptr** to **double** representation. First, it decomposes the input string into three parts: an initial, possibly empty, sequence of white-space characters (as specified by the **isspace** function), a subject sequence resembling a floating-point constant; and a final string of one or more unrecognized characters, including the terminating null character of the input string. Then, it attempts to convert the subject sequence to a floating-point number, and returns the result.

The expanded form of the subject sequence is an optional plus or minus sign, then a nonempty sequence of digits optionally containing a decimal-point character, then an optional exponent part, but no floating suffix. The subject sequence is defined as the longest initial subsequence of the input string, starting with the first non-white-space character, that is of the expected form. The subject sequence contains no characters if the input string is empty or consists entirely of white space, or if the first non-white-space character is other than a sign, a digit, or a decimal-point character.

If the subject sequence has the expected form, the sequence of characters starting with the first digit or the decimal-point character (whichever occurs first) is interpreted as a floating constant, except that the decimal-point character is used in place of a period, and that if neither an exponent part nor a decimal-point character appears, a decimal point is assumed to follow the last digit in the string. If the subject sequence begins with a minus sign, the value resulting from the conversion is negated. A pointer to the final string is stored in the object pointed to by **endptr**, provided that **endptr** is not a null pointer.

If the subject sequence is empty or does not have the expected form, no conversion is performed; the value of **nptr** is stored in the object pointed to by **endptr**, provided that **endptr** is not a null pointer.

The **strtod** function returns the converted value, if any. If no conversion could be performed, zero is returned. If the correct value is outside the range of representable values, plus or minus **HUGE_VAL** is returned (according to the sign of the value), and the value of the macro **ERANGE** is stored in **errno**. If the correct value would cause underflow, zero is returned and the value of the macro **ERANGE** is stored in **errno**.

`long int strtol(const char *nptr, char **endptr, int base);`

Converts the initial portion of the string pointed to by **nptr** to **long int** representation. First, it decomposes the input string into three parts: an initial, possibly empty, sequence of white-space characters (as specified by the **isspace** function), a subject sequence resembling an integer represented in some radix determined by the value of **base**, and a final string of one or more unrecognized characters, including the terminating null character of the input string. Then, it attempts to convert the subject sequence to an integer, and returns the result.

If the value of **base** is zero, the expected form of the subject sequence is that of an integer constant, optionally preceded by a plus or minus sign, but not including an integer suffix. If the value of **base** is between 2 and 36, the expected form of the subject sequence is a sequence of letters and digits representing an integer with the radix specified by **base**, optionally preceded by a plus or minus sign, but not including an integer suffix. The letters from **a** (or **A**) through **z** (or **Z**) are ascribed the values 10 to 35; only letters whose ascribed values are less than that of **base** are permitted. If the value of **base** is 16, the characters **0x** or **0X** may optionally precede the sequence of letters and digits, following the sign if present.

The subject sequence is defined as the longest initial subsequence of the input string, starting with the first non-white-space character, that is of the expected form. The subject sequence contains no characters if the input string is empty or consists entirely of white space, or if the first non-white-space character is other than a sign or a permissible letter or digit.

If the subject sequence has the expected form and the value of **base** is zero, the sequence of characters starting with the first digit is interpreted as an integer constant. If the subject sequence has the expected form and the value of **base** is between 2 and 36, it is used as the base for conversion, ascribing to each letter its value as given above. If the subject sequence begins with a minus sign, the value resulting from the conversion is negated. A pointer to the final string is stored in the object pointed to by **endptr**, provided that **endptr** is not null.

If the subject sequence is empty or does not have the expected form, no conversion is performed; the value **nptr** is stored in the object pointed to by **endptr**, provided that **endptr** is not a null pointer.

The **strtol** function returns the converted value, if any. If no conversion could be performed, zero is returned. If the correct value is outside the range of representable values, **LONG_MAX** or **LONG_MIN** is returned (according to the sign of the value), and the value of the macro **ERANGE** is stored in **errno**.

`unsigned long int strtoul(const char *nptr, char **endptr, int base);`

Converts the initial portion of the string pointed to by **nptr** to **unsigned long int** representation. The **strtoul** function works identically to the **strtol** function. The **strtoul** function returns the converted value, if any. If no conversion could be performed, zero is returned. If the correct value is outside the range of representable values, **ULONG_MAX** is returned, and the value of the macro **ERANGE** is stored in **errno**.

`int rand(void);`

The **rand** function computes a sequence of pseudo-random integers in the range 0 to **RAND_MAX**. The **rand** function returns a pseudo-random integer.

`void srand(unsigned int seed);`

Uses the argument as a seed for a new sequence of pseudo-random numbers to be returned by subsequent calls to **rand**. If **srand** is then called with the same seed value, the sequence of pseudo-random numbers shall be repeated. If **rand** is called before any calls to **srand** have been made, the same sequence shall be generated as when **srand** is first called with a seed value of 1. The following functions define a portable implementation of **rand** and **srand**.

```
static unsigned long int next = 1;

int rand(void)   /* RAND_MAX assumed to be 32767 */
{
    next = next * 1103515245 + 12345;
    return (unsigned int) (next/65536) % 32768;
}

void srand(unsigned int seed)
{
    next = seed;
}
```

void *calloc(size_t nmemb, size_t size);

Allocates space for an array of **nmemb** objects, each of whose size is **size**. The space is initialized to all bits zero. The **calloc** function returns either a null pointer or a pointer to the allocated space.

void free(void *ptr);

Causes the space pointed to by **ptr** to be deallocated, that is, made available for further allocation. If **ptr** is a null pointer, no action occurs. Otherwise, if the argument does not match a pointer earlier returned by the **calloc, malloc,** or **realloc** function, or if the space has been deallocated by a call to **free** or **realloc,** the behavior is undefined.

void *malloc(size_t size);

Allocates space for an object whose size is specified by **size** and whose value is indeterminate. The **malloc** function returns a null pointer or a pointer to the allocated space.

void *realloc(void *ptr, size_t size);

Changes the size of the object pointed to by **ptr** to the size specified by **size.** The contents of the object shall be unchanged up to the lesser of the new and old sizes. If the new size is larger, the value of the newly allocated portion of the object is indeterminate. If **ptr** is a null pointer, the **realloc** function behaves like the **malloc** function for the specified size. Otherwise, if **ptr** does not match a pointer earlier returned by the **calloc, malloc,** or **realloc** function, or if the space has been deallocated by a call to the **free** or **realloc** function, the behavior is undefined. If the space cannot be allocated, the object pointed to by **ptr** is unchanged. If **size** is zero and **ptr** is not null, the object it points to is freed. Function **realloc** returns either a null pointer or a pointer to the possibly moved allocated space.

void abort(void);

Causes abnormal program termination to occur, unless the signal **SIGABRT** is being caught and the signal handler does not return. Whether open output streams are flushed or open streams closed or temporary files removed is implementation-defined. An implementation-defined form of the status *unsuccessful termination* is returned to the host environment by means of the function call **raise(SIGABRT).** The **abort** function cannot return to its caller.

int atexit(void (*func)(void));

Registers the function pointed to by **func,** to be called without arguments at normal program termination. The implementation shall support the registration of at least 32 functions. The **atexit** function returns zero if the registration succeeds, nonzero if it fails.

```
void exit(int status);
```
Causes normal program termination to occur. If more than one call to the **exit** function is executed by a program, the behavior is undefined. First, all functions registered by the **atexit** function are called, in the reverse order of their registration. Each function is called as many times as it was registered. Next, all open streams with unwritten buffered data are flushed, all open streams are closed, and all files created by the **tmpfile** function are removed.

Finally, control is returned to the host environment. If the value of **status** is zero or **EXIT_SUCCESS**, an implementation-defined form of the status *successful termination* is returned. If the value of **status** is **EXIT_FAILURE**, an implementation-defined form of the status *unsuccessful termination* is returned. Otherwise the status returned is implementation-defined. The **exit** function cannot return to its caller.

```
char *getenv(const char *name);
```
Searches an *environment list,* provided by the host environment, for a string that matches the string pointed to by **name**. The set of environment names and the method for altering the environment list are implementation-defined. Returns a pointer to a string associated with the matched list member. The string pointed to shall not be modified by the program, but may be overwritten by a subsequent call to the **getenv** function. If the specified **name** cannot be found, a null pointer is returned.

```
int system(const char *string);
```
Passes the string pointed to by **string** to the host environment to be executed by a *command processor* in an implementation-defined manner. A null pointer may be used for **string** to inquire whether a command processor exists. If the argument is a null pointer, the **system** function returns nonzero only if a command processor is available. If the argument is not a null pointer, the **system** function returns an implementation-defined value.

```
void *bsearch(const void *key, const void *base, size_t nmemb,
         size_t size, int (*compar)(const void *, const void *));
```
Searches an array of **nmemb** objects, the initial element of which is pointed to by **base**, for an element that matches the object pointed to by **key**. The size of each element of the array is specified by **size**. The comparison function pointed to by **compar** is called with two arguments that point to the **key** object and to an array element, in that order. The function shall return an integer less than, equal to, or greater than zero if the **key** object is considered, respectively, to be less than, to match, or to be greater than the array element. The array shall consist of: all the elements that compare less than, all the elements that compare equal to, and all the elements that compare greater than the **key** object, in that order.

Function **bsearch** returns a pointer to a matching element of the array, or a null pointer if no match is found. If two elements compare as equal, the element matched is unspecified.

```
void qsort(void *base, size_t nmemb, size_t size, int
         (*compar)(const void *, const void *));
```
Sorts an array of **nmemb** objects. The initial element is pointed to by **base**. The size of each object is specified by **size**. The array contents are sorted into ascending order according to a comparison function pointed to by **compar**, which is called with two arguments that point to the objects being compared. The function returns an integer less than equal to, or greater than zero if the first argument is considered to be respectively less than, equal to, or greater than the second. If two elements compare as equal, their order in the sorted array is undefined.

```
int abs(int j);
```
Computes the absolute value of an integer **j**. If the result cannot be represented, the behavior is undefined. The **abs** function returns the absolute value.

`div_t div(int numer, int denom);`
> Computes the quotient and remainder of the division of the numerator **numer** by the denominator **denom**. If the division is inexact, the resulting quotient is the integer of lesser magnitude that is the nearest to the algebric quotient. If the result cannot be represented, the behavior is undefined; otherwise, **quot * denom + rem** shall equal **numer**. The **div** function returns a structure of type **div_t**, comprising both the quotient and the remainder. The structure shall contain the following members, in either order:
>
> ```
> int quot;    /* quotient */
> int rem;     /* remainder */
> ```

`long int labs(long int j);`
> Similar to the **abs** function, except that the argument and the returned value each have type **long int**.

`ldiv_t ldiv(long int numer, long int denom);`
> Similar to the **div** function, except that the arguments and the members of the returned structure (which has type **ldiv_t**) all have type **long int**.

`int mblen(const char *s, size_t n);`
> If **s** is not a null pointer, the **mblen** function determines the number of bytes contained in the multibyte character pointed to by **s**. If **s** is a null pointer, the **mblen** function returns a nonzero or zero value, if multibyte character encodings, respectively, do or do not have state-dependent encodings. If **s** is not a null pointer, the **mblen** function either returns 0 (if **s** points to the null character), or returns the number of bytes that are contained in the multibyte character (if the next **n** or fewer bytes form a valid multibyte character), or returns -1 (if they do not form a valid multibyte character).

`int mbtowc(wchar_t *pwc, const char *s, size_t n);`
> If **s** is not a null pointer, the **mbtowc** function determines the number of bytes that are contained in the multibyte character pointed to by **s**. It then determines the code for the value of type **wchar_t** that corresponds to that multibyte character. (The value of the code corresponding to the null character is zero.) If the multibyte character is valid and **pwc** is not a null pointer, the **mbtowc** function stores the code in the object pointed to by **pwc**. At most n bytes of the array pointed to by **s** will be examined.
>
> If **s** is a null pointer, the **mbtowc** function returns a nonzero or zero value, if multibyte character encodings, respectively, do or do not have state-dependent encodings. If **s** is not a null pointer, the **mbtowc** function either returns 0 (if **s** points to the null character), or returns the number of bytes that are contained in the converted multibyte character (if the next **n** or fewer bytes form a valid multibyte character), or returns -1 (if they do not form a valid multibyte character). In no case will the value returned be greater than n or the value of the **MB_CUR_MAX** macro.

`int wctomb(char *s, wchar_t wchar);`
> The **wctomb** function determines the number of bytes needed to represent the multibyte character corresponding to the code whose value is **wchar** (including any change in shift state). It stores the multibyte character representation in the array object pointed to by s (if **s** is not a null pointer). At most **MB_CUR_MAX** characters are stored. If the value of **wchar** is zero, the **wctomb** function is left in the initial shift state.
>
> If **s** is a null pointer, the **wctomb** function returns a nonzero or zero value, if multibyte character encodings, respectively, do or do not have state-dependent encodings. If **s** is not a null pointer, the **wctomb** function returns -1 if the value of **wchar** does not correspond to a

valid multibyte character, or returns the number of bytes that are contained in the multibyte character corresponding to the value of **wchar**. In no case will the value returned be greater than the value of the **MB_CUR_MAX** macro.

`size_t mbstowcs(wchar_t *pwcs, const char *s, size_t n);`

The **mbstowcs** function converts a sequence of multibyte characters that begins in the initial shift state from the array pointed to by **s** into a sequence of corresponding codes and stores not more than **n** codes into the array pointed to by **pwcs**. No multibyte characters that follow a null character (which is converted into a code with value zero) will be examined or converted. Each multibyte character is converted as if by a call to the **mbtowc** function, except that the shift state of the **mbtowc** function is not affected.

No more than **n** elements will be modified in the array pointed to by **pwcs**. The behavior of copying between objects that overlap is undefined. If an invalid multibyte character is encountered, function **mbstowcs** returns `(size_t)-1`. Otherwise, the **mbstowcs** function returns the number of array elements modified, not including a terminating zero code, if any.

`size_t wcstombs(char *s, const wchar_t *pwcs, size_t n);`

The **wcstombs** function converts a sequence of codes that correspond to multibyte characters from the array pointed to by **pwcs** into a sequence of multibyte characters that begins in the initial shift state and stores these multibyte characters into the array pointed to by **s**, stopping if a multibyte character would exceed the limit of **n** total bytes or if a null character is stored. Each code is converted as if by a call to the **wctomb** function, except that the shift state of the **wctomb** function is not affected.

No more than **n** bytes will be modified in the array pointed to by **s**. If copying takes place between objects that overlap, the behavior is undefined. If a code is encountered that does not correspond to a valid multibyte character, the **wcstombs** function returns `(size_t)-1`. Otherwise, the **wcstombs** function returns the number of bytes modified, not including a terminating null character, if any.

B.12 String Handling `<string.h>`

NULL

An implementation-defined null pointer constant.

size_t

The unsigned integral type of the result of the **sizeof** operator.

`void *memcpy(void *s1, const void *s2, size_t n);`

The **memcpy** function copies n characters from the object pointed to by **s2** into the object pointed to by **s1**. If copying takes place between objects that overlap, the behavior is undefined. The **memcpy** function returns the value of **s1**.

`void *memmove(void *s1, const void *s2, size_t n);`

The **memmove** function copies **n** characters from the object pointed to by **s2** into the object pointed to by **s1**. Copying takes place as if the **n** characters from the object pointed to by **s2** are first copied into a temporary array of **n** characters that does not overlap the objects pointed to by **s1** and **s2**, and then the **n** characters from the temporary array are copied into the object pointed to by **s1**. The **memmove** function returns the value of **s1**.

`char *strcpy(char *s1, const char *s2);`

The **strcpy** function copies the string pointed to by **s2** (including the terminating null character) into the array pointed to by **s1**. If copying takes place between objects that overlap, the behavior is undefined. The **strcpy** function returns the value of **s1**.

`char *strncpy(char *s1, const char *s2, size_t n);`

The `strncpy` function copies not more than n characters (characters that follow a null character are not copied) from the array pointed to by s2 to the array pointed to by s1. If copying takes place between objects that overlap, the behavior is undefined. If the array pointed to by s2 is a string that is shorter than n characters, null characters are appended to the copy in the array pointed to by s1, until n characters in all have been written. The `strncpy` function returns the value of s1.

`char *strcat(char *s1, const char *s2);`

The `strcat` function appends a copy of the string pointed to by s2 (including the terminating null character) to the end of the string pointed to by s1. The initial character of s2 overwrites the null character at the end of s1. If copying takes place between objects that overlap, the behavior is undefined. The `strcat` function returns the value of s1.

`char *strncat(char *s1, const char *s2, size_t n);`

The `strncat` function appends not more than n characters (a null character and characters that follow it are not appended) from the array pointed to by s2 to the end of the string pointed to by s1. The initial character of s2 overwrites the null character at the end of s1. A terminating null character is always appended to the result. If copying takes place between objects that overlap, the behavior is undefined. The `strncat` function returns the value of s1.

`int memcmp(const void *s1, const void *s2, size_t n);`

The `memcmp` function compares the first n characters of the object pointed to by s1 to the first n characters of the object pointed to by s2 The `memcmp` function returns an integer greater than, equal to, or less than zero, accordingly as the object pointed to by s1 is greater than, equal to, or less than the object pointed to by s2.

`int strcmp(const char *s1, const char *s2);`

The `strcmp` function compares the string pointed to by s1 to the string pointed to by s2. The `strcmp` function returns an integer greater than, equal to, or less than zero, accordingly as the string pointed to by s1 is greater than, equal to, or less than the string pointed to by s2.

`int strcoll(const char *s1, const char *s2);`

The `strcoll` function compares the string pointed to by s1 to the string pointed to by s2, both interpreted as appropriate to the `LC_COLLATE` category of the current locale. The `strcoll` function returns an integer greater than, equal to, or less than zero, accordingly as the string pointed to by s1 is greater than, equal to, or less than the string pointed to by s2 when both are interpreted as appropriate to the current locale.

`int strncmp(const char *s1, const char *s2, size_t n);`

The `strncmp` function compares not more than n characters (characters that follow a null character are not compared) from the array pointed to by s1 to the array pointed to by s2. The `strncmp` function returns an integer greater than, equal to, or less than zero, accordingly as the possibly null-terminated array pointed to by s1 is greater than, equal to, or less than the possibly null-terminated array pointed to by s2.

`size_t strxfrm(char *s1, const char *s2, size_t n);`

The `strxfrm` function transforms the string pointed to by s2 and places the resulting string into the array pointed to by s1. The transformation is such that if the `strcmp` function is applied to two transformed strings, it returns a value greater than, equal to, or less than zero, corresponding to the result of the `strcoll` function applied to the same two original strings. No more than n characters are placed into the resulting array pointed to by s1, including the terminating null character. If n is zero, s1 is permitted to be a null pointer. If copying takes place between objects that overlap, the behavior is undefined. The `strxfrm` function returns the length of the transformed string (not including the terminating null character). If the value is **n** or more, the contents of the array pointed to by **s1** are indeterminate.

`void *memchr(const void *s, int c, size_t n);`

The `memchr` function locates the first occurrence of **c** (converted to an **unsigned char**) in the initial **n** characters (each interpreted as **unsigned char**) of the object pointed to by **s**. The `memchr` function returns a pointer to the located character, or a null pointer if the character does not occur in the object.

`char *strchr(const char *s, int c);`

The `strchr` function locates the first occurrence of **c** (converted to a **char**) in the string pointed to by **s**. The terminating null character is considered to be part of the string. The `strchr` function returns a pointer to the located character, or a null pointer if the character does not occur in the string.

`size_t strcspn(const char *s1, const char *s2);`

The `strcspn` function computes the length of the maximum initial segment of the string pointed to by **s1** which consists entirely of characters not from the string pointed to by **s2**. The `strcspn` function returns the length of the segment.

`char *strpbrk(const char *s1, const char *s2);`

The `strpbrk` function locates the first occurrence in the string pointed to by **s1** of any character from the string pointed to by **s2**. The `strpbrk` function returns a pointer to the character, or a null pointer if no character from **s2** occurs in **s1**.

`char *strrchr(const char *s, int c);`

Function `strrchr` locates the last occurrence of **c** (converted to a **char**) in the string pointed to by **s**. The terminating null character is considered part of the string. The `strrchr` function returns a pointer to the character, or a null pointer if **c** does not occur in the string.

`size_t strspn(const char *s1, const char *s2);`

The `strspn` function computes the length of the maximum initial segment of the string pointed to by **s1** which consists entirely of characters from the string pointed to by **s2**. The `strspn` function returns the length of the segment.

`char *strstr(const char *s1, const char *s2);`

The `strstr` function locates the first occurrence in the string pointed to by **s1** of the sequence of characters (excluding the terminating null character) in the string pointed to by **s2**. The `strstr` function returns a pointer to the located string, or a null pointer if the string is not found. If **s2** points to a string with zero length, the function returns **s1**.

`char *strtok(char *s1, const char *s2);`

A sequence of calls to the `strtok` function breaks the string pointed to by **s1** into a sequence of tokens, each of which is delimited by a character from the string pointed to by **s2**. The first call in the sequence has **s1** as its argument, and is followed by calls with a null pointer as their first argument. The separator string pointed to by **s2** may be different from call to call.

The first call in the sequence searches the string pointed to by **s1** for the first character that is not contained in the current separator string pointed to by **s2**. If no such character is found, then there are no tokens in the string pointed to by **s1** and the `strtok` function returns a null pointer. If such a character is found, it is the start of the first token.

The `strtok` function then searches from there for a character that is contained in the current separator string. If no such character is found, the current token extends to the end of the string pointed to by **s1**, and subsequent searches for a token will return a null pointer. If

such a character is found, it is overwritten by a null character, which terminates the current token. The `strtok` function saves a pointer to the following character, from which the next
search for a token will start.

Each subsequent call, with a null pointer as the value of the first argument, starts searching from the saved pointer and behaves as described above. The implementation shall behave
as if no library function calls the `strtok` function. The `strtok` function returns a pointer to
the first character of a token, or a null pointer if there is no token.

```
void *memset(void *s, int c, size_t n);
```
Function `memset` copies the value of `c` (converted to an **unsigned char**) into each of the
first **n** characters in the object pointed to by **s**. The **memset** function returns the value of **s**.

```
char *strerror(int errnum);
```
The **strerror** function maps the error number in **errnum** to an error message string. The
implementation shall behave as if no library function calls the **strerror** function. The **strerror** function returns a pointer to the string, the contents of which are implementation-defined. The array pointed to shall not be modified by the program, but may be overwritten by a
subsequent call to the **strerror** function.

```
size_t strlen(const char *s);
```
The **strlen** function computes the length of the string pointed to by **s**. The **strlen** function returns the number of characters that precede the terminating null character.

B.13 Date and Time `<time.h>`

CLOCKS_PER_SEC
The number per second of the value returned by the **clock** function.

NULL
An implementation-defined null pointer constant.

clock_t
An arithmetic type capable of representing time.

time_t
An arithmetic type capable of representing time.

size_t
The unsigned integral type of the result of the **sizeof** operator.

struct tm
Holds the components of a calendar time, called the *broken-down time*. The structure shall
contain at least the following members, in any order. The semantics of the members and their
normal ranges are expressed in the comments.

```
int tm_sec;          /* seconds after the minute—[0, 61] */
int tm_min;          /* minutes after the hour—[0, 59] */
int tm_hour;         /* hours since midnight—[0, 23] */
int tm_mday;         /* day of the month—[1, 31] */
int tm_mon;          /* months since January—[0, 11] */
int tm_year;         /* years since 1900 */
int tm_wday;         /* days since Sunday—[0, 6] */
int tm_yday;         /* days since January 1—[0, 365] */
int tm_isdst;        /* Daylight Saving Time flag */
```

The value **tm_isdst** is positive if Daylight Saving Time is in effect, zero if Daylight Saving Time is not in effect, and negative if the information is not available.

`clock_t clock(void);`

The **clock** function determines the processor time used. The **clock** function returns the implementation's best approximation to the processor time used by the program since the beginning of an implementation-defined era related only to the program invocation. To determine the time in seconds, the value returned by the **clock** function should be divided by the value of the macro **CLOCKS_PER_SEC**. If the processor time used is not available or its value cannot be represented, the function returns the value **(clock_t)-1**.

`double difftime(time_t time1, time_t time0);`

The **difftime** function computes the difference between two calendar times: **time1 - time0**. The **difftime** function returns the difference expressed in seconds as a **double**.

`time_t mktime(struct tm *timeptr);`

The **mktime** function converts the broken-down time, expressed as local time, in the structure pointed to by **timeptr** into a calendar time value with the same encoding as that of the values returned by the **time** function. The original values of the **tm_wday** and **tm_yday** components of the structure are ignored, and the original values of the other components are not restricted to the ranges indicated above. On successful completion, the values of the **tm_wday** and **tm_yday** components of the structure are set appropriately, and the other components are set to represent the specified calendar time, but with their values forced to the ranges indicated above; the final value of **tm_mday** is not set until **tm_mon** and **tm_year** are determined. The **mktime** function returns the specified calendar time encoded as a value of type **time_t**. If the calendar time cannot be represented, the function returns the value **(time_t)-1**.

`time_t time(time_t *timer);`

The **time** function determines the current calendar time. The **time** function returns the implementation's best approximation to the current calendar time. The value **(time_t)-1** is returned if the calendar time is not available. If **timer** is not a null pointer, the return value is also assigned to the object it points to.

`char *asctime(const struct tm *timeptr);`

The **asctime** function converts the broken-down time in the structure pointed to by **timeptr** into a string in the form

```
    Sun Sep 16 01:03:52 1973\n\0
```
The **asctime** function returns a pointer to the string.

`char *ctime(const time_t *timer);`

The **ctime** function converts the calendar time pointed to by **timer** to local time in the form of a string. It is equivalent to

```
    asctime(localtime(timer))
```
The **ctime** function returns the pointer returned by the **asctime** function with that broken-down time as argument.

`struct tm *gmtime(const time_t *timer);`

The **gmtime** function converts the calendar time pointed to by **timer** into a broken-down time, expressed as Coordinated Universal Time (UTC). The **gmtime** function returns a pointer to that object, or a null pointer if UTC is not available.

`struct tm *localtime(const time_t *timer);`

> The `localtime` function converts the calendar time pointed to by `timer` into a broken-down time, expressed as local time. The `localtime` function returns a pointer to that object.

`size_t strftime(char *s, size_t maxsize, const char *format, const`
`              struct tm *timeptr);`

> The `strftime` function places characters into the array pointed to by `s` as controlled by the string pointed to by `format`. The `format` string consists of zero or more conversion specifiers and ordinary multibyte characters. All ordinary characters (including the terminating null character) are copied unchanged into the array. If copying takes place between objects that overlap, the behavior is undefined. No more than `maxsize` characters are placed into the array. Each conversion specifier is replaced by appropriate characters as described in the following list. The appropriate characters are determined by the `LC_TIME` category of the current locale and by the values contained in the structure pointed to by `timeptr`.

`%a`	is replaced by the locale's abbreviated weekday name.
`%A`	is replaced by the locale's full weekday name.
`%b`	is replaced by the locale's abbreviated month name.
`%B`	is replaced by the locale's full month name.
`%c`	is replaced by the locale's appropriate date and time representation.
`%d`	is replaced by the day of the month as a decimal number (`01-31`).
`%H`	is replaced by the hour (24-hour clock) as a decimal number (`00-23`).
`%I`	is replaced by the hour (12-hour clock) as a decimal number (`01-12`).
`%j`	is replaced by the day of the year as a decimal number (`001-366`).
`%m`	is replaced by the month as a decimal number (`01-12`).
`%M`	is replaced by the minute as a decimal number (`00-59`).

`%p`   is replaced by the locale's equivalent of the AM/PM designations associated with a 12-hour clock.

`%S`   is replaced by the second as a decimal number (`00-61`).

`%U`   is replaced by the week number of the year (the first Sunday as the first day of week 1) as a decimal number (`00-53`).

`%w`   is replaced by the weekday as a decimal number (`0-6`), where Sunday is `0`.

`%W`   is replaced by the week number of the year (the first Monday as the first day of week 1) as a decimal number (`00-53`).

`%x`	is replaced by the locale's appropriate date representation.
`%X`	is replaced by the locale's appropriate time representation.
`%y`	is replaced by the year without century as a decimal number (`00-99`).
`%Y`	is replaced by the year with century as a decimal number.

`%Z`   is replaced by the time zone name or abbreviation, or by no characters if no time zone is determinable.

`%%`   is replaced by `%`.

> If a conversion specifier is not one of the above, the behavior is undefined. If the total number of resulting characters including the terminating null character is not more than `max -`

size, the **strftime** function returns the number of characters placed into the array pointed to by **s** not including the terminating null character. Otherwise, zero is returned and the contents of the array are indeterminate.

B.14 Implementation Limits
`<limits.h>`

The following shall be defined equal to or greater than in magnitude (absolute value) to the values below.

```
#define CHAR_BIT                                    8
```
The number of bits for the smallest object that is not a bit-field (byte).

```
#define SCHAR_MIN                                -127
```
The minimum value for an object of type **signed char**.

```
#define SCHAR_MAX                                +127
```
The maximum value for an object of type **signed char**.

```
#define UCHAR_MAX                                 255
```
The maximum value for an object of type **unsigned char**.

```
#define CHAR_MIN                        0 or SCHAR_MIN
```
The minimum value for an object of type **char**.

```
#define CHAR_MAX              UCHAR_MAX or SCHAR_MAX
```
The maximum value for an object of type **char**.

```
#define MB_LEN_MAX                                  1
```
The maximum number of bytes in a multibyte character, for any supported locale.

```
#define SHRT_MIN                              -32767
```
The minimum value for an object of type **short int**.

```
#define SHRT_MAX                              +32767
```
The maximum value for an object of type **short int**.

```
#define USHRT_MAX                              65535
```
The maximum value for an object of type **unsigned short int**.

```
#define INT_MIN                               -32767
```
The minimum value for an object of type **int**.

```
#define INT_MAX                               +32767
```
The maximum value for an object of type **int**.

```
#define UINT_MAX                               65535
```
The maximum value for an object of type **unsigned int**.

```
#define LONG_MIN                         -2147483647
```
The minimum value for an object of type **long int**.

```
#define LONG_MAX                         +2147483647
```
The maximum value for an object of type **long int**.

```
#define ULONG_MAX                         4294967295
```
The maximum value for an object of type **unsigned long int**.

<float.h>

#define FLT_ROUNDS
> The rounding mode for floating-point addition.
>
> -1   indeterminable
>
> 0   toward zero
>
> 1   to nearest
>
> 2   toward positive infinity
>
> 3   toward negative infinity

The following shall be defined equal to or greater than in magnitude (absolute value) to the values below.

```
#define FLT_RADIX                                           2
```
> The radix of exponent representation, *b*.

```
#define FLT_MANT_DIG
#define LDBL_MANT_DIG
#define DBL_MANT_DIG
```
> The number of base-**FLT_RADIX** digits in the floating-point significand, *p*.

```
#define FLT_DIG                                             6
#define DBL_DIG                                            10
#define LDBL_DIG                                           10
```
> The number of decimal digits, *q*, such that any floating-point number with *q* decimal digits can be rounded into a floating-point number with *p* radix *b* digits and back again without change to the *q* decimal digits.

```
#define FLT_MIN_EXP
#define DBL_MIN_EXP
#define LDBL_MIN_EXP
```
> The minimum negative integer such that **FLT_RADIX** raised to that power minus 1 is a normalized floating-point number.

```
#define FLT_MIN_10_EXP                                    -37
#define DBL_MIN_10_EXP                                    -37
#define LDBL_MIN_10_EXP                                   -37
```
> The minimum negative integer such that 10 raised to that power is in the range of normalized floating point numbers.

```
#define FLT_MAX_EXP
#define DBL_MAX_EXP
#define LDBL_MAX_EXP
```
> The maximum integer such that **FLT_RADIX** raised to that power minus 1 is a representable finite floating-point number.

```
#define FLT_MAX_10_EXP                                    +37
#define DBL_MAX_10_EXP                                    +37
#define LDBL_MAX_10_EXP                                   +37
```
> The maximum integer such that 10 raised to that power is in the range of representable finite floating point numbers.

The following shall be defined equal to or greater than the values shown below.

```
#define FLT_MAX                          1E+37
#define DBL_MAX                          1E+37
#define LDBL_MAX                         1E+37
```
   The maximum representable finite floating-point number.

The following shall be defined equal to or less than the values shown below.

```
#define FLT_EPSILON                      1E-5
#define DBL_EPSILON                      1E-9
#define LDBL_EPSILON                     1E-9
```
   The difference between 1.0 and the least value greater than 1.0 that is representable in the given floating point type.

```
#define FLT_MIN                          1E-37
#define DBL_MIN                          1E-37
#define LDBL_MIN                         1E-37
```
   The minimum normalized positive floating-point number.

Appendix C
Operator Precedence and Associativity

Operator	Associativity
( ) [ ] -> .	left to right
++ -- + - ! ~ (type) * & sizeof	right to left
* / %	left to right
+ -	left to right
<< >>	left to right
< <= > >=	left to right
== !=	left to right
&	left to right
^	left to right
|	left to right
&&	left to right
||	left to right
? :	right to left
= += -= *= /= %= &= ^= |= <<= >>=	right to left
,	left to right

The operators are shown in decreasing order of precedence from top to bottom.

Appendix D
ASCII Character Set

	0	1	2	3	4	5	6	7	8	9
0	nul	soh	stx	etx	eot	enq	ack	bel	bs	ht
1	nl	vt	ff	cr	so	si	dle	dc1	dc2	dc3
2	dc4	nak	syn	etb	can	em	sub	esc	fs	gs
3	rs	us	sp	!	"	#	$	%	&	'
4	(	)	*	+	,	-	.	/	0	1
5	2	3	4	5	6	7	8	9	:	;
6	<	=	>	?	@	A	B	C	D	E
7	F	G	H	I	J	K	L	M	N	O
8	P	Q	R	S	T	U	V	W	X	Y
9	Z	[	\	]	^	_	'	a	b	c
10	d	e	f	g	h	i	j	k	l	m
11	n	o	p	q	r	s	t	u	v	w
12	x	y	z	{	|	}	~	del		

The digits at the left of the table are the left digits of the decimal equivalent (0-127) of the character code, and the digits at the top of the table are the right digits of the character code. For example, the character code for 'F' is 70, and the character code for '&' is 38.

APPENDIX E

Number Systems

Objectives

- To understand basic number systems concepts such as base, positional value, and symbol value.
- To understand how to work with numbers represented in the binary, octal, and hexadecimal number systems.
- To be able to abbreviate binary numbers as octal numbers or hexadecimal numbers.
- To be able to convert octal numbers and hexadecimal numbers to binary numbers.
- To be able to convert back and forth between decimal numbers and their binary, octal, and hexadecimal equivalents.
- To understand binary arithmetic, and how negative binary numbers are represented using two's complement notation.

Here are only numbers ratified.
William Shakespeare

Nature has some sort of arithmetic-geometrical coordinate system, because nature has all kinds of models. What we experience of nature is in models, and all of nature's models are so beautiful. It struck me that nature's system must be a real beauty, because in chemistry we find that the associations are always in beautiful whole numbers–there are no fractions.
Richard Buckminster Fuller

Outline

E.1 Introduction

In this appendix, we introduce the key number systems that C programmers use, especially when they are working on software projects that require close interaction with "machine-level" hardware. Projects like this include operating systems, computer networking software, compilers, database systems, and applications requiring high performance.

When we write an integer such as 227 or -63 in a C program, the number is assumed to be in the *decimal (base 10) number system.* The *digits* in the decimal number system are 0, 1, 2, 3, 4, 5, 6, 7, 8, and 9. The lowest digit is 0 and the highest digit is 9—one less than the *base* of 10. Internally, computers use the *binary (base 2) number system.* The binary number system has only two digits, namely 0 and 1. Its lowest digit is 0 and its highest digit is 1—one less than the base of 2.

As we will see, binary numbers tend to be much longer than their decimal equivalents. Programmers who work in assembly languages and in high-level languages like C that enable programmers reach down to the "machine level," find it cumbersome to work with binary numbers. So two other number systems—*octal number system (base 8)* and *hexadecimal number system (base 16)*—are popular primarily because they make it convenient to abbreviate binary numbers.

In the octal number system, the digits range from 0 to 7. Because both the binary number system and the octal number system have fewer digits than the decimal number system, their digits are the same as the corresponding digits in decimal.

The hexadecimal number system poses a problem because it requires sixteen digits—a lowest digit of 0 and a highest digit with a value equivalent to decimal 15 (one less than the base of 16). By convention, we use the letters A through F to represent the hexadecimal digits corresponding to decimal values 10 through 15. Thus in hexadecimal we can have numbers like 876 consisting solely of decimal-like digits, numbers like 8A55F consisting of digits and letters, and numbers like FFE consisting solely of letters. Occasionally, a hexadecimal number spells a common word such as FACE or FEED—this can appear strange to programmers accustomed to working with numbers.

Each of these number systems uses *positional notation*—each position in which a digit is written has a different *positional value.* For example, in the decimal number 937 (the 9, the 3, and the 7 are referred to as *symbol values*), we say that the 7 is written in the *ones position,* the 3 is written in the *tens position,* and the 9 is written in the *hundreds position.* Notice that each of these positions is a power of the base (base 10), and that these powers begin at 0 and increase by 1 as we move left in the number (Fig. E.3).

Binary digit	Octal digit	Decimal digit	Hexadecimal digit
0	0	0	0
1	1	1	1
	2	2	2
	3	3	3
	4	4	4
	5	5	5
	6	6	6
	7	7	7
		8	8
		9	9
			A (decimal value of 10)
			B (decimal value of 11)
			C (decimal value of 12)
			D (decimal value of 13)
			E (decimal value of 14)
			F (decimal value of 15)

Fig. E.1 Digits of the binary, octal, decimal, and hexadecimal number systems.

Attribute	Binary	Octal	Decimal	Hexadecimal
Base	2	8	10	16
Lowest digit	0	0	0	0
Highest digit	1	7	9	F

Fig. E.2 Comparison of the binary, octal, decimal, and hexadecimal number systems.

Positional values in the decimal number system			
Decimal digit	9	3	7
Position name	Hundreds	Tens	Ones
Positional value	100	10	1
Positional value as a power of the base (10)	10^2	10^1	10^0

Fig. E.3 Positional values in the decimal number system.

For longer decimal numbers, the next positions to the left would be the *thousands position* (10 to the 3rd power), the *ten-thousands position* (10 to the 4th power), the *hundred-thousands position* (10 to the 5th power), the *millions position* (10 to the 6th power), the *ten-millions position* (10 to the 7th power), and so on.

In the binary number 101, we say that the rightmost 1 is written in the *ones position,* the 0 is written in the *twos position,* and the leftmost 1 is written in the *fours position.* Notice that each of these positions is a power of the base (base 2), and that these powers begin at 0 and increase by 1 as we move left in the number (Fig E.4).

For longer binary numbers, the next positions to the left would be the *eights position* (2 to the 3rd power), the *sixteens position* (2 to the 4th power), the *thirty-twos position* (2 to the 5th power), the *sixty-fours position* (2 to the 6th power), and so on.

In the octal number 425, we say that the 5 is written in the *ones position,* the 2 is written in the *eights position,* and the 4 is written in the *sixty-fours position.* Notice that each of these positions is a power of the base (base 8), and that these powers begin at 0 and increase by 1 as we move left in the number (Fig. E.5).

For longer octal numbers, the next positions to the left would be the *five-hundred-and-twelves position* (8 to the 3rd power), the *four-thousand-and-ninety-sixes position* (8 to the 4th power), the *thirty-two-thousand-seven-hundred-and-sixty eights position* (8 to the 5th power), and so on.

In the hexadecimal number 3DA, we say that the A is written in the *ones position,* the D is written in the *sixteens position,* and the 3 is written in the *two-hundred-and-fifty-sixes position.* Notice that each of these positions is a power of the base (base 16), and that these powers begin at 0 and increase by 1 as we move left in the number (Fig. E.6).

Positional values in the binary number system			
Binary digit	1	0	1
Position name	Fours	Twos	Ones
Positional value	4	2	1
Positional value as a power of the base (2)	2^2	2^1	2^0

Fig. E.4   Positional values in the binary number system.

Positional values in the octal number system			
Decimal digit	4	2	5
Position name	Sixty-fours	Eights	Ones
Positional value	64	8	1
Positional value as a power of the base (8)	8^2	8^1	8^0

Fig. E.5   Positional values in the octal number system.

Positional values in the hexadecimal number system			
Decimal digit	3	D	A
Position name	Two-hundred-and-fifty-sixes	Sixteens	Ones
Positional value	256	16	1
Positional value as a power of the base (16)	16^2	16^1	16^0

Fig. E.6   Positional values in the hexadecimal number system.

For longer hexadecimal numbers, the next positions to the left would be the *four-thousand-and-ninety-sixes position* (16 to the 3rd power), the *thirty-two-thousand-seven-hundred-and-sixty-eights position* (16 to the 4th power), and so on.

E.2 Abbreviating Binary Numbers as Octal Numbers and Hexadecimal Numbers

The main use for octal and hexadecimal numbers in computing is for abbreviating lengthy binary representations. Figure E.7 highlights the fact that lengthy binary numbers can be expressed concisely in number systems with higher bases than the binary number system.

Decimal Number	Binary representation	Octal representation	Hexadecimal representation
0	0	0	0
1	1	1	1
2	10	2	2
3	11	3	3
4	100	4	4
5	101	5	5
6	110	6	6
7	111	7	7
8	1000	10	8
9	1001	11	9
10	1010	12	A
11	1011	13	B
12	1100	14	C
13	1101	15	D
14	1110	16	E
15	1111	17	F
16	10000	20	10

Fig. E.7 Decimal, binary, octal, and hexadecimal equivalents.

A particularly important relationship that both the octal number system and the hexadecimal number system have to the binary system is that the bases of octal and hexadecimal (8 and 16 respectively) are powers of the base of the binary number system (base 2). Consider the following 12-digit binary number and its octal and hexadecimal equivalents. See if you can determine how this relationship makes it convenient to abbreviate binary numbers in octal or hexadecimal. The answer follows the numbers.

Binary Number	Octal equivalent	Hexadecimal equivalent
100011010001	4321	8D1

To see how the binary number converts easily to octal, simply break the 12-digit binary number into groups of three consecutive bits each, and write those groups over the corresponding digits of the octal number as follows

```
100    011    010    001
4      3      2      1
```

Notice that the octal digit you have written under each group of three bits corresponds precisely to the octal equivalent of that 3-digit binary number as shown in Fig. E.7.

The same kind of relationship may be observed in converting numbers from binary to hexadecimal. In particular, break the 12-digit binary number into groups of four consecutive bits each and write those groups over the corresponding digits of the hexadecimal number as follows

```
1000    1101    0001
8       D       1
```

Notice that the hexadecimal digit you have written under each group of four bits corresponds precisely to the hexadecimal equivalent of that 4-digit binary number as shown in Fig. E.7.

E.3 Converting Octal Numbers and Hexadecimal Numbers to Binary Numbers

In the previous section, we saw how to convert binary numbers to their octal and hexadecimal equivalents by forming groups of binary digits and simply rewriting these groups as their equivalent octal digit values or hexadecimal digit values. This process may be used in reverse to produce the binary equivalent of a given octal or hexadecimal number.

For example, the octal number 653 is converted to binary simply by writing the 6 as its 3-digit binary equivalent 110, the 5 as its 3-digit binary equivalent 101, and the 3 as its 3-digit binary equivalent 011 to form the 9-digit binary number 110101011.

The hexadecimal number FAD5 is converted to binary simply by writing the F as its 4-digit binary equivalent 1111, the A as its 4-digit binary equivalent 1010, the D as its 4-digit binary equivalent 1101, and the 5 as its 4-digit binary equivalent 0101 to form the 16-digit 1111101011010101.

E.4 Converting from Binary, Octal, or Hexadecimal to Decimal

Because we are accustomed to working in decimal, it is often convenient to convert a binary, octal, or hexadecimal number to decimal to get a sense of what the number is "really" worth. Our diagrams in Section E.1 express the positional values in decimal. To convert a number to decimal from another base, multiply the decimal equivalent of each digit by its positional value, and sum these products. For example, the binary number 110101 is converted to decimal 53 as shown in Fig. E.8.

Converting a binary number to decimal					
Positional values:	32	16	8	4	2	1
Symbol values:	1	1	0	1	0	1
Products:	1*32=32	1*16=16	0*8=0	1*4=4	0*2=0	1*1=1
Sum:	= 32 + 16 + 0 + 4 + 0 + 1 = 53					

Fig. E.8   Converting a binary number to decimal.

To convert octal 7614 to decimal 3980, we use the same technique, this time using appropriate octal positional values as shown in Fig. E.9.

To convert hexadecimal AD3B to decimal 44347, we use the same technique, this time using appropriate hexadecimal positional values as shown in Fig. E.10.

E.5 Converting from Decimal to Binary, Octal, or Hexadecimal

The conversions of the previous section follow naturally from the conventions of positional notation. Converting from decimal to binary, octal, or hexadecimal also follows these conventions.

Suppose we wish to convert decimal 57 to binary. We begin by writing the positional values of the columns right to left until we reach a column whose positional value is greater than the decimal number. We do not need that column, so we discard it. Thus, we first write:

Converting an octal number to decimal			
Positional values:	512	64	8	1
Symbol values:	7	6	1	4
Products	7*512=3584	6*64=384	1*8=8	4*1=4
Sum:	= 3584 + 384 + 8 + 4 = 3980			

Fig. E.9   Converting an octal number to decimal.

Converting a hexadecimal number to decimal			
Positional values:	4096	256	16	1
Symbol values:	A	D	3	B
Products	A*4096=40960	D*256=3328	3*16=48	B*1=11
Sum:	= 40960 + 3328 + 48 + 11 = 44347			

Fig. E.10   Converting a hexadecimal number to decimal.

Positional values: 64   32   16   8   4   2   1

Then we discard the column with positional value 64 leaving:

Positional values: 32   16   8   4   2   1

Next we work from the leftmost column to the right. We divide 32 into 57 and observe that there is one 32 in 57 with a remainder of 25, so we write 1 in the 32 column. We divide 16 into 25 and observe that there is one 16 in 25 with a remainder of 9 and write 1 in the 16 column. We divide 8 into 9 and observe that there is one 8 in 9 with a remainder of 1. The next two columns each produce quotients of zero when their positional values are divided into 1 so we write 0s in the 4 and 2 columns. Finally, 1 into 1 is 1 so we write 1 in the 1 column. This yields:

Positional values: 32   16   8   4   2   1
Symbol values: 1   1   1   0   0   1

and thus decimal 57 is equivalent to binary 111001.

To convert decimal 103 to octal, we begin by writing the positional values of the columns until we reach a column whose positional value is greater than the decimal number. We do not need that column, so we discard it. Thus, we first write:

Positional values: 512   64   8   1

Then we discard the column with positional value 512, yielding:

Positional values: 64   8   1

Next we work from the leftmost column to the right. We divide 64 into 103 and observe that there is one 64 in 103 with a remainder of 39, so we write 1 in the 64 column. We divide 8 into 39 and observe that there are four 8s in 39 with a remainder of 7 and write 4 in the 8 column. Finally, we divide 1 into 7 and observe that there are seven 1s in 7 with no remainder so we write 7 in the 1 column. This yields:

Positional values: 64   8   1
Symbol values: 1   4   7

and thus decimal 103 is equivalent to octal 147.

To convert decimal 375 to hexadecimal, we begin by writing the positional values of the columns until we reach a column whose positional value is greater than the decimal number. We do not need that column, so we discard it. Thus, we first write

Positional values: 4096 256   16   1

Then we discard the column with positional value 4096, yielding:

Positional values: 256   16   1

Next we work from the leftmost column to the right. We divide 256 into 375 and observe that there is one 256 in 375 with a remainder of 119, so we write 1 in the 256 column. We divide 16 into 119 and observe that there are seven 16s in 119 with a remainder of 7 and write 7 in the 16 column. Finally, we divide 1 into 7 and observe that there are seven 1s in 7 with no remainder so we write 7 in the 1 column. This yields:

Positional values: 256   16   1
Symbol values: 1   7   7

and thus decimal 375 is equivalent to hexadecimal 177.

E.6 Negative Binary Numbers: Two's Complement Notation

The discussion in this appendix has been focussed on positive numbers. In this section, we explain how computers represent negative numbers using *two's complement notation.* First we explain how the two's complement of a binary number is formed, and then we show why it represents the negative value of the given binary number.

Consider a machine with 32-bit integers. Suppose

```
int value = 13;
```

The 32-bit representation of **value** is

```
00000000 00000000 00000000 00001101
```

To form the negative of **value** we first form its one's complement by applying C's bitwise complement operator (~):

```
ones_complement_of_value = ~value;
```

Internally, ~**value** is now **value** with each of its bits reversed—ones become zeros and zeros become ones as follows:

```
value:
00000000 00000000 00000000 00001101

~value (i.e., value's ones complement):
11111111 11111111 11111111 11110010
```

To form the two's complement of **value** we simply add one to **value**'s one's complement. Thus

```
Two's complement of value:
11111111 11111111 11111111 11110011
```

Now if this is in fact equal to -13, we should be able to add it to binary 13 and obtain a result of 0. Let us try this:

```
  00000000 00000000 00000000 00001101
 +11111111 11111111 11111111 11110011
 ------------------------------------
  00000000 00000000 00000000 00000000
```

The carry bit coming out of the leftmost column is discarded and we indeed get zero as a result. If we add the one's complement of a number to the number, the result would be all 1s. The key to getting a result of all zeros is that the twos complement is 1 more than the one's complement. The addition of 1 causes each column to add to 0 with a carry of 1. The carry keeps moving leftward until it is discarded from the leftmost bit, and hence the resulting number is all zeros.

Computers actually perform a subtraction such as

```
x = a - value;
```

by adding the two's complement of **value** to **a** as follows:

```
x = a + (~value + 1);
```

Suppose **a** is 27 and **value** is 13 as before. If the two's complement of **value** is actually the negative of **value**, then adding the two's complement of **value** to **a** should produce the result 14. Let us try this:

```
a (i.e., 27)       00000000 00000000 00000000 00011011
+(~value + 1)     +11111111 11111111 11111111 11110011
                  -----------------------------------
                   00000000 00000000 00000000 00001110
```

which is indeed equal to 14.

Summary

- When we write an integer such as 19 or 227 or -63 in a C program, the number is automatically assumed to be in the decimal (base 10) number system. The digits in the decimal number system are 0, 1, 2, 3, 4, 5, 6, 7, 8, and 9. The lowest digit is 0 and the highest digit is 9—one less than the base of 10.

- Internally, computers use the binary (base 2) number system. The binary number system has only two digits, namely 0 and 1. Its lowest digit is 0 and its highest digit is 1—one less than the base of 2.

- The octal number system (base 8) and the hexadecimal number system (base 16) have become popular primarily because they make it convenient to abbreviate binary numbers.

- The digits of the octal number system range from 0 to 7.

- The hexadecimal number system poses a problem because it requires sixteen digits—a lowest digit of 0 and a highest digit with a value equivalent to decimal 15 (one less than the base of 16). By convention, we use the letters A through F to represent the hexadecimal digits corresponding to decimal values 10 through 15.

- Each number system uses positional notation—each position in which a digit is written has a different positional value.

- A particularly important relationship that both the octal number system and the hexadecimal number system have to the binary system is that the bases of octal and hexadecimal (8 and 16 respectively) are powers of the base of the binary number system (base 2).

- To convert an octal number to a binary number, simply replace each octal digit with its three-digit binary equivalent.

- To convert a hexadecimal number to a binary number, simply replace each hexadecimal digit with its four-digit binary equivalent.

- Because we are accustomed to working in decimal, it is often convenient to convert a binary, octal, or hexadecimal number to decimal to get a better sense of what the number is "really" worth.

- To convert a number to decimal from another base, multiply the decimal equivalent of each digit by its positional value, and sum these products.

- Computers represent negative numbers using two's complement notation.

- To form the negative of a value in binary, first form its one's complement by applying C's bit-wise complement operator (~). This reverses the bits of the value. To form the two's complement of a value, simply add one to the value's one's complement.

Terminology

base	digit
base 2 number system	hexadecimal number system
base 8 number system	negative value
base 10 number system	octal number system
base 16 number system	one's complement notation
binary number system	positional notation
bitwise complement operator (~)	positional value
conversions	symbol value
decimal number system	two's complement notation

Self-Review Exercises

E.1   The bases of the decimal, binary, octal, and hexadecimal number systems are _____, _____, _____, and _____ respectively.

E.2   In general, the decimal, octal, and hexadecimal representations of a given binary number contain (more/fewer) digits than the binary number contains.

E.3   (True/False) A popular reason for using the decimal number system is that it forms a convenient notation for abbreviating binary numbers simply by substituting one decimal digit per group of four binary bits.

E.4   The (octal / hexadecimal / decimal) representation of a very large binary value is the most concise (of the given alternatives).

E.5   (True/False) The highest digit in any base is one more than the base.

E.6   (True/False) The lowest digit in any base is one less than the base.

E.7   The positional value of the rightmost digit of any number in either binary, octal, decimal, or hexadecimal is always _____.

E.8   The positional value of the digit to the left of the rightmost digit of any number in binary, octal, decimal, or hexadecimal is always equal to _____.

E.9   Fill in the missing values in this chart of positional values for the rightmost four positions in each of the indicated number systems:

decimal	1000	100	10	1
hexadecimal	...	256	...	...
binary	...	...	...	...
octal	512	...	8	...

E.10   Convert binary `110101011000` to octal and to hexadecimal.

E.11   Convert hexadecimal **FACE** to binary.

E.12   Convert octal `7316` to binary.

E.13   Convert hexadecimal **4FEC** to octal. (Hint: First convert **4FEC** to binary then convert that binary number to octal.)

E.14   Convert binary **1101110** to decimal.

E.15   Convert octal **317** to decimal.

E.16   Convert hexadecimal **EFD4** to decimal.

E.17   Convert decimal **177** to binary, to octal, and to hexadecimal.

E.18   Show the binary representation of decimal **417**. Then show the one's complement of **417**, and the two's complement of **417**.

E.19   What is the result when the one's complement of a number is added to itself?

Self-Review Answers

E.1   10, 2, 8, 16.

E.2   Fewer.

E.3   False.

E.4   Hexadecimal.

E.5   False—The highest digit in any base is one less than the base.

E.6   False— The lowest digit in any base is zero.

E.7   1 (the base raised to the zero power).

E.8   The base of the number system.

E.9   Fill in the missing values in this chart of positional values for the rightmost four positions in each of the indicated number systems:

decimal	1000	100	10	1
hexadecimal	4096	256	16	1
binary	8	4	2	1
octal	512	64	8	1

E.10   Octal **6530**; Hexadecimal **D58**.

E.11   Binary **1111 1010 1100 1110**.

E.12   Binary **111 011 001 110**

E.13   Binary **0 100 111 111 101 100**; Octal **47754** .

E.14   Decimal **2+4+8+32+64=110**.

E.15   Decimal **7+1*8+3*64=7+8+192=207**.

E.16   Decimal **4+13*16+15*256+14*4096=61396**.

E.17   Decimal **177**

      to binary:

```
256 128 64 32 16 8 4 2 1
128 64 32 16 8 4 2 1
(1*128)+(0*64)+(1*32)+(1*16)+(0*8)+(0*4)+(0*2)+(1*1)
10110001
```

to octal:

```
512 64 8 1
64 8 1
(2*64)+(6*8)+(1*1)
261
```

to hexadecimal:

```
256 16 1
16 1
(11*16)+(1*1)
(B*16)+(1*1)
B1
```

E.18   Binary:

```
512 256 128 64 32 16 8 4 2 1
256 128 64 32 16 8 4 2 1
(1*256)+(1*128)+(0*64)+(1*32)+(0*16)+(0*8)+(0*4)+(0*2)+
(1*1)
110100001
```

One's complement: `001011110`
Two's complement: `001011111`
Check: Original binary number + its two's complement

```
110100001
001011111
---------
000000000
```

E.19   Zero.

Exercises

E.20   Some people argue that many of our calculations would be easier in the base **12** number system because **12** is divisible by so many more numbers than **10** (for base **10**). What is the lowest digit in base **12**? What might the highest symbol for the digit in base **12** be? What are the positional values of the rightmost four positions of any number in the base **12** number system?

E.21   How is the highest symbol value in the number systems we discussed related to the positional value of the first digit to the left of the rightmost digit of any number in these number systems?

E.22   Complete the following chart of positional values for the rightmost four positions in each of the indicated number systems:

	1000	100	10	1
decimal	1000	100	10	1
base 6	...	...	6	...
base 13	...	169	...	...
base 3	27	...	...	...

E.23   Convert binary `100101111010` to octal and to hexadecimal.

E.24   Convert hexadecimal `3A7D` to binary.

E.25   Convert hexadecimal `765F` to octal. (Hint: First convert `765F` to binary, then convert that binary number to octal.)

E.26   Convert binary `1011110` to decimal.

E.27   Convert octal `426` to decimal.

E.28   Convert hexadecimal `FFFF` to decimal.

E.29   Convert decimal `299` to binary, to octal, and to hexadecimal.

E.30   Show the binary representation of decimal `779`. Then show the one's complement of `779`, and the two's complement of `779`.

E.31   What is the result when the two's complement of a number is added to itself?

E.32   Show the two's complement of integer value `-1` on a machine with 32-bit integers.

INDEX

Index